VW Passat
Service and Repair Manual

A K Legg LAE MIMI

Models covered

(4279 - 336 - 1AP2)

VW Passat Saloon & Estate models, including special/limited editions
Petrol engines: 1.8 litre (1781cc) & 2.0 litre (1984cc) 4-cylinder (inc. turbo)
Turbo-diesel engines: 1.9 litre (1896cc) 4-cylinder

Does NOT cover V5 (petrol), V6 (petrol & diesel) or W8 (petrol) engines, 'Tiptronic' transmission or 4-Motion models
Does NOT cover new range introduced June 2005

© Haynes Publishing 2010

ABCDE
FGHIJ
KLMN

A book in the **Haynes Service and Repair Manual Series**

ISBN **978 1 84425 279 4**

British Library Cataloguing in Publication Data
A catalogue record for this book is available from the British Library.

Printed in the USA .

Haynes Publishing
Sparkford, Yeovil, Somerset BA22 7JJ, England

Haynes North America, Inc
861 Lawrence Drive, Newbury Park, California 91320, USA

Haynes Publishing Nordiska AB
Box 1504, 751 45 UPPSALA, Sverige

Contents

LIVING WITH YOUR VW PASSAT

Introduction	Page	0•4
Safety first!	Page	0•6

Roadside Repairs

If your car won't start	Page	0•7
Jump starting	Page	0•8
Wheel changing	Page	0•9
Identifying leaks	Page	0•10
Towing	Page	0•10

Weekly Checks

Introduction	Page	0•11
Underbonnet check points	Page	0•11
Engine oil level	Page	0•12
Coolant level	Page	0•13
Brake (and clutch) fluid level	Page	0•13
Tyre condition and pressure	Page	0•14
Battery	Page	0•15
Electrical systems	Page	0•15
Washer fluid level	Page	0•16
Wiper blades	Page	0•16

Lubricants and fluids

	Page	0•17

Tyre pressures

	Page	0•17

MAINTENANCE

Routine maintenance and servicing

Petrol models	Page	**1A•1**
Servicing specifications	Page	1A•2
Maintenance schedule	Page	1A•3
Maintenance procedures	Page	1A•8
Diesel models	Page	**1B•1**
Servicing specifications	Page	1B•2
Maintenance schedule	Page	1B•3
Maintenance procedures	Page	1B•7

Contents

REPAIRS & OVERHAUL

Engine and associated systems

Petrol engine in-car repair procedures	Page	2A•1
Diesel engine in-car repair procedures	Page	2B•1
Engine removal and overhaul procedures	Page	2C•1
Cooling, heating and ventilation systems	Page	3•1
Fuel system – petrol injection	Page	4A•1
Fuel system – diesel	Page	4B•1
Emission control and exhaust systems	Page	4C•1
Starting and charging systems	Page	5A•1
Ignition system – petrol engines	Page	5B•1
Pre/post-heating systems – diesel models	Page	5C•1

Transmission

Clutch	Page	6•1
Manual transmission	Page	7A•1
Automatic transmission	Page	7B•1
Driveshafts	Page	8•1

Brakes and Suspension

Braking system	Page	9•1
Suspension and steering	Page	10•1

Body Equipment

Bodywork and fittings	Page	11•1
Body electrical system	Page	12•1
Wiring Diagrams	Page	12•21

REFERENCE

Dimensions and weights	Page	REF•1
Conversion factors	Page	REF•2
Jacking and vehicle support	Page	REF•3
Radio/CD/cassette unit anti-theft system - precaution	Page	REF•3
General repair procedures	Page	REF•4
Buying spare parts	Page	REF•5
Vehicle identification	Page	REF•5
Tools and working facilities	Page	REF•6
MOT test checks	Page	REF•8
Fault finding	Page	REF•12
Glossary of technical terms	Page	REF•20

Index

Index	Page	REF•24

The VW Passat models covered by this manual were introduced to the UK in December 2000. Saloon and Estate models are available, equipped with 1781 cc and 1984 cc petrol engines, and 1896 cc diesel engines. All engines are turbo-charged with the exception of the 1984 cc petrol engine. The diesel engines are equipped with unit injectors, where the injection pump is replaced by a rocker shaft and arm assembly which utilises a second set of camshaft lobes to compress each unit injector in turn; this provides higher injection pressures, and increased accuracy of injection timing.

Fully-independent front suspension is fitted, with the components attached to a subframe assembly; the rear suspension is semi-independent, with a torsion beam and trailing arms.

A five-speed manual gearbox is fitted as standard to all models, with a six-speed unit available as an option on the 1896cc 96 kW diesel Sport model. Automatic transmission was initially available as an option on all except 1984 cc petrol models, but was subsequently discontinued in May 2002.

A wide range of standard and optional equipment is available within the model range. Front and rear disc brakes, and ABS (Anti-lock Braking System) are fitted as standard on all models. ESP (Electronic Stability Program) was fitted as standard from December 2001 and was available as an option on earlier models. Air conditioning was fitted as standard equipment to all models.

For the home mechanic, the Passat is quite straightforward to maintain, and most of the items requiring frequent attention are easily accessible.

Your VW Passat Manual

The aim of this manual is to help you get the best value from your vehicle. It can do so in several ways. It can help you decide what work must be done (even should you choose to get it done by a garage). It will also provide information on routine maintenance and servicing, and give a logical course of action and diagnosis when random faults occur. However, it is hoped that you will use the manual by tackling the work yourself. On simpler jobs it may even be quicker than booking the car into a garage and going there twice, to leave and collect it. Perhaps most important, a lot of money can be saved by avoiding the costs a garage must charge to cover its labour and overheads.

The manual has drawings and descriptions to show the function of the various components so that their layout can be understood. Tasks are described and photographed in a clear step-by-step sequence. The illustrations are numbered by the Section number and paragraph number to which they relate – if there is more than one illustration per paragraph, the sequence is denoted alphabetically.

References to the 'left' or 'right' of the vehicle are in the sense of a person in the driver's seat, facing forwards.

Acknowledgements

Thanks are due to Draper Tools Limited, who provided some of the workshop tools, and to all those people at Sparkford who helped in the production of this manual.

This manual is not a direct reproduction of the vehicle manufacturer's data, and its publication should not be taken as implying any technical approval by the vehicle manufacturers or importers.

We take great pride in the accuracy of information given in this manual, but vehicle manufacturers make alterations and design changes during the production run of a particular vehicle of which they do not inform us. No liability can be accepted by the authors or publishers for loss, damage or injury caused by any errors in, or omissions from, the information given.

Project vehicles

The main vehicle used in the preparation of this manual, and which appears in many of the photographic sequences, was a 2002 VW Passat TDi Saloon. Other vehicles included a 2004 VW Passat 2.0 litre petrol Estate and a 2001 VW Passat TDi Estate.

Working on your car can be dangerous. This page shows just some of the potential risks and hazards, with the aim of creating a safety-conscious attitude.

General hazards

Scalding

• Don't remove the radiator or expansion tank cap while the engine is hot.
• Engine oil, automatic transmission fluid or power steering fluid may also be dangerously hot if the engine has recently been running.

Burning

• Beware of burns from the exhaust system and from any part of the engine. Brake discs and drums can also be extremely hot immediately after use.

Crushing

• When working under or near a raised vehicle, always supplement the jack with axle stands, or use drive-on ramps. *Never venture under a car which is only supported by a jack.*

• Take care if loosening or tightening high-torque nuts when the vehicle is on stands. Initial loosening and final tightening should be done with the wheels on the ground.

Fire

• Fuel is highly flammable; fuel vapour is explosive.
• Don't let fuel spill onto a hot engine.
• Do not smoke or allow naked lights (including pilot lights) anywhere near a vehicle being worked on. Also beware of creating sparks (electrically or by use of tools).
• Fuel vapour is heavier than air, so don't work on the fuel system with the vehicle over an inspection pit.
• Another cause of fire is an electrical overload or short-circuit. Take care when repairing or modifying the vehicle wiring.
• Keep a fire extinguisher handy, of a type suitable for use on fuel and electrical fires.

Electric shock

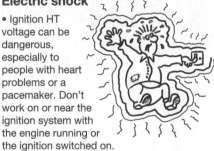

• Ignition HT voltage can be dangerous, especially to people with heart problems or a pacemaker. Don't work on or near the ignition system with the engine running or the ignition switched on.

• Mains voltage is also dangerous. Make sure that any mains-operated equipment is correctly earthed. Mains power points should be protected by a residual current device (RCD) circuit breaker.

Fume or gas intoxication

• Exhaust fumes are poisonous; they often contain carbon monoxide, which is rapidly fatal if inhaled. Never run the engine in a confined space such as a garage with the doors shut.

• Fuel vapour is also poisonous, as are the vapours from some cleaning solvents and paint thinners.

Poisonous or irritant substances

• Avoid skin contact with battery acid and with any fuel, fluid or lubricant, especially antifreeze, brake hydraulic fluid and Diesel fuel. Don't syphon them by mouth. If such a substance is swallowed or gets into the eyes, seek medical advice.
• Prolonged contact with used engine oil can cause skin cancer. Wear gloves or use a barrier cream if necessary. Change out of oil-soaked clothes and do not keep oily rags in your pocket.
• Air conditioning refrigerant forms a poisonous gas if exposed to a naked flame (including a cigarette). It can also cause skin burns on contact.

Asbestos

• Asbestos dust can cause cancer if inhaled or swallowed. Asbestos may be found in gaskets and in brake and clutch linings. When dealing with such components it is safest to assume that they contain asbestos.

Special hazards

Hydrofluoric acid

• This extremely corrosive acid is formed when certain types of synthetic rubber, found in some O-rings, oil seals, fuel hoses etc, are exposed to temperatures above 400°C. The rubber changes into a charred or sticky substance containing the acid. *Once formed, the acid remains dangerous for years. If it gets onto the skin, it may be necessary to amputate the limb concerned.*
• When dealing with a vehicle which has suffered a fire, or with components salvaged from such a vehicle, wear protective gloves and discard them after use.

The battery

• Batteries contain sulphuric acid, which attacks clothing, eyes and skin. Take care when topping-up or carrying the battery.
• The hydrogen gas given off by the battery is highly explosive. Never cause a spark or allow a naked light nearby. Be careful when connecting and disconnecting battery chargers or jump leads.

Air bags

• Air bags can cause injury if they go off accidentally. Take care when removing the steering wheel and/or facia. Special storage instructions may apply.

Diesel injection equipment

• Diesel injection pumps supply fuel at very high pressure. Take care when working on the fuel injectors and fuel pipes.

⚠ *Warning: Never expose the hands, face or any other part of the body to injector spray; the fuel can penetrate the skin with potentially fatal results.*

Remember...

DO

• Do use eye protection when using power tools, and when working under the vehicle.

• Do wear gloves or use barrier cream to protect your hands when necessary.

• Do get someone to check periodically that all is well when working alone on the vehicle.

• Do keep loose clothing and long hair well out of the way of moving mechanical parts.

• Do remove rings, wristwatch etc, before working on the vehicle – especially the electrical system.

• Do ensure that any lifting or jacking equipment has a safe working load rating adequate for the job.

DON'T

• Don't attempt to lift a heavy component which may be beyond your capability – get assistance.

• Don't rush to finish a job, or take unverified short cuts.

• Don't use ill-fitting tools which may slip and cause injury.

• Don't leave tools or parts lying around where someone can trip over them. Mop up oil and fuel spills at once.

• Don't allow children or pets to play in or near a vehicle being worked on.

The following pages are intended to help in dealing with common roadside emergencies and breakdowns. You will find more detailed fault finding information at the back of the manual, and repair information in the main chapters.

If your car won't start and the starter motor doesn't turn

- [ ] If it's a model with automatic transmission, make sure the selector is in P or N.
- [ ] Open the bonnet and make sure that the battery terminals are clean and tight.
- [ ] Switch on the headlights and try to start the engine. If the headlights go very dim when you're trying to start, the battery is probably flat. Get out of trouble by jump starting (see next page) using a friend's car.

If your car won't start even though the starter motor turns as normal

- [ ] Is there fuel in the tank?
- [ ] Is there moisture on electrical components under the bonnet? Switch off the ignition, then wipe off any obvious dampness with a dry cloth. Spray a water-repellent aerosol product (WD-40 or equivalent) on ignition and fuel system electrical connectors. (Note that diesel engines don't usually suffer from damp).

A Check the condition and security of the battery connections

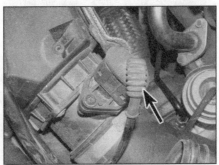

B Check the fuel injection system airflow meter wiring is secure

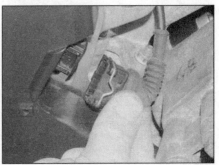

C Check the ignition system Hall sender wiring is secure

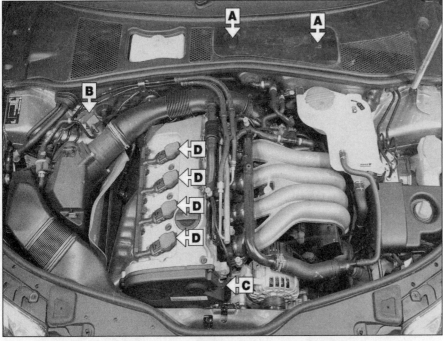

Check that electrical connections are secure (with the ignition switched off) and spray them with a water-dispersant spray like WD-40 if you suspect a problem due to damp

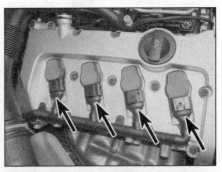

D Check that the HT leads are securely connected to the spark plugs on petrol engines. To do this, remove the engine top cover first

Jump starting

When jump-starting a car using a booster battery, observe the following precautions:

✔ Before connecting the booster battery, make sure that the ignition is switched off.

✔ Ensure that all electrical equipment (lights, heater, wipers, etc) is switched off.

✔ Take note of any special precautions printed on the battery case.

✔ Make sure that the booster battery is the same voltage as the discharged one in the vehicle.

✔ If the battery is being jump-started from the battery in another vehicle, the two vehicles MUST NOT TOUCH each other.

✔ Make sure that the transmission is in neutral (or PARK, in the case of automatic transmission).

 Jump starting will get you out of trouble, but you must correct whatever made the battery go flat in the first place. There are three possibilities:

1 The battery has been drained by repeated attempts to start, or by leaving the lights on.

2 The charging system is not working properly (alternator drivebelt slack or broken, alternator wiring fault or alternator itself faulty).

3 The battery itself is at fault (electrolyte low, or battery worn out).

1 Connect one end of the red jump lead to the positive (+) terminal of the flat battery

2 Connect the other end of the red lead to the positive (+) terminal of the booster battery.

3 Connect one end of the black jump lead to the negative (-) terminal of the booster battery

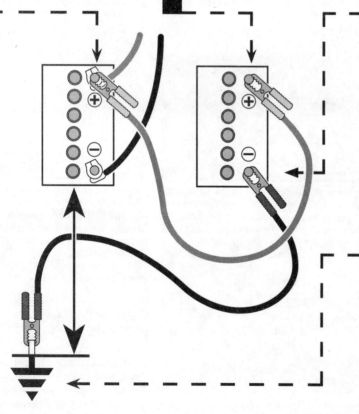

4 Connect the other end of the black jump lead to a bolt or bracket on the engine block, well away from the battery, on the vehicle to be started.

5 Make sure that the jump leads will not come into contact with the fan, drive-belts or other moving parts of the engine.

6 Start the engine using the booster battery and run it at idle speed. Switch on the lights, rear window demister and heater blower motor, then disconnect the jump leads in the reverse order of connection. Turn off the lights etc.

Wheel changing

Warning: Do not change a wheel in a situation where you risk being hit by other traffic. On busy roads, try to stop in a lay-by or a gateway. Be wary of passing traffic while changing the wheel – it is easy to become distracted by the job in hand.

Some of the details shown here will vary according to model. For instance, the location of the spare wheel and jack is not the same on all cars. However, the basic principles apply to all vehicles.

Preparation

☐ When a puncture occurs, stop as soon as it is safe to do so.
☐ Park on firm level ground, if possible, and well out of the way of other traffic.
☐ Use hazard warning lights if necessary.

☐ If you have one, use a warning triangle to alert other drivers of your presence.
☐ Apply the handbrake and engage first or reverse gear (or Park on models with automatic transmission).

☐ Chock the wheel diagonally opposite the one being removed – a couple of large stones will do for this.
☐ If the ground is soft, use a flat piece of wood to spread the load under the jack.

Changing the wheel

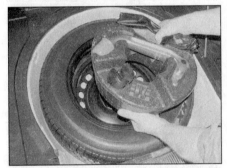

1 The spare is stored beneath the luggage compartment floor covering. The jack and tool kit are located in the spare wheel. Unscrew the bolt and remove the tool kit. Lift the spare wheel from the well in the floor.

2 Where fitted, insert a screwdriver into the slot and lever the cap from the wheel. Where fitted, use the hook in the tool kit to pull the cover from the wheel. If caps are fitted to each bolt, use the tool to pull off the covers.

3 Loosen each wheel bolt by half a turn. Use the special adapter where a locking wheel bolt is fitted.

4 Locate the jack head below the reinforced jacking point nearest the wheel to be changed. The jacking point is indicated by a diamond pressed into the sill. Turn the handle to raise the wheel clear of the ground.

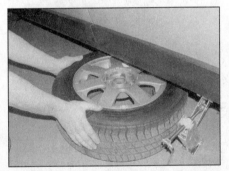

5 Remove the bolts and lift the wheel from the vehicle. After removing the first bolt, screw in the guide as an aid to fitting the spare wheel. Place the wheel beneath the sill as a precaution against the jack failing.

6 Fit the spare wheel and remove the guide pin, then tighten the bolts moderately with the wheelbrace. Lower the vehicle to the ground, then finally tighten the wheel bolts in a diagonal sequence. Refit the wheel cover/cap as applicable. Note that the wheel bolts should be tightened to the specified torque at the earliest opportunity.

Finally . . .

☐ Remove the wheel chocks.
☐ Stow the jack and tools in the correct locations in the car.
☐ Check the tyre pressure on the wheel just fitted. If it is low, or if you don't have a pressure gauge with you, drive slowly to the nearest garage and inflate the tyre to the right pressure.
☐ Have the damaged tyre or wheel repaired as soon as possible.

Note: *If a temporary 'space-saver' spare wheel has been fitted, special conditions apply to its use. This type of spare wheel is only intended for use in an emergency, and should not remain fitted any longer than it takes to get the punctured wheel repaired. While the temporary wheel is in use, do not exceed 50 mph (80 km/h), and avoid harsh acceleration, braking or cornering. Note that, besides being narrower than a normal roadwheel, the temporary spare wheel is of smaller diameter; therefore, since ground clearance will be slightly reduced with the temporary spare in use, take care when travelling over rough ground.*

Identifying leaks

Puddles on the garage floor or drive, or obvious wetness under the bonnet or underneath the car, suggest a leak that needs investigating. It can sometimes be difficult to decide where the leak is coming from, especially if the engine bay is very dirty already. Leaking oil or fluid can also be blown rearwards by the passage of air under the car, giving a false impression of where the problem lies.

 Warning: Most automotive oils and fluids are poisonous. Wash them off skin, and change out of contaminated clothing, without delay.

 The smell of a fluid leaking from the car may provide a clue to what's leaking. Some fluids are distinctively coloured. It may help to clean the car carefully and to park it over some clean paper overnight as an aid to locating the source of the leak.
Remember that some leaks may only occur while the engine is running.

Sump oil

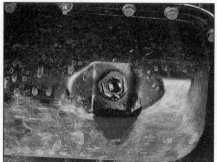

Engine oil may leak from the drain plug...

Oil from filter

...or from the base of the oil filter.

Gearbox oil

Gearbox oil can leak from the seals at the inboard ends of the driveshafts.

Antifreeze

Leaking antifreeze often leaves a crystalline deposit like this.

Brake fluid

A leak occurring at a wheel is almost certainly brake fluid.

Power steering fluid

Power steering fluid may leak from the pipe connectors on the steering rack.

Towing

When all else fails, you may find yourself having to get a tow home – or of course you may be helping somebody else. Long-distance recovery should only be done by a garage or breakdown service. For shorter distances, DIY towing using another car is easy enough, but observe the following points:

☐ Use a proper tow-rope – they are not expensive. The vehicle being towed must display an ON TOW sign in its rear window.
☐ Always turn the ignition key to the 'On' position when the vehicle is being towed, so that the steering lock is released, and the direction indicator and brake lights work.
☐ A rear towing eye is provided below the right-hand side of the bumper. The front

towing eye is fitted behind the cover on the right-hand side of the front bumper – see below. Only attach the tow-rope to the towing eyes provided.
☐ On some models, the front towing eye is supplied separately as part of the toolkit stored in the luggage compartment. To fit the eye, remove the vent/cover from the front bumper. Screw the eye into position anti-clockwise (it has a **left-handed** thread), and tighten using the wheelbrace handle.
☐ Before being towed, release the handbrake and select neutral on the transmission. **Note:** *On models with automatic transmission, special precautions apply. If in doubt, do not tow, or transmission damage may result.*

☐ Note that greater-than-usual pedal pressure will be required to operate the brakes, since the vacuum servo unit is only operational with the engine running.
☐ Because the power steering will not be operational, greater-than-usual steering effort will be required.
☐ The driver of the car being towed must keep the tow-rope taut at all times to avoid snatching.
☐ Make sure that both drivers know the route before setting off.
☐ Only drive at moderate speeds and keep the distance towed to a minimum. Drive smoothly and allow plenty of time for slowing down at junctions.

Introduction

There are some very simple checks which need only take a few minutes to carry out, but which could save you a lot of inconvenience and expense.

These *Weekly checks* require no great skill or special tools, and the small amount of time they take to perform could prove to be very well spent, for example:

☐ Keeping an eye on tyre condition and pressures, will not only help to stop them wearing out prematurely, but could also save your life.

☐ Many breakdowns are caused by electrical problems. Battery-related faults are particularly common, and a quick check on a regular basis will often prevent the majority of these.

☐ If your car develops a brake fluid leak, the first time you might know about it is when your brakes don't work properly. Checking the level regularly will give advance warning of this kind of problem.

☐ If the oil or coolant levels run low, the cost of repairing any engine damage will be far greater than fixing the leak, for example.

Underbonnet check points

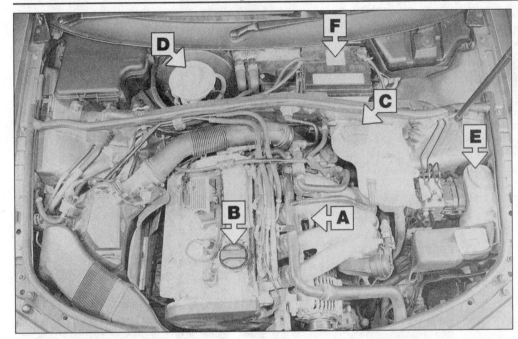

◀ 1.8 litre petrol

A *Engine oil level dipstick*

B *Engine oil filler cap*

C *Coolant expansion tank*

D *Brake fluid reservoir*

E *Screen washer fluid reservoir*

F *Battery*

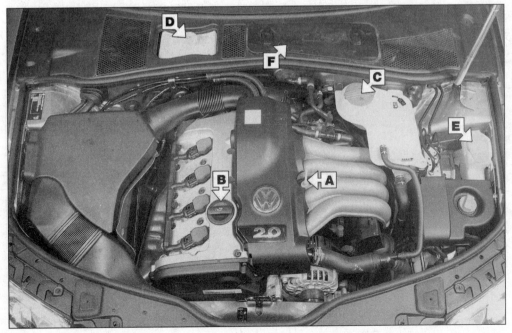

◀ 2.0 litre petrol

A *Engine oil level dipstick*

B *Engine oil filler cap*

C *Coolant expansion tank*

D *Brake fluid reservoir*

E *Screen washer fluid reservoir*

F *Battery*

◀ **1.9 litre diesel**

A *Engine oil level dipstick*

B *Engine oil filler cap*

C *Coolant expansion tank*

D *Brake fluid reservoir*

E *Screen washer fluid reservoir*

F *Battery*

Engine oil level

Before you start

✔ Make sure that the car is on level ground.

✔ Check the oil level before the car is driven, or at least 5 minutes after the engine has been switched off.

 If the oil is checked immediately after driving the vehicle, some of the oil will remain in the upper engine components, resulting in an inaccurate reading on the dipstick.

The correct oil

Modern engines place great demands on their oil. It is very important that the correct oil for your car is used (see *Lubricants and fluids*).

Car care

● If you have to add oil frequently, you should check whether you have any oil leaks. Place some clean paper under the car overnight, and check for stains in the morning. If there are no leaks, then the engine may be burning oil.

● Always maintain the level between the upper and lower dipstick marks (see photo 3). If the level is too low, severe engine damage may occur. Oil seal failure may result if the engine is overfilled by adding too much oil.

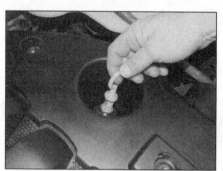

1 The dipstick is located on the left-hand side of the engine (see *Underbonnet check points* for exact location). Withdraw the dipstick.

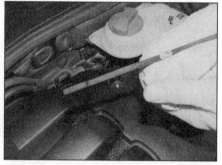

2 Using a clean rag or paper towel, wipe all oil from the dipstick. Insert the clean dipstick into the tube as far as it will go, then withdraw it again.

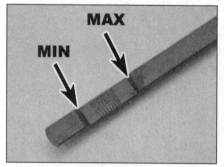

3 Note the oil level on the end of the dipstick, which should be between the upper and lower mark. Approximately 1.0 litre of oil will raise the level from the lower mark to the upper mark.

4 Oil is added through the filler cap on top of the engine. Turn the cap through a quarter-turn anti-clockwise and withdraw it. Top-up the level. A funnel may help to reduce spillage. Add the oil slowly, checking the level on the dipstick often. Do not overfill.

Coolant level

 Warning: Do not attempt to remove the expansion tank pressure cap when the engine is hot, as there is a very great risk of scalding. Do not leave open containers of coolant about, as it is poisonous.

Car Care

● With a sealed-type cooling system, adding coolant should not be necessary on a regular basis. If frequent topping-up is required, it is likely there is a leak. Check the radiator, all hoses and joint faces for signs of staining or wetness, and rectify as necessary.

● It is important that antifreeze is used in the cooling system all year round, not just during the winter months. Don't top up with water alone, as the antifreeze will become diluted.

1 The coolant level varies with the temperature of the engine. When the engine is cold, the coolant level should be between the MIN and MAX marks.

2 If topping-up is necessary, wait until the engine is cold. Slowly unscrew the cap to release any pressure present in the cooling system, and remove the cap.

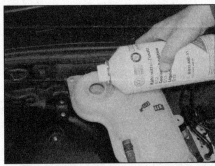

3 Add a mixture of water and antifreeze to the expansion tank until the coolant level is on the MAX mark.

Brake (and clutch) fluid level

Note: On manual transmission models, the fluid reservoir also supplies the clutch master cylinder with fluid.

Before you start

✔ Make sure that the car is on level ground.
✔ The fluid level in the reservoir will drop slightly as the brake pads wear down, but the fluid level must never be allowed to drop below the MIN mark.

Safety first!

● If the reservoir requires repeated topping-up, this is an indication of a fluid leak somewhere in the system, which should be investigated immediately.

● If a leak is suspected, the car should not be driven until the braking system has been checked. Never take any risks where brakes are concerned.

 Warning: Brake fluid can harm your eyes and damage painted surfaces, so use extreme caution when handling and pouring it. Do not use fluid which has been standing open for some time, as it absorbs moisture from the air, which can cause a dangerous loss of braking effectiveness.

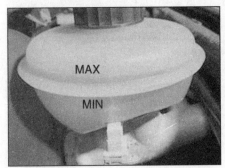

1 The MIN and MAX marks are indicated on the reservoir. The fluid level must be kept between the marks at all times.

2 If topping-up is necessary, first wipe clean the area around the filler cap to prevent dirt entering the hydraulic system. Unscrew the reservoir cap.

3 Carefully add fluid, taking care not to spill it onto the surrounding components. Use only the specified fluid; mixing different types can cause damage to the system. On completion, securely refit the cap and wipe away any spilt fluid.

Tyre condition and pressure

It is very important that tyres are in good condition, and at the correct pressure - having a tyre failure at any speed is highly dangerous. Tyre wear is influenced by driving style - harsh braking and acceleration, or fast cornering, will all produce more rapid tyre wear. As a general rule, the front tyres wear out faster than the rears. Interchanging the tyres from front to rear ("rotating" the tyres) may result in more even wear. However, if this is completely effective, you may have the expense of replacing all four tyres at once!

Remove any nails or stones embedded in the tread before they penetrate the tyre to cause deflation. If removal of a nail does reveal that the tyre has been punctured, refit the nail so that its point of penetration is marked. Then immediately change the wheel, and have the tyre repaired by a tyre dealer.

Regularly check the tyres for damage in the form of cuts or bulges, especially in the sidewalls. Periodically remove the wheels, and clean any dirt or mud from the inside and outside surfaces. Examine the wheel rims for signs of rusting, corrosion or other damage. Light alloy wheels are easily damaged by "kerbing" whilst parking; steel wheels may also become dented or buckled. A new wheel is very often the only way to overcome severe damage.

New tyres should be balanced when they are fitted, but it may become necessary to re-balance them as they wear, or if the balance weights fitted to the wheel rim should fall off. Unbalanced tyres will wear more quickly, as will the steering and suspension components. Wheel imbalance is normally signified by vibration, particularly at a certain speed (typically around 50 mph). If this vibration is felt only through the steering, then it is likely that just the front wheels need balancing. If, however, the vibration is felt through the whole car, the rear wheels could be out of balance. Wheel balancing should be carried out by a tyre dealer or garage.

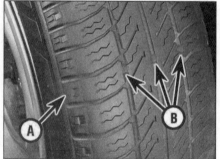

1 *Tread Depth - visual check*

The original tyres have tread wear safety bands (B), which will appear when the tread depth reaches approximately 1.6 mm. The band positions are indicated by a triangular mark on the tyre sidewall (A).

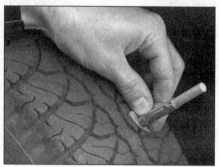

2 *Tread Depth - manual check*

Alternatively, tread wear can be monitored with a simple, inexpensive device known as a tread depth indicator gauge.

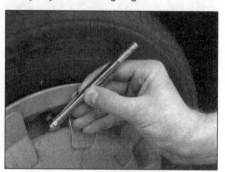

3 *Tyre Pressure Check*

Check the tyre pressures regularly with the tyres cold. Do not adjust the tyre pressures immediately after the vehicle has been used, or an inaccurate setting will result.

Tyre tread wear patterns

Shoulder Wear

Underinflation (wear on both sides)
Under-inflation will cause overheating of the tyre, because the tyre will flex too much, and the tread will not sit correctly on the road surface. This will cause a loss of grip and excessive wear, not to mention the danger of sudden tyre failure due to heat build-up.
Check and adjust pressures
Incorrect wheel camber (wear on one side)
Repair or renew suspension parts
Hard cornering
Reduce speed!

Centre Wear

Overinflation
Over-inflation will cause rapid wear of the centre part of the tyre tread, coupled with reduced grip, harsher ride, and the danger of shock damage occurring in the tyre casing.
Check and adjust pressures

If you sometimes have to inflate your car's tyres to the higher pressures specified for maximum load or sustained high speed, don't forget to reduce the pressures to normal afterwards.

Uneven Wear

Front tyres may wear unevenly as a result of wheel misalignment. Most tyre dealers and garages can check and adjust the wheel alignment (or "tracking") for a modest charge.
Incorrect camber or castor
Repair or renew suspension parts
Malfunctioning suspension
Repair or renew suspension parts
Unbalanced wheel
Balance tyres
Incorrect toe setting
Adjust front wheel alignment
Note: *The feathered edge of the tread which typifies toe wear is best checked by feel.*

Battery

Caution: Before carrying out any work on the vehicle battery, read the precautions given in 'Safety first!' at the start of this manual.

✔ Make sure that the battery tray is in good condition, and that the clamp is tight. Corrosion on the tray, retaining clamp and the battery itself can be removed with a solution of water and baking soda. Thoroughly rinse all cleaned areas with water. Any metal parts damaged by corrosion should be covered with a zinc-based primer, then painted.

✔ Periodically (approximately every three months), check the charge condition of the battery as described in Chapter 5A. A 'magic eye' charge indicator is fitted to the standard battery – if the indicator is green in colour, the battery is fully-charged, however, if it is colourless, it should be recharged. If it is yellow in colour, the battery should be renewed.

✔ If the battery is flat, and you need to jump start your vehicle, see *Roadside Repairs*.

1 The battery is located on the bulkhead at the rear of the engine compartment.

2 Check the tightness of battery clamps to ensure good electrical connections. You should not be able to move them. Also check each cable for cracks and frayed conductors.

3 If corrosion (white, fluffy deposits) is evident, remove the cables from the battery terminals, clean them with a small wire brush, then refit them. Automotive stores sell a tool for cleaning the battery post . . .

4 . . . as well as the battery cable clamps.
Note: *VW specifically prohibit the use of grease on the battery terminals.*

Electrical systems

✔ Check all external lights and the horn. Refer to the appropriate Sections of Chapter 12 for details if any of the circuits are found to be inoperative.

✔ Visually check all accessible wiring connectors, harnesses and retaining clips for security, and for signs of chafing or damage.

> **HAYNES HiNT**
> *If you need to check your brake lights and indicators unaided, back up to a wall or garage door and operate the lights. The reflected light should show if they are working properly.*

1 If a single indicator light, brake light or headlight has failed, it is likely that a bulb has blown and will need to be renewed. Refer to Chapter 12 for details. If both brake lights have failed, it is possible that the brake light switch operated by the brake pedal has failed. Refer to Chapter 9 for details.

2 If more than one indicator light or headlight has failed, it is likely that either a fuse has blown or that there is a fault in the circuit (see *Electrical fault finding* in Chapter 12). The main fuses are in the fusebox beneath a cover on the right-hand end of the facia panel. Use a small screwdriver to prise off the cover. The circuits protected by the fuses are shown on the inside of the cover. Additional heavy duty fuses and fusible links are in the fusebox located on top of the battery.

3 To renew a blown fuse, pull it from its location in the fusebox, using the plastic pliers provided. Fit a new fuse of the same rating, available from car accessory shops. It is important that you find the reason that the fuse blew (see *Electrical fault finding* in Chapter 12).

Washer fluid level

● Screenwash additives not only keep the windscreen clean during bad weather, they also prevent the washer system freezing in cold weather – which is when you are likely to need it most. Don't top-up using plain water, as the screenwash will become diluted, and will freeze in cold weather.

 Warning: On no account use engine coolant antifreeze in the screen washer system – this may damage the paintwork.

1 The reservoir for the windscreen and headlight washer systems is on the left-hand side of the engine compartment.

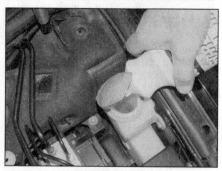

2 A screenwash additive should be added in the quantities recommended on the bottle.

Wiper blades

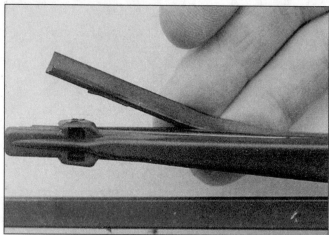

1 Check the condition of the wiper blades; if they are cracked or show any signs of deterioration, or if the glass swept area is smeared, renew them. For maximum clarity of vision, wiper blades should be renewed annually, as a matter of course.

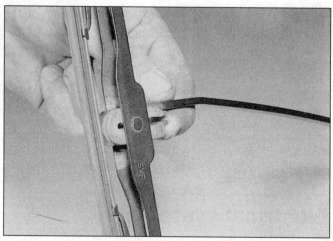

2 To remove a windscreen wiper blade, first pull the arm fully away from the screen until it locks – do not pull on the arm, especially the Aero type. When removing the standard wiper blade, swivel the blade through 90°, press the locking tab with your fingers, and slide the blade out of the hooked end of the arm.

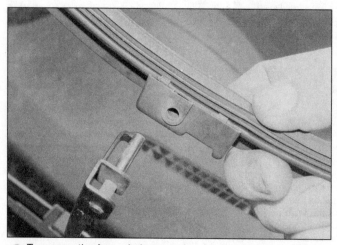

3 To remove the Aero windscreen wiper blade, turn it up to the stop, then withdraw it from the swivel pin.

4 Where applicable, don't forget to check the tailgate wiper blade as well. To remove the blade, depress the retaining tab and slide the blade out of the hooked end of the arm.

Lubricants and fluids

Engine (petrol)
    Standard (distance/time) service interval . . . .   Multigrade engine oil to VW 502.00 or better
    LongLife (variable) service interval . . . .   Multigrade engine oil to VW 504.00 or better*

Engine (diesel)
    Standard (distance/time) service interval . . . .   Multigrade engine oil to VW 505.01 or better
    LongLife (variable) service interval . . . .   Multigrade engine oil to VW 507.00 or better*

Cooling system. . . . .   VW additive G12 only (antifreeze and corrosion protection)

Manual transmission . . . .   VW G50 gear oil, viscosity SAE 75W/90 (synthetic)

Automatic transmission
    Main transmission. . . . .   VW ATF
    Final drive . . . .   VW G50 gear oil, viscosity SAE 75W/90 (synthetic)

Braking system. . . . .   Hydraulic fluid to SAE J1703F or DOT 4

Power steering reservoir . . . .   VW hydraulic oil G 002 000

* A maximum of 0.5 litres of standard oil may be used for topping-up when LongLife oil is unobtainable

Tyre pressures

Note: *The recommended tyre pressures for each vehicle are given on a sticker attached to the inside of the fuel filler flap. The pressures given are for the original equipment tyres – the recommended pressures may vary if any other make or type of tyre is fitted; check with the tyre manufacturer or supplier for latest recommendations. The following pressures are typical.*

	Front	Rear
Normal load	1.9 bars (28 psi)	1.9 bars (28 psi)
Full load	2.2 bars (32 psi)	2.7 bars (39 psi)

Note: *Where a space-saver spare tyre is fitted, its pressure must be 4.2 bars (61 psi).*

Chapter 1 Part A:
Routine maintenance and servicing – petrol models

Contents

Section number

Air filter element renewal 24
Airbag unit check 19
Antifreeze check 9
Automatic transmission final drive oil level check 29
Automatic transmission fluid renewal 28
Auxiliary drivebelt check and renewal 26
Auxiliary drivebelt check 8
Battery check 17
Brake (and clutch) fluid renewal 31
Brake hydraulic circuit check 10
Brake pad check 4
Coolant renewal 32
Driveshaft gaiter check 15
Engine management self-diagnosis memory fault check 21
Engine oil and filter renewal 3
Exhaust system check 6

Section number

Headlight beam adjustment 11
Hinge and lock lubrication 18
Hose and fluid leak check 7
Introduction 1
Manual transmission oil level check 13
Pollen filter element renewal 12
Power steering hydraulic fluid level check 27
Regular maintenance 2
Resetting the service interval display 5
Road test and exhaust emissions check 23
Spark plug renewal 25
Steering and suspension check 16
Sunroof check and lubrication 22
Timing belt check and renewal 30
Underbody protection check 14
Windscreen/tailgate/headlight washer system check 20

Degrees of difficulty

Easy, suitable for novice with little experience	**Fairly easy,** suitable for beginner with some experience	**Fairly difficult,** suitable for competent DIY mechanic	**Difficult,** suitable for experienced DIY mechanic	**Very difficult,** suitable for expert DIY or professional

Lubricants and fluids............................... Refer to end of *Weekly checks* on page 0•17

Capacities

Engine oil

	With filter	Without filter
Engine codes AWT and AZM.............................	3.5 litres	3.0 litres
Engine code ALT....................................	4.2 litres	3.7 litres

Cooling system

All models... 7.0 litres approx

Transmission

Manual transmission:
012/01W.. 2.25 litres
01E/0A1.. 2.5 litres
Automatic transmission fluid:
  4-speed transmission:
    Initial filling................................. 5.5 litres
    Fluid change.................................. 3.5 litres
  5-speed transmission:
    Initial filling................................. 9.0 litres
    Fluid change.................................. 2.6 litres
Automatic transmission final drive:
  4-speed transmission.............................. 1.0 litre
  5-speed transmission.............................. 0.75 litres

Power-assisted steering

All models... 1.5 litres (approx)

Fuel tank

All models... 62 litres (approx)

Washer reservoirs

Models with headlight washers............................. 5.5 litres
Models without headlight washers.......................... 3.0 litres

Cooling system

Antifreeze mixture:
  40% antifreeze................................... Protection down to -25°C
  50% antifreeze................................... Protection down to -35°C

Ignition system

Spark plugs:

	Type	Electrode gap
1.8 litre engine AWT...............................	NGK PFR6Q	0.8 mm
	VW 101000063AA	0.8 mm
2.0 litre engine:		
AZM.....................................	NGK BKUR6ET-10	1.1 mm
	VW 101000033AA	1.1 mm
ALT......................................	NGK BKUR5ET-10	1.1 mm
	VW 101000033AG	1.1 mm

Brakes

Front brake pad friction material minimum thickness.............. 2.0 mm
Rear brake pad friction material minimum thickness.............. 2.0 mm

Auxiliary drivebelt

Tension adjustment:
  Main drivebelt.................................... Automatically adjusted
  Air conditioning compressor drivebelt..................... Apply a torque of 25 Nm to the hexagon on the tensioner body

Torque wrench settings

	Nm	lbf ft
Automatic transmission:		
Drain plug (01V)	40	30
Final drive oil filler/level plug.	25	18
Inspection plug:		
01N	15	11
01V	80	59
Overflow pipe (01N)	2	1
Manual transmission filler/level plug	25	18
Power steering pump mounting.	25	18
Roadwheel bolts.	120	89
Spark plugs:		
Engine code AWT and ALT.	30	22
Engine code AZM.	25	18
Sump drain plug.	30	22

Maintenance schedule

The maintenance intervals (shown overleaf) in this manual are provided with the assumption that you, not the dealer, will be carrying out the work. These are the minimum intervals recommended by us for vehicles driven daily. If you wish to keep your vehicle in peak condition at all times, you may wish to perform some of these procedures more often. We encourage frequent maintenance, since it enhances the efficiency, performance and resale value of your vehicle.

When the vehicle is new, it should be serviced by a dealer service department, in order to preserve the factory warranty.

All models are equipped with a service interval display indicator in the instrument panel. Every time the engine is started the panel will illuminate for approximately 20 seconds with service information. With the standard non-variable display, the service intervals are in accordance with specific distances and time periods. With the LongLife display, the service interval is variable according to the number of starts, length of journeys, vehicle speeds, brake pad wear, bonnet opening frequency, fuel consumption, oil level and oil temperature, however the vehicle **must** be serviced at least every two years. At a distance of 2000 miles (3000 km) before the next service is due, 'Service in 2000 miles' (or '3000 km') will appear at the bottom of the speedometer, and this figure will reduce in steps of 100 units as the vehicle is used. Once the service interval has been reached, the display will flash 'Service' or 'Service Now'. Note that if the variable (LongLife) service interval is being used, the engine must **only** be filled with the recommended long-life engine oil (see *Recommended lubricants and fluids*).

After completing a service, VW technicians use a special instrument to reset the service display to the next service interval, and a print-out is put in the vehicle service record. The display can be reset by the owner as described in Section 5, but note that for models using the 'LongLife' interval, the procedure will automatically reset the display to the 10 000 miles/15 000 km 'distance' interval. To have the display reset to the 'variable' (LongLife) interval, it is necessary to take the vehicle to an VW dealer who will use a special instrument to encode the on-board computer.

Timing belt maintenance

The following schedules give the manufacturer's current recommended intervals for the replacement of the timing belt. However, in view of the fact that severe engine damage will result if the belt breaks, it is strongly recommended that the timing belt renewal interval is reduced to 40 000 miles or 4 years, whichever is the sooner, on vehicles which are subjected to intensive use, i.e., mainly short journeys or a lot of stop-start driving. The actual belt renewal interval is very much up to the individual owner, but shorter intervals of this sort are in line with the advice offered by many professionals.

At the very least, examine carefully the timing belt whenever the opportunity arises, renewing it if there is any doubt about its condition. Check also the sprockets for signs of wear or damage and ensure that the tensioner and idler pulleys rotate smoothly on their bearings; renew any worn or damaged components. **Note:** *It is considered good practice by many professional mechanics to renew tensioner and idler pulley assemblies as a matter of course, whenever the timing belt is renewed.*

Models using distance and time intervals

Note: *The following service intervals are only applicable to models using fixed distance and time intervals (shown in the vehicle Service Schedule booklet or on the Next Service sticker located on the driver's door pillar).*

Every 250 miles (400 km) or weekly

☐ Refer to *Weekly checks*

Every 5000 miles (7500 km) or 6 months

☐ Renew the engine oil and filter (Section 3)

Note: *Frequent oil and filter changes are good for the engine. We recommend changing the oil at the mileage specified here, or at least twice a year if the mileage covered is less.*

Every 10 000 miles (15 000 km) or 12 months, whichever comes first – OIL on display

In addition to the items listed above, carry out the following:

☐ Check the front and rear brake pad thickness (Section 4)
☐ Reset the service interval display (Section 5)

Every 20 000 miles (30 000 km) or 2 years, whichever comes first – 01 on display

In addition to the items listed above, carry out the following:

☐ Check the condition of the exhaust system and its mountings (Section 6)
☐ Check all underbonnet components and hoses for fluid and oil leaks (Section 7)
☐ Check the condition of the auxiliary drivebelt (Section 8)
☐ Check the coolant antifreeze concentration (Section 9)
☐ Check the brake hydraulic circuit for leaks and damage (Section 10)
☐ Check the headlight beam adjustment (Section 11)
☐ Renew the pollen filter element (Section 12)
☐ Check the manual transmission oil level (Section 13)
☐ Check the underbody protection for damage (Section 14)
☐ Check the condition of the driveshaft gaiters (Section 15)
☐ Check the steering and suspension components for condition and security (Section 16)
☐ Check the battery condition, security and electrolyte level (Section 17)

Every 20 000 miles (30 000 km) or 2 years, whichever comes first – 01 on display (continued)

☐ Lubricate all hinges and locks (Section 18)
☐ Check the condition of the airbag unit(s) (Section 19)
☐ Check the operation of the windscreen/tailgate/headlight washer system(s) (as applicable) (Section 20)
☐ Check the engine management self-diagnosis memory for faults (Section 21)
☐ Check the operation of the sunroof and lubricate the guide rails (Section 22)
☐ Carry out a road test and check exhaust emissions (Section 23)

Every 40 000 miles (60 000 km) or 4 years, whichever comes first

☐ Renew the air filter element (Section 24)
☐ Renew the spark plugs (Section 25)
☐ Check and renewal of the auxiliary drivebelt (Section 26)
☐ Check the power steering hydraulic fluid level (Section 27)
☐ Renew the automatic transmission fluid (Section 28)
☐ Check the automatic transmission final drive oil level (Section 29)

Every 60 000 miles (90 000 km)

☐ Renew the timing belt, SOHC engines (Section 30)

Note: *For SOHC engines, VW specify timing belt inspection at the first 60 000 miles (90 000 km) and then every 20 000 miles (30 000 km), with the belt being renewed whenever it is considered necessary. However, if the vehicle is used mainly for short journeys, we recommend that this shorter renewal interval is adhered to. The belt renewal interval is very much up to the individual owner but, bearing in mind that severe engine damage will result if the belt breaks in use, we recommend the shorter interval.*

Every 2 years

☐ Renew the brake (and clutch) fluid (Section 31)
☐ Renew the coolant (Section 32)*

* Note: *This work is not included in the VW schedule and should not be required if the recommended VW G12 LongLife coolant antifreeze/inhibitor is used.*

Every 120 000 miles (180 000 km)

☐ Renew the timing belt, DOHC engines (Section 30)

Models using LongLife variable intervals

The following variable service intervals are only applicable to models using the LongLife intervals (shown in the vehicle Service Schedule booklet or on the Next Service sticker located on the driver's door pillar). The occurrence of the service on the display unit will depend on how the vehicle is being used (number of starts, length of journeys, vehicle speeds, brake pad wear, bonnet opening frequency, fuel consumption, oil level and oil temperature). For example, if a vehicle is being used under extreme driving conditions, the 'oil' service may occur at 10 000 miles, whereas, if the vehicle is being used under moderate driving conditions, it may occur at 20 000 miles. It is important to realise that this system is completely variable according to how the vehicle is being used, and therefore the service should be carried out when indicated on the display. When an OIL CHANGE SERVICE or INSPECTION SERVICE (01) is due, follow the relevant procedure described for the normal 'distance and time' intervals.

Every 250 miles (400 km) or weekly
- ☐ Refer to *Weekly checks*

OIL on display
- ☐ Renew the engine oil and filter (Section 3)

Note: *Frequent oil and filter changes are good for the engine. We recommend changing the oil at least once a year.*
- ☐ Check the front and rear brake pad thickness (Section 4)
- ☐ Reset the service interval display (Section 5)

01 on display or every 2 years, whichever comes first

In addition to the items listed above, carry out the following:
- ☐ Check the condition of the exhaust system and its mountings (Section 6)
- ☐ Check all underbonnet components and hoses for fluid and oil leaks (Section 7)
- ☐ Check the condition of the auxiliary drivebelt (Section 8)
- ☐ Check the coolant antifreeze concentration (Section 9)
- ☐ Check the brake hydraulic circuit for leaks and damage (Section 10)
- ☐ Check the headlight beam adjustment (Section 11)
- ☐ Renew the pollen filter element (Section 12)
- ☐ Check the manual transmission oil level (Section 13)
- ☐ Check the underbody protection for damage (Section 14)
- ☐ Check the condition of the driveshaft gaiters (Section 15)
- ☐ Check the steering and suspension components for condition and security (Section 16)
- ☐ Check the battery condition, security and electrolyte level (Section 17)
- ☐ Lubricate all hinges and locks (Section 18)
- ☐ Check the condition of the airbag unit(s) (Section 19)
- ☐ Check the operation of the windscreen/tailgate/ headlight washer system(s) (as applicable) (Section 20)

01 on display or every 2 years, whichever comes first (continued)
- ☐ Check the engine management self-diagnosis memory for faults (Section 21)
- ☐ Check the operation of the sunroof and lubricate the guide rails (Section 22)
- ☐ Carry out a road test and check exhaust emissions (Section 23)

Every 40 000 miles (60 000 km) or 4 years, whichever comes first
- ☐ Renew the air filter element (Section 24)
- ☐ Renew the spark plugs (Section 25)
- ☐ Check the condition of the auxiliary drivebelt (Section 26)
- ☐ Check the power steering hydraulic fluid level (Section 27)
- ☐ Renew the automatic transmission fluid (Section 28)
- ☐ Check the automatic transmission final drive oil level (Section 29)

Every 60 000 miles (90 000 km)
- ☐ Renew the timing belt, SOHC engines (Section 30)

Note: *For SOHC engines, VW specify timing belt inspection at the first 60 000 miles (90 000 km) and then every 20 000 miles (30 000 km), with the belt being renewed whenever it is considered necessary. However, if the vehicle is used mainly for short journeys, we recommend that this shorter renewal interval is adhered to. The belt renewal interval is very much up to the individual owner but, bearing in mind that severe engine damage will result if the belt breaks in use, we recommend the shorter interval.*

Every 2 years
- ☐ Renew the brake (and clutch) fluid (Section 31)
- ☐ Renew the coolant (Section 32)*

* Note: This work is not included in the VW schedule and should not be required if the recommended VW G12 LongLife coolant antifreeze/inhibitor is used.

Every 120 000 miles (180 000 km)
- ☐ Renew the timing belt, DOHC engines (Section 30)

Underbonnet view (typical) of a 1.8 litre 20-valve turbocharged model (code AWT)

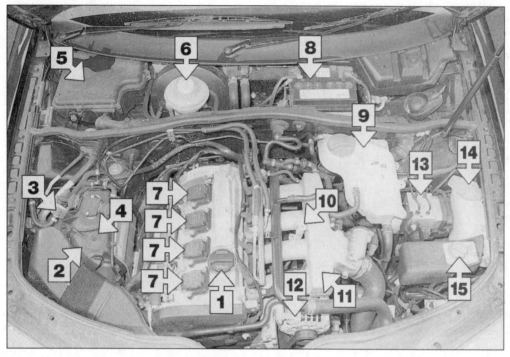

1 Engine oil filler cap
2 Air cleaner
3 Carbon canister solenoid valve
4 Airflow meter
5 Engine management ECM
6 Brake/clutch fluid reservoir
7 Ignition coils
8 Battery
9 Cooling system expansion tank
10 Engine oil level dipstick
11 Inlet manifold
12 Alternator
13 ABS unit
14 Washer fluid reservoir
15 Power steering fluid reservoir

Underbonnet view of a 2.0 litre model (code ALT)

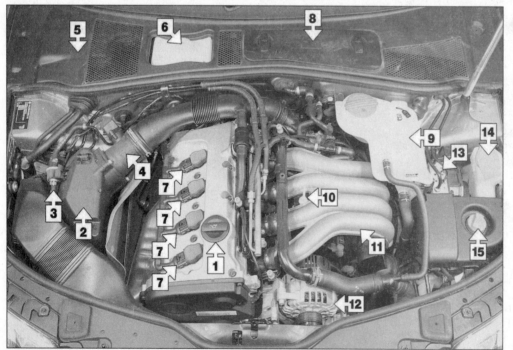

1 Engine oil filler cap
2 Air cleaner
3 Carbon canister solenoid valve
4 Airflow meter
5 Engine management ECM
6 Brake/clutch fluid reservoir
7 Ignition coils
8 Battery
9 Cooling system expansion tank
10 Engine oil level dipstick
11 Inlet manifold
12 Alternator
13 ABS unit
14 Washer fluid reservoir
15 Power steering fluid reservoir

Front underbody view of a 2.0 litre model (code ALT)

1 Exhaust front downpipe
2 Transmission mounting
3 Front suspension rear lower arm
4 Driveshaft
5 Anti-roll bar
6 Front suspension front lower arm
7 Engine mounting
8 Engine front torque arm
9 Engine sump oil drain plug
10 Power steering pump
11 Radiator bottom hose
12 Air conditioning compressor
13 Front subframe

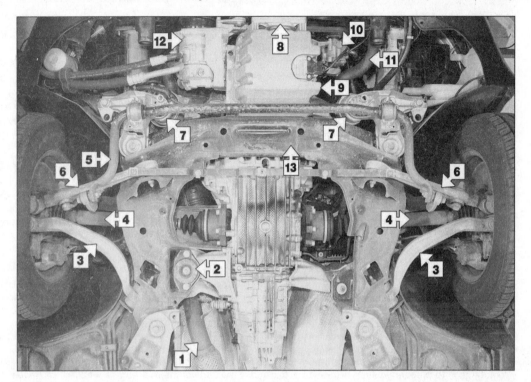

Rear underbody view

1 Intermediate exhaust pipe and silencer
2 Rear axle beam
3 Tail pipe and silencer
4 Fuel tank
5 Coil spring
6 Shock absorber strut

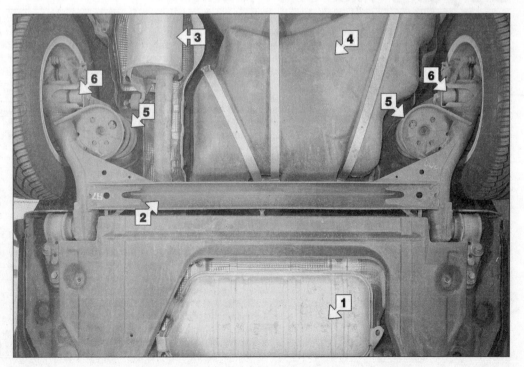

1 Introduction

This Chapter is designed to help the home mechanic maintain his/her vehicle for safety, economy, long life and peak performance.

The Chapter contains a master maintenance schedule, followed by Sections dealing specifically with each task in the schedule. Visual checks, adjustments, component renewal and other helpful items are included. Refer to the accompanying illustrations of the engine compartment and the underside of the vehicle for the locations of the various components.

Servicing your vehicle will provide a planned maintenance programme, which should result in a long and reliable service life. This is a comprehensive plan, so maintaining some items but not others will not produce the same results.

As you service your vehicle, you will discover that many of the procedures can – and should – be grouped together, because of the particular procedure being performed, or because of the proximity of two otherwise unrelated components to one another. For example, if the vehicle is raised for any reason, the exhaust can be inspected at the same time as the suspension and steering components.

The first step in this maintenance programme is to prepare yourself before the actual work begins. Read through all the Sections relevant to the work to be carried out, then make a list and gather all the parts and tools required. If a problem is encountered, seek advice from a parts specialist, or a dealer service department.

2 Regular maintenance

1 If, from the time the vehicle is new, the routine maintenance schedule is followed closely, and frequent checks are made of fluid levels and high-wear items, as suggested throughout this manual, the engine will be kept in relatively good running condition, and the need for additional work will be minimised.
2 It is possible that there will be times when the engine is running poorly due to the lack of regular maintenance. This is even more likely if a used vehicle, which has not received regular and frequent maintenance checks, is purchased. In such cases, additional work may need to be carried out, outside of the regular maintenance intervals.
3 If engine wear is suspected, a compression test (refer to the relevant Part of Chapter 2) will provide valuable information regarding the overall performance of the main internal components. Such a test can be used as a basis to decide on the extent of the work to be carried out. If, for example, a compression test indicates serious internal engine wear, conventional maintenance as described in this Chapter will not greatly improve the performance of the engine, and may prove a waste of time and money, unless extensive overhaul work is carried out first.
4 The following series of operations are those most often required to improve the performance of a generally poor-running engine:

Primary operations

a) Clean, inspect and test the battery (See 'Weekly checks').
b) Check all the engine-related fluids (See 'Weekly checks').
c) Check the condition and tension of the auxiliary drivebelt (Section 8).
d) Renew the spark plugs (Section 25).
e) Check the condition of the air filter, and renew if necessary (Section 24).
f) Check the condition of all hoses, and check for fluid leaks (Section 7).

5 If the above operations do not prove fully effective, carry out the following secondary operations:

Secondary operations

All items listed under Primary operations, plus the following:

a) Check the charging system (see Chapter 5A).
b) Check the ignition system (see Chapter 5B).
c) Check the fuel system (see Chapter 4A).
d) Renew the ignition HT leads (where applicable).

Every 5000 miles or 6 months

3 Engine oil and filter renewal

1 Frequent oil and filter changes are the most important maintenance procedures which can be undertaken by the DIY owner. As engine oil ages, it becomes diluted and contaminated, which leads to premature engine wear.
2 Before starting this procedure, gather all

3.3 The engine oil drain plug location on the sump

the necessary tools and materials. Also make sure that you have plenty of clean rags and newspapers handy, to mop up any spills. Ideally, the engine oil should be warm, as it will drain better, and more built-up sludge will be removed with it. Take care, however, not to touch the exhaust or any other hot parts of the engine when working under the vehicle. To avoid any possibility of scalding, and to protect yourself from possible skin irritants and other harmful contaminants in used engine oils, it is advisable to wear gloves when carrying out this work. Access to the underside of the vehicle is possible if it can be raised on a lift, driven onto ramps, or jacked up and supported on axle stands (see Jacking and vehicle support). Whichever method is chosen, make sure that the vehicle remains level, or if it is at an angle, that the drain plug is at the lowest point. With the vehicle raised, remove the engine compartment undershield.
3 Using a socket and wrench or a ring spanner, slacken the drain plug about half a turn. Position the draining container under the drain plug, then remove the plug completely (see Haynes Hint). Recover the sealing ring from the drain plug (see illustration).

4 Allow some time for the old oil to drain, noting that it may be necessary to reposition the container as the oil flow slows to a trickle.
5 After all the oil has drained, wipe off the drain plug with a clean rag, and fit a new sealing washer. Clean the area around the

Keep the drain plug pressed into the sump while unscrewing it by hand the last couple of turns. As the plug releases, move it away sharply so the stream of oil issuing from the sump runs into the container, not up your sleeve.

3.7 Unscrew the oil filter from the oil cooler

3.11a Remove the dipstick . . .

3.11b . . . then unscrew the oil filler cap

drain plug opening, and refit the plug. Tighten the plug securely.

6 If the filter is also to be renewed, move the container into position under the oil filter, which is located on the left-hand rear side of the cylinder block.

7 Using an oil filter removal tool if necessary, slacken the filter initially, then unscrew it by hand the rest of the way **(see illustration)**. Empty the oil in the filter into the container.

8 Use a clean rag to remove all oil, dirt and sludge from the filter sealing area on the engine. Check the old filter to make sure that the rubber sealing ring has not stuck to the engine. If it has, carefully remove it.

9 Apply a light coating of clean engine oil to the sealing ring on the new filter, then screw it into position on the engine. Tighten the filter firmly by hand only – **do not** use any tools.

10 Remove the old oil and all tools from under the car then refit the undershield and lower the car to the ground.

11 Remove the dipstick, then unscrew the oil filler cap from the cylinder head cover **(see illustrations)**. Fill the engine, using the correct grade and type of oil (see *Lubricants and fluids*). An oil can spout or funnel may help to reduce spillage. Pour in half the specified quantity of oil first, then wait a few minutes for the oil to settle in the sump. Continue adding oil a small quantity at a time until the level is up to the lower mark on the dipstick. Adding around 1.0 litre will bring the level up to the upper mark on the dipstick. Refit the filler cap.

12 Start the engine and run it at idle speed for a few minutes; check for leaks around the oil filter seal and the sump drain plug. Note that

there may be a few seconds delay before the oil pressure warning light goes out when the engine is started, as the oil circulates through the engine oil galleries and the new oil filter before the pressure builds up.

Caution: On models with a turbocharger, leave the engine idling until the oil pressure light goes out. Increasing the engine speed with the warning light on will damage the turbocharger.

13 Switch off the engine, and wait a few minutes for the oil to settle in the sump once more. With the new oil circulated and the filter completely full, recheck the level on the dipstick, and add more oil as necessary.

14 Dispose of the used engine oil safely, with reference to *General repair procedures* in the *Reference* section of this manual.

Every 10 000 miles, 12 months or OIL on display

4 Brake pad check

1 On some models, the outer brake pads can be checked without removing the wheels, by observing the brake pads through the holes in the wheels **(see illustration)**. If necessary, remove the wheel trim. The thickness of the pad lining must not be less than the dimension given in the Specifications.

2 If the outer pads are worn near their limits, it is worthwhile checking the inner pads as well. Apply the handbrake then jack up vehicle and support it on axle stands (see *Jacking and vehicle support*). Remove the roadwheels.

3 Use a steel rule to check the thickness of the brake pads (excluding the backing plate), and compare with the minimum thickness given in the Specifications **(see illustration)**.

4 For a comprehensive check, the brake pads should be removed and cleaned. The operation of the caliper can then also be checked, and the condition of the brake disc itself can be fully examined on both sides. Refer to Chapter 9.

5 If any pad's friction material is worn to the specified minimum thickness or less, *all four*

pads at the front or rear, as applicable, must be renewed as a set.

6 On completion of the check, refit the roadwheels and lower the vehicle to the ground.

5 Resetting the service interval display

1 After all necessary maintenance work has been completed, the service interval display must be reset. VW technicians use a special

4.1 The outer brake pads can be observed through the holes in the wheels

dedicated instrument to do this, and a print-out is then put in the vehicle service record. It is possible for the owner to reset the display as described in the following paragraphs, but note that the procedure will automatically reset the display to a 10 000 mile (15 000 km) interval. To continue with the 'variable' intervals which take into consideration the number of starts, length of journeys, vehicle speeds, brake pad wear, bonnet opening frequency, fuel consumption, oil level and oil temperature, the display must be reset by a VW dealership using the special dedicated instrument.

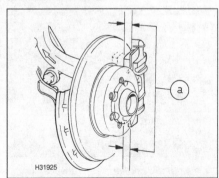

4.3 The thickness (a) of the brake pads must not be less than the specified amount

2 To reset the standard display manually, switch off the ignition, then press and hold down the trip reset button beneath the speedometer. Turn the digital clock reset knob clockwise, and the trip display will now show 'service - - -'. Depress the clock reset knob as required to alternate between individual services, however, do not zero the display otherwise incorrect readings will be shown.

3 To reset the LongLife display manually, switch off the ignition, then press and hold down the trip reset button beneath the speedometer. Switch on the ignition and release the reset button, and note that the relevant service will appear in the display. Turn the digital clock reset knob clockwise, and the display will now return to normal. Switch off the ignition to complete the resetting procedure. Do not zero the display otherwise incorrect readings will be shown.

Every 20 000 miles, 2 years or 01 on display

6 Exhaust system check

1 With the engine cold (at least an hour after the vehicle has been driven), check the complete exhaust system from the engine to the end of the tailpipe. The exhaust system is most easily checked with the vehicle raised on a hoist, or suitably supported on axle stands, so that the exhaust components are readily visible and accessible (see *Jacking and vehicle support*).

2 Check the exhaust pipes and connections for evidence of leaks, severe corrosion and damage. Make sure that all brackets and mountings are in good condition, and that all relevant nuts and bolts are tight. Leakage at any of the joints or in other parts of the system will usually show up as a black sooty stain in the vicinity of the leak.

3 Rattles and other noises can often be traced to the exhaust system, especially the brackets and mountings. Try to move the pipes and silencers. If the components are able to come into contact with the body or suspension parts, secure the system with new mountings. Otherwise separate the joints (if possible) and twist the pipes as necessary to provide additional clearance.

7 Hose and fluid leak check

1 Visually inspect the engine joint faces, gaskets and seals for any signs of water or oil leaks. Pay particular attention to the areas

A leak in the cooling system will usually show up as white- or rust-coloured deposits on the area adjoining the leak.

around the camshaft cover, cylinder head, oil filter and sump joint faces. Bear in mind that, over a period of time, some very slight seepage from these areas is to be expected – what you are really looking for is any indication of a serious leak. Should a leak be found, renew the offending gasket or oil seal by referring to the appropriate Chapters in this manual.

2 Also check the security and condition of all the engine-related pipes and hoses. Ensure that all cable-ties or securing clips are in place and in good condition. Clips which are broken or missing can lead to chafing of the hoses, pipes or wiring, which could cause more serious problems in the future.

3 Carefully check the radiator hoses and heater hoses along their entire length. Renew any hose which is cracked, swollen or deteriorated. Cracks will show up better if the hose is squeezed. Pay close attention to the hose clips that secure the hoses to the cooling system components. Hose clips can pinch and puncture hoses, resulting in cooling system leaks.

4 Inspect all the cooling system components (hoses, joint faces, etc) for leaks **(see Haynes Hint)**. Where any problems of this nature are found on system components, renew the component or gasket with reference to Chapter 3.

5 Where applicable, inspect the automatic transmission fluid cooler hoses for leaks or deterioration.

6 With the vehicle raised, inspect the petrol tank and filler neck for punctures, cracks and other damage. The connection between the filler neck and tank is especially critical. Sometimes a rubber filler neck or connecting hose will leak due to loose retaining clamps or deteriorated rubber.

7 Carefully check all rubber hoses and metal fuel lines leading away from the petrol tank. Check for loose connections, deteriorated hoses, crimped lines, and other damage. Pay particular attention to the vent pipes and hoses, which often loop up around the filler neck and can become blocked or crimped. Follow the lines to the front of the vehicle, carefully inspecting them all the way. Renew damaged sections as necessary.

8 From within the engine compartment, check the security of all fuel hose attachments and pipe unions, and inspect the fuel hoses and vacuum hoses for kinks, chafing and deterioration.

9 Where applicable, check the condition of the power steering fluid hoses and pipes.

8 Auxiliary drivebelt check

1 The main drivebelt drives the alternator, viscous coupling fan, and the power steering pump. Where air conditioning is fitted, a secondary drivebelt from the crankshaft pulley drives the air conditioning compressor.

2 For access to the drivebelts, apply the handbrake, then jack up the front of the vehicle and support it on axle stands (see *Jacking and vehicle support*). Remove the splash guard from under the engine, and where applicable remove the engine top cover as well.

3 Examine the auxiliary drivebelts along their entire length for damage and wear in the form of cuts and abrasions, fraying and cracking. The use of a mirror and possibly an electric torch will help, and the engine may be turned with a spanner on the crankshaft pulley in order to observe all areas of the belt **(see illustration)**.

4 If a drivebelt requires renewal, refer to Chapter 2A for the removal, refitting and adjustment procedure.

9 Antifreeze check

1 The cooling system should be filled with the recommended G12 antifreeze and corrosion protection fluid – **do not** mix this antifreeze with any other type. Over a period of time, the concentration of fluid may be reduced due to topping-up (this can be avoided by topping-up with the correct antifreeze mixture – see Specifications) or fluid loss. If loss of coolant has been evident, it is important to make the necessary repair before adding fresh fluid.

8.3 Checking the underside of the auxiliary drivebelt with a mirror

2 With the engine **cold**, carefully remove the cap from the expansion tank. If the engine is not completely cold, place a cloth rag over the cap before removing it, and remove it slowly to allow any pressure to escape.

3 Antifreeze checkers are available from car accessory shops. Draw some coolant from the expansion tank and observe how many plastic balls are floating in the checker. Usually, 2 or 3 balls must be floating for the correct concentration of antifreeze, but follow the manufacturer's instructions.

4 If the concentration is incorrect, it will be necessary to either withdraw some coolant and add antifreeze, or alternatively drain the old coolant and add fresh coolant of the correct concentration (see Section 32).

10 Brake hydraulic circuit check

1 Check the entire brake hydraulic circuit for leaks and damage. Start by checking the master cylinder in the engine compartment. At the same time, check the vacuum servo unit and ABS units for signs of fluid leakage.

2 Raise the front and rear of the vehicle and support it on axle stands (see *Jacking and vehicle support*). Check the rigid hydraulic brake lines for corrosion and damage. Also check the brake pressure regulator in the same manner.

3 At the front of the vehicle, check that the flexible hydraulic hoses to the calipers are not twisted or chafing on any of the surrounding suspension components. Turn the steering on full lock to make this check. Also check that the hoses are not brittle or cracked.

4 Lower the vehicle to the ground after making the checks.

11 Headlight beam adjustment

Halogen headlamps

1 Accurate adjustment of the headlight beam is only possible using optical beam setting equipment, and this work should therefore be carried out by a VAG dealer or suitably-equipped workshop.

2 For reference, the headlights can be adjusted using the adjuster screws, accessible at the top of each light unit (see Chapter 12).

3 Some models are equipped with an electrically-operated headlight beam adjustment system which is controlled through the switch in the facia. On these models, ensure that the switch is set to the basic 0 position before adjusting the headlight aim.

Electrical discharge headlights

4 The headlamp range is controlled dynamically by an electronic control unit which monitors the ride height of the vehicle by sensors fitted to the front and rear suspension.

12.3 Lift out the pollen filter

Beam adjustment can only be carried out using VW test equipment.

12 Pollen filter element renewal

1 The pollen filter is located on the bulkhead, in front of the windscreen – on RHD models it is on the left-hand side, and on LHD models it is on the right-hand side.

2 Pull up the rubber weatherstrip then lift the plastic lid from the air inlet plenum chamber cover.

3 Release the two retaining tabs, and lift out the pollen filter element **(see illustration)**. Note the airflow arrows on the element. Remove the element from the frame.

4 Fit the frame to the new element and locate it in the plenum chamber cover, making sure that the airflow arrows are pointing in the right direction.

5 Close the plastic lid, however, make sure it is fitted correctly, otherwise water may enter the filter or heater assembly.

13 Manual transmission oil level check

1 The oil filler/level plug is located on the left-hand side of the manual transmission, below the speedometer sender, and on some models it may be concealed by a heat shield **(see illustration)**. The plug may be either of

15.1 Check the condition of the driveshaft gaiters (arrowed)

13.1 The oil filler/level plug is located on the left-hand side of the manual transmission (arrowed)

17 mm Allen key type, or alternatively of multi-splined type.

2 Apply the handbrake, then jack up the front and rear of the vehicle and support it on axle stands (see *Jacking and vehicle support*). To ensure an accurate check, make sure that the vehicle is level.

3 Unscrew and remove the filler/level plug.

4 Check that the oil level is to the bottom lip of the filler hole.

5 If necessary, add the specified oil through the filler/level hole. If the level requires constant topping-up, check for leaks and repair.

6 Refit the plug and tighten to the specified torque, then lower the vehicle to the ground.

14 Underbody protection check

Raise and support the vehicle on axle stands (see *Jacking and vehicle support*). Using an electric torch or lead light, inspect the entire underside of the vehicle, paying particular attention to the wheel arches. Look for any damage to the flexible underbody coating, which may crack or flake off with age, leading to corrosion. Also check that the wheel arch liners are securely attached with any clips provided – if they come loose, dirt may get in behind the liners and defeat their purpose. If there is any damage to the underseal, or any corrosion, it should be repaired before the damage gets too serious.

15 Driveshaft gaiter check

1 With the vehicle raised and securely supported on stands, slowly rotate the roadwheel. Inspect the condition of the outer constant velocity (CV) joint rubber gaiters, squeezing the gaiters to open out the folds. Check for signs of cracking, splits or deterioration of the rubber, which may allow the grease to escape, and lead to water and grit entry into the joint. Also check the security and condition of the retaining clips. Repeat these checks on the inner joints **(see illustration)**. If any damage or deterioration is found, the gaiters should be renewed (see Chapter 8).

2 At the same time, check the general condition of the CV joints themselves by first holding the driveshaft and attempting to rotate the wheel. Repeat this check by holding the inner joint and attempting to rotate the driveshaft. Any appreciable movement indicates wear in the joints, wear in the driveshaft splines, or a loose driveshaft retaining nut.

16 Steering and suspension check

1 Raise the front and rear of the vehicle, and securely support it on axle stands (see *Jacking and vehicle support*).
2 Visually inspect the track rod end balljoint dust cover, the lower front suspension balljoint dust cover, and the steering rack-and-pinion gaiters for splits, chafing or deterioration. Any wear of these components will cause loss of lubricant, together with dirt and water entry, resulting in rapid deterioration of the balljoints or steering gear.
3 Check the power steering fluid hoses for chafing or deterioration, and the pipe and hose unions for fluid leaks. Also check for signs of fluid leakage under pressure from the steering gear rubber gaiters, which would indicate failed fluid seals within the steering gear.
4 Grasp the roadwheel at the 12 o'clock and 6 o'clock positions, and try to rock it **(see illustration)**. Very slight free play may be felt, but if the movement is appreciable, further investigation is necessary to determine the source. Continue rocking the wheel while an assistant depresses the footbrake. If the movement is now eliminated or significantly reduced, it is likely that the hub bearings are at fault. If the free play is still evident with the footbrake depressed, then there is wear in the suspension joints or mountings.
5 Now grasp the wheel at the 9 o'clock and 3 o'clock positions, and try to rock it as before. Any movement felt now may again be caused by wear in the hub bearings or the steering track rod balljoints. If the inner or outer balljoint is worn, the visual movement will be obvious.

16.4 Check for wear in the hub bearings by grasping the wheel and trying to rock it

6 Using a large screwdriver or flat bar, check for wear in the suspension mounting bushes by levering between the relevant suspension component and its attachment point. Some movement is to be expected as the mountings are made of rubber, but excessive wear should be obvious. Also check the condition of any visible rubber bushes, looking for splits, cracks or contamination of the rubber.
7 With the car standing on its wheels, have an assistant turn the steering wheel back-and-forth about an eighth of a turn each way. There should be very little, if any, lost movement between the steering wheel and roadwheels. If this is not the case, closely observe the joints and mountings previously described, but in addition, check the steering column universal joints for wear, and the rack-and-pinion steering gear itself.
8 Check for any signs of fluid leakage around the front suspension struts and rear shock absorber. Should any fluid be noticed, the suspension strut or shock absorber is defective internally, and should be renewed. **Note:** *Suspension struts/shock absorbers should always be renewed in pairs on the same axle to ensure correct vehicle handling.*
9 The efficiency of the suspension strut/shock absorber may be checked by bouncing the vehicle at each corner. Generally speaking, the body will return to its normal position and stop after being depressed. If it rises and returns on a rebound, the suspension strut/shock absorber is probably suspect. Examine also the suspension strut/shock absorber upper and lower mountings for any signs of wear.

17 Battery check

1 The battery is located beneath a cover at the rear of the engine compartment. Undo the clips and remove the cover.
2 Check that both battery terminals and all the fuse holder connections are securely attached and are free from corrosion.
3 Check the battery casing for signs of damage or cracking and check the battery retaining clamp bolt is securely tightened. If the battery casing is damaged in any way the battery must be renewed (see Chapter 5A).
4 If the vehicle is not fitted with a sealed-for-life maintenance-free battery, check the electrolyte level is between the MAX and MIN level markings on the battery casing. If topping-up is necessary, remove the battery (see Chapter 5A) from the vehicle then remove the cell caps/cover (as applicable). Using distilled water, top the electrolyte level of each cell up to the MAX level mark then securely refit the cell caps/cover. Ensure the battery has not been overfilled then refit the battery to the vehicle (see Chapter 5A).
5 On completion of the check, refit the cover.

18 Hinge and lock lubrication

1 Lubricate the hinges of the bonnet, doors and tailgate with a light general-purpose oil. Similarly, lubricate all latches, locks and lock strikers. At the same time, check the security and operation of all the locks, adjusting them if necessary (see Chapter 11).
2 Lightly lubricate the bonnet release mechanism and cable with a suitable grease.

19 Airbag unit check

Inspect the exterior condition of the airbag(s) for signs of damage or deterioration. If an airbag shows signs of damage, it must be renewed (see Chapter 12). Note that it is not permissible to attach any stickers to the surface of the airbag, as this may affect the deployment of the unit.

20 Windscreen/tailgate/ headlight washer system check

1 Check that each of the washer jet nozzles are clear and that each nozzle provides a strong jet of washer fluid.
2 The tailgate jet should be aimed to spray at the centre of the screen, using a pin.
3 The windscreen washer nozzles should be aimed slightly above the centre of the screen. Use a small screwdriver to turn the jet eccentric.
4 The headlight inner jet should be aimed slightly above the horizontal centreline of the headlight, and the outer jet should be aimed slightly below the centreline. VW technicians use a special tool to adjust the headlight jet after pulling the jet out onto its stop.
5 Especially during the winter months, make sure that the washer fluid frost concentration is sufficient.

21 Engine management self-diagnosis memory fault check

This work should be carried out by a VW dealer or diagnostic specialist using special equipment. The diagnostic socket is located beneath the right-hand side of the facia on RHD models, and beneath the left-hand side on LHD models.

22 Sunroof check and lubrication

1 Check the operation of the sunroof, and leave it in the fully open position.

2 Wipe clean the guide rails on each side of the sunroof opening, then apply lubricant to them. VW recommend lubricant spray G 052 778.

23 Road test and exhaust emissions check

Instruments and electrical equipment

1 Check the operation of all instruments and electrical equipment.
2 Make sure that all instruments read correctly, and switch on all electrical equipment in turn, to check that it functions properly.

Steering and suspension

3 Check for any abnormalities in the steering, suspension, handling or road feel.
4 Drive the vehicle, and check that there are no unusual vibrations or noises which may indicate wear in the driveshafts, wheel bearings, etc.
5 Check that the steering feels positive, with no excessive sloppiness, or roughness, and check for any suspension noises when cornering and driving over bumps.

Drivetrain

6 Check the performance of the engine, clutch (where applicable), gearbox/transmission and driveshafts.

7 Listen for any unusual noises from the engine, clutch and gearbox/transmission.
8 Make sure that the engine runs smoothly when idling, and that there is no hesitation when accelerating.
9 Check that, where applicable, the clutch action is smooth and progressive, that the drive is taken up smoothly, and that the pedal travel is not excessive. Also listen for any noises when the clutch pedal is depressed.
10 On manual gearbox models, check that all gears can be engaged smoothly without noise, and that the gear lever action is smooth and not abnormally vague or notchy.
11 On automatic transmission models, make sure that all gearchanges occur smoothly, without snatching, and without an increase in engine speed between changes. Check that all the gear positions can be selected with the vehicle at rest. If any problems are found, they should be referred to a VW dealer.
12 Listen for a metallic clicking sound from the front of the vehicle, as the vehicle is driven slowly in a circle with the steering on full-lock. Carry out this check in both directions. If a clicking noise is heard, this indicates wear in a driveshaft joint, in which case renew the joint if necessary.

Braking system

13 Make sure that the vehicle does not pull to one side when braking, and that the wheels do not lock when braking hard.

14 Check that there is no vibration through the steering when braking.
15 Check that the handbrake operates correctly without excessive movement of the lever, and that it holds the vehicle stationary on a slope.
16 Test the operation of the brake servo unit as follows. With the engine off, depress the footbrake four or five times to exhaust the vacuum. Hold the brake pedal depressed, then start the engine. As the engine starts, there should be a noticeable 'give' in the brake pedal as vacuum builds-up. Allow the engine to run for at least two minutes, and then switch it off. If the brake pedal is depressed now, it should be possible to detect a hiss from the servo as the pedal is depressed. After about four or five applications, no further hissing should be heard, and the pedal should feel considerably harder.
17 Under controlled emergency braking, the pulsing of the ABS unit must be felt at the footbrake pedal.

Exhaust emissions check

18 Although not part of the manufacturer's maintenance schedule, this check will normally be carried out on a regular basis according to the country the vehicle is operated in. Currently in the UK, exhaust emissions testing is included as part of the annual MOT test after the vehicle is 3 years old. In Germany the test is made when the vehicle is 3 years old, then repeated every 2 years.

Every 40 000 miles or 4 years

24 Air filter element renewal

1 Remove the air cleaner cover and air duct, then prise open the retaining clips and lift the upper cover from the air cleaner body. If necessary, temporarily remove the carbon canister solenoid valve from the cover **(see illustrations)**. Note that the airflow meter is attached to the upper cover.
2 Remove the air filter element, noting which way round it is fitted **(see illustration)**.
3 Wipe clean the main body, then fit the new air filter, making sure it is the correct way round.
4 Refit the upper cover and secure with the retaining clips.

25 Spark plug renewal

1 The correct functioning of the spark plugs is vital for the correct running and efficiency of the engine. It is essential that the plugs fitted are appropriate for the engine and if the engine is in good condition, the spark plugs should not need attention between scheduled

24.1a Remove the air cleaner cover . . .

24.1b . . . and air duct . . .

24.1c . . . then prise open the retaining clips, lift the cover . . .

24.2 . . . and remove the air filter element

25.4 Removing a spark plug

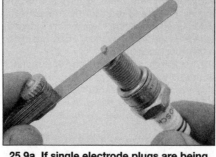

25.9a If single electrode plugs are being fitted, check the electrode gap using a feeler gauge . . .

With other spark plugs, the gap should be set to the value given by the manufacturer.

9 To set the gap, measure it with a feeler blade and then bend open, or closed, the outer plug electrode until the correct gap is achieved. The centre electrode should never be bent, as this may crack the insulator and cause plug failure, if nothing worse. If using feeler blades, the gap is correct when the appropriate-size blade is a firm sliding fit **(see illustrations)**.

10 Special spark plug electrode gap adjusting tools are available from most motor accessory shops, or from some spark plug manufacturers **(see illustration)**.

11 Before fitting the spark plugs, check that the threaded connector sleeves are tight, and that the plug exterior surfaces and threads are clean. It's often difficult to screw in new spark plugs without cross-threading them – this can be avoided using a piece of rubber hose **(see Haynes Hint)**.

12 Remove the rubber hose (if used), and tighten the plug to the specified torque using the spark plug socket and a torque wrench. Refit the remaining spark plugs in the same manner.

13 Reconnect the HT leads and where necessary refit the ignition coils with reference to Chapter 5B.

14 Refit the engine top cover.

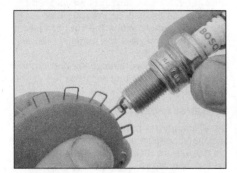

25.9b . . . or a wire gauge . . .

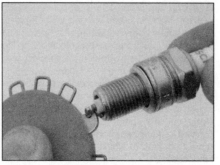

25.10 . . . and if necessary adjust the gap by bending the electrode

renewal intervals. Spark plug cleaning is rarely necessary, and should not be attempted unless specialised equipment is available, as damage can easily be caused to the firing ends.

2 First remove the engine top cover. On DOHC engines, remove the ignition HT coils (see Chapter 5B). On SOHC engines, if the marks on the original-equipment spark plug (HT) leads cannot be seen, mark the leads 1 to 4, to correspond to the cylinder the lead serves (No 1 cylinder is at the timing belt end of the engine). Pull the leads from the plugs by

HAYNES HiNT

It is very often difficult to insert spark plugs into their holes without cross-threading them. To avoid this possibility, fit a short length of rubber hose over the end of the spark plug. The flexible hose acts as a universal joint to help align the plug with the plug thread, the hose will slip on the spark plug, preventing thread damage to the aluminium cylinder head.

gripping the end fitting, not the lead, otherwise the lead connection may be fractured.

3 It is advisable to remove the dirt from the spark plug recesses using a clean brush, vacuum cleaner or compressed air before removing the plugs, to prevent dirt dropping into the cylinders.

4 Unscrew the plugs using a spark plug spanner, suitable box spanner or a deep socket and extension bar **(see illustration)**. Keep the socket aligned with the spark plug – if it is forcibly moved to one side, the ceramic insulator may be broken off. As each plug is removed, examine it as follows.

5 If the insulator nose of the spark plug is clean and white, with no deposits, this is indicative of a weak mixture or too hot a plug (a hot plug transfers heat away from the electrode slowly, a cold plug transfers heat away quickly).

6 If the tip and insulator nose are covered with hard black-looking deposits, then this is indicative that the mixture is too rich. Should the plug be black and oily, then it is likely that the engine is fairly worn, as well as the mixture being too rich.

7 If the insulator nose is covered with light tan to greyish-brown deposits, then the mixture is correct and it is likely that the engine is in good condition.

8 The spark plug electrode gap is of considerable importance as, if it is too large or too small, the size of the spark and its efficiency will be seriously impaired. On engines fitted with multi-electrode spark plugs, it is recommended that the plugs are renewed rather attempting to adjust the gaps.

26 Auxiliary drivebelt check and renewal

1 Refer to Section 8 for the checking procedure. If a drivebelt requires renewal, refer to Chapter 2A for the removal and refitting procedure.

27 Power steering hydraulic fluid level check

1 Refer to Chapter 10.

28 Automatic transmission fluid renewal

Note: *Although VW make no specific recommendation to renew the automatic transmission fluid, we consider it prudent to change the fluid every 40 000 miles or four years whichever occurs first.*

1 Apply the handbrake, then jack up the front of the vehicle and support it on axle stands (see *Jacking and vehicle support*). Remove the engine undershield. **Note:** *For an accurate fluid level check, VW technicians use an electronic tester which is plugged into the transmission electronic system, and which determines that the temperature of the fluid is between 35°C and 40°C. In view of this, it is recommended that the vehicle is taken to a VW dealer to have the work done. The following procedure*

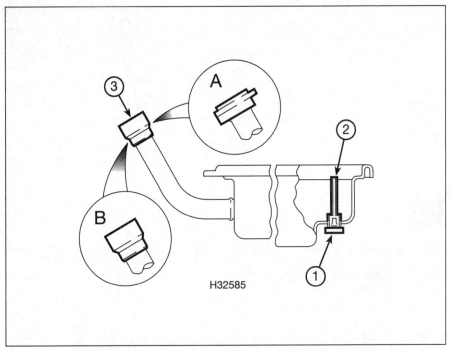

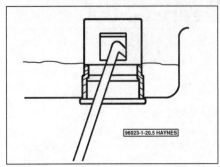

28.15 On 01V transmissions, the nozzle of the tool being used to add fluid must pass through the window in the deflector cap

28.3 Oil pan components on the 01N automatic transmission

1	Inspection plug	3 Sealing cap and plug	B Later sealing cap
2	Overflow pipe	A Early sealing cap

Note: Sealing cap B must be renewed after removal

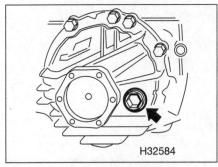

29.1 On automatic transmissions, the final drive filler/level plug is located on the left-hand side (arrowed)

is given on the understanding that the level is checked by a VW dealer on completion.

2 Note that the transmission must be refilled from below the vehicle, so make sure that the vehicle is supported in a level position.

01N 4-speed transmission

3 Position a suitable container beneath the transmission. Wipe clean the oil pan, then unscrew the inspection plug, followed by the overflow pipe, from the bottom of the oil pan **(see illustration)**. Allow the fluid to drain into the container.

4 Refit the overflow pipe and tighten to the specified torque.

5 Remove the sealing cap and plug from the filling tube attached to the side of the oil pan. **Note:** The later sealing cap and plug should be renewed whenever removed.

6 Add fluid to the oil pan until it runs out of the overflow pipe.

7 With P selected, run the engine at idling speed until it reaches normal temperature. If necessary add more fluid until it runs out of the overflow pipe.

8 Apply the footbrake pedal, then select each position with the selector lever, pausing for about 3 seconds in each position. Return the selector to position P.

9 At this stage, the VW technician connects the tester to confirm that the fluid temperature is between 35°C and 40°C. **Note:** If the fluid level is checked when the temperature is too low, overfilling will occur. If the fluid level is

checked when the temperature is too high, underfilling will occur.

10 With the engine still running at idle speed, allow any excess fluid to run out of the overflow pipe.

11 Switch off the engine, then refit the inspection plug together with a new seal, and tighten to the specified torque.

12 Fit a new sealing cap and plug to the filling tube.

01V 5-speed transmission

13 Position a suitable container beneath the transmission. Wipe clean the pan, then unscrew the drain plug located on the right-hand side of the pan. Allow the fluid to drain into the container.

14 Fit a new seal on the drain plug and tighten to the specified torque.

15 Unscrew the inspection plug at the rear of the pan, and add fluid until it runs out of the hole **(see illustration)**.

16 With P selected, run the engine at idling speed until it reaches normal temperature. If necessary add more fluid until it runs out of the inspection hole.

17 Apply the footbrake pedal, then select each position with the selector lever, pausing for about 3 seconds in each position. Return the selector to position P.

18 At this stage, the VW technician connects the tester to confirm that the fluid temperature is between 35°C and 40°C. **Note:** If the fluid level is checked when the temperature is too

low, overfilling will occur. If the fluid level is checked when the temperature is too high, underfilling will occur.

19 With the engine still running at idle speed, allow any excess fluid to run out of the overflow pipe.

20 Switch off the engine, then refit the inspection plug together with a new seal, and tighten to the specified torque.

All models

21 Lower the vehicle to the ground.

29 Automatic transmission final drive oil level check

1 The final drive oil filler/level plug is located on the left-hand side of the automatic transmission, behind the left-hand driveshaft inner joint **(see illustration)**. Apply the handbrake, then jack up the front of the vehicle and support it on axle stands (see *Jacking and vehicle support*). Remove the engine undershield. To ensure an accurate check, make sure that the vehicle is level.

2 Unscrew and remove the filler/level plug and check that the oil level is on the bottom lip of the filler hole. If necessary, add the specified oil through the filler/level hole. If the level requires constant topping-up, check for leaks and repair.

3 Refit the plug and tighten to the specified torque, then lower the vehicle to the ground.

Every 60 000 miles

30 Timing belt check and renewal

Inspection

1 Release the clips and remove the upper timing belt cover (refer to Chapter 2A).

2 Using a spanner or socket on the crankshaft pulley bolt, turn the engine slowly in a clockwise direction. **Do not** turn the engine on the camshaft bolt.

3 Check the complete length of the timing belt for signs of cracking, tooth separation, fraying, side glazing, and oil or grease contamination. Use a torch and mirror to check the underside of the belt.

4 If there is any evidence of wear or damage as described in the last paragraph, the timing belt **must** be renewed. A broken belt will cause major damage to the engine.

5 After making the check, refit the upper timing belt cover and remove the spanner/ socket from the crankshaft pulley bolt.

Renewal

6 Refer to Chapter 2A for details.

Every 2 years

31 Brake (and clutch) fluid renewal

⚠ *Warning: Brake hydraulic fluid can harm your eyes and damage painted surfaces, so use extreme caution when handling and pouring it. Do not use fluid that has been standing open for some time, as it absorbs moisture from the air. Excess moisture can cause a dangerous loss of braking effectiveness.*

1 The procedure is similar to that for the bleeding of the hydraulic system as described in Chapter 9, except that the brake fluid reservoir should be emptied by syphoning, using a clean poultry baster or similar before starting, and allowance should be made for the old fluid to be expelled when bleeding a section of the circuit. Since the clutch hydraulic system on manual gearbox models also uses fluid from the brake system reservoir, it should also be bled at the same time by referring to Chapter 6, Section 2.

2 Working as described in Chapter 9, open the first bleed screw in the sequence, and pump the brake pedal gently until nearly all the old fluid has been emptied from the master cylinder reservoir.

HAYNES HiNT *Old hydraulic fluid is often much darker in colour than the new, making it easy to distinguish the two.*

3 Top-up to the MAX level with new fluid, and continue pumping until only the new fluid remains in the reservoir, and new fluid can be seen emerging from the bleed screw. Tighten the screw, and top the reservoir level up to the MAX level line.

4 Work through all the remaining bleed screws in the sequence until new fluid can be seen at all of them. Be careful to keep the master cylinder reservoir topped-up to above the MIN level at all times, or air may enter the system and greatly increase the length of the task.

5 When the operation is complete, check that all bleed screws are securely tightened, and that their dust caps are refitted. Wash off all traces of spilt fluid, and recheck the master cylinder reservoir fluid level.

6 On models with a manual transmission unit, once the brake fluid has been changed the clutch fluid should also be renewed. Referring to Chapter 6, bleed the clutch until new fluid is seen to be emerging from the slave cylinder bleed screw, keeping the master cylinder fluid level above the MIN level line at all times to prevent air entering the system. Once the new fluid emerges, securely tighten the bleed screw then disconnect and remove the bleeding equipment. Securely refit the dust cap then wash off all traces of spilt fluid.

7 On all models, ensure the master cylinder fluid level is correct (see *Weekly checks*) and thoroughly check the operation of the brakes and (where necessary) clutch before taking the car on the road.

32 Coolant renewal

Note: *This work is not included in the VW schedule and should not be required if the recommended VW G12 LongLife coolant antifreeze/inhibitor is used. However, if standard antifreeze/inhibitor is used, the work should be carried out at the recommended interval.*

⚠ *Warning: Wait until the engine is cold before starting this procedure. Do not allow antifreeze to come in contact with your skin, or with the painted surfaces of the vehicle. Rinse off spills immediately with plenty of water. Never leave antifreeze lying around in an open container, or in a puddle in the driveway or on the garage floor. Children and pets are attracted by its sweet smell, but antifreeze can be fatal if ingested.*

Cooling system draining

1 With the engine completely cold, cover the expansion tank cap with a wad of rag, and slowly turn the cap anti-clockwise to relieve the pressure in the cooling system (a hissing sound will normally be heard). Wait until any pressure remaining in the system is released, then continue to turn the cap until it can be removed.

2 Where necessary, release the fasteners and remove the engine lower splash shield. Position a suitable container beneath the radiator bottom hose connection, then pull out the retaining clip and ease the hose from the radiator stub. If the hose joint has not been disturbed for some time, it will be necessary to gently manipulate the hose to break the joint. Do not use excessive force, or the radiator stub could be damaged. Allow the coolant to drain into the container. Note that the radiator is equipped with a drain tap, but this can only be accessed with the front bumper removed.

3 On engine codes AWT and AZM, unscrew the thermostat housing retaining bolts (refer to Chapter 3), and remove the thermostat to drain the engine block. Allow the coolant to drain. Refit the thermostat and housing using a new seal, and tighten the retaining bolts to the specified torque.

4 If the coolant has been drained for a reason other than renewal, then provided it is clean, it can be re-used, but this is not recommended.

5 Once all the coolant has drained, reconnect the hose to the radiator and ensure the retaining clip is properly seated.

Cooling system flushing

6 If coolant renewal has been neglected, or if the antifreeze mixture has become diluted, then in time, the cooling system may gradually lose efficiency, as the coolant passages become restricted due to rust, scale deposits, and other sediment. Flushing the system clean can restore the cooling system efficiency.

7 The radiator should be flushed independently of the engine, to avoid unnecessary contamination.

Radiator flushing

8 To flush the radiator, disconnect the top and bottom hoses and any other relevant hoses from the radiator, with reference to Chapter 3.

9 Insert a garden hose into the radiator top inlet. Direct a flow of clean water through the radiator, and continue flushing until clean water emerges from the radiator bottom outlet.

10 If after a reasonable period, the water still does not run clear, the radiator can be flushed with a good proprietary cooling system cleaning agent. It is important that their manufacturer's instructions are followed carefully. If the contamination is particularly bad, insert the hose in the radiator bottom outlet, and reverse-flush the radiator.

Engine flushing

11 To flush the engine, remove the thermostat as described in Chapter 3, then temporarily refit the thermostat cover.

12 With the top and bottom hoses disconnected from the radiator, insert a garden hose into the radiator top hose. Direct a clean flow of water through the engine, and continue flushing until clean water emerges from the radiator bottom hose.

13 On completion of flushing, refit the thermostat and reconnect the hoses with reference to Chapter 3.

Cooling system filling

14 Before attempting to fill the cooling system, make sure that all hoses and clips are in good condition, and that the clips/connections are secure. Note that an antifreeze mixture must be used all year round, to prevent corrosion of the engine components (see following sub-Section).

15 Slacken the clip and withdraw the heater unit supply hose from its bulkhead stub (see Chapter 3) until the bleed hole at the top of the hose is clear of the surface of the stub; do not disconnect the hose from the stub completely.

16 Remove the securing screws and detach the expansion tank from the engine compartment. Raise it approximately 100 mm above the engine compartment and support it there on a block of wood or using a length of wire.

17 Remove the expansion tank filler cap, and fill the system by slowly pouring the coolant into the expansion tank to prevent airlocks from forming.

18 If the coolant is being renewed, begin by pouring in a couple of litres of water, followed by the correct quantity of antifreeze, then top-up with more water.

19 Continue filling until coolant starts to run from the bleed hole in the heater hose. When this happens, refit the hose and tighten the clip securely.

20 Once the level in the expansion tank starts to rise, squeeze the radiator top and bottom hoses to help expel any trapped air in the system. Once all the air is expelled, top-up the coolant level to the MAX mark, refit the expansion tank cap, then refit the expansion tank to the bodywork.

21 Start the engine and run it at a fast idle for about three minutes. After this, allow the engine to idle normally until the bottom hose becomes hot.

22 Check for leaks, particularly around disturbed components. Check the coolant level in the expansion tank, and top-up if necessary. Note that the system must be cold before an accurate level is indicated in the expansion tank. If the expansion tank cap is removed while the engine is still warm, cover the cap with a thick cloth, and unscrew the cap slowly to gradually relieve the system pressure (a hissing sound will normally be heard). Wait until any pressure remaining in the system is released, then continue to turn the cap until it can be removed. Never remove the cap when the engine is still hot.

Antifreeze mixture

Caution: VW specify the use of G12 antifreeze (red in colour). DO NOT mix this with any other type of antifreeze, as severe engine damage may result. If the coolant visible in the expansion tank is brown in colour, then the cooling system may have been topped-up with coolant containing the wrong type of antifreeze. If you are unsure of the type of antifreeze used, or if you suspect that mixing may have occurred, the best course of action is to drain, flush and refill the cooling system.

23 If the recommended VW coolant is not being used, the antifreeze should always be renewed at the specified intervals. This is necessary not only to maintain the antifreeze properties, but also to prevent corrosion which would otherwise occur as the corrosion inhibitors become progressively less effective.

24 The quantity of antifreeze and levels of protection are indicated in the Specifications.

25 Before adding antifreeze, the cooling system should be completely drained, preferably flushed, and all hoses checked for condition and security.

26 After filling with antifreeze, a label should be attached to the expansion tank, stating the type and concentration of antifreeze used, and the date installed. Any subsequent topping-up should be made with the same type and concentration of antifreeze.

27 Do not use engine antifreeze in the windscreen/tailgate/headlight washer system, as it will cause damage to the vehicle paintwork.

Notes

Chapter 1 Part B:
Routine maintenance and servicing – diesel models

Contents

	Section number
Air filter element renewal	28
Airbag unit check	23
Antifreeze check	13
Automatic transmission final drive oil level check	33
Automatic transmission fluid renewal	32
Auxiliary drivebelt check and renewal	30
Auxiliary drivebelt check	12
Battery check	21
Brake (and clutch) fluid renewal	36
Brake hydraulic circuit check	14
Brake pad check	5
Coolant renewal	37
Driveshaft gaiter check	19
Engine management self-diagnosis memory fault check	25
Engine oil and filter renewal	3
Exhaust system check	8
Fuel filter renewal (vehicles using high sulphur diesel fuel)	11
Fuel filter renewal (vehicles using standard diesel fuel)	29
Fuel filter water draining (vehicles using high sulphur fuel)	4

	Section number
Fuel filter water draining (vehicles using standard fuel)	10
Headlight beam adjustment	15
Hinge and lock lubrication	22
Hose and fluid leak check	9
Introduction	1
Manual transmission oil level check	17
Pollen filter element renewal	16
Power steering hydraulic fluid level check	31
Regular maintenance	2
Resetting the service interval display	7
Road test and exhaust emissions check	27
Steering and suspension check	20
Sunroof check and lubrication	26
Timing belt and tensioning roller renewal (2000 to 2003 models)	34
Timing belt and tensioning roller renewal (2004-on models)	35
Timing belt check	6
Underbody protection check	18
Windscreen/tailgate/headlight washer system check	24

Degrees of difficulty

Easy, suitable for novice with little experience	**Fairly easy,** suitable for beginner with some experience	**Fairly difficult,** suitable for competent DIY mechanic	**Difficult,** suitable for experienced DIY mechanic	**Very difficult,** suitable for expert DIY or professional 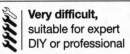

Lubricants and fluids. . . . .   Refer to the end of *Weekly checks* on page 0•18

Capacities

Engine oil (including filter)
All models . . . .   4.5 litres

Cooling system
All models. . . . .   6.0 litres

Transmission
Manual transmission:
  012/01W. . . . .   2.25 litres
  01E/0A1 . . . .   2.5 litres
Automatic transmission fluid:
  4-speed transmission:
    Initial filling . . . .   5.5 litres
    Fluid change. . . . .   3.5 litres
  5-speed transmission:
    Initial filling . . . .   9.0 litres
    Fluid change. . . . .   2.6 litres
Automatic transmission final drive:
  4-speed transmission. . . . .   1.0 litre
  5-speed transmission. . . . .   0.75 litres

Power-assisted steering
All models. . . . .   1.5 litres (approx)

Fuel tank
All models. . . . .   62 litres (approx)

Washer reservoirs
Models with headlight washers . . . .   5.5 litres
Models without headlight washers. . . . .   3.0 litres

Cooling system

Antifreeze mixture:
  40% antifreeze . . . .   Protection down to -25°C
  50% antifreeze . . . .   Protection down to -35°C

Engine

Timing belt wear limit . . . .   22.0 mm wide

Cooling system

Antifreeze mixture:
  40% antifreeze . . . .   Protection down to -25°C
  50% antifreeze . . . .   Protection down to -35°C
Note: *Refer to antifreeze manufacturer for latest recommendations.*

Brakes

Front brake pad friction material minimum thickness . . . .   2.0 mm
Rear brake pad friction material minimum thickness. . . . .   2.0 mm

Auxiliary drivebelt

Tension adjustment:
  Main drivebelt. . . . .   Automatically adjusted
  Air conditioning compressor drivebelt . . . .   Apply a torque of 25 Nm to the hexagon on the tensioner body

Torque wrench settings

	Nm	lbf ft
Automatic transmission:		
Drain plug (01V)	40	30
Final drive oil filler/level plug.	25	18
Inspection plug:		
01N.	15	11
01V.	80	59
Overflow pipe (01N)	2	1
Fuel filter top centre bolt (pre-01/2002 models).	8	6
Manual transmission filler/level plug	25	18
Oil filter cap	25	18
Power steering pump mounting.	25	18
Roadwheel bolts.	120	89
Sump drain plug.	30	22

Maintenance schedule

The maintenance intervals in this manual are provided with the assumption that you, not the dealer, will be carrying out the work. These are the minimum intervals recommended by us for vehicles driven daily. If you wish to keep your vehicle in peak condition at all times, you may wish to perform some of these procedures more often. We encourage frequent maintenance, since it enhances the efficiency, performance and resale value of your vehicle.

When the vehicle is new, it should be serviced by a dealer service department, in order to preserve the factory warranty.

All models are equipped with a service interval display indicator in the instrument panel. Every time the engine is started the panel will illuminate for approximately 20 seconds with service information. With the standard non-variable display, the service intervals are in accordance with specific distances and time periods. With the LongLife display, the service interval is variable according to the number of starts, length of journeys, vehicle speeds, brake pad wear, bonnet opening frequency, fuel consumption, oil level and oil temperature, however the vehicle **must** be serviced at least every two years. At a distance of 2000 miles (3000 km)

before the next service is due, 'Service in 2000 miles' (or '3000 km') will appear at the bottom of the speedometer, and this figure will reduce in steps of 100 units as the vehicle is used. Once the service interval has been reached, the display will flash 'Service' or 'Service Now'. Note that if the variable (LongLife) service interval is being used, the engine must **only** be filled with the recommended **long-life** engine oil (see *Recommended lubricants and fluids*).

After completing a service, VW technicians use a special instrument to reset the service display to the next service interval, and a print-out is put in the vehicle service record. The display can be reset by the owner as described in Section 6, but note that for models using the 'LongLife' interval, the procedure will automatically reset the display to the 10 000 miles/15 000 km 'distance' interval. To have the display reset to the 'variable' (LongLife) interval, it is necessary to take the vehicle to a VW dealer who will use a special instrument to encode the on-board computer.

Timing belt maintenance

The following schedules give the manufacturer's current recommended

intervals for the replacement of the timing belt and of its tensioning roller. Note that the manufacturer states specifically that it is NOT necessary to renew these components at earlier than the recommended mileage. However, in view of the fact that severe engine damage will result if the belt breaks, it is strongly recommended that the timing belt renewal interval is reduced to 40 000 miles or 4 years, whichever is the sooner, on vehicles which are subjected to intensive use, i.e., mainly short journeys or a lot of stop-start driving. The actual belt renewal interval is very much up to the individual owner, but shorter intervals of this sort are in line with the advice offered by many professionals.

At the very least, examine carefully the timing belt whenever the opportunity arises, renewing it if there is any doubt about its condition. Check also the sprockets for signs of wear or damage and ensure that the tensioner and idler pulleys rotate smoothly on their bearings; renew any worn or damaged components. **Note:** *It is considered good practice by many professional mechanics to renew tensioner and idler pulley assemblies as a matter of course, whenever the timing belt is renewed.*

Models using distance and time intervals

Note: *The following service intervals are only applicable to models with a PR number of QG0 or QG2 (shown in the vehicle Service Schedule booklet or on the Next Service sticker located on the driver's door pillar).*

Every 250 miles (400 km) or weekly

☐ Refer to *Weekly checks*

Every 5000 miles (7500 km) or 6 months

☐ Renew the engine oil and filter (Section 3)

Note: *Frequent oil and filter changes are good for the engine. We recommend changing the oil at the mileage specified here, or at least twice a year if the mileage covered is less.*

Every 10 000 miles (15 000 km) or 12 months, whichever comes first – OIL on display

In addition to the items listed above, carry out the following:

☐ Fuel filter water draining* (Section 4)
☐ Check the front and rear brake pad thickness (Section 5)
☐ Check the timing belt for wear (Section 6)
☐ Reset the service interval display (Section 7)

* *Only when using high sulphur diesel fuel not conforming to DIN EN 590 or when using RME fuel (diester).*

Every 20 000 miles (30 000 km) or 2 years, whichever comes first – 01 on display

In addition to the items listed above, carry out the following:

☐ Check the condition of the exhaust system and its mountings (Section 8)
☐ Check all underbonnet components and hoses for fluid and oil leaks (Section 9)
☐ Fuel filter water draining* (Section 10)
☐ Renew the fuel filter** (Section 11)
☐ Check the condition of the auxiliary drivebelt (Section 12)
☐ Check the coolant antifreeze concentration (Section 13)
☐ Check the brake hydraulic circuit for leaks and damage (Section 14)
☐ Check the headlight beam adjustment (Section 15)
☐ Renew the pollen filter element (Section 16)
☐ Check the manual transmission oil level (Section 17)
☐ Check the underbody protection for damage (Section 18)
☐ Check the condition of the driveshaft gaiters (Section 19)
☐ Check the steering and suspension components for condition and security (Section 20)
☐ Check the battery condition, security and electrolyte level (Section 21)

Every 20 000 miles (30 000 km) or 2 years, whichever comes first – 01 on display (continued)

☐ Lubricate all hinges and locks (Section 22)
☐ Check the condition of the airbag unit(s) (Section 23)
☐ Check the operation of the windscreen/tailgate/ headlight washer system(s) (as applicable) (Section 24)
☐ Check the engine management self-diagnosis memory for faults (Section 25)
☐ Check the operation of the sunroof and lubricate the guide rails (Section 26)
☐ Carry out a road test and check exhaust emissions (Section 27)

* *Only when using diesel fuel conforming to DIN EN 590.*
** *Only when using diesel fuel not conforming to DIN EN 590 or when using RME fuel (diester).*

Every 40 000 miles (60 000 km) or 4 years, whichever comes first

☐ Renew the air filter element (Section 28)
☐ Renew the fuel filter* (Section 29)
☐ Check and renewal of the auxiliary drivebelt (Section 30)
☐ Check the power steering hydraulic fluid level (Section 31)
☐ Renew the automatic transmission fluid (Section 32)
☐ Check the automatic transmission final drive oil level (Section 33)

* *Only when using diesel fuel conforming to DIN EN 590.*

Every 60 000 miles (90 000 km)

☐ Renew the timing belt and tensioning roller, 2000 to 2003 models (Section 34)

Every 80 000 miles (120 000 km)

☐ Renew the timing belt, 2004-on models (Section 34)

Every 2 years

☐ Renew the brake (and clutch) fluid (Section 36)
☐ Renew the coolant* (Section 37)

* **Note:** *This work is not included in the VW schedule and should not be required if the recommended VW G12 LongLife coolant antifreeze/inhibitor is used.*

Every 160 000 miles (240 000 km)

☐ Renew the timing belt and tensioning roller, 2004-on models (Section 35)

Models using LongLife variable intervals

The LongLife variable service intervals are only applicable to models with a PR number of QG1 (shown in the vehicle Service Schedule booklet or on the Next Service sticker located on the driver's door pillar). The occurrence of the service on the display unit will depend on how the vehicle is being used (number of starts, length of journeys, vehicle speeds, brake pad wear, bonnet opening frequency, fuel consumption, oil level and oil temperature). For example, if a vehicle is being used under extreme driving conditions, the 'oil' service may occur at 10 000 miles, whereas, if the vehicle is being used under moderate driving conditions, it may occur at 20 000 miles. It is important to realise that this system is completely variable according to how the vehicle is being used, and therefore the service should be carried out when indicated on the display. When an OIL CHANGE SERVICE or INSPECTION SERVICE (01) is due, follow the relevant procedure described for the normal 'distance and time' intervals

Every 250 miles (400 km) or weekly
- ☐ Refer to *Weekly checks*

OIL on display
- ☐ Renew the engine oil and filter (Section 3)

Note: *Frequent oil and filter changes are good for the engine. We recommend changing the oil at least once a year.*
- ☐ Fuel filter water draining* (Section 4)
- ☐ Check the front and rear brake pad thickness (Section 5)
- ☐ Check the timing belt for wear (Section 6)
- ☐ Reset the service interval display (Section 7)

* *Only when using high sulphur diesel fuel not conforming to DIN EN 590 or when using RME fuel (diester).*

01 on display or every 2 years, whichever comes first

In addition to the items listed above, carry out the following:
- ☐ Check the condition of the exhaust system and its mountings (Section 8)
- ☐ Check all underbonnet components and hoses for fluid and oil leaks (Section 9)
- ☐ Fuel filter water draining* (Section 10)
- ☐ Renew the fuel filter** (Section 11)
- ☐ Check the condition of the auxiliary drivebelt (Section 12)
- ☐ Check the coolant antifreeze concentration (Section 13)
- ☐ Check the brake hydraulic circuit for leaks and damage (Section 14)
- ☐ Check the headlight beam adjustment (Section 15)
- ☐ Renew the pollen filter element (Section 16)
- ☐ Check the manual transmission oil level (Section 17)
- ☐ Check the underbody protection for damage (Section 18)
- ☐ Check the condition of the driveshaft gaiters (Section 19)
- ☐ Check the steering and suspension components for condition and security (Section 20)
- ☐ Check the battery condition, security and electrolyte level (Section 21)
- ☐ Lubricate all hinges and locks (Section 22)
- ☐ Check the condition of the airbag unit(s) (Section 23)
- ☐ Check the operation of the windscreen/tailgate/headlight washer system(s) (as applicable) (Section 24)

01 on display or every 2 years, whichever comes first (continued)
- ☐ Check the engine management self-diagnosis memory for faults (Section 25)
- ☐ Check the operation of the sunroof and lubricate the guide rails (Section 26)
- ☐ Carry out a road test and check exhaust emissions (Section 27)

* *Only when using diesel fuel conforming to DIN EN 590.*
** *Only when using diesel fuel not conforming to DIN EN 590 or when using RME fuel (diester).*

Every 40 000 miles (60 000 km) or 4 years, whichever comes first
- ☐ Renew the air filter element (Section 28)
- ☐ Renew the fuel filter* (Section 29)
- ☐ Check and renewal of the auxiliary drivebelt (Section 30)
- ☐ Check the power steering hydraulic fluid level (Section 31)
- ☐ Renew the automatic transmission fluid (Section 32)
- ☐ Check the automatic transmission final drive oil level (Section 33)

* *Only when using diesel fuel conforming to DIN EN 590.*

Every 60 000 miles (90 000 km)
- ☐ Renew the timing belt and tensioning roller, 2000 to 2003 models (Section 34)

Every 80 000 miles (120 000 km)
- ☐ Renew the timing belt, 2004-on models (Section 35)

Every 2 years
- ☐ Renew the brake (and clutch) fluid (Section 36)
- ☐ Renew the coolant* (Section 37)

* **Note:** *This work is not included in the VW schedule and should not be required if the recommended VW G12 LongLife coolant antifreeze/inhibitor is used.*

Every 160 000 miles (240 000 km)
- ☐ Renew the timing belt and tensioning roller, 2004-on models (Section 35)

Underbonnet view of a diesel model

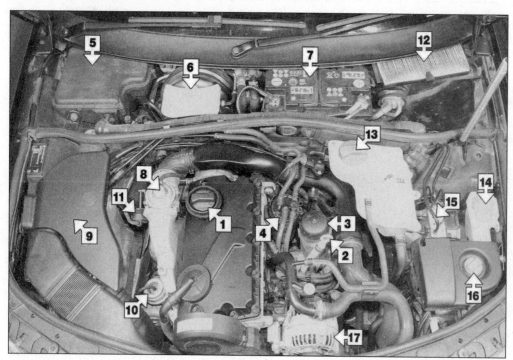

1   Engine oil filler cap
2   Engine oil level dipstick
3   Oil filter
4   Fuel filter
5   Engine management ECM
6   Brake fluid reservoir
7   Battery
8   EGR valve
9   Air cleaner
10 Turbocharger boost
    pressure control valve
11 Turbocharger and control
    unit
12 Pollen filter
13 Coolant expansion tank
14 Washer fluid reservoir
15 ABS unit
16 Power steering fluid
    reservoir
17 Alternator

Front underbody view of a diesel model

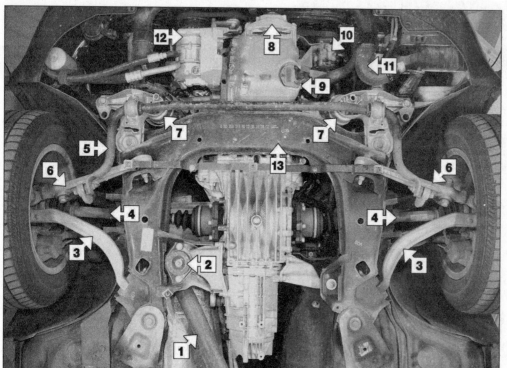

1   Exhaust front downpipe
2   Transmission mounting
3   Front suspension rear
    lower arm
4   Driveshaft
5   Anti-roll bar
6   Front suspension front
    lower arm
7   Engine mounting
8   Engine front torque arm
9   Engine sump oil drain
    plug
10 Power steering pump
11 Radiator bottom hose
12 Air conditioning
    compressor
13 Front subframe

Rear underbody view

1 Intermediate exhaust pipe and silencer
2 Rear axle beam
3 Tail pipe and silencer
4 Fuel tank
5 Coil spring
6 Shock absorber strut

Maintenance procedures

1 Introduction

This Chapter is designed to help the home mechanic maintain his/her vehicle for safety, economy, long life and peak performance.

The Chapter contains a master maintenance schedule, followed by Sections dealing specifically with each task in the schedule. Visual checks, adjustments, component renewal and other helpful items are included. Refer to the accompanying illustrations of the engine compartment and the underside of the vehicle for the locations of the various components.

Servicing your vehicle will provide a planned maintenance programme, which should result in a long and reliable service life. This is a comprehensive plan, so maintaining some items but not others will not produce the same results.

As you service your vehicle, you will discover that many of the procedures can – and should – be grouped together, because of the particular procedure being performed, or because of the proximity of two otherwise unrelated components to one another. For example, if the vehicle is raised for any reason, the exhaust can be inspected at the same time as the suspension and steering components.

The first step in this maintenance programme is to prepare yourself before the actual work begins. Read through all the Sections relevant to the work to be carried out, then make a list and gather all the parts and tools required. If a problem is encountered, seek advice from a parts specialist, or a dealer service department.

2 Regular maintenance

1 If, from the time the vehicle is new, the routine maintenance schedule is followed closely, and frequent checks are made of fluid levels and high-wear items, as suggested throughout this manual, the engine will be kept in relatively good running condition, and the need for additional work will be minimised.

2 It is possible that there will be times when the engine is running poorly due to the lack of regular maintenance. This is even more likely if a used vehicle, which has not received regular and frequent maintenance checks, is purchased. In such cases, additional work may need to be carried out, outside of the regular maintenance intervals.

3 If engine wear is suspected, a compression test (refer to the relevant Part of Chapter 2B) will provide valuable information regarding the overall performance of the main internal components. Such a test can be used as a basis to decide on the extent of the work to be carried out. If, for example, a compression test indicates serious internal engine wear, conventional maintenance as described in this Chapter will not greatly improve the performance of the engine, and may prove a waste of time and money, unless extensive overhaul work is carried out first.

4 The following series of operations are those most often required to improve the performance of a generally poor-running engine:

Primary operations

a) Clean, inspect and test the battery (See 'Weekly checks').
b) Check all the engine-related fluids (See 'Weekly checks').
c) Drain the water from the fuel filter (Section 4).
d) Check the condition and tension of the auxiliary drivebelt (Section 12).
e) Check the condition of the air filter, and renew if necessary (Section 28).
f) Check the condition of all hoses, and check for fluid leaks (Section 9).

5 If the above operations do not prove fully effective, carry out the following secondary operations:

Secondary operations

All items listed under Primary operations, plus the following:

a) Check the charging system (see Chapter 5A).
b) Check the preheating system (see Chapter 5C).
c) Renew the fuel filter (Section 11 or 29) and check the fuel system (see Chapter 4B).

Every 5000 miles or 6 months

3 Engine oil and filter renewal

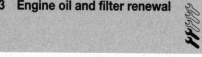

1 Frequent oil and filter changes are the most important preventative maintenance procedures which can be undertaken by the DIY owner. As engine oil ages, it becomes diluted and contaminated, which leads to premature engine wear.

2 Before starting this procedure, gather all the necessary tools and materials. Also make

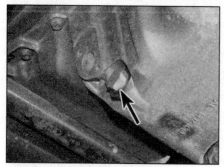

3.3 Sump drain plug

Keep the drain plug pressed into the sump while unscrewing it by hand the last couple of turns. As the plug releases, move it away sharply so the stream of oil issuing from the sump runs into the container, not up your sleeve.

sure that you have plenty of clean rags and newspapers handy, to mop-up any spills. Ideally, the engine oil should be warm, as it will drain better, and more built-up sludge will be removed with it. Take care, however, not to touch the exhaust or any other hot parts of the engine when working under the vehicle. To avoid any possibility of scalding, and to protect yourself from possible skin irritants and other harmful contaminants in used engine oils, it is advisable to wear gloves when carrying out this work. Access to the underside of the vehicle will be greatly improved if it can be raised on a lift, driven onto ramps, or jacked up and supported on axle stands (see *Jacking and vehicle support*). Whichever method is chosen, make sure that the vehicle remains level, or if it is at an angle, that the drain plug is at the lowest point. Undo the retaining screws and remove the engine undershield(s), then also remove the engine top cover where applicable.

3 Slacken the sump drain plug about half a turn. Position the draining container under the drain plug, then remove the plug completely **(see illustration and Haynes Hint)**. Recover the sealing ring from the drain plug.

4 Allow some time for the old oil to drain, noting that it may be necessary to reposition the container as the oil flow slows to a trickle.

5 After all the oil has drained, wipe off the drain plug with a clean rag, and fit a new sealing washer. Clean the area around the

drain plug opening, and refit the plug. Tighten the plug securely.

6 Remove the engine top cover(s) to gain access to the oil filter housing. Place absorbent cloths around the filter housing to catch any spilt oil.

7 Unscrew the oil filter housing cap, located to the left of the cylinder head. Although there is a special VW tool to undo the cap, a strap wrench is a suitable alternative. Lift the filter element from the housing, and discard the two O-rings **(see illustrations)**.

8 Wipe clean the inside of the oil filter housing and cap. Insert the new filter element into the housing. Note that the filter element is marked TOP on one end **(see illustration)**.

9 Fit the new O-rings, screw the cap into the housing, and tighten it to the specified torque.

10 Remove the old oil and all tools from under the car then refit the undershield(s) and lower the car to the ground. Also refit the engine top cover.

11 Remove the dipstick, then unscrew the oil filler cap from the cylinder head cover. Fill the engine, using the correct grade and type of oil (see *Lubricants and fluids*). An oil can spout or funnel may help to reduce spillage. Pour in half the specified quantity of oil first **(see illustrations)**, then wait a few minutes for the oil to run to the sump (see *Weekly checks*). Continue adding oil a small quantity at a time until the level is up to the maximum mark on the dipstick. Refit the filler cap.

3.7a If the special tool is not available, use a strap wrench to unscrew the oil filter cap

3.7b Remove the oil filter cap and discard the filter . . .

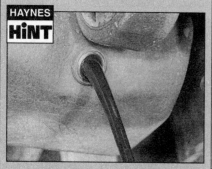

3.7c . . . then remove the upper . . .

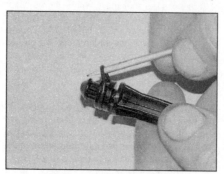

3.7d . . . and lower O-rings

3.8 Fit the oil filter element with the end marked TOP uppermost

12 Start the engine and run it for a few minutes; check for leaks around the oil filter cap and the sump drain plug. Note that there may be a few seconds delay before the oil pressure warning light goes out when the engine is started, as the oil circulates through the engine oil galleries and the new oil filter (where fitted) before the pressure builds-up.

⚠️ **Warning: Do not increase the engine speed above idling while the oil pressure light is illuminated, as considerable damage can be caused to the turbocharger.**

13 Switch off the engine, and wait a few minutes for the oil to settle in the sump once more. With the new oil circulated and the filter completely full, recheck the level on the dipstick, and add more oil as necessary.

14 Dispose of the used engine oil safely, with reference to *General repair procedures* in the *Reference* section of this manual.

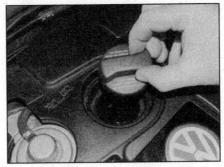

3.11a Unscrew the oil filler cap . . .

3.11b . . . pour in half the specified quantity of oil first, wait, then add the rest

Every 10 000 miles or OIL on display

4 Fuel filter water draining (vehicles using high sulphur fuel)

Note: *At this interval only when using high sulphur diesel fuel not conforming to DIN EN 590 or when using RME fuel (diester). This fuel is not available in the UK.*

1 Periodically, the water collected from the fuel by the filter unit must be drained out.

2 The fuel filter is located on the left-hand side of the engine **(see illustration)**. First remove the engine top cover, and place cloth rags around the area beneath the filter unit.

3 On pre-01/2002 models, unscrew the bolt from the centre of the filter unit, and position the upper part to one side leaving the hoses connected. The fuel filter on 01/2002-on models incorporates a control valve in its head, however, there is no requirement to remove this when draining the water.

Caution: Do not allow diesel fuel to contact any of the coolant hoses.

4 Position a container below the filter unit to catch escaping fuel, and fit a temporary hose onto the drain valve at the base of the filter.

5 Unscrew the drain valve at the base of the filter unit **(see illustration)**, until fuel starts to run out into the container. Keep the valve open until about 100 cc of fuel has been collected.

6 Close the drain valve, remove the drain hose, and wipe off any surplus fuel from the nozzle.

7 On pre-01/2002 models, fit the upper part of the filter and tighten the retaining bolt.

8 Remove the container and rags, then run the engine at idle and check around the fuel filter for fuel leaks.

9 Raise the engine speed to about 2000 rpm several times to purge air from the system, then stop the engine.

10 Check the filter for leaks, then refit the engine top cover.

5 Brake pad check

1 On some models, the outer brake pads can be checked without removing the wheels, by observing the brake pads through the holes in the wheels **(see illustration)**. If necessary, remove the wheel trim. The thickness of the pad lining must not be less than the dimension given in the Specifications.

4.2 Fuel filter (01/2002-on model)

5.1 The outer brake pads can be observed through the holes in the wheels

2 If the outer pads are worn near their limits, it is worthwhile checking the inner pads as well. Apply the handbrake then jack up vehicle and support it on axle stands (see *Jacking and vehicle support*). Remove the roadwheels.

3 Use a steel rule to check the thickness of the brake pads (excluding the backing plate), and compare with the minimum thickness given in the Specifications **(see illustration)**.

4 For a comprehensive check, the brake pads should be removed and cleaned. The operation of the caliper can then also be

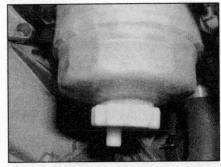

4.5 Unscrew the water drain tap on the bottom of the filter

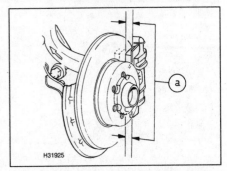

5.3 The thickness (a) of the brake pads must not be less than the specified amount

checked, and the condition of the brake disc itself can be fully examined on both sides. Refer to Chapter 9.

5 If any pad's friction material is worn to the specified minimum thickness or less, *all four pads at the front or rear, as applicable, must be renewed as a set.*

6 On completion of the check, refit the roadwheels and lower the vehicle to the ground.

6 Timing belt check

Note: *Although this does not form part of the VW maintenance schedule, it is recommended for vehicles completing short journeys or a lot of stop/starting.*

1 Release the clips and remove the upper timing belt cover (refer to Chapter 2B).

2 Using vernier calipers, measure the width of the timing belt where it is located on the camshaft sprocket, and compare with the wear limits in the Specifications. If the wear limit has been reached, the timing belt **must** be renewed.

3 Using a spanner or socket on the crankshaft pulley bolt, turn the engine slowly in a clockwise direction. **Do not** turn the engine on the camshaft bolt.

4 Check the complete length of the timing belt for signs of cracking, tooth separation, fraying, side glazing, and oil or grease contamination. Use an electric torch and mirror to check the underside of the belt.

5 If there is any evidence of wear or damage as described in the last paragraph, the timing belt **must** be renewed. A broken belt will cause major damage to the engine.

6 After making the check, refit the upper timing belt cover and remove the spanner/socket from the crankshaft pulley bolt.

7 Resetting the service interval display

1 After all necessary maintenance work has been completed, the service interval display must be reset. VW technicians use a special dedicated instrument to do this, and a print-out is then put in the vehicle service record. It is possible for the owner to reset the display as described in the following paragraphs, but note that the procedure will automatically reset the display to a 10 000 mile (15 000 km) interval. To continue with the 'variable' intervals which take into consideration the number of starts, length of journeys, vehicle speeds, brake pad wear, bonnet opening frequency, fuel consumption, oil level and oil temperature, the display must be reset by a VW dealership using the special dedicated instrument.

2 To reset the standard display manually, switch off the ignition, then press and hold down the trip reset button beneath the speedometer. Turn the digital clock reset knob clockwise, and the trip display will now show 'service - - -'. Depress the clock reset knob as required to alternate between individual services, however, do not zero the display otherwise incorrect readings will be shown.

3 To reset the LongLife display manually, switch off the ignition, then press and hold down the trip reset button beneath the speedometer. Switch on the ignition and release the reset button, and note that the relevant service will appear in the display. Turn the digital clock reset knob clockwise, and the display will now return to normal. Switch off the ignition to complete the resetting procedure. Do not zero the display otherwise incorrect readings will be shown.

Every 20 000 miles, 2 years or 01 on display

8 Exhaust system check

1 With the engine cold (at least an hour after the vehicle has been driven), check the complete exhaust system from the engine to the end of the tailpipe. The exhaust system is most easily checked with the vehicle raised on a hoist, or suitably supported on axle stands, so that the exhaust components are readily visible and accessible (see *Jacking and vehicle support*).

2 Check the exhaust pipes and connections for evidence of leaks, severe corrosion and damage. Make sure that all brackets and

A leak in the cooling system will usually show up as white- or rust-coloured deposits on the area adjoining the leak.

mountings are in good condition, and that all relevant nuts and bolts are tight. Leakage at any of the joints or in other parts of the system will usually show up as a black sooty stain in the vicinity of the leak.

3 Rattles and other noises can often be traced to the exhaust system, especially the brackets and mountings. Try to move the pipes and silencers. If the components are able to come into contact with the body or suspension parts, secure the system with new mountings. Otherwise separate the joints (if possible) and twist the pipes as necessary to provide additional clearance.

9 Hose and fluid leak check

1 Visually inspect the engine joint faces, gaskets and seals for any signs of water or oil leaks. Pay particular attention to the areas around the camshaft cover, cylinder head, oil filter and sump joint faces. Bear in mind that, over a period of time, some very slight seepage from these areas is to be expected – what you are really looking for is any indication of a serious leak. Should a leak be found, renew the offending gasket or oil seal by referring to the appropriate Chapters in this manual.

2 Also check the security and condition of all the engine-related pipes and hoses. Ensure that all cable-ties or securing clips are in place and in good condition. Clips which are broken or missing can lead to chafing of the hoses, pipes or wiring, which could cause more serious problems in the future.

3 Carefully check the radiator hoses and heater hoses along their entire length. Renew any hose which is cracked, swollen or deteriorated. Cracks will show up better if the hose is squeezed. Pay close attention to the hose clips that secure the hoses to the cooling system components. Hose clips can pinch and puncture hoses, resulting in cooling system leaks.

4 Inspect all the cooling system components (hoses, joint faces, etc) for leaks **(see Haynes Hint)**. Where any problems of this nature are found on system components, renew the component or gasket with reference to Chapter 3.

5 Where applicable, inspect the automatic transmission fluid cooler hoses for leaks or deterioration.

6 With the vehicle raised, inspect the petrol tank and filler neck for punctures, cracks and other damage. The connection between the filler neck and tank is especially critical. Sometimes a rubber filler neck or connecting hose will leak due to loose retaining clamps or deteriorated rubber.

7 Carefully check all rubber hoses and metal fuel lines leading away from the petrol tank. Check for loose connections, deteriorated hoses, crimped lines, and other damage. Pay particular attention to the vent pipes and hoses, which often loop up around the filler neck and can become blocked or crimped.

11.3 Undo the fuel filter central bolt (arrowed)

11.4 Loosen the fuel filter clamp screw

11.7a Release the clip . . .

Follow the lines to the front of the vehicle, carefully inspecting them all the way. Renew damaged sections as necessary.

8 From within the engine compartment, check the security of all fuel hose attachments and pipe unions, and inspect the fuel hoses and vacuum hoses for kinks, chafing and deterioration.

9 Where applicable, check the condition of the power steering fluid hoses and pipes.

10 Fuel filter water draining (vehicles using standard fuel)

Note: *At this interval only when using diesel fuel conforming to DIN EN 590 (standard fuel in the UK).*

Refer to Section 4.

11 Fuel filter renewal (vehicles using high sulphur diesel fuel)

Note: *At this interval only when using diesel fuel not conforming to DIN EN 590 or when using RME fuel (diester). This fuel is not available in the UK.*

1 The fuel filter is located on the left-hand side of the engine. First remove the engine top cover, and place cloth rags around the area beneath the filter unit.

2 Position a container underneath the filter unit and pad the surrounding area with rags to absorb any fuel that may be spilt.

Pre-01/2002 models

3 Unscrew the central bolt and position the upper part of the filter to one side leaving the hoses connected **(see illustration)**.

4 Slacken the clamp bolt and pull the filter upwards and out of the clamp **(see illustration)**.

Caution: Do not allow diesel fuel to contact any of the coolant hoses.

5 Fill the new filter with diesel fuel, and slide it into the clamp. Tighten the clamp screw securely.

6 Refit the upper part of the filter, and tighten the retaining bolt to the specified torque.

01/2002-on models

7 At the top of the filter unit, release the clip and lift out the control valve, leaving the fuel hoses attached to it **(see illustrations)**.

8 Slacken the hose clips and pull the fuel supply and delivery hoses from the ports on the top of the filter unit. If crimp-type clips are fitted, cut them off using snips, and use equivalent size worm-drive clips on refitting. Note the fitted position of each hose, to aid correct refitting later.

Caution: Be prepared for an amount of fuel loss.

9 Slacken the securing screw and raise the filter out of its retaining bracket **(see illustrations)**.

10 Fit a new fuel filter into the retaining bracket and tighten the securing screw.

11 Refit the control valve to the top of the filter and insert the retaining clip.

12 Reconnect the fuel supply and delivery hoses, using the notes made during removal – note the fuel flow arrow markings next to each port. Where crimp-type hoses were originally fitted, use equivalent size worm-drive clips on refitting **(see illustration)**.

All models

13 Start and run the engine at idle, then check around the fuel filter for fuel leaks. **Note:** *It may take a few seconds of cranking before the engine starts.*

14 Raise the engine speed to about 2000 rpm several times, then allow the engine to idle again.

15 Remove the collecting container and rags, then refit the engine top cover.

11.7b . . . and lift out the control valve, leaving the fuel hoses attached to it

11.9a Loosen the securing screw . . .

11.9b . . . and raise the filter out of its retaining bracket

11.12 Reconnect the fuel supply and delivery hoses

12.3 Checking the underside of the auxiliary drivebelt with a mirror

12 Auxiliary drivebelt check

1 The main drivebelt drives the alternator, viscous coupling fan, and the power steering pump. Where air conditioning is fitted, a secondary drivebelt from the crankshaft pulley drives the air conditioning compressor.

2 For access to the drivebelts, apply the handbrake, then jack up the front of the vehicle and support it on axle stands (see *Jacking and vehicle support*). Remove the splash guard from under the engine, and where applicable remove the engine top cover as well.

3 Examine the auxiliary drivebelts along their entire length for damage and wear in the form of cuts and abrasions, fraying and cracking. The use of a mirror and possibly an electric torch will help, and the engine may be turned with a spanner on the crankshaft pulley in order to observe all areas of the belt **(see illustration)**.

4 If a drivebelt requires renewal, refer to Chapter 2B for the removal, refitting and adjustment procedure.

13 Antifreeze check

1 The cooling system should be filled with the recommended G12 antifreeze and corrosion protection fluid – **do not** mix this antifreeze with any other type. Over a period of time, the concentration of fluid may be reduced due to topping-up (this can be avoided by topping-up with the correct antifreeze mixture – see Specifications) or fluid loss. If loss of coolant has been evident, it is important to make the necessary repair before adding fresh fluid.

2 With the engine **cold**, carefully remove the cap from the expansion tank. If the engine is not completely cold, place a cloth rag over the cap before removing it, and remove it slowly to allow any pressure to escape.

3 Antifreeze checkers are available from car accessory shops. Draw some coolant from the expansion tank and observe how many plastic balls are floating in the checker. Usually, 2 or 3 balls must be floating for the correct concentration of antifreeze, but follow the manufacturer's instructions.

4 If the concentration is incorrect, it will be necessary to either withdraw some coolant and add antifreeze, or alternatively drain the old coolant and add fresh coolant of the correct concentration (see Section 37).

14 Brake hydraulic circuit check

1 Check the entire brake hydraulic circuit for leaks and damage. Start by checking the master cylinder in the engine compartment. At the same time, check the vacuum servo unit and ABS units for signs of fluid leakage.

2 Raise the front and rear of the vehicle and support it on axle stands (see *Jacking and vehicle support*). Check the rigid hydraulic brake lines for corrosion and damage. Also check the brake pressure regulator in the same manner.

3 At the front of the vehicle, check that the flexible hydraulic hoses to the calipers are not twisted or chafing on any of the surrounding suspension components. Turn the steering on full lock to make this check. Also check that the hoses are not brittle or cracked.

4 Lower the vehicle to the ground after making the checks.

15 Headlight beam adjustment

Halogen headlamps

1 Accurate adjustment of the headlight beam is only possible using optical beam setting equipment, and this work should therefore be carried out by a VW dealer or suitably-equipped workshop.

2 For reference, the headlights can be adjusted using the adjuster screws, accessible at the top of each light unit (see Chapter 12).

3 Some models are equipped with an electrically-operated headlight beam adjustment system which is controlled through the switch in the facia. On these models, ensure that the switch is set to the basic 0 position before adjusting the headlight aim.

Electrical discharge headlights

4 The headlamp range is controlled dynamically by an electronic control unit which monitors the ride height of the vehicle by sensors fitted to the front and rear suspension. Beam adjustment can only be carried out using VW test equipment.

16 Pollen filter element renewal

1 The pollen filter is located on the bulkhead, in front of the windscreen – on RHD models it is on the left-hand side, and on LHD models it is on the right-hand side.

2 Pull up the rubber weatherstrip then lift the plastic lid from the air inlet plenum chamber cover.

3 Release the two retaining tabs, and lift out the pollen filter element **(see illustration)**. Note the airflow arrows on the element. Remove the element from the frame.

4 Fit the frame to the new element and locate it in the plenum chamber cover, making sure that the airflow arrows are pointing in the right direction.

5 Close the plastic lid, however, make sure it is fitted correctly, otherwise water may enter the filter or heater assembly.

17 Manual transmission oil level check

1 The oil filler/level plug is located on the left-hand side of the manual transmission, below the speedometer sender, and on some models it may be concealed by a heat shield **(see illustration)**. The plug may be either of 17 mm Allen key type, or alternatively of multi-splined type.

2 Apply the handbrake, then jack up the front and rear of the vehicle and support it on axle stands (see *Jacking and vehicle support*). To ensure an accurate check, make sure that the vehicle is level.

3 Unscrew and remove the filler/level plug.

16.3 Lift out the pollen filter

17.1 The oil filler/level plug is located on the left-hand side of the manual transmission (arrowed)

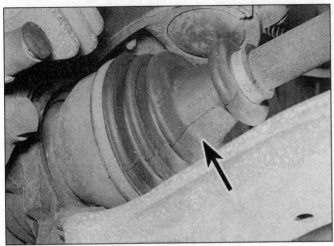

19.1 Check the condition of the driveshaft gaiters (arrowed)

20.4 Check for wear in the hub bearings by grasping the wheel and trying to rock it

4 Check that the oil level is to the bottom lip of the filler hole.

5 If necessary, add the specified oil through the filler/level hole. If the level requires constant topping-up, check for leaks and repair.

6 Refit the plug and tighten to the specified torque, then lower the vehicle to the ground.

18 Underbody protection check

Raise and support the vehicle on axle stands (see Jacking and vehicle support). Using an electric torch or lead light, inspect the entire underside of the vehicle, paying particular attention to the wheel arches. Look for any damage to the flexible underbody coating, which may crack or flake off with age, leading to corrosion. Also check that the wheel arch liners are securely attached with any clips provided – if they come loose, dirt may get in behind the liners and defeat their purpose. If there is any damage to the underseal, or any corrosion, it should be repaired before the damage gets too serious.

19 Driveshaft gaiter check

1 With the vehicle raised and securely supported on stands, slowly rotate the roadwheel. Inspect the condition of the outer constant velocity (CV) joint rubber gaiters, squeezing the gaiters to open out the folds. Check for signs of cracking, splits or deterioration of the rubber, which may allow the grease to escape, and lead to water and grit entry into the joint. Also check the security and condition of the retaining clips. Repeat these checks on the inner joints **(see**

illustration). If any damage or deterioration is found, the gaiters should be renewed (see Chapter 8).

2 At the same time, check the general condition of the CV joints themselves by first holding the driveshaft and attempting to rotate the wheel. Repeat this check by holding the inner joint and attempting to rotate the driveshaft. Any appreciable movement indicates wear in the joints, wear in the driveshaft splines, or a loose driveshaft retaining nut.

20 Steering and suspension check

1 Raise the front and rear of the vehicle, and securely support it on axle stands (see *Jacking and vehicle support*).

2 Visually inspect the track rod end balljoint dust cover, the lower front suspension balljoint dust cover, and the steering rack-and-pinion gaiters for splits, chafing or deterioration. Any wear of these components will cause loss of lubricant, together with dirt and water entry, resulting in rapid deterioration of the balljoints or steering gear.

3 Check the power steering fluid hoses for chafing or deterioration, and the pipe and hose unions for fluid leaks. Also check for signs of fluid leakage under pressure from the steering gear rubber gaiters, which would indicate failed fluid seals within the steering gear.

4 Grasp the roadwheel at the 12 o'clock and 6 o'clock positions, and try to rock it **(see illustration)**. Very slight free play may be felt, but if the movement is appreciable, further investigation is necessary to determine the source. Continue rocking the wheel while an assistant depresses the footbrake. If the movement is now eliminated or significantly reduced, it is likely that the hub bearings are at fault. If the free play is still evident with the

footbrake depressed, then there is wear in the suspension joints or mountings.

5 Now grasp the wheel at the 9 o'clock and 3 o'clock positions, and try to rock it as before. Any movement felt now may again be caused by wear in the hub bearings or the steering track rod balljoints. If the inner or outer balljoint is worn, the visual movement will be obvious.

6 Using a large screwdriver or flat bar, check for wear in the suspension mounting bushes by levering between the relevant suspension component and its attachment point. Some movement is to be expected as the mountings are made of rubber, but excessive wear should be obvious. Also check the condition of any visible rubber bushes, looking for splits, cracks or contamination of the rubber.

7 With the car standing on its wheels, have an assistant turn the steering wheel back-and-forth about an eighth of a turn each way. There should be very little, if any, lost movement between the steering wheel and roadwheels. If this is not the case, closely observe the joints and mountings previously described, but in addition, check the steering column universal joints for wear, and the rack-and-pinion steering gear itself.

8 Check for any signs of fluid leakage around the front suspension struts and rear shock absorber. Should any fluid be noticed, the suspension strut or shock absorber is defective internally, and should be renewed. **Note:** *Suspension struts/shock absorbers should always be renewed in pairs on the same axle to ensure correct vehicle handling.*

9 The efficiency of the suspension strut/shock absorber may be checked by bouncing the vehicle at each corner. Generally speaking, the body will return to its normal position and stop after being depressed. If it rises and returns on a rebound, the suspension strut/shock absorber is probably suspect. Examine also the suspension strut/shock absorber upper and lower mountings for any signs of wear.

21 Battery check

1 The battery is located beneath a cover at the rear of the engine compartment. Undo the clips and remove the cover.
2 Check that both battery terminals and all the fuse holder connections are securely attached and are free from corrosion.
3 Check the battery casing for signs of damage or cracking and check the battery retaining clamp bolt is securely tightened. If the battery casing is damaged in any way the battery must be renewed (see Chapter 5A).
4 If the vehicle is not fitted with a sealed-for-life maintenance-free battery, check the electrolyte level is between the MAX and MIN level markings on the battery casing. If topping-up is necessary, remove the battery (see Chapter 5A) from the vehicle then remove the cell caps/cover (as applicable). Using distilled water, top the electrolyte level of each cell up to the MAX level mark then securely refit the cell caps/cover. Ensure the battery has not been overfilled then refit the battery to the vehicle (see Chapter 5A).
5 On completion of the check, refit the cover.

22 Hinge and lock lubrication

1 Lubricate the hinges of the bonnet, doors and tailgate with a light general-purpose oil. Similarly, lubricate all latches, locks and lock strikers. At the same time, check the security and operation of all the locks, adjusting them if necessary (see Chapter 11).
2 Lightly lubricate the bonnet release mechanism and cable with a suitable grease.

23 Airbag unit check

Inspect the exterior condition of the airbag(s) for signs of damage or deterioration. If an airbag shows signs of damage, it must be renewed (see Chapter 12). Note that it is not permissible to attach any stickers to the surface of the airbag, as this may affect the deployment of the unit.

24 Windscreen/tailgate/headlight washer system check

1 Check that each of the washer jet nozzles are clear and that each nozzle provides a strong jet of washer fluid.
2 The tailgate jet should be aimed to spray at the centre of the screen, using a pin.

3 The windscreen washer nozzles should be aimed slightly above the centre of the screen using a small screwdriver to turn the jet eccentric.
4 The headlight inner jet should be aimed slightly above the horizontal centreline of the headlight, and the outer jet should be aimed slightly below the centreline. VW technicians use a special tool to adjust the headlight jet after pulling the jet out onto its stop.
5 Especially during the winter months, make sure that the washer fluid frost concentration is sufficient.

25 Engine management self-diagnosis memory fault check

This work should be carried out by a VW dealer or diagnostic specialist using special equipment. The diagnostic socket is located beneath the right-hand side of the facia on RHD models, and beneath the left-hand side on LHD models.

26 Sunroof check and lubrication

1 Check the operation of the sunroof, and leave it in the fully open position.
2 Wipe clean the guide rails on each side of the sunroof opening, then apply lubricant to them. VW recommend lubricant spray G 052 778.

27 Road test and exhaust emissions check

Instruments and electrical equipment

1 Check the operation of all instruments and electrical equipment.
2 Make sure that all instruments read correctly, and switch on all electrical equipment in turn, to check that it functions properly.

Steering and suspension

3 Check for any abnormalities in the steering, suspension, handling or road feel.
4 Drive the vehicle, and check that there are no unusual vibrations or noises which may indicate wear in the driveshafts, wheel bearings, etc.
5 Check that the steering feels positive, with no excessive sloppiness, or roughness, and check for any suspension noises when cornering and driving over bumps.

Drivetrain

6 Check the performance of the engine, clutch (where applicable), gearbox/transmission and driveshafts.
7 Listen for any unusual noises from the engine, clutch and gearbox/transmission.

8 Make sure that the engine runs smoothly when idling, and that there is no hesitation when accelerating.
9 Check that, where applicable, the clutch action is smooth and progressive, that the drive is taken up smoothly, and that the pedal travel is not excessive. Also listen for any noises when the clutch pedal is depressed.
10 On manual gearbox models, check that all gears can be engaged smoothly without noise, and that the gear lever action is smooth and not abnormally vague or notchy.
11 On automatic transmission models, make sure that all gearchanges occur smoothly, without snatching, and without an increase in engine speed between changes. Check that all the gear positions can be selected with the vehicle at rest. If any problems are found, they should be referred to a VW dealer.
12 Listen for a metallic clicking sound from the front of the vehicle, as the vehicle is driven slowly in a circle with the steering on full-lock. Carry out this check in both directions. If a clicking noise is heard, this indicates wear in a driveshaft joint, in which case renew the joint if necessary.

Braking system

13 Make sure that the vehicle does not pull to one side when braking, and that the wheels do not lock when braking hard.
14 Check that there is no vibration through the steering when braking.
15 Check that the handbrake operates correctly without excessive movement of the lever, and that it holds the vehicle stationary on a slope.
16 Test the operation of the brake servo unit as follows. With the engine off, depress the footbrake four or five times to exhaust the vacuum. Hold the brake pedal depressed, then start the engine. As the engine starts, there should be a noticeable 'give' in the brake pedal as vacuum builds-up. Allow the engine to run for at least two minutes, and then switch it off. If the brake pedal is depressed now, it should be possible to detect a hiss from the servo as the pedal is depressed. After about four or five applications, no further hissing should be heard, and the pedal should feel considerably harder.
17 Under controlled emergency braking, the pulsing of the ABS unit must be felt at the footbrake pedal.

Exhaust emissions check

18 Although not part of the manufacturer's maintenance schedule, this check will normally be carried out on a regular basis according to the country the vehicle is operated in. Currently in the UK, exhaust emissions testing is included as part of the annual MOT test after the vehicle is 3 years old. In Germany the test is made when the vehicle is 3 years old, then repeated every 2 years.

28.1a Remove the screws and lift off the air filter cover . . .

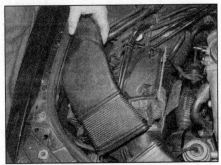

28.1b . . . pull off the air duct . . .

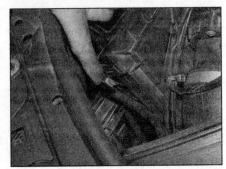

28.1c . . . release the retaining clips . . .

Every 40 000 miles or 4 years

28 Air filter element renewal

1 Remove the air filter cover and air duct, then prise open the retaining clips and lift the upper cover from the air filter body **(see illustrations)**. Note that the airflow meter is attached to the upper cover.
2 Remove the air filter element, noting which way round it is fitted **(see illustration)**.
3 Wipe clean the main body, then fit the new air filter, making sure it is the correct way round.
4 Refit the upper cover and secure with the retaining clips.

29 Fuel filter renewal (vehicles using standard diesel fuel)

Note: *At this interval only when using diesel fuel conforming to DIN EN 590 (standard fuel in the UK).*
1 Refer to Section 10.

30 Auxiliary drivebelt check and renewal

Check

1 See Section 12.

28.2 . . . and remove the air filter element

Renewal

2 Refer to Chapter 2B.

31 Power steering hydraulic fluid level check

1 Refer to Chapter 10.

32 Automatic transmission fluid renewal

Note: *Although VW make no specific recommendation to renew the automatic transmission fluid, we consider it prudent to change the fluid every 40 000 miles or four years whichever occurs first.*
1 Apply the handbrake, then jack up the front of the vehicle and support it on axle stands (see *Jacking and vehicle support*). Remove the engine undershield. **Note:** *For an accurate fluid level check, VW technicians use an electronic*

tester which is plugged into the transmission electronic system, and which determines that the temperature of the fluid is between 35°C and 40°C. In view of this, it is recommended that the vehicle is taken to a VW dealer to have the work done. The following procedure is given on the understanding that the level is checked by a VW dealer on completion.
2 Note that the transmission must be refilled from below the vehicle, so make sure that the vehicle is supported in a level position.

01N 4-speed transmission

3 Position a suitable container beneath the transmission. Wipe clean the oil pan, then unscrew the inspection plug, followed by the overflow pipe, from the bottom of the oil pan **(see illustration)**. Allow the fluid to drain into the container.
4 Refit the overflow pipe and tighten to the specified torque.
5 Remove the sealing cap and plug from the filling tube attached to the side of the oil pan. **Note:** *The later sealing cap and plug should be renewed whenever removed.*

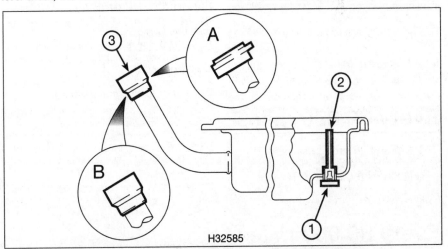

H32585

32.3 Oil pan components on the 01N automatic transmission

1 Inspection plug	3 Sealing cap and plug	A Early sealing cap
2 Overflow pipe		B Later sealing cap

Note: *Sealing cap B must be renewed after removal*

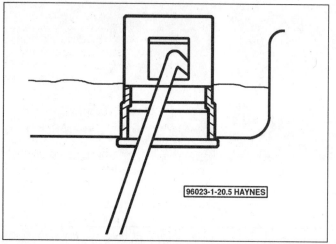

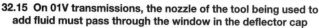

32.15 On 01V transmissions, the nozzle of the tool being used to add fluid must pass through the window in the deflector cap

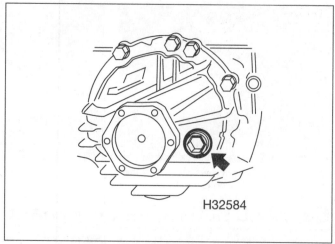

33.1 On automatic transmissions, the final drive filler/level plug is located on the left-hand side (arrowed)

6 Add fluid to the oil pan until it runs out of the overflow pipe.

7 With P selected, run the engine at idling speed until it reaches normal temperature. If necessary add more fluid until it runs out of the overflow pipe.

8 Apply the footbrake pedal, then select each position with the selector lever, pausing for about 3 seconds in each position. Return the selector to position P.

9 At this stage, the VW technician connects the tester to confirm that the fluid temperature is between 35°C and 40°C. **Note:** *If the fluid level is checked when the temperature is too low, overfilling will occur. If the fluid level is checked when the temperature is too high, underfilling will occur.*

10 With the engine still running at idle speed, allow any excess fluid to run out of the overflow pipe.

11 Switch off the engine, then refit the inspection plug together with a new seal, and tighten to the specified torque.

12 Fit a new sealing cap and plug to the filling tube.

01V 5-speed transmission

13 Position a suitable container beneath the transmission. Wipe clean the pan, then unscrew the drain plug located on the right-hand side of the pan. Allow the fluid to drain into the container.

14 Fit a new seal on the drain plug and tighten to the specified torque.

15 Unscrew the inspection plug at the rear of the pan, and add fluid until it runs out of the hole **(see illustration)**.

16 With P selected, run the engine at idling speed until it reaches normal temperature. If necessary add more fluid until it runs out of the inspection hole.

17 Apply the footbrake pedal, then select each position with the selector lever, pausing for about 3 seconds in each position. Return the selector to position P.

18 At this stage, the VW technician connects the tester to confirm that the fluid temperature is between 35°C and 40°C. **Note:** *If the fluid level is checked when the temperature is too low, overfilling will occur. If the fluid level is checked when the temperature is too high, underfilling will occur.*

19 With the engine still running at idle speed, allow any excess fluid to run out of the overflow pipe.

20 Switch off the engine, then refit the inspection plug together with a new seal, and tighten to the specified torque.

All models

21 Lower the vehicle to the ground.

33 Automatic transmission final drive oil level check

1 The final drive oil filler/level plug is located on the left-hand side of the automatic transmission, behind the left-hand driveshaft inner joint **(see illustration)**. Apply the handbrake, then jack up the front of the vehicle and support it on axle stands (see *Jacking and vehicle support*). Remove the engine undershield. To ensure an accurate check, make sure that the vehicle is level.

2 Unscrew and remove the filler/level plug and check that the oil level is on the bottom lip of the filler hole. If necessary, add the specified oil through the filler/level hole. If the level requires constant topping-up, check for leaks and repair.

3 Refit the plug and tighten to the specified torque, then lower the vehicle to the ground.

Every 60 000 miles

34 Timing belt and tensioning roller renewal (2000 to 2003 models)

1 Refer to Chapter 2B for details of renewing the timing belt and tensioning roller.

Every 80 000 miles

35 Timing belt and tensioning roller renewal (2004-on models)

1 Refer to Chapter 2B for details of renewing the timing belt.

2 Note that the tensioning roller must be renewed as a matter of course at every second timing belt renewal. Refer to Chapter 2B for details.

Every 2 years

36 Brake (and clutch) fluid renewal

⚠ *Warning: Brake hydraulic fluid can harm your eyes and damage painted surfaces, so use extreme caution when handling and pouring it. Do not use fluid that has been standing open for some time, as it absorbs moisture from the air. Excess moisture can cause a dangerous loss of braking effectiveness.*

1 The procedure is similar to that for the bleeding of the hydraulic system as described in Chapter 9, except that the brake fluid reservoir should be emptied by syphoning, using a clean poultry baster or similar before starting, and allowance should be made for the old fluid to be expelled when bleeding a section of the circuit. Since the clutch hydraulic system also uses fluid from the brake system reservoir, it should also be bled at the same time by referring to Chapter 6, Section 2.

2 Working as described in Chapter 9, open the first bleed screw in the sequence, and pump the brake pedal gently until nearly all the old fluid has been emptied from the master cylinder reservoir.

HAYNES HiNT *Old hydraulic fluid is often much darker in colour than the new, making it easy to distinguish the two.*

3 Top-up to the MAX level with new fluid, and continue pumping until only the new fluid remains in the reservoir, and new fluid can be seen emerging from the bleed screw. Tighten the screw, and top the reservoir level up to the MAX level line.

4 Work through all the remaining bleed screws in the sequence until new fluid can be seen at all of them. Be careful to keep the master cylinder reservoir topped-up to above the MIN level at all times, or air may enter the system and greatly increase the length of the task.

5 When the operation is complete, check that all bleed screws are securely tightened, and that their dust caps are refitted. Wash off all traces of spilt fluid, and recheck the master cylinder reservoir fluid level.

6 On models with a manual transmission unit, once the brake fluid has been changed the clutch fluid should also be renewed. Referring to Chapter 6, bleed the clutch until new fluid is seen to be emerging from the slave cylinder bleed screw, keeping the master cylinder fluid level above the MIN level line at all times to prevent air entering the system. Once the new fluid emerges, securely tighten the bleed screw then disconnect and remove the bleeding equipment. Securely refit the dust cap then wash off all traces of spilt fluid.

7 On all models, ensure the master cylinder fluid level is correct (see *Weekly checks*) and thoroughly check the operation of the brakes and (where necessary) clutch before taking the car on the road.

37 Coolant renewal

Note: *This work is not included in the VW schedule and should not be required if the recommended VW G12 LongLife coolant antifreeze/inhibitor is used. However, if standard antifreeze/inhibitor is used, the work should be carried out at the recommended interval.*

⚠ *Warning: Wait until the engine is cold before starting this procedure. Do not allow antifreeze to come in contact with your skin, or with the painted surfaces of the vehicle. Rinse off spills immediately with plenty of water. Never leave antifreeze lying around in an open container, or in a puddle in the driveway or on the garage floor. Children and pets are attracted by its sweet smell, but antifreeze can be fatal if ingested.*

Cooling system draining

1 With the engine completely cold, cover the expansion tank cap with a wad of rag, and slowly turn the cap anti-clockwise to relieve the pressure in the cooling system (a hissing sound will normally be heard). Wait until any pressure remaining in the system is released, then continue to turn the cap until it can be removed.

2 Release the fasteners and remove the engine lower splash shield. Position a suitable container beneath the radiator bottom hose connection, then pull out the retaining clip and ease the hose from the radiator stub. If the hose joint has not been disturbed for some time, it will be necessary to gently manipulate the hose to break the joint. Do not use excessive force, or the radiator stub could be damaged. Allow the coolant to drain into the container. Note that the radiator is equipped with a drain tap, but this can only be accessed with the front bumper removed.

3 Prise out the cover caps, undo the retaining nuts and remove the engine top cover. Release the securing clip, and disconnect one of the coolant hoses to the oil cooler to drain the engine block. Allow the coolant to drain. Reconnect the hose, retaining it with the securing clip, and refit the engine top cover. On pre-01/2002 models fitted with a fuel-cooling pump, disconnect the vacuum hose from the shut-off valve vacuum unit. **Note:** *After refilling the cooling system, the function of the shut-off valve must be checked by a VW dealer using special diagnostic equipment.*

4 If the coolant has been drained for a reason other than renewal, then provided it is clean, it can be re-used, but this is not recommended.

5 Once all the coolant has drained, reconnect the hose to the radiator and ensure the retaining clip is properly seated.

Cooling system flushing

6 If coolant renewal has been neglected, or if the antifreeze mixture has become diluted, then in time, the cooling system may gradually lose efficiency, as the coolant passages become restricted due to rust, scale deposits, and other sediment. Flushing the system clean can restore the cooling system efficiency.

7 The radiator should be flushed independently of the engine, to avoid unnecessary contamination.

Radiator flushing

8 To flush the radiator, disconnect the top and bottom hoses and any other relevant hoses from the radiator, with reference to Chapter 3.

9 Insert a garden hose into the radiator top inlet. Direct a flow of clean water through the radiator, and continue flushing until clean water emerges from the radiator bottom outlet.

10 If after a reasonable period, the water still does not run clear, the radiator can be flushed with a good proprietary cooling system cleaning agent. It is important that their manufacturer's instructions are followed carefully. If the contamination is particularly bad, insert the hose in the radiator bottom outlet, and reverse-flush the radiator.

Engine flushing

11 To flush the engine, remove the thermostat as described in Chapter 3, then temporarily refit the thermostat cover.

12 With the top and bottom hoses disconnected from the radiator, insert a garden hose into the radiator top hose. Direct a clean flow of water through the engine, and continue flushing until clean water emerges from the radiator bottom hose.

13 On completion of flushing, refit the thermostat and reconnect the hoses with reference to Chapter 3.

Cooling system filling

14 Before attempting to fill the cooling system, make sure that all hoses and clips are in good condition, and that the clips/connections are secure. Note that an antifreeze mixture must be used all year round, to prevent corrosion of the engine components (see following sub-Section).

15 Slacken the clip and withdraw the heater unit supply hose from its bulkhead stub (see Chapter 3) until the bleed hole at the top of the hose is clear of the surface of the stub; do not disconnect the hose from the stub completely.

16 Remove the securing screws and detach the expansion tank from the engine

compartment. Raise it approximately 100 mm above the engine compartment and support it there on a block of wood or using a length of wire.

17 Remove the expansion tank filler cap, and fill the system by slowly pouring the coolant into the expansion tank to prevent airlocks from forming.

18 If the coolant is being renewed, begin by pouring in a couple of litres of water, followed by the correct quantity of antifreeze, then top-up with more water.

19 Continue filling until coolant starts to run from the bleed hole in the heater hose. When this happens, refit the hose and tighten the clip securely.

20 Once the level in the expansion tank starts to rise, squeeze the radiator top and bottom hoses to help expel any trapped air in the system. Once all the air is expelled, top-up the coolant level to the MAX mark, refit the expansion tank cap, then refit the expansion tank to the bodywork.

21 On pre-01/2002 models, reconnect the vacuum hose to the shut-off valve vacuum unit.

22 Start the engine and run it at a fast idle for about three minutes. After this, allow the engine to idle normally until the bottom hose becomes hot.

23 Check for leaks, particularly around disturbed components. Check the coolant level in the expansion tank, and top-up if necessary. Note that the system must be cold before an accurate level is indicated in the expansion tank. If the expansion tank cap is removed while the engine is still warm, cover the cap with a thick cloth, and unscrew the cap slowly to gradually relieve the system pressure (a hissing sound will normally be heard). Wait until any pressure remaining in the system is released, then continue to turn the cap until it can be removed. Never remove the cap when the engine is still hot.

Antifreeze mixture

Caution: VW specify the use of G12 antifreeze (red in colour). DO NOT mix this with any other type of antifreeze, as severe engine damage may result. If the coolant visible in the expansion tank is brown in colour, then the cooling system may have been topped-up with coolant containing the wrong type of antifreeze. If you are unsure of the type of antifreeze used, or if you suspect that mixing may have occurred, the best course of action is to drain, flush and refill the cooling system.

24 If the recommended VW coolant is not being used, the antifreeze should always be renewed at the specified intervals. This is necessary not only to maintain the antifreeze properties, but also to prevent corrosion which would otherwise occur as the corrosion inhibitors become progressively less effective.

25 The quantity of antifreeze and levels of protection are indicated in the Specifications.

26 Before adding antifreeze, the cooling system should be completely drained, preferably flushed, and all hoses checked for condition and security.

27 After filling with antifreeze, a label should be attached to the expansion tank, stating the type and concentration of antifreeze used, and the date installed. Any subsequent topping-up should be made with the same type and concentration of antifreeze.

28 Do not use engine antifreeze in the windscreen/tailgate/headlight washer system, as it will cause damage to the vehicle paintwork.

Chapter 2 Part A:
Petrol engine in-car repair procedures

Contents

	Section number
Auxiliary drivebelts – removal and refitting	6
Balancer shaft/oil pump assembly – removal and refitting	17
Camshaft cover – removal and refitting	7
Camshaft oil seal – renewal	8
Crankshaft oil seals – renewal	9
Cylinder compression test	3
Cylinder head – dismantling and overhaul	See Chapter 2C
Cylinder head – removal and refitting	10
Engine mountings – inspection and renewal	13
Engine oil and filter – renewal	See Chapter 1A
Engine oil level – check	See Weekly checks

	Section number
Engine oil temperature sensor – removal and refitting	16
Engine valve timing marks – general information and usage	2
Flywheel/driveplate – removal, inspection and refitting	12
General information	1
Hydraulic tappets – operational check	11
Oil pump and pick-up – removal, inspection and refitting	15
Sump – removal and refitting	14
Timing belt – removal, inspection and refitting	4
Timing belt tensioner and sprockets – removal, inspection and refitting	5

Degrees of difficulty

Easy, suitable for novice with little experience	Fairly easy, suitable for beginner with some experience	Fairly difficult, suitable for competent DIY mechanic	Difficult, suitable for experienced DIY mechanic	Very difficult, suitable for expert DIY or professional

Specifications

General

Engine code by type*:
1781 cc, DOHC, Bosch Motronic ME7.5 injection, turbocharged	AWT
1984 cc, SOHC, Siemens Simos 3.2 injection, non-turbo	AZM
1984 cc, DOHC, Bosch Motronic ME7.5 injection, non-turbo	ALT

Power output:
1.8 litre (AWT)	110 kW (150 bhp)
2.0 litre (AZM)	85 kW (115 bhp)
2.0 litre (ALT)	96 kW (130 bhp)

Bore:
1.8 litre (AWT)	81.0 mm
2.0 litre (AZM, ALT)	82.5 mm

Stroke:
1.8 litre (AWT)	86.4 mm
2.0 litre (AZM and ALT)	92.8 mm

Compression ratio:
1.8 litre (AWT)	9.3 : 1
2.0 litre (AZM)	10.3 : 1
2.0 litre (ALT)	10.5 : 1

Compression pressures (wear limit):
1.8 litre (AWT)	7.0 bar
2.0 litre (AZM and ALT)	7.5 bar
Maximum difference between cylinders	3.0 bar
Firing order	1 – 3 – 4 – 2
No 1 cylinder location	Timing belt end

* **Note:** See 'Vehicle identification' at the end of this manual for the location of code marking on the engine.

Lubrication system

Oil pump type.	Sump-mounted, chain-driven from crankshaft

Oil pressure (oil temperature 80°C):
  1.8 litre (AWT):
    At idle speed. . . . .   1.2 to 1.6 bar
    At 2000 rpm . . . .   2.5 to 4.5 bar
  2.0 litre (AZM and ALT):
    At idle speed. . . . .   1.2 to 1.6 bar
    At 2000 rpm . . . .   2.7 to 4.5 bar
Oil pump backlash . . . .   0.2 mm (wear limit)
Oil pump endfloat. . . . .   0.15 mm (wear limit)

Torque wrench settings

	Nm	lbf ft
Air conditioning compressor drivebelt tensioner	20	15
Automatic camshaft adjuster bolt (Engine codes AWT and ALT).	10	7
Balancer shaft assembly (engine code ALT):		
Stage 1.	15	11
Stage 2.	Angle-tighten a further 90°	
Big-end bearing caps bolts/nuts*:		
Stage 1.	30	22
Stage 2.	Angle-tighten a further 90°	
Camshaft bearing cap:		
Engine code AZM.	20	15
Engine codes AWT and ALT.	10	7
Camshaft cover	10	7
Camshaft sprocket:		
Engine code AZM.	100	74
Engine codes AWT and ALT.	65	48
Coolant pump pulley halves.	25	18
Crankshaft front oil seal housing:		
M6 bolts	15	11
M8 bolts	25	18
Crankshaft pulley/vibration damper:		
Engine codes AZM and ALT.	25	18
Engine code AWT:		
Stage 1.	10	7
Stage 2.	Angle-tighten a further 90°	
Crankshaft rear oil seal housing.	15	11
Crankshaft sprocket*:		
Stage 1.	90	66
Stage 2.	Angle-tighten a further 90°	
Cylinder head bolts*:		
Stage 1.	40	30
Stage 2.	Angle-tighten a further 90°	
Stage 3.	Angle-tighten a further 90°	
Driveplate mounting bolts*:		
Stage 1.	60	44
Stage 2.	Angle-tighten a further 90°	
Engine mounting bracket to cylinder block	40	30
Engine mounting to subframe	25	18
Engine oil temperature sensor	10	7
Engine-to-transmission bolts:		
M10	45	33
M12	65	48
Exhaust pipe to manifold	30	22
Flywheel mounting bolts*:		
Stage 1.	60	44
Stage 2.	Angle-tighten a further 90°	
Main bearing cap bolts*:		
Stage 1.	65	48
Stage 2.	Angle-tighten a further 90°	
Oil jets.	27	20
Oil pump:		
Engine codes AWT and AZM	15	11
Engine code ALT.	8	6
Oil pump cover.	8	6
Oil pump sprocket (engine code ALT)	20	15

Torque wrench settings (continued)

	Nm	lbf ft
Sump:		
Stage 1 (all sump-to-block bolts)	Hand-tight	
Stage 2 (sump-to-transmission bolts)	Hand-tight	
Stage 3 (all bolts)	Lightly tighten in diagonal sequence	
Stage 4 (sump-to-transmission bolts)	45	33
Stage 5 (M7 sump-to-block bolts)	15	11
Stage 6 (M10 sump-to-block bolts)	45	33
Timing belt rear guard	20	15
Timing belt tensioner:		
Engine codes AWT and ALT	27	20
Engine code AZM	20	15

* Use new nuts/bolt(s)

---

1 General information

Using this Chapter

Chapter 2 is divided into three Parts; A, B and C. Repair operations that can be carried out with the engine in the vehicle are described in Part A (petrol engines) and Part B (diesel engines). Part C covers the removal of the engine/transmission as a unit, and describes the engine dismantling and overhaul procedures.

In Parts A and B, the assumption is made that the engine is installed in the vehicle, with all ancillaries connected. If the engine has been removed for overhaul, the preliminary dismantling information which precedes each operation may be ignored.

Access to the engine compartment can be improved by removing the bonnet as described in Chapter 11.

Engine description

Throughout this Chapter, engines are identified and referred to by the manufacturer's code letters, rather than capacity. A listing of all engines covered, together with their code letters, is given in the Specifications.

The engines are water-cooled, single or double overhead camshaft, in-line four-cylinder units, with cast-iron cylinder blocks and aluminium-alloy cylinder heads. All are mounted longitudinally at the front of the vehicle, with the transmission bolted to the rear of the engine.

The crankshaft is of five-bearing type, and thrustwashers are fitted to the centre main bearing to control crankshaft endfloat.

The camshaft is driven by a toothed timing belt from the crankshaft sprocket. On the AWT and ALT double overhead camshaft engines, the timing belt drives the exhaust camshaft, and the inlet camshaft is driven from the exhaust camshaft by chain at the rear of the camshafts. A hydraulic tensioner is fitted to the chain, and this takes the form of a mechanical camshaft adjuster to automatically vary the inlet camshaft valve timing. The valves are operated from the camshaft through hydraulic bucket type tappets, and the valve clearances are adjusted automatically.

The cylinder head carries the single or double camshafts and also houses the inlet and exhaust valves, which are closed by single coil springs, and which run in guides pressed into the cylinder head. The cylinder head contains integral oilways which supply and lubricate the tappets.

The coolant pump is driven by the timing belt. For details of the cooling system, refer to Chapter 3.

Lubricant is circulated under pressure by a pump, driven by a chain from the crankshaft. Oil is drawn from the sump through a strainer, and then forced through an externally-mounted, screw-on filter. From there, it is distributed to the cylinder head, where it lubricates the camshaft journals and hydraulic tappets, and also to the crankcase, where it lubricates the main bearings, connecting rod big-ends, gudgeon pins and cylinder bores. An oil pressure switch is located on the oil filter housing, operating at 1.4 bars. An oil cooler mounted above the oil filter is supplied with coolant from the cooling system to reduce the temperature of the oil before it re-enters the engine.

Repairs with engine installed

The following operations can be performed without removing the engine:

a) Auxiliary drivebelts – removal and refitting.
b) Camshaft(s) – removal and refitting*.
c) Camshaft oil seal – renewal.
d) Camshaft sprocket – removal and refitting.
e) Coolant pump – removal and refitting (refer to Chapter 3).
f) Crankshaft oil seals – renewal.
g) Crankshaft sprocket – removal and refitting.
h) Cylinder head – removal and refitting*.
i) Engine mountings – inspection and renewal.
j) Oil pump and pick-up assembly – removal and refitting.
k) Sump – removal and refitting.
l) Timing belt, sprockets and cover – removal, inspection and refitting.

* Cylinder head dismantling procedures are detailed in Chapter 2C, with details of camshaft and hydraulic tappet removal.

Note: *It is possible to remove the pistons and connecting rods (after removing the cylinder head and sump) without removing the engine. However, this is not recommended. Work of this nature is more easily and thoroughly completed with the engine on the bench, as described in Chapter 2C.*

2 Engine valve timing marks – general information and usage

General information

1 The crankshaft, camshaft and coolant pump sprockets are driven by the timing belt and, with the exception of the coolant pump, rotate in phase with each other. When the timing belt is removed during servicing or repair, it is possible for the sprockets to rotate independently of each other, and the correct phasing is then lost.

2 The design of the engines covered in this Chapter is such that piston-to-valve contact will occur if the crankshaft is turned with the timing belt removed. For this reason, it is important that the correct phasing between the camshaft and crankshaft is preserved whilst the timing belt is off the engine. This is achieved by setting the engine in a reference condition (known as Top Dead Centre or TDC) before the timing belt is removed, and then preventing the shafts from rotating until the belt is refitted. Similarly, if the engine has been dismantled for overhaul, the engine can be set to TDC during reassembly to ensure that the correct shaft phasing is restored. **Note:** *The coolant pump is also driven by the timing belt, but the pump alignment is not critical.*

3 TDC is the highest position a piston reaches within its respective cylinder – in a four-stroke engine, each piston reaches TDC twice per cycle; once on the compression stroke, and once on the exhaust stroke. In general, TDC normally refers to No 1 cylinder on the compression stroke. Note that the cylinders are numbered one to four, starting from the timing belt end of the engine.

2.4 TDC marks on the lower timing belt cover

2.5 TDC marks on the camshaft sprocket and timing inner cover

4 The crankshaft pulley has a marking which, when aligned with a reference marking on the timing belt cover, indicates that No 1 cylinder (and hence also No 4 cylinder) is at TDC **(see illustration)**.

5 The camshaft sprocket (exhaust camshaft on engine codes AWT and ALT) is also equipped with a timing mark **(see illustration)** – when this is aligned with a mark on the rear upper timing belt cover or camshaft cover, No 1 cylinder is at TDC compression.

6 In addition, the flywheel/driveplate has TDC markings which can be observed by removing a protective cover from the transmission bellhousing. Note however that the markings cannot be used if the transmission has been removed from the engine for repair or overhaul.

Setting TDC on No 1 cylinder

7 Before starting work, make sure that the ignition is switched off.

8 Where applicable, undo the retaining bolts and remove the engine top cover.

9 Remove all of the spark plugs as described in Chapter 1A.

10 Turn the engine clockwise with a spanner on the crankshaft pulley and use a suitable rubber plug over No 1 spark plug hole to determine when No 1 piston is on its compression stroke (pressure will be felt through the spark plug hole).

11 Continue turning the engine in a clockwise direction until the TDC mark on the crankshaft pulley or flywheel/driveplate is aligned with the corresponding mark on the timing cover or transmission casing. For an additional check, remove the upper timing belt outer cover to expose the camshaft timing belt sprocket TDC marks.

3 Cylinder compression test

1 When engine performance is down, or if misfiring occurs which cannot be attributed to the ignition or fuel systems, a compression test can provide diagnostic clues as to the engine's condition. If the test is performed regularly, it can give warning of trouble before any other symptoms become apparent.

2 The engine must be fully warmed-up to normal operating temperature, the battery must be fully-charged, and all the spark plugs must be removed (refer to Chapter 1A). The aid of an assistant will also be required. Where applicable, undo the retaining bolts and remove the engine top cover.

3 On engine code AZM (single coil unit) disconnect fuse 34 and also disconnect the wiring from the single coil unit located at the left-hand rear of the engine compartment; on engine codes AWT and ALT (one coil per spark plug) disconnect fuse 32.

4 Fit a compression tester to the No 1 cylinder spark plug hole – the type of tester which screws into the plug thread is preferable.

5 Have an assistant hold the throttle wide open. **Note:** *All models are fitted with an electronically-controlled throttle system where the throttle will not operate until the ignition is switched on.* Crank the engine on the starter motor for several seconds. After one or two revolutions, the compression pressure should build-up to a maximum figure, and then stabilise. Record the highest reading obtained.

6 Repeat the test on the remaining cylinders, recording the pressure in each. Keep the throttle wide open.

7 All cylinders should produce very similar pressures; a difference of more than 3 bars between any two cylinders indicates a fault. Note that the compression should build-up quickly in a healthy engine. Low compression on the first stroke, followed by gradually-increasing pressure on successive strokes, indicates worn piston rings. A low compression reading on the first stroke, which does not build-up during successive strokes, indicates leaking valves or a blown head gasket (a cracked head could also be the cause).

8 Refer to the Specifications section of this Chapter, and compare the recorded compression figures with those stated by the manufacturer.

9 If the pressure in any cylinder is low, carry out the following test to isolate the cause. Introduce a teaspoonful of clean oil into that cylinder through its spark plug hole, and repeat the test.

10 If the addition of oil temporarily improves the compression pressure, this indicates that bore or piston wear is responsible for the pressure loss. No improvement suggests that leaking or burnt valves, or a blown head gasket, may be to blame.

11 A low reading from two adjacent cylinders is almost certainly due to the head gasket having blown between them.

12 If one cylinder is about 20 percent lower than the others and the engine has a slightly rough idle, a worn camshaft lobe could be the cause.

13 On completion of the test, refit the spark plugs, fuses, wiring and top cover.

4 Timing belt – removal, inspection and refitting

General information

1 The primary function of the toothed timing belt is to drive the camshaft(s). Should the belt slip or break in service, the valve timing will be disturbed and piston-to-valve contact will occur, resulting in serious engine damage. For this reason, it is important that the timing belt is tensioned correctly.

Removal

2 Before starting work, disconnect the battery negative (earth) lead (see Chapter 5A).

3 Apply the handbrake, then jack up the front of the vehicle and support it on axle stands (see *Jacking and vehicle support*). Where applicable, remove the splash guard from under the engine compartment.

4.4a Use lengths of threaded rod for supporting the lock carrier

4.4b Unbolt the power steering fluid cooler . . .

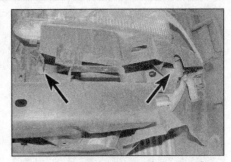

4.4c . . . then unscrew and remove the bumper guide bolts under each headlamp (arrowed) . . .

4.4d . . . and the one each side under the wing (arrowed) . . .

4.4e . . . then remove the bolt each side at the top of the wing . . .

4.4f . . . and the one alongside each headlamp

4 Access to the timing belt is achieved by moving the complete front panel (the lock carrier assembly) away from the front of the car as far as possible (into the 'Service' position – see Chapter 11, Section 10), but without disconnecting the radiator hoses or electrical wiring. To do this, first remove the front bumper as described in Chapter 11, then unscrew the three quick-release clips from the noise insulation panel and unbolt the air duct from between the lock carrier and the air cleaner. Unbolt the power steering oil cooler from the bottom of the radiator. On the left-hand side of the radiator, release the wiring from the clips. Unscrew the bolts securing the lock carrier/bumper bar assembly to the underbody channels, then unscrew and remove the two bolts securing the lock carrier to the top of the front wing on each side of the vehicle – one at the top/front of each wing, and one alongside each headlamp. Unscrew and remove the side-mounted bumper guides, located just below each headlamp, and unclip them from the front wings. Prise open the bonnet release cable connector in front of the driver's side bonnet hinge, and separate the two halves of the release cable. With the help of an assistant, pull the complete assembly away from the front of the car as far as possible. VW technicians use special tools to hold the assembly, however support bars may be made out of threaded metal rod and screwed into the underbody channels **(see illustrations)**.

5 Remove the auxiliary drivebelt(s) with reference to Section 6. Also unbolt the

tensioner from the front of the engine, using an Allen key **(see illustrations)**.

6 Remove the viscous fan unit with reference to Chapter 3, Section 5. Briefly, it is removed using an Allen key from behind, while holding

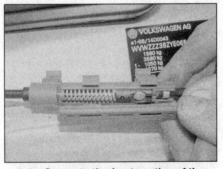

4.4g Separate the front section of the bonnet release cable

4.5b . . . and remove the tensioner

the unit stationary with a temporary bolt inserted from behind, resting on the engine cylinder block **(see illustrations)**.

7 Release the clips and remove the timing belt upper outer cover.

4.5a Unscrew the bolts . . .

4.6a Unscrew the bolt . . .

4.6b ... and remove the viscous fan unit

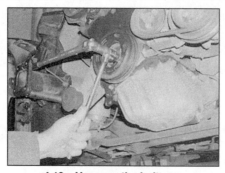

4.10a Unscrew the bolts ...

4.10b ... and withdraw the pulley/ vibration damper

8 If the timing belt is to be refitted, mark its normal direction of travel with chalk or a marker pen.

9 Set the engine at TDC with reference to Section 2. **Note:** *Check that* **all** *the TDC markings align exactly, as it is not unknown for the mark on the camshaft cover to be slightly out which may lead to confusion on refitting the timing belt. If there is a slight misalignment, make a temporary second mark to use during refitting.*

10 While holding the crankshaft stationary with a socket on the centre pulley bolt, unscrew and remove the bolts securing the pulley (or vibration damper) to the sprocket. Withdraw the pulley/vibration damper **(see illustrations)**.

11 Unscrew the bolts and remove the timing belt lower and centre covers from the cylinder block **(see illustrations)**.

Engine codes AWT and ALT

12 Using a 8.0 mm Allen key in the hole in the tensioner hub, slowly turn the tensioner anti-clockwise to compress the tensioner spring, until the tensioner can be locked with the locking plate. **Note:** *The tensioner has an oil damping element and it can only be compressed slowly by using even pressure.*

13 Loosen the centre nut of the tensioner, then turn the eccentric clockwise to release all tension from the timing belt. The eccentric has two small holes into which a special VW tool is inserted, however, a suitable tool can be fabricated from a length of metal and two

small bolts, or alternatively, 90° circlip pliers or two close-fitting drill bits and a lever can be used. **Note:** *Do not bend the small lug on the eccentric when turning it.*

Engine code AZM

14 Unscrew the centre nut of the semi-automatic tensioner, so that it releases all tension from the timing belt.

All engines

15 Slip the timing belt off of the crankshaft, camshaft, and coolant pump sprockets, and remove it from the engine. **Do not** bend the timing belt sharply if it is to be re-used.

Inspection

16 Examine the belt for evidence of contamination by coolant or lubricant. If this is the case, find the source of the contamination before progressing any further. Check the belt for signs of wear or damage, particularly around the leading edges of the belt teeth. Renew the belt if its condition is in doubt; the cost of belt renewal is negligible compared with potential cost of the engine repairs, should the belt fail in service. The belt must be renewed if it has covered the mileage stated by the manufacturer (see Chapter 1A), however, even if it has covered less, it is prudent to renew it regardless of condition as a precautionary measure. **Note:** *If the timing belt is not going to be refitted for some time, it is a wise precaution to hang a warning label on the steering wheel, to remind yourself (and others) not to turn the engine.*

Refitting

Engine codes AWT and ALT

17 Ensure that the timing mark on the camshaft sprocket is correctly aligned with the corresponding TDC reference mark on the timing belt inner cover; refer to Section 2 for details.

18 Loop the timing belt under the crankshaft sprocket loosely, observing the direction of rotation markings if the old timing belt is being refitted.

19 Temporarily refit the lower timing cover and the pulley for the auxiliary drivebelt to the crankshaft sprocket (using two of the retaining screws), noting that the offset mounting holes allow only one fitting position.

20 Check that the timing marks on the crankshaft pulley and lower timing cover are aligned with each other.

21 Engage the timing belt teeth with the crankshaft sprocket, then manoeuvre it into position over the coolant pump and camshaft sprockets. Observe the direction of rotation markings on the belt.

22 Pass the flat side of the belt over the tensioner roller – avoid bending the belt back on itself or twisting it excessively as you do this. Ensure that the front run of the belt is taut – ie, all the slack should be in the section of the belt that passes over the tensioner roller.

23 The tensioner locking plate (see paragraph 12) must now be removed and the setting procedure carried out. If a new tensioner has been fitted, or if the old unit has been removed and refitted, it must be turned anti-clockwise **gently** until the locking plate is not under tension and can be removed – **do not** bend the lug on the locking plate. Now turn the eccentric clockwise until an 8.0 mm drill can be inserted between the tensioner lever and housing **(see illustrations)**. With the tensioner held in this position, tighten the centre nut to the specified torque.

24 Using a spanner or wrench and socket on the crankshaft pulley centre bolt, rotate the crankshaft through two complete revolutions. Reset the engine to TDC on No 1 cylinder with reference to Section 2, and check that the crankshaft pulley and camshaft sprocket timing marks are correctly aligned.

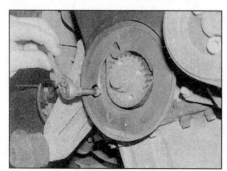

4.11a Unscrew the bolts ...

4.11b ... and remove the timing belt lower outer cover

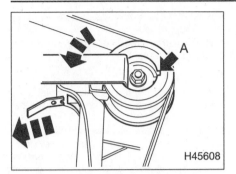

4.23a Removing the tensioner locking plate

Do not bend lug (A)

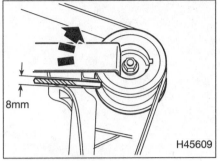

4.23b Turn the tensioner eccentric clockwise until a drill can be inserted

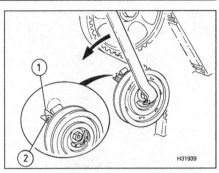

4.32 Timing belt tensioner setting (engine code AZM)

1 Notch   2 Pointer

25 Using the drill, check that the distance between the tensioner lever and housing is 6.0 to 10.0 mm. If necessary, repeat the procedure in paragraphs 23 and 24 and recheck the distance again.

Engine code AZM

26 Ensure that the timing mark on the camshaft sprocket is correctly aligned with the corresponding TDC reference mark on the timing belt inner cover; refer to Section 2 for details.

27 Loop the timing belt under the crankshaft sprocket loosely, observing the direction of rotation markings if the old timing belt is being refitted.

28 Temporarily refit the lower timing cover and the pulley for the auxiliary drivebelt to the crankshaft sprocket (using two of the retaining screws), noting that the offset mounting holes allow only one fitting position.

29 Check that the timing marks on the crankshaft pulley and lower timing cover are aligned with each other.

30 Engage the timing belt teeth with the crankshaft sprocket, then manoeuvre it into position over the coolant pump and camshaft sprockets. Observe the direction of rotation markings on the belt.

31 Pass the flat side of the belt over the tensioner roller – avoid bending the belt back on itself or twisting it excessively as you do this. Ensure that the front run of the belt is taut – ie, all the slack should be in the section of the belt that passes over the tensioner roller. Check that

the tag on the tensioner backplate is engaged with the recess in the cylinder head.

32 VW technicians use a special tool which engages the two holes in the tensioner wheel, however 90° circlip pliers or two close-fitting drill bits and a lever can be used. Turn the tensioner wheel five times fully onto the stops in both directions. Now turn the wheel fully anti-clockwise onto the stop, then turn it slowly clockwise until the pointer is aligned with the centre V of the notch (if necessary, use a mirror). Hold the wheel stationary and tighten the centre nut to the specified torque **(see illustration)**.

33 Using a spanner or wrench and socket on the crankshaft pulley centre bolt, rotate the crankshaft through two complete revolutions. Reset the engine to TDC on No 1 cylinder with reference to Section 2, and check that the crankshaft pulley and camshaft sprocket timing marks are correctly aligned. Recheck the timing belt tension and adjust it, if necessary. **Note:** *It is essential that when turning the crankshaft to TDC on No 1 cylinder, the last 45° is carried out without stopping.*

All engines

34 Refit the timing belt lower and centre covers, then refit the pulley/vibration damper and tighten the bolts to the specified torque.

35 Refit the timing belt upper outer cover.

36 Refit the viscous fan unit with reference to Chapter 3, then refit the auxiliary drivebelt tensioner and tighten the bolts. Refit the auxiliary drivebelt(s) with reference to Section 6.

37 Refit the lock carrier assembly using a reversal of the removal procedure.

38 Refit the splash guard under the engine compartment, then lower the vehicle to the ground.

39 Reconnect the battery negative (earth) lead (see Chapter 5A).

---

5 Timing belt tensioner and sprockets – removal, inspection and refitting

Removal

1 Remove the timing belt as described in Section 4. If necessary, unbolt the inner cover from the cylinder block.

Tensioner/roller

2 To remove the tensioner/roller assembly, unscrew the retaining nut and withdraw the tensioner from the location pin. On engine code AZM, note that the tensioner plate engages in a hole in the cylinder head.

Camshaft sprocket

3 To reduce the possibility of accidental contact between pistons and valves, turn the crankshaft against the normal direction of rotation (anti-clockwise) approximately 90°. Unscrew the camshaft sprocket bolt, while holding the sprocket stationary. Remove the bolt, sprocket, and on engine code AZM the key **(see illustrations)**.

5.3a Use a home-made tool to counterhold the camshaft sprocket

5.3b Remove the camshaft sprocket bolt

5.3c Remove the Woodruff key

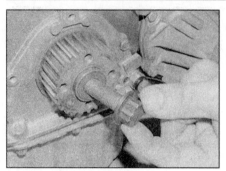

5.4a Unscrew the bolt . . .

5.4b . . . and remove the crankshaft sprocket

Crankshaft sprocket

4 To reduce the possibility of accidental contact between pistons and valves, turn the crankshaft against the normal direction of rotation (anti-clockwise) approximately 90°, where the pistons should all be half-way up the cylinder bores. Unscrew the crankshaft sprocket bolt, and remove the sprocket **(see illustrations)**. The bolt is very tight, and the crankshaft must be held stationary. On manual gearbox models, engage top gear and apply the footbrake pedal firmly. On automatic transmission models, unbolt the transmission front cover and use a wide-bladed screwdriver in the starter ring gear to hold the crankshaft stationary.

Inspection

5 Clean all the sprockets and examine them for wear and damage. Spin the tensioner roller, and check that it runs smoothly.
6 Check the tensioner for signs of wear and/or damage and renew if necessary.

Refitting

Crankshaft sprocket

7 Locate the sprocket on the crankshaft, then tighten the bolt to the specified torque while holding the crankshaft stationary using the method employed on removal. **Note:** *Do not turn the crankshaft as the pistons may contact the valves.*
8 Refit the timing belt as described in Section 4.

Camshaft sprocket

9 Locate the key (engine code AZM) on the

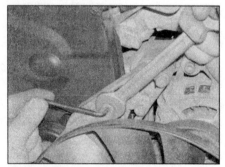

6.8a Move the tensioner clockwise with a spanner, then insert the metal rod to hold it

camshaft and refit the sprocket and bolt. Tighten the bolt to the specified torque while holding the sprocket using the method employed on removal. Note that on engine codes AWT and ALT the sprocket must be refitted with the narrow web facing forwards.
10 Refit the timing belt as described in Section 4.

Tensioner/roller

11 Refit the tensioner roller and spring assembly using a reversal of the removal procedure.
12 Refit the timing belt as described in Section 4.

---

6 Auxiliary drivebelts – removal and refitting

1 Depending on the vehicle specification and engine type, one or two auxiliary drivebelts may be fitted. The main drivebelt drives the alternator, viscous coupling fan, and the power steering pump. Where air conditioning is fitted, a secondary drivebelt from the crankshaft pulley drives the air conditioning compressor.
2 The main drivebelt and air conditioning drivebelt are both of multi-ribbed type. The main drivebelt tension is adjusted automatically by a spring-tensioned idler. Where fitted, the air conditioning compressor drivebelt is adjusted using a torque wrench on the idler.
3 To remove the drivebelts first apply the handbrake, then jack up the front of the vehicle

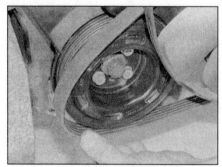

6.8b Remove the drivebelt from the crankshaft pulley

and support it on axle stands (see *Jacking and vehicle support*).
4 Remove the undershield from under the engine compartment.

Removal

5 If the drivebelt is to be re-used, mark it for clockwise direction to ensure it is refitted the same way round.
6 Although not essential, access to the drivebelt is best achieved by moving the complete front panel (the lock carrier assembly) away from the front of the car as far as possible, but without disconnecting the radiator hoses or electrical wiring. To do this, first remove the front bumper as described in Chapter 11, then unscrew the three quick-release clips from the noise insulation panel and unbolt the air duct from between the lock carrier and the air cleaner. On the left-hand side of the radiator, release the wiring from the clips. Unscrew the bolts securing the lock carrier/bumper bar assembly to the underbody channels, then unscrew the upper side bolts – one on the top/front of each wing, and one alongside each headlamp. Unscrew the bolts securing the bumper guides beneath each headlamp, and unclip them from the front wings. With the help of an assistant, pull the complete assembly away from the front of the car as far as possible. VW technicians use special tools to hold the assembly, however support bars may be made out of threaded metal rod and screwed into the underbody channels.
7 On models with air conditioning, loosen the pivot and tension bolts and move the tensioner roller upwards to release the tension on the drivebelt. Slip the drivebelt from the crankshaft, compressor and tensioner pulleys.
8 To remove the main drivebelt, the automatic tensioner must be released and held with a suitable pin or tool. Using a spanner on the flats, move the tensioner clockwise until the pin holes are aligned then insert a metal rod, bolt or drill bit to hold the tensioner in its released position. Remove the drivebelt from the crankshaft, alternator, viscous fan, and power steering pump pulleys **(see illustrations)**.

Refitting

9 Locate the coolant pump drivebelt on the power steering pump pulley, then loosely assemble the two halves of the pulley and the drivebelt on the coolant pump and insert the retaining bolts loosely. Press the two halves of the pulley together while turning the pulleys and progressively tighten the retaining bolts. The belt must not be allowed to become trapped between the two halves of the pulley. Finally, tighten the bolts to the specified torque.
10 Locate the main drivebelt on the pulleys, then initially turn the tensioner clockwise and remove the retaining pin. Release the tensioner to tension the drivebelt, making sure that it is correctly located in all the pulley grooves.

11 On models with air conditioning, locate the drivebelt on the compressor and crankshaft pulleys, making sure that it is correctly located in all the pulley grooves. Move the tensioner pulley downwards and engage the drivebelt with the pulley grooves. Tension the drivebelt by applying a torque of 30 Nm to the hexagon on the tensioner body. Hold this torque then tighten the adjustment and pivot bolts.

7 Camshaft cover – removal and refitting
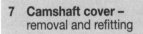

Removal

1 Where applicable, undo the retaining bolts and remove the engine top cover(s).
2 Loosen the clip and disconnect the crankcase ventilation hose from the camshaft cover. Recover the O-ring seal. Where applicable, unbolt the breather pipe and position it to one side.
3 Unclip and remove the upper timing cover with reference to Section 4.
4 On engine codes AWT and ALT, remove the ignition coils from the camshaft cover with reference to Chapter 5B.
5 Unscrew the nuts then lift the camshaft cover from the cylinder head. Recover the main gasket. On engine code AZM, note the location of the timing belt inner guard and the small support bracket, then remove the reinforcement strips and oil deflector. On engine codes AWT and ALT, recover the central spark plug tube gasket, and the oil deflector from between cylinders 1 and 2 above the inlet camshaft **(see illustrations)**.

Refitting

6 Clean the surfaces of the camshaft cover and cylinder head, then refit the oil deflector.
7 On engine code AZM, at the rear of the cylinder head apply suitable sealant to the top edges of the semi-circular cut out in the cylinder head. On engine codes AWT and ALT, at the rear of the cylinder head apply suitable sealant to the two points where the hydraulic tensioner contacts the cylinder head **(see illustration)**. Similarly, at the front of the cylinder head, apply suitable sealant to the two points where the camshaft bearing cap contacts the cylinder head.
8 Carefully lay the gasket on the cylinder head; on engine codes AWT and ALT also fit the new spark plug tube gaskets.
9 Refit the camshaft cover together with the oil deflector **(see illustration)**. On engine code AZM, refit the reinforcement strips, inner guard and support bracket. Tighten the nuts progressively to the specified torque, where given.
10 On engine codes AWT and ALT, refit each ignition coil together with their O-ring seals, making sure that they are located on the HT leads correctly, then tighten the retaining bolts

7.5a Remove the camshaft cover . . .

7.5b . . . then remove the spark plug tube gasket

securely. Reconnect the ignition coil wiring, then refit the earth wire and tighten the bolt.
11 Refit the upper timing cover and secure with the clips.
12 On engine code AZM, reconnect the crankcase ventilation hose together with a new O-ring seal, and secure with the clip. On engine codes AWT and ALT, reconnect the crankcase breather pipe to the ventilation hose, then attach the breather pipe to the camshaft cover and tighten the bolts.
13 Refit the engine top cover(s).

8 Camshaft oil seal – renewal

Engine code AZM

1 Remove the camshaft sprocket as described in Section 5.
2 Drill two small holes into the existing oil seal, diagonally opposite each other. Thread two self-tapping screws into the holes, and using two pairs of pliers, pull on the heads of the screws to extract the oil seal. Take great care to avoid drilling through into the seal housing or camshaft sealing surface.
3 Clean out the seal housing and sealing surface of the camshaft by wiping it with a lint-free cloth. Remove any swarf or burrs that may cause the seal to leak.
4 Lubricate the lip and outer edge of the new oil seal with clean engine oil, and push it over the camshaft until it is positioned above its housing. **Note:** *PTFE type oil seals may be*

7.7 Apply sealant to the joints on the cylinder head

*used with these engines – they must **not** be oiled prior to fitment. These seals are identified by having no coil spring.*
5 Using a hammer and a socket of suitable diameter, drive the seal squarely into its housing **(see illustration 8.16)**. **Note:** *Select a socket that bears only on the hard outer surface of the seal, not the inner lip which can easily be damaged.*
6 Refit the camshaft sprocket with reference to Section 5.

Engine codes AWT and ALT

7 To remove the exhaust camshaft oil seal proceed as described in paragraphs 1 to 6. The following paragraphs describe removing the inlet camshaft oil seal.
8 Remove the auxiliary drivebelt(s) as described in Section 6. Also unbolt the tensioner from the front of the engine, using an Allen key.
9 Disconnect the wiring from the Hall sender located on the front of the inlet camshaft.
10 Unclip and remove the upper timing cover.
11 Unscrew the retaining bolt and withdraw the Hall sender assembly from the cylinder head.
12 Note the location of the Hall sender rotor and convex washer. Unscrew the central bolt and remove the washer and rotor. The rotor engages with the slot in the end of the inlet camshaft.
13 Drill two small holes into the existing oil seal, diagonally opposite each other. Thread two self-tapping screws into the holes, and using two pairs of pliers, pull on the heads of

7.9 Refit the camshaft cover

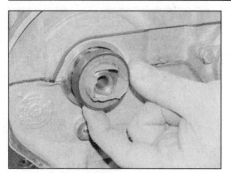

8.15 Fit the new camshaft oil seal

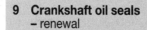

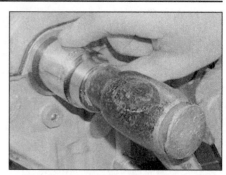

8.16 Use a socket to drive the oil seal squarely into the housing

the screws to extract the oil seal. Take great care to avoid drilling through into the seal housing or camshaft sealing surface.

14 Clean out the seal housing and sealing surface of the camshaft by wiping it with a lint-free cloth. Remove any swarf or burrs that may cause the seal to leak.

15 Lubricate the lip and outer edge of the new oil seal with clean engine oil, and push it over the camshaft until it is positioned above its housing. To prevent damage to the sealing lips, wrap some adhesive tape around the end of the camshaft **(see illustration)**. **Note:** *PTFE type oil seals may be used with these engines – they must **not** be oiled prior to fitment. These seals are identified by having no coil spring.*

16 Using a hammer and a socket of suitable diameter, drive the seal squarely into its housing **(see illustration)**. **Note:** *Select a socket that bears only on the hard outer*

surface of the seal, not the inner lip which can easily be damaged.

17 Locate the Hall sender rotor on the end of the inlet camshaft making sure that it engages the slot. Fit the convex washer and bolt, and tighten securely.

18 Locate the Hall sender assembly on the cylinder head, and retain with the bolt tightened securely.

19 Refit the upper timing cover, making sure that it engages the bottom cover correctly, and retain with the clips.

20 Reconnect the Hall sender wiring.

21 Refit the tensioner to the front of the engine and tighten the bolts securely.

22 Refit the auxiliary drivebelt(s) with reference to Section 6.

9 Crankshaft oil seals – renewal

Front oil seal

1 Remove the timing belt and crankshaft sprocket, with reference to Section 5.

2 The seal may be renewed without removing the housing by drilling two small holes diagonally opposite each other, inserting self-tapping screws, and pulling on the heads of the screws with pliers **(see illustration)**. Alternatively, unbolt and remove the housing (including the relevant sump bolts) then lever out the oil seal on the bench **(see illustration)**. If the sump gasket is damaged while removing the housing, it will be necessary to remove the

sump and fit a new gasket. However, refit the sump *after* fitting the housing.

3 Lubricate the sealing lips of the new seal with new engine oil and drive it into the housing with a block of wood or a socket until flush **(see illustration)**. Make sure that the closed end of the seal is facing outwards. **Note:** *PTFE type oil seals may be used with these engines – they must **not** be oiled prior to fitment. These seals are identified by having no coil spring.*

4 Clean the mating surfaces of the housing and cylinder block, then apply a 2.0 to 3.0 mm bead of silicone sealant to the housing, making sure that it is applied to the inside of the bolt holes **(see illustration)**.

5 Fit the housing, and tighten the bolts evenly in diagonal sequence. To prevent damage to the seal as it is being fitted, wrap some tape around the end of the crankshaft first **(see illustrations)**.

9.2a Remove the crankshaft front oil seal

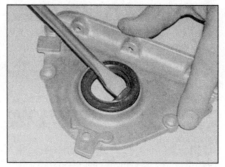

9.2b Use a screwdriver to lever out the crankshaft front oil seal from its housing

9.3 Use a socket to drive the crankshaft oil seal squarely into the housing

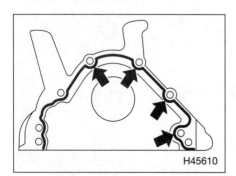

9.4 Apply sealant to the crankshaft front oil seal housing . . .

H45610

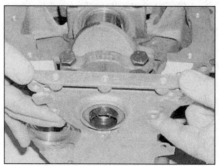

9.5a . . . refit the housing . . .

9.5b . . . and refit the bolts

9.9a Fit the new gasket . . .

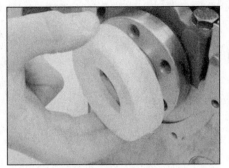

9.9b . . . then locate the tool over the end of the crankshaft

9.10 Fit the housing and oil seal over the fitting tool

6 Refit the timing belt and crankshaft sprocket, with reference to Section 5.

Rear oil seal

Note: *The oil seal is not available separately from the oil seal housing.*

7 Remove the flywheel/driveplate, with reference to Section 12.

8 Unbolt and remove the housing (including the relevant sump bolts) and remove the gasket. If the sump gasket is damaged while removing the housing, it will be necessary to remove the sump and fit a new gasket. However, refit the sump *after* fitting the housing.

9 New housings are provided with a fitting tool to prevent damage to the oil seal as it is being fitted. First fit the new gasket, then locate the tool on the end of the crankshaft **(see illustrations)**.

10 Fit the housing and oil seal, and tighten the bolts evenly in diagonal sequence to the specified torque, then remove the tool **(see illustration)**.

11 Refit the flywheel/driveplate, with reference to Section 12.

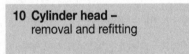

10 Cylinder head –
removal and refitting

Note: *Cylinder head dismantling and overhaul is covered in Chapter 2C.*

Removal

1 Before starting work, disconnect the battery negative (earth) lead (see Chapter 5A).

2 Apply the handbrake, then jack up the front of the vehicle and support it on axle stands (see *Jacking and vehicle support*).

3 Where applicable, undo the retaining bolts and remove the engine top cover(s).

4 Remove the timing belt as described in Section 4. This procedure includes removing the front bumper and positioning the front lock carrier away from the front of the car.

5 Drain the cooling system as described in Chapter 1A.

6 Refer to Chapter 4A and depressurise the fuel system, then disconnect the fuel supply and return lines from the fuel rail. Plug the lines to prevent entry of dust and dirt.

Engine codes AWT and ALT

7 Refer to Chapter 4A and unbolt the catalytic converter from the turbocharger.

8 Loosen the clips and disconnect the coolant hoses from the cylinder head.

9 Disconnect the crankcase ventilation hose and the secondary air injection hose.

10 Disconnect the turbocharger vacuum hose from the wastegate control.

11 Refer to Chapter 4A and disconnect all wiring to the injection and ignition systems.

12 Remove the camshaft cover as described in Section 7.

Engine code AZM

13 Disconnect the wiring from the following components:
a) Hall sender.
b) Injectors.
c) Coolant temperature sender.
d) Throttle valve control.
e) Inlet manifold change-over valve.

f) Air mass meter.
g) Activated charcoal filter system solenoid valve.

14 Loosen the clips and disconnect the coolant hoses from the cylinder head.

15 Disconnect all coolant and vacuum hoses from the cylinder head.

16 Refer to Chapter 4A and remove the air cleaner together with the air inlet ducting.

17 Refer to Chapter 4C and disconnect the catalytic converter from the exhaust manifold.

18 Unbolt the bracket from the inlet manifold.

19 Disconnect the HT leads from the spark plugs.

20 Where applicable, disconnect the vacuum pipe from the secondary air pump motor at the pressure pipe to the combi valve.

21 Remove the camshaft cover and oil deflector as described in Section 7 **(see illustration)**.

All engines

22 Using a multi-splined socket, unscrew the cylinder head bolts a turn at a time, in reverse order to the tightening sequence **(see illustration 10.30a or 10.30b)** and remove them together with their washers **(see illustration)**.

23 With all the bolts removed, lift the cylinder head from the block together with the exhaust manifold **(see illustration)**. If it is stuck, tap it free with a wooden mallet. Do not insert a lever into the gasket joint.

24 Remove the cylinder head gasket from the block **(see illustration)**.

25 Remove the inlet manifold (Chapter 4A),

10.21 Remove the oil splash guard

10.22 Unscrew the cylinder head bolts

10.23 Lift the cylinder head from the engine

10.24 Remove the cylinder head gasket

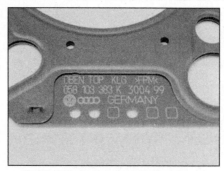

10.28 Cylinder head gasket markings

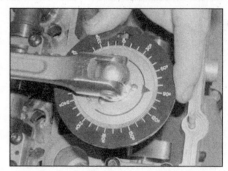

10.30a Angle-tighten the cylinder head bolts

exhaust manifold (Chapter 4C) and spark plugs (Chapter 1A) from the cylinder head.

Refitting

26 Thoroughly clean the contact faces of the cylinder head and block. Also clean any oil or coolant from the bolt holes in the block – if this precaution is not taken, not only will the tightening torque be incorrect but there is the possibility of damaging the block. The cylinder head bolts must be renewed whenever removed.

27 Refit the exhaust manifold (Chapter 4C), inlet manifold (Chapter 4A) and spark plugs (Chapter 1A) to the cylinder head.

28 Locate a new gasket on the block, with the part number or words OBEN TOP facing upwards **(see illustration)**. VW recommend that the gasket is not removed from its packaging until just prior to fitting it. On engine codes AWT and ALT, make sure that the location dowels are in position. There are no location dowels on engine code AZM, and it is recommended that two old cylinder head bolts are used as guides; cut off the heads of the bolts and cut slots in the bolts so that they can be unscrewed when the head is in position. Screw the bolts into the front corner positions of the block.

29 Carefully lower the head onto the block, making sure that it engages the location dowels or guides correctly. Do not use any jointing compound on the cylinder head joint. Insert the new cylinder head bolts, and initially hand-tighten them using a splined tool. On engine code AZM, unscrew and remove the guides, using a magnet to withdraw them.

30 Using the sequence shown tighten all the bolts to the Stage 1 torque given in the Specifications, then angle-tighten by the Stage 2 and 3 angles given in the Specifications **(see illustrations)**.

Engine codes AWT and ALT

31 Refit the camshaft cover with reference to Section 7.

32 Reconnect all wiring to the injection and ignition systems.

33 Reconnect the turbocharger vacuum hose to the wastegate control.

34 Reconnect the crankcase ventilation hose and secondary air injection hose.

35 Reconnect the coolant hoses and tighten the clips.

36 Refit the catalytic converter to the turbocharger.

Engine code AZM

37 Refit the camshaft cover and oil deflector with reference to Section 7.

38 Reconnect the vacuum pipe to the secondary air pump motor at the pressure pipe to the combi valve.

39 Reconnect the HT leads to the spark plugs.

40 Refit the bracket to the inlet manifold and tighten the bolts.

41 Reconnect the catalytic converter to the exhaust manifold with reference to Chapter 4C.

42 Refit the air cleaner and air ducting with reference to Chapter 4A.

43 Reconnect all coolant and vacuum hoses and tighten the clips.

44 Reconnect the wiring disconnected in paragraph 13.

All engines

45 Reconnect the fuel supply and return lines to the fuel rail.

46 Refit the timing belt with reference to Section 4.

47 Refill the cooling system with reference to Chapter 1A.

48 Refit the engine top cover(s).

49 Lower the car to the ground, then reconnect the battery negative (earth) lead.

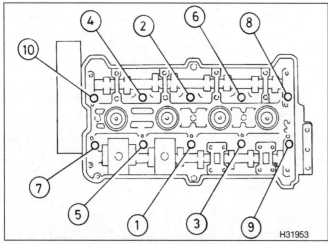

10.30b Cylinder head bolt tightening sequence (engine codes AWT and ALT)

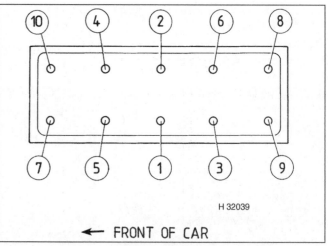

← FRONT OF CAR

10.30c Cylinder head bolt tightening sequence (engine code AZM)

11 Hydraulic tappets
– operational check

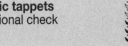

⚠️ **Warning: After fitting hydraulic tappets, wait a minimum of 30 minutes (or preferably, leave overnight) before starting the engine, to allow the tappets time to settle, otherwise the valve heads will strike the pistons.**

1 The hydraulic tappets are self-adjusting, and require no attention whilst in service.

2 If the hydraulic tappets become excessively noisy, their operation can be checked as described below.

3 Run the engine at 2500 rpm until it reaches its normal operating temperature. Switch off the engine, then refer to Section 7 and remove the camshaft cover.

4 Rotate the camshaft by turning the crank-shaft with a socket and wrench, until the first cam lobe over No 1 cylinder is pointing upwards.

5 Using a non-metallic tool, press the tappet downwards then use a feeler blade to check the free travel. If this is more than 0.2 mm before the valve starts to open, the tappet should be renewed.

6 Hydraulic tappet removal and refitting is described as part of the cylinder head overhaul sequence – see Chapter 2C for details.

7 If hydraulic tappet noise occurs repeatedly when travelling short distances, renew the oil retention valve located in the rear of the oil filter mounting housing. It will be necessary to remove the oil filter, then unbolt the housing from the cylinder block and recover the gasket. Use a suitable key to unscrew the valve, and tighten the new valve securely. Refit the housing together with a new gasket.

12 Flywheel/driveplate
– removal, inspection and refitting

Removal

1 On manual gearbox models, remove the gearbox (see Chapter 7A) and clutch (see Chapter 6).

2 On automatic transmission models, remove the automatic transmission as described in Chapter 7B.

3 The flywheel/driveplate bolts are offset to ensure correct fitment. Unscrew the bolts while holding the flywheel/driveplate stationary. Temporarily insert a bolt in the cylinder block, and use a screwdriver to hold the flywheel/driveplate, or make up a holding tool as shown **(see illustrations)**.

4 Lift the flywheel/driveplate from the crankshaft **(see illustration)**. If removing a driveplate, note the location of the shim (next to the crankshaft) and the spacer.

Inspection

5 Check the flywheel/driveplate for wear and damage. Examine the starter ring gear for

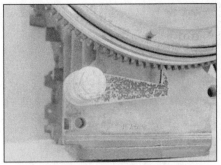

12.3a Tool for holding the flywheel/driveplate stationary

excessive wear to the teeth. If the driveplate or its ring gear are damaged, the complete driveplate must be renewed. The flywheel ring gear, however, may be renewed separately from the flywheel, but the work should be entrusted to a VW dealer. If the clutch friction face is discoloured or scored excessively, it may be possible to regrind it, but this work should also be entrusted to a VW dealer or specialist.

6 With the flywheel removed, check the spigot needle bearing in the end of the crankshaft for wear by turning it with a finger. If there is any evidence of excessive wear or if the bearing has been running dry, it must be renewed. To do this, use a bearing removal puller which engages the rear end of the bearing. Drive the new bearing into position until its outer end is 1.5 mm below the end of the crankshaft. The side of the bearing that is inscribed must be visible when the bearing is installed. **Note: A spigot needle bearing must not be fitted to the crankshaft on automatic transmission models.**

Refitting

7 Refitting is a reversal of removal, however on automatic transmission models temporarily refit the driveplate using the old bolts tightened to 30 Nm, and check that the distance from the rear face of the block to the outer face of the starter ring gear on the driveplate is 27 mm ± 1 mm. Alternatively, use vernier calipers through one of the torque converter mounting bolt holes to check that the distance from the rear face of the block to the outer face of the driveplate is 21.3 to 22.9 mm **(see illustration)**. If necessary, remove the driveplate, and fit a spacer behind it

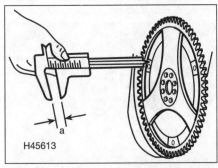

12.7 Checking the torque converter fitting dimension

a = 21.3 to 22.9 mm

12.3b Remove the flywheel bolts

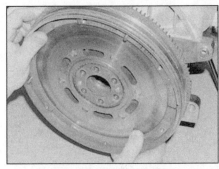

12.4 Remove the flywheel

to achieve the correct dimension. The raised pip on the outer shim must face the torque converter. Use new bolts when refitting the flywheel or driveplate, and coat the threads of the bolts with locking fluid if they are not already pre-coated. Tighten them to the specified torque.

13 Engine mountings
– inspection and renewal

Inspection

1 If improved access is required, raise the front of the car and support it securely on axle stands, and remove the undershield where applicable.

2 Check the mounting rubbers to see if they are cracked, hardened or separated from the metal at any point; renew the mounting if any such damage or deterioration is evident.

3 Check that all the mounting's fasteners are securely tightened; use a torque wrench to check if possible.

4 Using a large screwdriver or a crowbar, check for wear in the mounting by carefully levering against it to check for free play. Where this is not possible, enlist the aid of an assistant to move the engine/transmission back-and-forth, or from side-to-side, while you watch the mounting. While some free play is to be expected even from new components, excessive wear should be obvious. If excessive free play is found, check first that the fasteners are correctly secured, then renew any worn components as described below.

13.6 Remove the torque stop from the engine

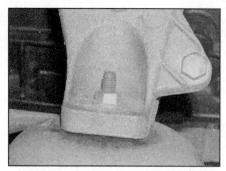

13.15a Remove the upper mounting nut

13.15b Left-hand engine mounting

13.16 Engine mounting bracket

Renewal

Front torque arm
(models without air conditioning)

5 Apply the handbrake then jack up the front of the vehicle and support it on axle stands (see *Jacking and vehicle support*). Remove the undershield where applicable. Support the weight of the engine/transmission using a trolley jack with a block of wood placed on its head.
6 Unscrew the bolts and remove the torque arm and rubber mounting from the front of the cylinder block **(see illustration)**. The rubber stop is available separately if required.
7 Unbolt the bracket from the front crossmember.
8 Fit the new torque arm and bracket using a reversal of the removal procedure.

Front torque bracket
(models with air conditioning)

9 Apply the handbrake then jack up the front of the vehicle and support it on axle stands (see *Jacking and vehicle support*). Remove the undershield where applicable. Support the weight of the engine/transmission using a trolley jack with a block of wood placed on its head.
10 Unscrew the bolts and remove the stop from the bracket on the front of the engine. Move the bracket over the rubber, then prise the rubber from the cross-tube and remove the bracket.
11 If necessary, the stop plate can be unbolted from the front of the engine, and the side supports also removed.

12 Fit the new rubber and bracket using a reversal of the removal procedure.

Right- or left-hand engine mounting

13 Apply the handbrake, then jack up the front of the vehicle and support it on axle stands (see *Jacking and vehicle support*).
14 Support the weight of the engine with a hoist. Alternatively, use a trolley jack and piece of wood beneath the sump.
15 Unscrew the mounting nuts, then raise the engine and withdraw the mounting from the engine bracket and subframe **(see illustrations)**. Note that the mounting has an integral hydro action, to absorb movement of the engine and prevent engine noise transmission inside the car.
16 If necessary, unbolt the mounting bracket from the side of the cylinder block **(see illustration)**.
17 Fit the new mounting using a reversal of the removal procedure.

14.3 Refit the sump drain plug

14 Sump – removal and refitting

Note: *When removing the sump on the 2.0 litre engine code ALT, the oil pump and balancer shaft assembly must also be removed and the intermediate plate renewed.*

Removal

1 Apply the handbrake, then jack up the front of the vehicle and support it on axle stands (see *Jacking and vehicle support*).
2 Unbolt and remove the undershield from under the front of the engine.
3 Position a container beneath the sump, then unscrew the drain plug and drain the engine oil. Clean the plug and if necessary renew the washer, then refit and tighten the plug after all the oil has drained **(see illustration)**. Remove the dipstick from the engine.
4 Access to the front of the engine is achieved by moving the complete front panel (the lock carrier assembly) away from the front of the car as far as possible, but without disconnecting the radiator hoses or electrical wiring. To do this, first remove the front bumper as described in Chapter 11, then unscrew the three quick-release clips from the noise insulation panel and unbolt the air duct from between the lock carrier and the air cleaner. On the left-hand side of the radiator, release the wiring from the clips. Unscrew the bolts securing the lock carrier/bumper bar assembly to the underbody channels, then unscrew the upper side bolts – one at the top/front of each wing, and one alongside each headlamp. Unscrew the bolts securing the bumper guides beneath each headlamp, and unclip them from the front wings. With the help of an assistant, pull the complete assembly away from the front of the car as far as possible. VW technicians use special tools to hold the assembly, however support bars may be made out of threaded metal rod and screwed into the underbody channels.
5 Remove the auxiliary drivebelt as described in Section 6. Mark the air conditioning compressor drivebelt for normal rotational direction, then unbolt the tensioner roller and remove the drivebelt.
6 Remove the viscous fan unit with reference to Chapter 3, Section 5. Briefly, it is removed by inserting an Allen key from behind, while holding the unit stationary with a temporary bolt inserted from behind, resting on the engine cylinder block.
7 Unbolt the engine front torque rod support bracket from the engine.
8 Unclip the lower part of the starter cable retainer.
9 Where applicable, unbolt the automatic transmission fluid cooling hose bracket from the sump.
10 Disconnect the wiring from the oil level/temperature sender.
11 On 2.0 litre models, remove the air intake pipe rear support.

12 The engine mountings must now be released, but first mark the positions of the mountings and location sleeves on the subframe to ensure correct refitting. Unscrew both mounting nuts.

13 Connect a suitable hoist to the engine, then raise it as far as possible without damaging or stretching the coolant hoses, intake hoses and wiring. Do not compress the crankcase breather T-piece to the bulkhead.

14 Support the front subframe with a trolley jack and length of wood. Mark the position of the subframe to ensure correct refitting and wheel alignment, then unscrew and remove the subframe mounting bolts. The front two bolts must be unscrewed first, then the rear bolts. Lower the subframe together with the anti-roll bar to the ground, or alternatively, lower the rear of the subframe to provide sufficient room to remove the sump.

15 On manual transmission models, unscrew the left-hand transmission mounting nut until it is flush with the end of the bolt (approximately four turns).

16 On automatic transmission models, loosen the rear bolt on the left-hand transmission mounting a few turns, then unscrew and remove the front bolt.

17 On manual and automatic transmission models, loosen the rear bolt on the right-hand transmission mounting a few turns, then unscrew and remove the front bolt.

18 On turbocharged engines, unscrew the flange bolts and disconnect the turbocharger oil return line from the sump. Recover the gasket.

19 Disconnect the oil level/temperature sensor wiring plug (where fitted). Unscrew and remove the sump bolts. Note that on manual transmission models, the two rear sump bolts are accessed through a cut-out in the flywheel – turn the flywheel as necessary to align the cut-out **(see illustrations)**.

20 Remove the sump and gasket. If it is stuck, tap it gently with a mallet to free it **(see illustrations)**.

21 On the 2.0 litre engine code ALT, remove the oil pump and balancer shaft gear assembly followed by the assembly-to-block intermediate plate as described in Section 17. This is necessary as the intermediate plate extends to the outer flange of the crankcase, where the sump is bolted, and the new plate must be sealed to both the crankcase and sump.

Refitting

22 Thoroughly clean the contact faces of the sump and block. VW recommend a rotary wire brush is used to clean away the sealant.

23 On the 2.0 litre engine code ALT, refit the oil pump and balancer shaft gear assembly together with a new assembly-to-block intermediate plate as described in Section 17. *Caution: Take care not to apply excessive amounts of sealant, in the hope of obtaining a better seal – if too much is applied, the excess may enter the sump and then block the oil pump strainer, causing oil starvation.*

14.19a Remove the rear sump bolts (flywheel removed)

14.20a Remove the sump . . .

24 Apply a 2 to 3 mm bead of suitable silicone sealant to the sump mating surface. Run the bead of sealant around the inside of the bolt holes, and take particular care at the rear of the sump to keep the bead near the inner edge of the sump, to avoid the two drillings in the block. The sump should be offered into position immediately, and the retaining bolts tightened hand-tight initially. If the engine is out of the car, make sure that the rear edge of the sump is flush with the transmission-to-engine intermediate plate on the rear of the cylinder block; the thickness of the plate is 0.8 mm **(see illustrations)**. Progressively tighten the sump bolts to the specified torque in the stages given in the Specifications. Refer to the sealant manufacturer's advice on the length of time required for the sealant to set. Typically, it is advisable to wait at least 30 minutes before filling the engine with oil. If the car is to be left for some time with no oil in the sump, ensure

14.19b Align the cut-outs in the flywheel with the sump for access to the rear sump bolts

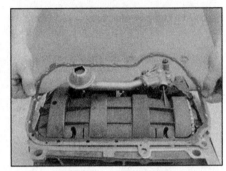

14.20b . . . and gasket

that the battery remains disconnected, so that no attempt is made to start the engine.

> **HAYNES HiNT** *To make aligning the sump easier, obtain two or three M6 studs, and screw them by a few threads into opposite sides of the cylinder block/crankcase mating surface. The sump can be offered into position and fitted over the studs, then the remaining sump bolts can be fitted and hand-tightened. Remove the studs, and fit the rest of the sump bolts.*

25 The remaining refitting procedure is a reversal removal, but tighten the nuts and bolts to the specified torque where given in the Specifications. On completion, fill the engine with the correct quantity of oil as described in Chapter 1A.

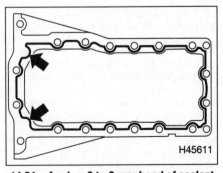

H45611

14.24a Apply a 2 to 3 mm bead of sealant to the sump

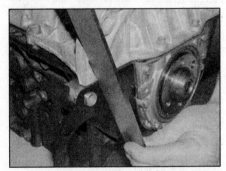

14.24b Using a straight-edge to align the sump with the rear of the engine

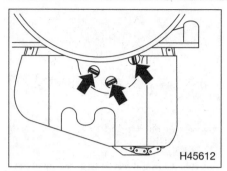

15.6 Release the cover locking lugs with a screwdriver

15 Oil pump and pick-up
– removal, inspection and refitting

Removal

1 Remove the sump as described in Section 14.
2 The oil pump is driven by chain from the front of the crankshaft. On the 2.0 litre engine code ALT, the oil pump is incorporated in the balancer shaft assembly between the sump and crankcase.

Engine codes AWT and AZM

3 Unscrew the bolt, release and remove the baffle plate from the bottom of the crankcase.
4 Unscrew and remove the remaining two mounting bolts, and release the oil pump from the dowels in the crankcase. Unhook the oil pump drive sprocket from the chain and withdraw the oil pump and suction pipe from the engine. Note that the tensioner will attempt to tighten the chain, and it may be necessary to use a screwdriver to hold it in its released position before releasing the oil pump sprocket from the chain.
5 Unscrew the flange bolts and remove the suction pipe from the oil pump. Recover the O-ring seal. Unscrew the bolts and remove the cover from the oil pump.

Engine code ALT

6 Release the locking lugs using a screwdriver through the slits provided, then withdraw the protector cover from the oil pump drive chain (**see illustration**).
7 Loosen the oil pump sprocket retaining bolt, then using a screwdriver carefully release the tension on the chain by pressing the tensioner in. Lock the tensioner in this position using an angled 3 mm Allen key through the hole provided.
8 Remove the retaining bolt and withdraw the oil pump sprocket, then release the chain from the balancer shaft drive sprocket.
9 Unbolt and remove the oil pump cover. Make sure that the location dowels remain in the balancer shaft assembly housing.

Inspection

10 Withdraw the inner and outer rotors, noting which way round they are fitted.

11 Examine the drive chain for wear and damage. To remove the chain, the timing belt must first be removed (see Section 4), then the crankshaft front oil seal housing unbolted from the cylinder block. With the housing removed, unbolt and remove the chain tensioner, then unhook the chain from the sprocket on the front of the crankshaft.
12 Clean the components and check them for wear and damage. Using a feeler blade, check the backlash between the rotors, and compare with that given in the Specifications. Similarly check the endfloat of the rotors, using a straight-edge across the end face of the housing. If outside the specified limits, the pump or balancer shaft housing should be renewed.

Refitting

13 On AWT and AZM code engines, prime the pump by pouring oil into the suction pipe aperture while turning the driveshaft. Due to the location of the suction pipe on engine code ALT, it is not possible to prime the pump.
14 Refit the oil pump cover and tighten the bolts to the specified torque.

Engine codes AWT and AZM

15 If the drive chain, crankshaft sprocket and tensioner have been removed, delay refitting them until after the oil pump has been mounted on the cylinder block. If they have not been removed, use a screwdriver to press the tensioner against its spring to provide sufficient slack in the chain to refit the oil pump.
16 Locate the oil pump on the dowels, then insert and tighten the two mounting bolts to the specified torque. Where applicable, engage the oil pump sprocket with the chain at this stage.
17 Where applicable, refit the drive chain, crankshaft sprocket and tensioner using a reversal of the removal procedure.
18 Refit the crankshaft front oil seal housing and timing belt where applicable. Apply suitable sealant to the front oil seal housing before fitting it.
19 Refit the baffle plate using the remaining oil pump mounting bolt and tighten it to the specified torque, followed by the sump with reference to Section 14.

Engine code ALT

20 If the drive chain, crankshaft sprocket and tensioner have been removed, refit them using a reversal of the removal procedure.
21 Locate the chain on the balancer shaft drive sprocket, then engage the oil pump sprocket in the chain and refit it to the oil pump inner rotor.
22 Use a screwdriver to press in the tensioner, then remove the Allen key and release the tensioner.
23 Tighten the sprocket retaining bolt to the specified torque.
24 Refit the protector cover over the oil pump drive chain and secure with the locking lugs.
25 Refit the sump with reference to Section 14.

16 Engine oil temperature sensor –
removal and refitting

Removal

1 Some models are equipped with an engine oil temperature sensor located on the underside of the sump. Apply the handbrake, then jack up the front of the vehicle and support it on axle stands (see *Jacking and vehicle support*).
2 Unbolt and remove the undershield from under the front of the engine.
3 Position a container beneath the sump, then unscrew the drain plug and drain the engine oil. Clean the plug and if necessary renew the washer, then refit and tighten the plug after all the oil has drained.
4 Disconnect the wiring plug from the oil temperature sensor.
5 Undo the two retaining bolts, and remove the sensor from the sump. Discard the O-ring, and new one must be used.

Refitting

6 Refitting is the reversal of removal, but always use a new O-ring and tighten the nuts and bolts to the specified torque as given in the Specifications. On completion, fill the engine with the correct quantity of oil as described in Chapter 1A.

17 Balancer shaft/
oil pump assembly –
removal and refitting

Removal

1 Models fitted with the 2.0 litre ALT engine are equipped with a balancer shaft assembly fitted to the bottom of the crankcase, inside the sump. The assembly consists of two counter-rotating balance shafts driven by the crankshaft, and the oil pump is also incorporated in the same housing (**see illustration**).
2 With reference to Section 3, set the crankshaft at TDC on No 1 cylinder at the end of the compression stroke.
3 Remove the sump as described in Section 14.
4 Release the securing clips and withdraw the protector cover from the oil pump drive chain.
5 Loosen the oil pump sprocket retaining bolt, then using a screwdriver carefully release the tension on the chain by pressing the tensioner in and locking it in position with a 3 mm Allen key (**see illustrations**).
6 Remove the retaining bolt and withdraw the oil pump sprocket, then release the chain from the balance shaft sprocket.
7 Working from the outside to the middle, loosen the retaining bolts, noting their fitted position (**see illustration**). Withdraw the balancer shaft assembly downwards from the crankcase. Recover the intermediate plate.

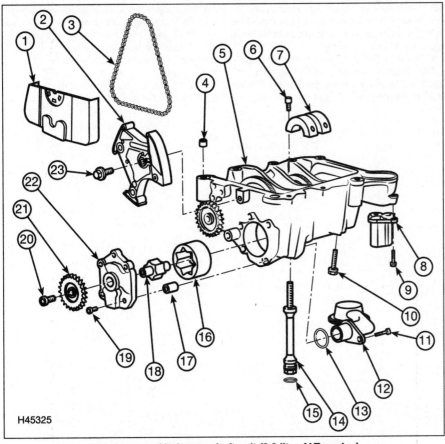

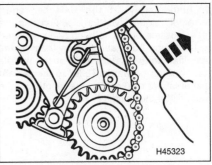

17.5a Press against the tensioner using a screwdriver – in direction of arrow . . .

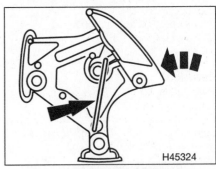

17.5b . . . then lock the tensioner in position with a 3 mm Allen key

H45325

17.1 Layout of balancer shaft unit (2.0 litre ALT engine)

1 Chain protector cover
2 Chain tensioner
3 Chain
4 Dowels
5 Oil pump/balancer shaft assembly
6 Bolt
7 Cover to prevent oil frothing
8 Oil return element with seal
9 Bolt
10 Bolt
11 Bolt
12 Oil strainer/suction pipe
13 O-ring/seal
14 Sealing bolt
15 O-ring/seal
16 Oil pump outer rotor
17 Dowels
18 Oil pump inner rotor
19 Bolt
20 Bolt
21 Oil pump drive sprocket
22 Oil pump cover
23 Bolt

Caution: The balance shaft assembly retaining bolts are of different lengths; make a note of their position for refitting.

Refitting

8 Check that the crankshaft is still at TDC on No 1 cylinder at the end of the compression stroke (see Section 3).

9 Position the balance shafts so that the timing mark on the sprocket is aligned with the hole in the housing and insert a locking pin **(see illustration)**.

10 Clean the mating surfaces of the balancer shaft assembly, intermediate plate (new) and crankcase, then apply a 2 to 3.0 mm thick bead of silicone sealant to the upper and lower surfaces of the intermediate plate, making sure that the bead runs along the inside of the bolt holes **(see illustration)**.

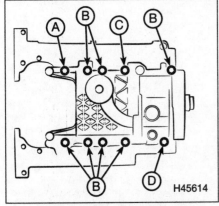

17.7 Balancer shaft assembly mounting bolt locations (engine code ALT)

A M7x40
B M7x55
C M7x90
D Bolt with sealing O-ring

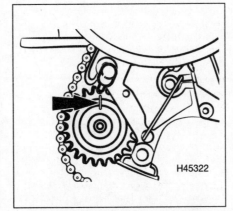

17.9 Align timing mark (arrowed) and insert locking pin – VW tool T10060

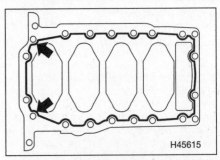

H45615

17.10 Apply a 2 to 3 mm bead of sealant to the balance shaft-to-crankcase intermediate plate

11 Immediately fit the balancer shaft assembly to the cylinder block, noting the fitted position of the bolts on removal. Insert the retaining bolts and tighten them to the specified torque, starting from the middle and working outwards. Refer to the sealant manufacturer's advice on the length of time required for the sealant to set.

12 With the locking pin still in position and the 3 mm Allen key locking the chain tensioner, refit the drive chain around the balance shaft sprocket.

13 Position the chamfered side of the oil pump shaft upwards and fit the oil pump sprocket, locating it in the drive chain. Tighten the retaining bolt by hand at this moment.

14 With the sprockets aligned, remove the locking keys from the balance shaft sprocket and chain tensioner, then tighten the oil pump sprocket to the specified torque.

15 Refit the protector cover to the oil pump drive chain.

16 Refit the sump as described in Section 14.

Chapter 2 Part B:
Diesel engine in-car repair procedures

Contents

Section number

Auxiliary drivebelts – removal, refitting and tensioning 6
Camshaft cover – removal and refitting 7
Camshaft oil seal – renewal 9
Camshaft(s) – removal and overhaul . . . . See Chapter 2C
Crankshaft oil seals – renewal 10
Cylinder compression test 3
Cylinder head – dismantling and overhaul . . . . See Chapter 2C
Cylinder head – removal and refitting 11
Engine mountings – inspection and renewal 14
Engine oil and filter – renewal . . . . See Chapter 1B

Section number

Engine oil level – check . . . . See Weekly checks
Engine valve timing marks – locating TDC on No 1 cylinder 2
Flywheel/driveplate – removal, inspection and refitting 13
General information 1
Hydraulic tappets – operation check 12
Oil pump and pick-up – removal, inspection and refitting 16
Pump injector rocker shaft assembly – removal and refitting 8
Sump – removal, inspection and refitting 15
Timing belt – removal, inspection and refitting 4
Timing belt tensioner and sprockets – removal and refitting 5

Degrees of difficulty

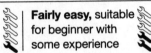

| Easy, suitable for novice with little experience | Fairly easy, suitable for beginner with some experience | Fairly difficult, suitable for competent DIY mechanic | Difficult, suitable for experienced DIY mechanic | Very difficult, suitable for expert DIY or professional |

Specifications

General

Power output:
 Engine code AVB* . . . . 74 kW (100 bhp)
 Engine codes AVF and AWX* . . . . 96 kW (130 bhp)
Bore . . . . 79.5 mm
Stroke . . . . 95.5 mm
Compression ratio:
 Engine code AVB* . . . . 19.5 : 1
 Engine code AVF and AWX* . . . . 19.0 : 1
Compression pressures (wear limit) . . . . 19.0 bar
Firing order . . . . 1 – 3 – 4 – 2
Cylinder No 1 location . . . . Timing belt end

* Note: *See 'Vehicle identification' for the location of the code marking on the engine.*

Lubrication system

Oil pump type . . . . Sump mounted, drive by chain from the timing end of the crankshaft
Oil pressure switch operating pressure:
 Brown . . . . 0.7 bar
 Grey . . . . 0.9 bar
Normal operating oil pressure (oil temperature 80°C):
 At 2000 rpm . . . . At least 2.0 bar
 Relief pressure valve . . . . 12.0 bar

Auxiliary drivebelt tension

Alternator/viscous fan/power steering pump/coolant pump . . . . Automatically adjusted by tensioner
Air conditioning compressor . . . . Apply 25 Nm to tensioner body

Torque wrench settings

	Nm	lbf ft
Air conditioning compressor/drivebelt bracket	45	33
Alternator	25	18
Alternator bracket to cylinder block	45	33
Auxiliary drivebelt tensioner	25	18
Big-end bearing caps bolts*:		
Stage 1	30	22
Stage 2	Angle-tighten a further 90°	
Brake vacuum exhauster clamp	20	15
Camshaft bearing cap:		
Stage 1	8	5
Stage 2	Angle-tighten a further 90°	
Camshaft cover	10	7
Camshaft sprocket bolt:		
Sprocket to hub	25	18
Hub to camshaft	100	74
Coolant pump	15	11
Cooling fan-to-viscous coupling bolts	10	7
Crankshaft front oil seal housing	15	11
Crankshaft pulley/vibration damper to sprocket:		
Stage 1	10	7
Stage 2	Angle-tighten a further 90°	
Crankshaft rear oil seal housing	15	11
Crankshaft sprocket bolt:		
Stage 1	120	89
Stage 2	Angle-tighten a further 90°	
Cylinder head bolts*:		
Stage 1	40	30
Stage 2	60	44
Stage 3	Angle-tighten a further 90°	
Stage 4	Angle-tighten a further 90°	
Driveplate (automatic transmission)*:		
Stage 1	60	44
Stage 2	Angle-tighten a further 90°	
Engine front mounting buffer stop	30	22
Engine lifting eye	20	15
Engine mounting to subframe	25	18
Engine-to-transmission bolts:		
M10	45	33
M12	65	48
Flywheel (manual transmission)*:		
Stage 1	60	44
Stage 2	Angle-tighten a further 90°	
Glow plug	15	11
Injector pump rocker shaft bolts*:		
Stage 1	20	15
Stage 2	Angle-tighten a further 90°	
Longitudinal strut:		
To bracket	25	18
To engine support	20	15
Lower timing cover	10	7
Main bearing cap bolts*:		
Stage 1	65	48
Stage 2	Angle-tighten a further 90°	
Oil drain plug	30	22
Oil filter cap:		
Top	25	18
Bottom	25	18
Oil filter housing to block*:		
Stage 1	15	11
Stage 2	Angle-tighten a further 90°	
Oil jets	25	18
Oil level/oil temperature sender	10	7
Oil pressure switch	20	15
Oil pump chain tensioner	15	11
Oil pump sprocket	25	18
Oil pump mounting bolt	15	11
Oil return pipe to cylinder block	40	30

Torque wrench settings (continued)

	Nm	lbf ft
Power steering pump	25	18
Power steering pump banjo bolt	30	22
Power steering pump pulley	25	18
Speed sender to crankshaft*:		
Stage 1	10	7
Stage 2	Angle-tighten a further 90°	
Suction tube to oil pump	15	11
Sump:		
Sump-to-block (M7)	15	11
Sump-to-block (M10)	40	30
Sump-to-transmission	45	33
Tandem pump	25	18
Thermostat housing	15	11
Timing belt small lower idler roller	20	15
Timing belt tensioner:		
Stage 1	20	15
Stage 2	Angle-tighten 45°	
Timing cover	10	7
Torque reaction bracket and stop	25	18
Viscous fan coupling	45	33

Use new nuts/bolt(s).

1 General information

Using this Chapter

Chapter 2 is divided into three Parts; A, B and C. Repair operations that can be carried out with the engine in the vehicle are described in Part A (petrol engines) and Part B (diesel engines). Part C covers the removal of the engine/transmission as a unit, and describes the engine dismantling and overhaul procedures.

In Parts A and B, the assumption is made that the engine is installed in the vehicle, with all ancillaries connected. If the engine has been removed for overhaul, the preliminary dismantling information which precedes each operation may be ignored.

Access to the engine bay can be improved by removing the bonnet as described in Chapter 11 and the lock carrier (front panel) as described in Section 2.

Engine description

The engines are water-cooled, single overhead camshaft, in-line four cylinder units with cast-iron cylinder blocks and aluminium-alloy cylinder heads. All are mounted longi-tudinally at the front of the vehicle, with the transmission bolted to the rear of the engine.

The cylinder head carries the camshaft, which is driven by a toothed timing belt. It also houses the inlet and exhaust valves, which are closed by double coil springs, and which run in guides pressed into the cylinder head. The camshaft actuates the valves directly via hydraulic tappets, mounted in the cylinder head. On all engines covered by this manual, a rocker shaft and roller rocker assembly mounted in the camshaft upper bearing caps uses an additional set of camshaft lobes to pressurise the 'Pump Injectors' – see Chapter 4B. The cylinder head

contains integral oilways which supply and lubricate the tappets.

The engines are of direct injection design. Unlike indirect injection engines where the cylinder head incorporates swirl chambers, the piston crowns are shaped to form combustion chambers.

The crankshaft is supported by five main bearings, and endfloat is controlled by thrust washers fitted each side of the centre (No 3) main bearing. A tandem pump, incorporating a vacuum pump and a fuel pump, is fitted to the rear of the cylinder head, and driven by the camshaft. The coolant pump is driven by the timing belt.

Lubricant is circulated under pressure by a pump, chain-driven from the crankshaft. Oil is drawn from the sump through a strainer, and then forced through an externally-mounted, screw-on filter. From there, it is distributed to the cylinder head, where it lubricates the camshaft journals and hydraulic tappets, and also to the crankcase, where it lubricates the main bearings, connecting rod big- and small-ends, gudgeon pins and cylinder bores. Oil jets are fitted to the base of each cylinder – these spray oil onto the underside of the pistons, to improve cooling. An oil cooler, supplied with engine coolant and mounted on the oil filter housing, reduces the temperature of the oil before it re-enters the engine.

Repairs with engine installed

The following operations can be performed without removing the engine:

a) Auxiliary drivebelts – removal and refitting.
b) Camshaft – removal and refitting*.
c) Camshaft oil seal – renewal.
d) Camshaft sprocket – removal and refitting.
e) Coolant pump – removal and refitting (refer to Chapter 3)
f) Crankshaft oil seals – renewal.
g) Crankshaft sprocket – removal and refitting.
h) Cylinder head – removal and refitting*.

i) Engine mountings – inspection and renewal.
j) Oil pump and pickup assembly – removal and refitting.
k) Pump injector rocker shaft assembly
l) Sump – removal and refitting.
m) Timing belt, sprockets and cover – removal, inspection and refitting.

* Cylinder head dismantling procedures are in Chapter 2C, and also contain details of camshaft and hydraulic tappet removal.

Note: It is possible to remove the pistons and connecting rods (after removing the cylinder head and sump) without removing the engine from the vehicle. However, this procedure is not recommended. Work of this nature is more easily and thoroughly completed with the engine on the bench – refer to Chapter 2C.

2 Engine valve timing marks – locating TDC on No 1 cylinder

General information

1 The crankshaft and camshaft sprockets are driven by the timing belt; the sprockets move in phase with each other to ensure correct valve timing.

2 The design of the engines covered in this Chapter is such that piston-to-valve contact will occur if the crankshaft is turned with the timing belt removed. For this reason, it is important that the correct phasing between the camshaft and crankshaft is preserved whilst the timing belt is off the engine. This is achieved by setting the engine in a reference condition (known as Top Dead Centre or TDC) before the timing belt is removed, and then preventing the shafts from rotating until the belt is refitted. Similarly, if the engine has been dismantled for overhaul, the engine can be set to TDC during reassembly to ensure that the correct shaft phasing is restored.

3 TDC is the highest position a piston reaches

2.4a Use lengths of threaded rod for supporting the lock carrier

2.4b Unbolt the power steering fluid cooler

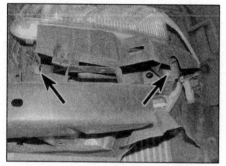

2.4c The bumper guides are held by two bolts under each headlamp (arrowed) . . .

2.4d . . . and on under each wing (arrowed) . . .

within its respective cylinder – in a four-stroke engine, each piston reaches TDC twice per cycle; once on the compression stroke, and once on the exhaust stroke. In general,

TDC normally refers to No 1 cylinder on the compression stroke. Note that the cylinders are numbered one to four, starting from the timing belt end of the engine.

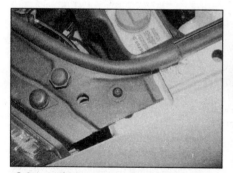

2.4e . . . then unscrew the carrier bolt on the top of the wing . . .

2.4f . . . and the one alongside each headlamp

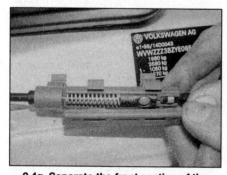

2.4g Separate the front section of the bonnet release cable

2.6 Unclip the upper timing belt cover

Setting TDC on No 1 cylinder

Note: *VAG special tool (T10050) is required to lock the crankshaft sprocket in the TDC position.*

4 In order to gain access to the TDC alignment marks on the crankshaft sprocket, it is necessary to position the complete front panel (lock carrier assembly) away from the front of the car as far as possible, but without disconnecting the radiator hoses or electrical wiring (in the service position). To do this, first remove the front bumper as described in Chapter 11, then unscrew the three quick-release clips from the noise insulation panel and unbolt the air duct from between the lock carrier and the air cleaner. Unscrew the bolts securing the lock carrier/bumper bar assembly to the underbody channels, unscrew and remove the side mounted bumper guides, just below each headlamp and unclip them from the front wings. Unscrew and remove the two bolts securing the lock carrier to the top of the front wing on each side of the vehicle – one at the top/front of each wing, and one alongside each headlamp. Prise open the bonnet release cable connector in front of the driver's side bonnet hinge, and separate the two halves of the release cable. With the help of an assistant, pull the complete assembly away from the front of the car as far as possible. VW technicians use special tools to hold the assembly, however support bars may be made out of threaded metal rod and screwed into the underbody channels **(see illustrations)**.

5 Remove the auxiliary drivebelt(s) as described in Section 6.

6 Release the retaining clips and remove the upper timing belt cover **(see illustration)**. Undo the two bolts securing the fuel coolant pipes to the cylinder head and the vacuum reservoir to the right of the cylinder head, and position them away from the front of the engine to give more clearance. There is no need to disconnect the coolant pipes.

7 Remove the viscous fan unit with reference to Chapter 3. Briefly, it is removed by inserting an Allen key from behind, while holding the unit stationary using a scissor-type tool engaged with two of the holes in the pulley – if the VW tool cannot be obtained, make up a similar tool out of two lengths of metal with bolts to engage the holes, or use a strap wrench around the pulley.

8 Unscrew the two retaining bolts and remove the auxiliary drivebelt tensioner assembly **(see illustration)**.

9 Undo the retaining bolts and remove the centre timing belt cover **(see illustration)**.

10 Remove the auxiliary drivebelt drive pulley from the crankshaft by prising out the centre cap and removing the four retaining bolts **(see illustration)**.

11 Unscrew the two retaining bolts and remove the lower timing belt cover.

12 Using a spanner or socket on the crankshaft sprocket bolt, turn the crankshaft

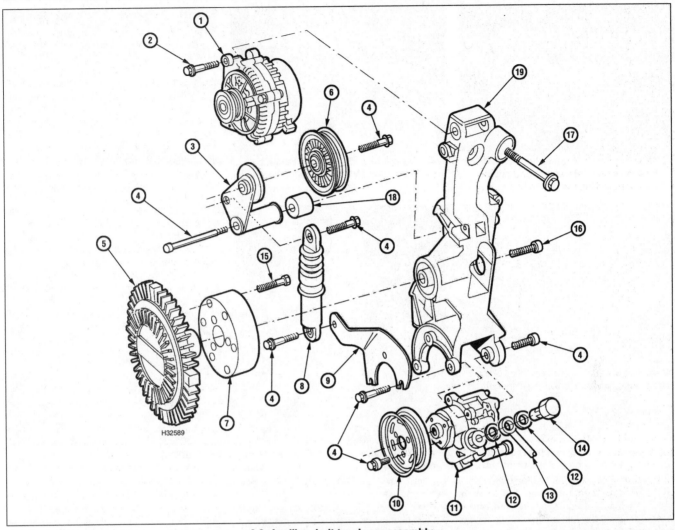

2.8 Auxiliary belt tensioner assembly

1 Alternator	5 Viscous fan coupling	9 Bracket	12 Washer	16 Bolt
2 Bolt	6 Pulley	10 Pulley	13 Pipe	17 Bolt
3 Lever	7 Pulley	11 Power steering	14 Banjo bolt	18 Spacer
4 Bolt	8 Tensioner	pump	15 Bolt	19 Bracket

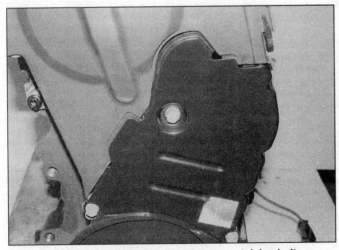

2.9 Undo the timing belt centre cover retaining bolts

2.10 Prise out the auxiliary drivebelt pulley centre cap

2.12a Position the crankshaft so that the mark on the sprocket is almost vertical (arrowed) . . .

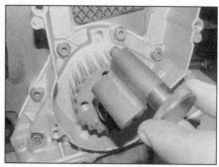

2.12b . . . and VW tool T10050 can be inserted . . .

2.12c . . . and the marks on the tool and sprocket align (arrowed)

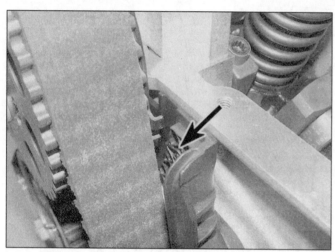

2.12d Align the arrow on the rear section of the timing belt upper cover with the lug on the camshaft hub sender wheel (arrowed) . . .

2.12e . . . and insert a 6 mm drill bit through the camshaft hub into the cylinder head to lock the camshaft (arrowed)

in the normal direction of rotation (clockwise) until the alignment mark on the face of the sprocket is as shown, and the arrow (marked 4Z) on the rear section of the timing belt upper cover aligns with the lug on the camshaft hub sender wheel. In this position it should be possible to insert VAG tool T10050 to lock the crankshaft, and 6 mm diameter rod to lock the camshaft **(see illustrations)**. **Note:** *The mark on the crankshaft sprocket and the mark on the VAG tool T10050 must align, whilst at the same time the shaft of tool T10050 must engage in the drilling in the crankshaft front oil seal housing.*
13 The engine is now set to TDC on No 1 cylinder.

3 Cylinder compression test

Compression test

Note: *A compression tester specifically designed for diesel engines must be used for this test.*
1 When engine performance is down, or if misfiring occurs, a compression test can provide diagnostic clues as to the engine's condition. If the test is performed regularly, it

can give warning of trouble before any other symptoms become apparent.
2 A compression tester specifically intended for diesel engines must be used, because of the higher pressures involved. The tester is connected to an adapter which screws into the glow plug hole. It is unlikely to be worthwhile buying such a tester for occasional use, but it may be possible to borrow or hire one – if not, have the test performed by a garage.
3 Unless specific instructions to the contrary are supplied with the tester, observe the following points:
a) *The battery must be in a good state of charge, the air filter must be clean, and the engine should be at normal operating temperature.*
b) *All the glow plugs should be removed before starting the test.*
c) *The stop solenoid and fuel metering control wiring must be disconnected, to prevent the engine from running or fuel from being discharged.* **Note:** *As a result of the wiring being disconnected, faults will be stored in the ECU memory. These must be erased after the compression test. Disconnect the injector solenoids by pulling apart the connector at the back of the cylinder head.*
4 There is no need to hold the accelerator pedal down during the test, because the diesel engine air inlet is not throttled.

5 The manufacturers specify a wear limit for compression pressure – refer to the Specifications. Seek the advice of a VW dealer or other diesel specialist if in doubt as to whether a particular pressure reading is acceptable.
6 The cause of poor compression is less easy to establish on a diesel engine than on a petrol one. The effect of introducing oil into the cylinders (wet testing) is not conclusive, because there is a risk that the oil will sit in the recess on the piston crown, instead of passing to the rings. However, the following can be used as a rough guide to diagnosis.
7 All cylinders should produce very similar pressures; a difference of more than 5.0 bars between any two cylinders indicates the existence of a fault. Note that the compression should build-up quickly in a healthy engine; low compression on the first stroke, followed by gradually-increasing pressure on successive strokes, indicates worn piston rings. A low compression reading on the first stroke, which does not build-up during successive strokes, indicates leaking valves or a blown head gasket (a cracked head could also be the cause).
8 A low reading from two adjacent cylinders is almost certainly due to the head gasket having blown between them; the presence of coolant in the engine oil will confirm this.

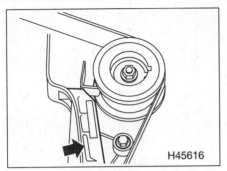

4.7 The hydraulic tensioner has a damper below it

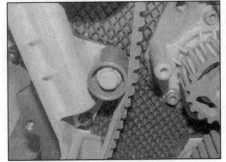

4.8 Unbolt the idler roller

4.9a Turn the tensioner arm anti-clockwise until it contacts the stop (A)

Leakdown test

9 A leakdown test measures the rate at which compressed air fed into the cylinder is lost. It is an alternative to a compression test, and in many ways it is better, since the escaping air provides easy identification of where pressure loss is occurring (piston rings, valves or head gasket).

10 The equipment needed for leakdown testing is unlikely to be available to the home mechanic. If poor compression is suspected, have the test performed by a suitably-equipped garage.

4	**Timing belt –** removal, inspection and refitting

Removal

1 The primary function of the toothed timing belt is to drive the camshaft, but it also drives the coolant pump. Should the belt slip or break in service, the valve timing will be disturbed and piston-to-valve contact may occur, resulting in serious engine damage. For this reason, it is important that the timing belt is tensioned correctly, and inspected regularly for signs of wear or deterioration.

2 Disconnect the battery (see Chapter 5A), then remove the engine top cover.

3 Apply the handbrake, then jack up the front of the vehicle and support it on axle stands (see *Jacking and vehicle support*). Where applicable, remove the splash guard from under the engine compartment.

4 Set the engine to TDC on No 1 cylinder as described in Section 2. This procedure includes moving the complete front panel (lock carrier assembly) away from the front of the car, and removing the auxiliary drivebelt(s), viscous fan and timing belt covers.

5 Unbolt the fuel cooler coolant hose support from the front of the engine and pull the hoses forwards slightly. **Do not** disconnect the hoses.

6 VW state that the camshaft sprocket **must** be reset each time the timing belt is removed – it is not acceptable to simply refit the belt to the sprocket without carrying out the resetting procedure. Hold the sprocket stationary using

the tool shown in Section 5, and loosen the three bolts by half a turn – **do not** unscrew them completely.

7 At this stage, it is necessary to determine which tensioning system is fitted to the timing belt. The hydraulic tensioner is identified by having a damper below it **(see illustration)**, whereas the friction-type incorporates a friction mechanism inside the tensioning roller.

Hydraulic tensioner

Note: VAG technicians use special tool T10008 to lock the timing belt tensioner in the released position. It is possible to manufacture a home-made alternative – see below.

8 Undo the bolt and remove the idler roller **(see illustration)**.

9 With reference to Section 5, relieve the tension on the timing belt by slackening the tensioner mounting nut slightly, and turning

the tensioner anti-clockwise with circlip pliers until it contacts the stop A. It may take a few moments for the tensioner plunger to fully compress. Alternatively, use an Allen key in the tensioner hub hole. Lock the plunger by inserting a locking plate (VAG tool No T10008). If this special tool is not available, an alternative can be manufactured by copying the design in the accompanying illustrations. Now turn the tensioner clockwise onto stop B **(see illustrations)**.

10 Examine the timing belt for manufacturer's markings that indicate the direction of rotation. If none are present, make your own using typist's correction fluid or a dab of paint – do not cut or score the belt in any way.

Caution: If the belt appears to be in good condition and can be re-used, it is essential that it is refitted the same way around, otherwise accelerated wear will result, leading to premature failure.

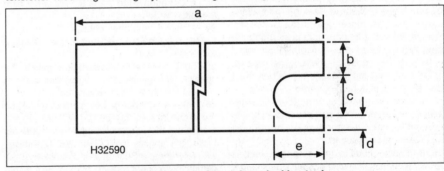

4.9b Home-made tensioner locking tool

a 52 mm   b 4.5 mm   c 5.5 mm   d 2 mm   e 7 mm

4.9c Insert the locking tool through the slot to lock the tensioner . . .

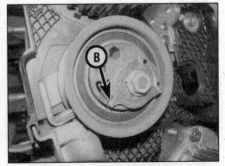

4.9d . . . and turn the tensioner arm clockwise until it contacts the stop (B)

4.18 Position the camshaft sprocket clockwise so that the securing bolts are against the ends of the elongated holes

4.21 Refit the idler roller

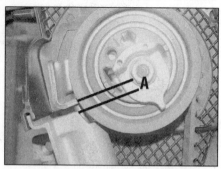

4.23 The gap between the top edge of the tensioner housing and the tensioner backplate arm (A) must be 4 mm

11 Slide the belt off the sprockets, taking care to avoid twisting or kinking it excessively if it is to be re-used.

Friction damper tensioner

12 Loosen the tensioner nut, then refer to Section 5 and turn the tensioner hub anti-clockwise with circlip pliers until it can be locked by inserting a suitable drill through the hole provided.
13 Turn the tensioner hub clockwise onto the stop, and hand-tighten the nut.
14 Slide the belt off the sprockets, taking care to avoid twisting or kinking it excessively if it is to be re-used.

Inspection

15 Examine the belt for evidence of contamination by coolant or lubricant. If this is the case, find the source of the contamination before progressing any further. Check the belt for signs of wear or damage, particularly around the leading edges of the belt teeth. Renew the belt if its condition is in doubt; the cost of belt renewal is negligible compared with potential cost of the engine repairs, should the belt fail in service. The belt must be renewed if it has covered the mileage stated by the manufacturer (see Chapter 1B); however, even if it has covered less, it is prudent to renew it regardless of condition as a precautionary measure.
16 If the timing belt is not going to be refitted for some time, it is a wise precaution to hang a warning label on the steering wheel, to remind yourself (and others) not to attempt to start the engine.

Refitting

17 Ensure that the crankshaft and camshaft are still set to TDC on No 1 cylinder, as described in Section 2.

Hydraulic tensioner

18 Turn the camshaft sprocket fully **clockwise** until the three bolts are against the ends of the elongated holes of the hub **(see illustration)**.
19 Loop the timing belt loosely under the crankshaft sprocket. **Note:** Observe any direction of rotation markings on the belt.
20 Engage the timing belt teeth with the camshaft sprocket, then manoeuvre it

into position around the tensioning roller, crankshaft sprocket, and finally around the coolant pump sprocket. Make sure that the belt teeth seat correctly on the sprockets. **Note:** Slight adjustment to the position of the camshaft sprocket may be necessary to achieve this. Avoid bending the belt back on itself or twisting it excessively as you do this.
21 Refit the idler roller and tighten the bolt to the specified torque **(see illustration)**.
22 Ensure that any slack in the belt is in the section of belt that passes over the tensioner roller.
23 Using a suitable tool (eg, circlip pliers) engaged with the two holes in the tensioner hub, turn the tensioner pulley anti-clockwise until the locking plate (T10008) is no longer under tension and can be removed. Turn the tensioner in a clockwise direction until gap of 4 mm exists between the tensioner backplate arm and the top edge of the tensioner housing **(see illustration)**.
24 With the tensioner held in this position, tighten the tensioner locknut to the specified torque and angle.
25 Tighten the camshaft sprocket bolts to the specified torque, remove the sprocket locking pin and the crankshaft locking tool.
26 Using a spanner or wrench and socket on the crankshaft pulley centre bolt, rotate the crankshaft through two complete revolutions. Reset the engine to TDC on No 1 cylinder, with reference to Section 2 and check that the camshaft sprocket locking pin (3359 or 6 mm rod) can still be inserted, and that the correct gap still exists between the tensioner backplate arm and top edge of the tensioner housing. If the tensioner gap is incorrect, carry out the tensioning procedure again. If the camshaft sprocket locking pin cannot be inserted, slacken the retaining bolts, turn the **hub** until the pin fits, and tighten the sprocket retaining bolts to the specified torque and angle.

Friction damper tensioner

27 Turn the camshaft sprocket fully anti-clockwise until the three bolts are against the ends of the elongated holes of the hub.
28 Loop the timing belt loosely under the crankshaft sprocket. **Note:** Observe any direction of rotation markings on the belt.
29 Engage the timing belt teeth with the

camshaft sprocket, then manoeuvre it into position around the tensioning roller, crankshaft sprocket, and finally around the coolant pump sprocket. Make sure that the belt teeth seat correctly on the sprockets. **Note:** Slight adjustment to the position of the camshaft sprocket may be necessary to achieve this. Avoid bending the belt back on itself or twisting it excessively as you do this.
30 Loosen the tensioner nut, but make sure that the arm on the rear plate remains engaged with the hole in the timing belt rear cover.
31 Using a suitable tool (eg, circlip pliers) engaged with the two holes in the tensioner hub, turn the tensioner pulley anti-clockwise until the locking drill can be removed.
32 Turn the tensioner pulley clockwise until the pointer is in the middle of the window in the rear plate.
33 Hold the tensioner pulley in this position and tighten the nut to the specified torque and angle.
34 Tighten the camshaft sprocket bolts to the specified torque, remove the sprocket locking pin and the crankshaft locking tool.
35 Using a spanner or wrench and socket on the crankshaft pulley centre bolt, rotate the crankshaft through two complete revolutions. Reset the engine to TDC on No 1 cylinder, with reference to Section 2 and check that the camshaft and crankshaft sprocket locking pins can still be inserted. If not, carry out the tensioning procedure again.

All models

36 Refit the fuel cooler coolant hose support to the front of the engine.
37 Refit the timing belt covers, viscous fan, auxiliary drivebelt(s) and lock carrier assembly using a reversal of the removal procedure.
38 Refit the engine top cover then reconnect the battery negative lead (see Chapter 5A).

5 Timing belt tensioner and sprockets – removal and refitting

1 Disconnect the battery (see Chapter 5A).
2 To gain access to the components detailed in this Section, first refer to Section 6 and remove the auxiliary drivebelts.

5.9 Hand tighten the camshaft sprocket bolts at this stage

5.12 Counter-hold the camshaft hub and undo the central retaining bolt about two turns

To make a camshaft sprocket holding tool, obtain two lengths of steel strip about 6 mm thick by 30 mm wide, one 600 mm long, the other 200 mm long (all dimensions are approximate). Bolt the two strips together to form a forked end, leaving the bolt slack so that the shorter strip can pivot freely. At the end of each 'prong' of the fork, secure a bolt with a nut and a locknut, to act as the fulcrums; these will engage with the cut-outs in the sprocket, and should protrude by about 30 mm.

Timing belt tensioner

3 With reference to the relevant paragraphs of Sections 2 and 4, set the engine to TDC on No 1 cylinder, then remove the upper section of the timing belt outer cover.

4 Relieve the tension on the timing belt with reference to Section 4.

5 Undo the retaining nut fully, and remove the tensioner pulley.

6 To remove the tensioner damper housing on models with an hydraulic tensioner, remove the right-hand cover (where fitted), and the housing retaining bolts.

Camshaft sprocket

7 Refer to Section 2 and 4, set the engine to TDC on No 1 cylinder. Slacken the three bolts securing the camshaft sprocket to the hub **(see Tool tip)**.

8 Remove the timing belt as described in Section 4. To eliminate any possibility of accidental piston-to-valve contact, turn the crankshaft 90° anti-clockwise. Unscrew the

three retaining bolts and remove the camshaft sprocket.

9 Locate the sprocket on the camshaft hub, and hand tighten the retaining bolts **(see illustration)**.

10 Turn the crankshaft clockwise 90° back to TDC. Refit and tension the timing belt as described in Section 4.

Camshaft hub

Note: *VAG technicians use special tool T10051 to counter-hold the hub, however it is possible to fabricate a suitable alternative – see below.*

11 Remove the camshaft sprocket as described in paragraphs 7 and 8.

12 Engage special tool T10051 with the three locating holes in the face of the hub to prevent the hub from turning. If this tool is not available, fabricate a suitable alternative as described in the *Tool tip* associated with paragraph 7. Whilst holding the tool, undo the central hub retaining bolt about two turns **(see illustration)**.

13 Leaving the central hub retaining bolt in place, attach VW tool T10052 (or a similar three-legged puller) to the hub, and evenly tighten the puller until the hub is free of the camshaft taper **(see illustration)**.

14 Ensure that the camshaft taper and the hub centre is clean and dry, locate the hub on the taper, noting that the built-in key in the hub taper must align with the keyway in the camshaft taper **(see illustration)**.

15 Hold the hub in this position with tool T10051 (or similar home-made tool), and tighten the central bolt to the specified torque.

16 The remainder of refitting is a reversal of removal.

Crankshaft sprocket

17 Remove the timing belt as described in Section 4. If the timing belt is to be re-used, make sure it is marked for direction of rotation.

18 The crankshaft sprocket must be held stationary whilst its retaining bolt is slackened. If access to the VW flywheel/driveplate locking tool is not available, lock the crankshaft in position by removing the starter motor, as described in Chapter 5A, to expose the ring gear. Get an assistant to insert a wide-bladed screwdriver between the ring gear teeth and the transmission bellhousing whilst the sprocket retaining bolt is slackened. Withdraw the bolt, recover the washer (where fitted) and lift off the sprocket.

19 With the sprocket removed, examine the crankshaft oil seal for signs of leaking. If necessary, refer to Section 10 and renew it.

20 Wipe the sprocket and crankshaft mating surfaces clean.

21 Offer up the sprocket to the crankshaft, engaging the lug on the inside of the sprocket with the recess in the end of the crankshaft. Insert the new retaining bolt and tighten it to the specified Stage 1 torque while holding the crankshaft stationary as described for removal. Then angle-tighten the bolt by the specified angle **(see illustration)**.

22 The remainder of refitting is a reversal of removal.

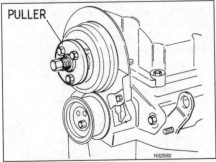

5.13 Attach a three-legged puller to the hub, and evenly tighten the puller until the hub is free of the camshaft taper

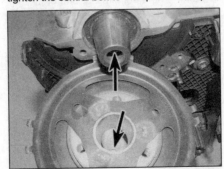

5.14 The built-in key in the hub taper must align with the keyway in the camshaft taper (arrowed)

5.21 Refit the crankshaft sprocket with a new retaining bolt, and tighten to the specified torque and angle setting

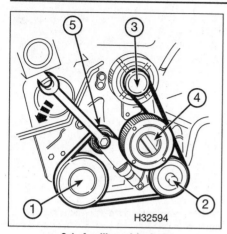

6.1 Auxiliary drivebelt

1 Crankshaft pulley
2 Power steering pump
3 Alternator
4 Viscous coupling
5 Tensioner

6 Auxiliary drivebelts – removal, refitting and tensioning

General information

1 One main auxiliary drivebelt is fitted to drive the alternator, viscous fan, and power steering pump. On models with air conditioning, a separate drivebelt drives the compressor. Both drivebelts are driven from pulleys mounted on the front of the crankshaft, and both drivebelts are of ribbed type **(see illustration)**.

2 The main drivebelt tension is adjusted automatically by a spring-tensioned idler. Where fitted, the air conditioning compressor drivebelt is adjusted using a torque wrench on the idler.

3 To remove the drivebelts first apply the handbrake, then jack up the front of the vehicle and support it on axle stands (see *Jacking and vehicle support*). Remove the undershield from under the engine compartment.

Removal

4 If any drivebelt is to be re-used, mark it for clockwise direction to ensure it is refitted the same way round.

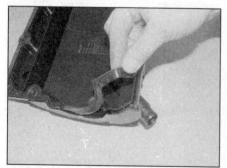

7.3 The camshaft cover gasket locates in a groove in the cover

5 Access to the drivebelt is best achieved by moving the complete front panel (the lock carrier assembly) away from the front of the car as far as possible, but without disconnecting the radiator hoses or electrical wiring. To do this, first remove the front bumper as described in Chapter 11, then unscrew the three quick-release clips from the noise insulation panel and unbolt the air duct from between the lock carrier and the air cleaner. On the left-hand side of the radiator, release the wiring from the clips. Unscrew the bolts securing the lock carrier/bumper bar assembly to the underbody channels, then unscrew the upper side bolts – one at the top/front of each wing, and one alongside each headlamp. Unscrew the bolts securing the bumper guides beneath each headlamp, and unclip them from the front wings. With the help of an assistant, pull the complete assembly away from the front of the car as far as possible. VW technicians use special tools to hold the assembly, however support bars may be made out of threaded metal rod and screwed into the underbody channels.

6 On models with air conditioning, loosen the pivot and tension bolts and move the tensioner roller upwards to release the tension on the drivebelt. Slip the drivebelt from the crankshaft, compressor and tensioner pulleys.

7 To remove the main drivebelt, first note how it is fitted to each pulley to ensure correct refitting. In particular note that the flat outer surface of the drivebelt is located on the viscous fan pulley. Use a 19 mm spanner on the hexagon cast into the tensioner pulley bracket, and push the tensioner pulley downwards (anti-clockwise).

Refitting

8 Locate the drivebelt on the alternator, viscous coupling fan, power steering pump, crankshaft and coolant pump (where applicable) pulleys, making sure that each rib is correctly located in a groove. Turn the automatic tensioner anti-clockwise and locate the drivebelt on the pulley, then release the tensioner to tension the drivebelt.

9 On models with air conditioning, locate the drivebelt on the compressor and crankshaft

7.5 Apply sealant to the points at the front and rear where the camshaft bearing cap contacts the cylinder head

pulleys, making sure that each rib is correctly located in a groove. Move the tensioner pulley downwards and engage the drivebelt with the pulley grooves. Tension the drivebelt by applying a torque of 25 Nm to the hexagon on the tensioner body. Hold this torque then tighten the adjustment and pivot bolts.

10 Refit the lock carrier assembly into position.

7 Camshaft cover – removal and refitting

Removal

1 Prise out the cover caps, undo the retaining nuts/bolts and remove the engine top cover, then disconnect the breather hose from the camshaft cover. Pull away the foam insulation around the camshaft cover.

2 Unscrew the camshaft cover retaining bolts and lift the cover away. If it sticks, do not attempt to lever it off – instead free it by working around the cover and tapping it lightly with a soft-faced mallet.

3 Recover the camshaft cover gasket **(see illustration)**. Inspect the gasket carefully, and renew it if damage or deterioration is evident.

4 Clean the mating surfaces of the cylinder head and camshaft cover thoroughly, removing all traces of oil and old gasket – take care to avoid damaging the surfaces as you do this.

Refitting

5 Refit the camshaft cover by following the removal procedure in reverse, noting the following points:

a) Apply suitable sealant to the points at the front and rear where the camshaft bearing cap contacts the cylinder head **(see illustration)**.

b) Tighten the camshaft cover retaining nuts/bolts to the specified torque.

8 Pump injector rocker shaft assembly – removal and refitting

Removal

1 Remove the camshaft cover as described in Section 7. In order to ensure that the rocker arms are refitted to their original locations, use a marker pen or paint and number the arms 1 to 4, with No 1 nearest the timing belt end of the engine. If the arms are not fitted to their original locations the injector basic clearance setting procedure must be carried out as described in Chapter 4B, Section 6.

2 Starting with the outer bolts first, carefully and evenly slacken the rocker shaft retaining bolts. Discard the rocker shaft bolts, new ones must be fitted **(see illustration)**.

Refitting

3 Carefully check the rocker shaft, rocker arms

and camshaft bearing cap seating surface for any signs of excessive wear or damage.

4 Ensure that the shaft seating surface is clean and position the rocker shaft assembly in the camshaft bearing caps, making sure that, if re-using the original rocker arms, they are in their original locations.

5 Insert the new rocker shaft retaining bolts, and starting from the inner bolts, gradually and evenly tighten the bolts to the Stage 1 torque setting.

6 Again, starting with the inner retaining bolts, tighten the bolts to the Stage 2 angle as listed in this Chapter's Specifications.

7 Refit the camshaft cover as described in Section 7.

9 Camshaft oil seal – renewal

1 Refer to Section 5 and remove the camshaft sprocket, and the camshaft hub.

2 Note the fitted position of the seal in the housing, and drill two small holes into the existing oil seal, diagonally opposite each other. Thread two self-tapping screws into the holes, and using two pairs of pliers, pull on the heads of the screws to extract the oil seal. Take great care to avoid drilling through into the seal housing or camshaft sealing surface.

3 Clean out the seal housing and sealing surface of the camshaft by wiping it with a lint-free cloth. Remove any swarf or burrs that may cause the seal to leak.

4 Do **not** lubricate the lip and outer edge of the new oil seal, and push it over the camshaft until it is positioned above its housing.

5 Using a hammer and a socket of suitable diameter, drive the seal squarely into its housing. **Note:** *Select a socket that bears only on the hard outer surface of the seal, not the inner lip which can easily be damaged.*

6 Refit the camshaft hub and sprocket as described in Section 5.

7 The remainder of refitting is a reversal of removal.

10 Crankshaft oil seals – renewal

Front oil seal

1 Remove the crankshaft sprocket with reference to Section 5.

2 Note the fitted location of the seal, drill two small holes into the existing oil seal, diagonally opposite each other. Thread two self-tapping screws into the holes and using two pairs of pliers, pull on the heads of the screws to extract the oil seal **(see illustration)**. Take great care to avoid drilling through into the seal housing or crankshaft sealing surface.

3 Clean out the seal housing and sealing surface of the crankshaft by wiping it with a

8.2 Starting with the outer bolts first, carefully and evenly slacken the rocker shaft retaining bolts

lint-free cloth – avoid using solvents that may enter the crankcase and affect component lubrication. Remove any swarf or burrs that could cause the seal to leak.

4 Note that the new oil seal must **not** be oiled or greased, as it is manufactured of special material.

5 Using a hammer and a socket of suitable diameter, drive the seal squarely into its housing. **Note:** *Select a socket that bears only on the hard outer surface of the seal, not the inner lip, which can easily be damaged.*

6 Refit the crankshaft sprocket with reference to Section 5.

Front oil seal housing gasket

7 Remove the crankshaft sprocket with reference to Section 5.

8 Unbolt the torque reaction bracket from the front of the engine.

10.2 Remove the crankshaft front oil seal using self-tapping screws

10.15 Apply a bead of sealant to the front oil seal housing

9 Remove the sump as described in Section 15.

10 Progressively slacken and then remove the oil seal housing retaining bolts.

11 Lift the housing away from the cylinder block, together with the crankshaft oil seal, using a twisting motion to ease the seal along the shaft.

12 Thoroughly clean the housing and block surfaces.

13 If necessary, prise the old oil seal from the housing using a screwdriver **(see illustration)**.

14 Wipe the oil seal housing clean, and check it visually for signs of distortion or cracking. Lay the housing on a work surface, with the mating surface face down. If removed, press in a new oil seal, using a block of wood as a press to ensure that the seal enters the housing squarely.

15 Apply a 2 to 3 mm wide bead of suitable sealant (available from VW dealers) to the oil seal housing sealing surface **(see illustration)**.

16 Wrap the end of the crankshaft with tape to protect the oil seal as the housing is being refitted.

17 Ease the seal along the shaft using a twisting motion, until the housing is flush with the crankcase **(see illustration)**. **Note:** *The oil seal must **not** be oiled or greased.*

18 Insert the bolts and tighten them progressively to the specified torque.

19 Refer to Section 15 and refit the sump.

20 Refit the torque reaction bracket to the front of the engine and tighten the bolts.

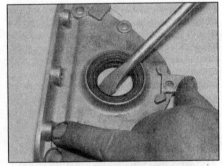

10.13 Prise the old oil seal from the crankshaft front oil seal housing

10.17 Offer up the seal and its housing to the end of the crankshaft

10.29 A protective cap is supplied with genuine VW crankshaft oil seals

21 Refit the crankshaft sprocket with reference to Section 5.

Rear oil seal and housing

Note: *The oil seal is integral with the housing and must be renewed as one complete assembly.*

22 Remove the transmission as described in Chapter 7A or 7B.

23 Refer to Section 13 of this Chapter and remove the flywheel (manual transmission) or driveplate (automatic transmission).

24 Remove the intermediate plate from the dowels on the cylinder block.

25 Remove the sump as described in Section 15.

26 Progressively slacken then remove the oil seal housing retaining bolts.

27 Lift the housing away from the cylinder block, together with the crankshaft oil seal, using a twisting motion to ease the seal off the shaft.

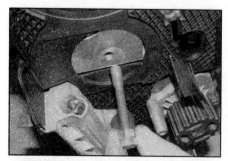

11.6a Undo the bolt on the front of the engine securing the timing belt inner cover to the cylinder head (arrowed) . . .

11.8 Using a stud extractor or two nuts locked together, unscrew the tensioner mounting stud from the cylinder head

10.30 Locate the crankshaft rear oil seal housing over the protective plastic cap

28 Wipe clean the block before fitting the new oil seal and housing. Note that no gasket is fitted as the housing incorporates sealant on its mating surface.

29 A protective plastic cap is supplied with genuine VW crankshaft oil seals; when fitted over the end of the crankshaft, the cap prevents damage to the inner lip of the oil seal as it is being fitted **(see illustration)**. Use adhesive tape wrapped around the end of the crankshaft if a cap is not available.

30 Offer up the seal and its housing to the end of the crankshaft. Carefully ease the seal along the shaft using a twisting motion, until the housing is flush with the crankcase **(see illustration)**. **Note:** *The oil seal must **not** be additionally oiled or greased.*

31 Insert the retaining bolts and tighten them progressively to the specified torque.

32 Refit the sump with reference to Section 15.

11.6b . . . and the one on the right-hand side

11.10 Unscrew the bolt and remove the camshaft position sensor

33 Refit the intermediate plate to the cylinder block, then insert and tighten the retaining bolts.

34 Refit the flywheel (manual transmission) or driveplate (automatic transmission) with reference to Section 13 of this Chapter.

35 Refit the transmission with reference to Chapter 7A or 7B.

---

11 Cylinder head –
removal and refitting

Note: *Cylinder head dismantling and overhaul is covered in Chapter 2C.*

Note: *In order to remove the cylinder head on diesel engines fitted with unit injectors, it is necessary to unplug the central connector for the injectors – this may cause a fault code to be logged by the engine management ECU. This code can only be erased by a VW dealer or suitably-equipped specialist.*

Removal

1 Disconnect the battery negative (earth) lead (see Chapter 5A).

2 Drain the engine oil with reference to Chapter 1B.

3 Drain the cooling system with reference to Chapter 1B.

4 Prise out the cover caps, undo the retaining nuts/bolts and remove the engine top cover.

5 Remove the timing belt with reference to Section 4, and the camshaft sprocket and hub as described in Section 5.

6 Undo the two bolts securing the timing belt inner cover to the cylinder head **(see illustrations)**.

7 With reference to Section 5, remove the timing belt tensioner pulley.

8 Using a stud extractor or two nuts locked together, unscrew and remove the timing belt tensioner pulley mounting stud **(see illustration)**.

9 Unscrew the retaining bolts and remove the camshaft cover as described in Section 7.

10 Remove the bolt securing the camshaft position sensor to the cylinder head. There is no need to disconnect it at this stage **(see illustration)**.

11 Disconnect the charge air pipe from the inlet manifold to the intercooler at the back of the engine and place to one side.

12 Undo the two bolts securing the coolant junction to the rear of the cylinder head **(see illustration)**. There is no need to disconnect the pipes or wiring plugs at this stage.

13 Unscrew the four retaining bolts and pull the tandem pump away from the cylinder head without disconnecting the fuel or vacuum hoses **(see illustration)**.

14 Disconnect the central connector for the unit injectors **(see illustration)**.

15 Disconnect and remove the hose connecting the upper coolant pipe to the pipe at the rear of the cylinder head **(see illustration)**.

11.12 Undo the two bolts (arrowed) and push the coolant outlet from the rear of the cylinder head

11.13 Undo the four tandem pump retaining bolts (arrowed)

16 Remove the turbocharger, as described in Chapter 4B, or remove it when the cylinder head is on the bench.

17 Slacken and remove the bolt securing the upper metal coolant pipe to the cylinder head.

18 With reference to Chapter 1B, remove the fuel filter.

19 Remove the upper bolt securing the fuel filter bracket to the cylinder head. Slacken the three bolts securing the fuel filter bracket to the cylinder block, pull the top of the bracket away from the cylinder head, and disconnect cylinder No 4 glow plug. Disconnect the rest of the glow plugs – if necessary, refer to Chapter 5C.

20 Disconnect vacuum pipes to the EGR valve and the manifold flap actuator **(see illustration)**.

21 Using a multi-splined tool, undo the cylinder head bolts, working from the outside-in, evenly and gradually. Check that nothing remains connected, and lift the cylinder head from the engine block. Seek assistance if possible, as it is a heavy assembly, especially as it is being removed complete with the manifolds.

22 Remove the gasket from the top of the block, noting the locating dowels. If the dowels are a loose fit, remove them and store them with the head for safe-keeping. Do not discard the gasket yet – it will be needed for identification purposes.

23 If the cylinder head is to be dismantled for overhaul, refer to Chapter 2C.

Manifold separation and reassembly

24 With the cylinder head on a workbench, if not done previously, remove the turbocharger with reference to Chapter 4B.

25 Remove the EGR valve (see Chapter 4C).

26 Where applicable, unscrew the nuts and remove the small heat shield from the front of the exhaust manifold **(see illustration)**.

27 Progressively unscrew the mounting bolts and remove the inlet manifold from the cylinder head. Remove the gasket and discard it.

28 If necessary, unbolt the oil supply pipe and bracket from the exhaust manifold.

29 Progressively unscrew the mounting nuts and remove the exhaust manifold from the cylinder head. Remove the gaskets and discard. Discard the self-locking mounting nuts and obtain new ones.

30 Ensure that the inlet and exhaust manifold mating surfaces are completely clean. Refit the exhaust manifold, using new gaskets and nuts. Ensure that the gaskets are fitted the correct way around, otherwise they will obstruct the inlet manifold gasket. Tighten the exhaust manifold retaining nuts to the specified torque (see Chapter 4C) **(see illustrations)**.

11.14 Disconnect the central connector for the unit injectors

11.15 Disconnect the coolant pipe from the rear of the cylinder head

11.20 Disconnect the vacuum pipes from the EGR valve and manifold flap actuator

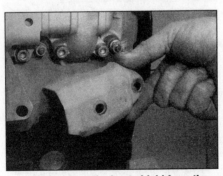

11.26 Remove the heat shield from the exhaust manifold

11.30a Fit the new exhaust manifold gasket

11.30b Refit the exhaust manifold and tighten the retaining nuts to the specified torque

11.32a Fit the new inlet manifold gasket to the cylinder head . . .

11.32b . . . then lift the inlet manifold into position

31 Where necessary, refit the oil supply pipe and bracket to the exhaust manifold and tighten the bolt.

32 Fit a new inlet manifold gasket to the cylinder head, then lift the inlet manifold into position. Insert the retaining bolts and tighten them to the specified torque (see Chapter 4B) **(see illustrations)**.

33 Refit the heat shield to the studs on the exhaust manifold, then fit and tighten the retaining nuts.

34 Refit the EGR valve with reference to Chapter 4C. Refit the turbocharger to the inlet and exhaust manifolds with reference to Chapter 4B.

Preparation for refitting

35 The mating faces of the cylinder head and cylinder block must be perfectly clean before refitting the head. Use a hard plastic or wood scraper to remove all traces of gasket and carbon; also clean the piston crowns. Take particular care during the cleaning operations, as aluminium alloy is easily damaged. Also, make sure that the carbon is not allowed to enter the oil and water passages – this is particularly important for the lubrication system, as carbon could block the oil supply

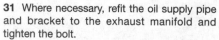

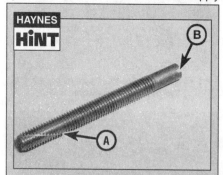

If a tap is not available, make a home-made substitute by cutting a slot (A) down the threads of one of the old cylinder head bolts. After use, the bolt head can be cut off, and the shank can then be used as an alignment dowel to assist cylinder head refitting, Cut a screwdriver slot (B) in the top of the bolt, to allow it to be unscrewed.

to the engine's components. Using adhesive tape and paper, seal the water, oil and bolt holes in the cylinder block/crankcase.

36 Check the mating surfaces of the cylinder block/crankcase and the cylinder head for nicks, deep scratches and other damage. If slight, they may be removed carefully with abrasive paper, but note that head machining will not be possible – refer to Chapter 2C.

37 If warpage of the cylinder head gasket surface is suspected, use a straight-edge to check it for distortion. Refer to Part C of this Chapter if necessary.

38 Clean out the cylinder head bolt drillings using a suitable tap. If a tap is not available, make a home-made substitute **(see Tool Tip)**.

39 On the engines covered in this Chapter, it is possible for the piston crowns to strike the valve heads, if the camshaft is rotated with the timing belt removed and the crankshaft set to TDC. For this reason, the camshaft must be locked at its TDC position using the locking bar engaged with the slot in the end of the camshaft while the cylinder head is being refitted. Turn the crankshaft to TDC on No 1 cylinder, and then anti-clockwise 90° so that all pistons are half-way up the cylinders.

Refitting

40 Examine the old cylinder head gasket for manufacturer's identification markings. These will either be in the form of notches or holes, and a part number, on the edge of the gasket **(see illustration)**. Unless new pistons have been fitted, the new cylinder head gasket must be the same type as the old one.

11.40 The thickness of the cylinder head gasket can be identified by notches or holes – see Chapter 2C

41 If new piston assemblies have been fitted as part of an engine overhaul, before purchasing the new cylinder head gasket, refer to Chapter 2C and measure the piston projection. Purchase a new gasket according to the results of the measurement (see Chapter 2C Specifications).

42 Lay the new head gasket on the cylinder block, engaging it with the locating dowels. Ensure that the manufacturer's TOP and part number markings are facing upwards.

43 Cut the heads from two of the old cylinder head bolts. Cut a slot, big enough for a screwdriver blade, in the end of each bolt. These can be used as alignment guides to assist in cylinder head refitting **(see illustration)**.

44 With the help of an assistant, place the cylinder head and manifolds centrally on the cylinder block, ensuring that the locating dowels engage with the recesses in the cylinder head.

45 Unscrew the home-made alignment dowels using a screwdriver and remove them.

46 Oil the bolt threads, then carefully enter each bolt (with washers where applicable) into its relevant hole (*do not drop them in*) and screw in, by hand only, until finger-tight **(see illustration)**.

47 Working progressively and in sequence, tighten the cylinder head bolts to the Stage 1 torque setting, using a torque wrench and socket **(see illustrations)**. Repeat the exercise in the same sequence for the Stage 2 torque setting.

48 Once all the bolts have been tightened to their Stage 2 settings, working again in

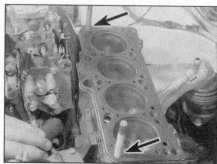

11.43 Two of the old head bolts (arrowed) can be used as cylinder head alignment guides

sequence, angle-tighten the bolts through the specified Stage 3 angle, using a socket and extension bar. It is recommended that an angle-measuring gauge is used during this stage of the tightening, to ensure accuracy. If a gauge is not available, use white paint to make alignment marks between the bolt head and cylinder head prior to tightening; the marks can then be used to check the bolt has been rotated through the correct angle during tightening. Repeat for the Stage 4 setting (see illustration). Note: *No further tightening of the cylinder head bolts is required after the engine has been started.*

49 Turn the crankshaft 90° clockwise (to TDC), and check that the TDC timing marks are still aligned with reference to Section 2.

50 The remainder of refitting is a reversal of the removal procedure, but on completion carry out the following:

a) *Refill the cooling system with the correct quantity of new coolant with reference to Chapter 1B.*

b) *Refill the engine with the correct grade and quantity of oil with reference to Chapter 1B.*

51 Have the engine management ECU's fault memory interrogated and erased by a VW dealer or suitably-equipped specialist.

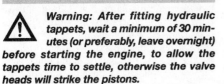

12 Hydraulic tappets –
operation check

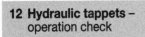

⚠️ *Warning: After fitting hydraulic tappets, wait a minimum of 30 minutes (or preferably, leave overnight) before starting the engine, to allow the tappets time to settle, otherwise the valve heads will strike the pistons.*

1 The hydraulic tappets are self-adjusting, and require no attention whilst in service.

2 If the hydraulic tappets become excessively noisy, their operation can be checked as described below.

3 Run the engine until it reaches its normal operating temperature, then increase the engine speed to approximately 2500 rpm for 2 minutes.

4 If irregular noisy tappets occur mainly when driving the car on short distances, but disappear after running the engine as described in paragraph 3, renew the oil retention valve located in the oil filter housing (see Chapter 2A, Section 11).

5 In the case of a regular noisy tappet, the faulty tappet must be renewed. To determine which one is faulty, switch off the engine, then refer to Section 7 and remove the camshaft cover.

6 Rotate the camshaft by turning the crankshaft with a socket and wrench, until the first cam lobe over No 1 cylinder is pointing upwards.

7 Using a non-metallic tool, press the tappet downwards then use a feeler blade to check the free travel. If this is more than 0.2 mm, the tappet should be renewed.

11.46 Oil the cylinder head bolt threads, then place each bolt into its relevant hole

11.47b Tighten the cylinder head bolts using a torque wrench

8 Hydraulic tappet removal and refitting is described as part of the cylinder head overhaul sequence – see Chapter 2C for details.

13 Flywheel/driveplate
– removal, inspection and refitting

Removal

1 On manual gearbox models, remove the gearbox (see Chapter 7A) and clutch (see Chapter 6).

2 On automatic transmission models, remove the automatic transmission as described in Chapter 7B.

3 The flywheel/driveplate bolts are offset to ensure correct fitment. Unscrew the bolts while holding the flywheel/driveplate stationary. Temporarily insert a bolt in the cylinder block, and use a screwdriver to hold the flywheel/driveplate, or make up a holding tool.

4 Lift the flywheel/driveplate from the crankshaft. If removing a driveplate, note the location of the shim and spacer.

Inspection

5 Check the flywheel/driveplate for wear and damage. Examine the starter ring gear for excessive wear to the teeth. If the driveplate or its ring gear are damaged, the complete driveplate must be renewed. The flywheel ring gear, however, may be renewed separately from the flywheel, but the work should be entrusted to a VW dealer. If the clutch friction face is discoloured or scored excessively, it

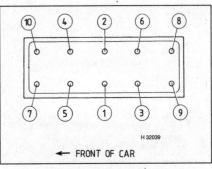

11.47a Cylinder head bolt tightening sequence

11.48 Angle-tighten the cylinder head bolts

may be possible to regrind it, but this work should also be entrusted to a VW dealer. Always renew the flywheel/driveplate bolts.

Refitting

6 Refitting is a reversal of removal, however on automatic transmission models temporarily refit the driveplate using the old bolts tightened to 30 Nm, then check that the distance from the rear face of the block to the outer face of the driveplate is 18.9 to 20.5 mm (see illustration). If necessary, remove the driveplate, and fit a spacer behind it to achieve the correct dimension. The raised pip on the outer shim must face the torque converter. Use new bolts when refitting the flywheel or driveplate, and coat the threads of the bolts with locking fluid if they are not already precoated. Tighten them to the specified torque.

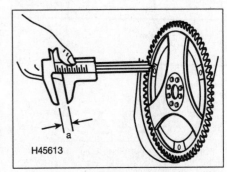

13.6 Checking the torque converter fitting dimension

a = 18.9 to 20.5 mm

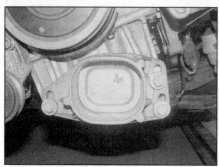

14.7 Unscrew the bolts and remove the bump stop from the front of the engine

14 Engine mountings
– inspection and renewal

Inspection

1 If improved access is required, raise the front of the car and support it securely on axle stands then remove the undershield.

2 Check the mounting rubbers to see if they are cracked, hardened or separated from the metal at any point; renew the mounting if any such damage or deterioration is evident.

3 Check that all the mounting's fasteners are securely tightened; use a torque wrench to check if possible.

4 Using a large screwdriver or a crowbar, check for wear in the mounting by carefully levering against it to check for free play. Where this is not possible, enlist the aid of an assistant to move the engine/transmission back-and-forth, or from side-to-side, while you watch the mounting. While some free play is to be expected even from new components, excessive wear should be obvious. If excessive free play is found, check first that the fasteners are correctly secured, then renew any worn components as described below.

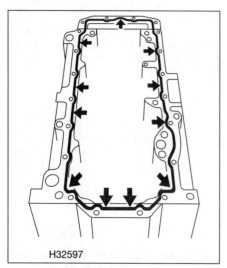

H32597

15.11 Evenly apply a 2 to 3 mm wide bead of silicone sealant to the sump

Renewal

Front torque arm

5 For improved access, apply the handbrake then jack up the front of the vehicle and support it on axle stands (see *Jacking and vehicle support*).

6 Where fitted, remove the engine undertray. Access is much improved if the lock carrier is placed in the Service Position (see Chapter 11).

7 Unscrew the bolts and remove the bump stop from the front of the engine **(see illustration)**.

8 Pull the rubber element from the front crossmember

9 Fit the rubber element and/or bump stop using a reversal of the removal procedure.

Right- or left-hand engine mounting

10 Apply the handbrake, then jack up the front of the vehicle and support it on axle stands (see *Jacking and vehicle support*).

11 Support the weight of the engine with a hoist.

12 Unscrew the upper mounting nut, then carefully raise the engine and unbolt the mounting from the bracket.

13 Fit the new mounting using a reversal of the removal procedure.

15 Sump –
removal, inspection and refitting

Removal

1 Apply the handbrake, then jack up the front of the vehicle and support it on axle stands (see *Jacking and vehicle support*). Also remove the undershield from under the engine and radiator, and where fitted the acoustic cover from over the sump.

2 Prise out the cover caps, undo the retaining nuts/bolts and remove the engine top cover.

3 In order to remove the sump, it is necessary to move the complete front panel (the lock carrier assembly) away from the front of the car as far as possible (into the 'Service' position – see Chapter 11, Section 10), but without disconnecting the radiator hoses or electrical wiring. To do this, first remove the front bumper as described in Chapter 11, then unscrew the three quick-release clips from the noise insulation panel and unbolt the air duct from between the lock carrier and the air cleaner. Unbolt the power steering oil cooler from the bottom of the radiator. On the left-hand side of the radiator, release the wiring from the clips. Unscrew the bolts securing the lock carrier/bumper bar assembly to the underbody channels, then unscrew and remove the two bolts securing the lock carrier to the top of the front wing on each side of the vehicle – one at the top/front of each wing, and one alongside each headlamp. Unscrew and remove the side mounted bumper

guides, located just below each headlamp, and unclip them from the front wings. Prise open the bonnet release cable connector in front of the driver's side bonnet hinge, and separate the two halves of the release cable. With the help of an assistant, pull the complete assembly away from the front of the car as far as possible. VW technicians use special tools to hold the assembly, however support bars may be made out of threaded metal rod and screwed into the underbody channels.

4 Support the weight of the engine using a suitable hoist.

5 Position a container beneath the sump, then unscrew the drain plug (refer to Chapter 1B) and drain the engine oil. Clean, refit, and tighten the plug after all the oil has drained. Remove the dipstick from the engine.

6 Detach the starter motor cables from under the engine mounting by cutting the plastic cable ties. Where fitted, disconnect the engine oil lever/temperature sensor wiring plug.

7 Mark the installation positions of the engine mountings on each side, then unscrew and remove the bottom nuts.

8 Make sure the engine is adequately supported on the hoist. Support the left- and right-hand front subframes with a trolley jack and length of wood. Mark the position of the subframes to ensure correct refitting and wheel alignment, then unscrew and remove the subframe mounting bolts. The front two bolts must be unscrewed first, then the rear bolts. Lower the subframes together with the anti-roll bar to the ground.

9 Unscrew and remove the sump bolts. Note that on manual transmission models, the two rear sump bolts are accessed through a cut-out in the flywheel – turn the flywheel as necessary to align the cut-out.

10 Remove the sump. If it is stuck, tap it gently with a mallet to free it.

Refitting

11 Clean the contact surfaces of the sump and block. Evenly apply a 2 to 3 mm wide bead of silicone sealant to the sump **(see illustration)**. Immediately install the sump, ensuring that the rear face of the sump is flush with the rear face of the cylinder block. **Note:** *If the sump is being fitted with the engine removed from the car and the transmission removed, make sure that the end face of the support bracket is flush with that of the intermediate plate. If the intermediate plate is removed, allow 0.8 mm for its thickness, and position the face of the bracket 0.8 mm protruding from the rear face of the cylinder block.* Tighten the bolts to the specified torque.

12 The remaining refitting procedure is a reversal removal, but tighten the nuts and bolts to the specified torque where given in the Specifications. On completion, fill the engine with the correct quantity of oil as described in Chapter 1B.

16.11a The oil pump sprocket will only fit in one position due to the flat machined on the oil pump shaft

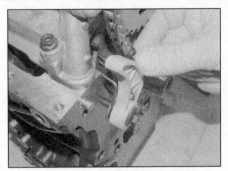

16.11b Refit the oil pump drive chain tensioner

16.13 Refit the baffle plate using the remaining oil pump mounting bolt

16 Oil pump and pick-up – removal, inspection and refitting

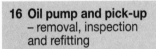

Removal

1 Remove the sump as described in Section 15.

2 Unscrew the bolt, release and remove the baffle plate from the bottom of the crankcase.

3 Slacken and remove the Torx screw securing the drive sprocket to the oil pump. Insert a screwdriver through one of the holes in the sprocket and against the oil pump body to prevent the sprocket from turning whilst the Torx screw is undone.

4 Unscrew and remove the remaining two mounting bolts, and release the oil pump from the dowels in the crankcase. Unhook the oil pump drive sprocket from the chain and withdraw it from the engine. Note that the tensioner will attempt to tighten the chain, and it may be necessary to use a screwdriver to hold it in its tensioned position before releasing the oil pump sprocket from the chain.

5 Unscrew the flange bolts and remove the suction pipe from the oil pump. Recover the O-ring seal. Unscrew the bolts and remove the cover from the oil pump. Before removing the rotors, mark them to ensure they are refitted the original way round.

6 Examine the drive chain for wear and damage. To remove the chain, the timing belt must first be removed (see Section 4), then the crankshaft front oil seal housing unbolted from the cylinder block. With the housing removed, unbolt and remove the chain tensioner, then unhook the chain from the sprocket on the front of the crankshaft.

Inspection

7 Clean the pump thoroughly, and inspect the rotors for signs of damage or wear. A suitable puller will be required to remove the sprocket from the front of the crankshaft, however note that it must be heated to 220°C for 15 minutes when refitting. Note that the broad collar of the sprocket faces the engine. Examine the pump rotors for signs of excessive wear and damage. If evident, renew the oil pump.

Refitting

8 Lubricate the rotors with fresh engine oil,

then refit the cover to the oil pump and tighten the bolts securely. Prime the pump by pouring oil into the suction pipe aperture while turning the driveshaft.

9 If the drive chain, crankshaft sprocket and tensioner have been removed, delay refitting them until after the oil pump has been mounted on the cylinder block.

10 Locate the oil pump on the dowels, then insert and tighten the two mounting bolts to the specified torque.

11 Where applicable, refit the drive chain, crankshaft sprocket, tensioner and oil pump sprocket using a reversal of the removal procedure. Note that the oil pump sprocket will only fit in one position due to the flat machined on the oil pump shaft **(see illustrations)**.

12 Refit the crankshaft front oil seal housing and timing belt where applicable. Apply suitable sealant to the front oil seal housing before fitting it.

13 Refit the baffle plate using the remaining oil pump mounting bolt and tighten it to the specified torque, followed by the sump with reference to Section 15 **(see illustration)**.

Chapter 2 Part C:
Engine removal and overhaul procedures

Contents

	Section number
Crankshaft – refitting and main bearing clearance check	12
Crankshaft – removal and inspection	8
Cylinder block/crankcase – cleaning and inspection	9
Cylinder head – dismantling, cleaning, inspection and reassembly	6
Engine – initial start-up after overhaul and reassembly	15
Engine – removal and refitting	4
Engine overhaul – general information	2
Engine overhaul – preliminary information	5
Engine overhaul – reassembly sequence	11
Engine removal – preparation and precautions	3
General information	1
Main and big-end bearings – inspection and selection	10
Piston/connecting rod assemblies – refitting and big-end bearing clearance check	14
Piston/connecting rod assemblies – removal and inspection	7
Pistons and piston rings – assembly	13

Degrees of difficulty

Easy, suitable for novice with little experience	**Fairly easy,** suitable for beginner with some experience	**Fairly difficult,** suitable for competent DIY mechanic	**Difficult,** suitable for experienced DIY mechanic	**Very difficult,** suitable for expert DIY or professional

Specifications

Engine codes*

Petrol engines

1781 cc, DOHC, Bosch Motronic ME7.5 injection, turbocharged	AWT
1984 cc, SOHC, Siemens Simos 3.2 injection, non-turbo	AZM
1984 cc, DOHC, Bosch Motronic ME7.5 injection, non-turbo	ALT

Diesel engines

Electronic direct injection, unit injectors, 74 kW (100 bhp)	AVB
Electronic direct injection, unit injectors, 96 kW (130 bhp)	AVF and AWX

* Note: See 'Vehicle identification' for the location of the code marking on the engine.

Cylinder head

Cylinder head gasket surface, maximum distortion	0.1 mm	
Minimum cylinder head height:		
Petrol engines:		
Engine code AZM	132.6 mm	
Engine codes AWT and ALT	139.25 mm	
Diesel engines	Head resurfacing not possible	
Cylinder head gasket selection (diesel engines):		
Piston projection 0.91 to 1.00 mm	1 hole/notch*	
Piston projection 1.01 to 1.10 mm	2 holes/notches*	
Piston projection 1.11 to 1.20 mm	3 holes/notches*	

	Inlet valve	**Exhaust valve**
Valve stem-to-cylinder head top face minimum dimension:		
Petrol engines:		
Engine code AZM	33.8 mm	34.1 mm
Engine codes AWT and ALT	31.0 mm (outer)	31.9 mm
	32.3 mm (centre)	
Diesel engines	43.4 mm	43.2 mm

* Disregard single and double oval holes.

Valves

	Inlet	Exhaust
Valve stem diameter:		
Petrol engines:		
Engine code AZM	6.98 ± 0.007 mm	6.96 ± 0.007 mm
Engine codes AWT and ALT	5.963 mm	5.943 mm
Diesel engines	6.980 mm	6.956 mm
Maximum valve head deflection (end of stem flush with top of guide):		
Petrol engines:		
Engine code AZM	1.0 mm	1.3 mm
Engine codes AWT and ALT	0.80 mm	0.80 mm
Diesel engines	1.3 mm	1.3 mm

Camshaft

Maximum endfloat:	
Petrol engines:	
Engine code AZM	0.15 mm
Engine codes AWT and ALT	0.20 mm
Diesel engines	0.15 mm
Maximum runout, all engines	0.01 mm
Maximum running clearance:	
Petrol engines	0.10 mm
Diesel engines	0.11 mm

Pistons and piston rings

Piston diameter:	
Petrol engines:	
Code AZM:	
Standard	82.465 mm
1st oversize	82.965 mm
Maximum deviation	0.04 mm
Code AWT:	
Standard	80.965 mm
1st oversize	81.465 mm
Maximum deviation	0.04 mm
Code ALT:	
Standard	80.965 mm
1st oversize	N/A
Maximum deviation	0.04 mm
Diesel engines:	
Standard	79.470 mm
1st oversize	79.720 mm
2nd oversize	79.970 mm
Maximum deviation	0.04 mm
Ring-to-groove clearance:	
Petrol engines:	
1st compression ring	0.06 to 0.09 mm
2nd compression ring	0.06 to 0.09 mm
Oil control ring	0.03 to 0.06 mm
Wear limit:	
Compression rings	0.20 mm
Oil control ring	0.15 mm
Diesel engines:	
1st compression ring	0.06 to 0.09 mm
2nd compression ring	0.05 to 0.08 mm
Oil control ring	0.03 to 0.06 mm
Wear limit:	
Compression rings	0.25 mm
Oil control ring	0.15 mm
Piston ring end gap clearance (ring 15 mm from bottom of bore):	
Petrol engines:	
New:	
Compression rings	0.20 to 0.40 mm
Oil scraper ring	0.25 to 0.50 mm
Wear limit	0.8 mm
Diesel engines:	
New:	
Compression rings	0.20 to 0.40 mm
Oil scraper ring	0.25 to 0.50 mm
Wear limit	1.0 mm

Cylinder block

Bore diameter:
  Petrol engines:
    Code AZM:
      Standard . . . . 82.51 mm
      Oversize . . . . 83.01 mm
      Maximum bore wear . . . . 0.08 mm
    Code AWT:
      Standard . . . . 81.01 mm
      Oversize . . . . 81.51 mm
      Maximum bore wear . . . . 0.08 mm
    Code ALT:
      Standard . . . . 81.01 mm
      Oversize . . . . N/A
      Maximum bore wear . . . . 0.08 mm
  Diesel engines:
    Standard . . . . 79.51 mm
    1st oversize . . . . 79.76 mm
    2nd oversize . . . . 80.01 mm
    Maximum bore wear . . . . 0.10 mm

Connecting rods

Big-end side clearance (maximum):
  Petrol engines:
    Code AZM . . . . 0.37 mm
    Code AWT . . . . 0.37 mm
    Code ALT . . . . 0.40 mm
  Diesel engines . . . . 0.37 mm

Crankshaft

Spigot needle bearing depth . . . . 1.5 mm

Endfloat:	New	Wear limit
Petrol engines	0.07 to 0.23 mm	0.30 mm
Diesel engines	0.07 to 0.17 mm	0.37 mm

Main bearing running clearance:
  Petrol engines:

Code AZM	0.01 to 0.04 mm	0.15 mm
Code AWT	0.02 to 0.04 mm	0.15 mm
Code ALT	0.02 to 0.04 mm	0.15 mm
Diesel engines	0.03 to 0.08 mm	0.17 mm

Main bearing journal diameter:
  Petrol engines:
    Standard size . . . . 54.00 mm -0.017 -0.037
    1st undersize . . . . 53.75 mm -0.017 -0.037
    2nd undersize . . . . 53.50 mm -0.017 -0.037
    3rd undersize . . . . 53.25 mm -0.017 -0.037
  Diesel engines:
    Standard size . . . . 54.00 mm -0.022 -0.042
    1st undersize . . . . 53.75 mm -0.022 -0.042
    2nd undersize . . . . 53.50 mm -0.022 -0.042
    3rd undersize . . . . 53.25 mm -0.022 -0.042

Big-end bearing journal diameter:
  Standard size . . . . 47.80 mm -0.022 -0.042
  1st undersize . . . . 47.55 mm -0.022 -0.042
  2nd undersize . . . . 47.30 mm -0.022 -0.042
  3rd undersize . . . . 47.05 mm -0.022 -0.042

Big-end bearing running clearance:	New	Wear limit
Petrol engines:		
Codes AZM and AWT	0.01 to 0.06 mm	0.12 mm
Code ALT	0.02 to 0.06 mm	0.09 mm
Diesel engines	0.03 to 0.08 mm	0.08 mm

Maximum journal out-of-round (typical) . . . . 0.03 mm

Torque wrench settings

Refer to Chapters 2A or 2B.

1 General information

Included in this Part of Chapter 2 are details of removing the engine from the car and general overhaul procedures for the cylinder head, cylinder block and all other engine internal components.

The information given ranges from advice concerning preparation for an overhaul and the purchase of parts, to detailed step-by-step procedures covering removal, inspection, renovation and refitting of engine internal components.

After Section 5, all instructions are based on the assumption that the engine has been removed from the car. For information concerning in-car engine repair, as well as the removal and refitting of those external components necessary for full overhaul, refer to the relevant in-car repair procedure section (Chapters 2A or 2B) and to Section 5 of this Chapter. Ignore any preliminary dismantling operations described in the relevant in-car repair sections that are no longer relevant once the engine has been removed from the car.

Apart from torque wrench settings, which are given at the beginning of the relevant in-car repair procedure in Chapters 2A or 2B, all specifications relating to engine overhaul are at the beginning of this Part of Chapter 2.

2 Engine overhaul – general information

It is not always easy to determine when, or if, an engine should be completely overhauled, as a number of factors must be considered.

High mileage is not necessarily an indication that an overhaul is needed, while low mileage does not preclude the need for an overhaul. Frequency of servicing is probably the most important consideration. An engine which has had regular and frequent oil and filter changes, as well as other required maintenance, should give many thousands of miles of reliable service. Conversely, a neglected engine may require an overhaul very early in its life.

Excessive oil consumption is an indication that piston rings, valve seals and/or valve guides are in need of attention. Make sure that oil leaks are not responsible before deciding that the rings and/or guides are worn. Perform a compression test, as described in the relevant Part A or B of this Chapter, to determine the likely cause of the problem.

Check the oil pressure with a gauge fitted in place of the oil pressure switch, and compare it with that specified (see Chapter 2A or 2B). If it is extremely low, the main and big-end bearings, and/or the oil pump, are probably worn out.

Loss of power, rough running, knocking or metallic engine noises, excessive valve gear noise, and high fuel consumption may also point to the need for an overhaul, especially if they are all present at the same time. If a complete service does not remedy the situation, major mechanical work is the only solution.

An engine overhaul involves restoring all internal parts to the specification of a new engine. During an overhaul, the pistons and the piston rings are renewed. New main and big-end bearings are generally fitted; if necessary, the crankshaft may be renewed, to restore the journals. The valves are also serviced as well, since they are usually in less-than-perfect condition at this point. While the engine is being overhauled, other components, such as the starter and alternator, can be overhauled as well. The end result should be an as-new engine that will give many trouble-free miles. **Note:** *Critical cooling system components such as the hoses, thermostat and coolant pump should be renewed when an engine is overhauled. The radiator should be checked carefully, to ensure that it is not clogged or leaking. Also, it is a good idea to renew the oil pump whenever the engine is overhauled.*

Before beginning the engine overhaul, read through the entire procedure, to familiarise yourself with the scope and requirements of the job. Overhauling an engine is not difficult if you follow carefully all of the instructions, have the necessary tools and equipment, and pay close attention to all specifications. It can, however, be time-consuming. Plan on the car being off the road for a minimum of two weeks, especially if parts must be taken to an engineering works for repair or reconditioning. Check on the availability of parts and make sure that any necessary special tools and equipment are obtained in advance. Most work can be done with typical hand tools, although a number of precision measuring tools are required for inspecting parts to determine if they must be renewed. Often the engineering works will handle the inspection of parts and offer advice concerning reconditioning and renewal. **Note:** *Always wait until the engine has been completely dismantled, and until all components (especially the cylinder block and the crankshaft) have been inspected, before deciding what service and repair operations must be performed by an engineering works. The condition of these components will be the major factor to consider when determining whether to overhaul the original engine, or to buy a reconditioned unit. Do not, therefore, purchase parts or have overhaul work done on other components until they have been thoroughly inspected.* As a general rule, time is the primary cost of an overhaul, so it does not pay to fit worn or sub-standard parts.

As a final note, to ensure maximum life and minimum trouble from a reconditioned engine, everything must be assembled with care, in a spotlessly-clean environment.

3 Engine removal – preparation and precautions

If you have decided that the engine must be removed for overhaul or major repair work, several preliminary steps should be taken.

Locating a suitable place to work is extremely important. Adequate work space, along with storage space for the vehicle, will be needed. If a workshop or garage is not available, at the very least a solid, level, clean work surface is required.

If possible, clear some shelving close to the work area and use it to store the engine components and ancillaries as they are removed and dismantled. In this manner, the components stand a better chance of staying clean and undamaged during the overhaul. Laying out components in groups together with their fixings bolts, screws, etc, will save time and avoid confusion when the engine is refitted.

Clean the engine compartment and engine before beginning the removal procedure; this will help visibility and help to keep tools clean.

The help of an assistant is essential; there are certain instances when one person cannot safely perform all of the operations required to remove the engine from the vehicle. Safety is of primary importance, considering the potential hazards involved in this kind of operation. A second person should always be in attendance to offer help in an emergency. If this is the first time you have removed an engine, advice and aid from someone more experienced would also be beneficial.

Plan the operation ahead of time. Before starting work, obtain (or arrange for the hire of) all of the tools and equipment you will need. Access to the following items will allow the task of removing and refitting the engine to be completed safely and with relative ease: a heavy-duty trolley jack – rated in excess of the weight of the engine, complete sets of spanners and sockets as described in the back of this manual, wooden blocks, and plenty of rags and cleaning solvent for mopping-up spilled oil, coolant and fuel. A selection of different sized plastic storage bins will also prove useful for keeping dismantled components grouped together. If any of the equipment must be hired, make sure that you arrange for it in advance, and perform all of the operations possible without it beforehand; this may save you time and money.

Plan on the vehicle being out of use for quite a while, especially if you intend to carry out an engine overhaul. Read through the whole of this Section and work out a strategy based on your own experience and the tools, time and workspace available to you. Some of the overhaul processes may have to be carried out by a VW dealer or an engineering works – these establishments often have busy schedules, so it would be prudent to consult

4.7 Radiator drain plug

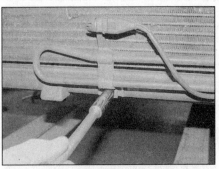

4.8 Undo the bolts and position the power steering fluid cooler pipe to one side

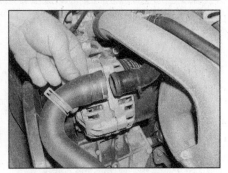

4.9 Disconnect the top hose from the engine

them before removing or dismantling the engine, to get an idea of the amount of time required to carry out the work.

When removing the engine from the vehicle, be methodical about the disconnection of external components. Labelling cables and hoses as they are removed will greatly assist the refitting process.

Always be extremely careful when lifting the engine from the engine bay. Serious injury can result from careless actions. If help is required, it is better to wait until it is available rather than risk personal injury and/or damage to components by continuing alone. By planning ahead and taking your time, a job of this nature, although major, can be accomplished successfully and without incident.

On all models described in this manual, the engine is lifted from the engine compartment leaving the gearbox in the car. Note that the engine should ideally be removed with the vehicle standing on all four roadwheels, but access to the exhaust system downpipe and lower bolts will be improved if the vehicle can be temporarily raised onto axle stands.

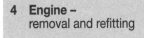

4 Engine –
  removal and refitting

Petrol engines

Removal

1 Select a solid, level surface to park the vehicle on. Give yourself enough space to move around it easily.
2 Disconnect the battery negative (earth) lead (see Chapter 5A).
3 Apply the handbrake, then jack up the front of the vehicle and support it on axle stands (see *Jacking and vehicle support*).
4 Remove the retaining clips and screws, and remove engine compartment undershield.
5 Where applicable, prise out the cover caps, undo the retaining bolts/nuts and remove the cover from the top of the engine.
6 Remove the front bumper with reference to Chapter 11.
7 With reference to Chapter 1A, carry out the following:
  a) Drain the cooling system. The drain plug

is located on the front left-hand side of the radiator **(see illustration)**, and on some engines a further plug is located on the coolant pump bearing housing. However, it may be quicker to simply disconnect the bottom radiator hose.
  b) Drain the engine oil.
8 Unscrew and remove the two bolts securing the power steering fluid cooling pipe to the front of the radiator, and position it to one side **(see illustration)**. Tie the outside temperature sensor in its original position.
9 Prise out the clips and disconnect the hoses from the top and bottom of the radiator, and from the thermostat housing. On engine codes AWT and ALT, it may be easier to disconnect the top hose from the engine **(see illustration)**. Where applicable, disconnect the hoses from the engine oil cooler and drain off the remaining coolant.
10 Unbolt the air duct leading to the air cleaner

from the lock carrier **(see illustration)**.
11 Disconnect the wiring from the headlights and headlight range control unit **(see illustrations)**.
12 Remove the front indicators with reference to Chapter 12, Section 7. Slide the plastic connection housing from the driver's side inner wing flange, and prise it open.
13 Disconnect the front section of the bonnet lock cable from rear section **(see illustration)**.
14 On turbocharged models, remove the connecting pipes between the turbocharger/intercooler, turbocharger/air cleaner, and intercooler/throttle control assembly. On models equipped with secondary air injection, remove the connecting pipes between the secondary air pump/combi valve, and the secondary air pump/air cleaner. On engine code AWT, remove the crankcase breather pipe, then detach the pressure pipe at the combination valve and detach from the

4.10 Unbolt the air intake duct from the top of the lock carrier

4.11a Disconnect the headlamp wiring plug . . .

4.11b . . . and the headlamp range control motor wiring plug

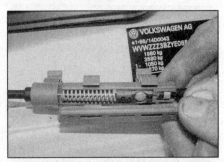

4.13 Disconnect the front section of the bonnet release cable by sliding the nipple and outer cable from the connector

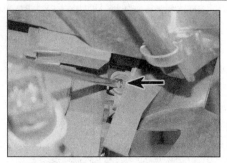

4.17a Press the lug into the centre, and pull the pin out to release the condenser (arrowed)

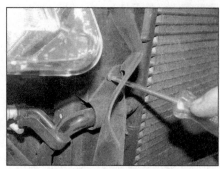

4.17b Undo the screws and remove the rubber cowlings

4.19 Remove the cover from the power steering fluid reservoir

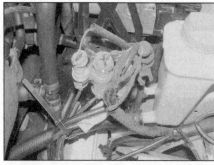

4.20 Disconnect the wiring plug beside the power steering fluid reservoir

17 On models equipped with air conditioning, to release the condenser from the lock carrier, press the lug in the end of the retaining pin, pull the pin from the mounting bracket either side of the condenser, and separate the two halves of the mounting brackets **(see illustration)**. Undo the retaining screws and remove the rubber shrouds either side of the condenser **(see illustration)**. Disconnect the pressure switch wiring as the condenser is removed. Disconnect the wiring from the low pressure switch, and also disconnect the magnetic clutch wiring from the bottom of the lock carrier. Lift the condenser from its bracket, rotate it to the side and tie it in place to secure it away from the engine compartment. Protect the condenser with card or cloth sheets to prevent damage to it when removing the engine.

⚠ *Warning: Do not disconnect the air conditioning refrigerant circuit.*

18 On models with automatic transmission, position a suitable container beneath the radiator, then loosen the union nuts and disconnect the transmission fluid pipes from the bottom of the radiator. Plug the pipes and radiator apertures to prevent entry of dust and dirt. Also unbolt the fluid pipe bracket from the engine.

19 Remove the cover from the power steering fluid reservoir **(see illustration)**.

20 Disconnect the five wiring plugs revealed by the power steering fluid reservoir cover removal **(see illustration)**.

21 On the top left-hand side of the lock carrier, disconnect the wiring for the anti-theft alarm system at the connectors.

22 Unscrew the lock carrier mounting bolts – one at the front/top of each wing, and one at the side of each headlamp. Unscrew the three bolts securing each bumper guide below each headlamp, and unclip them from the front wings. Unscrew the bolts retaining the lock carrier/bumper bar to the underbody channels and, with the help of an assistant, withdraw the complete lock carrier from the front of the car and place it in a safe position **(see illustrations)**.

23 Remove the air cleaner assembly complete with air duct with reference to Chapter 4A. On engine code ALT, also remove the air mass meter.

camshaft cover. Also, move the combination valve and bracket to one side, disconnect the wiring from the coolant temperature sender, and remove the crankcase breather T-piece.

15 On models fitted with an electric cooling fan, disconnect the wiring from the thermostat located on the bottom left-hand side of the radiator. Position the wiring to one side.

16 Disconnect the wiring from the horns, and move the wiring to one side.

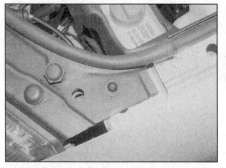

4.22a Remove the bolt at the top of each wing . . .

4.22b . . . and beside each headlamp

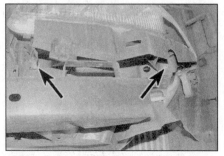

4.22c The bumper guides are retained by two bolts under each headlamp (arrowed) . . .

4.22d . . . and one under the front of each wing

4.22e Remove the bumper bar bolts

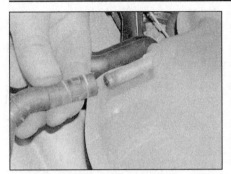

4.26a Disconnect the hoses from the coolant expansion tank . . .

4.26b . . . then remove the mounting screws . . .

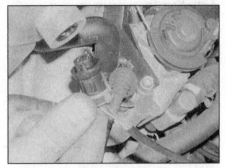

4.26c . . . and disconnect the low coolant warning switch

4.29a Disconnect the vacuum hose from the EVAP canister purge valve . . .

4.29b . . . and brake vacuum hose

4.32 Remove the intake pipe from the throttle housing

24 Disconnect the main ignition lead, disconnect the wiring and position the wiring on the engine. Also disconnect the oxygen sensor wiring.

25 Refer to Chapter 4A, and depressurise the fuel system, then disconnect the fuel supply and return lines at the fuel rail.

26 Loosen the clips and disconnect the small hoses from the coolant expansion tank on the left-hand side of the engine compartment. Disconnect the wiring from the low coolant warning switch, then unbolt the expansion tank and remove it (see illustrations).

27 On models equipped with cruise control, disconnect the actuator rod at the throttle valve control, and pull the vacuum hose from the vacuum unit.

28 Where fitted, disconnect the accelerator cable from the throttle housing and support bracket and position it to one side.

29 Disconnect the vacuum hoses from the

EVAP canister purge valve and brake vacuum servo (see illustrations).

30 On automatic transmission models, disconnect the wiring from the kick-down switch.

31 On left-hand drive models, remove the engine management ECU from the left-hand side of the bulkhead (see Chapter 4A). To do this, unbolt the cover from the electronics box first, then release the retainers and disconnect the wiring. On all models, release the engine wiring harness as required, and undo the earth cable screw, then position the wiring on the engine.

32 Remove the intake pipe and crankcase ventilation hoses from the throttle housing and engine valve cover (see illustration).

33 Loosen the clips and disconnect the heater hoses from the bottom hose coolant pipe and the outlet elbow on the rear of the cylinder head.

34 Disconnect the wiring from the speedometer sender on the left-hand side of the transmission.

35 On models with a manual transmission, disconnect the wiring from the reversing light switch on the left-hand side of the transmission.

36 Remove the auxiliary drivebelts with reference to Chapter 2A.

37 Refer to Chapter 3, and unbolt the air conditioning compressor from the engine. Tie the compressor to one side away from the engine compartment.

⚠️ Warning: Do not disconnect the air conditioning refrigerant circuit.

38 Unbolt the power steering pump from its mounting bracket and tie it to one side (see illustrations). Do not disconnect the hydraulic lines from the pump.

39 Disconnect the exhaust downpipe from

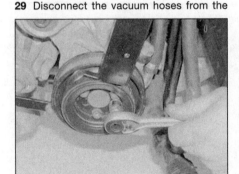

4.38a Unscrew the bolts . . .

4.38b . . . and remove the pulleys from the power steering pump . . .

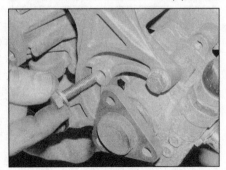

4.38c . . . then unscrew the bolts . . .

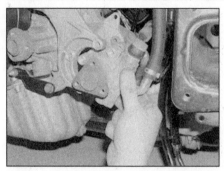

4.38d ... and move the power steering pump from its mounting, and tie it to one side

the exhaust manifold or catalytic converter with reference to Chapter 4C. Take care not to bend excessively the flexible section of the downpipe. On engine code ALT, remove the catalytic converter and front exhaust pipe.

40 Unbolt the heat shield from the right-hand engine mounting and lift it up. Unscrew the nuts from the tops of the right- and left-hand engine mountings. Also undo the screw and remove the earth cable from the right-hand engine mounting.

41 Remove the starter motor from the transmission with reference to Chapter 5A.

42 On automatic transmission models, unscrew and remove the three torque converter nuts accessible through the starter motor aperture. It will be necessary to turn the engine for access to each nut. To prevent the driveplate from turning while loosening the nuts, either counter-hold the crankshaft pulley bolt, or place a screwdriver in the teeth of the starter ring gear.

43 Mark the positions of the engine mountings in the subframe to ensure they are refitted correctly, then unscrew the lower nuts several turns.

44 Attach a suitable hoist to the engine, and lift the engine and transmission slightly. Make sure that the engine is adequately supported.

45 Unscrew and remove the bolts securing the transmission to the rear of the engine, then lower the engine to its original position. At this stage leave one of the bolts loosely fitted. Unbolt and remove the engine torque mounting bracket.

46 Using a trolley jack and piece of wood, support the front of the transmission.

4.47 Remove the engine from the engine compartment

Alternatively, a support bar for the transmission can be placed over the rear of the engine compartment.

47 Remove the last bolt, then check that all wiring and hoses have been disconnected, and lift the engine from the engine compartment **(see illustration)**. On automatic transmission models, make sure that the torque converter remains firmly in the transmission as the engine is being removed, and to prevent it falling out fit a metal bar across the bellhousing, secured with two bolts.

48 If they are loose, recover the location dowels from the rear of the cylinder block. Where necessary, remove the intermediate plate from the rear of the engine.

49 On manual transmission models, remove the clutch as described in Chapter 6.

Refitting

50 Refitting is a reversal of removal, but on manual transmission models first smear the splines of the input shaft with a little high melting-point grease. Lightly grease the contact surface of the release bearing, but **do not** grease the guide sleeve for the release bearing. On automatic transmission models, check that the torque converter is fully entered on the input shaft by checking that the distance between the bellhousing mounting flange and the torque converter is approximately 23.0 mm. If it is only 13.0 mm, the torque converter is not fully entered. Ensure that all engine and transmission mountings are fitted free of strain, and tighten all nuts and bolts to the specified torque. Refit, and where applicable adjust, all engine related components and systems with reference to the Chapters concerned. Ensure that the engine is filled with oil and that the cooling system is refilled as described in Chapter 1A before starting the engine.

Diesel engines

Removal

51 Select a solid, level surface to park the vehicle on. Give yourself enough space to move around it easily.

52 Disconnect the battery negative (earth) lead (see Chapter 5A).

53 Apply the handbrake, then jack up the front of the vehicle and support it on axle stands (see *Jacking and vehicle support*).

54 Remove the engine compartment undershield after undoing the screws.

55 Where applicable, prise out the cover caps, undo the retaining bolts/nuts and remove the cover from the top of the engine.

56 Remove the front bumper with reference to Chapter 11.

57 With reference to Chapter 1B, carry out the following:

a) *Drain the cooling system. A drain plug is located on the front left-hand side of the radiator, and any remaining coolant can be drained from the engine by unbolting the thermostat cover and removing the O-ring and thermostat.*

b) *If the engine is to be dismantled, drain the engine oil.*

58 Prise out the retaining clip, and disconnect the bottom hose from the radiator.

59 On models with an electric cooling fan, disconnect the wiring from the thermoswitch located on the bottom left-hand side of the radiator.

60 On automatic transmission models, position a suitable container beneath the engine compartment, then disconnect the automatic transmission fluid pipes at the lock carrier. Plug the ends of the pipes.

61 Loosen the clip and disconnect the air inlet duct from the intercooler at the bottom left of the lock carrier.

62 Loosen the clip and disconnect the turbocharger air hose at the bottom right-hand side of the lock carrier.

63 Unscrew the bolts and remove the air pipe to air cleaner duct from the lock carrier.

64 Remove the air cleaner assembly as described in Chapter 4B. Also, remove the inlet duct and manifold flap, and the EGR valve.

65 Disconnect the wiring from the headlights and headlight range control unit.

66 Remove the front indicators as described in Chapter 12, Section 7.

67 Release the clip and disconnect the top hose from the radiator.

68 Remove the air pipe and hose from the left-hand side of the engine. To do this, unscrew the retaining bolt, and loosen the clips.

69 Disconnect the bonnet lock cable from the lock carrier at the connection at the top of the driver's side inner wing.

70 Remove the cover from the power steering fluid reservoir.

71 At the left-hand front corner of the engine compartment lift the plastic cover and disconnect the five loom connectors.

72 On the top left-hand side of the lock carrier, disconnect the wiring for the anti-theft alarm system at the connectors.

73 Disconnect the wiring from the two horns and release the wiring from the support.

74 On models equipped with air conditioning, to release the condenser from the lock carrier, press the lug in the end of the retaining pin, pull the pin from the mounting bracket either side of the condenser, and separate the two halves of the mounting brackets. Undo the retaining screws and remove the rubber shrouds either side of the condenser. Disconnect the pressure switch wiring as the condenser is removed. Disconnect the wiring from the low pressure switch, and also disconnect the magnetic clutch wiring from the bottom of the lock carrier. Lift the condenser from its bracket, rotate it to the side and tie it in place to secure it away from the engine compartment. Protect the condenser with card or cloth sheets to prevent damage to it when removing the engine.

 Warning: Do not disconnect the air conditioning refrigerant circuit.

4.76 Remove the charge pressure duct from the rear of the engine compartment

75 Unscrew the lock carrier mounting bolts – one at the front/top of each wing, and one along side each headlamp. Unscrew the three bolts securing each bumper guide below each headlamp, and unclip them from the front wings. Unscrew the bolts securing the lock carrier/bumper bar to the underbody channels and, with the help of an assistant, withdraw the complete lock carrier from the front of the car and place it in a safe position.

76 Loosen the clips and remove the rear air intake duct from the rear of the engine. Disconnect the wiring from the sensors as applicable **(see illustration)**. Unscrew the mounting nut.

77 Loosen the clips and disconnect the hoses from the coolant expansion tank.

78 Unbolt the coolant expansion tank and disconnect the low coolant level switch wiring.

79 Disconnect the fuel supply and return lines from the filter cover on the left-hand side of the engine.

80 Refer to Chapter 1B and remove the fuel filter element. Undo the five retaining bolts and remove the fuel filter bracket from the engine block/cylinder head **(see illustration)**.

81 Disconnect the connectors for the camshaft position sensor, and engine speed sensor at the plenum chamber bulkhead **(see illustration)**.

82 The heater hoses are connected to the engine by quick-release couplings at the underside of the coolant junction at the rear of the cylinder head, and to the left of the cylinder head. Prise out the clip and pull the couplings apart.

83 Disconnect the brake vacuum hose from the plenum chamber connection.

84 Remove the auxiliary drivebelts with reference to Chapter 2B. Also remove the viscous fan with reference to Chapter 3.

85 Refer to Chapter 3, and unbolt the air conditioning compressor from the engine. Tie the compressor to one side away from the engine compartment.

 Warning: Do not disconnect the air conditioning refrigerant circuit.

86 Remove the starter motor as described in Chapter 5A. Release the starter motor wiring loom from its retaining bracket adjacent to the engine to transmission joint.

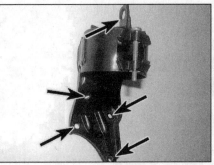

4.80 Undo the five retaining bolts and remove the fuel filter bracket from the engine block/cylinder head (arrowed)

87 Where fitted, disconnect the wiring plugs from the glow plugs, and the coolant temperature/level sensor fitted to the coolant junction on the rear of the cylinder head **(see illustrations)**.

88 Disconnect the wiring plugs fitted to the following components:

a) *Charge pressure sensor.*

b) *Fuel temperature sensor – located to the left of the cylinder head in the fuel return line.*

c) *Alternator (Chapter 5A).*

d) *Unit injector connector – located on the rear of the cylinder head* **(see illustration)**.

e) *Oil pressure switch – located in the front of the oil filter housing.*

89 Release the engine wiring loom from all retaining brackets/clips, and carefully position the loom away from the engine to one side. Note the routing of the loom to aid refitting.

4.87a Disconnect the heater system glow plugs . . .

4.88 Unscrew the cap and separate the unit injector connector

4.81 Disconnect the camshaft position sensor and engine speed sensor on the engine compartment bulkhead

90 Working on the right of the engine, undo the retaining bolts and remove the charge pressure control solenoid and spherical vacuum reservoir (where fitted) from the mounting bracket. There is no need to disconnect the vacuum hoses. Lay the components to one side **(see illustration)**.

91 Disconnect the fuel coolant supply and return hoses from the coolant pump and radiator in front of the right-hand side wheel arch. Disconnect the coolant hose from the thermostat cover by prising up the clip of the coupling and pulling the hose from the cover. Release the retaining clip and disconnect the fuel coolant hose between the shut-off valve and the engine. Release the hoses from any retaining clips. It should now be possible to move the coolant hoses as an assembly away from the engine and to one side **(see illustrations)**.

4.87b . . . and the coolant temperature sensor (arrowed)

4.90 Undo the retaining bolts and remove the charge pressure control solenoid and spherical vacuum reservoir (where fitted) from the mounting bracket

4.91a Disconnect the fuel coolant hoses . . .

4.91b . . . and the fuel coolant shut-off valve

92 Remove the three bolts and the power steering pump pulley. Unbolt the power steering pump from its mounting bracket and tie it to one side. Do not disconnect the hydraulic lines from the pump.

93 Unscrew the nuts securing the turbocharger to the catalytic converter. Loosen the exhaust front clamp and push it towards the rear to detach the exhaust pipes. Disconnect the exhaust front pipe and catalytic converter from the turbocharger. Take care not to bend excessively the flexible section of the downpipe. We found it preferable to completely remove the turbocharger as described in Chapter 4B.

94 Unbolt the earth wire from the right-hand engine mounting **(see illustration)**.

95 Where fitted, unbolt the turbocharger support bracket from the right-hand engine mounting.

96 On automatic transmission models, unscrew and remove the three torque converter nuts accessible through the starter motor aperture. It will be necessary to turn the engine for access to each nut. To prevent the driveplate from turning while loosening the nuts, either counter-hold the crankshaft pulley bolt, or place a screwdriver in the teeth of the starter ring gear.

97 On automatic transmission models, unbolt the hydraulic fluid pipe bracket from the left-

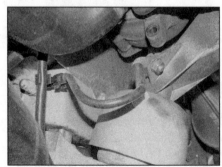

4.94 Unbolt the engine earth lead

hand side of the engine.

98 Remove the nuts on the top of each engine mounting, then unscrew the lower nuts several turns.

99 Attach a suitable hoist to the engine. Lifting eyes are provided at opposite corners of the cylinder head.

100 Unscrew and remove the bolts securing the transmission to the rear of the engine. At this stage leave one of the bolts loosely fitted. Also, unbolt and remove the engine torque mounting bracket.

101 Using a trolley jack and piece of wood, support the front of the transmission. Alternatively, a support bar for the transmission can be placed over the rear of the engine compartment.

102 Remove the last bolt, then check that all wiring and hoses have been disconnected, and lift the engine from the engine compartment. On automatic transmission models, make sure that the torque converter remains firmly in the transmission as the engine is being removed, and to prevent it falling out fit a metal bar across the bellhousing, secured with two bolts.

103 If they are loose, recover the location dowels from the rear of the cylinder block. Where necessary, remove the intermediate plate from the rear of the engine.

104 On manual transmission models, remove the clutch as described in Chapter 6.

Refitting

105 Refitting is a reversal of removal, but on manual transmission models first smear the splines of the input shaft with a little high melting-point grease. Lightly grease the contact surface of the release bearing, but **do not** grease the guide sleeve for the release bearing. On automatic transmission models, check that the torque converter is fully entered on the input shaft by checking that the distance between the bellhousing mounting flange and the torque converter is approximately 23.0 mm. If it is only 13.0 mm, the torque converter is not fully entered.

Ensure that all engine and transmission mountings are fitted free of strain, and tighten all nuts and bolts to the specified torque. Refit, and where applicable adjust, all engine related components and systems with reference to the Chapters concerned. Ensure that the engine is filled with oil and that the cooling system is refilled as described in Chapter 1B before starting the engine.

5 Engine overhaul – preliminary information

It is much easier to dismantle and work on the engine if it is mounted on a portable engine stand. These stands can often be hired from a tool hire shop. Before the engine is mounted on a stand, the flywheel should be removed, so that the stand bolts can be tightened into the end of the cylinder block/crankcase. **Note:** *Do not measure cylinder bore dimensions with the engine mounted on this type of stand.*

If a stand is not available, it is possible to dismantle the engine with it blocked up on a sturdy workbench, or on the floor. Be very careful not to tip or drop the engine when working without a stand.

If you intend to obtain a reconditioned engine, all ancillaries must be removed first, to be transferred to the new engine (just as they will if you are doing a complete engine overhaul yourself). These components include the following:

Petrol engines

a) *Alternator (including mounting brackets) and starter motor (Chapter 5A).*
b) *The ignition system including HT components, sensors, and spark plugs (Chapters 1A and 5B).*
c) *The fuel injection system components (Chapter 4A).*
d) *All electrical switches, actuators and sensors, and the engine wiring harness (Chapters 4A and 5B).*

e) *Inlet and exhaust manifolds (Chapters 4A and 4C).*
f) *Engine oil dipstick and tube.*
g) *Engine mountings (Chapter 2A).*
h) *Flywheel/driveplate (Chapter 2A).*
i) *Clutch components (Chapter 6).*

Diesel engines

a) *Alternator (including mounting brackets) and starter motor (Chapter 5A).*
b) *The glow plug/preheating system components (Chapter 5C)*
c) *All fuel system components, including all sensors and actuators (Chapter 4C)*
d) *The tandem pump (Chapter 4B)*
e) *All electrical switches, actuators and sensors, and the engine wiring harness (Chapters 4B and 5C).*
f) *Inlet and exhaust manifolds, and turbocharger (Chapters 4B and 4C).*
g) *The engine oil level dipstick and its tube.*
h) *Engine mountings (Chapter 2B).*
i) *Flywheel/driveplate (Chapter 2B).*
j) *Clutch components (Chapter 6).*

All engines

Note: *When removing the external components from the engine, pay close attention to details that may be helpful or important during refitting. Note the fitted position of gaskets, seals, spacers, pins, washers, bolts, and other small components.*

If you are obtaining a short engine (the engine cylinder block/crankcase, crankshaft, pistons and connecting rods, all fully assembled), then the cylinder head, sump, oil pump, timing belt (together with its tensioner and covers), auxiliary belt (together with its tensioner), coolant pump, thermostat housing, coolant outlet elbows, oil filter housing and where applicable oil cooler will also have to be removed.

If you are planning a full overhaul, the engine can be dismantled in the order given below:
a) *Inlet and exhaust manifolds (see the relevant part of Chapter 4).*

6.4 Keep groups of components together in labelled bags or boxes

b) *Timing belt, sprockets and tensioner (see Chapter 2A or 2B).*
c) *Cylinder head (see Chapter 2A or 2B).*
d) *Flywheel/driveplate (see Chapter 2A or 2B).*
e) *Sump (see Chapter 2A or 2B).*
f) *Oil pump or balancer shaft assembly (see Chapter 2A or 2B).*
g) *Piston/connecting rod assemblies (see Section 7).*
h) *Crankshaft (see Section 8).*

6 Cylinder head – dismantling, cleaning, inspection and reassembly

Note: *New and reconditioned cylinder heads are available from VW, and from engine specialists. Specialist tools are required for the dismantling and inspection procedures, and new components may not be readily available. It may, therefore, be more practical for the home mechanic to buy a reconditioned head, rather than to dismantle, inspect and recondition the original head.*

Dismantling

1 Remove the cylinder head from the engine block as described in Part A or B of this Chapter. Also remove the camshaft sprocket as described in Part A or B of this Chapter.

2 On diesel models, remove the injectors and glow plugs (see Chapters 4B and 5C).
3 Where applicable, remove the rear coolant outlet elbow together with its gasket/O-ring.
4 It is important that groups of components are kept together when they are removed and, if still serviceable, refitted in the same groups. If they are refitted randomly, accelerated wear leading to early failure will occur. Stowing groups of components in plastic bags or storage bins will help to keep everything in the right order – label them according to their fitted location, eg, No 1 exhaust, No 2 inlet, etc **(see illustration)**. Note that No 1 cylinder is nearest the timing belt end of the engine.
5 Check that the manufacturer's orientation markings are visible on camshaft bearing caps; if none can be found, make your own using a scriber or centre-punch.
6 The camshaft bearing caps must now be removed as follows.

Engine codes AWT and ALT

7 At the front of the inlet camshaft, unbolt the Hall sender then unscrew the bolt from the camshaft and remove the tapered washer and Hall sender plate.
8 The automatic camshaft adjuster must now be locked before removing it. VW technicians use special tool 3366 to do this. Alternatively, it is possible to make up a similar tool using a threaded rod, nuts and a small metal plate to keep the adjuster compressed. As a safety precaution, use a plastic cable tie to keep the home-made tool in position **(see illustrations)**.
9 Clean the chain and the camshaft sprockets in line with the arrows on the top of the camshaft rear bearing caps, then mark the sprockets and chain in relation to each other. Note that the distance between the two marks must be 16 rollers on the chain, but also note that the mark on the exhaust camshaft is slightly offset towards the centre of the cylinder head.

6.8a Home-made tool for holding the automatic adjuster in its compressed state

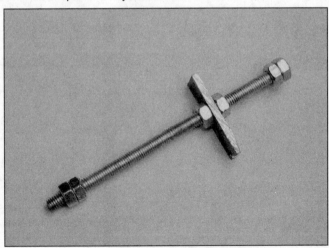
6.8b Home-made tool

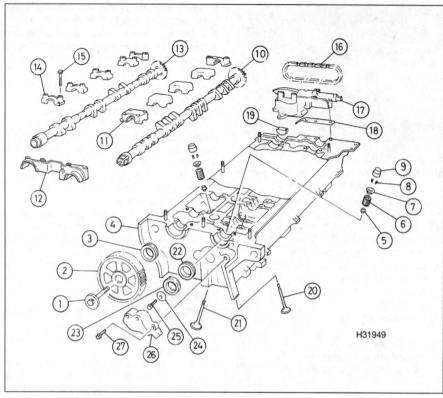

6.10 Cylinder head components (engine codes AWT and ALT)

1 Camshaft sprocket bolt
2 Camshaft sprocket
3 Oil seal
4 Cylinder head
5 Valve stem oil seal
6 Valve spring
7 Upper valve spring seat
8 Split collets
9 Hydraulic tappets
10 Inlet camshaft

11 Bearing cap, inlet camshaft
12 Front combined bearing cap
13 Exhaust camshaft
14 Bearing cap, exhaust camshaft
15 Camshaft bearing bolt
16 Drive chain
17 Automatic camshaft adjuster

18 Rubber seal
19 Half round rubber grommet
20 Exhaust valve
21 Inlet valve
22 Oil seal
23 Hall sender ring
24 Tapered washer
25 Ring retaining bolt
26 Hall sender
27 Hall sender retaining bolt

10 Progressively slacken the bolts from bearing caps 3 and 5 then 1 and 6 on both the inlet and exhaust camshafts **(see illustration). Note:** *The caps are numbered from the rear of the cylinder head, number 6 being the combined cap that straddles the front of both camshafts.*

11 Unscrew the automatic camshaft adjuster mounting bolts.

12 Progressively slacken the bolts from bearing caps 4 and 2 on both the inlet and exhaust camshafts, then lift both camshafts from the cylinder head together with the automatic adjuster and chain **(see illustration)**.

13 Release the adjuster from the chain and remove the chain from the camshaft sprockets. Remove the oil seals from the front of each camshaft **(see illustration)**.

Petrol engine code AZM and diesel engines

Note: *It is possible to remove the camshaft with the cylinder head still fitted to the engine in the vehicle. However access is severely restricted.*

14 On diesel engines, in order to ensure that the pump injector rocker arms are refitted to their original locations, use a marker pen or paint and number the arms 1 to 4, with No 1 nearest the timing belt end of the engine. If the arms are not fitted to their original locations the injector basic clearance setting procedure must be carried out as described in Chapter 4B. Starting with the outer bolts first, carefully and evenly slacken the rocker shaft retaining bolts. Discard the rocker shaft bolts, new ones must be fitted.

15 Slacken the nuts from bearing caps Nos 5, 1 and 3 first, then from bearing caps 2 and 4 **(see illustrations)**. Slacken the nuts alternately and diagonally half a turn at a time until they can be removed, then remove the bearing caps. Keep the caps in order and note their fitted positions. **Note:** *The camshaft bearing caps are numbered 1 to 5 from the timing belt end.*

16 On diesel engines, the camshaft rotates in shell bearings. As the camshaft bearing caps are removed, recover the shell bearing halves from the camshaft. Number the back of the bearings with a felt pen to ensure that, if re-used, the bearings are fitted to their original

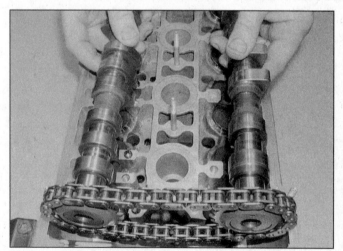

6.12 Lift the camshafts and chain from the cylinder head

6.13 Remove the camshaft adjuster

6.15a Cylinder head components (engine code AZM)

1 Camshaft bearing cap
2 Nut
3 Camshaft
4 Woodruff key
5 Camshaft sprocket bolt
6 Hydraulic tappet
7 Upper valve spring seat
8 Valve springs
9 Valve stem seals
10 Lower valve spring seat
11 Valve guides
12 Valves
13 Plug
14 Camshaft oil seal
15 Cylinder head

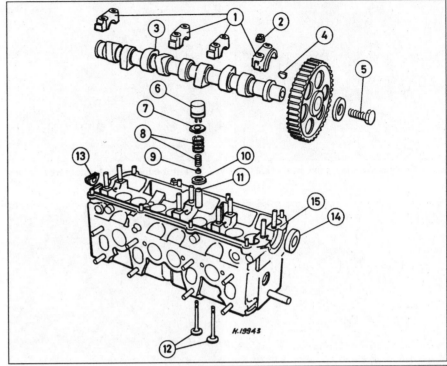

6.15b Cylinder head components (diesel engines)

1 Injector rocker shaft assembly
2 Bearing caps
3 Bearing shells
4 Camshaft
5 Cylinder head
6 Valves
7 Oil seal
8 Guide
9 Oil seal
10 Inner spring
11 Outer spring
12 Unit injector
13 Collets
14 Hydraulic tappet
15 Washers
16 Bolt
17 Bolt
18 Bolt
19 Unit injector

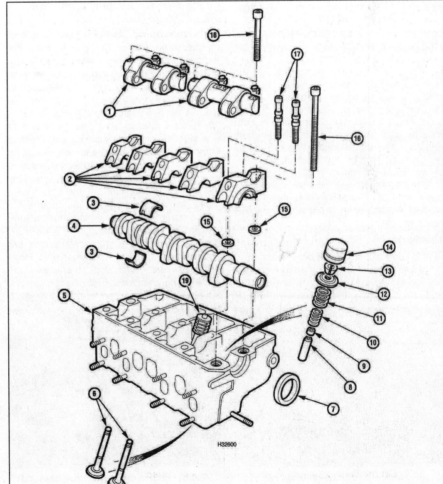

6.17 Remove the camshaft oil seal

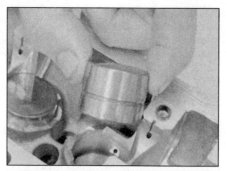

6.19 Lift the hydraulic tappets from their bores

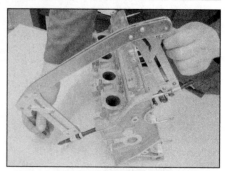

6.20a Compress the valve springs with a compressor tool

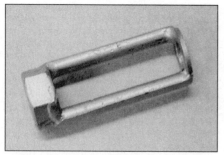

6.20b Home-made tool to access holes to the inlet valves on engine codes AWT and ALT

6.21a Remove the upper spring seat . . .

6.21b . . . and valve spring

locations. **Note:** *Fitted into the cylinder head, under each camshaft bearing cap, is a washer for each cylinder head bolt.*

17 Slide the oil seal from the front of the camshaft and discard it; a new one must be used on reassembly **(see illustration)**.

18 Carefully lift the camshaft from the cylinder head, keeping it level and supported at both ends as it is removed so that the journals and lobes are not damaged. Remove the oil seal from the front of the camshaft. On diesel engines recover the lower shell bearing halves from the cylinder head, number the back of the shells with a felt pen to ensure that, if re-used, the bearings are fitted to their original locations.

All engines

19 Lift the hydraulic tappets from their bores and store them with the valve contact surface facing downwards, to prevent the oil from draining out **(see illustration)**. It

is recommended that the tappets are kept immersed in oil for the period they are removed from the cylinder head. Make a note of the position of each tappet, as they must be fitted to the same valves on reassembly – accelerated wear leading to early failure will result if they are interchanged.

20 Turn the cylinder head over, and rest it on one side. Using a valve spring compressor, compress each valve spring in turn, extracting the split collets when the upper valve spring seat has been pushed far enough down the valve stem to free them. If the spring seat sticks, tap the upper jaw of the compressor with a hammer to free it **(see illustration)**. **Note:** *On engine codes AWT and ALT, the access holes to the inlet valves are considerably smaller in diameter than those to the exhaust valves, and the standard size valve spring compressor may be too large. If a tool cannot be obtained from a VW dealer, a*

home-made tool will have to be fabricated out of a suitable nut, washer and metal bar welded together (see illustration).

21 Release the valve spring compressor and remove the upper spring seat, and single valve spring (petrol engines) or double valve springs (diesel engines) **(see illustrations)**.

22 Use a pair of pliers or a special removal tool to extract the valve stem oil seal, then on diesel engines remove the lower spring seat from the valve guide. Withdraw the valve itself from the head gasket side of the cylinder head. Repeat this process for the remaining valves **(see illustrations)**.

Cleaning

23 Using a suitable degreasing agent, remove all traces of oil deposits from the cylinder head, paying particular attention to the journal bearings, hydraulic tappet bores, valve guides and oilways. Scrape off any

6.22a Use a removal tool . . .

6.22b . . . to remove the valve stem oil seals

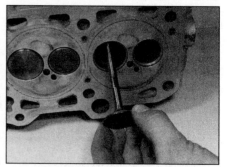

6.22c Remove the valves (typical)

traces of old gasket from the mating surfaces, taking care not to score or gouge them. If using emery paper, do not use a grade of less than 100. Turn the head over and using a blunt blade, scrape any carbon deposits from the combustion chambers and ports. Finally, wash the entire head casting with a suitable solvent to remove the remaining debris.

24 Clean the valve heads and stems using a fine wire brush. If the valve is heavily coked, scrape off the majority of the deposits with a blunt blade first, then use the wire brush.

25 Thoroughly clean the remainder of the components using solvent and allow them to dry completely. Discard the oil seals, as new ones must be fitted when the cylinder head is reassembled.

Inspection

Cylinder head

Note: *If the valve seats are to be recut, ensure that the maximum permissible reworking dimension is not exceeded (the maximum dimension will only allow minimal reworking to produce a perfect seal between valve and seat). If the maximum dimension is exceeded, the function of the hydraulic tappets cannot be guaranteed, and the cylinder head must be renewed. Refer to paragraph 28 for details of how to calculate the maximum permissible reworking dimension.*

26 Examine the head casting closely to identify any damage or cracks that may have developed. Pay particular attention to the areas around the valve seats and spark plug holes. If cracking is discovered in this area, VW state that the cylinder head may be re-used, provided the cracks are no larger than 0.3 mm wide on petrol engines or 0.5 mm wide on diesel engines. More serious damage will mean the renewal of the cylinder head.

27 Moderately pitted and scorched valve seats can be repaired by grinding in the valves in during reassembly, as described later in this Section.

28 On all petrol engines, recutting is not allowed as this has an adverse effect on the hydraulic tappets. On diesel engines, badly worn or damaged valve seats may be restored by recutting, however this work should be entrusted to an engineering works. After recutting and lapping, the maximum permissible reworking dimension **must** not be exceeded. To calculate the maximum permissible reworking dimension, proceed as follows **(see illustration)**:

a) *If a new valve is to be fitted, use the new valve for the following calculation.*

b) *Insert the valve into its guide in the cylinder head, and push the valve firmly on to its seat.*

c) *Using a flat edge placed across the top surface of the cylinder head, measure the distance between the top face of the valve stem, and the top surface of the cylinder head. Record the measurement obtained.*

d) *Consult the Specifications, and look up the value for the minimum permissible dimension between the top face of the valve stem and the top surface of the cylinder head.*

e) *Now take the measured distance and subtract the minimum permissible dimension, to give the maximum permissible reworking dimension; eg, Measured distance (34.4 mm) minus Minimum permissible dimension (34.0 mm) = Maximum permissible reworking dimension (0.4 mm).*

29 Measure any distortion of the gasket surfaces using a straight-edge and a set of feeler blades. Take one measurement longitudinally on both the inlet and exhaust manifold mating surfaces. Take several measurements across the head gasket surface, to assess the level of distortion in all planes **(see illustration)**. Compare the measurements with the figures in the Specifications.

30 On petrol engines, if the head is distorted out of specification, it may be possible to have it machined by an engineering works.

31 Minimum cylinder head heights (measured between the cylinder head gasket surface and the cylinder head cover gasket surface) are listed in Specifications.

Camshaft

32 Visually inspect the camshaft for evidence of wear on the surfaces of the lobes and journals. Normally their surfaces should be smooth and have a dull shine; look for scoring, erosion or pitting and areas that appear highly polished, indicating excessive wear. Accelerated wear will occur once the hardened exterior of the camshaft has been damaged, so always renew worn items. **Note:** *If these symptoms are visible on the tips of the camshaft lobes, check the corresponding tappet, as it will probably be worn as well.*

33 If the machined surfaces of the camshaft appear discoloured or blued, it is likely that it has been overheated at some point, probably due to inadequate lubrication. This may have distorted the shaft, so check the runout as follows: place the camshaft between two V-blocks and using a DTI gauge, measure the runout at the centre journal. If it exceeds the figure quoted in the Specifications at the start of this Chapter, renew the camshaft.

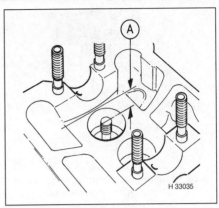

6.28 Measure the distance (A) between the top face of the valve stem and the top surface of the cylinder head

34 To measure the camshaft endfloat, temporarily refit the camshaft to the cylinder head, then fit the first and last bearing caps (and shell bearings where applicable) and tighten the retaining nuts to the specified first stage torque setting. Anchor a DTI gauge to the timing belt end of the cylinder head and align the gauge probe with the camshaft axis. Push the camshaft to one end of the cylinder head as far as it will travel, then rest the DTI gauge probe on the end of the camshaft, and zero the gauge display. Push the camshaft as far as it will go to the other end of the cylinder head, and record the gauge reading. Verify the reading by pushing the camshaft back to its original position and checking that the gauge indicates zero again **(see illustration)**. **Note:** *The hydraulic tappets must not be fitted whilst this measurement is being taken.*

35 Check that the camshaft endfloat measurement is within the limit listed in the Specifications. Wear outside of this limit is unlikely to be confined to any one component, so renewal of the camshaft, cylinder head and bearing caps must be considered.

Valves and associated components

Note: *On all engines, the valve heads cannot be recut, although they may be ground in. On 1.8 litre petrol engines, if new valves are to be fitted, the old valves must be disposed of carefully (do not dispose of them as normal scrap), as the valve stems are filled with sodium. Consult your local scrap or recycling centre for advice.*

6.29 Measure the distortion of the cylinder head

6.34 Check the camshaft endfloat using a DTI gauge

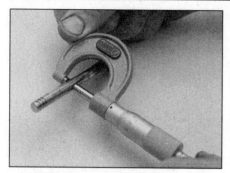

6.36 Measure the diameter of the valve stems with a micrometer

6.39 Measure the maximum deflection of the valve in its guide, using a DTI gauge

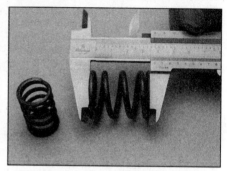

6.41 Measure the free length of each of the valve springs

36 Examine each valve closely for signs of wear. Inspect the valve stems for wear ridges, scoring or variations in diameter; measure their diameters at several points along their lengths with a micrometer **(see illustration)**.

37 The valve heads should not be cracked, badly pitted or charred. Note that light pitting of the valve head can be rectified by grinding in the valves during reassembly, as described later in this Section.

38 Check that the valve stem end face is free from excessive pitting or indentation; this would be caused by defective hydraulic tappets.

39 Insert each valve into its respective guide in the cylinder head and set up a DTI gauge against the edge of the valve head. With the valve end face flush with the top of the valve guide, measure the maximum side-to-side deflection of the valve in its guide **(see illustration)**.

40 If the measurement exceeds that given in the Specifications, the valve and valve guide should be renewed as a pair. **Note:** *Valve guides are an interference fit in the cylinder head and their removal requires access to a hydraulic press. For this reason, it would be wise to entrust the job to an engineering workshop.*

41 Using vernier calipers, measure the free length of each of the valve springs. As a manufacturer's figure is not quoted, the only way to check the length of the springs is by comparison with a new component. Note that valve springs are usually renewed during a major engine overhaul **(see illustration)**.

42 Stand each spring on its end on a flat surface, against an engineer's square **(see illustration)**. Check the squareness of the spring visually, and renew it if it appears distorted.

Reassembly

43 To achieve a gas-tight seal between the valves and their seats, it will be necessary to grind in (or lap in) the valves. To complete this process you will need a quantity of fine/coarse grinding paste and a grinding tool – this can either be of the rubber sucker type, or the automatic type which is driven by a rotary power tool.

44 Smear a small quantity of *fine* grinding paste on the sealing face of the valve head. Turn the cylinder head over so that the combustion chambers are facing upwards and insert the valve into the correct guide. Attach the grinding tool to the valve head and using a backward/forward rotary action, grind the valve head into its seat. Periodically lift the valve and rotate it to redistribute the grinding paste **(see illustration)**.

45 Continue this process until the contact between valve and seat produces an unbroken, matt grey ring of uniform width, on both faces. Repeat the operation on the remaining valves.

46 If the valves and seats are so badly pitted that coarse grinding paste must be used, bear in mind that there is a maximum protrusion of the end of the valve stem from the valve guide. Refer to the Specifications at the beginning of this Chapter for the minimum dimension from the end of the valve stem to the top face of the cylinder head. If this dimension is outside the limit due to excessive grinding-in, the hydraulic tappets may not operate correctly.

47 Assuming the repair is feasible, work as described previously but use coarse grinding paste initially, to achieve a dull finish on the valve face and seat. Wash off the coarse paste with solvent and repeat the process using fine grinding paste to obtain the correct finish.

48 When all the valves have been ground in, remove all traces of grinding paste from the cylinder head and valves with solvent, and allow them to dry completely.

49 Turn the head on its side. On diesel engines, fit the first lower spring seat into place, with the convex side facing the cylinder head **(see illustration)**.

50 Working on one valve at a time, lubricate the valve stem with clean engine oil, and insert it into the guide. Fit one of the protective plastic sleeves supplied with the new valve stem oil seals over the valve end face – this will protect the oil seal whilst it is being fitted **(see illustrations)**.

6.42 Check the squareness of the valve springs

6.44 Grind in the valves with a reciprocating rotary motion

6.49 Fit the lower spring seat with the convex face facing the cylinder head (diesel engines)

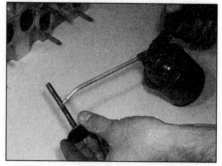

6.50a Lubricate the valve stem with clean engine oil before fitting it

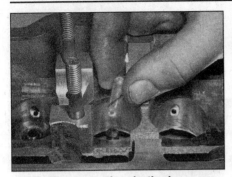

6.50b Fit a protective plastic sleeve over the valve stem before fitting the stem seal

6.51a Fit a new stem seal over the valve

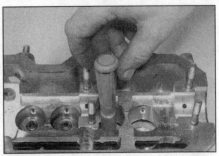

6.51b Use a special installer or suitable long reach socket to fit the valve stem oil seals

51 Dip a new valve stem seal in clean engine oil, and carefully push it over the valve and onto the top of the valve guide – take care not to damage the stem seal as it passes over the valve end face. Use a suitable long reach socket or special installer to press it firmly into position **(see illustrations)**. Remove the protective sleeve.

52 Locate the valve spring(s) over the valve stem **(see illustration)**. On diesel engines, ensure that the springs locate correctly on the lower seat.

53 Fit the upper seat over the top of the springs, then using a valve spring compressor, compress the springs until the upper seat is pushed beyond the collet grooves in the valve stem. Refit the split collet, using a dab of grease to hold the two halves in the grooves **(see illustrations)**. Gradually release the spring compressor, checking that the collet remains correctly seated as the spring

extends. When correctly seated, the upper seat should force the two halves of the collet together, and hold them securely in the grooves in the end of the valve.

54 Repeat this process for the remaining sets of valve components. To settle the components after installation, strike the end of each valve stem with a mallet, using a block of wood to protect the stem from damage. Check before progressing any further that the spilt collets remain firmly held in the end of the valve stem by the upper spring seat.

55 Smear some clean engine oil onto the sides of the hydraulic tappets, and fit them into position in their bores in the cylinder head. Push them down until they contact the valves, then lubricate the camshaft lobe contact surfaces **(see illustration)**.

Engine codes AWT and ALT

56 Locate the rubber/metal gasket for the automatic camshaft adjuster, together with

the half-round seal, on the front of the cylinder head. If the gasket does not have any sealant compound already on it, smear a little in the area shown **(see illustrations)**.

57 Lubricate the camshafts and cylinder head bearing journals with clean engine oil.

58 Engage the chain with the camshaft sprockets making sure that the distance between the marks on the sprockets is 16 rollers **(see illustration)**. Locate the adjuster between the chain runs, then carefully lower the camshafts into position on the cylinder head. Support the ends of the shafts as they are fitted, to avoid damaging the lobes and journals. Alternatively, it is possible to fit the camshafts together with the chain in the cylinder head, then slightly raise the sprocket ends of the camshafts in order to fit the adjuster.

59 The oil seals may be fitted at this stage, or alternatively fitted later. Dip the new oil seals

6.52 Fit the valve spring(s)

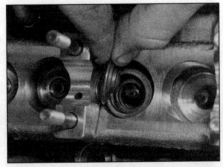

6.53a Fit the upper seat over the top of the valve spring

6.53b Use grease to hold the two halves of the split collet in the groove

6.55 Fit the tappets into their bores in the cylinder head

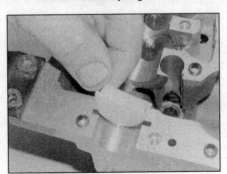

6.56a Fit the half-round seal

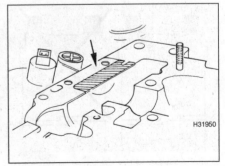

6.56b Apply sealant compound in the area shown

6.58 Engage the chain with the sprockets – note the marks indicating distance of 16 rollers

in engine oil, then locate them on the front of each camshaft. Make sure the closed ends of the seals face outwards from the camshafts and take care not to damage the seal lips. Locate the seals against the seats in the cylinder head.

60 Insert the automatic camshaft adjuster mounting bolts and tighten to the specified torque.

61 Oil the upper surfaces of the camshaft bearing journals, then fit Nos 2 and 4 bearing caps to both camshafts. Ensure that they are fitted the right way around and in the correct locations, then progressively tighten the retaining bolts to the specified torque. **Note:** *The bearing caps are numbered from the rear of the engine.*

62 Fit the No 1 bearing caps to each camshaft and progressively tighten the retaining bolts to the specified torque.

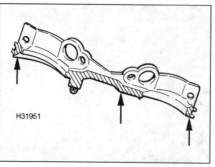

6.64 Apply a thin film of sealant to the contact face of the combined front bearing cap in the area shown

63 Remove the locking tool from the automatic camshaft adjuster.

64 Apply a thin film of sealant to the contact face of the combined front bearing cap, then fit the cap making sure that the oil seals locate against their seating **(see illustration)**. Progressively tighten the retaining bolts to the specified torque.

65 Fit Nos 3 and 5 bearing caps and progressively tighten the retaining bolts to the specified torque.

66 Refit the Hall sender plate and tapered washer to the front of the inlet camshaft and tighten the bolt to the specified torque.

67 Refit the Hall sender and tighten the retaining bolt.

Petrol engine code AZM and diesel engines

68 Lubricate the camshaft and cylinder head bearing journals with clean engine oil **(see illustrations)**. **Note:** *On diesel engines, fit the camshaft shell bearing lower halves into the cylinder head into their original locations, making sure that the locating lugs engage correctly with the corresponding cut-outs in the cylinder head. Once fitted, lubricate the bearing surfaces.*

69 Carefully lower the camshaft into position in the cylinder head making sure that the cam lobes for No 1 cylinder are pointing upwards. Support the ends of the shaft as it is fitted, to avoid damaging the lobes and journals **(see illustration)**.

70 Dip the new oil seal in engine oil, then locate it on the front of the camshaft. **Note:** *VW have gradually introduced oil seals made with PTFE, identified by the lack of annular spring. These type of seals must not be lubricated or greased.* Make sure the closed end of the seal faces outwards from the camshaft and take care not to damage the seal lip. Locate the seal against the seat in the cylinder head.

71 The bearing caps have their respective cylinder numbers stamped onto them, and have an elongated lug on one side. When correctly fitted, the numbers should be readable from the exhaust side of the cylinder head, and the lugs should face the inlet side of the cylinder head. Oil the upper surfaces of the camshaft bearing journals, then fit Nos 2 and 4 bearing caps. Ensure that they are fitted the right way around and in the correct locations, then progressively tighten the retaining bolts to the specified torque **(see illustrations)**. **Note:** *On diesel engines, insert the upper shell bearings into the camshaft bearing caps*

6.68a Lubricate the camshaft bearings with clean engine oil

6.68b On diesel engines, fit the camshaft shell bearing lower halves into the cylinder head into their original locations

6.69 Lower the camshaft into position on the cylinder head

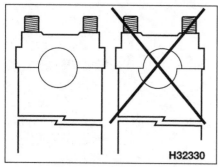

6.71a The camshaft bearing caps are drilled off-centre (engine code AZM)

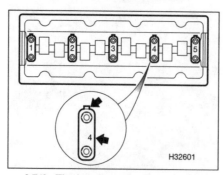

6.71b The bearing caps are fitted as shown (engine code AZM)

6.71c On diesel engines, insert the upper shell bearings into the camshaft bearing caps into their original locations

6.72a Smear the mating surfaces of cap No 1 with sealant on the AZM petrol engine . . .

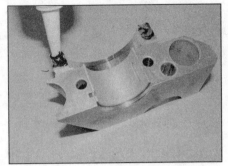

6.72b . . . and all diesel engines

6.74 Fit the coolant elbow using a new O-ring or gasket

into their original locations, making sure that the locating lugs engage correctly with the corresponding cut-outs in the bearing caps. If the camshaft is being refitted with the cylinder head removed from the engine, position the cylinder head bolt washers in their locating holes in the cylinder head.

72 Smear the mating surfaces of bearing cap No 1 with sealant then fit caps 1, 3 and 5 over the camshaft and progressively tighten the nuts to the specified torque **(see illustrations)**.

All engines

73 Where applicable, refit the coolant sensor and oil pressure switch to the cylinder head.

74 Where applicable, refit the coolant outlet elbow together with a new gasket/O-ring **(see illustration)**.

75 On diesel models, refit the injectors, pump injector rocker shaft and glow plugs (see Chapters 4B and 5C).

76 Refit the cylinder head with reference to Parts A or B of this Chapter. Also refit the camshaft sprocket as described in Part A or B of this Chapter.

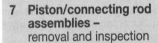

| 7 | Piston/connecting rod assemblies – removal and inspection |

Removal

1 Refer to Part A or B of this Chapter (as applicable) and remove the cylinder head, flywheel, sump and baffle plate, oil pump and pickup tube or balancer shaft assembly (engine code ALT).

2 Inspect the tops of the cylinder bores for ridges at the point where the pistons reach top dead centre. These must be removed otherwise the pistons may be damaged when they are pushed out of their bores. Use a scraper or ridge reamer to remove the ridges.

3 Using a set of feeler blades, measure the big-end to crankpin web thrust clearance at each connecting rod, and record the measurements for later reference.

4 Rotate the crankshaft until piston No 1 is at bottom dead centre; piston No 4 will also be at bottom dead centre. Unless they are already identified, mark the big-end bearing caps and

connecting rods with their respective piston numbers, using a centre-punch or a scribe **(see illustration)**. Note the orientation of the bearing caps in relation to the connecting rod; it may be difficult to see the manufacturer's markings at this stage, so scribe alignment arrows on them both to ensure correct reassembly.

5 Unscrew the bearing cap bolts/nuts, half a turn at a time, until they can be removed and the cap withdrawn **(see illustrations)**. Recover the bottom shell bearing, and tape it to the cap for safe-keeping. Note that if the shell bearings are to be re-used, they must be refitted to the same connecting rod.

6 Where the bearing caps are secured with nuts, wrap the threaded ends of the bolts with insulating tape to prevent them scratching the crankpins and bores when the pistons are removed **(see illustration)**.

7 Drive the piston out of the top of the bore

using a piece of wooden dowel or a hammer handle. As the piston and connecting rod emerge, recover the top shell bearing and tape it to the connecting rod for safe-keeping. On engines fitted with piston cooling jets at the bottom of the cylinders, take care not to allow the connecting rod to damage the jet as the piston is being removed.

8 Remove No 4 piston and connecting rod in the same manner, then turn the crankshaft through half a turn and remove No 2 and 3 pistons and connecting rods. Remember to maintain the components in their cylinder groups, whilst they are in a dismantled state.

9 If applicable, remove the retaining screws and withdraw the piston cooling jets from the bottom of the cylinder **(see illustrations)**.

Inspection

10 Insert a small flat-bladed screwdriver into the removal slot and prise the gudgeon

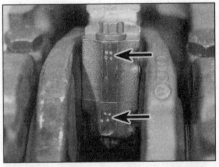

7.4 Mark the big-end caps and connecting rods with their numbers (arrowed)

7.5a Unscrew the big-end cap bolts . . .

7.5b . . . and remove the cap

7.6 Wrap the stud threads with tape

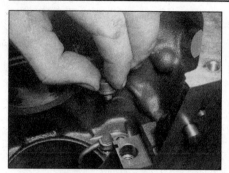

7.9a Remove the piston cooling jet retaining screws . . .

7.9b . . . and withdraw the jets from their mounting holes

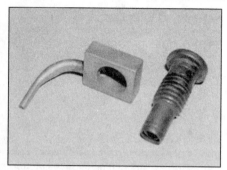

7.9c Piston cooling jet and retainer

pin circlips from each piston. Push out the gudgeon pin, and separate the piston and connecting rod **(see illustrations)**. Discard the circlips as new items must be fitted on reassembly. If the pin proves difficult to remove, heat the piston to 60°C with hot water – the resulting expansion will then allow the two components to be separated.

11 Before an inspection of the pistons can be carried out, the existing piston rings must be removed, using a removal/installation tool, or an old feeler blade if such a tool is not available. Always remove the upper piston rings first, expanding them to clear the piston crown. The rings are very brittle and will snap if they are stretched too much – sharp edges are produced when this happens, so protect your eyes and hands. Discard the rings on removal, as new items must be fitted when the engine is reassembled **(see illustration)**.

12 Use a section of old piston ring to scrape

the carbon deposits out of the ring grooves, taking care not to score or gouge the edges of the groove.

13 Carefully scrape away all traces of carbon from the tops of the pistons **(see illustration)**. A hand-held wire brush (or a piece of fine emery cloth) can be used, once the majority of the deposits have been scraped away. Be careful not to remove any metal from the piston, as it is relatively soft. **Note:** *Make sure each piston is kept identified for position during cleaning.*

14 Once the deposits have been removed, clean the pistons and connecting rods with paraffin or a suitable solvent, and dry thoroughly. Make sure that the oil return holes in the ring grooves are clear.

15 Examine the pistons for signs of excessive wear or damage. Some normal wear will be apparent, in the form of a vertical 'grain' on the piston thrust surfaces and a slight

looseness of the top compression ring in its groove. Abnormal wear should be carefully examined, to assess whether the component is still serviceable and what the cause of the wear might be.

16 Scuffing or scoring of the piston skirt may indicate that the engine has been overheating, through inadequate cooling or lubrication. Scorch marks on the skirt indicate that gas blow-by has occurred, perhaps caused by worn bores or piston rings. Burnt areas on the piston crown are usually an indication of pre-ignition, pinking or detonation. In extreme cases, the piston crown may be melted by operating under these conditions. Corrosion pit marks in the piston crown indicate that coolant has seeped into the combustion chamber. The faults causing these symptoms must be corrected before the engine is brought back into service, or the same damage will recur.

17 Check the pistons, connecting rods, gudgeon pins and bearing caps for cracks. Lay the connecting rods on a flat surface, and look along the length to see if it appears bent or twisted. If you have doubts about their condition, get them measured at an engineering workshop. Inspect the small-end bush bearing in the connecting rod for signs of wear or cracking.

18 Using a micrometer, measure the diameter of all four pistons at a point 10 mm from the bottom of the skirt, at right angles to the gudgeon pin axis **(see illustration)**. Compare the measurements with those listed in the Specifications. If the piston diameter is out of the tolerance band listed for its particular

7.10a Insert a small screwdriver into the slot and prise off the gudgeon pin circlips

7.10b Push out the gudgeon pin to separate the piston and connecting rod

7.11 Piston rings can be removed using an old feeler gauge

7.13 The piston crown on a diesel engine

7.18 Using a micrometer, measure the diameter of all four pistons

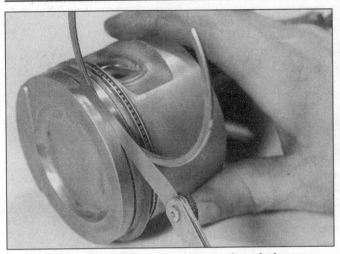

7.19 Measure the piston ring-to-groove using a feeler gauge

7.21a The piston crown is marked with an arrow which must point towards the timing belt end of the engine

size, then it must be renewed. **Note:** *If the cylinder block was rebored during a previous overhaul, oversize pistons may already have been fitted.* Record all of the measurements and use them to check the piston clearances when the cylinder bores are measured, later in this Chapter.

19 Locate a new piston ring in the appropriate groove and measure the ring-to-groove clearance using a feeler blade **(see illustration)**. Note that the rings are of different widths, so use the correct ring for the groove. Compare the measurements with those listed; if the clearances are outside of

the tolerance band, then the piston must be renewed. Confirm this by checking the width of the piston ring with a micrometer.

20 Examine the small-end bearing and gudgeon pin for wear and damage. If excessive, the gudgeon pin will have to be renewed and a new bush fitted to the connecting rod. This work must be entrusted to an engine overhaul specialist or engineering works.

21 The orientation of the piston with respect to the connecting rod must be correct when the two are reassembled. The piston crown is marked with an arrow (which may be obscured by carbon deposits); this must point

towards the timing belt end of the engine when the piston is installed. On diesel engines if the arrows are not visible, assemble the pistons to the connecting rods so that the combustion recess in the top of the piston is on the water pump side of the engine block. The connecting rod and its bearing cap both have recesses/lugs machined into them, close to their mating surfaces – these recesses/lugs must both face the same way as the arrow on the piston crown (ie, towards the timing belt end of the engine) when correctly installed **(see illustrations)**. Reassemble the two components to satisfy this requirement.

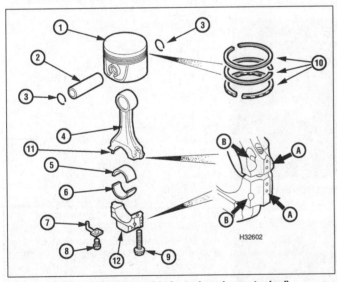

7.21b Piston assembly (petrol engines – typical)

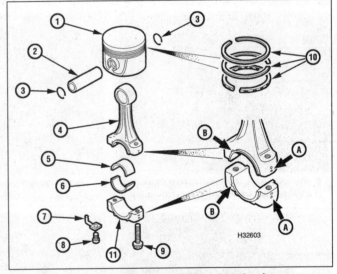

7.21c Piston assembly (diesel engines)

1 Piston	9 Big-end bearing cap
2 Gudgeon pin	bolts
3 Circlip	10 Piston rings
4 Connecting rod	11 Locating dowel
5 Big-end bearing shell	12 Big-end bearing cap
6 Big-end bearing shell	A Connecting rod/bearing cap
7 Oil jet for piston cooling	identification marks
(where applicable)	B Connecting rod/bearing cap
8 Oil jet retaining screw	orientation marks

1 Piston	9 Big-end bearing cap
2 Gudgeon pin	bolts
3 Circlips	10 Piston rings
4 Connecting rod	11 Bearing cap
5 Bearing shell	A Connecting rod/bearing cap
6 Bearing shell	identification marks
7 Oil jet for piston cooling	B Connecting rod/bearing cap
8 Oil jet retaining screw	orientation marks

8.1 Remove the baffle plate

8.3 Measure the crankshaft endfloat using a DTI gauge

8.4 If a DTI gauge is not available, measure the crankshaft endfloat using feeler gauges

22 Lubricate the gudgeon pin and small-end bush with clean engine oil. Slide the pin into the piston, engaging the connecting rod small-end. Fit two new circlips to the piston at either end of the gudgeon pin. Repeat this operation for the remaining pistons.

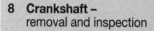

8 Crankshaft –
removal and inspection

Removal

Note: *If no work is to be done on the pistons and connecting rods, then removal of the cylinder head and pistons will not be necessary. Instead, the pistons need only be pushed far enough up the bores so that the connecting rods are positioned clear of the crankpins. The use of an engine stand is strongly recommended.*

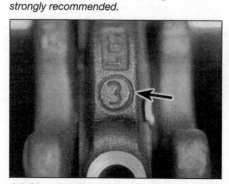

8.5 Manufacturer's identification markings on the main bearing caps (arrowed)

8.6b . . . then remove the main bearing caps

1 With reference to Chapter 2A or 2B as applicable, carry out the following:
 a) *Remove the timing belt and crankshaft sprocket.*
 b) *Remove the clutch components and flywheel or driveplate (as applicable).*
 c) *Remove the sump, baffle plate (see illustration), oil pump and pick-up tube or balancer shaft assembly (engine code ALT).*
 d) *Remove the front and rear crankshaft oil seals and housings.*

2 Remove the pistons and connecting rods or disconnect them from the crankshaft as described in Section 7 (see Note above).

3 With the cylinder block upside down on the bench, carry out a check of the crankshaft endfloat as follows. **Note:** *This can only be accomplished when the crankshaft is still installed in the cylinder block/crankcase, but is free to move.* Set up a DTI gauge so that the probe is in line with the crankshaft axis and

8.6a Loosen the main bearing cap bolts . . .

8.7 Lift the crankshaft from the crankcase

is in contact with a fixed point on the end of the crankshaft. Push the crankshaft along its axis to the end of its travel, and then zero the gauge. Push the crankshaft fully the other way, and record the endfloat indicated on the dial **(see illustration)**. Compare the result with the figure given in the Specifications and establish whether new thrustwashers are required.

4 If a dial gauge is not available, feeler blades can be used. First push the crankshaft fully towards the flywheel end of the engine, then use a feeler blade to measure the gap between cylinder No 3 crankpin web and the main bearing thrustwasher **(see illustration)**. Compare the results with the Specifications.

5 Observe the manufacturer's identification marks on the main bearing caps. The number indicates the cap position in the crankcase, as counted from the timing belt end of the engine **(see illustration)**.

6 Loosen the main bearing cap bolts half a turn at a time, until they can be removed **(see illustrations)**. Using a soft-faced mallet, strike the caps lightly to free them from the crankcase. Recover the lower main bearing shells, using tape to attach them to the cap for safe-keeping. Mark them to aid identification, but do not score or scratch them in any way.

7 Carefully lift the crankshaft out, taking care not to dislodge the upper main bearing shells **(see illustration)**.

8 Extract the upper main bearing shells from the crankcase, and tape them to their respective bearing caps. Remove the two thrustwasher bearings from either side of No 3 bearing saddle.

9 With the shell bearings removed, observe the recesses machined into the bearing caps and crankcase – these provide location for the lugs which protrude from the shell bearings and so prevent them from being fitted incorrectly.

Inspection

10 Wash the crankshaft in a suitable solvent and allow it to dry. Flush the oil holes thoroughly, to ensure they are not blocked.

11 Inspect the main bearing and crankpin journals carefully. If uneven wear, cracking, scoring or pitting are evident then the crankshaft should be reground by an engineering workshop, and refitted to the engine with undersize bearings.

12 Use a micrometer to measure the diameter of each main bearing journal (see illustration). Taking a number of measurements on the surface of each journal will reveal if it is worn unevenly. Differences in diameter measured at 90° intervals indicate that the journal is out of round. Differences in diameter measured along the length of the journal, indicate that the journal is tapered. Again, if wear is detected, the crankshaft must be reground by an engineering workshop, and undersize bearings will be needed.

13 Check the oil seal journals at either end of the crankshaft. If they appear excessively scored or damaged, they may cause the new seals to leak when the engine is reassembled. It may be possible to repair the journal; seek the advice of an engineering workshop or your VW dealer.

14 Measure the crankshaft runout by setting up a DTI gauge on the centre main bearing and rotating the shaft in V-blocks. The maximum deflection of the gauge will indicate the runout. Take precautions to protect the bearing journals and oil seal mating surfaces from damage during this procedure. A maximum runout figure is not quoted by the manufacturer, but use the figure of 0.03 mm as a rough guide. If the runout exceeds this figure, crankshaft renewal should be considered – consult your VW dealer or an engine rebuilding specialist for advice.

15 Refer to Section 10 for details of main and big-end bearing inspection.

---

9 Cylinder block/crankcase
– cleaning and inspection

Cleaning

1 Remove all external components as applicable including lifting eyes, mounting brackets, the coolant pump and housing, viscous fan idler, oil cooler and filter mounting housing (see illustrations) and electrical switches/sensors from the block. For complete cleaning, the core plugs should ideally be removed. Drill a small hole in the plugs, then insert a self-tapping screw into the hole. Extract the plugs by pulling on the screw with a pair of grips, or by using a slide hammer.

2 Scrape all traces of gasket and sealant from the cylinder block/crankcase, taking care not to damage the sealing surfaces.

3 Remove all oil gallery plugs (where fitted). The plugs are usually very tight – they may have to be drilled out, and the holes re-tapped. Use new plugs when the engine is reassembled.

4 If the casting is extremely dirty, it should be steam-cleaned. After this, clean all oil holes and galleries one more time. Flush all internal passages with warm water until the water runs clear. Dry thoroughly, and apply a light film of oil to all mating surfaces and cylinder bores,

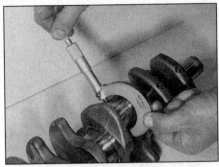

8.12 Use a micrometer to measure the diameter of each main bearing journal

to prevent rusting. If you have access to compressed air, use it to speed up the drying process, and to blow out all the oil holes and galleries.

> ⚠ **Warning: Wear eye protection when using compressed air.**

5 If the castings are not very dirty, you can do an adequate cleaning job with hot, soapy water and a stiff brush. Take plenty of time, and do a thorough job. Regardless of the cleaning method used, be sure to clean all oil holes and galleries very thoroughly, and to dry all components well. Protect the cylinder bores as described above, to prevent rusting.

6 All threaded holes must be clean, to ensure accurate torque readings during reassembly. To clean the threads, run the correct-size tap into each of the holes to remove rust, corrosion, thread sealant or sludge, and to restore damaged threads (see illustration).

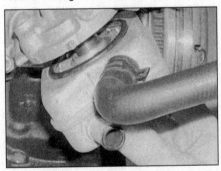

9.1a Remove the oil cooler . . .

9.1c Remove the coolant pump housing

If possible, use compressed air to clear the holes of debris produced by this operation. **Note:** *Take extra care to exclude all cleaning liquid from blind tapped holes, as the casting may be cracked by hydraulic action if a bolt is threaded into a hole containing liquid.*

7 Apply suitable sealant to the new oil gallery plugs, and insert them into the holes in the block. Tighten them securely. Similarly, apply sealant to the core plugs and tap them into the cylinder block using a close-fitting tube or socket.

8 If the engine is not going to be reassembled immediately, cover it with a large plastic bag to keep it clean; protect all mating surfaces and the cylinder bores as described above, to prevent rusting.

Inspection

9 Visually check the casting for cracks and corrosion. Look for stripped threads in the threaded holes. If there has been any history of internal water leakage, it may be worthwhile having an engine overhaul specialist check the cylinder block/crankcase with professional equipment. If defects are found, have them renewed or if possible, repaired.

10 Check the cylinder bores for scuffing or scoring. Any evidence of this kind of damage should be cross-checked with an inspection of the pistons (see Section 7 of this Chapter). If the damage is in its early stages, it may be possible to repair the block by reboring it. Seek the advice of an engineering workshop.

11 To allow an accurate assessment of the wear in the cylinder bores to be made, their

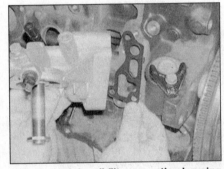

9.1b . . . and the oil filter mounting housing and gasket

9.6 To clean the cylinder block threads, run a correct-size tap into the holes

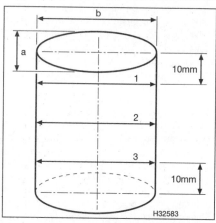

9.12 Bore measurement points

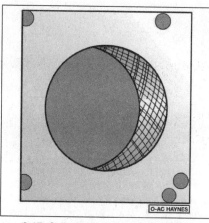

9.17 Cylinder bore honing pattern

diameter must be measured at a number of points, as follows. Insert a bore gauge into bore No 1 and take three measurements in line with the crankshaft axis; one at the top of the bore, roughly 10 mm below the top of the bore, one half-way down the bore and one at a point roughly 10 mm above the bottom of the bore. **Note:** *Stand the cylinder block squarely on a workbench during this procedure, inaccurate results may be obtained if the measurements are taken when the engine mounted on a stand.*

12 Rotate the bore gauge through 90°, so that it is at right angles to the crankshaft axis and repeat the measurements detailed in paragraph 11 **(see illustration)**. Record all six measurements, and compare them with the data listed in the Specifications. If the difference in diameter between any two cylinders exceeds the wear limit, or if any one cylinder exceeds its maximum bore diameter, then *all four* cylinders will have to be rebored and oversize pistons will have to be fitted (where available).

13 Use the piston diameter measurements recorded earlier (see Section 7) to calculate the piston-to-bore clearances. Figures are not available from the manufacturer, so seek the advice of your VW dealer or engine reconditioning specialist.

14 Place the cylinder block on a level work surface, crankcase downwards. Use a straight-edge and a set of feeler blades to measure the distortion of the cylinder head mating surface in both planes. A maximum figure is not quoted by the manufacturer, but use the figure of 0.05 mm as a rough guide. If the measurement exceeds this figure, repair may be possible by machining – consult your dealer for advice.

15 Before the engine can be reassembled, the cylinder bores must be honed. This process involves using an abrasive tool to produce a fine, cross-hatch pattern on the inner surface of the bore. This has the effect of seating the piston rings, resulting in a good seal between the piston and cylinder. There are two types of honing tool available to the home mechanic,

both are driven by a rotary power tool, such as a drill. The bottle brush hone is a stiff, cylindrical brush with abrasive stones bonded to its bristles. The more conventional surfacing hone has abrasive stones mounted on spring-loaded legs. For the inexperienced home mechanic, satisfactory results will be achieved more easily using the bottle brush hone. **Note:** *If you are unwilling to tackle cylinder bore honing, an engineering workshop will be able to carry out the job for you at a reasonable cost.*

16 Carry out the honing as follows; you will need one of the honing tools described above, a power drill, a supply of clean rags, some honing oil and a pair of safety glasses.

17 Fit the honing tool in the drill chuck. Lubricate the cylinder bores with honing oil and insert the honing tool into the first bore, compressing the stones to allow it to fit. Turn on the drill and as the tool rotates, move it up and down in the bore at a rate that produces

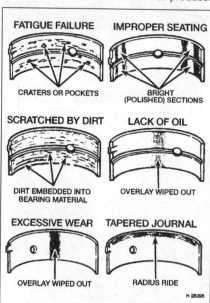

10.1 Typical bearing failures

a fine cross-hatch pattern on the surface. The lines of the pattern should ideally cross at about 50 to 60° **(see illustration)**, although some piston ring manufacturer's may quote a different angle; check the literature supplied with the new rings.

 Warning: Wear safety glasses to protect your eyes from debris flying off the honing tool.

18 Use plenty of oil during the honing process. Do not remove any more material than is necessary to produce the required finish. When removing the hone tool from the bore, do not pull it out whilst it is still rotating; maintain the up/down movement until the chuck has stopped, then withdraw the tool whilst rotating the chuck by hand, in the normal direction of rotation.

19 Wipe out the oil and swarf with a rag and proceed to the next bore. When all four bores have been honed, thoroughly clean the whole cylinder block in hot soapy water to remove all traces of honing oil and debris. The block is clean when a clean rag, moistened with new engine oil does not pick up any grey residue when wiped along the bore.

20 Apply a light coating of engine oil to the mating surfaces and cylinder bores to prevent rust forming.

21 Refit all the components removed in paragraph 1.

10 Main and big-end bearings – inspection and selection

Inspection

1 Even though the main and big-end bearings should be renewed during the engine overhaul, the old bearings should be retained for close examination, as they may reveal valuable information about the condition of the engine **(see illustration)**.

2 Bearing failure can occur due to lack of lubrication, the presence of dirt or other foreign particles, overloading the engine, or corrosion. Regardless of the cause of bearing failure, the cause must be corrected before the engine is reassembled, to prevent it from happening again.

3 When examining the bearing shells, remove them from the cylinder block/crankcase, the main bearing caps, the connecting rods and the connecting rod big-end bearing caps. Lay them out on a clean surface in the same general position as their location in the engine. This will enable you to match any bearing problems with the corresponding crankshaft journal. *Do not* touch any shell's internal bearing surface with your fingers while checking it, or the delicate surface may be scratched.

4 Dirt and other foreign matter gets into the engine in a variety of ways. It may be left in the engine during assembly, or it may pass through filters or the crankcase ventilation system. It may get into the oil, and from there into the bearings. Metal chips from machining operations and normal engine wear are often present. Abrasives are sometimes left in engine components after reconditioning, especially when parts are not thoroughly cleaned using the proper cleaning methods. Whatever the source, these foreign objects often end up embedded in the soft bearing material, and are easily recognised. Large particles will not embed in the bearing, but will score or gouge the bearing and journal. The best prevention for this cause of bearing failure is to clean all parts thoroughly, and keep everything spotlessly-clean during engine assembly. Frequent and regular engine oil and filter changes are also recommended.

5 Lack of lubrication (or lubrication breakdown) has a number of interrelated causes. Excessive heat (which thins the oil), overloading (which squeezes the oil from the bearing face) and oil leakage (from excessive bearing clearances, worn oil pump or high engine speeds) all contribute to lubrication breakdown. Blocked oil passages, which usually are the result of misaligned oil holes in a bearing shell, will also oil-starve a bearing, and destroy it. When lack of lubrication is the cause of bearing failure, the bearing material is wiped or extruded from the steel backing of the bearing. Temperatures may increase to the point where the steel backing turns blue from overheating.

6 Driving habits can have a definite effect on bearing life. Full-throttle, low-speed operation (labouring the engine) puts very high loads on bearings, tending to squeeze out the oil film. These loads cause the bearings to flex, which produces fine cracks in the bearing face (fatigue failure). Eventually, the bearing material will loosen in pieces, and tear away from the steel backing.

7 Short-distance driving leads to corrosion of bearings, because insufficient engine heat is produced to drive off the condensed water and corrosive gases. These products collect in the engine oil, forming acid and sludge. As the oil is carried to the engine bearings, the acid attacks and corrodes the bearing material.

8 Incorrect bearing installation during engine assembly will lead to bearing failure as well. Tight-fitting bearings leave insufficient bearing running clearance, and will result in oil starvation. Dirt or foreign particles trapped behind a bearing shell result in high spots on the bearing, which lead to failure.

9 *Do not* touch any shell's internal bearing surface with your fingers during reassembly as there is a risk of scratching the delicate surface, or of depositing particles of dirt on it.

10 As mentioned at the beginning of this Section, the bearing shells should be renewed as a matter of course during engine overhaul. To do otherwise is false economy.

Bearing selection

11 Main and big-end bearings for the engines described in this Chapter are available in standard sizes and a range of undersizes

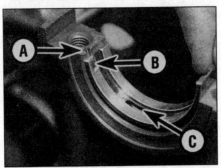

12.3 Upper main bearing shells correctly fitted

   A *Recess in bearing saddle*
   B *Lug on bearing shell*
   C *Oil hole*

to suit reground crankshafts. Refer to the Specifications for details.

12 The running clearances will need to be checked when the crankshaft is refitted with its new bearings (see Section 12).

11 Engine overhaul – reassembly sequence

1 Before reassembly begins, ensure that all new parts have been obtained, and that all necessary tools are available. Read through the entire procedure to familiarise yourself with the work involved, and to ensure that all items necessary for reassembly of the engine are at hand. In addition to all normal tools and materials, thread-locking compound will be needed. A suitable tube of liquid sealant will also be required for the joint faces that are without gaskets. It is recommended that the manufacturer's own products are used, which are specially formulated for this purpose; the relevant product names are quoted in the text of each Section where they are required.

2 In order to save time and avoid problems, engine reassembly should ideally be carried out in the following order:

a) *Crankshaft (see Section 12).*
b) *Piston/connecting rod assemblies (see Sections 13 and 14).*
c) *Oil pump or balancer shaft assembly (see Chapter 2A or 2B).*

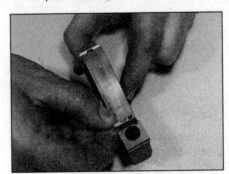

12.4 Fit the new lower half main bearing shells to the main bearing caps

d) *Sump (see Chapter 2A or 2B).*
e) *Flywheel/driveplate (see Chapter 2A or 2B).*
f) *Cylinder head (see Chapter 2A or 2B).*
g) *Timing belt tensioner, sprockets and timing belt (see Chapter 2A or 2B).*
h) *Inlet and exhaust manifolds (see the relevant part of Chapter 4).*
i) *Engine external components and ancillaries (see list in Section 5 of this Chapter).*

3 At this stage, all engine components should be absolutely clean and dry, with all faults repaired. The components should be laid out (or in individual containers) on a completely clean work surface.

12 Crankshaft – refitting and main bearing clearance check

Main bearing clearance check

1 The running clearance check can be carried out using the original bearing shells. However, it is preferable to use a new set, since the results obtained will be more conclusive. If new shells are being fitted, ensure that all traces of the protective grease are cleaned off using paraffin.

2 Clean the backs of the bearing shells, and the bearing locations in both the cylinder block/crankcase and the main bearing caps.

3 With the cylinder block positioned on a clean work surface, with the crankcase uppermost, press the bearing shells into their locations, ensuring that the tab on each shell engages in the notch in the cylinder block or bearing cap, and that the oil holes in the cylinder block and bearing shell are aligned **(see illustration)**. Take care not to touch any shell's bearing surface with your fingers. If the original bearing shells are being used for the check, ensure that they are refitted in their original locations.

4 Wipe off the rear surfaces of the new lower half main bearing shells and fit them to the main bearing caps, ensuring the locating lugs engage correctly **(see illustration)**.

5 The running clearance can be checked as follows, although this will be difficult to achieve without a range of internal micrometers or internal/external expanding calipers. Refit the main bearing caps to the cylinder block/ crankcase, with bearing shells in place. With the original cap retaining bolts tightened to the specified torque, measure the internal diameter of each assembled pair of bearing shells. If the diameter of each corresponding crankshaft journal is measured and then subtracted from the bearing internal diameter, the result will be the main bearing running clearance. Remove the main bearing caps and keep them identified for location.

Final crankshaft refitting

6 At this point, it is assumed that the crankshaft, cylinder block/crankcase and bearings have been cleaned, inspected and reconditioned or

12.8 Lubricate the upper main bearing shells . . .

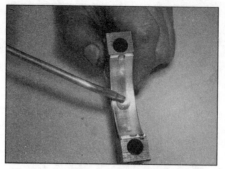

12.10a . . . and lower main bearing shells with clean engine oil . . .

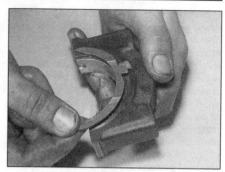

12.10b . . . then fit the thrustwashers each side of the bearing cap . . .

renewed. Where removed, the oil jets must be refitted at this stage and their mounting bolts tightened to the specified torque.

7 Give the newly-fitted main bearing shells and the crankshaft journals a final clean with a cloth. Check that the oil holes in the crankshaft are free from dirt, as any left here will become embedded in the new bearings when the engine is first started.

8 Liberally coat the bearing shells in the crankcase with clean engine oil of the appropriate grade **(see illustration)**.

9 Lower the crankshaft into position so that No 1 cylinder crankpin is at BDC, ready for fitting No 1 piston.

10 Lubricate the lower bearing shells in the main bearing caps with clean engine oil, then fit the thrustwashers to each side of No 3 bearing saddle and/or bearing cap. On petrol engine code AZM the thrustwashers are fitted to either side of the central bearing saddle,

on petrol engine codes AWT and ALT they are fitted to either side of the central main bearing cap, and on diesel engines they are fitted to either side of both the central bearing saddle and the central main bearing cap. Use a small quantity of grease to hold them in place. Ensure that they are seated correctly in the machined recesses, with the oil grooves facing outwards **(see illustrations)**.

11 Fit the main bearing caps in the correct order and orientation – No 1 bearing cap must be at the timing belt end of the engine and the bearing shell locating recesses in the bearing saddles and caps must be adjacent to each other **(see illustrations)**. Insert the bearing cap bolts and hand tighten them only.

12 Working from the centre bearing cap outwards, tighten the new retaining bolts to their specified torques and angles in the stages given **(see illustrations)**.

13 Check that the crankshaft rotates freely by

turning it manually. If resistance is felt, recheck the running clearances, as described above.

14 Carry out a check of the crankshaft endfloat as described at the beginning of Section 8. If the thrust surfaces of the crankshaft have been checked and new thrustwashers have been fitted, then the endfloat should be within specification.

15 Refit the pistons and connecting rods or reconnect them to the crankshaft as described in Section 14.

16 With reference to Chapter 2A or 2B as applicable, carry out the following:

a) *Refit the crankshaft front and rear oil seal housings, together with new oil seals.*

b) *Refit the oil pump and pickup tube or balancer shaft assembly (engine code ALT), baffle plate and sump.*

c) *Refit the flywheel and clutch or driveplate (as applicable).*

d) *Refit the crankshaft sprocket and timing belt.*

12.10c . . . and/or bearing saddle (see text)

12.11a Fit the No 3 main bearing cap

12.11b Fit the No 1 main bearing cap

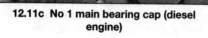

12.11c No 1 main bearing cap (diesel engine)

12.12a Tighten the main bearing cap bolts to the specified torque . . .

12.12b . . . and angle

13 Pistons and piston rings – assembly

1 At this point it is assumed that the pistons have been correctly assembled to their respective connecting rods and that the piston ring-to-groove clearances have been checked. If not, refer to the end of Section 7.

2 Before the rings can be fitted to the pistons, the end gaps must be checked with the rings fitted into the cylinder bores.

3 Lay out the piston assemblies and the new ring sets on a clean work surface so that the components are kept together in their groups during and after end gap checking. Place the crankcase on the work surface on its side, allowing access to the top and bottom of the bores.

4 Take the No 1 piston top ring and insert it into the top of the bore. Using the No 1 piston, push the ring close to the bottom of the bore, at the lowest point of the piston travel. Ensure that it is perfectly square in the bore.

5 Use a set of feeler blades to measure the gap between the ends of the piston ring. The correct blade will just pass through the gap with a minimal amount of resistance **(see illustration)**. Compare this measurement with that listed in Specifications. Check that you have the correct ring before deciding that a gap is incorrect. Repeat the operation for the remaining rings.

6 If new rings are being fitted, it is unlikely that the end gaps will be too small. If a measurement is found to be undersize, it must be corrected or there is the risk that the ends of the ring may contact each other during operation, possibly resulting in engine damage. This is achieved by gradually filing down the ends of the ring, using a file clamped in a vice. Fit the ring over the file such that both its ends contact opposite faces of the file. Move the ring along the file, removing small amounts of material at a time. Take great care as the rings are brittle and form sharp edges if they fracture. Remember to keep the rings and piston assemblies in the correct order.

7 When all the piston ring end gaps have been verified, they can be fitted to the pistons. Work from the lowest ring groove (oil control ring) upwards. Note that the oil control ring may comprise two side rails separated by a expander ring, or a one-piece oil control ring with a internal expander spring. Note also that the two compression rings are different in cross-section, and so must be fitted in the correct groove and the right way up, using a piston ring fitting tool. Both of the compression rings may have marks stamped on one side to indicate the top facing surface. Ensure that these marks face up when the rings are fitted **(see illustration)**.

8 Distribute the end gaps around the piston, spaced at 120° intervals to the each other.
Note: *If the piston ring manufacturer supplies specific fitting instructions with the rings, follow these exclusively.*

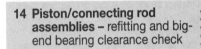

13.5 Check the piston ring end gap using a feeler gauge

14 Piston/connecting rod assemblies – refitting and big-end bearing clearance check

Note: *At this point, it is assumed that the crankshaft has been fitted to the engine, as described in Section 12. A piston ring compressor tool will be required for this operation.*

Big-end clearance check

1 The running clearance check can be carried out using the original bearing shells. However, it is preferable to use a new set, since the results obtained will be more conclusive.

2 Clean the backs of the bearing shells, and the bearing locations in both the connecting rods and the big-end bearing caps.

3 Press the bearing shells into their locations in the connecting rods and caps. On petrol engines, ensure that the tab on each shell engages in the notch in the connecting rod or cap. On diesel engines, note that the shells are not positively located by lugs and recesses – simply ensure the shells are fitted squarely into place **(see illustration)** – the upper bearing shell is more wear-resistant than the lower, and is identified by a black line on the bearing surface in the area of the bearing joint. Take care not to touch any shell's bearing surface with your fingers. If the original bearing shells are being used for the check, ensure that they are refitted in their original locations.

4 The running clearance can be checked, although this will be difficult to achieve without a range of internal micrometers or internal/

14.3 On diesel engines, ensure the shells are fitted squarely into place

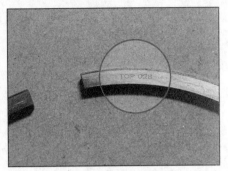

13.7 Piston ring top marking

external expanding calipers. Refit the big-end bearing cap to the connecting rod, using the marks made or noted on removal to ensure that they are fitted the correct way around, with the bearing shells in place. With the original cap retaining bolts or nuts (as applicable) correctly tightened, use an internal micrometer or vernier caliper to measure the internal diameter of each assembled pair of bearing shells. If the diameter of each corresponding crankshaft journal is measured, and then subtracted from the bearing internal diameter, the result will be the big-end bearing running clearance.

Final refitting

5 Ensure that the bearing shells are correctly fitted, as described at the beginning of this Section. If new shells are being fitted, ensure that all traces of the protective grease are cleaned off using paraffin. Wipe dry the shells and connecting rods with a lint-free cloth.

6 Lubricate the cylinder bores, the pistons, piston rings and upper bearing shells with clean engine oil **(see illustrations)**. Lay out each piston/connecting rod assembly in order on a work surface. Where the bearing caps are secured with nuts, pad the threaded ends of the bolts with insulating tape to prevent them scratching the crankpins and bores when the pistons are refitted.

7 Start with piston/connecting rod assembly No 1. Make sure that the piston rings are still spaced as described in Section 13, then clamp them in position with a piston ring compressor.

8 Insert the piston/connecting rod assembly into the top of cylinder No 1. Lower the big-

14.6a Lubricate the pistons . . .

14.6b ... and big-end upper bearing shells with clean engine oil

14.10 Use a hammer handle to tap the piston into its bore

end in first, guiding it to protect the cylinder bores. Where oil jets are located at the bottoms of the bores, take particular care not to break them off when guiding the connecting rods onto the crankpins.

9 Ensure that the orientation of the piston in its cylinder is correct – the piston crown, connecting rods and big-end bearing caps have markings, which must point towards the timing belt end of the engine when the piston is installed in the bore – refer to Section 7 for details.

10 Using a block of wood or hammer handle against the piston crown, tap the assembly into the cylinder until the piston crown is flush with the top of the cylinder (see illustration).

11 Ensure that the bearing shell is still correctly installed. Liberally lubricate the crankpin and both bearing shells with clean engine oil. Taking care not to mark the cylinder bores, tap the piston/connecting rod assembly down the bore and onto the crankpin. Remove the insulating tape from

the threaded ends of the bolts and oil the threads and undersides of the bolt heads. Fit the big-end bearing cap, tightening its new retaining bolts finger-tight at first. Note that the orientation of the bearing cap with respect to the connecting rod must be correct when the two components are reassembled. The connecting rod and its corresponding bearing cap both have recesses/lugs machined into them – these recesses/lugs must both face in the same direction as the arrow on the piston crown (ie, towards the timing belt end of the engine) when correctly installed – refer to the illustrations in Section 7 for details.

12 On diesel engines, the piston crowns are specially shaped to improve the engine's combustion characteristics. Because of this, pistons 1 and 2 are different to pistons 3 and 4. When correctly fitted, the larger inlet valve chambers on pistons 1 and 2 must face the flywheel/driveplate end of the engine, and the larger inlet valve chambers on the remaining pistons must face the timing belt end of the engine. New pistons have number markings on their crowns to indicate their type – 1/2 denotes piston 1 or 2, 3/4 indicates piston 3 or 4 (see illustration).

13 Tighten the retaining bolts to the specified Stage 1 torque (see illustration).

14 Angle-tighten the retaining bolts to the specified Stage 2 angle (see illustration).

15 Refit the remaining three piston/connecting rod assemblies in the same way.

16 Rotate the crankshaft by hand. Check that it turns freely; some stiffness is to be expected if new parts have been fitted, but there should be no binding or tight spots.

Diesel engines

17 If new pistons are fitted or if a new short engine is installed, the projection of the piston crowns above the cylinder head at TDC must be measured, to determine the type of head gasket that should be fitted.

18 Turn the cylinder block over (so that the crankcase is facing downwards) and rest it on a stand or wooden blocks. Anchor a DTI gauge to the cylinder block, and zero it on the head gasket mating surface. Rest the gauge probe on No 1 piston crown and turn the crankshaft slowly by hand so that the piston reaches TDC. Measure and record the maximum projection at TDC (see illustration).

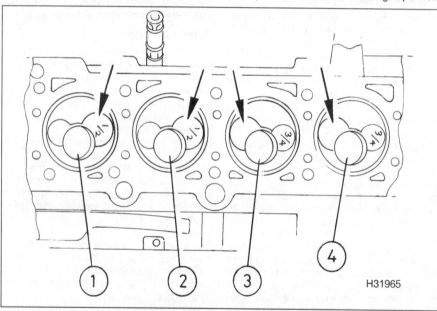

14.12 Piston orientation and coding on diesel engines

14.13 Tighten the big-end bearing cap bolts to the Stage 1 setting ...

14.14 ... and then angle-tighten them to the Stage 2 setting

14.18 Measure the piston projection with a dial gauge

19 Repeat the measurement for the remaining pistons and record.

20 If the measurements differ from piston to piston, take the highest figure and use this to determine the head gasket type that must be used – refer to the Specifications for details.

21 Note that if the original pistons have been refitted, then a new head gasket of the same type as the original item must be fitted.

All engines

22 Refer to Part A or B of this Chapter (as applicable) and refit the oil pump and pickup or balancer shaft assembly (engine code ALT), sump and baffle plate, flywheel and cylinder head.

15 Engine – initial start-up after overhaul and reassembly

1 Refit the remainder of the engine components in the order listed in Section 11 of this Chapter. Refit the engine to the vehicle as described in Section 4 of this Chapter. Double-check the engine oil and coolant levels and make a final check that everything has been reconnected. Make sure that there are no tools or rags left in the engine compartment.

Petrol models

2 Remove the spark plugs, referring to Chapter 1A for details.

3 The engine must be immobilised such that it can be turned over using the starter motor, without starting – disable the fuel pump by removing the fuel pump fuse (No 28) from the fusebox with reference to the relevant Part of Chapter 4, and also disable the ignition system by disconnecting the wiring from the ignition module.

Caution: To prevent damage to the catalytic converter, it is important to disable the fuel system.

4 Turn the engine using the starter motor until the oil pressure warning lamp goes out. If the lamp fails to extinguish after several seconds of cranking, check the engine oil level and oil filter security. Assuming these are correct, check the security of the oil pressure switch cabling – do not progress any further until you are satisfied that oil is being pumped around the engine at sufficient pressure.

5 Refit the spark plugs, the fuel pump fuse, and reconnect the wiring ignition module.

Diesel models

6 Disconnect the injector harness wiring plug at the rear of the cylinder head – refer to Chapter 4B for details.

7 Turn the engine using the starter motor until the oil pressure warning lamp goes out.

8 If the lamp fails to extinguish after several seconds of cranking, check the engine oil level and oil filter security. Assuming these are correct, check the security of the oil pressure switch cabling – do not progress any further until you are satisfied that oil is being pumped around the engine at sufficient pressure.

9 Reconnect the injector wiring plug.

All models

10 Start the engine, but be aware that as fuel system components have been disturbed, the cranking time may be a little longer than usual.

11 While the engine is idling, check for fuel, water and oil leaks. Don't be alarmed if there are some odd smells and the occasional plume of smoke as components heat up and burn off oil deposits.

12 Assuming all is well, keep the engine idling until hot water is felt circulating through the top hose.

13 After a few minutes, recheck the oil and coolant levels, and top-up as necessary.

14 There is no need to retighten the cylinder head bolts once the engine has been run following reassembly.

15 If new pistons, rings or crankshaft bearings have been fitted, the engine must be treated as new, and run-in for the first 600 miles (1000 km). *Do not* operate the engine at full-throttle, or allow it to labour at low engine speeds in any gear. It is recommended that the engine oil and filter are changed at the end of this period.

Notes

Chapter 3
Cooling, heating and ventilation systems

Contents
	Section number			Section number
Air conditioning compressor (auxiliary) drivebelt – checking and renewal	See Chapter 1A or 1B		Cooling system electrical switches and sensors – testing, removal and refitting	6
Air conditioning system – general information and precautions	10		Cooling system hoses – disconnection and renewal	2
Air conditioning system components – removal and refitting	11		Fuel cooling system components – removal and refitting	12
Antifreeze mixture	See Chapter 1A or 1B		General information and precautions	1
Coolant level check and top-up	See Weekly checks		Heater/ventilation components – removal and refitting	9
Coolant pump – removal and refitting	7		Heating and ventilation system – general information	8
Cooling fan(s) – testing, removal and refitting	5		Radiator – removal, inspection and refitting	3
Cooling system – draining, flushing and refilling	See Chapter 1A or 1B		Thermostat – removal, testing and refitting	4

Degrees of difficulty

Easy, suitable for novice with little experience	**Fairly easy,** suitable for beginner with some experience	**Fairly difficult,** suitable for competent DIY mechanic	**Difficult,** suitable for experienced DIY mechanic	**Very difficult,** suitable for expert DIY or professional

Specifications

Engine codes*

Petrol engines

1781 cc, DOHC, Bosch Motronic ME7.5 injection, turbocharged	AWT
1984 cc, SOHC, Siemens Simos 3.2 injection, non-turbo	AZM
1984 cc, DOHC, Bosch Motronic ME7.5 injection, non-turbo	ALT

Diesel engines

Electronic direct injection, unit injectors, 74 kW (100 bhp)	AVB
Electronic direct injection, unit injectors, 96 kW (130 bhp)	AVF and AWX

* Note: See 'Vehicle identification' for the location of the code marking on the engine.

General
Maximum system pressure	1.4 to 1.6 bar

Thermostat
Opening temperature	86°C (approx)

Cooling fan
Thermal switch:
1st speed cut-in	92 to 97°C
1st speed cut-out	91 to 84°C
2nd speed cut-in	99 to 105°C
2nd speed cut-out	98 to 91°C

Torque wrench settings

	Nm	lbf ft
Alternator/power steering pump bracket:		
Bracket to cylinder block	30	22
Strut to cylinder block	25	18
Strut to bracket	40	30
Coolant pump	15	11
Coolant pump drain plug	30	22
Coolant pump pulley bolts	25	18
Cooling fan switch	35	26
Fuel coolant pump bolt	7	5
Thermostat housing bolts:		
Petrol engine codes AWT and ALT	15	11
Petrol engine code AZM	10	7
Diesel engines	15	11
Viscous cooling fan coupling/drive pulley shaft bolt	45	33
Viscous cooling fan coupling-to-drive pulley bolts	10	7

1 General information and precautions

General information

The cooling system is of the pressurised type, comprising a coolant pump, an aluminium radiator, cooling fan(s), a thermostat, heater matrix, and all associated hoses and switches. The coolant pump is driven by the camshaft timing belt. All models are fitted with a viscous-coupled primary cooling fan, which is driven by the auxiliary drivebelt, and an auxiliary cooling fan which is electrically-operated. The system functions as follows.

When the engine is cold, the coolant in the engine is pumped around the cylinder block and head passages, and through an engine oil cooler (where fitted). After cooling the cylinder bores, combustion surfaces and valve seats, the coolant passes through the heater, and is returned via the cylinder block to the coolant pump. The thermostat is initially closed, preventing the cold coolant from the radiator entering the engine. Note: On the 2.0 litre DOHC petrol engine code ALT, the thermostat incorporates a heating element and is electronically-controlled and mapped by the engine management ECU. This system monitors engine load to determine the most efficient engine temperature.

When the coolant in the engine reaches a predetermined temperature, the thermostat opens. The cold coolant from the radiator is then allowed to enter the engine through the bottom hose and the hot coolant from the engine flows through the top hose to the radiator. As the coolant circulates through the radiator, it is cooled by the inrush of air when the car is in forward motion. The airflow is supplemented by the action of the cooling fan(s) when necessary. As the coolant reduces in temperature, it passes to the bottom of the radiator and the cycle is repeated.

The operation of the primary cooling fan is controlled by a viscous coupling. The coupling is driven by the auxiliary drivebelt and transmits drive to the fan through a temperature-sensitive fluid coupling arrangement. At lower temperatures the fan blade is allowed to spin freely on the coupling. At a predetermined temperature (around 75°C), an internal valve in the coupling opens, which effectively locks-up the coupling, and transmits drive to the fan. Once the temperature drops again, the valve closes and the fan is allowed to spin freely again.

The operation of the electrically-operated auxiliary cooling fan is controlled by a thermostatic switch. At a predetermined coolant temperature, the switch/sensor actuates the fan. The switch then cuts the power supply to the fan when the coolant temperature has reduced sufficiently.

On models with an automatic transmission unit, a transmission fluid cooler is built into the radiator. The transmission unit is linked to the radiator by two pipes and the fluid is circulated around the cooler to keep its temperature stable under arduous operating conditions.

On diesel engine models manufactured up to 01/2002, the fuel returning to the tank is cooled. The fuel cooling system comprises of a cooler built into the top of the fuel filter assembly, a separate radiator, a cooling circuit shut-off valve, a pump and temperature sensor. The fuel system cooling circuit is separate from the engine cooling circuit. The coolant pump operates at fuel temperatures in excess of 70°C, and is controlled by the engine ECU. On models manufactured from 01/2002-on, this system was discontinued.

Precautions

⚠️ **Warning: Do not attempt to remove the expansion tank filler cap, or to disturb any part of the cooling system, while the engine is hot, as there is a high risk of scalding. If the expansion tank filler cap must be removed before the engine and radiator have fully cooled (even though this is not recommended), the pressure in the cooling system must first be relieved. Cover the cap with a thick layer of cloth to avoid scalding, and slowly unscrew the filler cap until a hissing sound is heard. When the hissing has stopped, indicating that the pressure has reduced, slowly unscrew the filler cap until it can be removed; if more hissing sounds are heard, wait until they have stopped before unscrewing the cap completely. At all times, keep well away from the filler cap opening, and protect your hands.**

⚠️ **Warning: Do not allow antifreeze to come into contact with your skin, or with the painted surfaces of the vehicle. Rinse off spills immediately, with plenty of water. Never leave antifreeze lying around in an open container, or in a puddle in the driveway or on the garage floor. Children and pets are attracted by its sweet smell, but antifreeze can be fatal if ingested.**

⚠️ **Warning: If the engine is hot, the electric cooling fan may start rotating even if the engine is not running. Be careful to keep your hands, hair, and any loose clothing well clear when working in the engine compartment.**

⚠️ **Warning: Refer to Section 10 for precautions to be observed when working on models equipped with air conditioning.**

2 Cooling system hoses – disconnection and renewal

Note: Refer to the warnings given in Section 1 of this Chapter before proceeding. Hoses

should only be disconnected once the engine has cooled sufficiently to avoid scalding.

1 If the checks described in the relevant part of Chapter 1 reveal a faulty hose, it must be renewed as follows.

2 First drain the cooling system (see the relevant part of Chapter 1). If the coolant is not due for renewal, it may be re-used, providing it is collected in a clean container.

3 To disconnect a hose, release the retaining clips, then move them along the hose, clear of the relevant inlet/outlet. Carefully work the hose free. The hoses can be removed with relative ease when new – on an older car, they may have stuck.

4 In order to disconnect the radiator inlet and outlet hoses, and the heater hoses fitted to some models, apply pressure to hold the hose on to the relevant union, pull out the spring clip and pull the hose from the union. Note that the radiator inlet and outlet unions are fragile; do not use excessive force when attempting to remove the hoses. If a hose proves to be difficult to remove, try to release it by rotating the hose ends before attempting to free it.

5 If a hose proves to be difficult to remove, try to release it by rotating its ends before attempting to free it. Gently prise the end of the hose with a blunt instrument (such as a flat-bladed screwdriver), but do not apply too much force, and take care not to damage the pipe stubs or hoses. Note in particular that the radiator inlet stub is fragile; do not use excessive force when attempting to remove the hose. If all else fails, cut the hose with a sharp knife, then slit it so that it can be peeled off in two pieces. Although this may prove expensive if the hose is otherwise undamaged, it is preferable to buying a new radiator. Check first, however, that a new hose is readily available.

6 When fitting a hose, first slide the clips onto the hose, then work the hose into position. On some hose connections alignment marks are provided on the hose and union; if marks are present, ensure they are correctly aligned.

> **HAYNES HINT** *If the hose is stiff, use a little soapy water as a lubricant, or soften the hose by soaking it in hot water. Do not use oil or grease, which may attack the rubber.*

7 Ensure the hose is correctly routed, then slide each clip back along the hose until it passes over the flared end of the relevant inlet/outlet, before tightening the clip securely. Prior to refitting a radiator inlet or outlet hose, renew the connection O-ring regardless of condition. The connections are a push-fit over the radiator unions.

8 Refill the cooling system with reference to the relevant part of Chapter 1.

9 Check thoroughly for leaks as soon as possible after disturbing any part of the cooling system.

3 Radiator – removal, inspection and refitting

Removal

1 Disconnect the battery negative lead (see Chapter 5A) then remove the front bumper as described in Chapter 11. For improved access, place the lock carrier assembly in the 'service' position, as described in Chapter 11.

2 Drain the cooling system as described in the relevant part of Chapter 1.

3 Unplug the wiring connector from the cooling fan switch which is screwed into the radiator.

4 Disconnect the radiator top and bottom coolant hoses (see Section 2), noting the correct fitted locations **(see illustrations)**. **Note**: *On some later models, quick-release couplings are fitted to the hoses.*

5 On models with automatic transmission, wipe clean the area around the fluid pipe unions on the radiator. Slacken and remove the retaining bolts then carefully ease both pipes out from the radiator. Plug the pipe ends and cooler ports to minimise fluid loss and prevent the entry of dirt into the hydraulic system. Discard the sealing rings from the pipe end fittings, new ones must be used on refitting.

6 On models equipped with air conditioning, slacken and remove the nuts and bolts securing the condenser to the radiator and any nuts/bolts securing the refrigerant pipe clips in position. On some models the condenser is secured using plastic pins – depress the lug in the end of the pin and pull it free. Release the condenser from the radiator and support it to prevent excessive strain being placed on the pipes. **Do not** disconnect the refrigerant pipes (see Section 10).

7 On models equipped with air conditioning, unplug the wiring from the pressure switch at the right-hand side of the radiator.

8 Undo the retaining screws and remove the plastic covers from the left- and right-hand sides of the radiator. Where necessary also undo the retaining screws securing the intake duct to the top of the radiator **(see illustration)**.

9 Undo the bolts securing the power steering fluid cooler to the front of the radiator and position it clear **(see illustration)**. Tie the cooler to the body to prevent any strain being placed on the hoses.

10 Withdraw the upper radiator retaining pins, then pivot the radiator towards the front of the engine compartment and lift it away from its lower mountings. On models with air conditioning, take great care to avoid damaging the condenser as the radiator is removed.

Inspection

11 If the radiator has been removed due to suspected blockage, reverse-flush it as

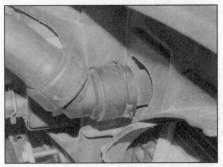
3.4a Prise out the retaining clip, and pull the top hose . . .

described in the relevant part of Chapter 1. Clean dirt and debris from the radiator fins, using an air line (in which case, wear eye protection) or a soft brush. Be careful, as the fins are sharp, and easily damaged.

12 If necessary, a radiator specialist can perform a flow test on the radiator, to establish whether an internal blockage exists.

13 A leaking radiator must be referred to a specialist for permanent repair. Do not attempt to weld or solder a leaking radiator, as damage to the plastic components may result.

14 If the radiator is to be sent for repair or renewed, remove all hoses and switches (where fitted).

15 Inspect the condition of the radiator mounting rubbers, and renew them if necessary.

Refitting

16 Refitting is a reversal of removal, bearing in mind the following points.

a) *Ensure that the radiator is correctly engaged with its mounting rubbers and that the upper retaining pins are securely refitted.*

b) *On models with automatic transmission, fit new sealing rings to the fluid pipe end fittings, lubricating them with fresh transmission fluid to ease installation. Ease both pipes fully into position before refitting the retaining bolts and tighten them securely.*

c) *Make sure all coolant hoses are correctly reconnected and securely retained by their clips.*

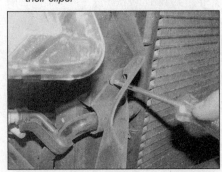
3.8 Undo the retaining screws and remove plastic covers from the left- and right-hand sides of the radiator

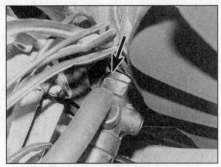
3.4b . . . and bottom hose from the radiator outlets (arrowed)

d) *Refill the cooling system as described in the relevant part of Chapter 1.*

e) *On models with automatic transmission, on completion check the transmission fluid level and, if necessary, top-up as described in the relevant part of Chapter 1.*

4 Thermostat – removal, testing and refitting

1 On petrol engines, the thermostat is fitted to a distribution housing on the left-hand side of the cylinder block, behind the coolant pump position. On diesel engines, the thermostat is fitted beneath an inlet elbow/cover on the left-hand side of the cylinder block.

Removal

2 Disconnect the battery negative lead (see Chapter 5A). Where applicable, undo the retaining bolts and remove the engine top cover.

3 Drain the cooling system as described in Chapter 1A or 1B.

Petrol engines

4 Disconnect the coolant hose from the thermostat housing.

5 On the petrol engine code ALT, disconnect the wiring from the thermostat housing.

6 Undo the bolts securing the housing to the engine block, and remove the housing along with the O-ring **(see illustration)**.

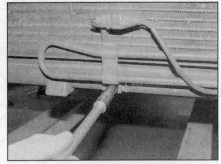
3.9 Undo the bolts securing the power steering fluid cooler to the front of the radiator

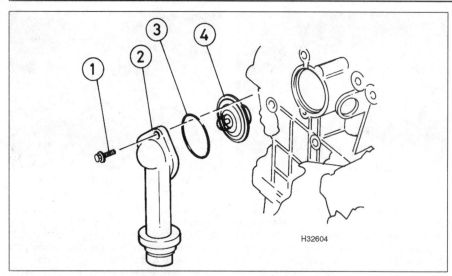

4.6 Thermostat and housing (petrol engines)

1 Bolt	2 Housing	3 Sealing ring	4 Thermostat

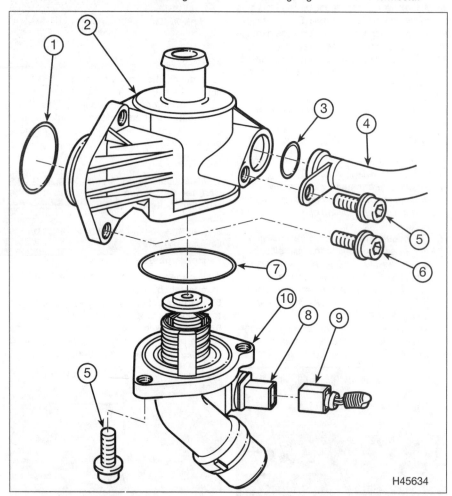

4.8 Thermostat and housing on the 2.0 litre petrol engine, code ALT

1	O-ring	4	Coolant pipe	8	Heating element socket
2	Distribution housing	5	Bolt	9	Wiring plug
3	O-ring	6	Bolt	10	Thermostat and housing
		7	O-ring		

7 Except on engine code ALT, turn the thermostat 90° anti-clockwise and remove the thermostat, noting which way around it is fitted.

8 On engine code ALT, unbolt the thermostat from the housing and recover the O-ring **(see illustration)**.

Diesel engines

9 If necessary, to improve access, release the retaining clip and disconnect the coolant hose from the thermostat cover.

10 Unscrew the retaining bolts and remove the thermostat housing cover and sealing ring from the engine **(see illustration)**. Discard the sealing ring; a new one must be used on refitting.

11 Remove the thermostat, noting which way around it is fitted **(see illustration)**.

Testing

All except petrol engine code ALT

12 A rough test of the thermostat may be made by suspending it with a piece of string in a container full of water. Heat the water to bring it to the boil – the thermostat must be fully open by the time the water boils. If not, renew it.

13 If a thermometer is available, the precise opening temperature of the thermostat may be determined; compare with the figures given in the Specifications. The opening temperature should also be marked on the thermostat.

14 A thermostat which fails to close as the water cools must also be renewed.

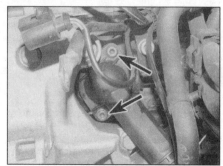

4.10 The thermostat flange is secured by two Allen screws (arrowed)

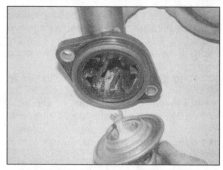

4.11 The thermostat rib aligns with the moulded interior of the flange (diesel engines)

Engine code ALT

15 With the thermostat cold, the large valve plate on the end of the spring must seal completely on the housing.

16 Place the thermostat vertically in a container of boiling water, then connect a 12 volt supply to the terminals. A minimum lift of 7.0 mm must occur within 10 minutes.

 Warning: Do not carry out the test with the thermostat out of water, otherwise it will be damaged.

17 If the thermostat does not perform as indicated, it must be renewed.

Refitting

18 Refitting is a reversal of removal, noting the following points:
a) Use new sealing ring(s).
b) On diesel engines, ensure that the curved brace of the thermostat body is positioned vertically.
c) Tighten the housing retaining bolts to the specified torque setting.
d) Refill the cooling system as described in Chapter 1A or 1B (as applicable)
e) On completion reconnect the battery.

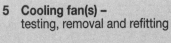

5 Cooling fan(s) – testing, removal and refitting

Electric auxiliary cooling fan

Testing

1 Current supply to the cooling fans is via the ignition switch, a fuse and a pair of series resistors. The circuit is completed by the cooling fan thermostatic switch, which is mounted in the left-hand side of the radiator.

2 If a fan does not appear to work, run the engine until normal operating temperature is reached, then allow it to idle. The fan should cut in within a few minutes (before the temperature gauge needle enters the red section, or before the coolant temperature warning light comes on).

3 If not, switch off the ignition and disconnect the wiring plug from the cooling fan switch. Bridge the relevant two contacts in the wiring plug (see *Wiring Diagrams* at the end of this Chapter 12 – most models have two-stage switches) using a length of spare wire, and switch on the ignition. If the fan now operates, the switch is probably faulty, and should be renewed.

4 If the fan still fails to operate, check that battery voltage is available at the feed wire to the switch; if not, then there is a fault in the feed wire (possibly due to a fault in the fan motor, or a blown fuse). If there is no problem with the feed, check that there is continuity between the switch earth terminal and a good earth point on the body; if not, then the earth connection is faulty, and must be remade.

5 If the switch and the wiring are in good condition, the fault must lie in the motor itself.

5.7a Slacken and remove the retaining bolts (arrowed) . . .

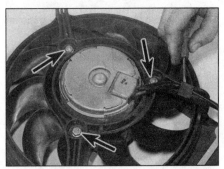

5.8a Unclip the motor wiring from the rear of the shroud then undo the retaining nuts (arrowed) and separate the motor and shroud

The motor can be checked by disconnecting it from the wiring loom and connecting a 12 volt supply directly to it.

Removal

6 Remove the radiator (see Section 3).

7 Slacken and remove the retaining bolts and remove the fan shroud assembly from the rear of the radiator **(see illustrations)**.

8 Unclip the motor wiring from the rear of the shroud then undo the retaining nuts and pull the motor assembly away from the shroud. On some models it will be necessary to detach the fan blade from the motor to gain the necessary clearance required; bend back the lockwasher tab and unscrew the retaining nut (the nut may have a left-hand thread on some models) to free the fan **(see illustrations)**. If the motor is faulty, the complete unit must be renewed, as no spares are available.

5.8c . . . and separate the motor and fan blades

5.7b . . . and remove the fan shroud assembly from the rear of the radiator

5.8b Where necessary, bend back the lockwasher tab and unscrew the retaining nut (Note: the nut may have a left-hand thread) . . .

Refitting

9 Fit the motor assembly to the shroud and securely tighten its retaining nuts. Ensure the motor wiring is correctly routed and clipped securely in position. Where necessary, seat the fan blade on the motor spindle then refit the lockwasher and retaining nut. Tighten the nut and secure it in position by bending up one of the lockwasher tabs.

10 Refit the shroud assembly to the radiator and securely tighten its retaining bolts.

11 Refit the radiator as described in Section 3.

Viscous-coupled cooling fan

Testing

12 The operation of the viscous coupling cannot be easily checked by the home mechanic. The only check which can be performed is a visual one to check the coupling assembly for signs of fluid leakage and the fan blade for signs of damage. When the coupling is cold, the fan should spin freely on the coupling and when it is hot (temperature above approximately 75ºC), the coupling should lock-up, causing the fan to rotate. If there is any doubt about the operation of the coupling, it should be renewed.

Removal

13 Place the lock carrier in the 'service' position as described in Chapter 11, Section 10.

14 Remove the auxiliary drivebelt as described in Chapter 2A or 2B as applicable.

5.15 Undo the retaining bolts and separate the fan blades from the coupling

15 Undo the retaining bolts and separate the fan blades from the coupling, noting which way around the fan blades are fitted (see illustration).

16 Counter-hold the drive pulley with a 5x60 mm bolt engaged with the small holes located around the pulley rim. Pass an 8 mm Allen key through the drive pulley mounting bracket, and engage it with the rear of the pulley shaft bolt. Slacken and withdraw the bolt and remove the drive pulley and viscous coupling from the engine (see illustration).

17 If required, the viscous coupling unit can be separated from the drive pulley by slackening and withdrawing the securing bolts.

Refitting

18 Refit the viscous coupling to the drive pulley (where removed) and tighten its retaining bolts to the specified torque.

19 Manoeuvre the drive pulley and coupling into position, then insert the shaft bolt and tighten it to the specified torque using a suitable 8 mm hex bit inserted through the rear of the drive pulley housing, whilst counter-holding the drive pulley with the 5x60 mm bolt, as during removal.

20 Refit the fan blade unit ensuring that it is mounted the correct way around.

21 Refit the auxiliary drivebelt as described in Chapter 2A or 2B as applicable.

22 Refit the lock carrier as described in Chapter 11.

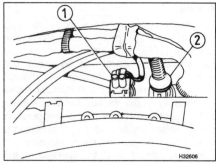

6.10a Cooling system sensor location (1.8 litre petrol engine)

1 Coolant temperature gauge/warning light sensor
2 Fuel injection system coolant temperature sensor

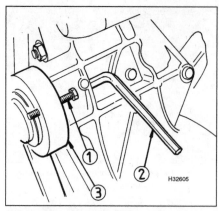

5.16 Viscous coupling drive pulley removal

1 5x60 mm bolt   3 Drive pulley
2 8 mm Allen key

6 Cooling system electrical switches and sensors
– testing, removal and refitting

Fan thermostatic switch

Testing

1 Testing of the switch is described in Section 5, as part of the electric cooling fan test procedure.

Removal

Note: *The engine and radiator should be allowed to cool completely before the switch is removed.*

2 The switch is located in the left-hand side of the radiator, just above the bottom hose stub, and on most models can be reached from above. Where this is not the case, firmly apply the handbrake then jack up the front of the vehicle and support it on axle stands. Remove the retaining screws and fasteners and remove the undercover to be able to access the switch from below.

3 Disconnect the battery negative lead (see Chapter 5A).

4 Drain the cooling system to just below the level of the switch (as described in the relevant part of Chapter 1). Alternatively, have ready a suitable bung to plug the switch aperture in the radiator when the switch is removed. If

6.10b Coolant temperature sensor – arrowed (diesel engines)

this method is used, take great care not to damage the radiator, and do not use anything which will allow foreign matter to enter the radiator.

5 Disconnect the wiring plug from the switch.

6 Carefully unscrew the switch from the radiator, and recover the sealing washer (where fitted). If the system has not been drained, plug the switch aperture to prevent further coolant loss.

Refitting

7 If the switch was originally fitted using a sealing ring, use a new sealing ring on refitting. Where no sealing ring was fitted, clean the switch threads thoroughly and coat them with fresh sealing compound.

8 Refitting is a reversal of removal. Tighten the switch securely and refill (or top-up) the cooling system as described in the relevant part of Chapter 1 (or *Weekly checks*).

9 On completion, start the engine and run it until it reaches normal operating temperature. Continue to run the engine, and check that the cooling fan cuts in and out correctly.

Temperature gauge/ warning light sensor

Testing

10 On all models, the coolant temperature gauge/warning light sensor is located in the coolant outlet union on the left-hand side/ rear of the cylinder head (see illustrations). Where two sensors are present, the outer of the two is the temperature gauge sensor (the inner sensor serves the engine management system).

11 The temperature gauge is fed with a stabilised voltage from the instrument panel feed (via the ignition switch and a fuse). The gauge earth is controlled by the sensor. The sensor contains a thermistor – an electronic component whose electrical resistance decreases at a predetermined rate as its temperature rises. When the coolant is cold, the sensor resistance is high, current flow through the gauge is reduced, and the gauge needle points towards the blue (cold) end of the scale. As the coolant temperature rises and the sensor resistance falls, current flow increases, and the gauge needle moves towards the upper end of the scale. If the sensor is faulty, it must be renewed.

12 The temperature warning light is fed with a voltage from the instrument panel. The light's earth is controlled by the sensor. The sensor is effectively a switch, which operates at a predetermined temperature to earth the light and complete the circuit.

13 The sensors for both the gauge and warning light are incorporated in a single, four-pin unit.

14 If the gauge develops a fault, first check the other instruments; if they do not work at all, check the instrument panel electrical feed. If the readings are erratic, there may be a fault in the voltage stabiliser, which will necessitate renewal of the stabiliser (the stabiliser is

integral with the instrument panel printed circuit board – see Chapter 12). If the fault lies in the temperature gauge alone, check it as follows.

15 If the gauge needle remains at the cold end of the scale when the engine is hot, disconnect the sensor wiring plug, and earth the relevant wire to the cylinder head. If the needle then deflects when the ignition is switched on, the sensor unit is proved faulty, and should be renewed. If the needle still does not move, remove the instrument panel (Chapter 12) and check the continuity of the wire between the sensor unit and the gauge, and the feed to the gauge unit. If continuity is shown, and the fault still exists, then the gauge is faulty, and the gauge unit should be renewed.

16 If the gauge needle remains at the hot end of the scale when the engine is cold, disconnect the sensor wire. If the needle then returns to the cold end of the scale when the ignition is switched on, the sensor unit is proved faulty, and should be renewed. If the needle still does not move, check the remainder of the circuit as described previously.

17 The same basic principles apply to testing the warning light. The light should illuminate when the relevant sensor wire is earthed.

Removal

18 Either partially drain the cooling system to just below the level of the sensor (as described in Chapter 1A or 1B), or have ready a suitable plug which can be used to plug the sensor aperture whilst it is removed. If a plug is used, take great care not to damage the sensor unit aperture, and do not use anything which will allow foreign matter to enter the cooling system.

19 On diesel engines, prise out the cover caps then unscrew the retaining nuts and remove the top cover from the engine to gain access to the sensor.

20 On all engines, disconnect the wiring connector from the sensor and identify whether the sensor is a push-fit or a screw-fit.

21 On screw-fit sensors, unscrew the sensor from the engine and recover its sealing washer.

22 On push-fit sensors, depress the sensor unit and slide out its retaining clip. Withdraw the sensor from the engine and recover its sealing ring.

Refitting

23 On screw-fit sensors, fit a new sealing washer then fit the sensor, tightening it securely.

24 On push-fit sensor units, fit a new sealing ring then push the sensor fully into its aperture and secure it in position with the retaining clip.

25 Reconnect the wiring connector then refill the cooling system as described in the relevant part of Chapter 1 or top-up as described in *Weekly checks*. On diesel engines, refit the top cover to the engine unit.

Engine management system temperature sensor

26 On all models, the engine management system coolant temperature sensor is located in the coolant outlet union on the rear of the cylinder head. Where two sensors are present the temperature gauge one is the outer one (the inner sensor serves the fuel gauge/warning light).

27 The sensor is a thermistor (see paragraph 11) housed in a two-pin unit. The fuel injection/engine management electronic control unit (ECU) supplies the sensor with a set voltage and then, by measuring the current flowing in the sensor circuit, it determines the engine's temperature. This information is then used, in conjunction with other inputs, to control the injector timing, the idle speed, etc. It is also used to determine the glow plug preheating and post-heating times.

28 If the sensor circuit should fail to provide adequate information, the ECU's back-up facility will override the sensor signal. In this event, the ECU assumes a predetermined setting which will allow the fuel injection/engine management system to run, albeit at reduced efficiency. When this occurs, the warning light on the instrument panel will come on, and the advice of a VW dealer should be sought. The sensor itself can only be tested using special VW diagnostic equipment. *Do not* attempt to test the circuit using any other equipment, as there is a high risk of damaging the ECU.

Removal and refitting

29 Refer to the information given in paragraphs 18 to 25.

7 Coolant pump – removal and refitting

Petrol engine

Removal

1 Disconnect the battery negative cable (see Chapter 5A), then drain the cooling system as described in Chapter 1A.

2 Place the lock carrier in the 'service' position, as described in Chapter 11.

7.7b Remove the bolts and withdraw the coolant pump from the cylinder block

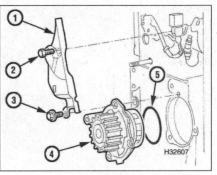

7.7a Coolant pump mounting details (petrol engines)

1 Timing belt cover	*3 Bolt*
2 Bolt	*4 Coolant pump*
	5 Seal

3 Remove the auxiliary drivebelt as described in Chapter 2A.

4 Remove the viscous-coupled cooling fan unit as described in Section 5.

5 With reference to Chapter 2A remove the timing belt. **Note:** *There is no need to remove the lower timing belt cover – the timing belt can be left in position on the crankshaft sprocket.*

6 On the petrol engine code AZM, undo the upper screw securing the timing belt inner cover to the cylinder head.

7 Unscrew and remove the coolant pump securing bolts. Carefully withdraw the pump from the cylinder block and recover the sealing O-ring. On engine code AZM, the upper coolant pump mounting bolt also secures the inner timing belt cover **(see illustrations)**.

Refitting

8 Ensure that the pump and housing mating surfaces are clean and free from all traces of corrosion.

9 Obtain a new sealing O-ring and moisten it with undiluted antifreeze of the specified type (see *Recommended lubricants and fluids*). Position the sealing ring in its housing on the cylinder block **(see illustration)**.

10 Fit the coolant pump to the cylinder block, ensuring that the plug insert in the pump flange faces downwards **(see illustration)**.

11 Insert the mounting bolts and tighten them evenly and progressively to the specified torque. On engine code AZM, locate the inner cover on the upper mounting bolt.

7.9 Fit a new O-ring to the coolant pump

7.10 Refit the coolant pump with the flange plug facing down

12 On engine code AZM, refit and tighten the inner cover upper bolt.

13 Refit the timing belt as described in Chapter 2A.

14 Refit the viscous-coupled cooling fan unit and the auxiliary drivebelt.

15 Refit the lock carrier and tighten the securing bolts to the specified torque (see Chapter 11).

16 On completion refill the cooling system as described in Chapter 1A, then reconnect the battery.

Diesel engine

Removal

17 Disconnect the battery negative cable (see Chapter 5A), then drain the cooling system as described in Chapter 1B.

18 Place the lock carrier in the 'service' position, as described in Chapter 11.

19 Remove the auxiliary drivebelt as described in Chapter 2A.

20 Remove the viscous-coupled cooling fan unit as described in Section 5.

21 With reference to Chapter 2B remove the timing belt.

22 Unscrew and remove the coolant pump securing bolts.

23 Carefully withdraw the pump from the cylinder block and recover the sealing O-ring.

Refitting

24 Ensure that the pump and housing mating surfaces are clean and free from all traces of corrosion.

25 Obtain a new sealing O-ring and moisten it with undiluted antifreeze of the specified type (see *Recommended lubricants and fluids*). Position the sealing O-ring in its housing on the cylinder block.

26 Fit the coolant pump to the cylinder block, ensuring that the plug insert in the pump flange faces downwards **(see illustration 7.10)**.

27 Insert the retaining bolts and tighten them evenly and progressively to the specified torque.

28 Refit the timing belt as described in Chapter 2B.

29 Refit the viscous-coupled cooling fan unit and auxiliary drivebelt.

30 Refit the lock carrier and tighten the securing bolts to the specified torque (see Chapter 11).

31 On completion refill the cooling system as described in Chapter 1B, then reconnect the battery.

8 Heating and ventilation system – general information

1 The heating/ventilation system consists of a fully adjustable blower motor (housed behind the facia), face level vents in the centre and at each end of the facia, and air ducts to the front footwells.

2 The heater control unit is located in the facia, and the controls operate flap valves to deflect and mix the air flowing through the various parts of the heating/ventilation system. The flap valves are contained in the air distribution housing, which acts as a central distribution unit, passing air to the various ducts and vents.

3 Cold air enters the system through the grille at the rear of the engine compartment. If required, the airflow is boosted by the blower, and then flows through the various ducts, according to the settings of the controls. Stale air is expelled through ducts at the rear of the vehicle. If warm air is required, the cold air is passed over the heater matrix, which is heated by the engine coolant.

4 The outside air supply to the vehicle can be closed off which is useful to prevent unpleasant odours entering from outside the vehicle. This is achieved either by setting the blower motor switch to position 0 or by operating the recirculation switch (depending on model). This facility should only be used briefly, as the recirculated air inside the vehicle will soon become stale.

5 On models with a solar sunroof, the sliding roof incorporates solar panels which energise the air conditioning blower motor to cool the interior of the car.

9 Heater/ventilation components – removal and refitting

General information

1 The information in this Section is only applicable to models equipped with a manually-operated conventional heating system, without air conditioning. On models with air conditioning, removal and refitting of the heater/ventilation/air conditioning system components is described in Section 11.

Heater/ventilation control unit

Removal

2 Disconnect the battery negative lead (see Chapter 5A). Remove the audio unit as described in Chapter 12.

3 Carefully pull the knobs from the heater control rotary switch shafts **(see illustration)**.

4 Using a small flat-bladed screwdriver, carefully prise off the control unit surround. Pad the screwdriver blade with tape to avoid damaging the trim panel and facia.

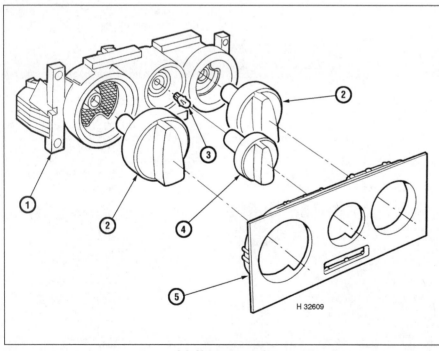
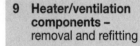

H 32609

9.3 Heater controls

1 Control unit	3 Bulb	5 Trim panel
2 Control knob	4 Rotary control	

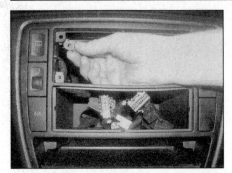

9.5 Note the location of the captive spire nuts

5 Slacken and withdraw the four screws from the corners of the heater control unit aperture. Note the fitted locations of the captive spire nuts (see illustration).

6 Undo the two screws in the storage compartment under the audio compartment, and lift off the centre console switch panel. Disconnect the various switch wiring plugs as the panel is withdrawn. On later models, there is no need to remove the switch panel as the heater control unit releases from the front; note the fitted locations of the spring clips.

7 Note the correct fitted location of each control cable (the cable end fittings are colour-coded) then detach them from the control panel (see illustrations). The outer cables are either clipped in position, and can be released by carefully levering back the panel retaining tangs from below using a flat-bladed screwdriver, or are retained by a self-tapping screw.

8 Once the wiring and cables are detached, remove the control panel from the vehicle.

Refitting

9 Refitting is a reversal of removal, but ensure that the control cables (where fitted) are securely reconnected to their original locations. Check the operation of the controls prior to refitting the centre console.

Blower motor

10 Disconnect the cable from the battery negative terminal (see Chapter 5A).

11 Refer to Chapter 11 and remove the glovebox assembly from the facia.

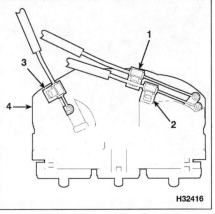

9.7a Cable connections at the control panel

1 Central flap
  RHD: Yellow
  LHD: Black
2 Footwell/defrost
  flap
  RHD: Green
  LHD: White
3 Temperature
  flap
  RHD: Orange
  LHD: Red
4 Controls

12 Remove the series resistor/thermal fuse unit, as described in the next sub-section.

13 Unplug the motor wiring connector from the side of the motor housing (see illustration).

14 Grasp the motor mounting plate and slide it downwards to release it from its housing. Undo the securing screws and separate

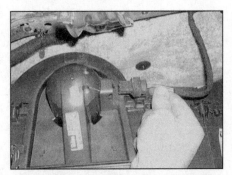

9.13 Unplug the motor wiring connector from the side of the motor housing

9.14b . . . and slide it downwards to release it from its housing

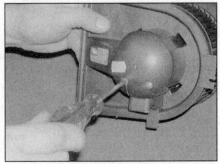

9.14c Undo the securing screws . . .

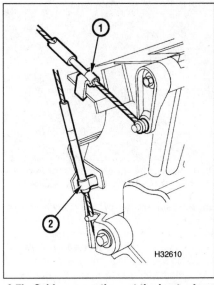

9.7b Cable connections at the heater box

1 Temperature flap
  RHD: Orange
  LHD: Red
2 Central flap
  RHD: Yellow
  LHD: Black

the motor from the mounting plate (see illustrations).

Blower motor resistor/ thermal fuse

Removal

15 Remove the glovebox as described in Chapter 11. The resistor/fuse unit is mounted

9.14a Grasp the motor mounting plate . . .

9.14d . . . and separate the motor from the mounting plate

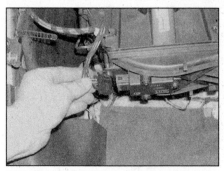

9.16 Unplug the wiring connector from the rear of the resistor/fuse unit baseplate

9.17a Undo the securing screws . . .

9.17b . . . and remove the baseplate from the blower motor housing

on the underside of the blower motor housing.

16 Unplug the wiring connector from the resistor/fuse unit baseplate **(see illustration)**.

17 Undo the securing screws and remove the baseplate from the blower motor housing **(see illustrations)**.

18 The resistor/fuse unit is not available separately, and if faulty, must be renewed complete with the baseplate.

Refitting

19 Refitting is the reverse of removal.

Heater unit

Removal

20 Ensure that engine has cooled completely before starting work.

21 Open the bonnet and at the rear of the engine compartment, locate the heater matrix

hoses and trace them back to the point where they connect to bulkhead stub pipes.

22 Place a draining container underneath the hoses, to catch the coolant that will escape when they are disconnected.

23 Apply proprietary hose clamps to both heater hoses, then release the clips and disconnect the hoses from the bulkhead stubs **(see illustrations)**. Allow the coolant from the heater circuit to collect in the draining container.

24 If you have access to a source of compressed air, apply it carefully at *low pressure* to the left hand bulkhead stub and blow the remainder of the coolant from the heater matrix.

⚠️ **Warning: Always wear eye protection when working with compressed air.**

25 If you do not have access to compressed air, bear in mind that a larger volume of coolant will remain in the heater circuit and that this

may escape as the heater unit is removed from the inside of the car.

26 Prise the rubber grommet from the bulkhead aperture, then slide it off the pipe stubs and remove it from the engine compartment **(see illustration)**.

27 Remove the entire facia panel and crossmember as described in Chapter 11.

28 Undo the bolts and remove the left and right-hand facia support brackets from the floorpan **(see illustrations)**.

29 Unclip the rear passenger air ducts from the front of the footwell vent unit. Remove the securing screws and detach the footwell vent unit from the base of the heater unit **(see illustrations)**.

30 Unplug the wiring heater unit wiring at the multiway connectors. Label each connection to avoid confusion on refitting. Release the wiring from the support clips on the side of the heater unit.

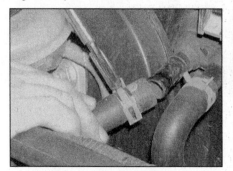

9.23a Release the clips . . .

9.23b . . . and disconnect the heater hoses from the bulkhead stubs

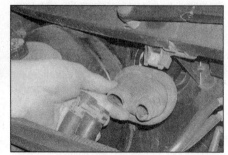

9.26 Prise the rubber grommet from the bulkhead aperture, then slide it off the pipe stubs

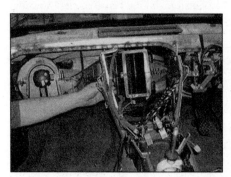

9.28a Undo the bolts and remove the left . . .

9.28b . . . and right-hand facia support brackets from the floorpan

9.29a Unclip the rear passenger air ducts from the front of the footwell vent unit

31 Slacken and withdraw the securing screws and lift the heater unit away from the bulkhead, towards the passenger's side of the vehicle. The heater unit gasket may be stuck to the bulkhead – carefully rock the housing from side-to-side until the gasket releases.

32 Remove the unit from the vehicle, keeping it upright to avoid spilling the residual coolant.

Refitting

33 Refitting is the reverse of removal, noting the following points.

a) *Use a new housing gasket if the original is damaged.*

b) *Ensure the ducts, elbows and gaiter are all securely joined to the housing and the wiring/cables are correctly routed before securing the housing in position.*

c) *Ensure the coolant hoses are securely reconnected to the matrix; the feed hose from the cylinder head must be connected to the left-hand union and the return hose to the coolant pump to the right-hand union.*

d) *Ensure that the rubber grommet is securely seated over the bulkhead stub pipes.*

e) *On completion, top-up and bleed the cooling system as described in the relevant part of Chapter 1.*

Heater matrix

Removal

34 Remove the heater unit as described earlier in this Section.

35 With the housing on a bench, undo the screw, depress the locking catches and withdraw the heater matrix from the top of the heater unit **(see illustrations)**. Protect your hands as you do this – the matrix fins are sharp and can cause injury.

Refitting

36 Refitting is a reversal of removal. New heater matrices will be supplied with self-adhesive foam padding strips – these should be affixed to the edges of the core and the upper flange before the matrix is inserted into the heater unit.

Fresh/recirculating air flap valve motor

Removal

37 Disconnect the negative cable from the battery terminal (see Chapter 5A).

38 Remove the glovebox assembly as described in Chapter 11.

39 The flap valve motor is located on the left-hand side (LHD: right-hand side) of the blower motor housing.

40 Unplug the wiring connector from the side of the motor.

41 Undo the securing screw and carefully withdraw the motor from the housing, manoeuvring the control lever through the housing aperture.

9.29b Remove the securing screws and detach the footwell vent unit from the base of the heater unit

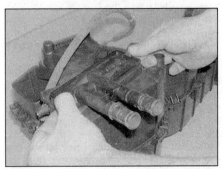

9.35b . . . depress the locking catches . . .

Refitting

42 Refitting is a reversal of removal. If the position of the motor control lever makes refitting difficult, temporarily reconnect the battery and operate the recirculation switch, until the control lever is positioned horizontally with respect to the motor body.

---

10 Air conditioning system – general information and precautions

General information

1 Air conditioning is fitted as standard equipment on all models. It combines a conventional air heating system with an air cooling and dehumidifying system. This allows greater control over the temperature and humidity of the air inside the car, giving increased comfort and rapid window demisting.

2 The cooling side of the system works in the same way as a domestic refrigerator. Refrigerant gas, contained in a sealed network of alloy pipes, is drawn into a belt-driven compressor, and is forced through a condenser mounted on the front of the radiator. On entering the condenser, the refrigerant changes state from gas to liquid and releases heat, which is absorbed by the air flowing into the front of the engine compartment through the condenser. The liquid refrigerant passes through an expansion valve to an evaporator, where it changes from liquid under high pressure to gas under low pressure. This

9.35a With the housing on a bench, undo the screw . . .

9.35c . . . and withdraw the heater matrix from the top of the heater unit

change in state is accompanied by a drop in temperature, which cools the evaporator. Air passing through the evaporator is cooled before flowing into the air distribution unit. The refrigerant then returns to the compressor, and the cycle begins again.

3 The cooled air passes to the air distribution unit, where it is blended with hot air blown through the heater matrix, to achieve the desired temperature in the passenger compartment. When the air conditioning system is operating in Automatic mode, a series of air valves controlled by servo motors automatically regulate the cabin temperature by blending hot and cold air.

4 The heating side of the system operates as described in Section 8.

5 The operation of the air conditioning system is managed by an electronic control unit, which controls the electric cooling fan, the compressor, and the facia-mounted warning light. Any problems with the system should be referred to a VW dealer. The system has a built-in, self-diagnostic capability, but specialist equipment is needed to interpret the information it produces.

Precautions

6 When working on the air conditioning system, it is necessary to observe special precautions. If for any reason the refrigerant lines must be disconnected, you must entrust this task to a VW dealer or an air conditioning specialist. Similarly, the system can only be evacuated and recharged by a dealer or air conditioning specialist.

Warning: The air conditioning system contains a pressurised liquid refrigerant. If the system is discharged in an uncontrolled manner without the aid of specialist equipment, the refrigerant will boil as soon as it is exposed to the atmosphere, causing severe frostbite if it comes into contact with unprotected skin. In addition, certain refrigerants, in the presence of a naked flame (including a lit cigarette), will oxidise to form a highly poisonous gas. It is therefore extremely dangerous to disconnect any part of the air conditioning system without specialised knowledge and equipment.

7 Uncontrolled discharging of the refrigerant can also be damaging to the environment, as certain refrigerants contain CFCs.

8 Do not operate the air conditioning system if it is known to be short of refrigerant, as this will damage the compressor.

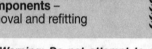

11 Air conditioning system components – removal and refitting

 Warning: Do not attempt to discharge the refrigerant circuit yourself (refer to the precautions given in Section 10). Have the air conditioning system discharged by a qualified refrigeration engineer. On completion, have the engineer fit new O-rings to the line connections and evacuate and recharge the system.

Compressor

Removal

1 Disconnect the negative cable from the battery terminal (see Chapter 5A).

2 Place the lock carrier in the 'service' position (see Chapter 11).

3 Have the air conditioning system discharged by a qualified engineer.

4 Remove the auxiliary drivebelt as described in the relevant part of Chapter 2.

5 Unscrew the retaining bolts and disconnect the refrigerant lines from the compressor. Remove the O-ring seals and discard them – new ones must be used on reconnection. Plug the open pipes and ports to prevent the ingress of moisture.

6 Unplug the wiring for the clutch unit, and where applicable, the shaft speed sensor at the connectors at the rear of the compressor.

7 Unscrew the three (Nippondenso compressor) or four (Zexel compressor) securing bolts from the front of the compressor, then remove the compressor from its mounting bracket.

Refitting

8 Refitting is a reversal of the removal procedure; ensure that all fixings are tightened to the specified torque, where given. On completion, have the refrigerant engineer fit new O-rings to the line connections and then evacuate and recharge the refrigerant circuit.

Evaporator/heater matrix housing

Caution: Before removing the evaporator/ heater matrix housing, the air conditioning control system components must be set in a reference position. This work should be entrusted to a VW dealer as it requires access to dedicated test equipment.

Removal

9 Ensure that engine has cooled completely before starting work.

10 Have the air conditioning system discharged by a qualified engineer, then have the air conditioning control system components set in a reference position by a VW dealer.

11 Disconnect the negative cable from the battery terminal (see Chapter 5A).

12 Open the bonnet and at the rear of the engine compartment, locate the heater matrix hoses and trace them back to the point where they connect to bulkhead stub pipes.

13 Place a draining container underneath the hoses, to catch the coolant that will escape when they are disconnected.

14 Apply proprietary hose clamps to both heater hoses, then slacken the clips and disconnect the hoses from the bulkhead stubs. Allow the coolant from the heater circuit to collect in the draining container.

15 If you have access to a source of compressed air, apply it carefully at *low pressure* to the left-hand bulkhead stub and blow the remainder of the coolant from the heater matrix.

 Warning: Always wear eye protection when working with compressed air.

16 If you do not have access to compressed air, bear in mind that a larger volume of coolant will remain in the heater circuit and that this may escape as the housing is removed from the inside of the car.

17 Prise the rubber grommet from the bulkhead aperture, then slide it off the pipe stubs and remove it from the engine compartment.

18 Locate the aluminium air conditioning refrigerant pipes and trace them back to the engine compartment bulkhead. Unscrew the centre bolt and disconnect the pipes at the union. Remove the O-ring seals and

11.29 Disconnect the wiring plug, undo the screws, rotate the motor slightly and withdraw it from the housing

discard them – new ones must be used on reconnection. Plug the open pipes to prevent the ingress of moisture.

19 Release the rubber grommet from the bulkhead aperture and slide it off the refrigerant pipe unions.

20 Remove the entire facia panel, crossmember and centre bracket as described in Chapter 11.

21 Unclip the rear passenger air ducts from the front of the footwell vent unit. Remove the securing screws and detach the footwell vent unit from the base of the evaporator/heater matrix housing.

22 Unplug the wiring for the evaporator/ heater matrix housing at the multiway connectors. Label each connection to avoid confusion on refitting. Release the wiring from the support clips on the side of the housing.

23 Lift the evaporator/heater matrix housing away from the bulkhead, towards the passenger's side of the vehicle. The housing gasket may be stuck to the bulkhead – carefully rock the housing from side-to-side until the gasket releases.

24 Remove the housing from the vehicle, keeping it upright to avoid spilling the residual coolant.

Refitting

25 Refitting is the reverse of removal, noting the following points.

  a) Use a new housing gasket if the original is damaged.
  b) Ensure that the condenser drain pipe is correctly positioned on the rear of the evaporator/heater matrix housing.
  c) Ensure the ducts, elbows and gaiter are all securely joined to the housing and the wiring/cables are correctly routed before securing the housing in position.
  d) Ensure the coolant hoses are securely reconnected to the matrix; the feed hose from the cylinder head must be connected to the left hand union and the return hose to the coolant pump to the right hand union (with the vent hole incorporated).
  e) Ensure that the rubber grommets are securely seated in the bulkhead apertures.
  f) Top-up and bleed the cooling system as described in the relevant part of Chapter 1.
  g) On completion, have the refrigerant engineer fit new O-rings to the line connections and then evacuate and recharge the refrigerant circuit.

Blower motor

Removal

26 Disconnect the negative cable from the battery terminal (see Chapter 5A).

27 Refer to Chapter 11 and remove the glovebox from the facia.

28 Working under the facia in the passenger footwell, unplug the wiring connectors from the rear of the blower motor unit.

29 Remove the screws, then rotate the blower motor unit slightly and withdraw it from the heater matrix/evaporator housing. The motor can now be detached from its baseplate by unplugging the wiring connectors and releasing the retaining catches. Note that on vehicles equipped with a passenger side airbag, the airbag and its support bracket (nearest the door) must be removed in order to gain access to the uppermost blower motor retaining screw (see illustration).

Removal

30 Refitting is a reversal of removal.

Blower motor control unit

Removal

31 Disconnect the negative cable from the battery terminal (see Chapter 5A).
32 With reference to paragraphs 27 to 29, remove the blower motor.
33 The control unit is located alongside the blower motor fan. Undo the three retaining screws and pull the control unit out and slightly away from the blower fan.
34 Disconnect the control unit wiring connector.

Refitting

35 Refitting is a reversal of removal.

Control panel

Manual air conditioning

36 Using a small flat-bladed screwdriver as a lever, detach the trim panel around the heater rotary controls.
37 Undo the four screws, one in each corner of the heater control panel aperture.
38 Remove the audio unit as described in Chapter 12.
39 The control panel trim is secured in position by two retaining screws and four spring clips, and is removed by reaching through the audio unit aperture and pushing the control panel trim forwards.
40 Pull the control panel with the cables attached out of the facia panel.
41 Note their fitted locations, and disconnect the control cables and wiring connectors..
42 Refitting is a reversal of removal.

Climatronic air conditioning

Note: *After refitting/renewing the control panel, access to VW dedicated test equipment is needed to establish the 'Basic setting' of the unit.*
43 Disconnect the battery negative terminal (see Chapter 5A).
44 Using a small flat-bladed screwdriver, carefully prise out the control/display panel outer trim.
45 Undo the four retaining screws, one in each corner of the control panel aperture (see illustration).
46 Pull the control panel out of the facia and disconnect the wiring connectors.
47 No further dismantling of the control panel is possible.
48 Refitting is a reversal of removal, but the unit needs to be reset using dedicated VW test equipment.

Fresh/recirculating air flap motors

Manual air conditioning

49 Remove the passenger glovebox as described in Chapter 11.
50 Using a mirror to identify their location, undo the two Torx screws, unclip the fresh/recirculation air lever, pull off the connector, and pull the motor downwards and away from the passenger side of the heater assembly.
51 Refitting is a reversal of removal.

Climatronic air conditioning

Note: *After refitting/renewing the flap valve positioning motors, access to VW dedicated test equipment is needed to establish the 'Basic setting' of the units.*
52 Remove the facia and crossmember as described in Chapter 11.
53 Disconnect the footwell air distribution vent from the base of the evaporator/heater matrix housing.
54 The flap valve positioning motors are located on the side of the evaporator/heater matrix housing and is identified as follows:
  a) *Footwell/defroster valve – yellow wiring connector*
  b) *Temperature flap valve – violet wiring connector*
  c) *Centre flap valve – green wiring connector*
55 Unplug the wiring connector, then disconnect the operation lever from the motor shaft.
56 Remove the retaining screws and withdraw the motor from the housing. Note that the footwell/defroster valve is retained by a bracket.
57 Refitting is a reversal of removal. On completion, the air conditioning control system must be re-initialised by a VW dealer using dedicated test equipment.

Temperature sensors

58 Temperature sensors are mounted in the individual air ducts leading to the footwell and

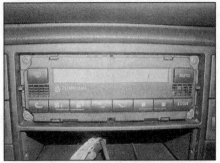

11.45 Undo the four retaining screws, one in each corner of the control panel aperture

face level vents. These can be removed by disconnecting the wiring, then rotating the sensor unit and withdrawing it from the ducting.

Sunlight photo-sensor

Removal

59 Carefully prise from the defrosting vent in the centre of the facia. Disconnect the wiring and tie the connector back to prevent it from disappearing down inside the facia.

Refitting

60 Refitting is a reversal of removal.

12 Fuel cooling system components – removal and refitting

1 On diesel engines manufactured up to 01/2002, the temperature of the returning fuel from the engine is reduced prior to re-entering the plastic fuel tank. This is achieved by cooling the fuel filter housing with a separate cooling circuit, which includes a radiator, cooling pump, shut-off valve and fuel temperature sensor. Although the cooling circuit is supplied with coolant by the main engine coolant circuit, the engine ECU

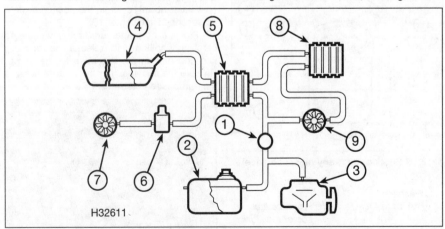

12.1 Fuel cooling circuit (diesel engines manufactured before 01/2002)

1 *Coolant shut-off valve*	4 *Fuel tank*	7 *Fuel pump*
2 *Expansion tank*	5 *Fuel cooler*	8 *Fuel cooling circuit radiator*
3 *Engine cooling circuit*	6 *Fuel temperature sensor*	9 *Fuel cooling pump*

H32611

12.5 Undo the four nuts and manoeuvre the radiator out from the mounting bracket

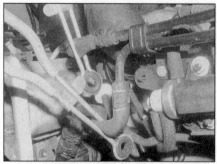

12.9 Clamp the coolant supply and return hoses

12.10 Release the securing clips and disconnect the hoses to the coolant pump

controlled shut-off valve prevents the engine cooling circuit heating the fuel cooling circuit. Once the temperature of the fuel rises to 70°C, the engine ECU operates the fuel coolant pump, and coolant flows through the fuel filter housing to the radiator mounted in front of the right-hand wheel arch liner **(see illustration)**. Engines manufactured from 01/2002-on are not fitted with the fuel cooling system.

Radiator

Removal

2 With reference to Chapter 11, place the lock carrier in the 'service' position. The fuel coolant radiator is located behind the bumper bar at the right-hand side front of the vehicle.

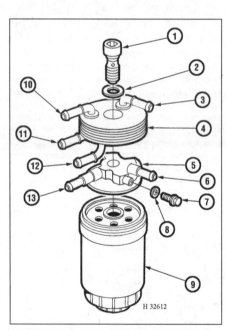

12.15 Fuel cooler (early diesel engines)

1 *Bolt*	8 *Washer*
2 *Washer*	9 *Filter*
3 *Return to fuel tank*	10 *From the fuel cooler radiator*
4 *Cooler*	11 *To the fuel cooler radiator*
5 *Filter head*	12 *From the fuel pump*
6 *From the fuel tank*	13 *To the fuel pump*
7 *Bleed screw*	

3 Clamp the supply hose to the fuel coolant pump, and the return hose from the radiator, or drain the cooling system as described in Chapter 1B.

4 Place a container under the vehicle to catch any spilled fluid, release the retaining clip and detach the top hose from the radiator. Release the clip securing the bottom hose to the radiator.

5 Undo the four retaining nuts and manoeuvre the radiator out of the mounting bracket, disconnecting the bottom hose as the radiator is withdrawn **(see illustration)**.

6 If required, the mounting bracket can be removed by pulling it out from the mounting grommets.

Refitting

7 Refitting is the reversal of removal. Top-up the cooling system through the engine cooling system expansion tank.

Cooling pump

Removal

8 With reference to Chapter 11, place the lock carrier in the 'service' position. The fuel cooling pump is located behind the bumper bar at the right-hand side front of the vehicle.

9 Clamp the supply hose to the fuel cooling pump, and the return hose from the radiator **(see illustration)**, or drain the cooling system as described in Chapter 1B.

10 Place a container under the vehicle to catch any spilled fluid, release the retaining clip and detach the top hose to the pump. Release the clip securing the bottom hose to the pump **(see illustration)**.

12.19 Clamp the hoses either side of the valve, release the retaining clips and disconnect the hoses

11 Disconnect the wiring plug from the pump.

12 Undo the single retaining bolt, and remove the pump. Disconnect the bottom hose as the pump is withdrawn.

Refitting

13 Refitting is the reversal of removal. Top-up the cooling system through the engine cooling system expansion tank.

Fuel cooler unit

Removal

14 The fuel cooler unit is incorporated into the fuel filter. Lever out the cover caps, undo the retaining nuts/bolts, and remove the engine top cover.

15 Clamp the coolant hoses, and fuel return hoses leading to and from the fuel filter **(see illustration)**, or be prepared for fuel/coolant spillage. Noting their fitted locations, release the retaining clips and disconnect the hoses.

Caution: Ensure that no fuel contacts the coolant hoses. Mop-up any spilt fuel immediately.

16 Undo the central bolt and separate the top cooler part of the filter housing from the rest of the filter assembly.

Refitting

17 Refitting is a reversal of removal. Top-up the cooling system through the engine cooling system expansion tank.

Shut-off valve

Removal

18 The coolant shut-off valve is located in the coolant hose between the fuel cooler and the expansion tank. Lever out the cover caps, undo the retaining nuts/bolts, and remove the engine top cover.

19 Clamp the hoses either side of the valve, release the retaining clips and disconnect the hoses **(see illustration)**.

20 Disconnect the vacuum pipe and remove the valve. No further dismantling of the valve is recommended.

Refitting

21 Refitting is a reversal of removal. Top-up the cooling system through the engine cooling system expansion tank.

Fuel temperature sensor

Removal

22 The fuel temperature sensor is located in the hose from the fuel pump to the cooler. Lever out the cover caps, undo the retaining nuts/bolts, and remove the engine top cover. Remove the intercooler-to-inlet manifold pipe at the rear of the cylinder head.

23 Clamp the hose either side of the sensor.

24 Unplug the wiring connector, release the retaining clip, and remove the sensor **(see illustration)**.

25 The sensor can be tested using a multimeter. Connect the multimeter leads to the terminals of the sensor and set the meter to measure resistance (ohms). As the temperature increases, the resistance of the sensor decreases. So at 30°C the resistance should be 1500 to 2000 ohms, and at 80°C the resistance should be 275 to 375 ohms. If the resistance value of the sensor does not match these values, or fails to change, it must be renewed.

Refitting

26 Refitting is a reversal of removal. Top-up the cooling system through the engine cooling system expansion tank.

12.24 Release the retaining clip and withdraw the temperature sensor

Chapter 4 Part A:
Fuel system – petrol injection

Contents

Section number

Air cleaner and inlet ducts – removal and refitting 2
Bosch Motronic engine management components – removal and
  refitting 3
Fuel filter – renewal. 5
Fuel injection system – depressurisation 8
Fuel injection system – testing and adjustment 10
Fuel pump and gauge sender unit – removal and refitting. 6

Section number

Fuel tank – removal and refitting 7
General information and precautions. 1
Inlet manifold – removal and refitting 9
Intercooler – removal and refitting 12
Simos engine management components – removal and refitting . . . 4
Turbocharger – general information, removal and refitting. 11

Degrees of difficulty

Easy, suitable for novice with little experience 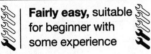	Fairly easy, suitable for beginner with some experience 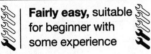	Fairly difficult, suitable for competent DIY mechanic 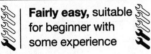	Difficult, suitable for experienced DIY mechanic	Very difficult, suitable for expert DIY or professional

Specifications

General

Engine code by type*

1781 cc, DOHC, Bosch Motronic ME7.5 injection, turbocharged	AWT
1984 cc, SOHC, Siemens Simos 3.2 injection, non-turbo	AZM
1984 cc, DOHC, Bosch Motronic ME7.5 injection, non-turbo	ALT

* Note: *See 'Vehicle identification' at the end of this manual for the location of code marking on the engine.*

Recommended fuel

Minimum octane rating.	95 RON unleaded (91 RON unleaded may be used, but with reduced performance)

Fuel system data

Fuel pump type	Electric, immersed in fuel tank
Fuel pump delivery rate (battery voltage 12V)	260 cm³/15 secs
Regulated fuel pressure at idling speed:	
Vacuum hose fitted.	3.5 bar (approx)
Vacuum hose disconnected	4.0 bar (approx)
Minimum holding pressure (after 10 minutes)	2.0 bar
Engine idle speed (non-adjustable, electronically controlled):	
Engine code AWT.	740 to 920 rpm
Engine code AZM.	740 to 860 rpm
Engine code ALT.	700 to 960 rpm
Idle CO content (non-adjustable, electronically controlled)	0.1 to 1.1 %
Injector electrical resistance (at room temperature):	
Engine code AWT.	12 to 17 ohms
Engine code AZM.	14 to 17 ohms
Engine code ALT.	12 to 17 ohms
Engine coolant temperature sensor resistance:	
At 30°C.	1500 to 2000 ohms
At 80°C.	275 to 375 ohms
Engine speed sensor resistance	730 to 1000 ohms

Torque wrench settings

	Nm	lbf ft
Accelerator pedal sender	10	7
Air cleaner	10	7
Air temperature sensor	10	7
Catalytic converter to turbocharger	30	22
Coolant pipe to inlet manifold	10	7
Coolant return pipe to turbocharger	30	22
Coolant supply pipe to turbocharger	25	18
Engine speed sender	10	7
Engine speed sensor	10	7
Fuel filter bracket	10	7
Fuel pump/sender unit ring	60	44
Fuel rail to inlet manifold	10	7
Fuel tank filler neck	25	18
Fuel tank mounting bolts	25	18
Fuel tank	25	19
Inlet manifold and support bracket	20	15
Inlet manifold flange to cylinder head	20	15
Inlet manifold support brackets	20	15
Inlet manifold	10	7
Oil return pipe to turbocharger	10	7
Oil supply pipe to turbocharger	25	18
Oxygen sensor	50	37
Throttle body	10	7
Turbocharger bracket:		
To turbocharger	40	30
To cylinder block	45	33
Turbocharger to exhaust manifold	35	26

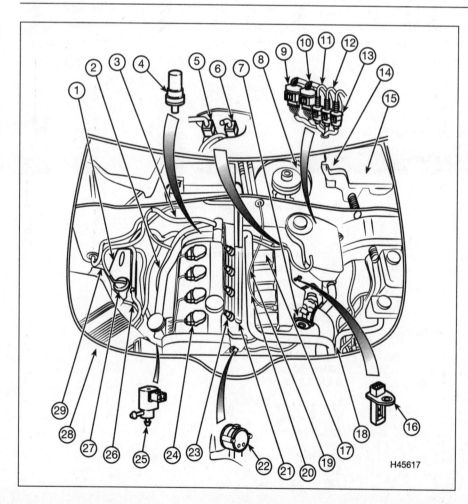

1.1a Bosch Motronic components – engine code AWT

1 Air cleaner
2 Oxygen sensor (before catalytic converter)
3 Oxygen sensor (after catalytic converter)
4 Coolant temperature sender
5 Divert air valve
6 Secondary air inlet valve
7 Throttle body/control unit
8 Clutch pedal switch, brake light switch, brake pedal switch and accelerator position senders
9 Oxygen sensor (before catalytic converter) connector (brown)
10 Oxygen sensor (after catalytic converter) connector (black)
11 Engine speed sender connector (grey)
12 Knock sensor 1 connector (green)
13 Knock sensor 2 connector (blue)
14 Secondary air pump motor
15 Engine management control unit (ECU)
16 Intake air temperature sender
17 Engine speed sender
18 Charge pressure sender
19 Knock sensor 2
20 Knock sensor 1
21 Fuel pressure regulator
22 Hall sender
23 Injectors
24 Ignition coil with output stage
25 Charge pressure control solenoid valve
26 Earth
27 Airflow meter
28 Secondary air pump motor
29 Activated charcoal filter solenoid valve

H45617

1 General information and precautions

General information

The Bosch and Simos multipoint petrol injection systems described in this Chapter are self-contained engine management systems, which control both the fuel injection and ignition **(see illustrations)**. This Chapter deals with the fuel system components only; refer to Chapter 5B for details of the ignition system.

The fuel injection system comprises a fuel tank, an electric fuel pump, a fuel filter, fuel supply and return lines, a throttle body, an air mass sensor, a fuel rail and four electronic injectors, a fuel pressure regulator, and an electronic control unit (ECU), together with its associated sensors, actuators and wiring. The component layout varies according to the system – refer to the relevant Section for details.

A turbocharger is fitted to engine code AWT. Engine code ALT has a variable geometry inlet manifold, where the length of the inlet track is varied to emphasise the torque or power characteristics of the engine dependant on engine speed and load, etc. The inlet path is controlled by a vacuum-operated valve which can operate in one of two positions. At low engine speed/high torque the valve position forces the incoming air through a long inlet track, thus increasing the torque output and low speed driveability. At high engine speed/high power the valve position forces the incoming air through a short inlet track, thus increasing the power output and throttle response. The vacuum supply to the valve is controlled by the engine management ECM.

All models are equipped with an electronically-controlled throttle system referred to as Electronic Power Control (EPS). A sensor on the accelerator pedal informs the engine management ECU of the position and rate-of-change of the pedal, which then determines the optimum position for the throttle valve in the throttle body. There is no accelerator cable. The position of the accelerator pedal is transmitted to the engine control unit by two variable resistors, and the throttle valve is operated by an electric motor on the throttle body. When the engine is stopped but the ignition is switched on, the throttle valve moves exactly as dictated by the throttle pedal, however, when the engine is running, the control unit can open or close the throttle valve independently. The control unit calculates the most efficient opening of the throttle valve according to a number of parameters, so it is possible under certain conditions that the throttle valve may be completely open even though the pedal is only depressed half way.

The air mass sensor is located on the air cleaner outlet to the throttle body. Fuel is supplied under pressure to a fuel rail, and then passes to four electronic injectors. The duration of the injection period is determined by the ECU which switches the injectors on and off as required.

The fuel pump delivers a constant supply of fuel through a cartridge filter. The fuel is supplied to a fuel rail, and the fuel pressure regulator maintains a constant fuel pressure to the fuel injectors and returns excess fuel to the tank via the return line. The constant fuel flow system helps to reduce fuel temperature and prevents vaporisation.

The ECU controls starting and warm-up enrichment together with idle speed regulation and lambda control. Idle speed control is achieved partly by an electronic throttle valve positioning module, on the side of the throttle body and partly by the ignition system. Manual adjustment of the idle speed is not possible.

Inlet air is drawn into the engine through the air cleaner, which contains a renewable paper filter element.

**1.1b Simos components –
engine code AZM**

1 Activated charcoal filter solenoid
2 Airflow meter with intake air temperature sensor
3 Secondary air injection combi valve
4 Coolant temperature sender
5 Ignition transformer
6 Throttle body/control unit
7 Oxygen sensor connector (brown)
8 Oxygen sensor connector (black)
9 Engine speed sensor connector (grey)
10 Knock sensor 1 connector (green)
11 Knock sensor 2 connector (brown)
12 Earth
13 Secondary air pump motor
14 Relay for Simos control unit
15 Fuse for secondary air pump
16 Engine management control unit (ECU)
17 Cover
18 Intake manifold change-over valve
19 Vacuum control element
20 Engine speed sender
21 Knock sensor 1
22 Knock sensor 2
23 Fuel pressure regulator
24 Hall sender connector (black)
25 Injectors
26 Hall sender
27 Oxygen sensor (after catalytic converter)
28 Oxygen sensor (before catalytic converter)
29 Secondary air pump motor
30 Air cleaner

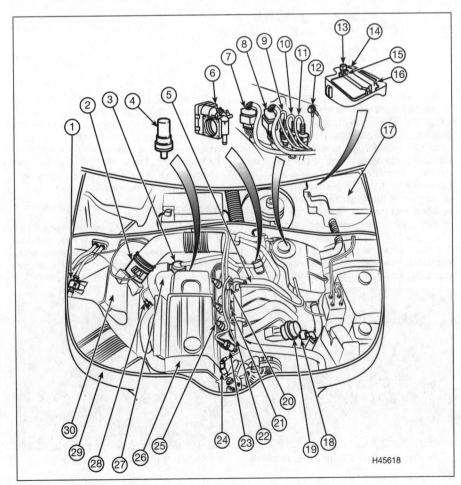

H45618

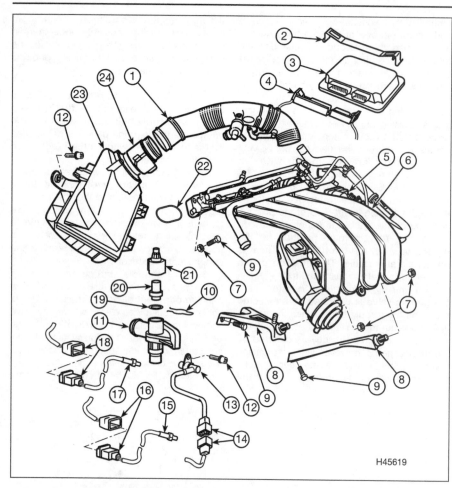

H45619

1.1c Bosch Motronic components – engine code ALT

1   Inlet duct
2   Retaining plate
3   ECU
4   Wiring connector
5   Throttle valve control
6   Inlet manifold
7   Nuts
8   Support brackets
9   Bolt
10 Spring clip
11 Elbow
12 Bolt
13 Engine speed sender
14 Wiring connector
15 Oxygen sensor (after catalytic converter)
16 Wiring connector
17 Oxygen sensor (before catalytic converter)
18 Wiring connector
19 O-ring
20 Coolant temperature sender
21 Wiring connector
22 Gasket
23 Air cleaner
24 Airflow meter

the fuel system, refer to the precautions given in 'Safety First!' at the beginning of this manual, and follow them implicitly. Always switch off the ignition before working on the fuel system. Petrol is a highly dangerous and volatile liquid, and the precautions necessary when handling it cannot be overstressed.

Note: Residual pressure will remain in the fuel lines long after the vehicle was last used. Before disconnecting any fuel line, first depressurise the fuel system as described in Section 8.

Caution: Before working on the fuel system components, always remove fuse 28, otherwise the fuel pump can be activated by the door contact switch.

The exhaust gas oxygen content is constantly monitored by the ECU via the two oxygen sensors, which are mounted each side of the catalytic converter. The ECU then uses this information to adjust the air/fuel ratio. Manual adjustment of the idle speed exhaust CO content is not possible. A catalytic converter is fitted to the exhaust system on all models. A fuel evaporative control system is fitted, and the ECU controls the operation of the activated charcoal canister – refer to Chapter 4C for further details.

It should be noted that fault diagnosis of all the engine management systems described in this Chapter is only possible with dedicated electronic test equipment. Problems with the system operation should therefore be referred to a VW dealer or engine management specialist for assessment. Once the fault has been identified, the removal and refitting sequences detailed in the following Sections will then allow the appropriate component(s) to be renewed as required.

Precautions

⚠️ **Warning: Many of the procedures in this Chapter require the removal of fuel lines and connections, which may result in some fuel spillage. Before carrying out any operation on**

2   Air cleaner and inlet ducts – removal and refitting

Removal

1 Remove the air cleaner cover and air ducts, then prise open the retaining clips and lift the upper cover from the air cleaner body **(see illustrations)**. Note that the airflow meter is attached to the upper cover. On turbo models, where fitted, remove the heat shield from the side of the air cleaner housing.
2 Remove the air cleaner filter element (see Chapter 1A for more details).
3 Where fitted, disconnect the crankcase ventilation hoses.
4 Disconnect the wiring from the airflow meter and remove the upper cover from the engine compartment. If necessary, remove the airflow meter from the upper cover with reference to Section 4 or 5. On turbo models, disconnect

2.1a Release the air filter cover retaining clips . . .

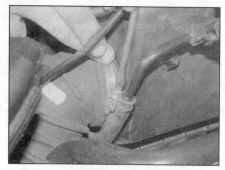

2.1b . . . and disconnect the air ducts

the ignition output stage on the top of the air cleaner cover, and the airflow meter located on the underside of the air cleaner cover.

5 Unscrew the mounting bolt and remove the air cleaner body from the engine compartment **(see illustration)**. If necessary remove the rubber mountings from the body. Check the condition of the mountings and renew them if necessary.

6 On non-turbo models, remove the air duct from between the air cleaner and throttle body by releasing the clips **(see illustrations)**.

7 On turbo models, remove the air duct from between the air cleaner and intercooler.

Refitting

8 Refitting is a reversal of removal.

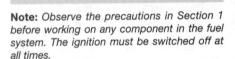

3 Bosch Motronic engine management components – removal and refitting

Note: *Observe the precautions in Section 1 before working on any component in the fuel system. The ignition must be switched off at all times.*

Airflow meter

Removal

1 The airflow meter is located on or under the air cleaner upper cover depending on model. On non-turbo models the meter is mounted on the top, whilst turbo models have the meter mounted on the underside of the cover. First prise open the retaining clips, disconnect the air ducts, and lift the upper cover from the air cleaner body.

2 On turbo models, undo the screws and remove the heat shield.

3 Disconnect the wiring from the airflow meter.

4 Undo the mounting screws then remove the airflow meter. Recover the gasket.

Refitting

5 Refitting is a reversal of removal, but fit a new gasket or O-ring as applicable.

Throttle valve potentiometer

Note: *The potentiometer is an integral part of the throttle body and cannot be renewed separately.*

Air temperature sensor

Removal

6 The sensor is located on the inlet manifold on engine codes AWT and ALT **(see illustration)**, and is integral with the airflow meter on engine code AZM.

7 Unplug the harness connector from the sensor.

8 Unscrew the bolt and remove the sensor from the manifold. The sensor can be tested using a multimeter. Connect the multimeter leads to the terminals of the sensor and set the meter to measure resistance (ohms). As the temperature increases, the resistance of the

2.1c Where fitted, remove the heat shield

2.6a Loosen the clips . . .

sensor decreases. So at 30°C the resistance should be 1500 to 2000 ohms, and at 80°C the resistance should be 275 to 375 ohms. If the resistance value of the sensor does not match these values, or fails to change, it must be renewed.

Refitting

9 Refitting is a reversal of removal, however observe the correct tightening torque.

Throttle valve positioner

Note: *The throttle valve positioner is incorporated in the throttle body and is not available as a separate part.*

Roadspeed sensor

Removal and refitting

10 The roadspeed sensor is fitted into the back of the gearbox. Refer to Chapter 7A for the removal and refitting procedure. Any fault

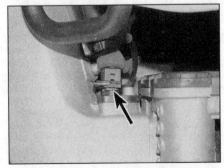

3.6 The inlet manifold air temperature sensor is fitted near the throttle body

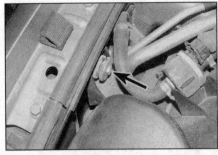

2.5 Unscrew the bolt (arrowed) and remove the air cleaner body from the engine compartment

2.6b . . . and remove the air duct from between the air cleaner and throttle body

with the sensor must be checked by a VW dealer, and if necessary renewed.

Coolant temperature sensor

Removal

11 The coolant temperature sensor is located on the rear of the cylinder head on all engines.

12 Drain approximately one quarter of the coolant from the engine with reference to Chapter 1A.

13 Disconnect the wiring from the sensor.

14 Unscrew the sensor or extract the retaining clip and remove the sensor. Recover the sealing washer/O-ring. A handheld diagnostic instrument will be required to test the sensor, and it may be necessary to take the car to a VW dealer.

Refitting

15 Refitting is a reversal of removal, but fit a new washer/O-ring. Where applicable, tighten the sensor securely. Refer to Chapter 1A and top-up the cooling system.

Engine speed sensor

Removal

16 The engine speed sensor is mounted on the rear, left-hand side of the cylinder block, adjacent to the mating surface of the block and transmission bellhousing, just behind the oil filter.

17 If necessary, drain the engine oil and remove the oil filter and cooler to improve access with reference to Chapter 1A.

18 Unplug the harness connector from the sensor.

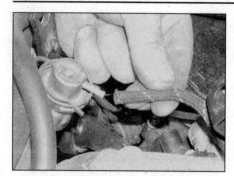

3.28 Disconnect the vacuum hose from the fuel pressure regulator

3.30 Fuel supply line union (arrowed)

Fuel injectors and fuel rail

Removal

27 Disconnect the battery negative (earth) lead (see Chapter 5A). Undo the retaining bolts and remove the engine top cover.
28 Disconnect the vacuum hose from the fuel pressure regulator on the fuel rail **(see illustration)**.
29 Temporarily remove the fuel tank filler cap and refit it in order to release any pressure/vacuum.
30 Wrap some rag around the fuel supply line union located over the fuel rail **(see illustration)**, and also place a suitable container beneath the union to catch any spilt fuel. Unscrew the union nut while holding the union bolt with another spanner, and allow the fuel to drain into the container. Remove the rag.
31 Unscrew the return union and disconnect the return fuel line.
32 Disconnect the wiring from each of the injectors. Label the wiring to aid correct refitting later.
33 Disconnect the wiring from the Hall sender.
34 Unscrew the mounting bolts, then carefully lift the fuel rail together with the injectors from the inlet manifold **(see illustrations)**.
35 With the assembly on the bench, pull out the clips and release each of the injectors from the fuel rail. Recover the O-ring seals **(see illustrations)**.

3.34a Unscrew the mounting bolts . . .

3.34b . . . and remove the fuel rail with injectors from the inlet manifold

19 Unscrew the retaining bolt and withdraw the sensor from the cylinder block.

Refitting

20 Refitting is a reversal of removal. Tighten the securing bolt to the specified torque.

Throttle body/control unit

Note: *In order for a new throttle body/control unit to function correctly, it must be matched to the engine management ECU using a dealer scan tool.*

Removal

21 Loosen the clips and detach the air cleaner air ducting from the throttle body.
22 Unplug the harness connector from the throttle body.
23 Note their fitted locations, disconnect the vacuum and coolant hoses (where fitted) from

the throttle body. Where necessary release the wiring harness from the guide clip.
24 Unscrew and remove the securing bolts, then lift the throttle body/control unit away from the inlet manifold. Recover and discard the seal.
25 Further dismantling of the throttle body is not recommended. No parts are available separately. If any part of the throttle body is defective, the completely assembly must be renewed.

Refitting

26 Refitting is a reversal of removal, noting the following:
 a) Use a new throttle body-to-inlet manifold seal.
 b) Ensure that all vacuum hoses, coolant hoses (where applicable) and electrical connectors are refitted securely.

Refitting

36 Refit the injectors and fuel rail by following the removal procedure in reverse, noting the following points:
 a) Renew the injector O-ring seals, and smear them with a little clean engine oil before fitting them. When fitting the front O-ring, do not remove the plastic cap from the head of the injector but leave it in position and lift the O-ring over it.
 b) Ensure that the injector retaining clips are securely seated.
 c) Check that the fuel supply and return lines are reconnected correctly. Check the sealing washers and if necessary renew them.
 d) Check that all vacuum and electrical

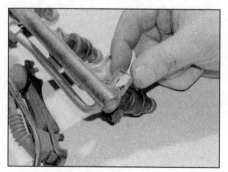

3.35a Pull out the clip . . .

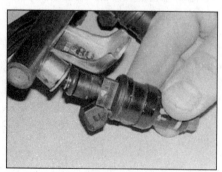

3.35b . . . and withdraw the injectors from the fuel rail

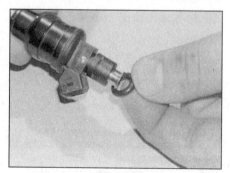

3.35c Remove the O-ring from the injectors

connections are remade correctly and securely.
e) *Reconnect the battery as described in Chapter 5A.*
f) *On completion, start the engine and check for fuel leaks.*

Fuel pressure regulator

Removal

37 Undo the securing bolts and remove the engine top cover. Depressurise the fuel system as described in Section 8.
38 Disconnect the vacuum hose from the pressure regulator **(see illustration)**.
39 Place a cloth rag beneath the regulator to catch any spilt fuel.
40 Pull out the retaining spring clip, then lift the regulator from the fuel rail. Recover the O-ring seals.

Refitting

41 Refit the fuel pressure regulator by following the removal procedure in reverse, but renew the O-ring seals and ensure that the regulator retaining clip is secure.

Hall sender

Removal

42 Remove the timing belt outer cover with reference to Chapter 2A.
43 Release the clip and disconnect the wiring multiplug from the Hall sender **(see illustration)**.
44 Unscrew the mounting bolts and withdraw the Hall sender from the front of the cylinder head. Recover the gasket.

Refitting

45 Refitting is a reversal of removal, but renew the gasket and tighten the mounting bolts securely.

Oxygen sensors

Removal

46 On all engines covered in this Manual, the two oxygen sensors are located at each end of the catalytic converter on the right-hand side of the engine. One is located on the front-top of the catalytic converter, and one on the rear-top of the catalytic converter. On the ALT non-turbocharged engine, the catalytic converter is attached to the rear of the exhaust

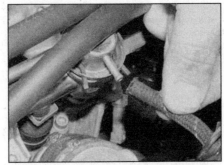

3.38 Disconnect the vacuum hose from the pressure regulator

manifold. On the turbocharged AWT engine, it is attached to the rear of the turbocharger.
47 The wiring connector for the oxygen sensors is located on the left-hand side of the bulkhead, beneath the coolant expansion tank. Undo the tank mounting screws and disconnect the low coolant wiring, then position the tank to one side. **Do not** disconnect any of the coolant hoses from the tank. Disconnect the oxygen sensor wiring and release the cables from the plastic ties.
48 Unscrew and remove the sensor, taking care to avoid damaging the sensor probe as it is removed. **Note:** *As the wiring flying lead remains connected to the sensor, a special slotted socket needs to be used to remove the sensor.*

Refitting

49 Apply a little anti-seize grease to the sensor threads, but avoid contaminating the probe tip. **Note:** *New oxygen sensors may be supplied with fitting paste on the threads.*
50 Refit the sensor and tighten it to the correct torque.
51 Reconnect the wiring and secure with the plastic ties.

Electronic control unit (ECU)

Caution: The ECU is programmed and identified specifically for the vehicle it is fitted to, and the identity coding must be tranferred to any new unit. This process requires the use of dedicated instruments only available to VW dealers. For this reason, it is recommended that ECU renewal is carried out by a VW dealer,

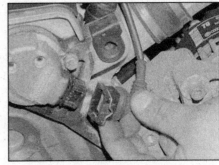

3.43 Disconnect the wiring from the Hall sensor

however removal and refitting of the original ECU is possible by the home mechanic. Note also that if the ECU is renewed, the identification of the new ECU must be transferred to the immobiliser control unit by a VW dealer or specialist. Caution: Always wait at least 30 seconds after switching off the ignition before disconnecting the wiring from the ECU. When the wiring is disconnected, all the learned values may be erased, although any contents of the fault memory are retained. After reconnecting the wiring, the vehicle must be driven for several miles so that the ECU can learn its basic settings. If the engine still runs erratically, the basic settings may be reinstated by a VW dealer or specialist using a special test instrument.

Removal

52 The electronic control unit is located on the bulkhead at the rear of the engine compartment. On RHD models it is on the right-hand side, and on LHD models it is on the left-hand side.
53 Disconnect the battery negative (earth) lead (see Chapter 5A).
54 Undo the screws and lift off the cover **(see illustrations)**. **Note:** *On early LHD models, a hole is provided in the cowl panel for access to the rear mounting bolt, however on later models it is necessary to unclip the cowl panel for access to the bolt.*
55 Release the spring retainer with a screwdriver and lift up the electronic control unit **(see illustrations)**.

3.54a Undo the screws . . .

3.54b . . . and lift off the ECU cover

3.55a Release the spring retainer . . .

3.55b ... to release the ECU

56 Prise open the clip and release the wiring connector from the ECU.

> ⚠ **Warning: Wait a minimum of 30 seconds after switching off the ignition, before disconnecting the ECU wiring connector.**

57 Withdraw the ECU from the bulkhead.

Refitting

58 Refitting is a reversal of removal, but press the clip down until it snaps into position **(see illustration)**. Reconnect the battery as described in Chapter 5A. Note that the vehicle must be driven for several miles so that the ECU can learn its basic settings. In order to store its learnt values (and faults where present), the ECU continues to be supplied with voltage for up to 15 minutes via the supply relay terminal 87. Once this period is finished, the ECU disconnects the earth wire via contact 21 terminal.

4 Simos engine management components – removal and refitting

Note: *Observe the precautions in Section 1 before working on any component in the fuel system. The ignition must be switched off at all times.*

Airflow meter

Removal

1 Disconnect the battery negative (earth) lead (see Chapter 5A). Also undo the retaining bolts and remove the engine top cover where necessary.

3.58 Press down firmly on the ECU retaining clip

2 With reference to Section 2, slacken the clips and disconnect the air ducting from the airflow meter, at the rear of the air cleaner housing.
3 Unplug the harness connector from the airflow meter.
4 Remove the retaining screws and extract the meter from the air cleaner housing. Recover the O-ring seal.
Caution: Handle the airflow meter carefully – its internal components are easily damaged.

Refitting

5 Refitting is a reversal of removal. Renew the O-ring seal if it appears damaged.

Throttle valve potentiometer

6 The throttle valve potentiometer is an integral part of the throttle body – refer to the information in the relevant sub-Section.

Air temperature sensor

7 The sensor is incorporated into the airflow meter, and is not available as a separate part.

Roadspeed sensor

8 The roadspeed sensor is mounted on the transmission – refer to Chapter 7A.

Coolant temperature sensor

Removal

9 The coolant temperature sensor is mounted in the coolant outlet elbow on the rear of the cylinder head. Undo the retaining bolts and remove the engine top cover where necessary.
10 Disconnect the wiring from the sensor.
11 Refer to Chapter 1A, and drain approximately one quarter of the coolant from the engine.
12 Extract the retaining clip and lift the sensor from the coolant elbow – be prepared for an amount of coolant loss. Recover the O-ring. The sensor can be tested using a multimeter. Connect the multimeter leads to the terminals of the sensor and set the meter to measure resistance (ohms). As the temperature increases, the resistance of the sensor decreases. So at 30°C the resistance should be 1500 to 2000 ohms, and at 80°C the resistance should be 275 to 375 ohms. If the resistance value of the sensor does not match these values, or fails to change, it must be renewed.

Refitting

13 Refit the sensor by reversing the removal procedure, using a new O-ring. Refer to Chapter 1A and top-up the cooling system.

Engine speed sensor

Removal

14 The engine speed sensor is mounted on the rear, left-hand side of the cylinder block, adjacent to the mating surface of the block and transmission bellhousing, just behind the oil filter. If necessary, drain the engine oil

and remove the oil filter and cooler to improve access with reference to Chapter 1A.
15 Unplug the harness connector from the sensor.
16 Unscrew the retaining bolt and withdraw the sensor from the cylinder block. The sensor can be tested using a multimeter. Connect the multimeter to the outer pins of the sensor connector and set the meter to measure resistance (ohms). A reading of 730 to 1000 ohms indicates that the sensor is serviceable.

Refitting

17 Refitting is a reversal of removal.

Throttle body

Note: *In order for a new throttle body assembly to function correctly, it must be matched to the engine management ECU using a dealer scan tool. On automatic transmission models, it must also be adapted for the transmission.*

Removal

18 Slacken the clips and detach the inlet air ducting from the throttle body.
19 Unplug the harness connector from the throttle positioning valve module.
20 Disconnect the vacuum hose from the port on the throttle body, then release the wiring harness from the guide clip.
21 Refer to Chapter 1A, and drain approximately one quarter of the coolant from the engine. Slacken the clips and disconnect the coolant hoses from the ports on the throttle body, making a careful note of their fitted positions.
22 Disconnect the charcoal filter emission control system vacuum hose from the port on the throttle body.
23 Unscrew and remove the bolts, then lift the throttle body away from the inlet manifold. Recover and discard the gasket.

Refitting

24 Refitting is a reversal of removal, noting the following:
a) Use a new throttle body-to-inlet manifold gasket.
b) Ensure that all the vacuum hoses and electrical connectors are refitted securely.
c) Refer to Chapter 1A and top-up the cooling system.

Fuel injectors and fuel rail

Note: *In order for new injectors to function correctly, the existing injector 'learnt' values stored in the engine management ECU must be erased using a dealer scan tool. Failure to do so could cause erratic engine performance, and reduced efficiency.*

Removal

25 Disconnect the battery negative (earth) lead (see Chapter 5A). Undo the retaining bolts and remove the engine top cover where necessary.
26 Disconnect the vacuum hose from the fuel pressure regulator on the fuel rail.
27 Temporarily remove the fuel tank filler cap and refit it in order to release any pressure.

28 Wrap some rag around the fuel supply line union located over the fuel rail, and also place a suitable container beneath the union to catch any spilt fuel. Unscrew the union nut while holding the union bolt with another spanner, and allow the fuel to drain into the container. Remove the rag.

29 Unscrew the return union and disconnect the return fuel line.

30 Disconnect the wiring from each of the injectors. Label the wiring to aid correct refitting later.

31 Unscrew the mounting bolts, then carefully lift the fuel rail together with the injectors from the inlet manifold.

32 With the assembly on the bench, pull out the clips and release each of the injectors from the fuel rail. Recover the O-ring seals.

Refitting

33 Refit the injectors and fuel rail by following the removal procedure in reverse, noting the following points:

a) Renew the injector O-ring seals if they appear worn or damaged.

b) Ensure that the injector retaining clips are securely seated.

c) Check that the fuel supply and return hoses are reconnected correctly. Check the sealing washers and if necessary renew them.

d) Check that all vacuum and electrical connections are remade correctly and securely.

e) Reconnect the battery (Chapter 5A).

f) On completion, start the engine and check for fuel leaks.

Fuel pressure regulator

Note: *In order for new fuel pressure regulator to function correctly, the existing 'learnt' values stored in the engine management ECU must be erased using a dealer scan tool. Failure to do so could cause erratic engine performance, and reduced efficiency.*

Removal

34 Undo the retaining bolts and remove the engine top cover where necessary, then depressurise the fuel system as described in Section 9.

35 Disconnect the vacuum hose from the pressure regulator.

36 Place a cloth rag beneath the regulator to catch any spilt fuel.

37 Pull out the retaining spring clip, then lift the regulator from the fuel rail. Recover the O-ring seals.

Refitting

38 Refit the fuel pressure regulator by following the removal procedure in reverse, but renew the O-ring seals and ensure that the regulator retaining clip is secure.

Hall sender

Removal

39 Remove the camshaft sprocket with reference to Chapter 2A.

40 Note the location of the Hall sender and if necessary mark it in relation to the cylinder head. Disconnect the wiring from the sender.

41 Unbolt the rear timing cover from the cylinder head.

42 Unscrew the remaining bolts and remove the Hall sender from the cylinder head.

Refitting

43 Refitting is a reversal of removal, but make sure that the sender base plate is central before tightening the retaining bolts.

Oxygen sensors

Note: *In order for a new oxygen sensor to function correctly, the existing sensor 'learnt' values stored in the engine management ECU must be erased using a dealer scan tool. Failure to do so could cause erratic engine performance, and reduced efficiency.*

Removal

44 The two oxygen sensors are located at the front and rear of the catalytic converter.

45 The wiring connector for the oxygen sensors is located on the left-hand side of the bulkhead, beneath the coolant expansion tank.

46 Undo the tank mounting screws and disconnect the low coolant wiring, then position the tank to one side. **Do not** disconnect any of the coolant hoses from the tank. Disconnect the oxygen sensor wiring and release the cables from the plastic ties.

47 Unscrew and remove the sensor, taking care to avoid damaging the sensor probe as it is removed. **Note:** *As the wiring flying lead remains connected to the sensor, a special slotted socket needs to be used to remove the sensor.*

Refitting

48 Apply a little anti-seize grease to the sensor threads, but avoid contaminating the probe tip. **Note:** *New oxygen sensors may be supplied with fitting paste on the threads.*

49 Refit the sensor and tighten it to the correct torque.

50 Reconnect the wiring and secure with the plastic ties.

Electronic control unit (ECU)

Caution: *The ECU is programmed and identified specifically for the vehicle it is fitted to, and the identity coding must be tranferred to any new unit. This process requires the use of dedicated instruments only available to VW dealers. For this reason, it is recommended that ECU renewal is carried out by a VW dealer, however removal and refitting of the original ECU is possible by the home mechanic. Note also that if the ECU is renewed, the identification of the new ECU must be transferred to the immobiliser control unit by a VW dealer or specialist.*

Caution: *Always wait at least 30 seconds after switching off the ignition before disconnecting the wiring from the ECU.*

When the wiring is disconnected, all the learned values may be erased, although any contents of the fault memory are retained. After reconnecting the wiring, the vehicle must be driven for several miles so that the ECU can learn its basic settings. If the engine still runs erratically, the basic settings may be reinstated by a VW dealer or specialist using a special test instrument.

Removal

51 The electronic control unit is located on the bulkhead at the rear of the engine compartment. On RHD models it is on the right-hand side, and on LHD models it is on the left-hand side.

52 Disconnect the battery negative (earth) lead (see Chapter 5A).

53 Undo the screws and lift off the cover. **Note:** *On early LHD models, a hole is provided in the cowl panel for access to the rear mounting bolt, however on later models it is necessary to unclip the cowl panel for access to the bolt.*

54 Release the spring retainer and lift up the electronic control unit.

55 Prise open the clip and release the wiring connector from the ECU.

⚠ **Warning: Wait a minimum of 30 seconds after switching off the ignition, before disconnecting the ECU wiring connector.**

56 Withdraw the ECU from the bulkhead.

Refitting

57 Refitting is a reversal of removal. Reconnect the battery as described in Chapter 5A. Note that the vehicle must be driven for several miles so that the ECU can learn its basic settings. In order to store its learnt values (and faults where present), the ECU continues to be supplied with voltage for approximately 40 seconds via the supply relay terminal 23. Once this period is finished, the ECU disconnects the supply via the voltage supply relay J363.

5 Fuel filter – renewal

Note: *Observe the precautions in Section 1 before working on fuel system components.*

1 The fuel filter is situated underneath the rear of the vehicle, in front of the fuel tank (**see illustration**). To gain access to the filter, chock the front wheels, then jack up the rear of the vehicle and support it securely on axle stands.

2 Depressurise the fuel system with reference to Section 8.

3 If available, fit hose clamps to the filter inlet and outlet hoses. These are not essential, but even with the system depressurised, there will still be an amount of petrol in the pipes (and the old filter), and this will drain out when the pipes are disconnected. Even with hose clamps fitted, the old filter will contain some

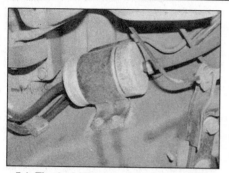

5.1 The fuel filter is located underneath the rear of the vehicle

fuel, so have some rags ready to soak up any spillage.

4 Loosen the hose clips and detach the hoses from the filter. If crimp-type clips are used, discard them and fit worm-type clips when reassembling. Similarly, if the fuel hoses show any sign of perishing or cracking, particularly at the hose ends or where the hose enters the metal end fitting, renew the hoses.

5 Before removing the filter, note the direction-of-flow marking on the filter body, and check against the new filter – the arrow should point in the direction of fuel flow (towards the front of the car).

6 It may be possible to slide the filter from the mounting at this stage, but if it is tight unbolt the mounting from the underbody and remove the filter on the bench.

7 Fit the new filter into position, with the flow marking arrow correctly orientated. With the filter located in the mounting, insert and tighten the mounting bolts.

8 Reconnect the fuel hoses using new clips if necessary. Ensure that no dirt is allowed to enter the hoses or filter connections. Remove the hose clamps.

9 Start the engine noting that there may be a delay as the system repressurises and the new filter fills with fuel. Let the engine run for several minutes while you check the filter hose connections for leaks, then switch it off.

 Warning: Dispose the old filter safely; it will be highly flammable, and may explode if thrown on a fire.

6 Fuel pump and gauge sender unit – removal and refitting

Note: Observe the precautions in Section 1 before working on fuel system components. A special VW tool is required to unscrew the inner section of the baffle housing.
Caution: The fuel tank must not be more than half full when carrying out this work.

Removal

1 The fuel pump and gauge sender unit are combined in one assembly, mounted in the fuel tank. Access is via a hatch provided in the load space floor. Removal of the unit exposes the contents of the tank to the atmosphere, so extreme care must be exercised to prevent fire. The area inside and around the car must be well-ventilated to prevent a build-up of fuel fumes. If possible, remove the unit when the fuel tank is nearly empty, or alternatively syphon the fuel from the tank into a suitable container.

2 Ensure that the vehicle is parked on a level surface, then disconnect the battery negative (earth) lead (see Chapter 5A).

3 Depressurise the fuel system as described in Section 8.

4 Refer to Chapter 11, Section 33, and remove the trim from the load space floor.

5 Slacken and remove the access hatch screws and lift the hatch away from the floorpan **(see illustration)**.

6 Unplug the wiring connector from the pump/sender unit **(see illustration)**.

7 Place rags beneath the fuel hoses to catch spilt fuel. Depress the retaining circlips and disconnect the fuel supply and return hoses **(see illustration)**. Identify each hose for position. Also release the pipes from the clips on the support ring.

8 Note the location of the arrows and support ring, then unscrew the plastic ring securing the pump/sender unit in the tank. VW technicians use a special tool to unscrew the ring, however two screwdrivers engaged with the slots in the ring and crossed over each other may be used with success. Alternatively use a pair of large water pump pliers **(see illustrations)**.

6.5 Remove the access hatch to expose the fuel tank aperture cap

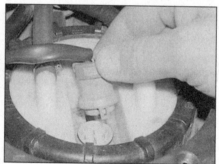

6.6 Disconnect the wiring plug

6.7 Disconnect the fuel supply and return hoses

6.8a Note the alignment screws

6.8b Use a large pair of water pump pliers to loosen the plastic ring

6.8c Remove the plastic ring

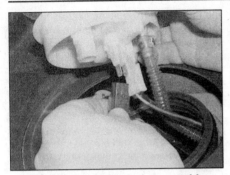

6.10 Disconnect the fuel gauge wiring from the underside of the flange

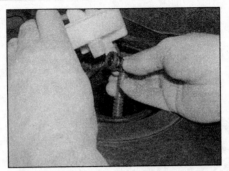

6.11 Disconnect the fuel return pipe from the underside of the flange

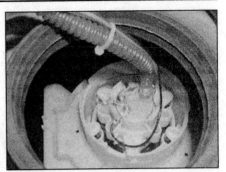

6.12 View of the baffle housing inner section through the top of the fuel tank

9 Remove the flange and seal from the fuel tank aperture.

10 Disconnect the fuel gauge sender wiring and release it from the inside of the flange **(see illustration)**.

11 Squeeze the ferrule and pull the fuel return pipe from the bottom of the flange **(see illustration)**.

12 Turn the inner section of the baffle housing anti-clockwise approximately 15°, then lift out the fuel pump together with the inner section of the baffle housing **(see illustration)**. VW technicians use a special tool which engages the cut-outs in the top of the fuel pump, and it is recommended that this tool is obtained if at all possible. It may be possible to use an alternative tool, however the plastic is quite flexible and may be broken easily. If the fuel pump is to be renewed, drain all fuel from the old unit. The flange may be removed from the fuel pump if necessary by loosening the clip and disconnecting the intermediate supply pipe, however, note the fitted position of the pipe to ensure correct refitting.

13 To remove the fuel gauge sender, reach inside the fuel tank and depress the retaining tab on the side of the baffle housing. Carefully lift out the sender **(see illustrations)**.

14 Inspect the float on the sender unit swinging arm for punctures and fuel ingress, and renew it if it appears damaged. Inspect the rubber seal from the fuel tank aperture and renew it if necessary. Inspect the sender unit wiper and track; clean off any dirt and debris that may have accumulated and look for breaks in the track.

Refitting

15 Insert the fuel gauge sender in the baffle housing and press it down until it engages the retaining clip.

16 If the flange was removed from the fuel pump, reconnect the intermediate supply pipe and tighten the clip. Position the pipe **(see illustration)**.

17 Insert the fuel pump and inner baffle housing in the outer baffle housing so that the notch in the upper edge is aligned with the first mark on the housing. Using the spanner, push the fuel pump/housing down and turn it clockwise until it is aligned with the second mark on the housing.

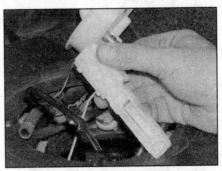

6.13a Remove the fuel gauge sender from the fuel tank

18 Reconnect the fuel return pipe to the bottom of the flange.

19 Attach the fuel gauge sender wiring to the inside of the flange, and reconnect it to the bottom of the flange. The wiring must be wrapped once around the fuel return pipe.

20 Smear the new rubber seal with clean fuel, then locate it on the flange and refit the flange in the tank aperture.

21 Refit the support ring, then screw on and tighten the plastic ring. To ensure the alignment arrows are opposite each other

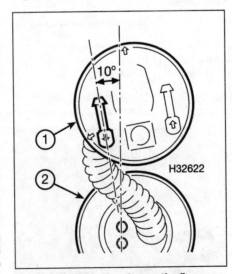

6.16 Position the pipe on the flange

1 Flange
2 Inner section of baffle housing

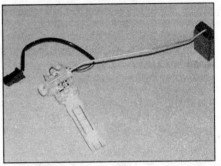

6.13b Fuel gauge sender removed from the fuel tank

when the ring is fully tight, turn the flange slightly anti-clockwise while the ring is being tightened.

22 Reconnect the fuel supply and return hoses.

23 Reconnect the wiring connector to the pump/sender unit.

24 Refit the access hatch and tighten the screws.

25 Refit the trim to the load space floor.

26 Reconnect the battery negative (earth) lead (see Chapter 5A).

7 Fuel tank – removal and refitting

Note: *Observe the precautions in Section 1 before working on fuel system components.*

Removal

1 Before the tank can be removed, it must be drained of as much fuel as possible. As no drain plug is provided, it is preferable to remove the tank when it is nearly empty. Alternatively, syphon or hand-pump the fuel from the tank into a suitable safe container **(see illustration overleaf)**.

2 Disconnect the battery negative (earth) lead (see Chapter 5A).

3 Refer to Chapter 11, Section 33, and remove the trim from the load space floor.

4 Slacken and remove the access hatch screws and lift the hatch away from the floorpan.

5 Unplug the wiring connector from the pump/sender unit. **Do not** disconnect the

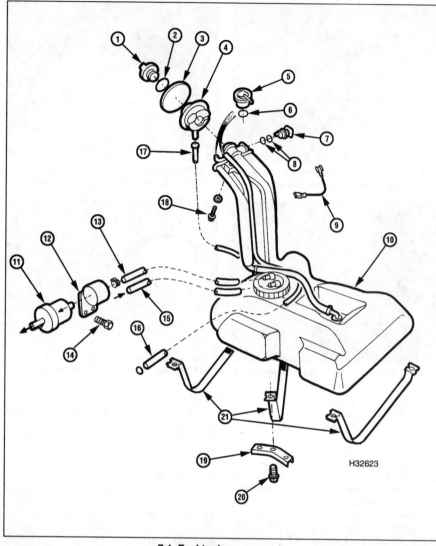

7.1 Fuel tank components

1 Filler cap	9 Earth lead	16 Breather pipe to activated
2 Gasket	10 Fuel tank	charcoal canister
3 Retaining ring	11 Fuel filter	17 Overflow hose
4 Rubber cap	12 Mounting bracket	18 Bolt
5 Gravity valve	13 Fuel feed from fuel rail	19 Bracket
6 O-ring seal	14 Bolt	20 Bolt
7 Vent valve	15 Fuel return from fuel	21 Fuel tank mounting
8 O-ring seals	rail	straps

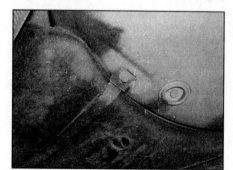

7.13a Fuel tank rear mounting . . .

7.13b . . . and front mounting

fuel supply and return hoses as they are disconnected later on the underbody in front of the fuel tank.

6 Chock the front wheels, then jack up the rear of the vehicle and support on axle stands (see *Jacking and vehicle support*). Remove the right-hand rear roadwheel.

7 Remove the right-hand rear wheel arch liner with reference to Chapter 11.

8 Open the fuel tank filler flap and wipe clean the area around the filler neck. Unscrew the bolts and remove the tank flap unit and rubber cup.

9 Unscrew the bolt securing the filler neck and protection plate to the body. Note that the bolt also secures the earth wire.

10 On models with engine code AWT, remove the rear underbody splash guard from in front of the rear axle.

11 On all models, disconnect the fuel supply hose from the fuel filter inlet. At the front of the tank, identify the positions of the return hose, and the fuel evaporative carbon canister hose on the underbody. Loosen the clips and disconnect the hoses. Be prepared for some loss of fuel by placing a suitable container beneath the tank. Tape over or plug the hoses to prevent entry of dust and dirt.

12 Support the fuel tank with a trolley jack and piece of wood.

13 Mark the positions of the support straps to ensure correct refitting, then unbolt and remove them **(see illustrations)**. Note the position of the earth cable on the rearmost mounting.

14 With the help of an assistant, lower the fuel tank to the ground and remove from under the vehicle.

15 If the tank is contaminated with sediment or water, remove the fuel pump/sender unit (see Section 6) and swill the tank out with clean fuel. The tank is injection moulded from a synthetic material and if damaged, it should be renewed. However, in certain cases it may be possible to have small leaks or minor damage repaired by a suitable specialist.

Refitting

16 Refitting is the reverse of the removal procedure noting the following points:

a) When lifting the tank back into position take care to ensure none of the hoses get trapped between the tank and vehicle underbody.

b) Ensure that all pipes and hoses are correctly routed and secured.

c) It is important that the earth cable is correctly refitted to the strap and filler neck. Connect an ohmmeter between the metal ring on the filler neck and a bare metal part of the body, and check that the reading is zero resistance.

d) Tighten the tank retaining strap bolts.

e) On completion, refill the tank with fuel and thoroughly check for signs of leakage prior to taking the vehicle out on the road.

f) Reconnect the battery as described in Chapter 5A.

8 Fuel injection system – depressurisation

Note: *Observe the precautions in Section 1 before working on fuel system components.*

⚠️ **Warning: The following procedure will merely relieve the pressure in the fuel system – remember that fuel will still be present in the system components and take precautions accordingly before disconnecting any of them. Before working on the fuel system components, it is recommended that fuse 28 is removed, otherwise the fuel pump can be activated by the door contact switch.**

1 The fuel system referred to in this Section comprises the tank-mounted fuel pump and sender, the fuel filter, the fuel rail and injectors, the fuel pressure regulator and the metal pipes and flexible hoses of the fuel lines between these components. All these contain fuel which will be under pressure while the engine is running, while the ignition is switched on, or if a door contact switch is operated. The pressure will remain for some time after the ignition has been switched off and must be relieved before any of these components are disturbed for servicing work.

2 Disconnect the battery negative (earth) lead (see Chapter 5A).

3 Open the fuel filler flap and briefly remove the filler cap to relieve any pressure in the fuel tank. Refit the cap.

4 Where applicable, undo the retaining bolts and remove the engine top cover.

5 Place some cloth rags beneath the fuel supply pipe union located over the fuel rail on the inlet manifold. Also wrap a cloth around the union.

6 Using two spanners, loosen the union nut and release the fuel pressure. Leave the union nut loose and the rags in position while working on the fuel system.

7 On completion of the work, tighten the union nut using the two spanners.

9 Inlet manifold – removal and refitting

Note: *Observe the precautions in Section 1 before working on fuel system components.*

Removal

1 Disconnect the battery negative (earth) lead (see Chapter 5A).

2 Where applicable, undo the retaining bolts, and remove the engine top cover(s).

3 Drain the cooling system as described in Chapter 1A. Alternatively on non-turbo models, fit hose clamps to the two hoses leading to the throttle body.

4 If the coolant has been drained, loosen the clips and disconnect the two coolant hoses

9.15 Remove the support bracket from the inlet manifold

from the coolant expansion tank located on the left-hand side of the engine.

5 Undo the screws and lift the expansion tank, then disconnect the wiring from the low level warning switch. Remove the tank from the engine compartment. Where the coolant has not been drained, position the tank to the rear of the engine compartment away from the inlet manifold.

6 Disconnect the wiring from the throttle body/control unit.

7 Disconnect the vacuum hose from the ACF (activated charcoal filter) valve at the inlet manifold.

8 Disconnect the brake servo vacuum hose from the inlet manifold.

9 On non-turbo models, remove the air inlet duct from between the air cleaner and throttle body/control unit, and where necessary also disconnect the crankcase breather hose. Withdraw the duct from the engine compartment.

10 On turbo models, loosen the clip and disconnect the inlet duct from the throttle body/control unit on the left-hand side of the engine.

11 Disconnect the wiring and fuel pressure regulator hose from the throttle body/control unit. If not already done so, loosen the clips and disconnect the coolant hoses from the throttle body/control unit. Remove the throttle body/control unit from the inlet manifold with reference to Sections 3 or 4.

12 Disconnect the wiring from the air temperature sensor and inlet manifold change-over valve.

13 Unscrew the fuel rail mounting bolts, then

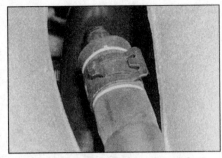

9.16 On 1.8 litre engines, the coolant hose is located between the inlet manifold branches

carefully remove the fuel rail and injectors from the inlet manifold and position to the rear of the engine compartment on a clean cloth. Where applicable, disconnect the wiring from the Hall sender on the front of the engine.

14 Unbolt the upper coolant pipe from the top of the inlet manifold, then loosen the clips and disconnect the hoses from each end of the pipe. Remove the pipe from the engine.

15 Unscrew and remove the bolts/nuts securing the support brackets to the inlet manifold. Also unscrew the nuts from the mounting rubbers **(see illustration)**.

16 Pull out the engine oil level dipstick from its tube. Where applicable, note the location of the coolant hose between the central tubes of the inlet manifold **(see illustration)**.

17 Unscrew the nuts and bolts securing the inlet manifold to the cylinder head. Withdraw the inlet manifold and recover the gasket **(see illustrations)**.

9.17a Unscrew the nuts and bolts . . .

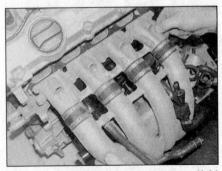

9.17b . . . then withdraw the inlet manifold from the cylinder head . . .

9.17c . . . and recover the gasket

18 The manifold is fitted with rubber connecting boots between the manifold and the manifold flange. If necessary, release the retaining clips and ease the manifold from the connecting boots. If split or damaged, the boots must be renewed.

19 Although the variable inlet manifold vacuum control element and/or control solenoid can be removed with the inlet manifold in place (by disconnecting the vacuum hoses, disconnecting the wiring plug and unscrewing the retaining screws), in order to remove the change-over barrel the inlet manifold must be removed **(see illustration)**.

Refitting

20 Refitting is the reverse of the removal procedure noting the following points:
a) *Clean the contact faces of the inlet manifold, flange and cylinder head, and fit new gaskets.*
b) *Tighten nuts and bolts to the specified torque.*
c) *Refill/top-up the cooling system with reference to Chapter 1A.*
d) *Reconnect the battery as described in Chapter 5A.*

10 Fuel injection system – testing and adjustment

1 If a fault appears in the fuel injection system first ensure that all the system wiring connectors are securely connected and free of corrosion. Then ensure that the fault is not due to poor maintenance; ie, check that the air cleaner filter element is clean, the spark plugs are in good condition and correctly gapped, the cylinder compression pressures are correct, the ignition system wiring is in good condition and securely connected and the engine breather hoses are clear and undamaged, referring to Chapters 1A, 2A and 5B.

2 If these checks fail to reveal the cause of the problem the vehicle should be taken to a VW dealer for testing. A diagnostic connector, located under a trim in the centre console under the handbrake lever handle, is incorporated in the engine management system wiring harness, into which dedicated electronic test equipment can be plugged. The test equipment is capable of 'interrogating' the engine management system ECU electronically and accessing its internal fault log (reading fault codes).

3 Fault codes can only be extracted from the ECU using a dedicated fault code reader. A VW dealer will obviously have such a reader, but they are also available from other suppliers. It is unlikely to be cost-effective for the private owner to purchase a fault code reader, but a well-equipped local garage or auto-electrical specialist will have one.

4 Using this equipment, faults can be pinpointed quickly and simply, even if their occurrence is intermittent. Testing all the system components individually in an attempt to locate the fault by elimination is a time-consuming operation that is unlikely to be fruitful (particularly if the fault occurs dynamically), and carries a high risk of damage to the ECU's internal components.

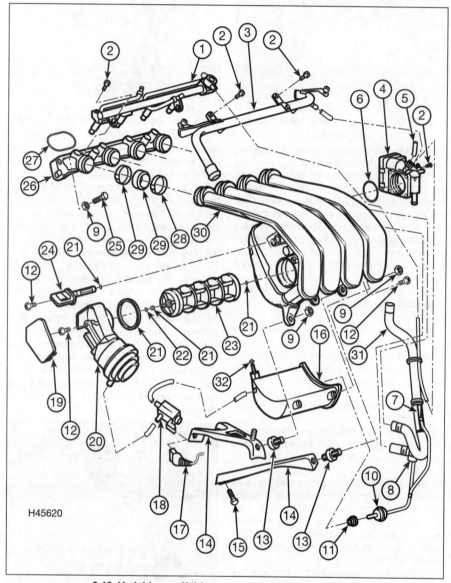

H45620

9.19 Variable manifold components (engine code ALT)

1 Fuel rail with injectors
2 Coolant pipe mounting bolts
3 Coolant pipe
4 Throttle body/control unit
5 From activated charcoal filter solenoid valve
6 Seal
7 Vacuum booster
8 Non-return valve
9 Rubber mounting nut
10 Non-return valve
11 Gasket
12 Bolt
13 Rubber mounting
14 Inlet manifold support
15 Support retaining bolt
16 Vacuum reservoir

17 Wiring connector
18 Inlet manifold change-over valve
19 Cover
20 Vacuum control element
21 O-ring
22 Spring
23 Change-over roller
24 Intake air temperature sender
25 Clamp bolt
26 Inlet connecting pipe
27 Seal
28 Clip
29 Connecting boots
30 Inlet manifold
31 From crankcase breather valve
32 Rubber bush

5 Experienced home mechanics equipped with an accurate tachometer and a carefully-calibrated exhaust gas analyser may be able to check the exhaust gas CO content and the engine idle speed; if these are found to be out of specification, then the vehicle must be taken to a suitably-equipped VW dealer for assessment. Neither the air/fuel mixture (exhaust gas CO content) nor the engine idle speed are manually adjustable; incorrect test results indicate the need for maintenance (possibly, injector cleaning) or a fault within the fuel injection system.

11 Turbocharger – general information, removal and refitting

General information

1 The turbocharger is mounted directly on the exhaust manifold. Lubrication is provided by an oil supply pipe that runs from the engine oil filter mounting. Oil is returned to the sump via a return pipe that connects to the side of the sump. Early turbocharger units incorporate a conventional wastegate valve, however later units have several internal vanes connected to a control ring; both types are controlled by a vacuum actuator diaphragm by the engine management ECU in order to vary the boost pressure applied to the inlet manifold.

2 The turbocharger's internal components rotate at a very high speed, and as such are very sensitive to contamination; a great deal of damage can be caused by small particles of dirt, particularly if they strike the delicate turbine blades.

Caution: Thoroughly clean the area around all oil pipe unions before disconnecting them, to prevent the ingress of dirt. Store dismantled components in a sealed container to prevent contamination. Cover the turbocharger air inlet ducts to prevent debris entering, and clean using lint-free cloths only.

Removal

3 Apply the handbrake, then jack up the front of the vehicle and support it on axle stands (see *Jacking and vehicle support*). Remove the engine compartment undershield.

4 Undo the retaining bolts, and remove the engine top cover where applicable.

5 Remove the air cleaner as described in Section 2.

6 On models with air conditioning, loosen the pivot and tension bolts and move the

tensioner roller upwards to release the tension on the drivebelt. Slip the drivebelt from the crankshaft, compressor and tensioner pulleys. Unbolt the compressor and tie it to one side with reference to Chapter 3. **Do not** disconnect the refrigerant lines from the compressor.

7 Unbolt and remove the turbocharger support bracket.

8 Unbolt the oil return pipe either from the turbocharger or sump and recover the gasket.

9 Loosen the clips and disconnect the air supply and feed hoses from the turbocharger.

10 Fit hose clamps to the coolant supply and return hoses on the turbocharger. Alternatively, drain the cooling system with reference to Chapter 1A.

11 Unscrew the union bolt and disconnect the coolant supply pipe. Recover the gaskets.

12 Disconnect the vacuum hose from the pressure regulating valve capsule.

13 Unscrew the bolt securing the coolant supply pipe to the pressure regulating valve bracket.

14 Unbolt the crankcase breather pipe at the cylinder head cover and heat shield.

15 Unscrew the two bolts securing the oil supply pipe to the heat shield, then remove the heat shield.

16 Loosen the clip and disconnect the coolant return pipe from the rigid pipe on the turbocharger. Leave the rigid pipe in position on the turbocharger.

17 Unscrew the union nut and disconnect the oil supply pipe. Use two spanners to do this, one to hold the adapter stationary in the turbocharger.

18 Unscrew the nuts and disconnect the exhaust front pipe/catalytic converter from the turbocharger. Push the front pipe to the rear and recover the gasket.

19 Unscrew the bolts securing the turbocharger to the exhaust manifold. Swivel the turbocharger to one side, then unscrew the union bolt and remove the coolant supply pipe and gasket. Withdraw the turbocharger from the engine compartment.

Refitting

20 Refit the turbocharger by following the removal procedure in reverse, noting the following points:

a) *Renew all gaskets.*

b) *Renew all self-locking nuts.*

c) *Before reconnecting the oil supply pipe, fill the oil gallery in the turbocharger with fresh oil using an oil can.*

d) *Tighten all nuts and bolts to the specified torque where given.*

e) *When the engine is started after refitting, allow it to idle for approximately one minute to give the oil time to circulate around the turbine shaft bearings.*

f) *Top-up and bleed the cooling system with reference to Chapter 1A.*

12 Intercooler – removal and refitting

Removal

1 Apply the handbrake, then jack up the front of the vehicle and support it on axle stands (see *Jacking and vehicle support*). Remove the engine compartment undertray.

2 The intercooler is located on the left-hand side of the engine compartment, and access to it is achieved by moving the complete front panel (the lock carrier assembly) away from the front of the car as far as possible, but without disconnecting the radiator hoses or electrical wiring. To do this, first remove the front bumper as described in Chapter 11, then unscrew the three quick-release clips from the noise insulation panel and unbolt the air duct from between the lock carrier and the air cleaner. On the left-hand side of the radiator, release the wiring from the clips. Unscrew the bolts securing the lock carrier assembly to the underbody channels, then unscrew the upper side bolts – one at the top/front of each wing, and one alongside each headlamp. Unscrew the three bolts securing each bumper guide, beneath each headlamp, and unclip them from the wings. With the help of an assistant, pull the complete assembly away from the front of the car as far as possible. VW technicians use special tools to hold the assembly, however support bars may be made out of threaded metal rod screwed into the underbody channels.

3 Loosen the clip and disconnect the top hose from the intercooler.

4 Remove the air duct from the front of the intercooler. Recover the rubber grommets.

5 Loosen the clip and disconnect the bottom hose from the intercooler.

6 Pull the bottom of the intercooler out from the mounting grommet, then unhook it from the upper mounting grommets. Withdraw it downwards from under the car. If necessary, remove the grommets from the mounting bracket.

Refitting

7 Refitting is a reversal of removal.

Notes

Chapter 4 Part B:
Fuel system – diesel

Contents

	Section number
Accelerator position sender – removal, refitting and adjustment	3
Air cleaner and inlet ducts – removal and refitting	2
Diesel engine management components – removal and refitting	7
Fuel gauge sender unit – removal and refitting	4
Fuel tank – removal and refitting	5
General information and precautions	1

	Section number
Injectors – general information, removal and refitting	6
Inlet manifold – removal and refitting	10
Inlet manifold change-over flap and valve – removal and refitting	12
Intercooler – removal and refitting	9
Tandem fuel pump – removal and refitting	11
Turbocharger – general information, removal and refitting	8

Degrees of difficulty

Easy, suitable for novice with little experience	**Fairly easy,** suitable for beginner with some experience	**Fairly difficult,** suitable for competent DIY mechanic	**Difficult,** suitable for experienced DIY mechanic	**Very difficult,** suitable for expert DIY or professional

Specifications

General

Engine code by type:*
Electronic direct injection, unit injectors, 74 kW (100 bhp) .... AVB
Electronic direct injection, unit injectors, 96 kW (130 bhp) .... AVF and AWX
Maximum engine speed .... Non-adjustable (ECU controlled)
Engine idle speed .... 820 to 900 rpm
* **Note:** *See 'Vehicle identification' for the location of the code marking on the engine.*

Fuel injectors
Injection pressure .... 180 to 2050 bar

Tandem pump
Fuel pressure at 1500 rpm .... 3.5 bar

Turbocharger
Type .... Garrett
Maximum boost pressure .... 1.7 to 2.2 bar

Torque wrench settings

	Nm	lbf ft
Accelerator pedal position sender	10	7
Camshaft position sensor	10	7
EGR pipe to exhaust manifold	25	18
EGR valve to inlet manifold	10	7
Fuel filler neck	10	7
Fuel pipe unions to injection pump and injectors	25	18
Fuel pump/sender retaining ring	80	59
Fuel tank retaining strap bolts	25	18
Heat shield to exhaust manifold	25	18
Injector rocker arm adjustment screw locknut	30	22
Inlet manifold flange housing	10	7
Inlet manifold to cylinder head*	25	18
Intercooler	10	7
Oil supply pipe to turbocharger	25	18
Pump injector clamp bolt*:		
Stage 1	12	9
Stage 2	Angle-tighten a further 270°	
Pump injector rocker shaft bolts*:		
Stage 1	20	15
Stage 2	Angle-tighten a further 90°	
Tandem pump bolts:		
Upper	20	15
Lower	10	7
Turbocharger oil return pipe to cylinder block	40	30
Turbocharger to catalytic converter	25	18
Turbocharger to exhaust manifold	25	18

* *Use new fasteners*

1 General information and precautions

General information

The fuel system consists of a rear-mounted fuel tank, an engine-bay mounted fuel filter with an integral water separator, fuel supply and return lines and four pump injectors (one for each cylinder) operated mechanically by a separate camshaft and electronically by a solenoid. The fuel is delivered to the injectors (known as 'Unit injectors') by a camshaft driven 'tandem pump' – the pump is called a 'tandem pump' as it also incorporates the brake vaccuum pump. From the pump, the fuel is channelled through a distributor pipe located within the cylinder head to the injectors. A 'roller rocker' assembly, mounted above the camshaft bearing caps, uses an extra set of camshaft lobes to compress the top of each injector once per firing cycle. This arrangement creates far higher injection pressures. The injection lobes incorporate a steep leading edge and a flat trailing edge in order to achieve high injection pressure quickly and allow good recharging. The precise timing of the pre-injection and main injection is controlled by the engine management ECU and a solenoid on each injector – in its normal open position, the solenoid effectively diverts the fuel to the tank return circuit, however, when the solenoid is activated, it closes the return to enable the fuel pressure necessary for injection to be achieved. The resultant effect of this system is improved engine torque and power output, greater combustion efficiency, and lower exhaust emissions. Because the fuel injection pressures are very high, the fuel is heated considerably, and therefore it is channelled through a cooler located on the top of the filter before it is returned to the fuel tank.

All engines are fitted with a turbocharger and an intercooler.

The direct injection fuelling system is controlled electronically by a diesel engine management system, comprising an Electronic Control Unit (ECU) and its associated sensors, actuators and wiring.

Injection timing and duration are controlled by the ECU and are dependant on engine speed, throttle position and rate of opening, inlet air flow, inlet air temperature, coolant temperature, fuel temperature, ambient pressure (altitude) and manifold depression information, received from sensors mounted on and around the engine.

On all engines, the ECU also manages the operation of the Exhaust Gas Recirculation (EGR) emission control system, the turbocharger boost pressure control system and the glow plug control system.

It should be noted that fault diagnosis of the diesel engine management system is only possible with dedicated electronic test equipment. Problems with the system's operation should therefore be referred to a VW dealer or suitably-equipped specialist for assessment. Once the fault has been identified, the removal/refitting sequences detailed in the following Sections will then allow the appropriate component(s) to be renewed as required.

Precautions

Many of the operations described in this Chapter involve the disconnection of fuel lines, which may cause an amount of fuel spillage. Before commencing work, refer to the warnings below and the information in *Safety first!* at the beginning of this manual.

⚠ *Warning: When working on any part of the fuel system, avoid direct contact skin contact with diesel fuel – wear protective clothing and gloves when handling fuel system components. Ensure that the work area is well-ventilated to prevent the build-up of diesel fuel vapour.*
* *Fuel injectors operate at extremely high pressures and the jet of fuel produced at the nozzle is capable of piercing skin, with potentially fatal results. However, note that with the pump injector system fitted to all diesel engines in this manual the injectors can only be operated when fully fitted in the cylinder head, so there is no real danger of personal injury as they cannot be operated while connected to a fuel line away from the engine (as is the case with injectors on an engine with an injector pump).*

Nevertheless, where pressure testing of the fuel system components is involved, it is highly recommended that a diesel fuel systems specialist carries out this work.
* *Under no circumstances should diesel fuel be allowed to come into contact with coolant hoses – wipe off accidental spillage immediately. Hoses that have been contaminated with fuel for an extended period should be renewed. Diesel fuel systems are particularly sensitive to contamination from dirt, air and water. Pay particular attention to cleanliness when working on any part of the fuel system, to prevent the ingress of dirt. Thoroughly clean the area around fuel unions before disconnecting them. Store dismantled components in sealed containers to prevent contamination and the formation of condensation. Only use lint-free cloths and clean fuel for component cleansing.*

2 Air cleaner and inlet ducts – removal and refitting

Removal

1 Disconnect the wiring from the airflow meter on the air cleaner cover. Also disconnect the small hose.
2 Release the wiring and hose from the clip on the air cleaner cover.
3 Loosen the clip and disconnect the air inlet duct from the air cleaner cover.
4 Release the spring clips and withdraw the air cleaner cover, then remove the filter element (see Chapter 1B for more details). Handle the airflow meter carefully, as it is a delicate component.
5 Unscrew the mounting bolt and remove the air cleaner from the right-hand side of the engine compartment **(see illustrations)**.
6 To remove the remaining ducting, apply the handbrake, then jack up the front of the vehicle and support it on axle stands (see *Jacking and vehicle support*). Remove the splash guard from under the radiator.
7 Loosen the clips and disconnect the U-shaped hose from the intercooler and air pipe on the left-hand side of the engine compartment **(see illustration)**.

2.5a Unscrew the mounting bolt and remove the air cleaner body

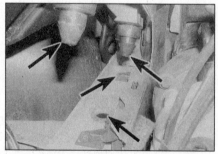

2.5b The base of the air cleaner housing has two locating lugs which engage in corresponding holes in the body (arrowed)

2.7 Loosen the clips and disconnect the hose on the left-hand side of the engine compartment

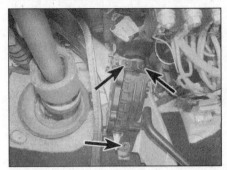

3.3 Undo the three Allen screws (arrowed) and remove the accelerator position sensor

4.4 Remove the three screws and lift away the access cover

4.5 Disconnect the wiring from the sender unit

8 Loosen the clip and disconnect the air cleaner hose from the right-hand side of the air pipe, then unbolt and remove the air pipe.

9 Loosen the clips and disconnect the rear air ducts from the intercooler and inlet manifold. Disconnect the wiring and hoses as applicable, then unscrew the mounting bolts and remove the ducts.

Refitting

10 Refitting is a reversal of removal.

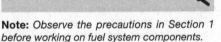

3 Accelerator position sender
– removal, refitting and adjustment

Note: *In order for a new accelerator position sender to function correctly, it must be matched to the engine management ECU using a dealer scan tool.*

Removal

1 Refer to Chapter 11, Section 29, and remove the trim panels from under the steering column area of the facia, to gain access to the pedal cluster.

2 Disconnect the wiring from the accelerator position sender.

3 Undo the three Allen bolts, and remove

the sender from its mounting bracket **(see illustration)**.

4 No further dismantling of the sender is recommended – no component parts are available. If the sender if faulty, a new one must be fitted.

Refitting

5 Position the sender on the mounting bracket, ensuring that the two locating pins engage with their corresponding holes in the bracket.

6 Insert and tighten the three Allen bolts to the specified torque. Reconnect the wiring plug, and refit the under dash trim panel.

4 Fuel gauge sender unit
– removal and refitting

Note: *Observe the precautions in Section 1 before working on fuel system components.*

Removal

1 The fuel gauge sender unit is mounted in the fuel tank. Access is via a hatch provided in the load space floor. Removal of the unit exposes the contents of the tank to the atmosphere, so extreme care must be exercised to prevent

fire. The area inside and around the car must be well-ventilated to prevent a build-up of fuel fumes. If possible, remove the unit when the fuel tank is nearly empty, or alternatively syphon the fuel from the tank into a suitable container.

2 Ensure that the vehicle is parked on a level surface, then disconnect the battery negative (earth) lead (see Chapter 5A).

3 Refer to Chapter 11, Section 33, and remove the trim from the load space floor.

4 Unscrew and remove the access hatch screws and lift the hatch away from the floorpan **(see illustration)**.

5 Unplug the wiring connector from the tank hatch **(see illustration)**.

6 Place rags beneath the fuel supply and return hoses to catch spilt fuel. Loosen the clips and disconnect the fuel supply and return hoses. Identify each hose for position **(see illustration)**.

7 Note the location of the arrows and then unscrew the plastic ring securing the tank hatch to the tank. VW technicians use a special tool to unscrew the ring, however two screwdrivers engaged with the slots in the ring and crossed over each other may be used with success. Alternatively use a pair of large water pump pliers **(see illustration)**.

4.6 The arrows moulded into the plastic by the pipe indicate whether the connection is for the supply or return hose (fuel return hose shown disconnected)

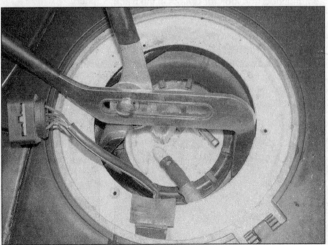

4.7 Using a pair of grips, unscrew the plastic securing ring and remove it

4.8 Disconnect the sender unit wiring plug

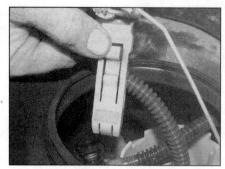

4.9a Depress the retaining clip . . .

4.9b . . . and slide the sender unit up and out of the tank

4.11a Fit a new seal to the tank aperture

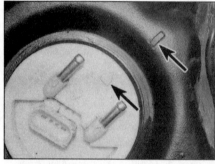

4.11b Align the sender unit marks before fitting the securing ring (arrowed)

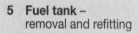

5 Fuel tank – removal and refitting

Note: *Observe the precautions in Section 1 before working on fuel system components.*

Removal

1 Before the tank can be removed, it must be drained of as much fuel as possible. As no drain plug is provided, it is preferable to remove the tank when it is nearly empty. Alternatively, syphon or hand-pump the fuel from the tank into a suitable safe container.

2 Disconnect the battery negative (earth) lead (see Chapter 5A).

3 Refer to Chapter 11, Section 33, and remove the trim from the load space floor.

4 Unscrew and remove the access hatch screws and lift the hatch away from the floorpan **(see illustration)**.

5 Unplug the wiring connector for the sender unit. **Do not** disconnect the fuel supply and return hoses.

6 Open the fuel tank filler flap and wipe clean the area around the filler neck. Using a screwdriver, carefully lever out the rubber cup around the filler neck.

7 Pull the rubber cup through the body aperture.

8 Chock the front wheels, then jack up the rear of the vehicle and support on axle stands (see *Jacking and vehicle support*). Remove the right-hand rear roadwheel.

9 Remove the right-hand rear wheel arch liner.

10 Unscrew the bolt securing the filler neck and protection plate to the body. Note that the bolt also secures the earth wire **(see illustration)**.

11 Where fitted, remove the rear underbody splash guard from in front of the rear axle (four nuts and one cross-head screw).

12 At the front of the tank, identify the positions of the supply and return hoses. Loosen the clips and disconnect the hoses. Be prepared for some loss of fuel by placing a suitable container beneath the tank **(see illustration)**.

13 Support the fuel tank with a trolley jack and piece of wood.

8 Carefully lift the fuel tank hatch and seal from the fuel tank. Disconnect the sender unit wiring plug from the hatch underside **(see illustration)**.

9 Reach inside the tank, depress the retaining clip on the side of the sender unit, and slide the unit up and out of the tank. Inspect the float on the sender unit swinging arm for punctures and fuel ingress, and renew the sender unit if it appears damaged. Inspect the rubber seal from the fuel tank aperture and renew it if necessary. Inspect the sender unit wiper and track; clean off any dirt and debris that may have accumulated and look for breaks in the track **(see illustrations)**.

Refitting

10 Insert the fuel gauge sender unit into the slot on the side of the pick-up module in the

tank. Reconnect the sender unit wiring plug to the hatch underside.

11 Position the new seal in the tank aperture, and refit the hatch into the fuel tank aligning the arrows **(see illustrations)**. Note that the seal must be fitted dry.

12 Screw on and tighten the plastic ring. To ensure the alignment arrows are opposite each other when the ring is fully tight, turn the flange slightly anticlockwise while the ring is being tightened.

13 Reconnect the fuel supply and return hoses and tighten the clips.

14 Reconnect the wiring connector to the hatch.

15 Refit the access hatch and tighten the screws.

16 Refit the trim to the load space floor.

17 Reconnect the battery negative (earth) lead (see Chapter 5A).

5.4 Undo the screws and remove the fuel tank access hatch

5.10 The filler neck is secured to the body by one bolt

14 Mark the positions of the support straps to ensure correct refitting, then unbolt and remove them **(see illustration)**.

15 With the help of an assistant, lower the fuel tank to the ground and remove from under the vehicle.

16 If the tank is contaminated with sediment or water, remove the sender unit (see Section 4) and swill the tank out with clean fuel. The tank is injection moulded from a synthetic material and if damaged, it should be renewed. However, in certain cases it may be possible to have small leaks or minor damage repaired by a suitable specialist.

Refitting

17 Refitting is the reverse of the removal procedure noting the following points:
- a) *When lifting the tank back into position take care to ensure none of the hoses get trapped between the tank and vehicle underbody.*
- b) *Ensure that all pipes and hoses are correctly routed and secured.*
- c) *Before fully tightening the fuel tank mounting strap bolts, push the fuel tank fully to the right-hand side.*
- d) *It is important that the earth cable is correctly refitted to the strap and filler neck. Connect an ohmmeter between the metal ring on the filler neck and a bare metal part of the body, and check that the reading is zero resistance.*
- e) *On completion, refill the tank with fuel and thoroughly check for signs of leakage prior to taking the vehicle out on the road.*
- f) *Reconnect the battery as described in Chapter 5A.*

6 Injectors – general information, removal and refitting

Note: *Observe the precautions in Section 1 before working on fuel system components.*

General information

1 Injectors deteriorate with prolonged use and it is reasonable to expect them to need reconditioning or renewal after 100 000 miles (160 000 km) or so. Accurate testing, overhaul and calibration of the injectors must be left to a specialist.

Removal

Note: *Take care not to allow dirt into the injectors or fuel pipes during this procedure. Do not drop the injectors or allow the needles at their tips to become damaged. The injectors are precision-made to fine limits and must not be handled roughly.*

2 With reference to Chapter 2B, remove the upper timing belt cover and camshaft cover.

3 Using a spanner or socket, turn the crankshaft pulley until the rocker arm for the injector which is to be removed is at its

5.12 Identify the fuel return and supply hoses before disconnecting them

highest, ie, the injector plunger spring is under the least amount of tension.

4 Slacken the locknut of the adjustment screw on the end of the rocker arm above the injector, and undo the adjustment screw until the rocker arm lies against the plunger pin of the injector **(see illustration)**.

5 Starting at the outside and working in, gradually and evenly slacken and remove the rocker shaft retaining bolts. Lift off the rocker shaft. Check the contact face of each adjustment screw, and renew any that show signs of wear.

6 Undo the clamping block securing bolt and remove the block from the side of the injector **(see illustration)**.

7 Using a small screwdriver, carefully prise the wiring connector from the injector.

6.4 Undo the adjustment screw until the rocker arm lies against the plunger pin of the injector

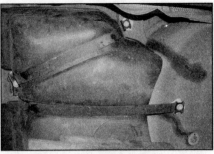

5.14 Mark the positions of the support straps to ensure correct refitting, then unbolt and remove them

8 VW technicians use a slide hammer (tool No T10055) to pull the injector from the cylinder head. This is a slide hammer which engages in the side of the injector. If this tool is not available, it is possible to fabricate an equivalent using a short section of angle-iron, a length of threaded rod, a cylindrical weight, and two locknuts. Weld/braze the rod to the angle-iron, slide the weight over the rod, and lock the two nuts together at the end of the rod to provide the stop for the weight **(see illustration)**. Seat the slide hammer/tool in the slot on the side on the injector, and pull the injector out using a few gently taps. Recover circlip, the heat shield and O-rings and discard. New ones must be used for refitting **(see illustration)**.

9 If required, the injector wiring loom/rail can

6.6 Remove the clamping block securing bolt

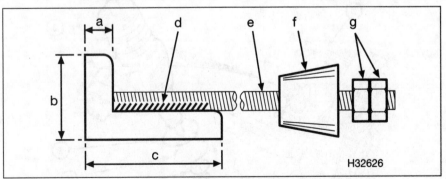

6.8a Unit injector removal tool

a 5 mm	d Weld/braze the rod to
b 15 mm	the angle-iron
c 25 mm	e Threaded rod
	f Cylindrical weight
	g Locknuts

H32626

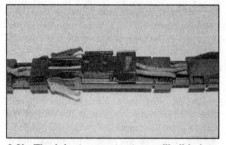

6.8b Seat the slide hammer/tool in the slot on the side on the injector, and pull the injector out

6.9a Undo the two nuts at the back of the head and slide the injector loom/rail out

6.9b The injector connectors will slide into the loom/rail to prevent them from being damaged as the assembly is withdrawn/inserted into the cylinder head

6.10 Great care must be used to ensure that the injector O-rings are fitted without being twisted

be removed from the cylinder head by undoing the two retaining nuts/bolts at the back of the head. To prevent the wiring connectors fouling the cylinder head casting as the assembly is withdrawn, insert the connectors into the storage slots in the plastic wiring rail. Carefully push the assembly to the rear, and out of the casting **(see illustrations)**.

Refitting

10 Prior to refitting the injectors, the three O-rings, heat insulation washer and clip must be renewed. Due to the high injection pressures, it is essential that the O-rings are fitted without being twisted. VW recommend the use of three special assembly sleeves to install the O-rings squarely. It may be prudent to entrust O-ring renewal to a VW dealer or suitably-equipped injection specialist, rather than risk subsequent leaks **(see illustration)**. If a new pump injector is fitted, the adjustment screw in the rocker arm must also be renewed. Whenever the pump injector is adjusted, the adjustment screw and the pump injector ball-pin must be examined for wear, and if necessary renewed.

11 After renewing the O-rings, fit the heat shield and secure it in place with the circlip **(see illustration)**.

12 Smear clean engine oil onto the O-rings, and push the injector evenly down into the cylinder head onto its stop.

13 Fit the clamping block alongside the injector, but only hand-tighten the new retaining bolt at this stage.

14 It is essential that the injectors are fitted at right-angles to the clamping block. In order to achieve this, measure the distance from the rear face of the cylinder head to the rounded section of the injector **(see illustrations)**. The dimensions (a) are as follows:

Old type solenoid valve nut
(hexagon flats same width as collar)
Cylinder 1 = 332.2 ± 0.08 mm
Cylinder 2 = 244.2 ± 0.08 mm
Cylinder 3 = 152.8 ± 0.08 mm
Cylinder 4 = 64.8 ± 0.08 mm
New type solenoid valve nut
(hexagon flats narrower than collar)
Cylinder 1 = 333.0 ± 0.08 mm
Cylinder 2 = 245.0 ± 0.08 mm
Cylinder 3 = 153.6 ± 0.08 mm
Cylinder 4 = 65.6 ± 0.08 mm

15 Once the injector(s) are aligned correctly, tighten the clamping bolt to the specified Stage one torque setting, and the Stage two angle tightening setting. **Note:** *If an injector has been*

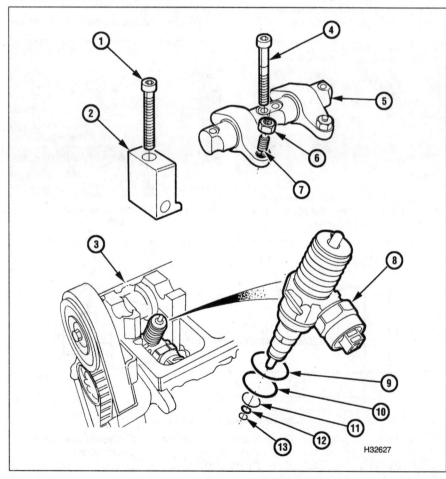

6.11 Unit injector

1	*Bolt*	*7*	*Adjuster*
2	*Clamping block*	*8*	*Unit injector*
3	*Cylinder head*	*9*	*O-ring*
4	*Bolt*	*10*	*O-ring*
5	*Rocker arm*	*11*	*O-ring*
6	*Nut*	*12*	*Heat shield*
		13	*Circlip*

H32627

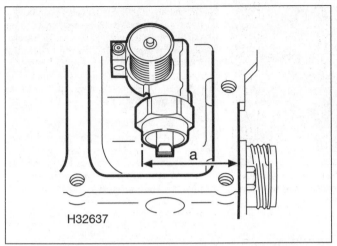

6.14a Measure the distance (a) from the rear of the cylinder head to the rounded section of the injector (old-type nut, see text)

6.14b Use a set square against the rounded edge of the injector . . .

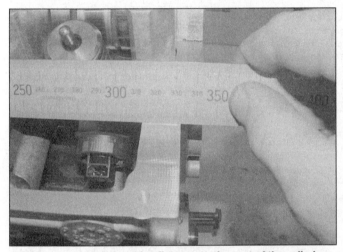

6.14c . . . and measure the distance to the rear of the cylinder head

6.17 Attach a DTI (Dial Test Indicator) gauge to the cylinder head upper surface, and position the DTI probe against the top of the adjustment screw

renewed, it is essential that the adjustment screw, locknut of the corresponding rocker and ball-pin are renewed at the same time. The ball-pins simply pull out of the injector spring cap. There is an O-ring in each spring cap to stop the ball-pins from falling out.

16 Smear some grease (VW No G000 100) onto the contact face of each rocker arm adjustment screw, and refit the rocker shaft assembly to the camshaft bearing caps, tightening the retaining bolts as follows. Starting from the inside out, hand-tighten the bolts. Again, from the inside out, tighten the bolts to the Stage one torque setting. Finally, from the inside out, tighten the bolts to the Stage two angle tightening setting.

17 The following procedure is only necessary if an injector has been removed. Attach a DTI (Dial Test Indicator) gauge to the cylinder head upper surface, and position the DTI probe against the top of the adjustment screw **(see illustration)**. Turn the crankshaft until the rocker arm roller is on the highest point of its corresponding camshaft lobe, and the

adjustment screw is at its lowest. Once this position has been established, remove the DTI gauge, screw the adjustment screw in until firm resistance is felt and the injector spring cannot be compressed further. Turn the adjustment screw **anti-clockwise** 225°, and tighten the locknut to the specified torque. Repeat this procedure for any other injectors that have been removed.

7.1 Disconnect the wiring plug (arrowed), pull out the retaining clip, and remove the coolant temperature sensor

18 Reconnect the wiring plug to the injector.
19 Refit the camshaft cover and upper timing belt cover, as described in Chapter 2B.
20 Start the engine and check that it runs correctly.

7 Diesel engine management system components – removal and refitting

Note: *Observe the precautions in Section 1 before working on the fuel system.*

Coolant temperature sensor

Removal

1 The coolant temperature sensor is located on the rear of the cylinder head **(see illustration)**. Prise out the cover caps, undo the retaining nuts/bolts and remove the engine cover.
2 Refer to Chapter 1B and drain approximately one quarter of the coolant from the engine.
3 Disconnect the wiring, pull out the retaining

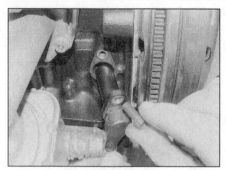

7.5 Engine speed sensor (shown with engine removed)

7.9 Disconnect the charge pressure control valve vacuum pipes, and unscrew the mounting nuts

7.14 Air intake charge pressure/ temperature sensor

clip, and remove the sensor. The sensor can be tested using a multimeter. Connect the multimeter leads to the terminals of the sensor and set the meter to measure resistance (ohms). As the temperature increases, the resistance of the sensor decreases. So at 30°C the resistance should be 1500 to 2000 ohms, and at 80°C the resistance should be 275 to 375 ohms. If the resistance value of the sensor does not match these values, or fails to change, it must be renewed.

Refitting

4 Refitting is a reversal of removal. Top-up the cooling system with reference to Chapter 1B.

Engine speed sensor

Removal

5 The engine speed sensor is mounted on the rear left-hand side of the cylinder block, adjacent to the mating surface of the block and transmission bellhousing (see illustration). Prise out the cover caps, undo the retaining nuts/bolts and remove the engine cover.

6 Trace the wiring back from the sensor to the connector and disconnect it.

7 Undo the retaining screw and withdraw the sensor from the cylinder block. The sensor can be tested using a multimeter. Connect the multimeter leads to terminals 1 (adjacent to the square side of the plug) and 2 (centre terminal) of the sensor plug, and set the meter to measure resistance (ohms). If the sensor is usable, the resistance should 450 to 550 ohms. If the sensor resistance is outside this range, renew the sensor.

7.17 Air mass meter

Refitting

8 Refitting is a reversal of removal.

Charge pressure control valve

Removal

9 The charge pressure control valve is located behind and slightly to the left of the right-hand headlight (see illustration). First disconnect the plastic air duct from the inlet duct and intermediate duct leading to the air cleaner.

10 Disconnect the wiring from the valve.

11 Remove the vacuum hoses, noting their order of connection carefully to aid correct refitting.

12 Unscrew the mounting nuts and withdraw the valve.

Refitting

13 Refitting is a reversal of removal.

Air intake charge pressure/temperature sensor

Removal

14 The air intake charge pressure/temperature sensor is located on the air duct leading from the intercooler to the inlet manifold, at the left-hand rear of the engine compartment (see illustration). First disconnect the wiring.

15 Undo the screws and remove the sensor from the air duct.

Refitting

16 Refitting is a reversal of removal.

Air mass meter

Removal

17 The air mass meter is located in the air cleaner upper cover (see illustration).

18 Disconnect the plastic air duct from the inlet duct and intermediate duct leading to the air cleaner.

19 Loosen the clip and disconnect the air inlet hose from the airflow meter.

20 Prise open the retaining clips and lift the upper cover from the air cleaner body together with the airflow meter. Disconnect the wiring from the meter and remove the assembly.

21 The airflow meter and shield may be unbolted from the upper cover and also the intermediate air duct removed. Handle the airflow meter carefully, as it is a delicate component. Recover the sealing collar.

Refitting

22 Refitting is a reversal of removal.

Electronic control unit (ECU)

Caution: Always wait at least 30 seconds after switching off the ignition before disconnecting the wiring from the ECU. When the wiring is disconnected, all the learned values may be erased, although any contents of the fault memory are retained. After reconnecting the wiring, the basic settings may be reinstated by a VW dealer or specialist using a special test instrument. Note also that if the ECU is renewed, the identification of the new ECU must be transferred to the immobiliser control unit by a VW dealer or specialist.

Removal

23 The electronic control unit is located on the bulkhead at the rear of the engine compartment (see illustration). On RHD models it is on the right-hand side, and on LHD models it is on the left-hand side.

24 Disconnect the battery negative (earth) lead (see Chapter 5A).

25 Undo the screws and lift off the cover. **Note:** *On early LHD models, a hole is provided in the cowl panel for access to the rear mounting bolt, however on later models it is necessary to unclip the cowl panel for access to the bolt.*

26 Using a screwdriver, release the spring retainer from the top of the ECU. Lift the

7.23 The ECU is located on the bulkhead at the rear of the engine compartment

electronic control unit from the mounting box for access to the wiring connector **(see illustration)**. Note: *On some models it may be necessary to remove the auxiliary relay carrier together with the auxiliary fusebox.*

27 Prise open the clip and release the wiring connector from the ECU.

 Warning: Wait a minimum of 30 seconds after switching off the ignition, before disconnecting the ECU wiring connector.

28 Withdraw the ECU from the bulkhead. If necessary, the mounting box can be removed by unscrewing the retaining nuts and releasing the peg from the location hole.

Refitting

29 Refitting is a reversal of removal. When refitting the cover, press it down firmly by hand, then progressively tighten the retaining screws. Reconnect the battery as described in Chapter 5A.

System relay and glow plug fusebox

Removal

30 The system relay is located beneath the ECU cover. First disconnect the battery negative (earth) lead (see Chapter 5A).

31 Undo the screws and lift off the cover.

32 To remove the relay, pull it directly from the fusebox. To remove the fusebox, remove the ECU (without disconnecting it), and slide the fusebox up.

Refitting

33 Refitting is a reversal of removal.

Clutch and brake pedal switches

Removal and refitting

34 The clutch and brake pedal switches send signals to the ECU which automatically adjusts the injection pump timing. Refer to Chapters 6 and 9 for information on their removal and refitting.

Fuel temperature sensor

35 The fuel temperature sensor is located in the fuel return pipe beside the fuel filter assembly on the left-hand side of the engine compartment **(see illustration)**. Clamp the fuel return hoses either side of the sensor.

36 Release the retaining clips and disconnect the hoses from the sensor. Be prepared for fuel spillage.

37 Disconnect the wiring plug from the sensor. The sensor can be tested using a multimeter. Connect the multimeter leads to the terminals of the sensor and set the meter to measure resistance (ohms). As the temperature increases, the resistance of the sensor decreases. So at 30°C the resistance should be 1500 to 2000 ohms, and at 80°C the resistance should be 275 to 375 ohms. If the resistance value of the sensor does not match these values, or fails to change, it must be renewed.

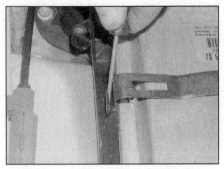

7.26 Use a screwdriver to release the spring retainer from the top of the ECU

38 Refitting is a reversal of removal.

Altitude sensor

39 The altitude sensor is built into the engine management ECU. It is not available as a separate part. If the sensor is defective, the ECU must be renewed.

Camshaft position sensor

Removal

40 With reference to Chapter 2B, remove the timing belt upper cover.

41 Undo the retaining bolt, and remove the sensor from the cylinder head.

42 Trace the sensor wiring back to the connector on the engine bulkhead and unplug.

43 Prise out the grommet in the timing belt rear cover and manoeuvre the sensor out through the hole.

Refitting

44 Refitting is a reversal of removal, noting that the sensor has a locating peg which must be fitted into the hole in the cylinder head **(see illustration)**. Tighten the sensor retaining bolt to the specified torque.

8 Turbocharger – general information, removal and refitting

General information

1 A turbocharger is fitted to all diesel engines in this Manual, and it is mounted directly on the exhaust manifold. Lubrication is provided by an oil supply pipe that runs from the engine oil filter mounting. Oil is returned to the sump by a return pipe that connects to the side of the cylinder block. The turbocharger unit has an integral wastegate valve and vacuum actuator diaphragm, which is used to control the boost pressure applied to the inlet manifold.

2 The turbocharger's internal components rotate at a very high speed, and as such are very sensitive to contamination; a great deal of damage can be caused by small particles of dirt, particularly if they strike the delicate turbine blades.

Caution: Thoroughly clean the area around

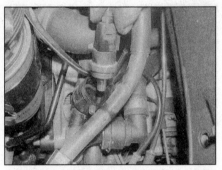

7.35 The fuel temperature sensor is in the fuel return line, beside the oil filter housing

all oil pipe unions before disconnecting them, to prevent the ingress of dirt. Store dismantled components in a sealed container to prevent contamination. Cover the turbocharger air inlet ducts to prevent debris entering, and clean using lint-free cloths only.

Removal

3 Apply the handbrake, then jack up the front of the vehicle and support it on axle stands (see *Jacking and vehicle support*). Remove the engine compartment undershield. With reference to Chapter 11, place the lock carrier in the 'service' position.

4 Prise out the cover caps, undo the retaining bolts/nuts and remove the engine top cover where applicable.

5 On models with air conditioning, loosen the pivot and tension bolts and move the tensioner roller upwards to release the tension on the drivebelt. Slip the drivebelt from the crankshaft, compressor and tensioner pulleys. Unbolt the compressor and tie it to one side with reference to Chapter 3. **Do not** disconnect the refrigerant lines from the compressor.

6 Loosen the clips and disconnect the right-hand air inlet hose. Undo the bolts/nuts and remove the exhaust manifold support bracket.

7 Unscrew the union bolt and disconnect the oil return pipe from the right-hand side of the cylinder block. Disconnect the oil return pipe from the turbocharger only **(see illustration)**. Plug or cover the pipe and aperture to prevent entry of dust and dirt.

7.44 The camshaft position sensor has a locating peg which must be fitted into the hole in the cylinder head

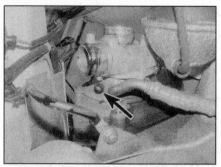

8.7 Undo the union nut and disconnect the turbocharger oil return pipe (arrowed)

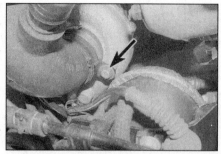

8.10 On some models, the air pipe to the turbocharger is secured by screws as well as a clip (arrowed – one hidden)

8.11 Turbocharger oil supply pipe and union nut

8.12 Vacuum pipe on the turbocharger wastegate control unit

8.13 Turbocharger-to-catalytic converter mounting nuts

9 Intercooler – removal and refitting

8 Unscrew the turbocharger-to-exhaust manifold mounting bolts but leave the two front bolts loose to support the unit.

9 Remove the air cleaner assembly as described in Section 2.

10 Loosen the clips and disconnect the front air inlet hose from the turbocharger. Note that on some engines, the inlet pipe is secured to the turbocharger by two bolts as well as clips **(see illustration)**.

11 Unscrew the union nut and disconnect the oil supply pipe from the turbocharger **(see illustration)**. Release the oil supply pipe supporting bracket from its mounting point.

12 Note the location of the vacuum hose then disconnect it from the wastegate/vane control unit **(see illustration)**.

13 Unscrew and remove the nuts securing the turbocharger to the catalytic converter **(see illustration)**.

14 Remove the last two mounting bolts, and withdraw the turbocharger from the exhaust manifold and catalytic converter. Recover the gasket.

Refitting

15 Refit the turbocharger by following the removal procedure in reverse, noting the following points:

a) Renew the gasket.

b) Renew all self-locking nuts.

c) Before reconnecting the oil supply pipe, fill the turbocharger with fresh oil using an oil can.

d) Tighten all nuts and bolts to the specified torque where given.

e) When the engine is started after refitting, allow it to idle for approximately one minute to give the oil time to circulate around the turbine shaft bearings.

Removal

1 Apply the handbrake, then jack up the front of the vehicle and support it on axle stands (see *Jacking and vehicle support*). Remove the engine compartment undertray.

2 The intercooler is located on the left-hand side of the engine compartment, and access to it is achieved by moving the complete front panel (the lock carrier assembly) away from the front of the car as far as possible, but without disconnecting the radiator hoses or electrical wiring. To do this, first remove the front bumper as described in Chapter 11, then unscrew the three quick-release clips from the noise insulation panel and unbolt the air duct from between the lock carrier and the air cleaner. On the left-hand side of the radiator, release the wiring from the clips. Remove the three bolts securing each bumper guide beneath each headlamp, and unclip them from the front wings. Unscrew the bolts securing the lock carrier/bumper bar assembly to the underbody channels, then unscrew the upper side bolts – one on the top/front of each wing, and one alongside each headlamp. With the help of an assistant, pull the complete assembly away from the front of the car as far as possible. VW technicians use special tools to hold the assembly, however support bars may be made out of threaded metal rod screwed into the underbody channels.

3 Loosen the clip and disconnect the top hose from the intercooler.

4 Remove the air duct from the front of the intercooler. Recover the rubber grommets.

5 Loosen the clip and disconnect the bottom hose from the intercooler **(see illustration)**.

6 Pull the bottom of the intercooler out from the mounting grommet, then unhook it from the upper mounting grommets. Withdraw it downwards from under the car **(see illustration)**. If necessary, remove the grommets from the mounting bracket.

Refitting

7 Refitting is a reversal of removal.

9.5 Loosen the clip and disconnect the intercooler bottom hose

9.6 Intercooler mounting bracket and grommet

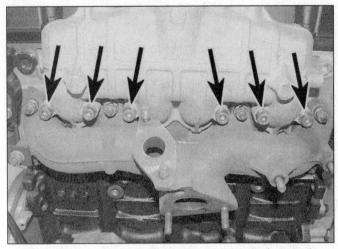

10.5 Unscrew the inlet manifold mounting bolts (arrowed)

11.2 Disconnect the injector connectors

10 Inlet manifold – removal and refitting

Removal

1 Prise out the cover caps, undo the retaining nuts/bolts and remove the engine top cover.
2 Undo the bolts securing the EGR pipe to the inlet manifold flap assembly.
3 Undo the retaining screws and separate the inlet manifold flap assembly from the inlet manifold (see Section 12). Recover the O-ring.
4 Unbolt the EGR pipe from the exhaust manifold. On automatic transmission models, also release the three retaining bolts and manoeuvre the EGR cooler away from the inlet manifold.
5 Remove the heat shield from the manifold, then unscrew the mounting nuts/bolts and remove the inlet manifold from the cylinder head. Recover the gaskets from the inlet manifold **(see illustration)**.

Refitting

6 Refitting is a reversal of removal, using new manifold, EGR pipe and manifold flap assembly gaskets.

11 Tandem fuel pump – removal and refitting

Note: *Disconnecting the central connector for the unit injectors may cause a fault code to be logged by the engine management ECU. This code can only be erased by a VW dealer or suitably-equipped specialist.*

Removal

1 Prise out the cover caps, unscrew the retaining nuts/bolts and remove the engine top cover.
2 Disconnect the charge air pipe at the back of the cylinder head, and place it to one side. Disconnect the central connector for the unit injectors **(see illustration)**.
3 Release the retaining clip (where fitted) and

disconnect the brake servo pipe from the tandem pump **(see illustration)**.
4 Disconnect the fuel supply hose (marked white) from the tandem pump **(see illustration 11.3)**. Be prepared for fuel spillage.
5 Unscrew the four retaining bolts and move the tandem pump away from the cylinder head **(see illustration 11.3)**. As the pump is lifted up, disconnect the fuel return hose (marked blue). Be prepared for fuel spillage. There are no serviceable parts within the tandem pump. If the pump is faulty, it must be renewed.

Refitting

6 Reconnect the fuel return hose to the pump and refit the pump to the cylinder head, using new rubber seals, and ensuring that the pump pinion engages correctly with the drive slot in the camshaft **(see illustration)**.
7 Refit the pump retaining bolts, and tighten them to the specified torque.
8 Re-attach the fuel supply hose and brake servo hose to the pump.
9 Reconnect the central connector for the unit injectors.
10 Refit the charge air pipe.
11 Disconnect the fuel filter return hose (marked blue), and connect the hose to a hand vacuum pump. Operate the vacuum pump until fuel comes out of the return hose.

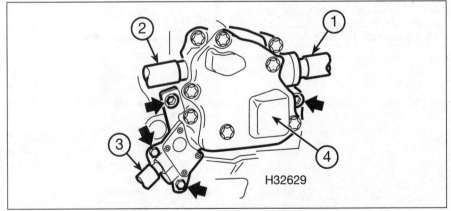

11.3 Fuel tandem pump securing bolts (arrowed)

1 Brake servo hose	3 Fuel return hose
2 Fuel supply hose	4 Tandem pump

11.6 Ensure that the tandem pump pinion engages correctly with the drive slot in the camshaft

12.6 Unscrew the three retaining bolts and remove the inlet manifold flange housing

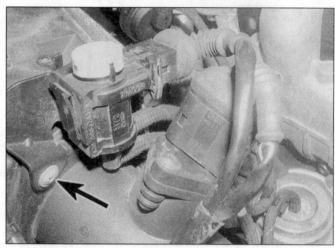

12.10 Disconnect the vacuum pipes, and unscrew the inlet manifold flap control valve mounting screw (arrowed)

This primes the tandem pump. Take care not to suck any fuel into the vacuum pump. Reconnect the return hose to the fuel filter.
12 Refit the engine top cover.
13 Have the engine management ECU's fault memory interrogated and erased by a VW dealer or suitably-equipped specialist.

12 Inlet manifold change-over flap and valve – removal and refitting

Change-over flap housing and vacuum control element

Removal

1 As diesel engines have a very high compression ratio, when the engine is turned off, the pistons still compress a large quantity of air for a few revolutions and cause the engine unit to shudder. The inlet manifold change-over flap is located in the inlet flange housing bolted to the inlet manifold. When the ignition switch is turned to the 'off' position, the engine management ECU-controlled valve actuates the flap, which shuts off the air supply to the cylinders. This allows the pistons to compress very little air, and the engine runs

softly to a halt. The flap must open again approximately 3 seconds after switching off the ignition switch. The EGR (Exhaust Gas Recirculation) valve is also incorporated into the flap housing.
2 Where fitted, prise out the cover caps, undo the retaining nuts/bolts, and remove the engine top cover.
3 Release the retaining clips, and disconnect the air inlet trucking from the inlet manifold flange housing.
4 Undo the two retaining bolts and disconnect the EGR pipe from the underside of the inlet flange. Recover the gasket.
5 Disconnect the vacuum pipe to the actuator. Disconnect the vacuum pipe for the EGR valve.
6 Unscrew the three retaining bolts and remove the inlet manifold flange housing. Discard the sealing O-ring, a new one must be used **(see illustration)**.
7 Although it is possible to remove the vacuum actuator from the inlet flange housing, by unscrewing the two bracket retaining bolts and disengaging the actuating arm from the flap spindle, at the time of writing the inlet manifold flange was only available as a unit complete with the vacuum actuator and EGR valve. Consult your VW dealer.

Refitting

8 Refitting is a reversal of removal. Tighten the inlet manifold flange housing bolts to the specified torque.

Change-over valve

Removal

9 The change-over valve controls the supply of vacuum to the change-over flap. The electrical supply to the valve is controlled by the engine management ECU. When the ignition key is turned to the 'off' position, the ECU signals the valve, which allows vacuum to pull the flap shut. Approximately three seconds later, the power supply to the valve is cut, the vacuum to the actuator collapses, and the flap opens.
10 The valve is located on the right-hand side of the engine compartment, on the top of the air filter housing. Note their fitted positions and disconnect the vacuum pipes from the valve **(see illustration)**.
11 Disconnect the wiring plug from the valve.
12 Undo the retaining screw and remove the valve.

Refitting

13 Refitting is a reversal of removal.

Chapter 4 Part C:
Emission control and exhaust systems

Contents

	Section number
Catalytic converter – general information and precautions	7
Crankcase emission system – general information	3
Evaporative loss emission control system – information and component renewal	2
Exhaust Gas Recirculation (EGR) system – information and component removal	4
Exhaust manifold – removal and refitting	5
Exhaust system – component renewal	6
General information	1
Secondary air injection system – information and component renewal	8

Degrees of difficulty

Easy, suitable for novice with little experience	**Fairly easy,** suitable for beginner with some experience	**Fairly difficult,** suitable for competent DIY mechanic	**Difficult,** suitable for experienced DIY mechanic	**Very difficult,** suitable for expert DIY or professional

Specifications

Engine codes*

Petrol engines

1781 cc, DOHC, Bosch Motronic ME7.5 injection, turbocharged	AWT
1984 cc, SOHC, Siemens Simos 3.2 injection, non-turbo	AZM
1984 cc, DOHC, Bosch Motronic ME7.5 injection, non-turbo	ALT

Diesel engines

Electronic direct injection, unit injectors, 74 kW (100 bhp)	AVB
Electronic direct injection, unit injectors, 96 kW (130 bhp)	AVF and AWX

* **Note:** *See 'Vehicle identification' for the location of the code marking on the engine.*

Torque wrench settings	Nm	lbf ft
Catalytic converter to front pipe:		
SOHC petrol engines	40	30
DOHC petrol engines	25	18
Diesel engines	25	18
Catalytic converter to turbocharger	30	22
EGR valve to inlet manifold:		
Petrol engines	25	18
Diesel engines	10	7
Exhaust clamp bolts	40	30
Exhaust manifold*	25	18
Exhaust mounting brackets to underbody	25	18
Front exhaust pipe to manifold:		
Petrol engines	30	22
Front pipe to bracket on gearbox:		
Petrol engines	25	18
Semi-flexible pipe to EGR valve and exhaust manifold	25	18

** Use new fasteners*

1 General information

Emission control systems

All petrol engine models are designed to use unleaded petrol and are controlled by engine management systems that are programmed to give the best compromise between driveability, fuel consumption and exhaust emission production. In addition, a number of systems are fitted that help to minimise other harmful emissions. A crankcase emission control system is fitted, which reduces the release of pollutants from the engine's lubrication system, and a catalytic converter is fitted which reduces exhaust gas pollutant. An evaporative loss emission control system reduces the release of gaseous hydrocarbons from the fuel tank, and a secondary injection system is fitted to some models to reduce the catalytic converter warm-up time.

All diesel-engined models have a crankcase emission control system, and in addition are fitted with a catalytic converter, and an

Exhaust Gas Recirculation (EGR) system to reduce exhaust emissions.

Crankcase emission control

To reduce the emission of unburned hydrocarbons from the crankcase into the atmosphere, the engine is sealed and the blow-by gases and oil vapour are drawn from inside the crankcase, through a wire mesh oil separator, into the inlet tract to be burned by the engine during normal combustion.

Under all conditions the gases are forced out of the crankcase by the (relatively) higher crankcase pressure. All diesel engines have a pressure-regulating valve on the camshaft cover to control the flow of gases from the crankcase.

Exhaust emission control – petrol models

To minimise the amount of pollutants which escape into the atmosphere, all petrol models are fitted with a three-way catalytic converter in the exhaust system. The fuelling system is of the closed-loop type, in which an oxygen sensor in the exhaust system provides the engine management system ECU with constant feedback, enabling the ECU to adjust the air/fuel mixture to optimise combustion. A second oxygen sensor is also fitted after the catalytic converter, to inform the ECU of the oxygen content of the post-catalyst gases.

The oxygen sensors have a heating element built-in that is controlled by the ECU through the oxygen sensor relay to quickly bring the sensor's tip to its optimum operating temperature. The sensor's tip is sensitive to oxygen and relays a voltage signal to the ECU that varies according on the amount of oxygen in the exhaust gas. If the inlet air/fuel mixture is too rich, the exhaust gases are low in oxygen so the sensor sends a low-voltage signal, the voltage rising as the mixture weakens and the amount of oxygen rises in the exhaust gases. Peak conversion efficiency of all major pollutants occurs if the inlet air/fuel mixture is maintained at the chemically-correct ratio for the complete combustion of petrol of 14.7 parts (by weight) of air to 1 part of fuel (the stoichiometric ratio). The sensor output voltage alters in a large step at this point, the ECU using the signal change as a reference point and correcting the inlet air/fuel mixture accordingly by altering the fuel injector pulse width. Details of the oxygen sensor removal and refitting are given in Chapter 4A.

In order to work efficiently, the catalytic converter needs to be heated to a temperature of at least 300°C. So that the exhaust gases can heat the catalyst up faster, some models are equipped with a secondary air injection system. During the initial warm-up stage, fresh air is injected behind the exhaust valves, this enriches the exhaust gases with oxygen, which causes an 'afterburning' effect, which shortens the catalyst warm-up phase. The activation of the secondary air injection pump and inlet valve, is controlled by the engine management ECU.

Exhaust emission control – diesel models

An oxidation catalyst is fitted in the exhaust system of all diesel engined models. This has the effect of removing a large proportion of the gaseous hydrocarbons, carbon monoxide and particulates present in the exhaust gas.

An Exhaust Gas Recirculation (EGR) system is also fitted to all diesel engined models. This reduces the level of nitrogen oxides produced during combustion by introducing a proportion of the exhaust gas back into the inlet manifold, under certain engine operating conditions, via a plunger valve. The system is controlled electronically by the diesel engine management ECU.

Evaporative emission control – petrol models

To minimise the escape of unburned hydrocarbons into the atmosphere, an evaporative loss emission control system (EVAP) is fitted to all petrol models. The fuel tank filler cap is sealed and a charcoal canister is mounted underneath the right-hand wing to collect the petrol vapours released from the fuel contained in the fuel tank. It stores them until they can be drawn from the canister (under the control of the engine management system ECU) via the purge valve(s) into the inlet tract, where they are then burned by the engine during normal combustion.

To ensure that the engine runs correctly when it is cold and/or idling and to protect the catalytic converter from the effects of an over-rich mixture, the purge control valve(s) are not opened by the ECU until the engine has warmed-up, and the engine is under load; the valve solenoid is then modulated on and off to allow the stored vapour to pass into the inlet tract.

Exhaust systems

On petrol models the exhaust system comprises the exhaust manifold, turbocharger (engine code AWT only), catalytic converter (with 'before' and 'after' oxygen sensors), front pipe, intermediate pipe and silencer, and tailpipe and silencer.

On all diesel models, the exhaust system comprises the exhaust manifold, turbocharger, front pipe and integral catalytic converter, a

2.9 The charcoal canister is located behind the front right-hand wheel arch liner

short connecting pipe, intermediate pipe and silencer, and tailpipe and silencer. The system is supported by rubber bushes and/or rubber mounting rings.

Initially, the exhaust intermediate and rear sections are manufactured as one unit, however they are available separately as service items.

2 Evaporative loss emission control system – information and component renewal

Information

1 The evaporative loss emission control system is only fitted to petrol models, and consists of a purge valve, activated charcoal filter canister and a series of connecting vacuum hoses.

2 The purge valve is located in the front right-hand corner of the engine compartment, in the vacuum line between the charcoal canister and the inlet manifold. The charcoal canister is mounted inside the right-hand front wheel housing behind the wheel arch liner, in front of the A-pillar.

Component renewal

Purge valve

3 Ensure that the ignition is switched off, then unplug the wiring harness from the purge valve at the connector.

4 Loosen the clips and disconnect the vacuum hoses. Note which way round the valve is fitted.

5 Refitting is a reversal of removal.

Charcoal canister

6 Apply the handbrake, then jack up the front of the vehicle and support it on axle stands (see *Jacking and vehicle support*). Remove the right-hand front roadwheel.

7 Refer to Chapter 11, and partially remove the rear of the right-hand front wheel arch liner to give access to the charcoal canister.

8 Disconnect the vacuum and breather hoses, noting which ports they connect to.

9 Undo the mounting screws and remove the charcoal canister **(see illustration)**.

10 Refitting is a reversal of removal.

3 Crankcase emission system – general information

1 The crankcase emission control system consists of hoses connecting the crankcase to the air cleaner or inlet manifold. A pressure regulating valve is fitted to all diesel engines. Oil separator units are fitted to some petrol engines.

2 The system requires no attention other than to check at regular intervals that the hoses, valve and oil separator are free of blockages and in good condition.

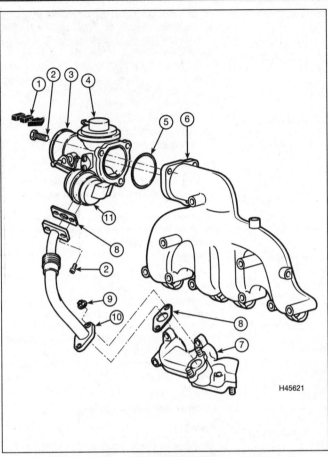

4.1a Exhaust gas recirculation (EGR) valve components – manual transmission models

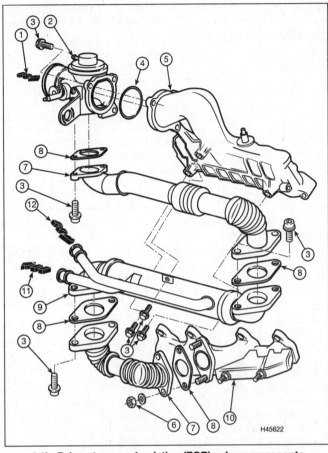

4.1b Exhaust gas recirculation (EGR) valve components – automatic transmission models

1	Air from intercooler	4	EGR valve	8	Gasket
2	Bolt	5	O-ring	9	Nut
3	Inlet connecting pipe	6	Inlet manifold	10	EGR connecting pipe
		7	Exhaust manifold	11	Vacuum actuator

1	Air from intercooler	6	Nut	10	Exhaust manifold
2	EGR valve	7	EGR connecting pipes	11	To heat exchanger
3	Retaining bolt			12	From connection
4	O-ring	8	Gasket	13	Inlet connecting pipe
5	Inlet manifold	9	Cooling radiator		

4 Exhaust Gas Recirculation (EGR) system – information and component removal

Information

1 An Exhaust Gas Recirculation (EGR) system is fitted to all diesel engines; it consists of an EGR valve, modulator valve, delivery pipe(s), and a series of connecting vacuum hoses **(see illustrations)**.

2 The EGR valve is controlled by the engine management control unit (ECU), and is incorporated into the inlet manifold flange housing, which also contains the manifold change-over flap.

EGR valve renewal

3 Disconnect the vacuum hose from the port on the EGR valve.

4 Unscrew the bolts securing the EGR flexible pipe to the underside of the inlet manifold flange housing. Recover the gasket **(see illustration)**.

5 Disconnect the vacuum pipe to the inlet manifold change-over flap actuator.

6 Release the retaining clips and disconnect the inlet trunking from the inlet manifold flange housing.

7 Undo the three retaining bolts and remove the inlet manifold flange housing, complete with EGR valve **(see illustration)**. As the EGR valve is integral with the inlet manifold flange housing, it is not available as a separate part.

8 Refitting is a reversal of removal, but use new flange joint gaskets and self-locking nuts.

EGR control valve renewal

9 The EGR control valve is located on the connecting pipe between the intercooler and

4.4 Unscrew the bolts securing the EGR flexible pipe to the underside of the inlet manifold flange housing, and recover the gasket

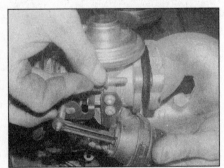

4.7 Undo the three retaining bolts and remove the inlet manifold flange housing, complete with EGR valve

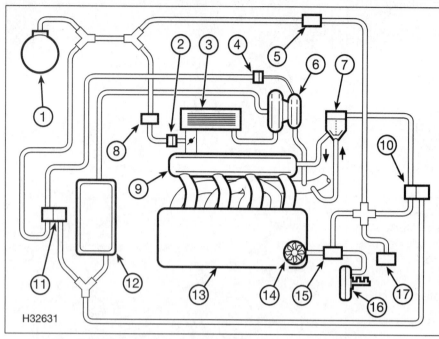

4.12 Undo the two retaining bolts and remove the EGR control valve

H32631

4.10 Turbocharger air system/EGR system – diesel engines

1 Vacuum reservoir	6 Turbocharger	12 Air cleaner
2 Inlet manifold change-over flap actuator	7 EGR valve	13 Cylinder head
3 Intercooler	8 Inlet manifold change-over flap control valve	14 Tandem pump
4 Wastegate actuator	9 Inlet manifold	15 Non-return valve
5 Charge pressure control solenoid valve	10 EGR control valve	16 Brake servo
	11 Non-return valve	17 Fuel cooling circuit shut-off valve

the inlet manifold to the left of the engine. The valve controls the vacuum supply to the EGR valve. The EGR control valve is in turn controlled by the engine management ECU.

10 Note their fitted locations, and disconnect the vacuum pipes from the control valve **(see illustration)**.

11 Disconnect the wiring plug from the control valve.

12 Undo the two retaining bolts and remove the control valve **(see illustration)**.

13 Refitting is a reversal of removal.

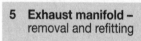

5 Exhaust manifold –
removal and refitting

Petrol engine models

Removal

1 Apply the handbrake, then jack up the front of the vehicle and support it on axle stands (see *Jacking and vehicle support*). Remove the splash guard from the bottom of the engine compartment.

2 Remove the air cleaner and trunking as described in Chapters 4A. Also, undo the retaining bolts and remove the engine top cover where necessary.

3 On turbocharged engines, unscrew the turbocharger support bracket bolts several

turns only. Also unbolt the oil supply pipe from the heat shield.

4 Unbolt the heat shield from over the exhaust manifold where necessary.

5 On non-turbocharged engines, unscrew the nuts and disconnect the exhaust front pipe from the exhaust manifold. Recover the gasket and push the front pipe to the rear away from the manifold.

6 On turbocharged engines, unscrew the three bolts securing the turbocharger to the exhaust manifold, and lower the turbocharger, then recover the gasket. Plug the opening in the turbocharger with rag to prevent entry of any foreign objects.

7 Progressively unscrew and remove the

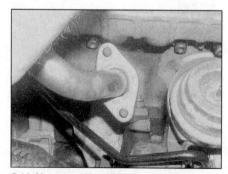

5.14 Unscrew the two bolts and disconnect the EGR pipe from the exhaust manifold

nuts and washers, and withdraw the exhaust manifold from the studs on the cylinder head. Recover the gasket(s).

Refitting

8 Clean thoroughly the mating surfaces of the manifold and cylinder head.

9 Refitting is a reversal of removal, but fit new gaskets, renew self-locking nuts, and tighten the nuts to the specified torque. On turbocharged engines, fit the exhaust manifold, then the turbocharger to the manifold, and finally the turbocharger to the cylinder block. Refer to Chapter 4A for additional tightening torques.

Diesel engine models

Removal

10 Remove the turbocharger as described in Chapter 4B.

11 Unbolt and remove the heat shield.

12 Remove the inlet manifold as described in Chapter 4B.

13 Unscrew the bolt securing the oil supply pipe to the exhaust manifold.

14 Unbolt and remove the EGR recirculation pipe **(see illustration)**. Recover the gaskets.

Note: *On models fitted with automatic transmission, undo the bolts securing the EGR flexible pipe to the inlet flange housing and the exhaust manifold, undo the bolts securing the EGR cooler to the inlet manifold and position it to one side.*

15 Progressively unscrew and remove the nuts and washers, and withdraw the exhaust manifold from the studs on the cylinder head. Recover the gaskets.

Refitting

16 Clean thoroughly the mating surfaces of the manifold and cylinder head.

17 Refitting is a reversal of removal, but fit new gaskets, renew self-locking nuts, and tighten the nuts to the specified torque.

6 Exhaust system –
component renewal

Warning: Allow ample time for the exhaust system to cool before starting work. In particular, note

that the catalytic converter runs at very high temperatures. If there is any chance that the system may still be hot, wear suitable gloves.

Removal

1 Each exhaust section can be removed individually, however because the system is located above the rear axle, the system cannot be removed complete.

2 To remove part of the system, first jack up the front or rear of the car and support it on axle stands (see *Jacking and vehicle support*). Alternatively, position the car over an inspection pit or on car ramps.

Front pipe (SOHC engines)

Note: *Handle the flexible, braided section of the front pipe carefully, and do not bend it excessively.*

3 Working under the car, unbolt the floor crossmember from the underbody.

4 Remove the air cleaner assembly as described in Chapter 4A or 4B.

5 Unscrew the nuts and disconnect the front pipe from the exhaust manifold. Recover the gasket **(see illustrations)**.

6 Support the intermediate (or catalytic converter/short pipe) exhaust section on a trolley jack, then unscrew the flange bolts and separate the front pipe. Recover the gasket.

Catalytic converter (SOHC engines)

7 This is part of the front pipe removal procedure in paragraphs 3 to 6.

Catalytic converter (non-turbo DOHC engines)

8 Working under the car, support the front pipe and intermediate section on axle stands or trolley jacks. Unscrew the flange bolts and separate the catalytic converter from the front pipe. Recover the gasket.

9 Note the fitted position of the clamp (the bolts should be on the left-hand side of the clamp, and the lower ends of the bolts should not be below the bottom of the intermediate pipe), then unscrew the clamp bolts and separate the catalytic converter from the intermediate section **(see illustration)**.

Catalytic converter (turbo DOHC engines)

10 Remove the oxygen sensors as described in Chapter 4A.

11 Unscrew and remove the bolts securing the catalytic converter to the front pipe. Recover the gasket.

12 Unbolt the exhaust system bracket from the gearbox and lower the front pipe.

13 Unscrew the flange nuts and remove the catalytic converter from the turbocharger. Recover the gasket. Withdraw the catalytic converter from under the car.

Short pipe (diesel engines)

14 Unscrew the flange bolts and separate the short pipe from the catalytic converter.

15 Unscrew the clamp bolts and separate

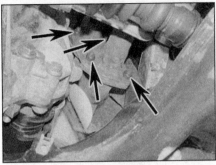

6.5a Unscrew the exhaust front pipe-to-manifold bolts . . .

the short pipe from the intermediate section. Withdraw the short pipe from under the car.

Intermediate pipe and silencer

16 Working under the car, support the front pipe on an axle stand or trolley jack.

17 If the original intermediate/tail pipe is fitted, it will be necessary to cut through the middle pipe in order to separate it from the tailpipe and silencer. The pipe has an indentation to indicate where the cut must be made approximately 160 to 180 mm before the rear silencer. Using a hacksaw, cut through the pipe at right-angles.

18 If the service pipe has been fitted, unscrew the clamp bolts and separate the intermediate pipe from the tailpipe.

19 Note the fitted position of the clamp attaching the intermediate pipe to the catalytic converter or short pipe (the bolts should be on the left-hand side of the clamp, and the lower ends of the bolts should not be below the bottom of the pipe), then unscrew the clamp bolts and separate the catalytic converter.

20 Disconnect the rubber mounting and withdraw the intermediate pipe and silencer from under the car.

Tailpipe and silencer

21 If the original intermediate/tail pipe is fitted, it will be necessary to cut through the middle pipe in order to separate it from the tailpipe and silencer. The pipe has an indentation to indicate where the cut must be made. Using a hacksaw, cut through the pipe at right-angles.

22 If the service pipe has been fitted, unscrew the clamp bolts and separate the tailpipe from the intermediate pipe. Note that the fitted

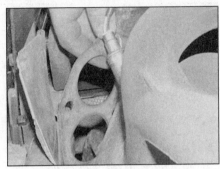

6.5b . . . and remove the gasket

position of the clamp should be with the bolts facing the rear of the car, and the bolt ends should not be below the bottom of the pipe.

23 Disconnect the rubber mountings and withdraw the tailpipe and silencer from under the car **(see illustrations)**.

Refitting

24 Each section is refitted by a reversal of the removal sequence, noting the following points.

  a) Ensure that all traces of corrosion have been removed from the flanges or pipe ends and renew all necessary gaskets.

  b) Inspect the rubber mountings for signs of damage or deterioration and renew as necessary.

  c) Prior to tightening the exhaust system mounting, ensure that all rubber mountings are correctly located and that there is adequate clearance between the exhaust system and vehicle underbody.

6.9 Intermediate section clamp – non-turbo petrol engine

6.23a Tailpipe and silencer front mounting

6.23b Tailpipe and silencer rear mounting

7 Catalytic converter – general information and precautions

1 The catalytic converter is a reliable and simple device which needs no maintenance in itself, but there are some facts which an owner should be aware of if the converter is to function properly for its full service life.

Petrol models

a) *DO NOT use leaded petrol (or LRP) – the lead will coat the internal precious metals, reducing their converting efficiency and will eventually destroy the converter.*
b) *Always keep the ignition and fuel systems well-maintained in accordance with the manufacturer's schedule.*
c) *If the engine develops a misfire, do not drive the car at all (or at least as little as possible) until the fault is cured.*
d) *DO NOT push- or tow-start the car – this will soak the catalytic converter in unburned fuel, causing it to overheat when the engine does start.*
e) *DO NOT switch off the ignition at high engine speeds.*

f) *The catalytic converter, used on a well-maintained and well-driven car, should last between 50 000 and 100 000 miles – if the converter is no longer effective it must be renewed.*

Petrol and diesel models

a) *DO NOT use fuel or engine oil additives – these may contain substances harmful to the catalytic converter.*
b) *Remember that the catalytic converter operates at very high temperatures. DO NOT, therefore, park the car in dry undergrowth, over long grass or piles of dead leaves after a long run.*
c) *Remember that the catalytic converter is FRAGILE – do not strike it with tools during servicing work.*

8 Secondary air injection system – information and component renewal

Information

1 Engine codes AWT (1.8 litre) and AZM (2.0 litre) are equipped with a secondary air injection system which is designed to promote afterburning of the exhaust gases in order to reduce harmful emissions. The system also shortens the amount of time the catalytic converter takes to warm-up. In order to function correctly, the catalytic converter needs to be at a temperature of at least 300°C, and this temperature level is normally achieved by the action of the exhaust gases passing through. In order to reduce the catalyst warm-up phase, a secondary air injection pump injects fresh air just behind the exhaust valves in the cylinder head. This oxygen rich mixture causes an 'afterburning' effect in the exhaust, and greatly increases the gas temperature, and therefore the catalyst temperature. The system is only active during cold starts (up to 33°C coolant temperature), and only operates for approximately 2 minutes.

Component renewal

2 At the time of writing, no information concerning the removal and refitting of the secondary air injection system components was available.

Chapter 5 Part A:
Starting and charging systems

Contents

Section number

Alternator – brush holder/voltage regulator module renewal 6
Alternator – removal and refitting 5
Alternator/charging system – testing in vehicle 4
Battery – disconnection, removal and refitting 3
Battery – testing and charging 2
Battery check . . . . See *Weekly checks*
Electrical system check . . . . See *Weekly checks*

Section number

General information and precautions 1
Oil level/temperature sensor – removal and refitting 11
Oil pressure warning light switch – removal and refitting 10
Starter motor – removal and refitting 8
Starter motor – testing and overhaul 9
Starting system – testing 7

Degrees of difficulty

Easy, suitable for novice with little experience 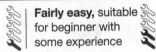	Fairly easy, suitable for beginner with some experience	Fairly difficult, suitable for competent DIY mechanic	Difficult, suitable for experienced DIY mechanic	Very difficult, suitable for expert DIY or professional

Specifications

Engine codes*

Petrol engines

1781 cc, DOHC, Bosch Motronic ME7.5 injection, turbocharged	AWT
1984 cc, SOHC, Siemens Simos 3.2 injection, non-turbo	AZM
1984 cc, DOHC, Bosch Motronic ME7.5 injection, non-turbo	ALT

Diesel engines

Electronic direct injection, unit injectors, 74 kW (100 bhp)	AVB
Electronic direct injection, unit injectors, 96 kW (130 bhp)	AVF and AWX

* **Note:** *See 'Vehicle identification' for the location of the code marking on the engine.*

General
System type . . . . 12 volt, negative earth

Starter motor
Type . . . . Pre-engaged

Battery
Rating . . . . 44 to 80 Ah (depending on model and market)

Alternator
Type	Bosch or Valeo
Rating	70, 90 or 120 amp
Minimum brush length	5.0 mm

Torque wrench settings

	Nm	lbf ft
Alternator connections:		
B+ connection	15	11
D+ connection (where applicable)	3	2
Alternator mounting bolt	25	18
Battery clamp bolt	15	11
Oil level/temperature sensor bolts	10	7
Starter motor:		
Bracket to cylinder block	22	16
To transmission	65	48

1.5a The battery negative terminal earth strap . . .

1 General information and precautions

General information

The engine electrical system consists mainly of the charging and starting systems. Because of their engine-related functions, these are covered separately from the body electrical devices such as the lights, instruments, etc, which are covered in Chapter 12. On petrol engine models refer to Part B of this Chapter for information on the ignition system, and on diesel models refer to Part C for the preheating system.

The electrical system is of the 12 volt negative earth type.

The battery, which may be of the low maintenance or maintenance-free (sealed for life) type, is charged by the alternator, which is belt-driven from the crankshaft pulley.

The starter motor is of the pre-engaged type, with an integral solenoid. On starting, the solenoid moves the drive pinion into engagement with the flywheel/driveplate ring gear before the starter motor is energised. Once the engine has started, a one-way clutch prevents the motor armature being driven by the engine until the pinion disengages from the flywheel.

Two primary earth straps are fitted; one from the battery negative terminal to the body, and one from the engine to the body **(see illustrations)**.

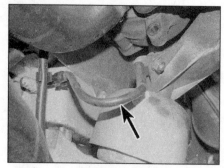

1.5b . . . and the engine-to-body earth strap

Further details of the various systems are given in the relevant Sections of this Chapter. While some repair procedures are given, the usual course of action is to renew the component concerned. The owner whose interest extends beyond mere component renewal should obtain a copy of the *Automotive Electrical & Electronic Systems Manual*, available from the publishers of this manual.

Precautions

⚠️ *Warning: It is necessary to take extra care when working on the electrical system to avoid damage to semi-conductor devices (diodes and transistors), and to avoid the risk of personal injury. In addition to the precautions given in 'Safety first!', observe the following when working on the system:*

• *Always remove rings, watches, etc, before working on the electrical system.* Even with the battery disconnected, capacitive discharge could occur if a component's live terminal is earthed through a metal object. This could cause a shock or nasty burn.

• *Do not reverse the battery connections.* Components such as the alternator, electronic control units, or any other components having semi-conductor circuitry could be irreparably damaged.

• *Never disconnect the battery terminals, the alternator, any electrical wiring or any test instruments when the engine is running.*

• *Do not allow the engine to turn the alternator when the alternator is not connected.*

• *Never test for alternator output by 'flashing' the output lead to earth.*

• *Always ensure that the battery negative lead is disconnected when working on the electrical system.*

• *If the engine is being started using jump leads and a slave battery, connect the batteries negative-to-negative and positive-to-positive (see Jump starting at the beginning of the manual). This also applies when connecting a battery charger.*

• *Before using electric-arc welding equipment on the car, disconnect the battery, alternator and components such as electronic control units to protect them from the risk of damage.*

Caution: The radio/cassette fitted as standard equipment has a built-in security code to deter thieves. If the power source to the unit is cut, the anti-theft system will activate. Even if the power source is immediately reconnected, the radio/cassette unit will not function until the correct security code has been entered. Therefore, if you do not know the correct security code for the radio/cassette unit, do not disconnect the battery negative terminal or remove the radio/cassette unit from the vehicle.

2 Battery – testing and charging

Testing

Standard and low-maintenance battery

1 If the vehicle covers a small annual mileage, it is worthwhile checking the specific gravity of the electrolyte every three months to determine the state of charge of the battery. Use a hydrometer to make the check, and compare the results with the following table. Note that the specific gravity readings assume an electrolyte temperature of 15°C (60°F); for every 10°C (18°F) below 15°C (60°F) subtract 0.007. For every 10°C (18°F) above 15°C (60°F) add 0.007.

	Above 25°C	Below 25°C
Fully-charged	1.210 to 1.230	1.270 to 1.290
70% charged	1.170 to 1.190	1.230 to 1.250
Discharged	1.050 to 1.070	1.110 to 1.130

2 If the battery condition is suspect, first check the specific gravity of electrolyte in each cell. A variation of 0.040 or more between any cells indicates loss of electrolyte or deterioration of the internal plates.

3 If the specific gravity variation is 0.040 or more, the battery should be renewed. If the cell variation is satisfactory but the battery is discharged, it should be charged as described later in this Section.

Maintenance-free battery

4 In cases where a sealed for life maintenance-free battery is fitted, topping-up and testing of the electrolyte in each cell is not possible. The condition of the battery can therefore only be tested using a battery condition indicator or a voltmeter.

5 Certain models may be fitted with a maintenance-free battery with a built-in charge condition indicator. The indicator is located in the top of the battery casing and indicates the condition of the battery from its colour. If the indicator shows green, then the battery is in a good state of charge. If the indicator turns darker, eventually to black, then the battery requires charging, as described later in this Section. If the indicator shows clear/yellow, then the electrolyte level in the battery is too low to allow further use, and the battery should be renewed. **Do not** attempt to charge, load or jump start a battery when the indicator shows clear/yellow.

All battery types

6 If testing the battery using a voltmeter, connect the voltmeter across the battery and note the voltage. The test is only accurate if the battery has not been subjected to any kind of charge for the previous six hours. If this is not the case, switch on the headlights for 30 seconds, then wait four to five minutes before testing the battery after switching off the headlights. All other electrical circuits must

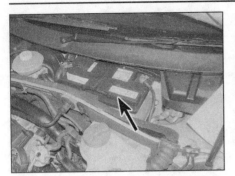

3.1 The battery is located at the rear of the engine compartment

3.2a Loosen the clamp nut . . .

3.2b . . . and disconnect the battery negative (–) lead from the terminal

be switched off, so check that the doors and tailgate are fully shut when making the test.

7 If the voltage reading is less than 12.2 volts, then the battery is discharged, whilst a reading of 12.2 to 12.4 volts indicates a partially-discharged condition.

8 If the battery is to be charged, remove it from the vehicle and charge it as described later in this Section.

Charging

Note: *The following is intended as a guide only. Always refer to the manufacturer's recommendations (often printed on a label attached to the battery) before charging a battery.*

Standard and low-maintenance battery

9 Charge the battery at a rate equivalent to 10% of the battery capacity (eg, for a 45 Ah battery charge at 4.5 A) and continue to charge the battery at this rate until no further rise in specific gravity is noted over a four-hour period.

10 Alternatively, a trickle charger charging at the rate of 1.5 amps can safely be used overnight.

11 Specially rapid boost charges which are claimed to restore the power of the battery in 1 to 2 hours are not recommended, as they can cause serious damage to the battery plates through overheating.

12 While charging the battery, note that the temperature of the electrolyte should never exceed 37.8°C (100°F).

Maintenance-free battery

13 This battery type takes considerably longer to fully recharge than the standard type, the time taken being dependent on the extent of discharge, but it can take anything up to three days.

14 A constant voltage type charger is required, to be set, when connected, to 13.9 to 14.9 volts with a charger current below 25 amps. Using this method, the battery should be useable within three hours, giving a voltage reading of 12.5 volts, but this is for a partially-discharged battery and, as mentioned, full charging can take far longer.

15 If the battery is to be charged from a fully-discharged state (condition reading less than 12.2 volts), have it recharged by your local

automotive electrician, as the charge rate is higher and constant supervision during charging is necessary.

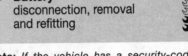

3 Battery – disconnection, removal and refitting

Note: *If the vehicle has a security-coded radio, check that you have a copy of the code number before disconnecting the battery cable; refer to the caution in Section 1.*

Disconnection and removal

1 The battery is located at the rear of the engine compartment, on the bulkhead **(see illustration)**.

2 Loosen the clamp nut and disconnect the battery negative (-) lead from the terminal **(see illustrations)**.

3 Lift the plastic flap where fitted, then loosen the clamp nut and disconnect the battery positive (+) lead from the terminal.

4 At the base of the battery, unscrew the retaining clamp bolt and remove the clamp **(see illustration)**.

5 Where fitted, disconnect the vent pipe from the battery. Note on some models the vent incorporates a flashback arrester.

6 Remove the wiper arms, as described in Chapter 12.

7 Carefully prise the windscreen cowl panel up and out of its slot in the base of the windscreen.

8 Lift out the battery and withdraw it from the engine compartment **(see illustration)**

3.4 Unscrew the battery retaining clamp bolt (arrowed)

Refitting

9 Clean the battery mounting and apply a little grease to the threads of the clamp bolt.

10 Place the battery in position and refit the clamp. Tighten the bolt to the specified torque.

11 Where fitted, refit the vent pipe.

12 Reconnect the battery positive (+) lead to the terminal and tighten the clamp nut.

13 Reconnect the battery negative (-) lead to the terminal and tighten the clamp nut.

14 Smear petroleum jelly around the battery terminals to prevent corrosion – corroded connections are amongst the most frequent causes of electrical system faults.

15 Refit the windscreen cowl panel and wiper blades.

16 Re-activate the radio by inserting the security code.

4 Alternator/charging system – testing in vehicle

Note: *Refer to Section 1 of this Chapter before starting work.*

1 If the charge warning light fails to illuminate when the ignition is switched on, first check the alternator wiring connections for security. If satisfactory, check that the warning light bulb has not blown, and that the bulbholder is secure in its location in the instrument panel. If the light still fails to illuminate, check the continuity of the warning light feed wire from the alternator to the bulbholder. Check the condition of the auxiliary drivebelt. If all

3.8 Remove the battery from the engine compartment

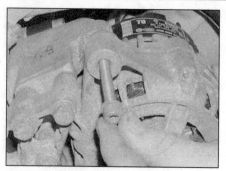

5.5 Unscrew and remove the upper alternator mounting bolt

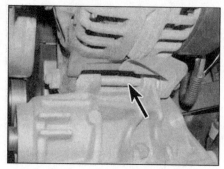

5.6a Alternator lower mounting bolt

5.6b Alternator lower mounting nut

5.7 Alternator connections

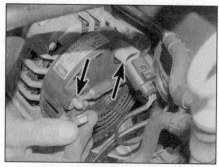

5.10 Alternator connections (arrowed)

5.12 Undo the mounting bolts and remove the alternator

is satisfactory, the alternator is at fault and should be renewed or taken to an auto-electrician for testing and repair.

2 Similarly, if the charge warning light comes on with the ignition, but is then slow to go out when the engine is started, this may indicate an impending alternator problem. Check all the items listed in the preceding paragraph, and refer to an auto-electrical specialist if no obvious faults are found.

3 If the charge warning light illuminates when the engine is running, stop the engine and check that the drivebelt is correctly tensioned (see Chapter 2A or 2B) and that the alternator connections are secure. If all is so far satisfactory, check the alternator brushes and slip-rings as described in Section 6. If the fault persists, the alternator should be renewed, or taken to an auto-electrician for testing and repair.

4 If the alternator output is suspect even though the warning light functions correctly, the regulated voltage may be checked as follows.

5 Connect a voltmeter across the battery terminals, and start the engine.

6 Increase the engine speed until the voltmeter reading remains steady; the reading should be approximately 12 to 13 volts, and no more than 14 volts.

7 Switch on as many electrical accessories (eg, the headlights, heated rear window and heater blower) as possible, and check that the alternator maintains the regulated voltage at around 13 to 14 volts.

8 If the regulated voltage is not as stated, this may be due to worn brushes, weak brush springs, a faulty voltage regulator, a faulty diode, a severed phase winding or worn or damaged slip-rings. The brushes and slip-rings may be checked (see Section 6), but if the fault persists, the alternator should be renewed or taken to an auto-electrician.

5 Alternator – removal and refitting

Removal

1 The alternator is fitted to the left-hand front of the engine. First, disconnect the battery negative lead and position it away from the terminal – refer to the precautions in Section 1. Where applicable, prise out the cover caps, undo the retaining nuts/bolts, and remove the engine top cover.

2 On turbocharged petrol engines, loosen the clip and disconnect the intercooler air duct from the throttle housing.

3 Remove the auxiliary drivebelt as described in Chapter 2A or 2B as applicable.

4 Remove the viscous fan unit with reference to Chapter 3. Briefly, it is removed by inserting an Allen key from behind, while holding the unit stationary with a temporary bolt inserted from behind, resting on the engine cylinder block, or a strap wrench around the pulley.

Petrol engines

5 Unscrew and remove the alternator upper mounting bolt (see illustration).

6 Unscrew the nut from the alternator lower mounting bolt, then swivel the alternator to one side and withdraw the lower mounting bolt from the front (see illustrations).

7 Carefully release the support plastic tie from the alternator wiring (see illustration).

8 Undo the nuts and disconnect the main cable and charging warning light wire from the rear of the alternator. **Note:** On some models the D+ connection is a push-on plug.

9 Push the coolant pipe to one side, and withdraw the alternator from the engine.

Diesel engines

10 Undo the nuts and disconnect the main cable and charging warning light wire from the rear of the alternator (see illustration). **Note:** On some models the D+ connection is a push-on plug.

11 Carefully release the support plastic tie from the alternator wiring.

12 Support the alternator, then unscrew and remove the mounting bolts (see illustration).

13 Push the coolant pipe to one side, and withdraw the alternator from the engine.

Refitting

14 Refitting is a reversal of removal. Refer to Chapter 2A or 2B as applicable for details of refitting the main drivebelt. Tighten the alternator mounting bolts, and the alternator wiring connections to the specified torque.

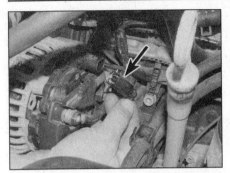

6.3 Disconnecting the warning lamp wiring

6.4a Prise off the rubber cap . . .

6.4b . . . then unscrew the nut and disconnect the battery cable from the alternator terminal

6 Alternator – brush holder/voltage regulator module renewal

1 It is not necessary to remove the alternator from the engine. First, disconnect the battery negative lead (refer to Section 3).
2 Remove the engine top cover.
3 Disconnect the warning lamp wiring **(see illustration)**.
4 Prise off the rubber cap, then unscrew the nut and disconnect the battery cable from the alternator terminal **(see illustrations)**.
5 Undo the upper nuts and lower screw, and remove the protective cover from the alternator **(see illustrations)**.
6 Undo the three screws, and withdraw the brush holder/voltage regulator module from the alternator **(see illustrations)**.

7 Measure the free length of the brushes and compare with the measurement given in the Specifications **(see illustration)**; renew the module if the brushes are worn below the minimum limit.
8 Clean and inspect the surfaces of the slip-rings on the end of the alternator shaft, working through the module location hole. If they are excessively worn, or damaged, the alternator must be renewed.
9 Reassemble the alternator by following the dismantling procedure in reverse.

7 Starting system – testing

Note: *Refer to Section 1 of this Chapter before starting work.*

1 If the starter motor fails to operate when the ignition key is turned to the appropriate position, the following possible causes may be to blame:
 a) The battery is faulty.
 b) The electrical connections between the switch, solenoid, battery and starter motor are somewhere failing to pass the necessary current from the battery through the starter to earth.
 c) The solenoid is faulty.
 d) The starter motor is mechanically or electrically defective.
2 To check the battery, switch on the headlights. If they dim after a few seconds, this indicates that the battery is discharged – recharge (see Section 2) or renew the battery. If the headlights glow brightly, operate the ignition switch and observe the lights. If they dim, then this indicates that current is reaching the starter

6.5a Unscrew the upper nuts . . .

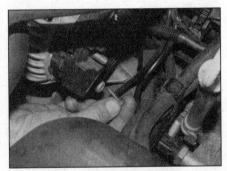

6.5b . . . and lower screw . . .

6.5c . . . and remove the protective cover

6.6a Undo the three screws . . .

6.6b . . . and withdraw the brush holder/ voltage regulator module

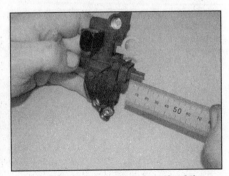

6.7 Measuring the free length of the brushes

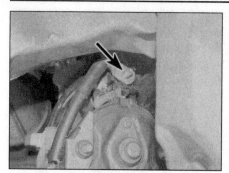

8.4a Disconnect the main cable from the starter motor

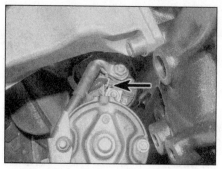

8.4b Starter motor solenoid terminal

motor, therefore the fault must lie in the starter motor. If the lights continue to glow brightly (and no clicking sound can be heard from the starter motor solenoid), this indicates that there is a fault in the circuit or solenoid – see following paragraphs. If the starter motor turns slowly when operated, but the battery is in good condition, then this indicates that either the starter motor is faulty, or there is considerable resistance somewhere in the circuit.

3 If a fault in the circuit is suspected, disconnect the battery leads (including the earth connection to the body), the starter/solenoid wiring and the engine/transmission earth strap. Thoroughly clean the connections, and reconnect the leads and wiring, then use a voltmeter or test light to check that full battery voltage is available at the battery positive lead connection to the solenoid, and that the earth is sound. Smear petroleum jelly around the battery terminals to prevent corrosion – corroded connections are amongst the most frequent causes of electrical system faults.

4 If the battery and all connections are in good condition, check the circuit by disconnecting the wire from the solenoid blade terminal. Connect a voltmeter or test light between the wire end and a good earth (such as the battery negative terminal), and check that the wire is live when the ignition switch is turned to the start position. If it is, then the circuit is sound – if not the circuit wiring can be checked as described in Chapter 12.

5 The solenoid contacts can be checked by connecting a voltmeter or test light between the battery positive feed connection on the starter side of the solenoid, and earth. When the

ignition switch is turned to the start position, there should be a reading or lighted bulb, as applicable. If there is no reading or lighted bulb, the solenoid is faulty and should be renewed.

6 If the circuit and solenoid are proved sound, the fault must lie in the starter motor. Begin checking the starter motor by removing it (see Section 8), and checking the brushes. If the fault does not lie in the brushes, the motor windings must be faulty. In this event, it may be possible to have the starter motor overhauled by a specialist, but check on the availability and cost of spares before proceeding, as it may prove more economical to obtain a new or exchange motor.

8 Starter motor – removal and refitting

Removal

1 The starter motor is fitted to the right-hand rear of the engine cylinder block on all diesel engines, and petrol engine codes AWT and AZM. It is on the left-hand side of the engine on petrol engine code ALT. First, disconnect the battery negative (earth) lead (see Section 3).

2 Apply the handbrake, then jack up the front of the vehicle and support it on axle stands (see *Jacking and vehicle support*). Where fitted, remove the splash guard from under the engine compartment.

3 On models with air conditioning, for improved access, it may be necessary to loosen the refrigerant hose supports. Similarly,

on automatic transmission models, it may be necessary to loosen or remove the supports for the hoses leading from the automatic transmission to the oil cooler.

4 Disconnect the wiring from the solenoid on the top of the starter motor. The battery positive cable is retained by a nut, and the trigger wiring is a push-fit **(see illustrations)**.

5 Where fitted, loosen the clip and remove the heat shield.

6 Where a mounting bracket is fitted to the front of the starter motor, undo the retaining nuts and remove it **(see illustration)**.

7 Unscrew and remove the upper and lower starter motor mounting bolts, then lift the starter motor and withdraw it forwards from the bellhousing aperture **(see illustration)**.

Refitting

8 Refit the starter motor by following the removal procedure in reverse. Tighten the mounting bolts to the specified torque.

9 Starter motor – testing and overhaul

If the starter motor is thought to be defective, it should be removed from the vehicle and taken to an auto-electrician for assessment. In the majority of cases, new starter motor brushes can be fitted at a reasonable cost. However, check the cost of repairs first as it may prove more economical to purchase a new or exchange motor.

10 Oil pressure warning light switch – removal and refitting

Removal

1 The oil pressure light switch is screwed into the oil filter housing, located on the left-hand side of the engine block. Undo the retaining bolts/nuts, and remove the engine top cover.

2 Disconnect the switch wiring plug.

3 Unscrew the switch from the housing and (where fitted) recover the sealing washer **(see illustration)**. Be prepared for fluid spillage, and if the switch is to be left removed from the

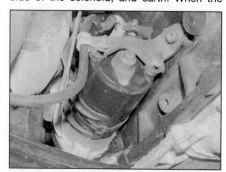

8.6 Starter motor and mounting bracket

8.7 Undo the starter mounting bolt (arrowed)

10.3 Unscrew the oil pressure switch from the oil filter housing

engine for any length of time, plug the switch aperture.

Refitting

4 Examine the sealing washer for signs of damage or deterioration and if necessary renew it.

5 Refit the switch and washer, tightening it securely, and reconnecting the wiring plug.

6 Refit the engine top cover then check, and if necessary, top-up the engine oil level.

11 Oil level/temperature sensor – removal and refitting

Removal

1 Where fitted, the engine oil level/temperature sensor is located in the base of the oil sump. Apply the handbrake, then jack up the front of the vehicle and support it on axle stands (see *Jacking and vehicle support*). Remove the splash guard from under the engine compartment.

2 Position a container beneath the sump, then unscrew the drain plug (refer to the relevant part of Chapter 1) and drain the engine oil. Clean, refit, and tighten the plug after all the oil has drained.

3 Disconnect the oil level/temperature sensor wiring plug.

4 Undo the securing bolts, and lower the sensor from the sump. Discard the O-ring seal, a new one must be fitted **(see illustration)**.

Refitting

5 Clean the mating surfaces of the sensor and the sump. Smear the new O-ring seal with clean engine oil, and position it on the sensor.

6 Fit the sensor to the sump, insert the securing bolts and tighten them to the specified torque.

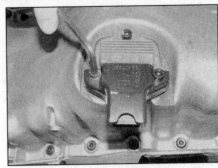

11.4 Undo the bolts and lower the sensor from the sump

7 Reconnect the sensor wiring plug

8 Refit the engine splash guard, lower the vehicle to the ground.

9 Refill the engine with new oil as described in the relevant part of Chapter 1. Start the engine and check for leaks.

Notes

Chapter 5 Part B:
Ignition system – petrol engines

Contents

Section number

General information 1
HT coil(s) – removal and refitting 3
Ignition switch removal and refitting . . . . See Chapter 10
Ignition system – testing. 2

Section number

Ignition timing – checking and adjusting 4
Knock sensors – removal and refitting. 5
Spark plug renewal. . . . . See Chapter 1A

Degrees of difficulty

Easy, suitable for novice with little experience	**Fairly easy,** suitable for beginner with some experience	**Fairly difficult,** suitable for competent DIY mechanic	**Difficult,** suitable for experienced DIY mechanic	**Very difficult,** suitable for expert DIY or professional

Specifications

General

Engine code by type*:
1781 cc, DOHC, turbocharged.	AWT
1984 cc, SOHC, non-turbo.	AZM
1984 cc, DOHC, non-turbo	ALT

* Note: *See 'Vehicle identification' at the end of this manual for the location of the code marking on the engine.*

Ignition type

1781 cc engine code AWT	Bosch Motronic ME7.5 injection
1984 cc engine code AZM	Siemens Simos 3.2 injection
1984 cc engine code ALT	Bosch Motronic ME7.5 injection

Ignition coil

Type:
Engine codes AWT and ALT	One coil per spark plug
Engine code AZM	Single DIS coil unit with four HT lead outputs

Coil winding resistance:
Primary	N/A

Secondary:
Engine codes AWT and ALT	N/A
Engine code AZM (cylinders 1/4 and 2/3)	4000 to 6000 ohms

Ignition timing

All engines	Controlled by engine management system

HT leads

HT lead resistance*	4000 to 8000 ohms

* Including suppression connector and spark plug connector.

Spark plugs

See Chapter 1A Specifications

Torque wrench setting	**Nm**	**lbf ft**
Knock sensor mounting bolt	20	15

1 General information

The Bosch and Simos systems described in this Chapter are self-contained engine management systems, which control both the fuel injection and ignition. This Chapter deals with the ignition system components only – refer to Chapter 4A for details of the fuel system components.

The ignition system fitted to engine codes AWT and ALT includes four separate coils, one fitted to each spark plug, whereas the system fitted to engine code AZM is of the 'distributorless' (DIS – Distributorless Ignition System) type. With both types, the ignition timing is adjusted automatically by the Electronic Control Unit (ECU). The ECU calculates and controls the ignition timing according to engine speed, crankshaft position, camshaft position, and inlet airflow rate information, received from sensors mounted on and around the engine. Other parameters that affect ignition timing are throttle position and rate of opening, inlet air temperature, coolant temperature and engine knock. Note that most of these sensors have a dual role, in that the information they provide is equally useful in determining the fuelling requirements as in deciding the optimum ignition or firing point – therefore, removal of some of the sensors mentioned below is described in Chapter 4A.

On engine codes AWT and ALT, each spark plug has its own dedicated 'plug-top' HT coil which fits directly onto the spark plug (no HT leads are therefore needed). Unlike the 'wasted spark' system in the next paragraph, on these models a spark is only generated at each plug once every engine cycle. On these engines the coil dwell angle is controlled by a Hall transmitter on the end of the inlet camshaft at the front of the engine.

The single coil unit fitted to engine code AZM operates on the 'wasted spark' principle. The coil unit in fact contains two separate coils – one for cylinders 1 and 4, the other for cylinders 2 and 3. Each of the two coils produces an HT voltage at both outputs every time its primary coil voltage is interrupted – ie, cylinders 1 and 4 always 'fire' together, then 2 and 3 'fire' together. When this happens, one of the two cylinders concerned will be on the compression stroke (and will ignite the fuel/air mixture), while the other one is on the exhaust stroke – because the spark on the exhaust stroke has no effect, it is effectively wasted, hence the term 'wasted spark'.

A knock sensor is mounted on the cylinder block in order to detect engine pre-ignition (or 'pinking') before it actually becomes audible. If pre-ignition occurs, the ECU retards the ignition timing of the cylinder that is pre-igniting in steps until the pre-ignition ceases. The ECU then advances the ignition timing of that cylinder in steps until it is restored to normal, or until pre-ignition occurs again. On Motronic-equipped vehicles, two knock sensors are fitted.

On engines fitted with the Motronic engine management systems, idle speed control is achieved partly by an electronic throttle valve positioning module, mounted on the side of the throttle body and partly by the ignition system, which gives fine control of the idle speed by altering the ignition timing. On the Simos system, the ECU controls the idle speed through ignition timing and injection period. Manual adjustment of the engine idle speed is not necessary or possible.

In the event of a fault in the system due to loss of a signal from one of the sensors, the ECU reverts to an emergency ('limp-home') program. This will allow the car to be driven, although engine operation and performance will be limited. A warning light on the instrument panel will illuminate if the fault is likely to cause an increase in harmful exhaust emissions.

It should be noted that comprehensive fault diagnosis of all the engine management systems described in this Chapter is only possible with dedicated electronic test equipment. In the event of a sensor failing or other fault occurring, a fault code will be stored in the ECU's fault log, which can only be extracted from the ECU using a dedicated fault code reader. A VW dealer will obviously have such a reader, but they are also available from other suppliers. It is unlikely to be cost-effective for the private owner to purchase a fault code reader, but a well-equipped local garage or auto-electrical specialist will have one. Once the fault has been identified, the removal and refitting sequences detailed in the following Sections will then allow the appropriate component(s) to be renewed as required.

2 Ignition system – testing

Warning: Extreme care must be taken when working on the system with the ignition switched on; it is possible to get a substantial electric shock from a vehicle's ignition system. Persons with cardiac pacemaker devices should keep well clear of the ignition circuits, components and test equipment. Always switch off the ignition before disconnecting or connecting any component and when using a multimeter to check resistances.

Engines with one coil per plug

1 If a fault appears in the engine management (fuel injection/ignition) system which is thought to ignition related, first ensure that the fault is not due to a poor electrical connection or poor maintenance; ie, check that the air cleaner filter element is clean, the spark plugs are in good condition and correctly gapped, that the engine breather hoses are clear and undamaged, referring to Chapter 1A for further information. If the engine is running very roughly, check the compression pressures as described in Chapter 2A or 2B (as applicable).

2 If these checks fail to reveal the cause of the problem the vehicle should be taken to a suitably-equipped VW dealer for testing. A diagnostic connector is incorporated in the engine management circuit into which a special electronic diagnostic tester can be plugged (see Chapter 4A). The tester will locate the fault quickly and simply, alleviating the need to test all the system components individually which is a time-consuming operation that carries a high risk of damaging the ECU.

3 The only ignition system checks which can be carried out by the home mechanic are those described in Chapter 1A, relating to the spark plugs. If necessary, the system wiring and wiring connectors can be checked as described in Chapter 12 ensuring that the ECU wiring connector(s) have first been disconnected.

Engines with single DIS coil

4 Refer to the information given in paragraphs 1 to 3. The only other likely cause of ignition trouble is the HT leads, linking the HT coil to the spark plugs. Check the leads as follows. Never disconnect more than one HT lead at a time to avoid possible confusion.

5 Pull the first lead from the plug by gripping the end fitting, not the lead, otherwise the lead connection may be fractured. Check inside the end fitting for signs of corrosion, which will look like a white crusty powder. Push the end fitting back onto the spark plug, ensuring that it is a tight fit on the plug. If not, remove the lead again and use pliers to carefully crimp the metal connector inside the end fitting until it fits securely on the end of the spark plug.

6 Using a clean rag, wipe the entire length of the lead to remove any built-up dirt and grease. Once the lead is clean, check for burns, cracks and other damage. Do not bend the lead excessively, nor pull the lead lengthwise – the conductor inside is quite fragile, and might break.

7 Disconnect the other end of the lead from the HT coil. Again, pull only on the end fitting. Check for corrosion and a tight fit in the same manner as the spark plug end.

8 If an ohmmeter is available, check for continuity between the HT lead terminals. If there is no continuity the lead is faulty and must be renewed (as a guide, the resistance of each lead should be in the region of 4 to 8 kΩ).

9 Refit the lead securely on completion of the check then check the remaining leads one at a time, in the same way. If there is any doubt about the condition of any HT leads, renew them as a complete set.

3.1 Removing an HT coil on an engine with a single coil per plug

3.2 Single DIS ignition coil

3.5 Disconnect the LT wiring plug from the ignition coil

3.7a Note their positions, then disconnect the HT leads . . .

3.7b . . . unscrew the three Allen bolts, and remove the coil unit

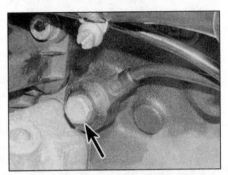

5.3 Unscrew the knock sensor mounting bolt

3 HT coil(s) – removal and refitting

Removal

Note: *The action of simply disconnecting and re-connecting the ignition coil(s) - even if no other work is done on any of the system's components - may cause a fault code to be logged and the engine management system warning light to illuminate. This will require the system to be re-set by a VW dealer or similarly-equipped expert.*

DOHC engines - one coil per plug

2 Unscrew the retaining bolts and/or nuts and withdraw the engine top cover. Unscrew the two bolts to release the wiring from the camshaft cover, then very carefully raise the ignition coils far enough until the wiring can be disconnected. VW supply a special tool, a puller which grips only on the thicker top rim of the coil, thus avoiding the risk of damage to the coil's thinner lower ribs. Disconnect the wiring from the coil (press the connector towards the coil, depress the locking catch and carefully pull the connector off the coil) and withdraw it.

SOHC engines - single DIS coil

2 The ignition coil unit is mounted at the left-hand rear of the engine compartment **(see illustration)**.

3 Make sure the ignition is switched off (take out the key).

4 Where applicable, remove the engine top cover(s). Removal details vary according to model, but the cover retaining nuts are concealed under circular covers, which are prised out of the main cover. Where plastic screws or turn-fasteners are used, these can be removed using a wide-bladed screwdriver. Remove the nuts or screws, and lift the cover from the engine, releasing any wiring or hoses attached.

5 Unplug the main wiring plug (LT connector) at the base of the ignition coil **(see illustration)**.

6 The original HT leads should be marked from 1 to 4, corresponding to the cylinder/spark plug they serve (No 1 is at the timing belt end of the engine). Some leads are also marked from A to D, and corresponding markings are found on the ignition coil HT terminals – in this case, cylinder A corresponds to No 1, B to No 2, and so on. If there are no markings present, label the HT leads before disconnecting, and either paint a marking on the ignition coil terminals or make a sketch of the lead positions for use when reconnecting.

7 Disconnect the HT leads from the ignition coil terminals, then unscrew the mounting bolts and remove the coil unit **(see illustrations)**.

Refitting

8 Refitting is a reversal of the relevant removal procedure. If wished, spray a little water-dispersant (such as WD-40) on to each of the connectors as it is reconnected.

9 On SOHC engines, use the marks noted or made on disconnection when reconnecting the

HT leads. On DOHC engines, press each coil carefully down on to its spark plug, rotating it as necessary so that it locates correctly in the camshaft cover, until it is felt to engage fully on the spark plug terminal. Reconnect the coil wiring and fasten the two bolts securing the wiring to the camshaft cover. Refit the engine top cover.

4 Ignition timing – checking and adjusting

The ignition timing is controlled by the engine management system ECU and cannot be adjusted manually. The vehicle must be taken to a VW dealer if the timing requires checking.

5 Knock sensors – removal and refitting

Removal

1 The two knock sensors are located on the left-hand rear of the cylinder block.

2 Unplug the wiring from the sensor at the connector.

3 Unscrew the mounting bolt and remove the sensor **(see illustration)**.

Refitting

4 Refitting is a reversal of removal, but note that the sensor's operation will be affected if its mounting bolt is not tightened to exactly the right torque.

Chapter 5 Part C:
Pre/post-heating systems – diesel models

Contents

Section number

General description 1

Glow plugs – testing, removal and refitting 2

Section number

Degrees of difficulty

Easy, suitable for novice with little experience	**Fairly easy,** suitable for beginner with some experience	**Fairly difficult,** suitable for competent DIY mechanic	**Difficult,** suitable for experienced DIY mechanic	**Very difficult,** suitable for expert DIY or professional

Specifications

General

Engine code by type* :

Electronic direct injection, unit injectors, 74 kW (100 bhp)	AVB
Electronic direct injection, unit injectors, 96 kW (130 bhp)	AVF and AWX

* Note: See 'Vehicle identification' for the location of the code marking on the engine.

Glow plugs

Current consumption . . . . 8 amps per glow plug

Torque wrench setting	Nm	lbf ft
Glow plug to cylinder head	15	11

1 General information

To assist cold starting, diesel engined models are fitted with a preheating system, which comprises four glow plugs, a glow plug control unit (incorporated in the ECU), a facia-mounted warning lamp and the associated electrical wiring.

The glow plugs are miniature electric heating elements, encapsulated in a metal case with a probe at one end and electrical connection at the other. Each combustion chamber has a glow plug threaded into it, which is positioned directly in line with the incoming spray of fuel. When the glow plug is energised, the air in the combustion chamber is heated, allowing optimum combustion temperature to be achieved more quickly.

The duration of the preheating period is governed by the ECU, which monitors the temperature of the engine via the coolant temperature sensor and alters the preheating time to suit the conditions. Preheating only takes place at coolant temperatures above 9°C.

A facia-mounted warning light informs the driver that preheating is taking place. The light extinguishes when sufficient preheating has taken place to allow the engine to be started, but power will still be supplied to the glow plugs for a further period until the engine is started. If no attempt is made to start the engine, the power supply to the glow plugs is switched off to prevent battery drain and glow plug burn-out. After the engine is started, there is a period of post-heating which takes place irrespective of whether it is preceded by preheating or not. This period lasts for a maximum of 4 minutes after the engine has been started, at engine speeds of under 2500 rpm. The heating is switched off after this period, or if the engine speed exceeds 2500 rpm. Post-heating reduces combustion noise and improves idling quality, and additionally reduces hydrocarbon emissions.

The warning light comes on when the ignition is initially switched on with a cold engine, and indicates that the glow plugs are being energised. If the light does not come on in these conditions, there is a defect in the glow plug system which should be investigated. When the engine is warm, the light may not come on, and the engine can be started straight away, and any post-heating will take place automatically.

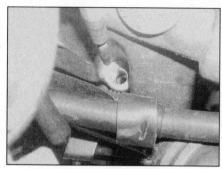

2.13 The fuel filter bracket is attached to the cylinder block/head at five points (arrowed)

2.16a Glow plug location on the cylinder head

2.16b Removing No 4 glow plug

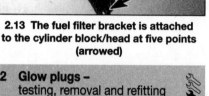

2 Glow plugs –
testing, removal and refitting

Testing

1 If the system malfunctions, testing is ultimately by substitution of known good units, but some preliminary checks may be made as described in the following paragraphs.

2 Before testing the system, check that the battery voltage is at least 11.5 volts, using a voltmeter. Switch off the ignition.

3 Where necessary for access, remove the engine top cover(s). Removal details vary according to model, but the cover retaining nuts are concealed under circular covers, which are prised out of the main cover. Remove the nuts, and lift the cover from the engine, releasing any wiring or hoses attached.

4 Disconnect the wiring plug from the coolant temperature sender at the rear of the engine. Disconnecting the sender in this way simulates a cold engine, which is a requirement for the glow plug system to activate.

5 Disconnect the wiring connector from the most convenient glow plug, and connect a suitable voltmeter between the wiring connector and a good earth.

6 Have an assistant switch on the ignition. Battery voltage should be displayed for

approximately 20 seconds – note that the voltage will drop to zero when the pre- and post-heating periods end.

7 If no supply voltage can be detected at the glow plug, then either the glow plug relay (where applicable) or the supply wiring must be faulty. Also check that the glow plug fuse or fusible link (usually located on top of the battery) has not blown – if it has, this may indicate a serious wiring fault; consult a VW dealer for advice.

8 To locate a faulty glow plug, first disconnect the battery negative cable and position it away from the terminal.

9 Disconnect the wiring plug from the glow plug terminal. Measure the electrical resistance between the glow plug terminal and the engine earth. At the time of writing, this information is not available – as a guide, a resistance of more than a few ohms indicates that the plug is defective.

10 If a suitable ammeter is available, connect it between the glow plug and its wiring connector, and measure the steady-state current consumption (ignore the initial current surge, which will be about 50% higher). As a guide, high current consumption (or no current draw at all) indicates a faulty glow plug.

11 As a final check, remove the glow plugs and inspect their stems for signs of damage. A badly burned or charred stem may be an indication of a faulty fuel injector.

Removal

12 Disconnect the battery negative (earth) lead (see Chapter 5A). Prise out the cover caps, undo the retaining nuts/bolts, and remove the engine top cover.

13 To improve access to No 4 glow plug, undo the central 13 mm hexagon socket head bolt, and move the fuel filter head (with hoses still connected) to one side (see Chapter 1B). Undo the clamp screw, and slide the fuel filter up and out of the bracket (see Chapter 1B). Slacken and remove the five nuts/bolts securing the filter bracket to the engine **(see illustration)**.

14 Pull the coolant pipe away from the No 4 glow plug.

15 Carefully pull the connector(s) from the top of the glow plug(s).

16 Using a deep 10 mm socket, unscrew and remove the glow plug(s) from the cylinder head **(see illustrations)**.

Refitting

17 Refitting is the reversal of removal, noting the following points:

a) *Tighten the glow plugs to the specified torque.*

b) *When refitting cylinder No 4 glow plug, slacken the metal coolant pipe retaining nut at the front of the engine to facilitate the fitting of the fuel filter bracket to the engine. Fill the filter with fuel prior to refitting the filter head.*

Chapter 6
Clutch

Contents

Section number

Clutch friction disc and pressure plate – removal, inspection and
   refitting 6
Clutch pedal – removal and refitting 3
Clutch pedal switch – removal, refitting and adjustment 8
General information 1

Section number

Hydraulic system – bleeding 2
Master cylinder – removal, overhaul and refitting 4
Release bearing and lever – removal, inspection and refitting. 7
Slave cylinder – removal, overhaul and refitting. 5

Degrees of difficulty

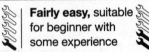

Easy, suitable for novice with little experience	Fairly easy, suitable for beginner with some experience	Fairly difficult, suitable for competent DIY mechanic	Difficult, suitable for experienced DIY mechanic	Very difficult, suitable for expert DIY or professional

Specifications

Engine codes*

Petrol engines

1781 cc, DOHC, Bosch Motronic ME7.5 injection, turbocharged	AWT
1984 cc, SOHC, Siemens Simos 3.2 injection, non-turbo	AZM
1984 cc, DOHC, Bosch Motronic ME7.5 injection, non-turbo	ALT

Diesel engines

Electronic direct injection, unit injectors, 74 kW (100 bhp)	AVB
Electronic direct injection, unit injectors, 96 kW (130 bhp)	AVF and AWX

* Note: *See 'Vehicle identification' for the location of the code marking on the engine.*

General

Type	Single dry friction disc, diaphragm spring with spring-loaded hub
Operation	Hydraulic with slave and master cylinders
Friction disc diameter.	N/A

Torque wrench settings

	Nm	lbf ft
Clutch master cylinder mounting bolts	20	15
Clutch pedal bracket mounting bolts (from inside engine compartment):		
Long Torx bolt (also secures brake master cylinder and servo).	25	18
Short hex socket-head bolt	25	18
Clutch pedal shaft securing bolt	25	18
Clutch release lever leaf spring retaining bolt*:		
01E/0A1 transmission.	25	18
Clutch slave cylinder mounting bolt*	20	15
Hydraulic pipe unions.	15	11
Pressure plate-to-flywheel bolt	25	18

* Use new fasteners

1 General information

The clutch is of single dry plate type, incorporating a diaphragm spring pressure plate, and is hydraulically-operated.

The clutch cover (pressure plate) is bolted to the rear face of the flywheel, and the friction disc is located between the pressure plate and the flywheel friction surface. The disc hub is splined to the transmission input shaft and is free to slide along the splines. Friction lining material is riveted to each side of the disc and the disc hub incorporates cushioning springs to absorb transmission shocks and ensure a smooth take-up of drive. The flywheel is manufactured in two parts instead of the conventional single unit; the friction surface has a limited buffered movement in relation to the main flywheel mass bolted to the rear of the crankshaft. This has the effect of absorbing the initial clutch engagement shock and makes for a smoother gearchange.

When the clutch pedal is depressed, the slave cylinder pushrod moves the release lever forwards, and the release bearing is forced onto the diaphragm spring fingers. As the centre of the spring is pushed in, the outer part of the spring moves out and releases the pressure plate from the friction disc. Drive then ceases to be transmitted to the transmission.

When the clutch pedal is released, the diaphragm spring forces the pressure plate into contact with the linings on the friction disc, and at the same time pushes the disc slightly forward along the input shaft splines into engagement with the flywheel. The friction disc is now firmly sandwiched between the pressure plate and flywheel. This causes drive to be taken up.

An over-centre spring is fitted to the clutch pedal to equalise the operating effort over the full pedal stroke.

As the linings wear on the friction disc, the pressure plate rest position moves closer to the flywheel resulting in the 'rest' position of the diaphragm spring fingers being raised. The hydraulic system requires no adjustment since the quantity of hydraulic fluid in the circuit automatically compensates for wear every time the clutch pedal is operated.

2.10 Use a length of plastic or rubber tubing that is a tight fit over the end of the bleed screw (arrowed)

2 Hydraulic system – bleeding

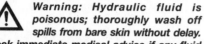

⚠ *Warning: Hydraulic fluid is poisonous; thoroughly wash off spills from bare skin without delay. Seek immediate medical advice if any fluid is swallowed or gets into the eyes. Certain types of hydraulic fluid are inflammable and may ignite when brought into contact with hot components. Hydraulic fluid is also an effective paint stripper. If spillage occurs onto painted bodywork or fittings, it should be washed off immediately, using copious quantities of cold water. It is also hygroscopic (it absorbs moisture from the air) therefore old fluid should never be re-used.*

1 The correct operation of any hydraulic system is only possible after removing all air from the components and circuit; this is achieved by bleeding the system.

2 During the bleeding procedure, add only clean, unused hydraulic fluid of the recommended type; never re-use fluid that has already been bled from the system. Ensure that sufficient fluid is available before starting work.

3 If there is any possibility of incorrect fluid being already in the system, the hydraulic circuit must be flushed completely with uncontaminated, correct fluid.

4 If hydraulic fluid has been lost from the system, or air has entered because of a leak, ensure that the fault is cured before continuing further.

5 The bleed screw is located on the slave cylinder located on the left-hand upper side of the transmission. As access to the bleed screw is limited it will be necessary to jack up the front of the vehicle and support it on axle stands so that the screw can be reached from below.

6 Check that all pipes and hoses are secure, unions tight and the bleed screw is closed. Clean any dirt from around the bleed screw.

7 Unscrew the master cylinder fluid reservoir cap (the clutch shares the same fluid reservoir as the braking system), and top the master cylinder reservoir up to the upper (MAX) level line. Refit the cap loosely, and remember to maintain the fluid level at least above the lower (MIN) level line throughout the procedure, or there is a risk of further air entering the system.

8 There is a number of one-man, do-it-yourself bleeding kits currently available from motor accessory shops. It is recommended that one of these kits is used whenever possible, as they greatly simplify the bleeding operation, and reduce the risk of expelled air and fluid being drawn back into the system. If such a kit is not available, the basic (two-man) method must be used, which is described in detail below.

9 If a kit is to be used, prepare the vehicle as described previously, and follow the kit manufacturer's instructions, as the procedure may vary slightly according to the type being used; generally, they are as outlined below in the relevant sub-section.

Bleeding

Basic (two-man) method

10 Collect a clean glass jar, a suitable length of plastic or rubber tubing which is a tight fit over the bleed screw (see illustration), and a ring spanner to fit the screw. The help of an assistant will also be required.

11 Remove the dust cap from the bleed screw. Fit the spanner and tube to the screw, place the other end of the tube in the jar, and pour in sufficient fluid to cover the end of the tube.

12 Ensure that the fluid level is maintained at least above the lower level line in the reservoir throughout the procedure.

13 Have the assistant fully depress the clutch pedal several times to build-up pressure, then maintain it on the final downstroke.

14 While pedal pressure is maintained, unscrew the bleed screw (approximately one turn) and allow the compressed fluid and air to flow into the jar. The assistant should maintain pedal pressure and should not release it until instructed to do so. When the flow stops, tighten the bleed screw again, have the assistant release the pedal slowly, and recheck the reservoir fluid level.

15 Repeat the steps given in paragraphs 13 and 14 until the fluid emerging from the bleed screw is free from air bubbles. If the master cylinder has been drained and refilled allow approximately five seconds between cycles for the master cylinder passages to refill.

16 When no more air bubbles appear, tighten the bleed screw securely, remove the tube and spanner, and refit the dust cap. Do not overtighten the bleed screw.

Using a one-way valve kit

17 As their name implies, these kits consist of a length of tubing with a one-way valve fitted, to prevent expelled air and fluid being drawn back into the system; some kits include a translucent container, which can be positioned so that the air bubbles can be more easily seen flowing from the end of the tube.

18 The kit is connected to the bleed screw, which is then opened. The user returns to the driver's seat, depresses the clutch pedal with a smooth, steady stroke, and slowly releases it; this is repeated until the expelled fluid is clear of air bubbles.

19 Note that these kits simplify work so much that it is easy to forget the fluid reservoir level; ensure that this is maintained at least above the lower level line at all times.

Using a pressure-bleeding kit

20 These kits are usually operated by the reservoir of pressurised air contained in the spare tyre. However, note that it will probably be necessary to reduce the pressure to a lower level than normal; refer to the instructions supplied with the kit.

21 By connecting a pressurised, fluid-filled container to the fluid reservoir, bleeding can be carried out simply by opening the bleed screw and allowing the fluid to flow out until no more air bubbles can be seen in the expelled fluid.

22 This method has the advantage that the large reservoir of fluid provides an additional safeguard against air being drawn into the system during bleeding.

All methods

23 When bleeding is complete, and correct pedal feel is restored, tighten the bleed screw securely and wash off any spilt fluid. Refit the dust cap to the bleed screw.

24 Check the hydraulic fluid level in the master cylinder reservoir, and top-up if necessary (see *Weekly Checks*).

25 Discard any hydraulic fluid that has been bled from the system; it will not be fit for re-use.

26 Check the operation of the clutch pedal. If the clutch is still not operating correctly, air must still be present in the system, and further bleeding is required. Failure to bleed satisfactorily after a reasonable repetition of the bleeding procedure may be due to worn master cylinder/release cylinder seals.

---

3 Clutch pedal – removal and refitting

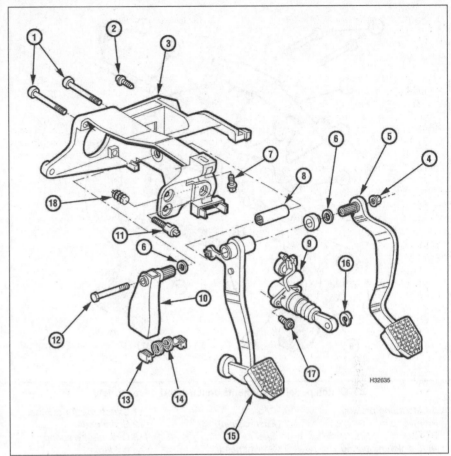

3.5 Clutch pedal components on right-hand drive models

1 Bolt	6 Shim	11 Clutch pedal	14 Over-centre
2 Bolt	7 Bolt	switch	spring
3 Mounting	8 Bush	12 Bolt	15 Clutch pedal
bracket	9 Master	13 Over-centre	16 Clip
4 Nut	cylinder	spring	17 Bolt
5 Brake pedal	10 Lever	holders	18 Clip

Right-hand drive models

Removal

1 Remove the storage compartment/panel from below the steering column. Unclip the cover then undo the retaining screws and pull the storage compartment from the clips in the facia. This will allow access to the pedal bracket.

2 Where fitted, disconnect the wiring and unscrew the switch above the clutch pedal, counting the number of turns, to aid refitment.

3 Using a screwdriver, extract the clip and release the clutch master cylinder pushrod from the pedal.

4 Unscrew the pivot bolt from the left-hand end of the pedal pivot, then withdraw the lever, push the centre bush towards the passenger side, and lower the clutch pedal from the bracket, at the same time releasing it from the over-centre spring. Note the position of the bush, bearings, spacers and caps to ensure correct reassembly.

5 If necessary, the bearings can be renewed individually **(see illustration).**

Refitting

6 Refitting is a reversal of removal but grease the bearings and bush first, and apply locking fluid to the pivot bolt before tightening it to the specified torque. Refer to Chapter 9 and make sure that the brake pedal is refitted correctly.

Left-hand drive models

Removal

7 Remove the storage compartment/panel from below the steering column. Unclip the cover then undo the retaining screws and pull the storage compartment from the clips in the facia. This will allow access to the pedal bracket.

8 Where fitted, disconnect the wiring and unscrew the switch above the clutch pedal. **Do not** press the switch out of the clip otherwise the threads will be damaged and the switch will have to be renewed.

9 Using a screwdriver, release the clutch master cylinder pushrod pin securing clip from the pedal by twisting it upwards then pulling it from the pedal. Pull up the pedal to disconnect it from the pushrod **(see illustration overleaf).**

10 Prise the pedal retaining clip from the groove in the left-hand end of the pivot shaft.

11 Unscrew the shaft retaining bolt, then press the shaft to the right until the clutch pedal can be removed from the bracket.

12 Prise the over-centre spring from the slots in the pedal bracket.

Refitting

13 Refitting is a reversal of removal, but do not refit the shaft retaining bolt until the pedal pivot shaft clip has been fitted.

---

4 Master cylinder – removal, overhaul and refitting

Note: *Refer to the warning at the beginning of Section 2 regarding the hazards of working with hydraulic fluid.*

Removal

1 The clutch master cylinder is located inside the car on the clutch and brake pedal mounting bracket. Hydraulic fluid for the unit

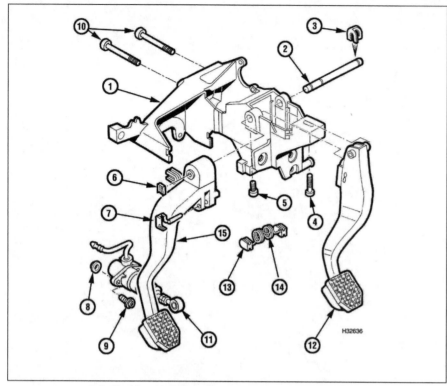

3.9 Clutch pedal components on left-hand drive models

1 Mounting bracket	6 Clip	11 Clutch master cylinder
2 Pivot pin	7 Pushrod pin	12 Brake pedal
3 Clip	8 Seal	13 Over-centre spring
4 Bracket mounting	9 Socket head	holders
bolt	bolt	14 Over-centre spring
5 Pivot pin locking bolt	10 Torx bolts	15 Clutch pedal

is supplied from the brake master cylinder reservoir.

2 Disconnect the battery negative lead (refer to Chapter 5A).

3 With the bonnet open, place cloth rags beneath the clutch master cylinder fluid supply hose where it enters the bulkhead, then fit a hose clamp to the hose and disconnect it from the master cylinder **(see illustration)**. The hose supplies the master cylinder with fluid from the brake master cylinder reservoir.

4 Remove the supply hose grommet from the bulkhead.

5 Using a screwdriver, ease out the pressure pipe retaining clip and slightly pull out the hydraulic pressure line from the master cylinder. Tape over or plug the line to prevent loss of fluid or entry of dust.

6 Disconnect the wiring from the brake fluid reservoir level sensor, then unscrew the bolt securing the reservoir to the brake master cylinder. Using a Torx key, unscrew the bolt securing the master cylinder to the brake servo unit.

7 Inside the car, remove the storage compartment/panel from below the steering

column. Unclip the cover then undo the retaining screws and pull the storage compartment from the clips in the facia. This will allow access to the pedal switch.

8 Disconnect the master cylinder pushrod from the peg on the clutch pedal by prising off the retaining clip **(see illustration)**.

9 Using an Allen key, unscrew and remove the clutch master cylinder mounting bolts **(see illustration)**.

10 Unscrew the pedal bracket mounting bolt located directly above the brake pedal switch, then pull the bracket slightly away from the bulkhead.

11 Withdraw the clutch master cylinder from inside the car, noting the location of the rubber seal and washer, and the position of the fluid supply pipe.

Overhaul

12 Repair kits are not available from VW, but they may be available from a motor factor. To overhaul the master cylinder, first clean the exterior surfaces.

13 Prise off the rubber boot and remove the pushrod. If necessary, loosen the locknut, unscrew the clevis and locknut, and remove the pushrod from the rubber boot. Note the distance between the pushrod eye centre and the mounting flange to ensure correct refitting.

14 Extract the circlip from the mouth of the cylinder, and withdraw the washer, piston and spring noting that the smaller end of the spring contacts the piston.

15 Clean the components, and examine them for wear and deterioration. If the piston and bore are worn excessively, or if corrosion is evident, renew the complete cylinder. If they are in good condition, remove the seals from the piston and renew them.

16 Dip the new seals in hydraulic fluid, and fit them on the piston, using the fingers only to manipulate them into position. Make sure that the seal lips face the spring end of the piston.

17 Insert the spring in the cylinder, then dip the piston in hydraulic fluid and carefully insert it.

18 Fit the washer, then locate the circlip in the groove.

19 Apply a little grease to the end of the

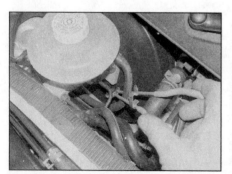

4.3 Clamp the supply hose from the fluid reservoir to the clutch master cylinder using a brake hose clamp

4.8 Prise off the retaining clip and disconnect the master cylinder pushrod (arrowed)

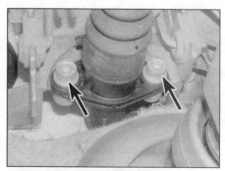

4.9 Unscrew the master cylinder screws with an Allen key

pushrod, then locate it on the piston and fit the rubber boot.

20 Screw on the locknut and clevis then adjust the distance between the centre of the eye and the bulkhead face of the mounting flange to 139.0 ± 0.5 mm on RHD models, or 165.0 ± 0.5 mm on LHD models.

Refitting

21 Refitting is a reversal of removal, but tighten all nuts and bolts to the specified torques where given. When repositioning the pedal bracket onto the bulkhead, have an assistant guide the clutch master cylinder pipe through the location hole from the engine compartment side. When reconnecting the fluid pressure line, the clip must engage audibly. Bleed the clutch hydraulic system as described in Section 2. On completion, check the setting of the clutch pedal switch as follows. With the pedal released, the gap between the switch plunger and the main body of the switch must not be more than 0.5 mm. Also the gap between the pedal bracket and the retaining tabs of the switch must not be more than 0.5 mm. To adjust the switch, turn it as required while holding the clip.

---

5 Slave cylinder –
removal, overhaul and refitting

Note: *Refer to the warning at the beginning of Section 2 regarding the hazards of working with hydraulic fluid.*
Note: *A new slave cylinder mounting bolt will be required.*

Removal

1 The slave cylinder is located on top of the transmission. Although access is possible from the engine compartment, it may be considered better to raise the front of the car for access from below.
2 Apply the handbrake, then jack up the front

of the vehicle and support it on axle stands (see *Jacking and vehicle support*). Remove the engine undertray.
3 Clamp the rubber section of the hydraulic hose leading from the master cylinder to the slave cylinder using a brake hose clamp, to prevent loss of hydraulic fluid.
4 Using a screwdriver, prise out the spring clip and disconnect the hydraulic line from the slave cylinder. Tape over or plug the end of the line and the slave cylinder aperture **(see illustration)**.
5 Unscrew the mounting bolt and withdraw the slave cylinder. As the cylinder is being removed, recover the hose support bracket.

Overhaul

6 Repair kits are not available from VW, but they may be available from a motor factor.
7 To overhaul the slave cylinder, first clean the exterior surfaces.
8 Prise off the rubber boot and remove the pushrod.
9 Extract the special spring clip from the mouth of the cylinder, and withdraw the piston and spring.
10 Clean the components, and examine them for wear and deterioration. If the piston and bore are worn excessively, or if corrosion is evident, renew the complete cylinder. If they are in good condition, remove the seal from the piston and renew it.
11 Dip the new seal in hydraulic fluid, and fit it on the piston, using the fingers only to manipulate it into position. Make sure that the seal lip faces the spring end of the piston.
12 Insert the spring in the cylinder, then dip the piston in hydraulic fluid and carefully insert it.
13 Hold the piston depressed with a screwdriver then press a new spring clip into the mouth of the cylinder, making sure that the legs of the clip grip the cylinder.
14 Fit the pushrod, followed by the rubber boot.

Refitting

15 Refitting is a reversal of removal, but smear a little lithium-based grease to the outer surface of the rubber boot before locating the slave cylinder in the transmission aperture **(see illustration)**. Tighten the new mounting bolt and union to the specified torque and finally bleed the system as described in Section 2. The end of the pushrod which contacts the release lever should be lightly lubricated with a molybdenum disulphide grease and care must be taken to ensure that the pushrod actually engages with the depression in the lever. The slave cylinder must be pressed into the transmission casing before the mounting bolt can be inserted. Due to the limited access and the fact that the slave cylinder must be pushed against the considerable force of the internal return spring, refitting should be made in stages. First fully insert the cylinder (without the hose support bracket), ensuring that the bolt hole is correctly aligned, then refit the hose support bracket so that the front tags are engaged with the cut-out in the cylinder. With the cylinder held in this position, insert the mounting bolt and tighten to the specified torque. Finally locate the hydraulic line on the support bracket.

---

6 Clutch friction disc and
pressure plate – removal, inspection and refitting

Warning: Dust created by clutch wear and deposited on the clutch components may contain asbestos, which is a health hazard. DO NOT blow it out with compressed air or inhale any of it. DO NOT use petrol or petroleum-based solvents to clean off the dust. Brake system cleaner or methylated spirit should be used to flush the dust into a suitable receptacle. After the clutch components are wiped clean with clean rags, dispose of the contaminated rags and cleaner in a sealed container.

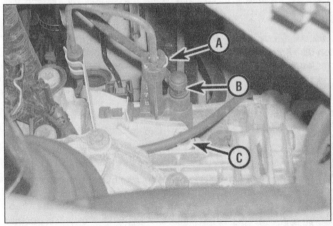

5.4 Clutch slave cylinder

A *Hydraulic line retaining clip*
B *Bleed nipple*
C *Mounting bolt*

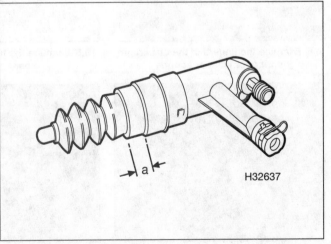

5.15 Apply a thin layer of lithium grease to the area (a) of the slave cylinder before inserting it into the transmission housing

H32637

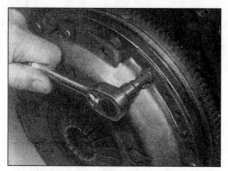

6.3a Using a diagonal pattern, slacken the pressure plate bolts evenly . . .

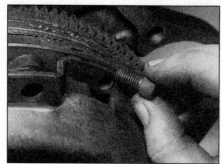

6.3b . . . and then remove them

6.4 Remove the pressure plate and friction disc from the flywheel

Removal

1 Access to the clutch is obtained by removing the transmission as described in Chapter 7A.

2 Mark the clutch pressure plate and flywheel in relation to each other. Note that on some models, VW used a white spot on the flywheel and pressure plate cover to indicate the correct assembly position.

3 Hold the flywheel stationary, then unscrew the clutch pressure plate bolts progressively in diagonal sequence using an Allen key **(see illustrations)**. With the bolts unscrewed two or three turns, check that the pressure plate is not binding on the dowel pins. If necessary, use a screwdriver to release the pressure plate.

4 Remove all the bolts, then lift the clutch pressure plate and friction disc from the flywheel **(see illustration)**.

Inspection

Note: *Due to the amount of work necessary to remove and refit clutch components, it is usually considered good practice to renew the clutch friction disc, pressure plate assembly and release bearing as a matched set, even if only one of these is actually worn enough to require renewal. It is also worth considering the renewal of the clutch components on a preventative basis if the engine and/or transmission have been removed for some other reason.*

5 Clean the pressure plate, disc and flywheel. Do not inhale the dust, as it may contain asbestos which is dangerous to health.

6 Examine the fingers of the diaphragm spring for wear or scoring **(see illustration)**. If the depth of wear exceeds half the thickness of the fingers, a new pressure plate assembly must be fitted.

7 Examine the pressure plate for scoring, cracking and discoloration. Light scoring is acceptable, but if excessive, a new pressure plate assembly must be fitted.

8 Examine the friction disc linings for wear and cracking, and for contamination with oil or grease **(see illustration)**. The linings are worn excessively if they are worn down to, or near, the rivets. Check the disc hub and splines for wear by temporarily fitting it on the transmission input shaft. Renew the friction disc as necessary.

9 Examine the flywheel friction surface for scoring, cracking and discoloration (caused by overheating). If excessive, it may be possible to have the flywheel machined by an engineering works, otherwise it should be renewed.

10 Ensure that all parts are clean, and free of oil or grease, before reassembling. Apply just a small amount of lithium-based grease to the splines of the friction disc hub. **Do not** use copper-based grease. Note that new pressure plates and clutch covers may be coated with protective grease. It is only permissible to clean the grease away from the friction disc lining contact area. Removal of the grease from other areas will shorten the service life of the clutch.

Refitting

11 Commence reassembly by locating the friction disc on the flywheel, with the raised, torsion spring side of the hub facing outwards. If possible, the centralising tool (see paragraph 14) should be used to hold the disc on the flywheel at this stage **(see illustration)**.

12 Locate the clutch pressure plate on the disc, and fit it onto the location dowels **(see illustration)**. If refitting the original pressure plate, make sure that the previously-made marks are aligned.

13 Insert the bolts finger-tight to hold the pressure plate in position.

14 The friction disc must now be centralised, to ensure correct alignment of the transmission input shaft with the spigot bearing in the crankshaft. To do this, a proprietary tool may be used, or alternatively, use a wooden mandrel made to fit inside the friction disc and flywheel spigot bearing. Insert the tool through the friction disc into the spigot bearing, and make sure that it is central.

6.6 Examine the fingers of the diaphragm spring for wear or scoring

6.8 Examine the friction disc linings for wear and cracking

6.11 Locate the friction disc on the flywheel

6.12 Locate the clutch pressure plate over the friction disc

6.15 Tighten the clutch pressure plate bolts evenly and gradually

15 Tighten the pressure plate bolts progressively and in diagonal sequence, until the specified torque setting is achieved, then remove the centralising tool **(see illustration)**.
16 Check the release bearing in the transmission bellhousing for smooth operation, and if necessary renew it with reference to Section 7.
17 Refit the transmission with reference to Chapter 7A.

7 Release bearing and lever – removal, inspection and refitting

Removal

1 Remove the transmission as described in Chapter 7A.
2 On 012/01W transmissions, use a screwdriver to prise the release lever from the

7.2a Push the spring clip to release the arm from the pivot stud – 012 transmission

ball-stud inside the transmission bellhousing. If this proves difficult, push the spring clip from the pivot end of the release lever by pushing it through the hole. This will release the pivot end of the lever from the ball-stud. Now withdraw the lever together with the release bearing from the guide sleeve **(see illustrations)**. On 01E/0A1 transmissions, undo the single bolt and remove the leaf spring. Withdraw the release lever complete with release bearing and intermediate piece.
3 Use a screwdriver to depress the plastic tabs and separate the bearing from the lever **(see illustrations)**.
4 On 012/01W transmissions, remove the plastic pivot from the ball-stud. The release lever locates on the plastic pivot.

Inspection

5 Spin the release bearing by hand, and check it for smooth running. Any tendency to seize

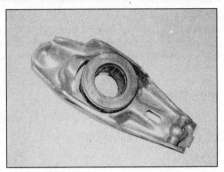

7.2b Release lever and bearing removed from the 012 transmission

or run rough will necessitate renewal of the bearing. If it is to be re-used, wipe it clean with a dry cloth; on no account should the bearing be washed in a liquid solvent, otherwise the internal grease will be removed.

Refitting

6 On 012/01W transmissions, commence refitting by lubricating the ball-stud and plastic pivot with a little lithium-based grease **(see illustration)**. On all transmissions, smear a little grease on the release bearing surface which contacts the diaphragm spring fingers and the release lever, and also on the guide sleeve.
7 On 012/01W transmissions, fit the spring onto the release lever, and make sure the plastic pivot is in place on the ball-stud. Refit the lever together with the bearing and press the release lever onto the ball-stud until the spring holds it in position **(see illustrations)**. On

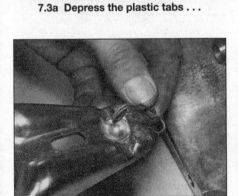

7.3a Depress the plastic tabs . . .

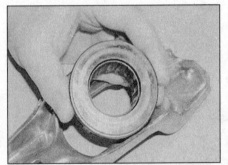

7.3b . . . and remove the bearing from the arm

7.6 Lubricate the ball-stud with a little lithium grease

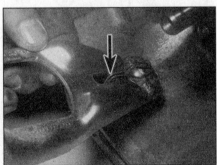

7.7a Locate the spring over the end of the release lever . . .

7.7b . . . and press the spring into the hole (arrowed) . . .

7.7c . . . then press the release lever onto the ball-stud until the spring clip holds it in position

01E/0A1 transmissions, re-glue the plastic ring to the bearing race, and engage the retaining lugs of the release bearing with the release lever. Set the release lever on the intermediate piece, fit the leaf spring, and tighten the retaining bolt to the specified torque (see illustration).

8 Clutch pedal switch – removal, refitting and adjustment

Removal

1 Inside the car, remove the storage compartment/panel from below the steering column. Unclip the cover then undo the retaining screws and pull the storage compartment from the clips in the facia. This will allow access to the pedal switch.

2 The design of the threads of the clutch switch are such that it can be pushed approximately into place, and then screwed in or out for fine adjustment. Consequently, there are two methods of removal. The first is to unplug the wiring connector from the switch, and unscrew the switch from the bracket/clip. The second method is to unplug the wiring connector from the switch, and pull the switch out from the bracket/clip. Whilst the latter method is quicker, it also risks damaging the threads of the switch, which may necessitate a new unit.

Refitting

3 Press the switch into the mounted securing clip, until it contacts the clutch pedal.

4 Carry out the adjustment procedure in paragraph 7, before proceeding.

5 Reconnect the wiring plug. The remainder of refitting is a reversal of removal.

Adjustment

6 With the storage compartment/panel below the steering column removed, disconnect the wiring plug to the switch.

7 With the pedal released, the gap between the switch plunger and the main body of the switch must not be more than 0.5 mm. Also the gap between the pedal bracket and the retaining tabs of the switch must not be more than 0.5 mm. To adjust the switch, turn it as required (see illustration).

8 Reconnect the wiring plug, and refit the storage compartment/panel.

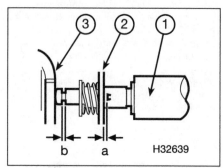

8.7 Clutch pedal switch adjustment

1 Switch
2 Mounting bracket
3 Clutch pedal
a and b = 0.5 mm maximum

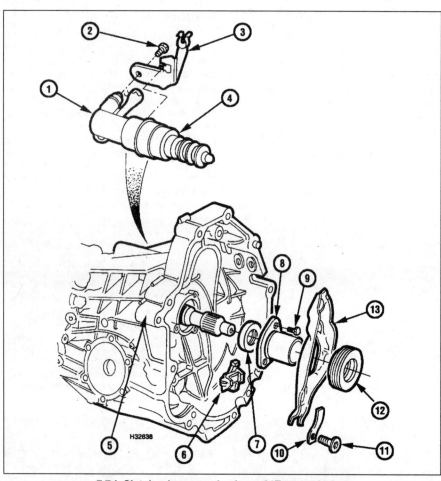

7.7d Clutch release mechanism – 01E transmission

1	Slave cylinder	5	Gearbox
2	Bolt	6	Intermediate
3	Hose support		piece
	bracket	7	Oil seal
4	Plunger	8	Guide sleeve

9 Bolt
10 Leaf spring
11 Bolt
12 Release bearing
13 Release lever

Chapter 7 Part A:
Manual transmission

Contents

	Section number			Section number
Gearchange linkage – adjustment	2	Manual transmission overhaul – general information		4
General information	1	Multi-function switch – removal and refitting		5
Manual transmission – removal and refitting	3	Oil seals – renewal		7
Manual transmission oil level check	See Chapter 1A or 1B	Roadspeed sensor – removal and refitting		6

Degrees of difficulty

Easy, suitable for novice with little experience 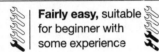	Fairly easy, suitable for beginner with some experience	Fairly difficult, suitable for competent DIY mechanic	Difficult, suitable for experienced DIY mechanic	Very difficult, suitable for expert DIY or professional

Specifications

Engine codes*

Petrol engines

1781 cc, DOHC, Bosch Motronic ME7.5 injection, turbocharged	AWT
1984 cc, SOHC, Siemens Simos 3.2 injection, non-turbo	AZM
1984 cc, DOHC, Bosch Motronic ME7.5 injection, non-turbo	ALT

Diesel engines

Electronic direct injection, unit injectors, 74 kW (100 bhp)	AVB
Electronic direct injection, unit injectors, 96 kW (130 bhp)	AVF and AWX

* **Note:** *See 'Vehicle identification' for the location of the code marking on the engine.*

General

Type	Transmission mounted on rear of engine, with drive flanges to front wheels. Five or six forward speeds and reverse, synchromesh on all gears, integral final drive
Lubricant capacities	See Chapter 1A or 1B

Torque wrench settings	Nm	lbf ft
Drive flange:		
M10	80	59
M8	45	33
Driveshaft cover plates	25	18
Engine speed sensor	10	7
Engine-to-transmission bolts:		
M10	45	33
M12	65	48
Gearchange adjustment bolt	23	17
Guide sleeve bolt*:		
Aluminium casing	35	26
Magnesium casing	25	18
Multi-function switch*:		
Aluminium casing	25	18
Magnesium casing	15	11
Oil drain plug (01E/0A1 transmission)	40	30
Oil filler plug:		
01E/0A1 transmission	40	30
012/01W transmission	25	18
Selector lever bolt	25	18

* *On magnesium casings the code MgAl9Zn1 appears just in front of the left-hand driveshaft, and on the bottom of the casing behind the left-hand driveshaft.*

1 General information

Two different transmissions may be fitted to vehicles covered by this manual – 012/01W is a five-speed transmission, and 01E/0A1 is a five- or six-speed transmission. Both units may have aluminium or magnesium casings. The 01E/0A1 six-speed transmission is only fitted to the 1.9 litre 96 kW (130 bhp) diesel engine, however, the 01E/0A1 and 012/01W five-speed transmissions may be fitted to any of the engines covered by this manual. The transmission identification marks are stamped into the casing on the mounting flange in front of the left-hand driveshaft.

The transmissions are bolted to the rear of the in-line engines. The front-wheel-drive configuration transmits the power to a differential unit located at the front of the transmission, through driveshafts, to the front wheels. All gears, including reverse, incorporate a synchromesh engagement.

Gearchange is by a floor-mounted lever. A rod connects the bottom of the lever to a shift rod which protrudes from the rear of the transmission (see illustrations).

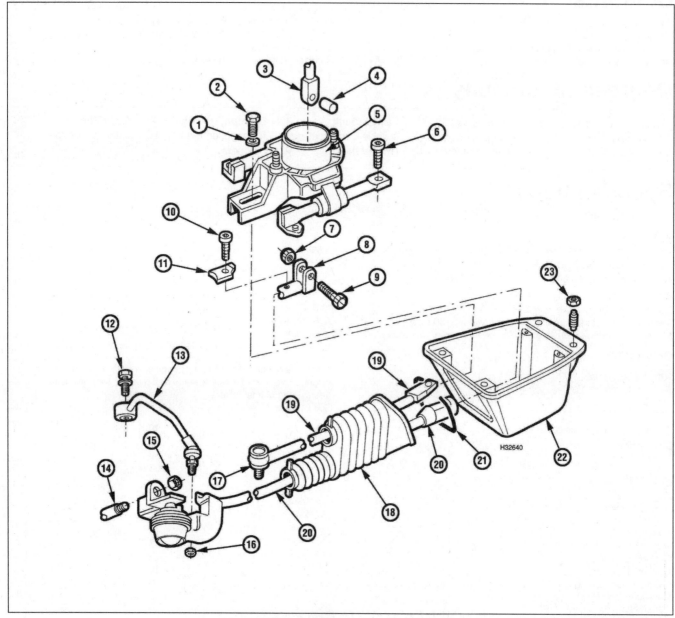

1.3a 01E/0A1 transmission selector components

1 Washer	6 Bolt	11 Clamp
2 Bolt	7 Nut*	12 Bolt
3 Gear lever	8 Selector	13 Connecting rod
4 Spacer	fork	14 Transmission
5 Rear housing with	9 Bolt	selector shaft
pushrod	10 Bolt	15 Nut*

16 Nut	21 Tensioning
17 Washer	ring
18 Bellows	22 Gear lever
19 Front	housing
pushrod	23 Nut
20 Selector rod	* Always renew

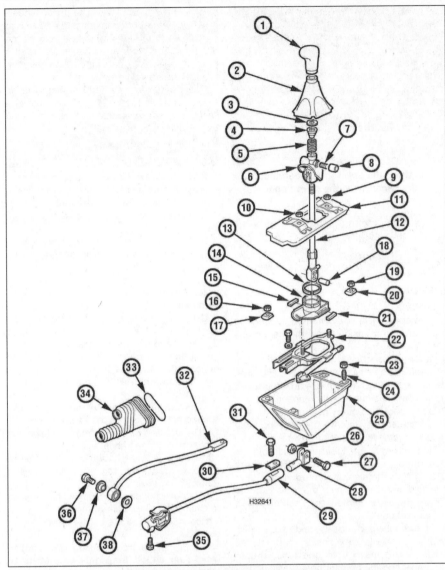

1.1b 012/01W transmission selector components

1 Gear knob	12 Gear lever	21 Buffer	30 Clamp
2 Gaiter	13 Circlip*	22 Rear housing and	31 Bolt
3 Clip*	14 Ball housing	pushrod	32 Front pushrod
4 Spacer	15 Buffer	23 Nut	33 Tensioning
5 Spring	16 Nut	24 Stud	ring
6 Ball-stop	17 Connecting	25 Gear lever	34 Bellows
7 Spring	piece	housing	35 Bolt*
8 Bush	18 Spacer	26 Nut*	36 Bolt
9 Nut	19 Nut	27 Bolt	37 Washer
10 Nut	20 Connecting	28 Selector fork	38 Washer
11 Cover	piece	29 Selector rod	* Always renew

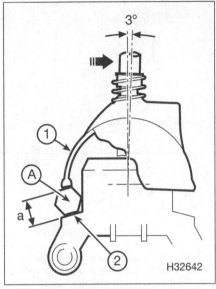

2.5 Insert the Allen key (A) between the ball-stop left-hand lug (1) and the sloped shoulder (2)

a = 14 mm

5 Insert a 14 mm Allen key between the left lug of the ball-stop and the sloped shoulder alongside the ball-stop. The key must be in contact along the entire shoulder (see illustration). Position the gear lever slightly to the rear and tighten the selector rod bolt.

6 Check the correct operation of the selector mechanism, and refit the gear lever housing cover, gaiter and gear knob.

012/01W transmission

7 Working inside the car, unscrew and remove the knob from the top of the gear lever, then unclip and remove the gaiter.

8 Remove the noise insulation around the bottom of the gear lever housing.

9 Measure the distance between the selector mechanism and body (see illustrations). If the distance is not correct, loosen the pushrod bolt, reposition the pushrod, and tighten the bolt.

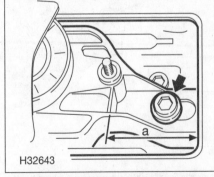

2.9a Measure the distance between the selector mechanism and body (a)

On 012 transmissions where the gear lever is not pressed down for reverse the dimension is 41 mm

2 Gearchange linkage
– adjustment

01E/0A1 transmission

1 Working inside the car, unscrew and remove the knob from the top of the gear lever, then unclip and remove the gaiter.

2 Unscrew the retaining nuts and remove the gear lever housing cover.

3 Measure the distance between the rear pushrod and body (see illustration 2.9b). If the distance is not 43 mm, loosen the pushrod bolt, reposition the pushrod, and tighten the bolt.

4 Working through the gear lever aperture, loosen the selector rod bolt. Do not remove the bolt.

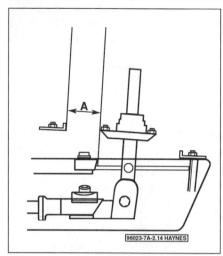

2.9b On 012 transmissions where the gear lever must be pressed down for reverse, the dimension (A) is 37 mm

On 01E transmissions the dimension is 43 mm

10 Working through the gear lever aperture, loosen the clamp bolt attaching the gearchange rod to the adjustment fork on the gearchange lever. Do not remove the bolt.

11 Check that the ball housing is horizontal. If not, loosen the two nuts, adjust the position of the housing, and retighten the nuts.

12 Have an assistant hold the gear lever in a vertical position so that the distance between the ends of the curved ball-stop are the same on both sides with the lever positioned slightly to the rear. The gear lever is now in the 3rd/4th neutral position.

13 Make sure the transmission gear selector rod is positioned in neutral, then tighten the adjustment bolt.

14 Check the correct operation of the selector mechanism, and refit the noise insulation, gaiter and gear knob.

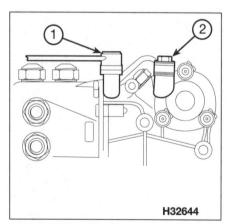

3.17a Unbolt the connecting rod from the right-hand side of the gearbox (2), undo the Allen screw and detach the front pushrod from the top of the gearbox casing (1) . . .

3.10 Undo the bolts and disconnect the driveshaft from the drive flange

3 Manual transmission
– removal and refitting

Removal

1 Select a solid, level surface to park the vehicle upon. Give yourself enough space to move around it easily. Apply the handbrake and chock the rear wheels.

2 Apply the handbrake, then jack up the front of the vehicle and support it on axle stands (see *Jacking and vehicle support*). Remove the splash guard from under the engine compartment.

3 Disconnect the battery negative (earth) lead (see Chapter 5A). Remove the retaining nuts/bolts and remove the engine cover.

4 Remove the air cleaner assembly as described in Chapter 4A or 4B. On the 012/01W transmissions remove the inlet manifold cover, disconnect the hose from the airflow meter, and where applicable remove the air inlet duct.

5 On turbocharged models, undo the screws and lift the coolant expansion tank from its location and move it to one side without disconnecting the coolant hoses. Disconnect the lambda sensor wiring on the bulkhead (petrol models).

6 Refer to Chapter 4C, and remove the exhaust front pipe and catalytic converter.

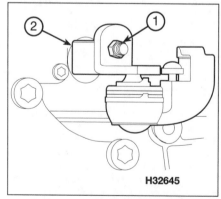

3.17b . . . then undo the retaining nut (1) and pull the selector lever from the selector shaft (2)

3.16 Unscrew the bolt and disconnect the gearchange rod from the rear of the transmission (arrowed)

Take care not to bend excessively the flexible section of the front pipe.

7 Unscrew and remove the transmission-to-engine bolts accessible from above (ie, the engine compartment).

8 Unbolt the splash guard support bracket from under the front of the engine compartment.

9 Using an Allen key, unbolt the heat shields from over the inner end of the right-hand driveshaft and left-hand driveshaft (if fitted).

10 Refer to Chapter 8 and detach the driveshafts from the transmission flanges **(see illustration)**. Rest the driveshafts on the suspension links.

11 Disconnect the wiring from the speedometer sender on the transmission.

12 Disconnect the wiring from the reversing light switch on the transmission.

13 Check that all wiring has been disconnected from the transmission and transmission-to-engine bolts.

14 Remove the starter motor with reference to Chapter 5A. If preferred, the wiring may be left connected, and the starter supported to one side.

15 Support the transmission on a trolley jack, then unbolt the right- and left-hand transmission mountings complete with rubber bushes.

16 On 012/01W transmissions, unscrew the bolt and disconnect the gearchange rod from the rear of the transmission **(see illustration)**. Note the securing bolt engages with a dimple in the transmission rod. Lower the transmission slightly and undo the Allen screw and detach the front pushrod from the transmission case.

17 On 01E/0A1 transmissions, lower the gearbox slightly and unbolt the connecting rod from the right-hand side of the gearbox, undo the Allen screw and detach the front pushrod from the top of the gearbox casing, undo the retaining nut and detach the selector lever from the selector shaft **(see illustrations)**.

18 Make sure that the transmission is adequately supported, then unscrew the remaining bolts securing the transmission to the engine.

19 With the help of an assistant, withdraw the transmission from the locating dowels on the rear of the engine, making sure that the input shaft does not hang on the clutch.

5.1 Multi-function switch

Lower the transmission sufficient to gain access to the clutch slave cylinder. Make sure that the driveshafts are supported clear of the transmission.

⚠ *Warning: Make sure that the transmission remains steady on the jack head. Keep the transmission level until the input shaft is fully withdrawn from the clutch friction disc.*

20 Unbolt the slave cylinder from the transmission, and tie it to one side. **Note:** *Do not depress the clutch pedal with the slave cylinder removed.*
21 Lower the transmission to the ground.

Refitting

22 Before refitting the transmission, make sure that the location dowels are correctly positioned in the engine cylinder block rear face. Also make sure that the starter motor lower mounting bolt is positioned in the transmission, as it cannot be inserted with the transmission in its normal position. It is recommended that the clutch friction disc and release bearing are checked as described in Chapter 6, and renewed if necessary.
23 Refitting the transmission is a reversal of the removal procedure, but note the following points:
a) *Check the rear rubber mountings and renew them if necessary.*
b) *Apply a little high melting-point grease to the splines of the transmission input shaft.*
c) *Tighten all nuts and bolts to the specified torque where given.*
d) *On completion, refer to Section 2 and check the gearchange linkage adjustment.*

4 Manual transmission overhaul – general information

1 Overhauling a manual transmission unit is a difficult and involved job for the DIY home mechanic. In addition to dismantling and reassembling many small parts, clearances must be precisely measured and, if necessary, changed by selecting shims and spacers. Internal transmission components are also often difficult to obtain and in many instances, extremely expensive. Because of this, if the transmission develops a fault or becomes

noisy, the best course of action is to have the unit overhauled by a specialist repairer or to obtain an exchange reconditioned unit.
2 Nevertheless, it is not impossible for the more experienced mechanic to overhaul the transmission if the special tools are available and the job is carried out in a deliberate step-by-step manner, to ensure that nothing is overlooked.
3 The tools necessary for an overhaul include internal and external circlip pliers, bearing pullers, a slide hammer, a set of pin punches, a dial test indicator and possibly a hydraulic press. In addition, a large, sturdy workbench and a vice will be required.
4 During dismantling of the transmission, make careful notes of how each component is fitted to make reassembly easier and accurate.
5 Before dismantling the transmission, it will help if you have some idea of where the problem lies. Certain problems can be closely related to specific areas in the transmission which can make component examination and renewal easier. Refer to the *Fault finding* Section in this manual for more information.

5 Multi-function switch – removal and refitting

Removal

1 The multi-function switch is located on top of the 012/01W transmission only **(see illustration)**.
2 Apply the handbrake, then jack up the front of the vehicle and support it on axle stands (see *Jacking and vehicle support*).
3 Disconnect the wiring connector, then unscrew the bolts securing the switch lead to the top of the transmission.
4 Note the fitted position of the switch, then unscrew the bolt and remove the switch retainer plate.
5 Withdraw the multi-function switch from the transmission. Recover the O-ring seal.

Refitting

6 To refit the switch first clean the switch location in the transmission. Fit a new O-ring seal, then insert the switch in the previously noted position.
7 Refit the retainer plate and tighten the bolt.
8 Secure the lead to the top of the transmission and tighten the bolts.
9 Reconnect the wiring, then lower the vehicle to the ground.

6 Roadspeed sensor – removal and refitting

Removal

1 All transmissions are fitted with an electronic roadspeed sensor on the left-hand side of the transmission, just above the driveshaft drive

6.1 The roadspeed sensor is mounted on the left-hand side of the transmission

flange **(see illustration)**. This device measures the rotational speed of the transmission final drive and converts the information into an electronic signal, which is then sent to the speedometer module in the instrument panel. On certain models, the signal is also used as an input by the engine management system ECU.
2 Apply the handbrake, then jack up the front of the vehicle and support it on axle stands (see *Jacking and vehicle support*).
3 Remove the left-front road wheel, and the cover above the left-hand driveshaft.
4 Disconnect the wiring plug from the sensor.
5 Depress the retainer, then turn the speedometer drive and withdraw it from the transmission. Take care not to damage the drive, as the electronic components are delicate. Recover the seal **(see illustration)**.

Refitting

6 Refitting is a reversal of removal, but renew the seal.

7 Oil seals – renewal

Driveshaft flange oil seals

1 Apply the handbrake, then jack up the front of the vehicle and support it on axle stands (see *Jacking and vehicle support*). Remove the relevant roadwheel. Undo the retaining bolts/nuts and remove the engine undertray.

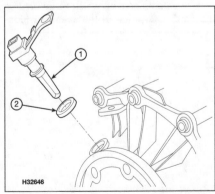

6.5 Roadspeed sensor (1) and seal (2)

7.4 Screw a bolt through the driveshaft flange and onto a distance piece placed against the transmission casing

7.5 Note the depth of the fitted seal, then prise it out using a flat-bladed screwdriver

7.7 Using a suitable tubular drift (such as a socket) tap the seal squarely into position

2 Refer to Chapter 8 and unbolt the heat shield, then unscrew the bolts and remove the relevant driveshaft from the transmission drive flange. Tie the driveshaft away from the transmission, and wrap the inner joint in a plastic bag, in order to prevent entry of dust and dirt. Turn the steering as necessary to move the driveshaft away from the flange.

3 Position a suitable container beneath the transmission to catch spilled oil.

012/01W transmissions

4 The drive flange is held in the differential sun gear by an internal circlip, and the flange must be pulled outwards to release the circlip. To do this, locate a suitable distance piece (such as a chisel) between the flange and the final drive cover or transmission casing (as applicable), then screw a bolt through the flange onto the distance piece. As the bolt is tightened, the flange will be forced outwards and the circlip released from its groove **(see illustration)**. If the flange is tight, turn it 180° and repeat the removal procedure.

5 With the flange out, note the fitted depth of the oil seal in the housing, then prise it out using a large flat-bladed screwdriver **(see illustration)**.

6 Clean all traces of dirt from the area around the oil seal aperture, then apply a smear of grease to the lips of the new oil seal.

7 Ensure the seal is correctly positioned, with its sealing lip facing inwards, and tap it squarely into position, using a suitable tubular drift (such as a socket) which bears only on the hard outer edge of the seal **(see illus-**

tration). If the surface of the flange is good, make sure the seal is fitted at the same depth in its housing as originally noted; it should be 5.5 mm below the outer edge of the transmission. If the surface of the flange is worn, fit the oil seal at a depth of 6.5 mm.

8 Clean the oil seal and apply a smear of multi-purpose grease to its lips.

9 It is recommended that the circlip on the inner end of the drive flange is renewed whenever the flange is removed. To do this, mount the flange in a soft-jawed vice, then prise off the old circlip and fit the new one **(see illustration)**. Lightly grease the circlip.

10 Insert the drive flange through the oil seal and engage it with the differential gear. Using a suitable drift, drive the flange fully into the gear until the circlip is felt to engage.

01E/0A1 transmissions

11 The drive flange is held in place by a M8 or M10 bolt. Undo the bolt and pull the flange out. If necessary, counterhold the flange by inserting two bolts into its circumference and using a lever.

12 With the flange out, note the fitted depth of the oil seal in the housing, then prise it out using a large flat-bladed screwdriver.

13 Clean all traces of dirt from the area around the oil seal aperture, then apply a smear of grease to the lips of the new oil seal.

14 Ensure the seal is correctly positioned, with its sealing lip facing inwards, and tap it squarely into position, using a suitable tubular drift (such as a socket) which bears only on the hard outer edge of the seal. If the surface of the

flange is good, make sure the seal is fitted at the same depth in its housing as originally noted; it should be 5.5 mm below the outer edge of the transmission. If the surface of the flange is worn, fit the oil seal at a depth of 6.5 mm.

15 Clean the oil seal and apply a smear of multi-purpose grease to its lips. Refit the drive flange and tighten the retaining bolt to the specified torque setting.

All transmissions

16 Refit the driveshaft (see Chapter 8), and the engine undertray.

17 Refit the roadwheel, then lower the vehicle to the ground. Check and if necessary top-up the transmission oil level (refer to the relevant part of Chapter 1).

Input shaft oil seal

18 The transmission must be removed for access to the input shaft oil seal. Refer to Section 3 of this Chapter.

19 Remove the clutch release bearing and lever with reference to Chapter 6.

012/01W transmission

20 Unscrew the bolts and remove the guide sleeve from inside the bellhousing. Recover the O-ring. Do not disturb any shims located on the input shaft. Discard the O-ring, a new one must be fitted **(see illustration)**.

21 Using a punch or drift, carefully drive the oil seal from its fitted position in the guide sleeve **(see illustration)**.

22 Wipe clean the oil seal seating.

23 Smear a little multi-purpose grease on the lips of the new oil seal, and locate the seal in

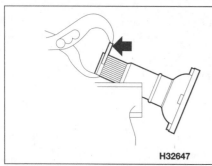

7.9 Fit a new circlip to the groove in the transmission's drive flange

H32647

7.20 Unscrew the bolts and remove the guide sleeve from inside the bellhousing

7.21 Carefully drive the input shaft oil seal from the guide tube

the guide sleeve with the sealing lip facing the gearbox side **(see illustration)**. Tap the seal squarely into position, using a suitable drift which bears only on the hard outer edge of the seal, until it is against the stop.

24 Using a new O-ring and new bolts, refit the guide sleeve to the transmission, tightening the bolts to the specified torque **(see illustration)**.

01E/0A1 transmission

25 Unscrew the bolts and remove the guide sleeve from inside the bellhousing. Recover the gasket. Do not disturb any shims located on the input shaft.

26 Note the fitted depth of the oil seal in the transmission housing, then use a screwdriver to prise it out taking care not to damage the input shaft.

27 Wipe clean the oil seal seating and input shaft.

28 Smear a little multi-purpose grease on the lips of the new oil seal, then locate the seal over the input shaft with its sealing lip facing inwards. Tap the oil seal squarely into position to a depth of 3.5 mm, using a suitable tubular drift which bears only on the hard outer edge of the seal. If the surface of the input shaft is worn excessively, position the oil seal at a depth of 4.5 mm.

29 Refit the guide sleeve, and tighten the bolts to the specified torque.

All transmissions

30 Refit the clutch release bearing and lever with reference to Chapter 6.

31 Refit the transmission with reference to Section 3 of this Chapter.

Selector shaft oil seal

32 Apply the handbrake, then jack up the front of the vehicle and support it on axle stands

7.23 Locate the seal in the guide sleeve with the sealing lip facing the gearbox side

(see *Jacking and vehicle support*). Where applicable, remove the engine undertray.

012/01W transmission

33 Unscrew the locking bolt and slide the gear lever coupling from the transmission selector shaft.

34 Using a small screwdriver, carefully prise the oil seal from the transmission housing taking care not to damage the surface of the selector shaft or housing.

35 Wipe clean the oil seal seating and selector shaft, then smear a little multi-purpose grease on the new oil seal lips and locate the seal over the end of the shaft. Make sure the closed side of the seal faces outwards. To prevent damage to the oil seal, temporarily wrap some adhesive tape around the end of the shaft.

36 Tap the oil seal squarely into position, using a suitable tubular drift which bears only on the hard outer edge of the seal. The seal should be inserted until it is 1.0 mm below the surface of the transmission.

37 Refit the gear lever coupling and tighten the locking bolt.

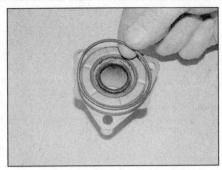

7.24 Fit a new O-ring to the guide sleeve

01E/0A1 transmission

38 Unscrew the retaining nut, and pull the selector lever from the selector shaft. **Note:** *Access to the selector lever with the transmission fitted is limited. It may be improved by lowering the transmission a little – see Section 3.*

39 Using a small screwdriver, carefully prise the oil seal from the housing, taking care not to damage the surface of the selector shaft or housing.

40 Wipe clean the oil seal seating and selector shaft, then smear a little multi-purpose grease on the new oil seal lips and locate the seal over the end of the shaft. Make sure the closed side of the seal faces outwards.

41 Tap the seal squarely into position, using a suitable drift which bears only on the outer edge of the seal.

42 Refit the selector lever to the shaft and tighten the nut to the specified torque.

All transmissions

43 Refit the engine undertray.

44 Lower the vehicle to the ground.

Chapter 7 Part B:
Automatic transmission

Contents

	Section number		Section number
Automatic transmission – removal and refitting	2	General information	1
Automatic transmission fluid – renewal ....See Chapter 1A or 1B		Locking cable – removal, refitting and adjustment	5
Automatic transmission overhaul – general information	3	Selector cable – removal, refitting and adjustment	4

Degrees of difficulty

Easy, suitable for novice with little experience	Fairly easy, suitable for beginner with some experience	Fairly difficult, suitable for competent DIY mechanic	Difficult, suitable for experienced DIY mechanic	Very difficult, suitable for expert DIY or professional

Specifications

General

Type . . . . Electro-hydraulically controlled planetary gearbox providing four or five forward speeds and one reverse speed. Drive transmitted through hydrodynamic torque converter

Designation:
Four-speed 01N
Five-speed 01V
Automatic transmission fluid capacity . . . . See Chapter 1A or 1B

Torque wrench settings

	Nm	lbf ft
Automatic transmission selector cable support bolt	23	17
Bracket for fluid pipe	10	7
Fluid pipe union	25	18
Fluid pipes to transmission	20	15
Torque converter to driveplate	85	63
Transmission bellhousing-to-engine bolts:		
M10.	45	33
M12.	65	48
Transmission mounting:		
Centre bolt	40	30
To body.	23	17
To transmission.	40	30

1 General information

The automatic transmission is a four- or five-speed unit, incorporating a hydrodynamic torque converter with a planetary gearbox. The four-speed unit is only fitted to early UK diesel models covered by this Manual, although it is also fitted to other non-UK petrol and diesel models.

Gear selection is achieved by means of a floor-mounted, seven position selector lever. The positions are P (Park), R (Reverse), N (Neutral), D (Drive), 3 (3rd gear lock), 2 (2nd gear lock), 1 (1st gear lock). The transmission has a kick-down feature which provides greater acceleration when the accelerator pedal is depressed to the floor.

The overall operation of the transmission is managed by the engine management electronic control unit (ECU) and as a result there are no manual adjustments.

Comprehensive fault diagnosis can therefore only be carried out using dedicated electronic test equipment.

Due to the complexity of the transmission and its control system, major repairs and overhaul operations should be left to a VW dealer, who will be equipped to carry out fault diagnosis and repair. The information in this Chapter is therefore limited to a description of the removal and refitting of the transmission as a complete unit. The removal, refitting and adjustment of the selector cable is also described.

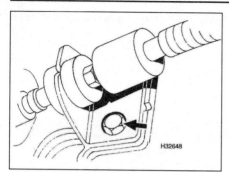

2.9 Undo the bolt (arrowed) and release the selector cable support bracket

2 Automatic transmission
– removal and refitting

Removal

1 Select a solid, level surface to park the vehicle upon. Give yourself enough space to move around it easily. Apply the handbrake and chock the rear wheels.

2 Apply the handbrake, then jack up the front of the vehicle and support it on axle stands (see *Jacking and vehicle support*). Remove both front roadwheels. On five-speed transmission models, unclip the vehicle level sender from the front suspension lower arm.

3 Remove the engine undershield panel and remove the noise insulation and bracket.

4 Disconnect the battery negative (earth) lead (see Chapter 5A) and position it away from the terminal.

5 Where necessary, unscrew the nuts/bolts and remove the top cover from the engine. On five-speed transmission models, also remove the cover from the air filter and disconnect the inlet hose from the inlet manifold.

6 Remove the exhaust front downpipe and

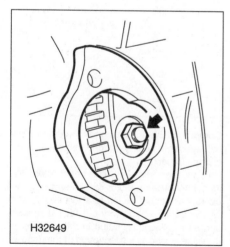

H32649

2.16 The torque converter-to-driveplate nuts are accessed through the starter motor aperture

catalytic converter with reference to Chapter 4C, taking care not to bend the flexible coupling. Also, where necessary, unbolt the downpipe mounting bracket from the transmission. On five-speed transmission models, remove the suction connecting piece together with the inlet manifold flap and exhaust gas recirculation valve.

7 Disconnect the wiring from the roadspeed sensor located in front of the left-hand drive flange.

8 Identify the wiring connections on the rear of the transmission, then unplug them. Loosen and detach the wiring support, and position the wiring to one side.

9 With the selector lever in position P, carefully disconnect the inner cable from the transmission lever, then unbolt the support bracket **(see illustration)**. Position the cable to one side.

10 Using an Allen key, unbolt the heat shields from over the inner end of the right-hand driveshaft.

11 Refer to Chapter 8 and detach the driveshafts from the transmission flanges. Tie the driveshafts away from the transmission.

12 Unbolt the right-hand transmission mounting complete with rubber bush and shield.

13 Position a suitable container beneath the transmission to collect spilt hydraulic fluid.

14 Detach the hydraulic pipes from the transmission, and recover the sealing rings. On petrol models without air conditioning, unscrew the bolts and withdraw the pipes. On all other models, unscrew the union nuts located beneath the left-hand side of the radiator and also the nuts located beneath the front of the transmission, and remove the pipes completely. Plug the apertures in the transmission housing to prevent entry of dust and dirt.

15 Remove the starter motor as described in Chapter 5A.

16 Turn the engine to locate one of the torque converter-to-driveplate nuts in the starter motor aperture **(see illustration)**. Unscrew and remove the nut while preventing the engine from turning using a wide-bladed screwdriver engaged with the ring gear teeth on the driveplate. Unscrew the remaining two nuts, turning the engine a third of a turn at a time to locate them.

17 Unscrew the transmission-to-engine mounting bolts accessible from under the car.

18 Support the engine with a hoist or support bar located on the front wing inner channels. If necessary, remove the bonnet as described in Chapter 11 in order to position the hoist over the engine. Due to the weight of the automatic transmission, the engine should be supported using both the front and rear lifting eyes. Depending on the engine, temporarily remove components as necessary to attach the hoist.

19 Support the transmission with a trolley jack or stand. Unbolt the left-hand transmission mounting complete with rubber bush and shield.

20 On five-speed transmission models, mark the location of the subframe beneath the engine compartment, then loosen only the front subframe bolts. Remove the remaining subframe bolts and lower the rear of the subframe. **Note:** *It is important that the subframe is refitted in its correct position otherwise the handling of the car will be affected and excessive tyre wear will occur.*

21 Unscrew and remove the transmission-to-engine mounting bolts accessible from over the engine.

22 With the help of an assistant, withdraw the transmission from the locating dowels on the rear of the engine, making sure that the torque converter remains fully engaged with the transmission input shaft. If necessary, use a lever to release the torque converter from the driveplate.

23 When the locating dowels are clear of their mounting holes, lower the transmission to the ground using the jack. Strap a restraining bar across the front of the bellhousing to keep the torque converter in position.

⚠ **Warning: Make sure that the transmission remains steady on the jack head. Take care to prevent the torque converter from falling out as the transmission is removed.**

24 Where necessary, remove the intermediate plate from the locating dowels.

Refitting

25 Refitting the transmission is a reversal of the removal procedure, but note the following points:

a) As the torque converter is refitted, ensure that the drive pins at the centre of the torque converter hub engage with the recesses in the automatic transmission fluid pump inner wheel.

b) Tighten the bellhousing bolts and torque converter-to-driveplate nuts to the specified torque. Always renew self-locking nuts and bolts.

c) Renew the O-ring seals on the fluid pipes and filler tube attached to the transmission casing.

d) Tighten the transmission mounting bolts to the correct torque.

e) Check the final drive oil level and transmission fluid level as described in Chapter 1A or 1B.

f) On completion, refer to Section 4 and check the gear selector cable adjustment.

g) On five-speed transmission models, renew the front subframe bolts and make sure that the front subframe is positioned exactly as removed. Finally have the wheel alignment checked and if necessary adjusted.

h) If the transmission does not perform as expected after refitting, have the ECU basic setting re-introduced by a VW dealer or automatic transmission specialist.

3 Automatic transmission overhaul – general information

In the event of a fault occurring, it will be necessary to establish whether the fault is electrical, mechanical or hydraulic in nature, before repair work can be contemplated. Diagnosis requires detailed knowledge of the transmission's operation and construction, as well as access to specialised test equipment, and so is deemed to be beyond the scope of this manual. It is therefore essential that problems with the automatic transmission are referred to a VW dealer for assessment.

Note that a faulty transmission should not be removed before the vehicle has been assessed by a dealer, as fault diagnosis is carried out with the transmission *in situ*.

4 Selector cable – removal, refitting and adjustment

Removal

1 Move the selector lever to the P position.
2 Apply the handbrake, then jack up the front of the vehicle and support it on axle stands (see *Jacking and vehicle support*).
3 Working under the vehicle, undo the screws and lower the heat shield from the gear selector mounting bracket onto the exhaust. Slide the heat shield to the rear.

4.4 Selector components – 4-speed 01N transmission

1 *Knob*
2 *Sleeve*
3 *Display*
4 *Light guide*
5 *Guide*
6 *Selector lever*
7 *Spring*
8 *Connecting rod*
9 *Ignition/starter switch*
10 *Lock solenoid*
11 *Spring*
12 *Nut*
13 *Spring clip*
14 *Washer*
15 *Lever*
16 *Support bracket*
17 *Bolt*
18 *Selector lever cable*
19 *Clip*
20 *Rubber housing*
21 *Locking element*
22 *Cover*
23 *Pin*
24 *Pivot*
25 *Bracket*
26 *Engagement element*
27 *Locking cable*

Four-speed transmission

4 Release the cover from the bottom of the selector lever bracket by pressing the fastener to the front **(see illustration)**.
5 Disconnect the inner cable by squeezing the clip to release the cable from the selector lever. Pull the outer cable from the support, then pull out the locking element and remove the cover and cable from the bottom of the selector lever assembly. Take care not to bend the cable excessively.

Five-speed transmission

6 Support the weight of the transmission with a trolley jack and piece of wood, then

unbolt and remove the left-hand transmission mounting.
7 Undo the retaining nuts and remove the cover from the underside of the lever housing **(see illustration overleaf)**.
8 Disconnect the inner cable by squeezing the clip to release the cable from the selector lever.
9 Pull down the locking plate securing the outer cable to the housing, and withdraw the cable.

All transmissions

10 At the transmission end of the cable, use a screwdriver to prise the end of the inner cable up from the transmission lever.

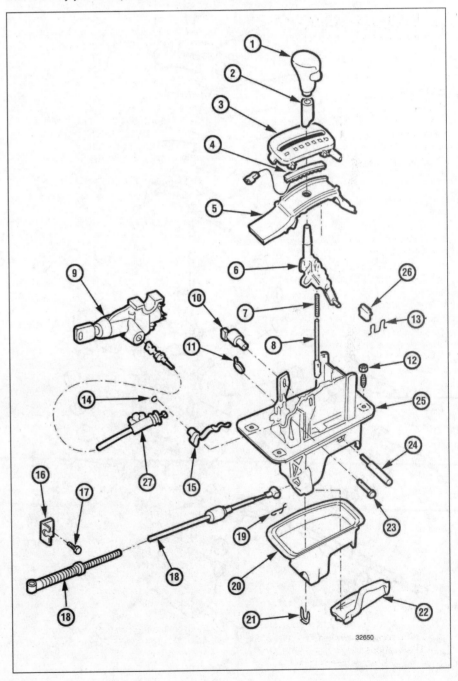

32650

11 Unscrew the bolt(s) and detach the support bracket with cable from the side of the transmission.

12 Loosen the locknuts (where fitted) and detach the cable from the bracket. Withdraw the cable from under the car.

Refitting

13 Refitting is a reversal of removal, but lightly grease the cable end fittings. Before lowering the car to the ground and *before* reconnecting the cable to the transmission lever, adjust the cable as follows.

Adjustment

14 Move the selector lever inside the car to the P position.

15 Move the selector lever on the transmission to the P position, which is the rear stop. Make sure that both front wheels are locked by attempting to turn them in the same direction at the same time. **Note:** *Even though the transmission is locked, it will still be possible to turn the front wheels in* **opposite** *directions, since the differential gears are able move in relation to each other.*

16 Loosen the bolt(s) securing the selector cable bracket to the transmission.

17 Press the cable end onto the selector lever, then check that the cable is free of any stress by moving it side-to-side several times. Now tighten the cable bracket securing bolt(s) to the specified torque.

18 Check the adjustment by selecting P. With the brake pedal released, check that the selector lever cannot be moved out of the P position with the lever button pressed. Now depress the brake pedal and check that the

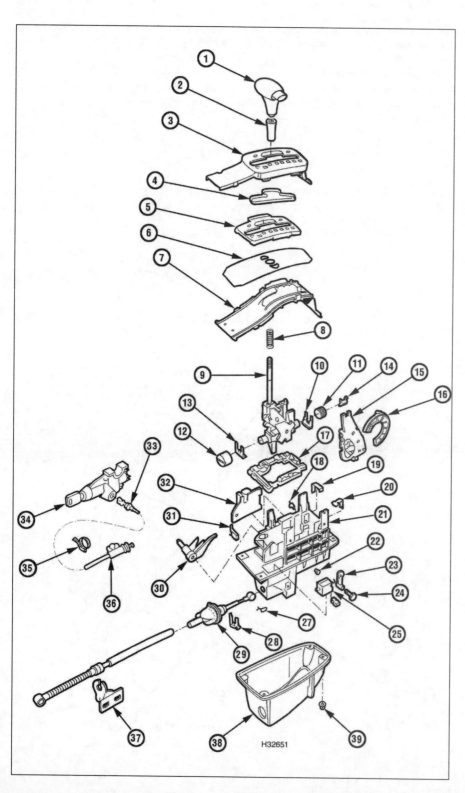

4.7 Selector components – 5-speed 01V transmission

1 *Selector lever handle*
2 *Sleeve*
3 *Cover moulding*
4 *Trim piece*
5 *Symbol panel*
6 *Masking panel*
7 *Guide*
8 *Spring*
9 *Pull rod*
10 *Locking clip*
11 *Mounting bush*
12 *Mounting bush*
13 *Locking clip*
14 *Stop buffer*
15 *Cable lever*
16 *Detent*
17 *Frame*
18 *Fulcrum pin*
19 *Spring clip with roller*
20 *Spring clip with roller*
21 *Mounting bracket*
22 *Fulcrum pin*
23 *Locking pawl*
24 *Fulcrum pin*
25 *Selector lever lock solenoid*
27 *Securing clip*
28 *Locking plate*
29 *Selector lever cable*
30 *Locking lever*
31 *Securing spring*
32 *Mounting*
33 *Locking cable*
34 *Ignition/starter switch*
35 *Cable tie*
36 *Locking cable*
37 *Support bracket*
38 *Cover*
39 *Nut*

H32651

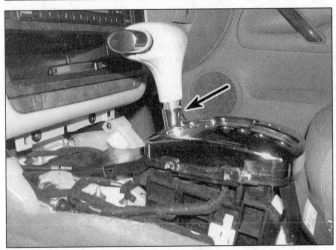

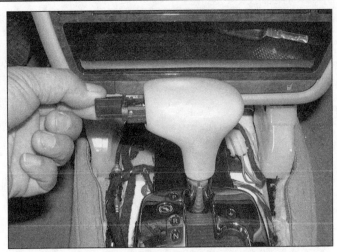

5.2a To remove the selector lever handle, slide this sleeve down as far as it will go . . .

5.2b . . . then pull the button on the handle out and slide the handle off the lever

lock solenoid releases enabling the selector lever to be moved to any position with the lever button pressed. Check that the display agrees with the position of the lever.

19 Select position N. With the brake pedal released, check that the selector lever is locked. Depress the pedal and check that the selector lever can be moved to any position. Note that it is only possible to select R with the button pressed.

20 On RHD models, check that it is only possible to operate the starter motor in positions P and N with the button released.

21 Lower the car to the ground.

| 5 | Locking cable – removal, refitting and adjustment |

Note: *VW tool number 3352 will be required to adjust the locking cable.*

Removal

1 Disconnect the battery negative terminal (see Chapter 5A).

2 Check the colour of the selector lever handle. To remove the selector lever handle coloured red and black, first move the gear selector lever to position 1, then press the lever sleeve down, possibly using a tool to lever it **(see illustrations)**, pull the knob outwards to its stop, and pull the handle off – **do not** depress the button.

3 To remove the selector lever handle coloured black, first move the gear selector lever to position 3, then press down the lever sleeve located beneath the handle. Pull out the handle button just enough to allow the internal lever to hang down, then pull the handle upwards from the selector lever.

4 With reference to Chapter 11, remove the centre console, then refer to Chapter 10 and remove the steering wheel together with airbag.

5 Remove the steering column combination switch as described in Chapter 12.

6 Turn the ignition switch to the 'On' position.

7 Move the selector lever to position P.

8 Lift up the locking clip (1) on the outer cable, and pull the cable from the ignition switch **(see illustration)**.

9 Remove the selector lever cover and guide.

10 Lift the securing spring slightly, and unclip the locking cable. Release the cable from the cable tie.

11 Note the routing of the cable and withdraw it from the passenger compartment.

Refitting

12 Refit the cable, using the routing noted during removal.

13 Ensure that the ignition switch is in the 'On' position, and the selector lever is in the P position.

14 Fit the cable to the ignition switch, ensuring that the locking device engages correctly. Turn the ignition switch to the 'Off' position.

15 Clip the locking cable into the securing spring in the mounting bracket.

16 Engage the locking cable support bracket into the selector mechanism, and the locking inner cable eye into the lever. Carry out the following adjustment procedure.

17 The remainder of refitting is a reversal of removal.

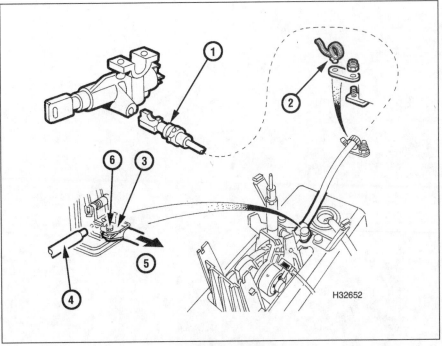

5.8 Locking cable

1 Locking clip	3 Support bracket	5 Towards the engine
2 Cable tie	4 VW setting bar (3352)	6 Bolt

H32652

Adjustment

18 Loosen the support bracket clamp bolt **(see illustration 5.8)**. It must be possible to move the support bracket forward by hand.

19 Move the steering column down and to the rear, then position VW special tool 3352 (setting bar) between the locking cable lever and the locking cable eye.

20 Pull the outer cable forwards towards the engine, and tighten the support bracket clamp bolt securely. Remove the setting bar.

21 Check the operation of the locking cable.

Chapter 8
Driveshafts

Contents

Section number

Driveshaft and CV joint check . . . . .See Chapter 1A or 1B
Driveshaft overhaul – general information 4
Driveshafts – overhaul 3

Section number

Driveshafts – removal and refitting. 2
General information 1

Degrees of difficulty

Easy, suitable for novice with little experience

Fairly easy, suitable for beginner with some experience

Fairly difficult, suitable for competent DIY mechanic

Difficult, suitable for experienced DIY mechanic

Very difficult, suitable for expert DIY or professional

Specifications

Lubrication

Type	G 000 603 grease*
Amount per joint:	
Outer joint:	
88 mm diameter joint	90 g
98 mm diameter joint	120 g
Inner joint:	
100 mm diameter joint	90 g
108 mm diameter joint	120 g

* Note from 08/04 a different type of grease was introduced which must not be mixed with the previous type. See your VW dealer for details.

Torque wrench settings

	Nm	lbf ft
Driveshaft-to-transmission flange socket-head bolts:		
M8 bolts	40	30
M10 bolts	77	57
Hub bolt*:		
M14 bolt:		
Stage 1	115	85
Stage 2	Angle-tighten a further 180°	
M16 bolt:		
Stage 1	190	140
Stage 2	Angle-tighten a further 180°	
Upper suspension arm pinch-bolt nut*	40	30

* Use new fasteners

1 General information

Drive is transmitted from the differential to the front wheels by means of two steel driveshafts of either solid or hollow construction (depending on model). Both driveshafts are splined at their outer ends, to accept the wheel hubs, and are secured to the hub by a large bolt. The inner end of each driveshaft is bolted to the transmission drive flanges.

Constant velocity (CV) joints are fitted to each end of the driveshafts, to ensure the smooth and efficient transmission of drive at all the angles possible as the roadwheels move up-and-down with the suspension, and as they turn from side-to-side under steering. On petrol engine models with a manual transmission unit, both inner and outer constant velocity joints are of the ball-and-cage type. On all diesel engine models, and petrol engine models with automatic transmission, the outer joint is of the ball-and-cage type, but the inner joint is of the tripod type. On diesel engines with a manual transmission, the outer tripod joint may be removed separately, but on petrol models with automatic transmission, the tripod joint is integral with the driveshaft.

Rubber or plastic gaiters are secured over both CV joints with steel clips. These contain the grease that is packed into the joint, and also protect the joint from the ingress of dirt and debris.

2.1 Hexagon-type hub bolt securing the driveshaft

2.12a Manoeuvre the driveshaft into position, engaging the splined with those of the hub . . .

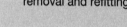

2 Driveshafts –
removal and refitting

Removal

1 Remove the wheel trim/hub cap (as applicable) then partially slacken the hub bolt with the vehicle resting on its wheels – either a hexagon or multi-point socket head bolt is fitted **(see illustration)**. Also slacken the wheel bolts.

2 Chock the rear wheels of the car, firmly apply the handbrake, then jack up the front of the car and support it on axle stands. Remove the appropriate front roadwheel. Whilst the wheel is removed, refit at least one of the wheel bolts to ensure the brake disc remains correctly positioned on the hub.

3 Remove the retaining screws and fasteners and remove the undercover from beneath the

2.8 Withdraw the driveshaft from the wheel arch

2.12b . . . and fit the new hub bolt

engine/transmission unit to gain access to the driveshafts. Where necessary, also unbolt the heat shield from the transmission housing to improve access to the inner joint.

4 Remove the ABS wheel sensor from the hub as described in Chapter 9. Release the sensor wiring from the locating bracket on the brake caliper.

5 Unscrew the pinch-bolt and separate the front and rear upper suspension arm balljoints from the top of the hub carrier (see Chapter 10). Discard the nut, a new one should be used on refitting.

Caution: Do not unbolt the steering track rod from the hub carrier.

6 Slacken and remove the hub bolt. If the bolt was not slackened with the wheels on the ground, refit at least two roadwheel bolts to the front hub, tightening them securely, then have an assistant firmly depress the brake pedal to prevent the front hub from rotating, whilst you

slacken and remove the hub bolt. Alternatively, a tool can be fabricated from two lengths of steel strip (one long, one short) and a nut and bolt; the nut and bolt forming the pivot of a forked tool.

7 Slacken and remove the bolts securing the inner driveshaft joint to the transmission drive flange and recover the reinforcing plates (where fitted) from underneath the bolts. Support the driveshaft by suspending it with wire or string – do not allow it to hang under its weight, or the joint may be damaged.

8 Swivel the hub carrier towards the rear of the wheel arch to free the driveshaft inner joint from transmission flange. Move the joint to one side then free the outer joint splines from the hub and manoeuvre the driveshaft out from underneath the vehicle **(see illustration)**. On driveshafts where the inner joint is exposed, remove the gasket from the driveshaft inner joint face and discard it; a new one should be used on refitting. **Note:** *Do not allow the vehicle to rest on its wheels with one or both driveshafts removed, as damage to the wheel bearings may result. If moving the vehicle is unavoidable, temporarily insert the outer end of the driveshaft in the hubs and tighten the driveshaft bolts. Support the inner ends of the driveshafts to avoid damage.*

Refitting

9 Before installing the driveshaft, examine the driveshaft oil seal in the transmission for signs of damage or deterioration. If necessary, on manual transmissions, renew it as described in Chapter 7A.

10 Thoroughly clean the driveshaft outer joint and hub splines and the mating surfaces of the inner joint and transmission flange. Check that all gaiter clips are securely fastened.

11 On a driveshaft where the inner joint is exposed (ball-and-cage type), fit a new gasket to the inner joint face by peeling off its backing foil and sticking it securely to the joint.

12 Manoeuvre the driveshaft into position, engaging the splines with those of the hub, and slide the outer joint into position. Fit the new hub bolt, tightening it by hand only at this stage **(see illustrations)**.

13 Align the driveshaft inner joint with the transmission flange then refit the retaining bolts and where fitted (on ball-and-cage type joints) the reinforcing plates. Tighten all bolts by hand then, working in a diagonal sequence,

2.13a Align the driveshaft inner joint with the transmission drive flange . . .

2.13b . . . then refit the retaining bolts and the reinforcing plates . . .

2.13c . . . then tighten the driveshaft bolts to the specified torque

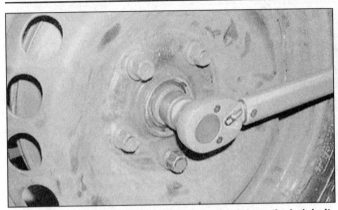

2.17a With the vehicle resting on its wheels, tighten the hub bolt to the specified Stage 1 torque . . .

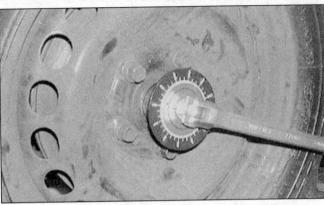

2.17b . . . then angle-tighten it through the specified Stage 2 angle

tighten them to the specified torque **(see illustrations)**. Where necessary, refit the heat shield to the transmission housing and securely tighten its retaining bolts.

14 Refit the front and rear upper suspension arms to top of the hub, insert the pinch-bolt, then fit the new retaining nut and tighten it to the specified torque.

15 Refit the ABS wheel sensor to the hub as described in Chapter 9. Refit the ABS wiring to the brake caliper bracket.

16 Refit the undercover and roadwheel then lower the vehicle to the ground and tighten the wheel bolts to the specified torque (see Chapter 1A or 1B).

17 With the vehicle resting on its wheels, tighten the hub bolt to the specified Stage 1 torque then angle-tighten it through the specified Stage 2 angle, using an angle-measuring gauge to ensure accuracy **(see illustrations)**. If an angle gauge is not available, use white paint to make alignment marks between the bolt head and hub/wheel prior to tightening; the marks can then be used to check that the bolt has been rotated through the correct angle.

18 Refit the wheel trim/hub cap (as applicable).

3 Driveshafts – overhaul

1 Remove the driveshaft from the vehicle as described in Section 2 and proceed as described under the relevant sub-heading.

Outer joint

Note: *A long M16 bolt/threaded rod will be useful during this procedure (see paragraph 4).*

2 Secure the driveshaft in a vice equipped with soft jaws, and release the gaiter retaining clips. If necessary, the retaining clips can be cut to release them.

3 Fold back the rubber gaiter to expose the outer constant velocity joint. Scoop out the excess grease and dispose of it.

4 It is now necessary to remove the outer constant velocity joint from the driveshaft.

This is most easily achieved using a hammer and suitable soft metal drift to sharply strike the inner member of the outer joint to drive it off the end of the shaft, taking great care not to damage the joint. On models with hollow driveshafts, it will first be necessary to displace the inner circlip (using circlip pliers) from its groove at the inner surface of the joint, to allow the dished washer and the plastic spacer ring to be slid along the driveshaft, away from the joint.

5 Once the joint assembly has been removed, remove the circlip from the groove in the driveshaft splines, and discard it. A new circlip must be fitted on reassembly.

6 Slide the spacer and dished washer off from the driveshaft, noting their correct fitted locations, and remove the rubber gaiter.

7 With the constant velocity joint removed from the driveshaft, thoroughly clean the joint using paraffin, or a suitable solvent, and dry it thoroughly. Carry out a visual inspection of the joint.

8 Move the inner splined driving member from side-to-side, to expose each ball in turn at the top of its track. Examine the balls for cracks, flat spots, or signs of surface pitting.

9 Inspect the ball tracks on the inner and outer members. If the tracks have widened, the balls will no longer be a tight fit. At the same time, check the ball cage windows for wear or cracking between the windows.

10 If the constant velocity joint is found to be worn or damaged, it will be necessary to renew

the joint, or the complete driveshaft (where the joint is not available separately). Refer to your VW dealer for further information on parts availability. If the joint is in satisfactory condition, obtain a repair kit; the genuine VW kit consists of a new gaiter, circlip, spring washer and spacer, retaining clips, and the correct type and quantity of grease. **Note:** *As of 08/04 a new type of grease was introduced.* **Do not** *mix this type with the earlier type. Thoroughly clean away all old grease before working-in the new type.*

11 Tape over the splines on the end of the driveshaft, then slide the new gaiter onto the shaft **(see illustration)**. Remove the tape.

12 Fit the dished washer, ensuring its convex surface is facing inwards, then slide on the spacer with its flatter surface facing the dished washer **(see illustrations)**.

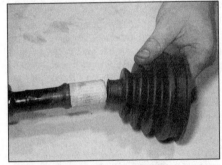

3.11 Tape over the driveshaft splines then slide the new gaiter along the shaft

3.12a Fit the dished washer with its convex surface facing inwards . . .

3.12b . . . then slide on the spacer with its flatter surface facing the dished washer

3.13 Fit the new circlip to the driveshaft groove

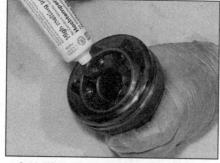

3.14 Work the grease will into the ball tracks of the outer joint

3.15a Locate the outer joint on the driveshaft splines . . .

3.15b . . . and tap it over the circlip

3.16 Seat the gaiter on the outer joint and driveshaft then lift its inner lip to equalise air pressure inside the gaiter

3.17a Fit the inner and outer retaining clips . . .

13 Fit the new circlip, making sure it is correctly located in the driveshaft groove **(see illustration)**.

14 Work the grease well into the ball tracks of the outer joint then fill the gaiter with any excess **(see illustration)**.

15 Locate the outer joint on the driveshaft splines and slide it on until the inner member abuts the circlip. Tap the joint outer member sharply with hammer and soft-metal drift to force the inner member over the circlip and fully onto the driveshaft **(see illustrations)**. Pull on the joint assembly to make sure the joint is securely retained by the circlip.

16 Locate the outer lip of the gaiter in the groove on the joint outer member then lift the inner lip of the gaiter to equalise the air pressure inside **(see illustration)**.

17 Fit both the inner and outer retaining

clips to the gaiter and secure each one in position by compressing its raised section. In the absence of the special tool, carefully compress each clip using a pair of side-cutters taking great care not to cut through the clip **(see illustrations)**.

18 Check that the constant velocity joint moves freely in all directions, then refit the driveshaft to the vehicle as described in Section 2.

Inner joint

Ball-and-cage type

Note: *The inner joint is a very tight fit on the driveshaft and removal/refitting will therefore require the use of a hydraulic press and suitable adapters. If this equipment is not available, gaiter renewal must be entrusted to a VW dealer or other suitably-equipped garage.*

19 Secure the driveshaft in a vice equipped with soft jaws then, using a hammer and punch, carefully tap the gaiter locating plate off from the inner constant velocity joint outer member **(see illustration)**.

20 Remove the circlip from the inner end of the driveshaft.

21 Remove the inner constant velocity joint from the driveshaft by securely supporting the joint outer member and pressing the driveshaft out from the inner member. Note which way around the joint outer member is fitted.

22 Release the gaiter inner retaining clip and remove the gaiter from the driveshaft.

23 Clean and inspect the inner joint as described in paragraphs 7 to 9.

24 If the constant velocity joint is found to be worn or damaged, it will be necessary to renew the joint, or the complete driveshaft (where no joint components are available separately). Refer to your VW dealer for further information on parts availability. If the joint is in satisfactory condition, obtain a repair kit; the genuine VW kit consists of a new gaiter, locating plate, circlip, retaining clips, and the correct type and quantity of grease. **Note:** *As of 08/04 a new type of grease was introduced.* **Do not** *mix this type with the earlier type. Thoroughly clean away all old grease before working-in the new type.*

25 Tape over the splines on the end of the driveshaft, then slide the new gaiter onto the shaft. Remove the tape and fit the locating plate to the driveshaft gaiter.

26 Securely clamp the driveshaft then press the inner joint onto the shaft, ensuring it is

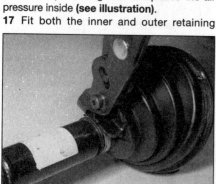

3.17b . . . and secure them in position by carefully compressing their raised sections . . .

3.17c . . . taking great care not to cut through the clip

fitted the right way around. Secure the joint in position with the new circlip making sure it is correctly located in the driveshaft groove.

27 Work the grease well into the ball tracks of the joint then fill the gaiter with any excess.

28 Wipe clean the mating surfaces of the gaiter locating plate and joint. Apply a smear of sealant (VW recommend D 454 300 A2 sealant – available from your VW dealer) to the locating plate then align the locating plate holes with those on the joint outer member and tap the plate firmly onto the joint.

29 Ensure the outer lip is correctly engaged with the locating plate then lift the inner lip of the gaiter to equalise the air pressure inside.

30 Fit both the inner and outer retaining clips to the gaiter and secure each one in position by compressing its raised section. In the absence of the special tool, carefully compress each clip using a pair of side-cutters taking great care not to cut through the clip.

31 Check that the constant velocity joint moves freely in all directions, then refit the driveshaft to the vehicle as described in Section 2.

Tripod type

32 On manual transmission models, loosen the clips and slide the gaiter away from the joint, then use a screwdriver to lever off the joint protective cover. If necessary remove the large O-ring seal from the groove. Mark the driveshaft, tripod and joint housing in relation to each other, then slowly withdraw the housing from the tripod, making sure that the rollers remain in position – if necessary, mark the rollers to ensure correct refitting. Extract the circlip, then press or drive off the tripod from the driveshaft, and finally remove the gaiter.

33 On automatic transmission models, remove the outer constant velocity joint as described above in paragraphs 2 to 6, then release the retaining clips and slide the inner gaiter from the driveshaft. If necessary, cut the gaiter to release it from the shaft.

34 Thoroughly clean the joint using paraffin, or a suitable solvent, and dry it thoroughly. Check the tripod joint bearings and joint outer member for signs of wear, pitting or scuffing on their bearing surfaces. Check that the bearing

rollers rotate smoothly and easily around the tripod joint, with no traces of roughness **(see illustration)**.

35 If on inspection the tripod joint or outer member reveal signs of wear or damage, it will be necessary to renew the complete driveshaft assembly, since the joint is not available separately. If the joint is in satisfactory condition, obtain a repair kit consisting of a new gaiter, retaining clips, and the correct type and quantity of grease. **Note:** As of 08/04 a new type of grease was introduced. **Do not** mix this type with the earlier type. Thoroughly clean away all old grease before working-in the new type. Although not strictly necessary, it is also recommended that the outer constant velocity joint gaiter is renewed, regardless of its apparent condition.

36 On reassembly, pack the inner joint with the grease supplied. Work the grease well into the bearing tracks and rollers, while twisting the joint **(see illustration)**.

37 Clean the shaft, using emery cloth to remove any rust or sharp edges which may damage the gaiter. Tape over the splines on the end of the driveshaft and grease the driveshaft ridges to prevent possible damage to the inner gaiter on installation.

38 Ease the inner gaiter and small clip onto and along the driveshaft and carefully lever it over driveshaft ridge, taking care not to damage it **(see illustrations)**.

39 On manual transmission models, refit the tripod on the driveshaft splines in its previously-noted position, and fit the circlip.

3.34 Check the inner joint rollers and bearings for wear

3.36 Work the grease well into the bearing tracks and rollers

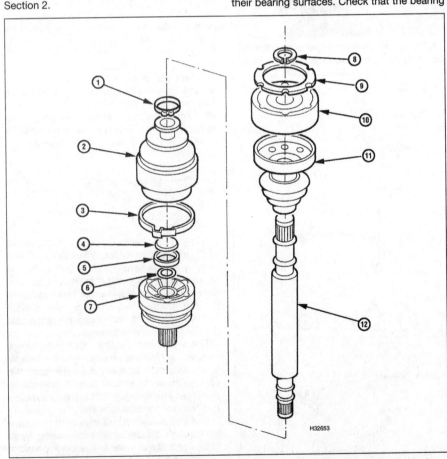

H32653

3.19 Exploded view of the driveshaft – petrol engine models with manual transmission

1 Retaining clip	6 Circlip	10 Inner constant velocity joint
2 Outer gaiter	7 Outer constant velocity joint	11 Locking plate and gaiter
3 Retaining clip	8 Circlip	12 Driveshaft
4 Dished washer	9 Gasket	
5 Spacer		

3.38a Tape over the driveshaft splines then slide the inner gaiter into position . . .

3.38b . . . levering it carefully over the driveshaft ridge

3.41a Seat the gaiter in position, then lift the inner lip to equalise the air pressure inside

3.41b Fit the retaining clips to the gaiter . . .

3.41c . . . and secure them in position by carefully compressing their raised sections

Locate the housing over the tripod and rollers, again in its previously-noted position. Fit a new O-ring seal and press on the cover.

40 On automatic transmission models, locate the outer lip in the groove on the joint outer member and seat the inner lip correctly on the driveshaft.

41 Lift the inner lip of the gaiter to equalise the air pressure inside then fit both the inner and outer retaining clips. Secure each clip in position by compressing its raised section **(see illustrations)**. In the absence of the special tool, carefully compress each clip using a pair of side-cutters taking great care not to cut through the clip.

42 Refit the outer constant velocity joint as described in paragraphs 11 to 17 **(see illustration)**.

43 Check that both constant velocity joints move freely in all directions, then refit the driveshaft to the vehicle as described in Section 2.

4 Driveshaft overhaul – general information

If any of the checks described in Chapter 1A or 1B reveal wear in any driveshaft joint, first remove the roadwheel trim or centre cap (as appropriate) and check that the hub bolt is tight. If the bolt is loose, obtain a new bolt and tighten it to the specified torque (see Section 2). If the bolt is tight, refit the centre cap/trim and repeat the check on the other hub bolt.

Road test the vehicle, and listen for a metallic clicking from the front as the vehicle is driven slowly in a circle on full-lock. If a clicking noise is heard, this indicates wear in the outer constant velocity joint; this means that the joint must be renewed.

If vibration, consistent with road speed, is felt through the car when accelerating, there is a possibility of wear in the inner constant velocity joints.

To check the joints for wear, remove the driveshafts, then dismantle them as described in Section 3; if any wear or free play is found, the affected joint must be renewed. Refer to your VW dealer for information on the availability of driveshaft components.

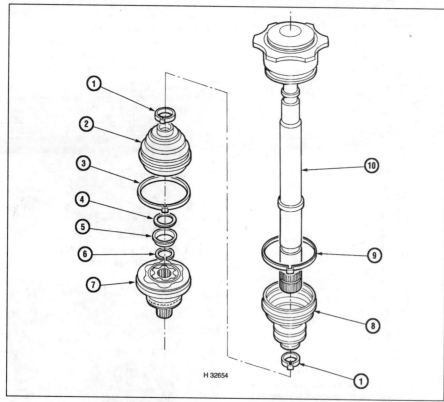

3.42 Exploded view of driveshaft – diesel engine and automatic transmission petrol engine models

1 Retaining clip
2 Outer gaiter
3 Retaining clip
4 Dished washer
5 Spacer
6 Circlip
7 Outer joint
8 Inner gaiter
9 Retaining clip
10 Driveshaft

Chapter 9
Braking system

Contents

	Section number
Anti-lock braking system (ABS) – general information	18
Anti-lock braking system (ABS) components – removal and refitting	19
Brake pedal – removal and refitting	11
ESP system components – removal and refitting	21
Front brake caliper – removal, overhaul and refitting	8
Front brake disc – inspection, removal and refitting	6
Front brake pad wear check	See Chapter 1A or 1B
Front brake pads – renewal	4
General information	1
Handbrake – adjustment	14
Handbrake cables – removal and refitting	16
Handbrake lever – removal and refitting	15
Hydraulic fluid – level check	See Weekly checks

	Section number
Hydraulic fluid – renewal	See Chapter 1A or 1B
Hydraulic pipes and hoses – renewal	3
Hydraulic system – bleeding	2
Master cylinder – removal, overhaul and refitting	10
Rear brake caliper – removal, overhaul and refitting	9
Rear brake disc – inspection, removal and refitting	7
Rear brake pad wear check	See Chapter 1A or 1B
Rear brake pads – renewal	5
Stop-light and brake pedal switches – removal, refitting and adjustment	17
Vacuum pump (diesel engine models) – removal and refitting	20
Vacuum servo unit – testing, removal and refitting	12
Vacuum servo unit check valve – removal, testing and refitting	13

Degrees of difficulty

Easy, suitable for novice with little experience	**Fairly easy,** suitable for beginner with some experience	**Fairly difficult,** suitable for competent DIY mechanic	**Difficult,** suitable for experienced DIY mechanic	**Very difficult,** suitable for expert DIY or professional

Specifications

Engine codes*

Petrol engines

1781 cc, DOHC, Bosch Motronic ME7.5 injection, turbocharged	AWT
1984 cc, SOHC, Siemens Simos 3.2 injection, non-turbo	AZM
1984 cc, DOHC, Bosch Motronic ME7.5 injection, non-turbo	ALT

Diesel engines

Electronic direct injection, unit injectors, 74 kW (100 bhp)	AVB
Electronic direct injection, unit injectors, 96 kW (130 bhp)	AVF and AWX

* **Note:** See 'Vehicle identification' for the location of the code marking on the engine.

Front brakes

Type	Disc, with single-piston sliding caliper

	FN3 (ATE) calipers	C54 (Lucas) calipers
Disc diameter	282.5 or 288 mm	280 mm
Disc (ventilated) thickness:		
New	25 mm	22 mm
Minimum	23 mm	20 mm
Maximum disc run-out	0.05 mm	0.05 mm
Brake pad wear limit (friction material only – not including backing plate)	2 mm	2 mm

Rear brakes

Type	Disc, with single-piston sliding caliper
Disc diameter	245 mm
Disc thickness:	
New	10 mm
Minimum thickness	8 mm
Maximum disc run-out	0.05 mm
Brake pad wear limit (friction material only – not including backing plate)	2 mm

Servo

Pushrod balljoint-to-servo unit mating surface dimension:	
LHD models	159.0 ± 0.5 mm
RHD models	173.5 ± 0.5 mm

Torque wrench settings

	Nm	lbf ft
ABS hydraulic unit mounting nuts	12	9
Brake pedal shaft to operating lever bolt*	25	18
Front brake caliper (FN3/ATE):		
Guide pins	25	18
Mounting bracket bolts	125	92
Wiring/brake hose bracket bolt	10	7
Front brake caliper (C54/Lucas):		
Guide pin bolts*	30	22
Mounting bracket bolts	125	92
Wiring/brake hose bracket bolt	10	7
Handbrake lever mounting nuts	25	18
Hydraulic pipe union nuts	24	18
Master cylinder retaining nuts	49	36
Rear brake caliper:		
Guide pin bolts*	30	22
Mounting bracket bolt	95	70
Road wheel bolt	120	89
Tandem vacuum/fuel pump bolts:		
Upper	20	15
Lower	10	7
Vacuum servo to bulkhead/pedal bracket bolts (T45)	25	18

* Use new fasteners

1 General information

All models have disc brakes fitted at the front and rear wheels as standard. ABS (Anti-lock Braking System) is also fitted as standard on all models (refer to Section 18 for further information on ABS operation).

The front and rear disc brakes are actuated by single-piston sliding type calipers, which ensure that equal pressure is applied to each disc pad. The handbrake mechanism is built into the rear calipers.

On all models, the handbrake provides an independent mechanical (rather than hydraulic) means of rear brake application.

Because the diesel engines have no throttle valve, there is insufficient vacuum in the inlet manifold to operate the braking system servo effectively at all times. To overcome this problem, a vacuum pump is fitted to models with diesel engines, to provide sufficient vacuum to operate the servo unit. The vacuum pump is mounted on the rear of the cylinder head and driven by the camshaft.

ESP (Electronic Stability Program) was fitted as standard from December 2001, and was available as an option on earlier models. The ESP (Electronic Stability Program) incorporates the ABS, EDL (Electronic Differential Lock) system and TCS (Traction Control System). It stabilises the vehicle when oversteering or understeering by applying the brake, or applying increased power to the relevant roadwheel, to increase the driver's control of the vehicle. In order for the ESP system to function, it utilises sensors which provide data concerning the speed of the vehicle around a vertical axis, the lateral movement of the vehicle, the brake pressure and the angle of the front wheels.

Note: *When servicing any part of the system, work carefully and methodically; also observe scrupulous cleanliness when overhauling any part of the hydraulic system. Always renew components (in axle sets, where applicable) if in doubt about their condition, and use only genuine VW parts, or at least those of known good quality. Note the warnings given in 'Safety first!' and at relevant points in this Chapter concerning the dangers of asbestos dust and hydraulic fluid.*

2 Hydraulic system – bleeding

⚠ **Warning: Hydraulic fluid is poisonous; wash off immediately and thoroughly in the case of skin contact, and seek immediate medical advice if any fluid is swallowed or gets into the eyes. Certain types of hydraulic fluid are inflammable, and may ignite when allowed into contact with hot components; when servicing any hydraulic system, it is safest to assume that the fluid is inflammable, and to take precautions against the risk of fire as though it is petrol that is being handled. Hydraulic fluid is also an effective paint stripper, and will attack plastics; if any is spilt, it should be washed off immediately, using copious quantities of fresh water. Finally, it is hygroscopic (it absorbs moisture from the air) – old fluid may be contaminated and unfit for further use. When topping-up or renewing the fluid, always use the recommended type, and ensure that it comes from a freshly-opened sealed container.**

Note: *VW specify that at least 0.2 litre of hydraulic is bled through each caliper.*

General

1 The correct operation of any hydraulic system is only possible after removing all air from the components and circuit; this is achieved by bleeding the system.

2 During the bleeding procedure, add only clean, unused hydraulic fluid of the recommended type; *never* re-use fluid that has already been bled from the system. Ensure that a sufficient quantity of new fluid is available before starting work.

3 If there is any possibility of incorrect fluid being already in the system, the brake components and circuit must be flushed completely with uncontaminated, correct fluid, and new seals should be fitted to the various components.

4 If hydraulic fluid has been lost from the system, or air has entered because of a leak, ensure that the fault is cured before proceeding further.

5 Park the vehicle on level ground, securely chock the wheel then release the handbrake.

6 Check that all pipes and hoses are secure, unions tight and bleed screws closed. Clean any dirt from around the bleed screws.

7 Unscrew the master cylinder reservoir cap, and top the master cylinder reservoir up to the MAX level line; refit the cap loosely, and remember to maintain the fluid level at least above the MIN level line throughout the procedure, or there is a risk of further air entering the system.

8 There is a number of one-man, do-it-yourself brake bleeding kits currently available from motor accessory shops. It is recommended that one of these kits is used whenever possible, as they greatly simplify the bleeding operation, and also reduce the risk of expelled air and fluid being drawn back into the system. If such a kit is not available, the basic (two-man) method must be used, which is described in detail below.

9 If a kit is to be used, prepare the vehicle as described previously, and follow the kit manufacturer's instructions, as the procedure may vary slightly according to the type being used; generally, they are as outlined below in the relevant sub-section.

10 Whichever method is used, the same sequence must be followed (see paragraphs 11 and 12) to ensure the removal of all air from the system.

Bleeding

Sequence

11 If the system has been only partially disconnected, and suitable precautions were taken to minimise fluid loss, it should be necessary only to bleed that part of the system (ie, the primary or secondary circuit).

12 If the complete system is to be bled, then it should be done working in the following sequence:

   a) Right-hand rear brake.
   b) Left-hand rear brake.
   c) Right-hand front brake.
   d) Left-hand front brake.

Basic (two-man) method

13 Collect a clean glass jar, a suitable length of plastic or rubber tubing which is a tight fit over the bleed screw, and a ring spanner to fit the screw. The help of an assistant will also be required.

14 Remove the dust cap from the first screw in the sequence. Fit the spanner and tube to the screw, place the other end of the tube in the jar, and pour in sufficient fluid to cover the end of the tube.

15 Ensure that the master cylinder reservoir fluid level is maintained at least above the MIN level line throughout the procedure.

16 Have the assistant fully depress the brake pedal several times to build-up pressure, then maintain it on the final downstroke.

17 While pedal pressure is maintained, unscrew the bleed screw (approximately one turn) and allow the compressed fluid and air to flow into the jar.

18 The assistant should maintain pedal pressure, following it down to the floor if necessary, and should not release it until instructed to do so. When the flow stops, tighten the bleed screw again, have the assistant release the pedal slowly, and recheck the reservoir fluid level.

19 Repeat the steps given in paragraphs 16 to 18 inclusive until the fluid emerging from the bleed screw is free from air bubbles. If the master cylinder has been drained and refilled, and air is being bled from the first screw in the sequence, allow approximately five seconds between cycles for the master cylinder passages to refill.

20 When no more air bubbles appear, tighten the bleed screw securely, remove the tube and spanner, and refit the dust cap. Do not overtighten the bleed screw.

21 Repeat the procedure on the remaining screws in the sequence, until all air is removed from the system and the brake pedal feels firm again. On completion, lower the vehicle to the ground (where necessary).

Using a one-way valve kit

22 As their name implies, these kits consist of a length of tubing with a one-way valve fitted, to prevent expelled air and fluid being drawn back into the system; some kits include a translucent container, which can be positioned so that the air bubbles can be more easily seen flowing from the end of the tube.

23 The kit is connected to the bleed screw, which is then opened **(see illustration)**. The user returns to the driver's seat, depresses the brake pedal with a smooth, steady stroke, and slowly releases it; this is repeated until the expelled fluid is clear of air bubbles.

24 Note that these kits simplify work so much that it is easy to forget to watch the master cylinder reservoir fluid level; ensure that this is maintained at least above the MIN level line at all times, otherwise air will be reintroduced into the system.

Using a pressure-bleeding kit

25 These kits are usually operated by the reservoir of pressurised air contained in the spare tyre. However, note that it will probably be necessary to reduce the pressure to a lower level than normal; refer to the instructions supplied with the kit.

26 By connecting a pressurised, fluid-filled container to the master cylinder reservoir, bleeding can be carried out simply by opening each screw in turn (in the specified sequence), and allowing the fluid to flow out until no more air bubbles can be seen in the expelled fluid.

27 This method has the advantage that the large reservoir of fluid provides an additional safeguard against air being drawn into the system during bleeding.

28 Pressure-bleeding is particularly effective when bleeding difficult systems, or when bleeding the complete system at the time of routine fluid renewal.

All methods

29 When bleeding is complete, and firm pedal feel is restored, wash off any spilt fluid, tighten the bleed screws securely, and refit their dust caps.

30 Check the hydraulic fluid level in the master cylinder reservoir, and top-up if necessary (see *Weekly checks*).

31 Discard any hydraulic fluid that has been

2.23 Connect the brake bleeding kit hose to the caliper bleed nipple, then open the nipple using a spanner

bled from the system; it will not be fit for re-use.

32 Check the feel of the brake pedal. If it feels at all spongy, air must still be present in the system, and further bleeding is required. Failure to bleed satisfactorily after a reasonable repetition of the bleeding procedure may be due to worn master cylinder seals.

33 Because the clutch hydraulic system shares the same fluid reservoir, we recommend that the clutch is bled at the same time (see Chapter 6).

3 Hydraulic pipes and hoses – renewal

Note: *Before starting work, refer to the note at the beginning of Section 2 concerning the dangers of hydraulic fluid.*

1 If any pipe or hose is to be renewed, minimise fluid loss by first removing the master cylinder reservoir cap, then tightening it down onto a piece of polythene to obtain an airtight seal. Alternatively, flexible hoses can be sealed, if required, using a proprietary brake hose clamp; metal brake pipe unions can be plugged (if care is taken not to allow dirt into the system) or capped immediately they are disconnected. Place a wad of rag under any union that is to be disconnected, to catch any spilt fluid.

2 If a flexible hose is to be disconnected, unscrew the brake pipe union nut and remove the spring clip which secures the hose to its mounting bracket **(see illustration)**.

3 To unscrew the union nuts, it is preferable to obtain a brake pipe spanner of the correct size; these are available from most large motor accessory shops. Failing this, a close-fitting open-ended spanner will be required, though if the nuts are tight or corroded, their flats may be rounded-off if the spanner slips. In such a case, a self-locking wrench is often the only way to unscrew a stubborn union, but it follows that the pipe and the damaged nuts must be renewed on reassembly. Always clean a union and surrounding area before disconnecting it. If disconnecting a component with more than one union, make a careful note of the connections before disturbing any of them.

3.2 Undo the brake pipe union and recover the spring clip

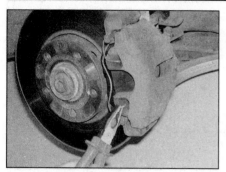

4.2 Unclip the pad retaining spring and remove it from the brake caliper

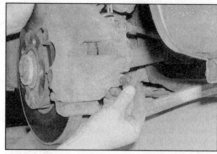

4.4a Remove the end caps from the guide bushes to gain access to the caliper guide pin

4.4b Slacken . . .

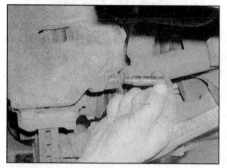

4.4c . . . and remove the caliper guide pins . . .

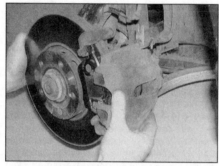

4.4d . . . then lift the caliper away from the mounting bracket

4 If a brake pipe is to be renewed, it can be obtained, cut to length with the union nuts and end flares in place, from VW dealers. All that is then necessary is to bend it to shape, following the line of the original, before fitting it to the car. Alternatively, most motor accessory shops can make up brake pipes from kits, but this requires very careful measurement of the original, to ensure that the new one is of the correct length. The safest answer is usually to take the original to the shop as a pattern.

5 On refitting, do not overtighten the union nuts. It is not necessary to exercise brute force to obtain a sound joint.

6 Ensure that the pipes and hoses are correctly routed, with no kinks, and that they are secured in the clips or brackets provided. After fitting, remove the polythene from the reservoir, and bleed the hydraulic system as described in Section 2. Wash off any spilt fluid, and check carefully for fluid leaks.

4 Front brake pads – renewal

> ⚠️ **Warning: Renew both sets of front brake pads at the same time – never renew the pads on only one wheel, as uneven braking may result. Note that the dust created by wear of the pads may contain asbestos, which is a health hazard. Never blow it out with compressed air, and don't inhale any of it. An approved filtering mask should be worn when working on the brakes. DO NOT use petrol or petroleum-based solvents to clean brake parts; use brake cleaner or methylated spirit only.**

1 Apply the handbrake, then jack up the front of the vehicle and support it on axle stands.

Remove the front roadwheels. Whilst the wheels are removed, refit at least one wheel bolt to each hub to ensure the brake discs remain correctly positioned on the hubs.

FN3 (ATE) calipers

2 Carefully unclip the pad retaining spring and remove it from the brake caliper **(see illustration)**.

3 Where fitted, disconnect the brake pad wear indicator wiring at the connector by lifting the locking tab and turning it through 90°.

4 Remove the end caps from the guide bushes, then unscrew and remove the caliper guide pins and lift the caliper away from the mounting bracket **(see illustrations)**. Tie the caliper to the suspension strut using a suitable piece of wire; do not allow it to hang unsupported from the flexible brake hose.

5 Unclip the inner pad from the caliper piston and remove the outer pad from the mounting bracket **(see illustrations)**.

6 First measure the thickness of each brake pad's friction material **(see illustration)**. If any pad is worn at any point to the specified minimum thickness or less, all four pads must be renewed. Also, the pads should be renewed if any are fouled with oil or grease; there is no satisfactory way of degreasing friction material, once contaminated. If any of the brake pads are worn unevenly, or are fouled with oil or grease, trace and rectify the cause before reassembly.

7 If the brake pads are still serviceable, carefully clean them using a clean, fine wire brush or similar, paying particular attention to the sides and back of the metal backing.

4.5a Unclip the inner pad from the caliper piston . . .

4.5b . . . and remove the outer pad from the mounting bracket

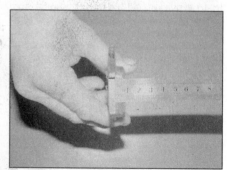

4.6 Measure the thickness of each pads friction material

4.9 Using a retraction tool to push the piston back into the caliper

Note the clamp connected to the brake hose and the brake bleeding kit connected to the caliper bleed nipple

Clean out the grooves in the friction material, and pick out any large embedded particles of dirt or debris. Carefully clean the pad locations in the caliper mounting bracket.

8 Prior to fitting the pads, check that the guide pins are free to slide easily in the caliper body bushes, and are a reasonably tight fit. Brush the dust and dirt from the caliper and piston, but **do not** inhale it, as it is injurious to health. Inspect the dust seal around the piston for damage, and the piston for evidence of fluid leaks, corrosion or damage. If any of these components requires attention, refer to Section 8.

9 If new brake pads are to be fitted, the caliper piston must be pushed back into the cylinder to make room for them. Either use a piston retraction tool, a G-clamp or use suitable pieces of wood as levers. Clamp off the flexible brake hose leading to the caliper then connect a brake bleeding kit to the caliper bleed nipple. Open the bleed nipple as the piston is retracted; the surplus brake fluid will then be collected in the bleed kit vessel **(see illustration)**.

Caution: The ABS unit contains hydraulic components that are very sensitive to impurities in the brake fluid. Even the smallest particles can cause the system to fail through blockage. The pad retraction method described here prevents any debris in the brake fluid expelled from the caliper from being passed back to the ABS hydraulic unit.

10 Clip the inner pad into the caliper piston and fit the outer pad to the mounting bracket, ensuring its friction material is against the brake disc. Note that the outer pad has an arrow stamped onto its outer lower edge; this should point in the normal direction of rotation of the brake disc. If new pads are being fitted, remove the adhesive foil backing (where fitted) from the outer pad and clean off any sticky residue.

11 Manoeuvre the caliper into position then refit the caliper guide pins and tighten them to the specified torque setting **(see illustration)**.

12 Refit the end caps to the caliper guide bushes and clip the wear sensor wiring onto the lower cap.

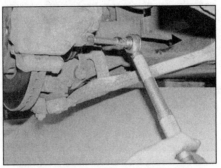

4.11 Refit the caliper guide pins and tighten them to the specified torque setting

4.20a Lift the caliper away from the mounting bracket

13 Fit the pad retaining spring, ensuring its ends are correctly located in the caliper body holes. Press the inner edge of the spring into position so that its ends are firmly in contact with the surface of the brake pad. **Note:** *If the spring is not located correctly, the outer pad will not sit properly, resulting in increased pedal travel.*

14 Depress the brake pedal repeatedly, until the pads are pressed into firm contact with the brake disc, and normal (non-assisted) pedal pressure is restored.

15 Repeat the above procedure on the remaining front brake caliper.

16 Refit the roadwheels, then lower the vehicle to the ground and tighten the roadwheel bolts to the specified torque setting.

17 Check (and if necessary top-up) the hydraulic brake fluid level as described in *Weekly checks*.

⚠️ *Warning: New pads will not give full braking efficiency until they have bedded-in. Be prepared for this, and avoid hard braking as much as possible for the first hundred miles or so after pad renewal.*

C54 (Lucas) calipers

Note: *The caliper guide pin bolts must be renewed whenever they are unscrewed.*

18 Unscrew and remove the caliper upper and lower guide pin bolts whilst counter-holding the guide pins with an open-ended spanner **(see illustration)**. Note that new bolts must be used on refitting. Alternatively, just the lower guide pin bolt can be removed, and

4.18 Slacken and remove the caliper guide pin bolts whilst counter-holding the guide pins with an open-ended spanner

4.20b Tie the caliper to the suspension strut using a suitable piece of wire; do not allow it to hang unsupported from the flexible brake hose

the caliper then swivelled upwards to expose the brake pads.

19 Where fitted, disconnect the brake pad wear indicator wiring at the connector by lifting the locking tab and turning it through 90°.

20 Lift the caliper away from the mounting bracket and tie the caliper to the suspension strut using a suitable piece of wire; do not allow it to hang unsupported from the flexible brake hose **(see illustrations)**.

21 Remove the inner and outer pads from the caliper mounting bracket. Ensure that the circular heat shield plate remains clipped into the end face of the piston **(see illustrations)**.

22 First measure the thickness of each brake pad's friction material. If either pad is worn at any point to the specified minimum thickness

4.21a Remove the inner . . .

4.21b ... and outer pads from the caliper mounting bracket

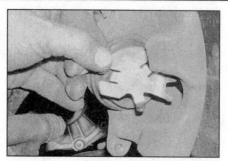

4.21c Ensure that the circular heat shield plate remains clipped into the end face of the piston

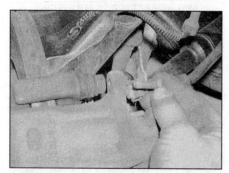

4.29a Fit the new caliper guide pin bolts ...

4.29b ... and tighten them to the specified torque setting

or less, all four pads must be renewed. Also, the pads should be renewed if any are fouled with oil or grease; there is no satisfactory way of degreasing friction material, once contaminated. If any of the brake pads are worn unevenly, or are fouled with oil or grease, trace and rectify the cause before reassembly.
23 If the brake pads are still serviceable, carefully clean them using a clean, fine wire brush or similar, paying particular attention to the sides and back of the metal backing. Clean out the grooves in the friction material, and pick out any large embedded particles of dirt or debris. Carefully clean the pad locations in the caliper mounting bracket.
24 Prior to fitting the pads, check that the guide pins are free to slide easily in the caliper body bushes.
25 Brush the dust and dirt from the caliper and piston, but **do not** inhale it, as it is injurious to health. Inspect the dust seal around the piston

for damage, and the piston for evidence of fluid leaks, corrosion or damage. If any of these components requires attention, refer to Section 8.
26 If new brake pads are to be fitted, the caliper piston must be pushed back into the cylinder to make room for them; refer to the information given in paragraph 9.
27 Locate the inner and outer pads in the caliper mounting bracket, ensuring its friction material is against the brake disc.
28 Fit the caliper over the brake pads, ensuring that the butterfly clips on the outer edge of the brake pads bear against the inner surface of the caliper body without jamming in the caliper inspection aperture. **Note**: *New caliper guide pin bolts must be used.*
29 Fit the new caliper guide pin bolts and tighten them to the specified torque setting, counter-holding the guide pin with an open-ended spanner **(see illustrations)**.

30 Reconnect the brake pad wear indicator wiring, making sure that it is routed between the caliper and hose.
31 Depress the brake pedal repeatedly, until the pads are pressed into firm contact with the brake disc, and normal (non-assisted) pedal pressure is restored.
32 Repeat the above procedure on the remaining front brake caliper.
33 Refit the roadwheels, then lower the vehicle to the ground and tighten the roadwheel bolts to the specified torque setting.
34 Check (and if necessary top-up) the hydraulic brake fluid level as described in *Weekly checks.*

> ⚠ *Warning: New pads will not give full braking efficiency until they have bedded-in. Be prepared for this, and avoid hard braking as much as possible for the first hundred miles or so after pad renewal.*

5 Rear brake pads – renewal

> ⚠ *Warning: Renew both sets of rear brake pads at the same time – never renew the pads on only one wheel, as uneven braking may result. Note that the dust created by wear of the pads may contain asbestos, which is a health hazard. Never blow it out with compressed air, and don't inhale any of it. An approved filtering mask should be worn when working on the brakes. DO NOT use petrol or petroleum-based solvents to clean brake parts; use brake cleaner or methylated spirit only.*

Note: *The caliper guide pin bolts must be renewed whenever they are unscrewed.*

1 Chock the front wheels, then jack up the rear of the vehicle and support it on axle stands. Remove the rear wheels. Whilst the wheels are removed, refit at least one wheel bolt to each hub to ensure the brake discs remain correctly positioned on the hubs.
2 With the handbrake lever fully released, disconnect the handbrake cable from the rear brake caliper by pulling out the outer cable retaining circlip and unhooking the inner cable from the lever on the caliper.
3 Unscrew and remove the caliper guide pin bolts, counter-holding the guide pins with an open-ended spanner to prevent them from rotating **(see illustration)**. Discard the guide pin bolts – new bolts must be used on refitting.
4 Lift the caliper away from the brake pads, and tie it to the suspension strut using a suitable piece of wire. Do not allow the caliper to hang unsupported on the flexible brake hose **(see illustration)**.
5 Withdraw the two brake pads from the caliper mounting bracket **(see illustrations)**.
6 First measure the thickness of each brake pad (excluding the backing plate). If either

5.3 Slacken and remove the caliper guide pin bolts

5.4 Lift the caliper away from the brake pads

pad is worn at any point to the specified minimum thickness or less, **all four** pads must be renewed. Also, the pads should be renewed if any are fouled with oil or grease; there is no satisfactory way of degreasing friction material, once contaminated. If any of the brake pads are worn unevenly, or fouled with oil or grease, trace and rectify the cause before reassembly.

7 If the brake pads are still serviceable, carefully clean them using a clean, fine wire brush or similar, paying particular attention to the sides and back of the metal backing. Clean out the grooves in the friction material (where applicable), and pick out any large embedded particles of dirt or debris. Carefully clean the pad locations in the caliper body/mounting bracket.

8 Prior to fitting the pads, check that the guide pins are free to slide easily in the caliper bracket, and check that the rubber guide pin gaiters are undamaged. Brush the dust and dirt from the caliper and piston, but **do not** inhale it, as it is injurious to health. Inspect the dust seal around the piston for damage, and the piston for evidence of fluid leaks, corrosion or damage. If attention to any of these components is necessary, refer to Section 9.

9 If new brake pads are to be fitted, it will be necessary to retract the piston fully into the caliper bore, by rotating it in a clockwise direction and pressing the piston in at the same time, using a retraction tool, or a pair of circlip pliers **(see illustration)**. The excess brake fluid must be ejected from the caliper bleed nipple; refer to the information given in Section 4.

10 Where applicable, peel the protective sheet from the new pad backing plates, then fit the pads in the mounting bracket, ensuring that the friction material is facing the brake disc.

11 Slide the caliper back into position over the pads ensuring the pad anti-rattle springs are correctly positioned against the inner surface of the caliper body and are not jammed in the inspection aperture **(see illustration)**.

12 Press the caliper into position, then install the new guide pin bolts, tightening them to the specified torque setting whilst retaining the guide pins with an open-ended spanner.

13 Repeat the above procedure on the remaining rear brake caliper.

14 Depress the brake pedal repeatedly to force the pads into firm contact with the discs. Once normal pedal feel has returned, check that the discs rotate freely. Adjust the handbrake as described in Section 14.

15 Refit the roadwheels then lower the vehicle to the ground and tighten the roadwheel bolts to the specified torque setting.

16 Check (and if necessary top-up) the hydraulic fluid level as described in *Weekly checks*.

 Warning: New pads will not give full braking efficiency until they have bedded-in. Be prepared for

5.5a **Withdraw the outer . . .**

5.9 **Use a retraction tool to push and turn screw the piston back into the caliper**

this, and avoid hard braking as much as possible for the first hundred miles or so after pad renewal.

6 Front brake disc – inspection, removal and refitting

Note: *Before starting work, refer to the note at the beginning of Section 4 concerning the dangers of asbestos dust.*

Inspection

Note: *If either disc requires renewal, BOTH should be renewed at the same time, to ensure even and consistent braking. New brake pads should also be fitted.*

1 Apply the handbrake, then jack up the front of the car and support it on axle stands. Remove the appropriate front roadwheel. Whilst the wheel is removed, refit at least one

6.5 **Use a DTI gauge to measure disc run-out**

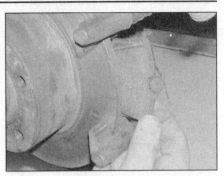

5.5b **. . . and inner pad from the caliper mounting bracket**

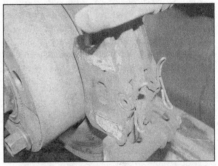

5.11 **Ensure that the anti-rattle springs are correctly positioned, and do not jam in the inspection aperture when the caliper is refitted**

of the wheel bolts to ensure the brake disc remains correctly positioned on the hub; if necessary fit spacers to the wheel bolts to clamp the disc firmly in position.

2 Slowly rotate the brake disc so that the full area of both sides can be checked; remove the brake pads if better access is required to the inboard surface. Light scoring is normal in the area swept by the brake pads, but if heavy scoring or cracks are found, the disc must be renewed.

3 It is normal to find a lip of rust and brake dust around the disc's perimeter; this can be scraped off if required. If, however, a lip has formed due to excessive wear of the brake pad swept area, then the disc's thickness must be measured using a micrometer. Take measurements at several places around the disc, at the inside and outside of the pad swept area; if the disc has worn at any point to the specified minimum thickness or less, the disc must be renewed.

4 If the disc is thought to be warped, it can be checked for run-out. Secure the disc firmly to the hub by refitting at least two roadwheel bolts – fit plain washers to the roadwheel bolts to ensure that the disc is properly seated on the hub.

5 Either use a dial gauge mounted on any convenient fixed point, while the disc is slowly rotated, or use feeler blades to measure (at several points all around the disc) the clearance between the disc and a fixed point, such as the caliper mounting bracket **(see illustration)**. If the measurements obtained are

6.8 After marking the position of the disc to the hub, remove the front brake disc

at the specified maximum or beyond, the disc is excessively warped, and must be renewed, however, it is worth checking first that the hub bearing is in good condition (Chapter 10).
6 Check the disc for cracks, especially around the wheel bolt holes, and any other wear or damage, and renew if necessary.

Removal

7 Unscrew and remove the two bolts securing the brake caliper mounting bracket to the strut. Slide the whole caliper assembly off the hub and away from the disc and tie the assembly to the front coil spring, using a piece of wire or string, to avoid placing any strain on the hydraulic brake hose. The caliper mounting bracket can be unbolted and removed separately if required (see Section 8).
8 Use chalk or paint to mark the relationship of the disc to the hub, then remove all the wheel bolts and washers used to secure the disc in position and remove the disc **(see illustration)**. If it is tight, lightly tap its rear face with a hide or plastic mallet to free it from the hub.

Refitting

9 Refitting is the reverse of the removal procedure, noting the following points:
   a) *Ensure that the mating surfaces of the disc and hub are clean and flat.*
   b) *On refitting, align (if applicable) the marks made on removal.*
   c) *If a new disc has been fitted, use a suitable solvent to wipe any preservative coating from the disc, before refitting the caliper. Note that new brake pads should always be fitted when the disc is renewed.*

7.4 Before removing the rear disc, mark the position of the disc in relation to the hub

   d) *Prior to installation, clean the caliper bracket mounting bolts. Slide the caliper into position, making sure the pads pass either side of the disc, and tighten the caliper bracket bolts to the specified torque setting.*
   e) *Refit the roadwheel then lower the vehicle to the ground and tighten the wheel bolts to the specified torque. Apply the footbrake several times to force the pads back into contact with the disc before driving the vehicle.*

7 Rear brake disc – inspection, removal and refitting

Note: *Before starting work, refer to the note at the beginning of Section 5 concerning the dangers of asbestos dust.*

Inspection

Note: *If either disc requires renewal, BOTH should be renewed at the same time, to ensure even and consistent braking. New brake pads should be fitted also.*
1 Firmly chock the front wheels, engage 1st gear (or P), then jack up the rear of the car and support it on axle stands (see *Jacking and vehicle support*). Remove the appropriate rear roadwheel.
2 Inspect the disc as described in Section 6.

Removal

3 Unscrew the two bolts securing the brake caliper mounting bracket in position, then slide the whole caliper, bracket and pads off the disc. If preferred, the caliper and pads can be removed separately before unbolting the mounting bracket. Using a piece of wire or string, tie the caliper to the rear suspension coil spring, to avoid placing any strain on the hydraulic brake hose.
4 Use chalk or paint to mark the relationship of the disc to the hub, then remove the disc **(see illustration)**. If it is tight, lightly tap its rear face with a hide or plastic mallet to free it from the hub.

Refitting

5 Refitting is the reverse of the removal procedure, noting the following points:
   a) *Ensure that the mating surfaces of the disc and hub are clean and flat.*
   b) *On refitting, align (if applicable) the marks made on removal.*
   c) *If a new disc has been fitted, use a suitable solvent to wipe any preservative coating from the disc, before refitting the caliper. Note that new brake pads should always be fitted when the disc is renewed.*
   d) *Prior to installation, clean the caliper bracket mounting bolts. Slide the caliper into position, making sure the pads pass either side of the disc, and tighten the caliper bracket bolts to the specified torque setting.*

   e) *Refit the roadwheel then lower the vehicle to the ground and tighten the wheel bolts to the specified torque. Apply the footbrake several times to force the pads back into contact with the disc before driving the vehicle.*

8 Front brake caliper – removal, overhaul and refitting

Note: *Before starting work, refer to the note at the beginning of Section 2 concerning the dangers of hydraulic fluid, and to the warning at the beginning of Section 4 concerning the dangers of asbestos dust.*
Note: *The guide pin bolts on C54 (Lucas) calipers must be renewed whenever they are unscrewed.*

Removal

1 Apply the handbrake, then jack up the front of the vehicle and support it on axle stands. Remove the front roadwheels. Whilst the wheels are removed, refit at least one wheel bolt to the hub to ensure the brake disc remains correctly positioned on the hub.
2 Minimise fluid loss by first removing the master cylinder reservoir cap, and then tightening it down onto a piece of polythene, to obtain an airtight seal. Alternatively, use a brake hose clamp, a G-clamp or a similar tool to clamp the flexible hose.
3 Where applicable, disconnect the wiring connector from the brake pad wear sensor connector. Unclip the connector from the caliper bracket.
4 Clean the area around the caliper brake pipe union then unscrew the union nut. Unbolt the mounting bracket from the caliper and position the pipe clear. Plug/cover the pipe end and caliper union to minimise fluid loss and prevent the entry of dirt into the hydraulic system. Wash off any spilt fluid immediately with cold water.
5 On models with FN3 (ATE) calipers, carefully lever the pad retaining spring out position and remove it from the brake caliper using a flat-bladed screwdriver **(see illustration)**. Remove the end caps from the guide bushes then unscrew and remove the caliper guide pins.

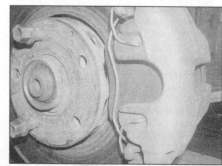

8.5 Carefully lever the pad retaining spring out of position

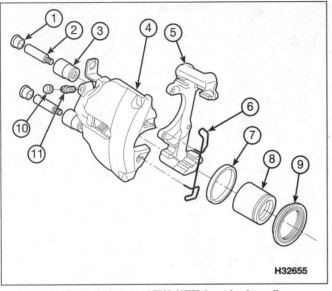

H32655

8.14a Exploded view of FN3 (ATE) front brake caliper

1 Dust cap
2 Guide pins
3 Guide sleeves
4 Caliper
5 Caliper mounting
bracket

6 Pad retaining spring
7 Piston seal
8 Piston
9 Dust seal
10 Dust cap
11 Bleed screw

H32656

8.14b Exploded view of C54 (Lucas) front brake caliper

1 Guide pin bolts
2 Bleed screw
3 Caliper
4 Dust cap

5 Piston seal
6 Piston
7 Dust seal
8 Caliper mounting bracket

6 On models with C54 (Lucas) calipers, counter-hold the guide pins with an open-ended spanner, then unscrew and remove both guide pin bolts.

7 Lift the caliper out of position, freeing it from the pad wear sensor wiring (where applicable). Remove the inner and outer brake pads with reference to Section 4, then unbolt and remove the caliper mounting bracket.

Overhaul

8 With the caliper on the bench, wipe away all traces of dust and dirt, but *avoid inhaling the dust, as it is injurious to health.*

9 Withdraw the partially ejected piston from the caliper body, and remove the dust seal.

 HAYNES HiNT *If the piston cannot be withdrawn by hand, it can be forced out by applying compressed air to the brake hose union hole. Only low pressure should be required, such as that generated by a foot pump. Even using low pressure, the piston will be ejected with considerable force; place a block of soft wood in the caliper to prevent damage to the end of the piston, and avoid getting your fingers trapped between the piston and caliper.*

10 Using a soft flat-bladed instrument, such as a plastic spatula, extract the piston hydraulic seal, taking great care not to damage the caliper bore.

11 Thoroughly clean all components, using only methylated spirit, isopropyl alcohol or clean brake fluid as a cleaning medium. Never use mineral-based solvents such as petrol or paraffin, as they will attack the hydraulic system's rubber components. Dry the components immediately, using compressed air or a clean, lint-free cloth. Use compressed air to blow clear the fluid passages.

12 Check all components, and renew any that are worn or damaged. Check particularly the cylinder bore and piston; these should be renewed if they are scratched, worn or corroded in any way (note that this means the renewal of the complete body assembly). Similarly check the condition of the guide pins and the bushes in the caliper body; both pins should be undamaged and (when cleaned) a reasonably tight sliding fit in the bushes. If there is any doubt about the condition of any component, renew it.

13 If the caliper is fit for further use, obtain the appropriate repair kit; the components are available from VW dealers in various combinations. All rubber seals should be renewed as a matter of course; these should never be re-used.

14 On commencement of reassembly, ensure that all components are clean and dry **(see illustrations)**.

15 Soak the piston and the new piston (fluid) seal in clean hydraulic fluid. Smear clean fluid on the cylinder bore surface.

16 Fit the new piston (fluid) seal, using only your fingers (no tools) to manipulate it into the cylinder bore groove.

17 Fit the new dust seal to the rear of the piston and seat the outer lip of the seal in the caliper body groove. Carefully ease the piston squarely into the cylinder bore using a twisting motion. Press the piston fully into position and seat the inner lip of the dust seal in the piston groove.

18 If the guide bushes are being renewed, push the old bushes out from the body and press the new ones into position, making sure they are correctly seated.

19 Prior to refitting, fill the caliper with fresh hydraulic fluid by unscrewing the bleed screw and pumping the fluid through the caliper until bubble-free fluid is expelled from the union hole.

Refitting

20 Refit the caliper mounting bracket to the hub carrier using cleaned bolts, and tighten them to the specified torque **(see illustrations)**. Refit the brake pads with reference to Section 4, then manoeuvre the caliper into position over the brake pads.

8.20a Fit the caliper mounting bracket to the hub carrier . . .

8.20b . . . use cleaned bolts . . .

8.20c . . . and tighten them to the specified torque

21 Fit the caliper guide pins/guide pin bolts (as applicable), tightening them to the specified torque setting, and refit the end caps to the guide bushes. **Note:** *On models with C54 (Lucas) calipers, new guide pin bolts must be fitted.*

22 Reconnect the brake pipe to the caliper and refit the mounting bracket to the caliper. Tighten the bracket retaining bolt and the brake pipe union nut to their specified torque settings.

23 On models with the FN3 (ATE) calipers, refit the pad retaining spring, ensuring its ends are correctly located in the caliper body holes.

24 Ensure the wiring is correctly routed through the loop on the lower cap then clip the pad wear sensor wiring connector onto its bracket on the caliper. Securely reconnect the wiring connector.

25 Remove the brake hose clamp or polythene (where fitted) and bleed the hydraulic system

as described in Section 2. Note that, providing the precautions described were taken to minimise brake fluid loss, it should only be necessary to bleed the relevant front brake.

26 Refit the roadwheel, then lower the vehicle to the ground and tighten the roadwheel bolts to the specified torque.

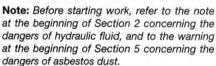

9 Rear brake caliper –
removal, overhaul and refitting

Note: *Before starting work, refer to the note at the beginning of Section 2 concerning the dangers of hydraulic fluid, and to the warning at the beginning of Section 5 concerning the dangers of asbestos dust.*

Note: *New guide pin bolts must be used on refitting.*

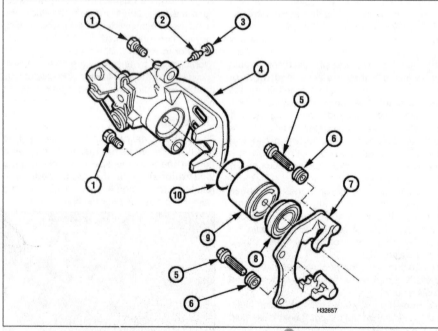

9.12 Exploded view of the rear brake caliper

1 Guide pin bolt	5 Guide pin	8 Dust seal
2 Bleed screw	6 Dust sleeve	9 Piston
3 Dust cap	7 Caliper mounting	10 Piston seal
4 Caliper	bracket	

Removal

1 Chock the front wheels, then jack up the rear of the vehicle and support it on axle stands. Remove the relevant rear wheel. Whilst the wheel is removed, refit at least one wheel bolt to the hub to ensure the brake disc remains in position.

2 With the handbrake lever fully released, disconnect the handbrake cable from the rear brake caliper by pulling out the outer cable retaining circlip and unhooking the inner cable from the lever on the caliper.

3 Minimise fluid loss by first removing the master cylinder reservoir cap, and then tightening it down onto a piece of polythene, to obtain an airtight seal. Alternatively, use a brake hose clamp, a G-clamp or a similar tool to clamp the flexible hose.

4 Clean the area around the caliper brake hose then unscrew the union.

5 Unscrew and remove the caliper guide pin bolts, using a slim open-ended spanner to prevent the guide pins from rotating. Discard the guide pin bolts – new bolts must be used on refitting.

6 Lift the brake caliper away from the its mounting bracket and unscrew it from the end of the brake hose. Plug/cover the hose end and caliper union to minimise fluid loss and prevent the entry of dirt into the hydraulic system. Wash off any spilt fluid immediately with cold water. Remove the inner and outer brake pads from the caliper mounting bracket. Unbolt and remove the caliper mounting bracket.

Overhaul

Note: *It is not possible to overhaul the brake caliper handbrake mechanism. If the mechanism is faulty, or fluid is leaking from the handbrake lever seal the caliper assembly must be renewed.*

7 With the caliper on the bench, wipe away all traces of dust and dirt, but avoid inhaling the dust, as it is injurious to health.

8 Remove the piston from the caliper bore by rotating it in an anti-clockwise direction. This can be achieved using a suitable pair of circlip pliers engaged in the caliper piston slots. Once the piston turns freely but does not come out any further, the piston is held in only by its seal and can be withdrawn by hand.

9 Remove the dust seal from the piston then, using a blunt flat-bladed instrument, carefully extract the piston hydraulic seal from the caliper bore. Take great care not to mark the caliper surface.

10 Withdraw the guide pins from the caliper mounting bracket, and remove the guide sleeve gaiters.

11 Inspect all the caliper components (as described for the front brake caliper in Section 8), and renew as necessary, noting that the handbrake mechanism must **not** be dismantled.

12 On reassembly, ensure all components are clean and dry **(see illustration)**.

9.17 Secure the rear caliper mounting bracket with new bolts (arrowed)

9.21 Reconnect the handbrake cable to the rear caliper, securing it in position with the retaining clip (arrowed)

13 Soak the piston and the new piston (fluid) seal in clean hydraulic fluid. Smear clean fluid on the cylinder bore surface. Fit the new piston (fluid) seal, using only your fingers (not tools) to manipulate into the cylinder bore groove.

14 Fit the new dust seal to the rear of the piston and seat the outer lip of the seal in the caliper body groove. Carefully ease the piston squarely into the cylinder bore using a twisting motion. Turn and push the piston in a clockwise direction, using the method employed on dismantling, until it is fully retracted into the caliper bore then seat the inner lip of the dust seal in the piston groove.

15 Apply the grease supplied in the repair kit, or a copper-based brake grease or anti-seize compound, to the guide pins. Fit the new gaiters to the guide pins and fit the pins to the caliper mounting bracket, ensuring that the gaiters are correctly located in the grooves on both the pins and caliper bracket.

16 Prior to refitting, fill the caliper with fresh hydraulic fluid by unscrewing the bleed screw and pumping the fluid through the caliper until bubble-free fluid is expelled from the union hole.

Refitting

17 Refit the caliper mounting bracket to the rear hub carrier using cleaned bolts, and tighten them to the specified torque **(see illustration)**. Refit the brake pads to the caliper mounting bracket with reference to Section 5.

18 Screw the caliper fully onto the brake hose, then manoeuvre the caliper into position over the pads then fit the new guide pin bolts, tightening them to the specified torque setting.

19 Remove the brake hose clamp or polythene (where used) and securely tighten the brake hose union.

20 Bleed the hydraulic system as described in Section 2. Note that, providing the precautions described were taken to minimise brake fluid loss, it should only be necessary to bleed the relevant rear brake.

21 Reconnect the handbrake cable to the caliper **(see illustration)**, securing it in position with the retaining clip, and adjust the cable as described in Section 14.

22 Refit the roadwheel, then lower the vehicle to the ground and tighten the roadwheel bolts to the specified torque.

10 Master cylinder – removal, overhaul and refitting

Note: *Before starting work, refer to the warning at the beginning of Section 2 concerning the dangers of hydraulic fluid. A T45 Torx socket head key will be needed to unscrew the master cylinder retaining nuts.*

Removal

1 Remove the plenum chamber cover and water deflector, then place cloth rags beneath the master cylinder to catch any spilt fluid. Syphon the hydraulic brake fluid from the reservoir into a suitable container using an old poultry baster or similar. Discard the fluid as it must not be re-used.

2 Disconnect the clutch master cylinder feed hose from the side of the brake master cylinder reservoir. Tape over or plug the outlet.

3 Disconnect the wiring plug from the brake fluid level sender unit **(see illustration)**.

4 On 2001 models, unscrew the clamp bolt, then depress the locking tab and remove the reservoir from the rubber seals on the right-hand side of the master cylinder. On later models, unscrew the trunnion bolt which secures the reservoir, and pull the reservoir from the top of the master cylinder. The reservoir will be quite tight in the rubber seals.

5 Wipe clean the area around the brake pipe unions on the side of the master cylinder, and make a note of the correct fitted positions of the unions, then unscrew the union nuts and carefully withdraw the pipes. Plug or tape over the pipe ends and master cylinder apertures, to minimise the loss of brake fluid, and to prevent the entry of dirt into the system. Wash off any spilt fluid immediately with cold water.

6 The master cylinder is secured to the vacuum servo by two large hexagon nuts, and the vacuum servo is secured to the bulkhead by two long through-bolts; there is no need to loosen the through-bolts. Unscrew the hexagon nuts and withdraw the master cylinder from the threaded extensions on the servo unit. Recover the sealing ring fitted to the rear of the master cylinder and discard it; a new one must be used on refitting **(see illustrations)**.

10.3 Disconnect the wiring plug from the brake fluid level sender unit (arrowed)

10.6a Undo the master cylinder securing nuts

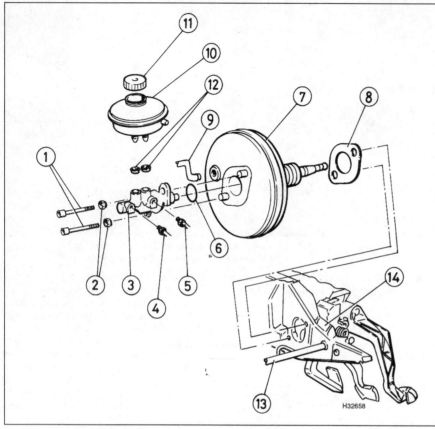

10 Fit the master cylinder to the servo unit, ensuring that the servo unit pushrod enters the master cylinder bore centrally. Have an assistant depress the brake pedal slightly, so that pushrod is moved towards the master cylinder.

11 Refit the master cylinder mounting nuts and tighten them to the specified torque.

12 Wipe clean the brake pipe unions, then refit them to the master cylinder ports and tighten them to the specified torque.

13 Refit the fluid reservoir making sure that the outlets are fully entered in the rubber seals. On 2001 models, tighten the clamp bolt.

14 Reconnect the clutch master cylinder hose to the fluid reservoir and securely tighten the retaining clip.

15 Reconnect the fluid level sender unit wiring connector.

16 Clip the wiring loom into position and refit the sealing strip to the upper edge of the bulkhead.

17 Refill the master cylinder reservoir with new fluid, and bleed the brake and (if necessary) the clutch hydraulic systems, as described in Section 2 and Chapter 6 respectively.

---

11 Brake pedal –
removal and refitting

Removal

1 Remove the driver's side lower trim below the dashboard.

2 Release the stop-light switch from its mounting bracket and position it to one side. Also, where fitted, remove the brake pedal/cruise control switches.

3 On right-hand drive models, unscrew the brake pedal pivot bolt, and push the pedal to the right and remove it. Note that the pivot bolt is locked with locking fluid.

4 On left-hand drive models, pull off the securing clip from the right-hand end of the pedal pivot pin, unscrew the pivot pin securing bolt, and slide the pivot pin to the left.

5 On right-hand drive models, the brake pedal pivot pin is connected to a remote operating lever to the left of the clutch pedal, which then acts upon the brake servo pushrod. On left-hand drive models the brake pedal acts directly upon the servo pushrod. On both models it is necessary to separate the servo pushrod from the pedal/remote lever. The end of the pushrod is shaped as a ball, and engages with a retaining clip in the back of the lever/pedal. To release the clip a special VW tool is available, but a suitable alternative can be improvised as shown. Note that the plastic lugs are very stiff, and it will not be possible to release them by hand, Using the tool, release the securing lugs and pull the pedal/lever from the servo pushrod **(see illustrations).**

6 Examine all components for signs of wear or damage, renewing them as necessary.

10.6b Exploded view of the master cylinder/brake vacuum servo

1	T45 Torx bolt	5	Brake pipe
2	Self-locking nut	6	Seal
3	Master cylinder	7	Servo
4	Brake pipe	8	Gasket

9	Vacuum hose	13	Fluid supply hose
10	Fluid reservoir	14	Engine
11	Cap		compartment
12	Sealing plugs		bulkhead

Overhaul

7 If the master cylinder is faulty, it must be renewed. Repair kits are not available from VW dealers, so the cylinder must be treated as a sealed unit.

8 The only items which can be renewed are the mounting seals for the fluid reservoir; if these show signs of deterioration, carefully lever out the old seals with the aid of a screwdriver. Lubricate the new seals with clean brake fluid, and ease them into the master cylinder ports. When fitting the rear seal, take care to ensure that the seal engages correctly with the pushrod circuit filling tube and ensure that the seal projects from the rear of its housing by approximately 1 mm. Once both seals are correctly fitted, ease the fluid reservoir into position and push it fully home.

Refitting

9 Remove all traces of dirt from the master cylinder and servo unit mating surfaces, and fit a new sealing ring to the rear of the master cylinder body.

11.5a The end of the servo pushrod is shaped as a ball, and engages in the back of the lever/pedal

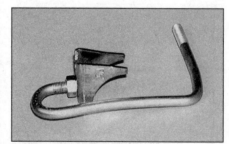

11.5b Improvised special tool constructed from a modified exhaust clamp, used to release the brake pedal/lever from the servo pushrod

11.5c Exploded view of the brake/clutch pedal assembly – RHD models

1 Tork screw	10 Remote
2 Bolt	operating lever
3 Mounting	11 Bush
bracket	12 Bolt
4 Seal	13 Mounting
5 Brake	14 Over-centre
pedal	spring
6 Washer	15 Clutch pedal
7 Bolt	16 Circlip
8 Sleeve	17 Bolt
9 Clutch master	18 Bush
cylinder	19 Cap

Refitting

7 Apply a smear of multi-purpose grease to the pedal pivot bore and the pushrod ball.

8 The remainder of the refitting procedure is a reversal of the removal procedure, noting the following points:

a) On RHD models, the remote lever will only engage the brake pedal pivot in one position, thanks to a larger master spline **(see illustration)**.

b) Apply locking fluid to the threads of the brake pedal pivot bolt before tightening it to the specified torque.

c) Tighten all fixings to the correct torque, where specified.

d) Refit and adjust the stop-light and pedal switch as described in Section 17.

e) Refit the cruise control system vacuum valves.

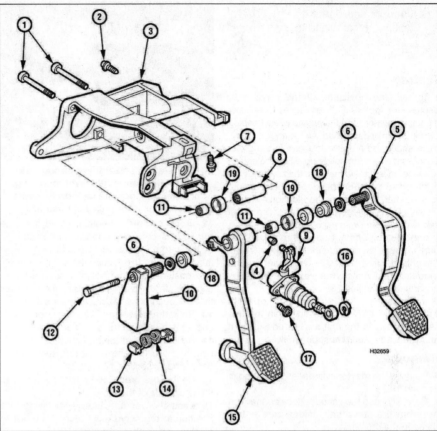

11.5d Exploded view of the brake/clutch pedal assembly – LHD models

1 Mounting	9 Bolt
bracket	10 Bolt
2 Pivot pin	11 Clutch master
3 Clip	cylinder
4 Bolt	12 Brake pedal
5 Bolt	13 Mounting
6 Clip	14 Over-centre
7 Pin	spring
8 Seal	15 Clutch pedal

11.8 Note the master spline on the brake operating lever – RHD models

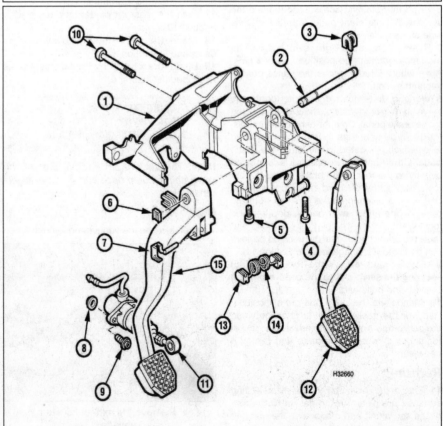

12 Vacuum servo unit –
testing, removal and refitting

Testing

1 To test the operation of the servo unit, depress the footbrake several times to exhaust the vacuum, then start the engine whilst keeping the pedal firmly depressed. As the engine starts, there should be a noticeable give in the brake pedal as the vacuum builds-up. Allow the engine to run for at least two minutes, then switch it off. If the brake pedal is now depressed it should feel normal, but further applications should result in the pedal feeling firmer, with the pedal stroke decreasing with each application.

2 If the servo does not operate as described, first inspect the servo unit check valve as described in Section 13. On diesel engine models, also check the vacuum pump as described in Section 20.

3 If the servo unit still fails to operate satisfactorily, the fault may lie within the unit itself. Repairs to the unit are not possible – if faulty, the servo unit must be renewed.

Removal

4 Remove the master cylinder as described in Section 10.

5 Carefully ease the vacuum hose connection out from the servo unit, taking care not to damage the grommet.

6 Undo the retaining screws and remove the storage compartment panel from the driver's side of the facia.

7 Release the stop-light switch from its mounting bracket and position it to one side. Also, where fitted, remove the cruise control vacuum switch.

8 Working underneath the facia, locate the servo unit pushrod and note how it is connected to the brake pedal. On right-hand drive models, the pushrod connects to a remote operating lever, which is located to the left of the clutch pedal. On left-hand drive models it is connected directly to the rear of the brake pedal. In both installations, the pushrod is equipped with a balljoint. To disconnect the pushrod from the remote operating lever/pedal, depress the locking tabs of the balljoint retaining clip and raise the brake pedal, until the pushrod balljoint can be felt to disengage (refer to Section 11).

9 Unscrew and remove the Torx bolts (T45) securing the servo unit to the pedal mounting bracket and bulkhead.

10 Manoeuvre the servo unit out of position. Recover the gasket which is fitted between the servo and bulkhead. Examine the gasket for signs of wear or damage and renew if necessary.

Refitting

11 Ensure the servo unit and bulkhead mating surfaces are clean, fit the gasket to the rear of the servo unit and manoeuvre the unit into position.

14.4 Pass a screwdriver through the hole in the handbrake lever mounting bracket and lock the handbrake cable compensator pulley in position

12 From inside the vehicle, make sure the pushrod is correctly engaged with the rear of the pedal, or the remote operating lever (as applicable) then press the pushrod firmly into position until the balljoint can be felt to engage. Lift the brake pedal by hand to check that the pushrod is securely reconnected.

13 Refit the servo unit securing Torx bolts and tighten them to the specified torque.

14 Refit and adjust the operation of the stop-light and cruise control vacuum switches as described in Section 17.

15 Refit the storage compartment panel to the underside of the facia.

16 Ease the vacuum hose end fitting into position in the servo unit, taking care not to displace the rubber grommet.

17 Refit the master cylinder as described in Section 10.

18 Bleed the brake hydraulic system as described in Section 2.

19 Bleed the clutch hydraulic system as described in Chapter 6.

13 Vacuum servo unit check valve –
removal, testing and refitting

Note: *The valve is an integral part of the servo unit vacuum hose and is not available separately.*

Removal

1 Carefully ease the vacuum hose connection

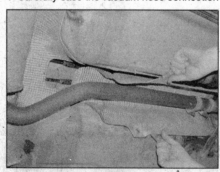

14.5a Remove the exhaust system heat shields . . .

out from the servo unit, taking care not to damage the grommet.

2 Work back along the hose, freeing it from all the relevant retaining clips whilst noting its correct routing.

3 Slacken the retaining clip then disconnect the vacuum hose from the manifold and/or vacuum pump (as applicable) and remove it from the vehicle.

Testing

4 Examine the vacuum hose for signs of damage, and renew if necessary. The valve may be tested by blowing through it in both directions. Air should flow through the valve in one direction only – when blown through from the servo unit end of the valve. Renew the valve if this is not the case.

5 Examine the servo unit rubber sealing grommet and hose(s) linking the main hose to the manifold/pump (as applicable) for signs of damage or deterioration, and renew as necessary.

Refitting

6 Ensure the sealing grommet is in position in the servo unit then carefully ease the vacuum hose end fitting into position, taking care not to displace or damage the grommet.

7 Ensure the hose is correctly routed then connect it to the pump/manifold and securely tighten the retaining clip.

8 On completion, start the engine and check the check valve-to-servo unit connection for signs of air leaks.

14 Handbrake –
adjustment

Note: *Handbrake adjustment is normally only required after renewing the cables, brake calipers or brake discs.*

1 Depress the brake pedal firmly, to settle the rear brake self-adjustment mechanism.

2 Chock the front wheels, then jack up the rear of the vehicle and support it on axle stands. Fully release the handbrake lever.

3 Remove the ashtray unit from the rear section of the centre console as described in Chapter 11.

4 Pass a screwdriver through the hole in the handbrake lever mounting bracket and lock the handbrake cable compensator pulley in position, to prevent it from turning (**see illustration**).

5 Working underneath the vehicle, locate the handbrake adjuster collars, which are located above the exhaust pipe. Access can be gained by removing the exhaust system centre heat shields (**see illustrations**).

6 Working on the first adjustment collar, remove the locking ring, then rotate the collar clockwise until it reaches its end stop. Counterhold the rear section of the handbrake cable using an open-ended spanner on the hex nut provided as you do this (**see illustrations**).

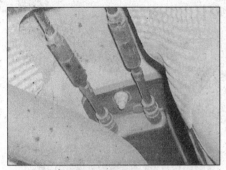

14.5b ... to gain access to the handbrake cable adjuster collars

7 Grasp the handbrake cable either side of the adjustment collar and push them together firmly.

8 Rotate the adjustment collar anti-clockwise, until the slot for the locking ring is just visible, then insert the locking ring into its slot.

9 Repeat the steps in paragraphs 6 to 8 on the remaining adjustment collar.

10 Pull the two sections of the adjustment collar apart on either cable until the slack in both handbrake cables has been taken up. Ensure that the brake caliper handbrake levers remain seated on their stops as you do this.

11 Working inside the vehicle, remove the screwdriver to free the handbrake cable compensator pulley, then apply and release the handbrake lever firmly at least three times.

12 Return to the underside of the vehicle and turn the adjustment collars on both handbrake cables until a gap of approximately 1 mm (but not greater than 1.5 mm) can seen between the caliper handbrake levers and their end stops **(see illustration)**.

13 Check on both handbrake cables that the adjustment collars have not been turned to the extent that the coloured rubber O-rings inside the collars have been exposed. If this is the case, the handbrake cables may be stretched beyond the limit of adjustment, or the rear brake pads may be excessively worn.

14 Check the operation of the handbrake and repeat the adjustment procedure as necessary.

15 Once the handbrake is correctly adjusted (both brakes securely lock the wheels with the lever applied and spin freely when the lever is released), lower the vehicle to the ground.

15 Handbrake lever – removal and refitting

Removal

1 Remove the rear section of the centre console as described in Chapter 11.

2 Unscrew the two nuts that secure the handbrake lever to the floorpan **(see illustration)**.

3 Disengage the handbrake cable from the base of the lever, then free the handbrake

14.6a Remove the locking ring ...

lever from its mountings and remove it from the vehicle.

Refitting

4 Refitting is a reversal of removal, but adjust the handbrake, as described in Section 14, before the rear section of the centre console is refitted.

16 Handbrake cables – removal and refitting

Removal

1 The handbrake cable consists of two sections, a right- and a left-hand section, which are linked to the lever by a compensator plate. Each section can be removed individually as follows. Chock the front wheels, then jack up the rear of the vehicle, support it on axle stands, and remove the rear wheels. Fully release the handbrake lever.

2 Undo the nuts and remove the exhaust system heat shields to gain access to the front end of the handbrake cable.

3 With reference to Section 14, remove the locking ring from the first handbrake cable adjustment collar and rotate the collar anti-clockwise as far as possible. Grasp the front and rear sections of the handbrake cable either side of the adjustment collar and push them firmly together. Repeat this on the other cable.

4 Working at the first rear brake caliper, remove the metal clip and disconnect the

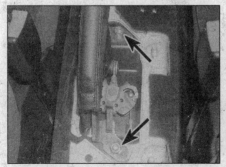

15.2 Unscrew the two nuts that secure the handbrake lever to the floorpan (arrowed)

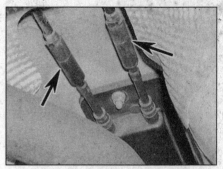

14.6b ... then rotate the collar anti-clockwise until it reaches its end stop, whilst counter-holding the rear section of the handbrake cable using a spanner

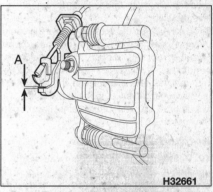

H32661

14.12 Turn the adjustment collar until a gap of between 1.0 and 1.5 mm (A) can be seen between the caliper handbrake lever and the end stop

handbrake cable outer from its mounting lug. Release the cable inner from its lever and withdraw the cable from the caliper **(see illustrations)**. Repeat this operation at the remaining caliper.

5 Work back along the length of each handbrake cable, noting its correct routing, and free it from all the relevant retaining clips and fixings, including those on the rear suspension beam. Note the location of the ABS sensor wiring on the clips.

6 Undo the nuts and remove the exhaust system rear silencer heat shield to gain access to the handbrake cable clamp plate. Release the spring clips and free the cables from the floorpan.

16.4a Remove the metal clip and disconnect the handbrake cable outer from its mounting lug

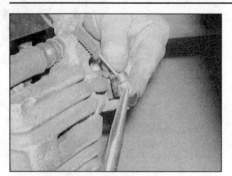

16.4b Release the cable inner from its lever and withdraw the cable from the caliper

7 Carefully prise the handbrake cable grommets from the underside of the handbrake lever housing.

8 Working inside the vehicle, remove the centre console, then unhook the handbrake cables from the compensator pulley at the rear of the handbrake lever, by inserting a screwdriver through the hole provided in the handbrake lever mounting bracket **(see illustration)**.

9 Withdraw the handbrake cables from under the car.

Refitting

10 Refitting is a reversal of the removal procedure, ensuring that the cable is correctly routed and retained by all the necessary clips and ties. In particular, make sure that the cable grommets seat correctly in the underside of the handbrake lever housing. On completion, adjust the operation of the handbrake as described in Section 14.

---

17 Stop-light and brake pedal switches – removal, refitting and adjustment

Note: *VW recommend that the switch is renewed every time it is removed, to ensure secure fitment.*

Removal

1 The stop-light and brake pedal switches are located on the pedal bracket behind the facia.

2 Undo the retaining screws and remove the storage compartment panel/trim panel from the underside of the facia on the driver's side.

3 Note the adjustment of the relevant switch, then disconnect the wiring connector from the switch body **(see illustration)**.

4 On models up to and including 2002, depress the brake pedal, then unscrew and remove the lower locknut from the switch. Withdraw the switch and remove it from the bracket. If the switch retaining clip and washer are a loose fit, remove them and store with the switch.

5 On 2003-on models, press in the operating rod, then turn the switch 45° anti-clockwise to remove it.

Refitting and adjustment

Models up to and including 2002

6 Ensure the clip is securely fitted to the pedal bracket. On early models, where adjustment of the switch has not previously been carried out, an upper locknut may not be fitted. To permit adjustment, an M12x1.5 nut must be threaded onto the switch shaft before the switch is refitted to its mounting bracket.

7 Fit the spring washer to the switch, then depress the brake pedal and engage the switch with its retaining clip, pushing it fully into position.

8 Fit the lower locknut to the switch, then allow the brake pedal to slowly pivot back to its rest position, so that the pedal just bears against the switch plunger.

9 Adjust the position of the switch in its bracket by turning the upper and lower locknuts such that the protrusion of the plunger from the front of the switch is between 0.5 and 1.2 mm. Tighten the lower locknut when this dimension is correct.

Models from 2003-onwards

10 Pull the plunger fully out of the switch, then, with the brake pedal released, guide the plunger through the hole against the pedal, and secure by turning it 45° clockwise.

All models

11 Reconnect the wiring connector, and check the operation of the stop-lights.

12 Refit the storage compartment panel/trim panel to the facia.

---

18 Anti-lock braking system (ABS) – general information

1 ABS is fitted as standard to all models in the range. The system comprises a hydraulic unit, an electronic control unit (ECU) and four roadwheel sensors. The hydraulic unit contains the eight hydraulic solenoid valves (two for each brake – one inlet and one outlet) and the electrically-driven return pump. The purpose of the system is to prevent the roadwheels locking during heavy braking. This is achieved by automatic release of the brake on the relevant wheel, followed by re-application of the brake. In the case of the rear wheels, both rear brakes are released and applied at the same time.

2 The solenoid valves are controlled by the ECU, which itself receives signals from the four wheel sensors (front sensors are fitted to the hubs and the rear sensors are fitted to the rear axle), which monitor the speed of rotation of each wheel. By comparing these signals, the ECU can determine the speed at which the vehicle is travelling. It can then use this speed to determine when a wheel is decelerating at an abnormal rate, compared to the speed of the vehicle, and therefore predicts when a wheel is about to lock. During normal operation, the system functions in the same way as a non-ABS braking system.

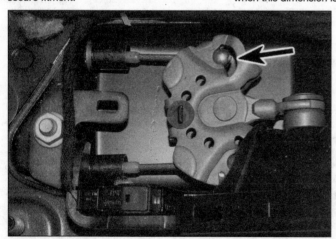

16.8 Unhook the handbrake cables from the rear of the handbrake lever, by inserting a screwdriver through the hole in the handbrake lever mounting bracket

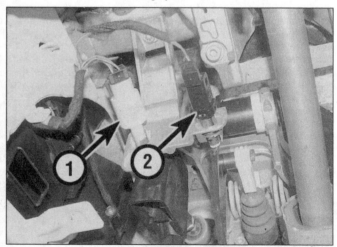

17.3 Stop-light switch (1) and clutch pedal switch (2)

3 If the ECU senses that a wheel is about to lock, it closes the relevant outlet solenoid valves in the hydraulic unit, which then isolates the relevant brake on the wheel which is about to lock from the master cylinder, effectively sealing-in the hydraulic pressure.

4 If the speed of rotation of the wheel continues to decrease at an abnormal rate, the ECU opens the inlet solenoid valves on the relevant brake and operates the electrically-driven return pump which pumps the hydraulic fluid back into the master cylinder, releasing the brake. Once the speed of rotation of the wheel returns to an acceptable rate, the pump stops; the solenoid valves switch again, allowing the hydraulic master cylinder pressure to return to the caliper, which then re-applies the brake. This cycle can be carried out many times a second.

5 The action of the solenoid valves and return pump creates pulses in the hydraulic circuit. When the ABS system is functioning, these pulses can be felt through the brake pedal.

6 The operation of the ABS system is entirely dependent on electrical signals. To prevent the system responding to any inaccurate signals, a built-in safety circuit monitors all signals received by the ECU. If an inaccurate signal or low battery voltage is detected, the ABS system is automatically shut down, and the warning light on the instrument panel is illuminated, to inform the driver that the ABS system is not operational. Normal braking should still be available, however.

7 On models with a traction control system, the ABS system is expanded to include Electronic Differential Lock (EDL) and traction control/Anti-Slip Regulation (ASR) functions. If under acceleration the ECU senses that a wheel is spinning, it uses the hydraulic unit to gradually apply the brake on that wheel until traction is regained. Once the wheel regains traction, the brake is released.

8 The ESP (Electronic Stability Program) function is a further expansion of the ABS system which takes into consideration the angle of the steering wheel, using a steering angle sender and Yaw Rate Sender. Additionally, the system monitors lateral acceleration with a Lateral Acceleration Sender.

9 Models covered in this Manual are fitted with Bosch type 5.3 ABS for 2001 models, and Bosch type 5.7 ABS for 2002-on models – the ECU and hydraulic unit are combined into one unit.

10 If a fault does develop in the ABS system, the vehicle must be taken to a VW dealer for fault diagnosis and repair.

19 Anti-lock braking system (ABS) components – removal and refitting

Hydraulic unit

Note: *VW state that the operation of the hydraulic unit should be checked using special test equipment after refitting. Bearing this in*

19.14a Remove the wheel speed sensor . . .

mind, it is recommended that removal and refitting of the unit is entrusted to a VW dealer. If you decide to remove/refit the unit yourself, ensure that the operation of the braking system is checked at the earliest opportunity by a VW dealer.

Removal

1 Disconnect the battery negative terminal (see Chapter 5A). Where necessary, remove the engine upper cover.

2 Release the locking bar and disconnect the main wiring connector from the hydraulic unit.

3 Raise the front of the vehicle and rest it securely on axle stands, then remove the left-hand front roadwheel.

4 Connect a length of hose to the left-hand front brake caliper bleed screw, then direct the other end of the hose into a suitable receptacle, as described in Section 2. Open the bleed screw and then depress the brake pedal through one full stroke and hold it in this position, using a suitable weight, or a wedge such as a block of wood. When the expelled brake fluid has collected into the receptacle, close the bleed screw. **Note:** *The brake pedal must be held in the depressed position until the brake pipes have been reconnected to the hydraulic unit, at the end of this procedure.*

5 Wipe clean the area around all the pipes unions and mark the locations of the hydraulic fluid pipes to ensure correct refitting. Unscrew the union nuts and disconnect the pipes from the regulator assembly. Be prepared for fluid spillage, and plug the open ends of the pipes and the hydraulic unit unions to prevent dirt ingress and further fluid loss.

6 Unscrew the hydraulic unit mounting nuts and remove the assembly from the engine compartment. If necessary, the mounting bracket can then be unbolted and removed from the vehicle. Renew the regulator mountings if they show signs of wear or damage. **Note:** *Keep the hydraulic unit upright to minimise the risk of fluid loss, and to prevent air locks inside the unit.*

Refitting

Note: *New hydraulic units are supplied prefilled with brake fluid and fully bled; it is vitally important that the union plugs are not removed until the brake pipes are reconnected as loss of fluid will introduce air into the unit.*

7 Manoeuvre the hydraulic unit into position

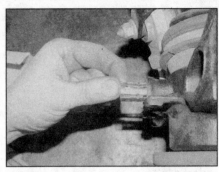

19.14b . . . and sleeve from the hub carrier

in the mounting bracket and tighten the mounting nuts to the specified torque setting.

8 Remove the plugs and reconnect the hydraulic pipes to the correct unions on the hydraulic unit and tighten the union nuts to the specified torque.

9 Securely reconnect the wiring connector to the hydraulic unit.

10 Fill the brake fluid reservoir with fresh fluid (see *Weekly checks*) and reconnect the battery.

11 Remove the weight/wedge from the brake pedal and then bleed the entire braking hydraulic system as described in Section 2. Thoroughly check the operation of the braking system before using the vehicle on the road. Have the operation of the ABS system checked by a VW dealer at the earliest possible opportunity.

Front wheel sensor

Removal

12 Apply the handbrake, then jack up the front of the vehicle and support securely on axle stands. To improve access, remove the roadwheel.

13 Trace the wiring back from the sensor, releasing it from all the relevant clips and ties whilst noting its correct routing, and disconnect the wiring connector.

14 Carefully pull the sensor out from the hub carrier assembly and remove it from the vehicle. With the sensor removed, slide the rubber seal and clamping sleeve out from the hub carrier **(see illustrations)**.

Refitting

15 Ensure that the mating faces of the sensor, clamping ring and hub carrier are clean and dry then lubricate clamping sleeve and wheel sensor surfaces with a small quantity of copper-based grease.

16 Press the clamping sleeve fully into the hub carrier then insert the wheel sensor together with the rubber seal. Ensure the sensor wiring is correctly positioned then push the sensor firmly into position until it is fully home in the hub carrier.

17 Ensure the sensor is securely retained then work along the sensor wiring, making sure it is correctly routed, securing it in position with all the relevant clips and ties. Reconnect the wiring connector.

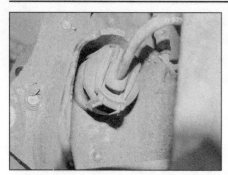

19.22 Release the speed sensor retaining clip, and carefully prise the sensor from the axle assembly

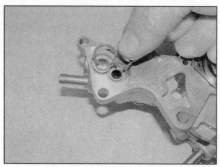

20.6a Fit new rubber seals . . .

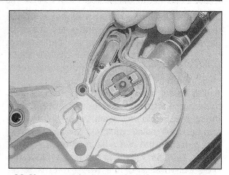

20.6b . . . and ensure that the pump drive aligns with the slot in the camshaft

18 Refit the wheel then lower the vehicle and tighten the wheel bolts to the specified torque.

Rear wheel sensor

Removal

19 Remove the rear seat cushion and side trim (see Chapter 11), and locate the rear wheel sensor ABS wiring connectors. Unplug the relevant connector and free the wiring from its retaining clips.
20 Chock the front wheels, then jack up the rear of the vehicle and support it on axle stands. To improve access, remove the appropriate roadwheel.
21 Working underneath the vehicle, trace the wiring back from the sensor, releasing it from all the relevant clips. Undo the retaining bolts and remove the wiring protective cover from the rear axle (where fitted) then release the wiring grommet from body and pull the wiring through so that it is free to be removed with the sensor.
22 Note the fitted position of the speed sensor, then release the retaining clip and carefully prise the sensor from the axle assembly **(see illustration)**.

Refitting

23 Ensure that the mating faces of the sensor and axle are clean and dry, then lubricate the wheel sensor surfaces with a little copper-based grease.
24 Ensure the sensor wiring is correctly positioned then push the sensor firmly into position until it is fully home in the axle. Note that the left-hand sensor must have the lug pointing forwards, and the right-hand sensor must have the lug pointing to the rear. Refit the retaining clip.
25 Ensure the sensor is securely retained then work along the sensor wiring, making sure it is correctly routed, securing it in position with all the relevant clips and ties. Refit the wiring protective cover to the axle (where fitted), tighten its retaining screws securely, then feed the wiring connector up through the body and seat the wiring grommet correctly in position.
26 Refit the roadwheel then lower the vehicle to the ground and tighten the wheel bolts to the specified torque.

27 Reconnect the sensor wiring connect then refit the seat cushion and trim panel.

20 Vacuum pump (diesel engine models) – removal and refitting

Note: *Disconnecting the central connector for the unit injectors will cause a fault code to be logged by the engine management ECU. This code can only be erased by a VW dealer or suitably-equipped specialist.*

Removal

1 Prise out the cover caps, unscrew the retaining nuts/bolts and remove the engine top cover.
2 Disconnect the charge air pipe at the back of the cylinder head, and place it to one side. Disconnect the central connector for the unit injectors.
3 Release the retaining clip (where fitted) and disconnect the brake servo pipe from the tandem pump.
4 Disconnect the fuel supply hose (marked white) from the tandem pump. Be prepared for fuel spillage.
5 Unscrew the four retaining bolts and move the tandem pump away from the cylinder head. As the pump is lifted up, disconnect the fuel return hose (marked blue). Be prepared for fuel spillage. There are no serviceable parts within the tandem pump. If the pump is faulty, it must be renewed.

Refitting

6 Reconnect the fuel return hose to the pump and refit the pump to the cylinder head, using new rubber seals, and ensuring that the pump pinion engages correctly with the drive slot in the camshaft **(see illustrations)**.
7 Refit the pump retaining bolts, and tighten them to the specified torque.
8 Re-attach the fuel supply hose and brake servo hose to the pump.
9 Reconnect the central connector for the unit injectors.
10 Refit the charge air pipe.
11 Disconnect the fuel filter return hose (marked blue), and connect the hose to a hand vacuum pump. Operate the vacuum

pump until fuel comes out of the return hose. This primes the tandem pump. Take care not to suck any fuel into the vacuum pump. Reconnect the return hose to the fuel filter.
12 Refit the engine top cover.
13 Have the engine management ECU's fault memory interrogated and erased by a VW dealer or suitably-equipped specialist.

21 ESP system components – removal and refitting

1 The ESP system comprises of the ABS, TCS and EDL system. The ESP, TCS and EDL systems rely on the ABS system components for measuring and reducing wheel speed. In addition to the wheel speed sensors and brake pressure sensors, the ESP receives information concerning the steering wheel angle, lateral acceleration and vehicle rotational speed (yaw rate). Testing of the various system components should be entrusted to a VW dealer or specialist.

Lateral acceleration sensor/ yaw rate sensor

Warning: Handle the sensor with great care. Severe shakes/jolts can destroy the sensors.

2 The lateral acceleration sensor and the Yaw rate sensor are integrated in one housing, located under the rear seat bench. Remove the rear seat bench as described in Chapter 11.
3 Disconnect the wiring plug, unscrew the two retaining screws and remove the housing. No further dismantling is possible.
4 Refitting is a reversal of removal. Ensure the housing is correctly seated before securely tightening the retaining bolts.

Electronic control unit

5 The electronic control unit (ECU) is located under the carpet below the glovebox **(see illustration)**. Slide the passenger's seat fully to the rear, and remove the glovebox as described in Chapter 11.
6 Remove the A-pillar trim from the passenger's side footwell (see Chapter 11)
7 Fold back the carpet under the facia to reveal the ECU.

8 Remove the two securing nuts, and release the locking device to disconnect the wiring plug as the ECU is removed.

ESP hydraulic pump and brake pressure sensor

9 The brake pressure sensor is integral with the ESP hydraulic pump, and if defective, must be renewed together. The pump is located in the lower part of the ABS hydraulic unit mounting bracket. To remove the pump, remove the ABS hydraulic unit and mounting bracket as described in Section 19, labelling all pipe unions to aid refitment. Separate the hydraulic pump from the mounting bracket.

10 Whilst refitting is a reversal of removal, it will be necessary to have the assembly initialised/adapted by a dedicated diagnostic tester – see your local VW dealer or specialist.

Steering angle sensor

11 The steering angle sensor is incorporated into the airbag contact unit between the steering wheel and column switch. To remove the sensor, refer to Chapter 12, Section 5, and remove the steering column switch. Then the steering angle sensor can be detached from the combination switch, but after re-installation, specialist equipment is required to perform a 'zero comparison'. Therefore we recommend that removal and refitting of the angle sensor is entrusted to a VW dealer or specialist.

21.5 ESP control unit

Chapter 10
Suspension and steering

Contents

Section number

Front hub bearings – renewal. 2
Front suspension anti-roll bar – removal and refitting 6
Front suspension strut – overhaul 4
Front suspension strut – removal and refitting. 3
Front suspension subframe – removal and refitting. 7
Front suspension transverse arms – removal, overhaul and refitting 5
General information 1
Ignition switch/steering column lock – removal and refitting. 14
Power steering fluid level check. . . . . See *Weekly checks*
Power steering pump – removal and refitting 18
Power steering pump drivebelt check, adjustment and
  renewal. . . . . .See Chapter 1A or 1B
Power steering system – level check and bleeding 17
Rear axle assembly – removal and refitting 11

Section number

Rear hub, bearings and housing – renewal 8
Rear suspension strut – overhaul. 10
Rear suspension strut and spring – removal and refitting 9
Steering column – removal, inspection and refitting 13
Steering gear – adjustment 21
Steering gear assembly – removal, overhaul and refitting 15
Steering gear rubber bellows – renewal. 16
Steering wheel – removal and refitting. 12
Suspension and steering check. . . . . See Chapter 1A or 1B
Track rod – removal and refitting 20
Track rod balljoint – removal and refitting 19
Wheel alignment and steering angles – general information 22
Wheel and tyre maintenance and tyre pressure
  checks . . . . .See *Weekly checks*

Degrees of difficulty

Easy, suitable for novice with little experience	**Fairly easy,** suitable for beginner with some experience	**Fairly difficult,** suitable for competent DIY mechanic	**Difficult,** suitable for experienced DIY mechanic	**Very difficult,** suitable for expert DIY or professional

Specifications

Engine codes*

Petrol engines
1781 cc, DOHC, Bosch Motronic ME7.5 injection, turbocharged . . . . . AWT
1984 cc, SOHC, Siemens Simos 3.2 injection, non-turbo. . . . . AZM
1984 cc, DOHC, Bosch Motronic ME7.5 injection, non-turbo. . . . . . . ALT

Diesel engines
Electronic direct injection, unit injectors, 74 kW (100 bhp) . . . . AVB
Electronic direct injection, unit injectors, 96 kW (130 bhp) . . . . AVF and AWX
* Note: See 'Vehicle identification' for the location of the code marking on the engine.

Roadwheels
Type . . . . Pressed-steel or aluminium alloy (depending on model)
Size:
  Normal roadwheels. . . . . 6J x 15, 7J x 15 or 7J x 16 (depending on model)
  Spare wheel (space saver type) . . . . 4B x 15
Tyre pressures . . . . Refer to *Weekly checks* on page 0•17

Wheel alignment and steering angles
Front wheel alignment:
  Toe setting (per wheel) . . . . +10' ± 2'
  Camber:
    Standard setting*:
      Standard suspension (code 1BA/1BC). -35' ± 25'
      Sports suspension (code 1BE) . . . . -50' ± 25'
      Heavy duty suspension (code 1BP) . . . . -35' ± 25'
      Heavy duty suspension (code 1BB) . . . . -20' ± 25'
      Heavy duty suspension (code 1BF) . . . . -20' ± 25' (unladen), -35' ± 25' (laden)
    Maximum difference between sides. . . . . ± 30'

Wheel alignment and steering angles (continued)

Rear wheel alignment
  Toe setting*:
    Standard suspension (code 1BA/1BC) . . . . +20' +15' -10'
    Sports suspension (code 1BE) . . . . +28' +15' -10'
    Heavy duty suspension (code 1BP) . . . . +14' +15' -10'
    Heavy duty suspension (code 1BB) . . . . +20' +15' -10'
    Heavy duty suspension (code 1BF) . . . . -1° 30' ±20'
  Camber:
    Standard setting . . . . -1° 30' ± 20'
    Maximum difference between sides . . . . 30'
The suspension type code is stamped on the vehicle identification (VIN) plate.

Torque wrench settings

	Nm	lbf ft
Front suspension		
Anti-roll bar:		
Drop link (earlier models with balljoints):		
Lower joint-to-anti-roll bar nut*	100	74
Upper joint-to-suspension arm nut*:		
Stage 1	40	30
Stage 2	Angle-tighten a further 90°	
Drop link (later models with rubber bushes):		
Lower joint-to-anti-roll bar nut*:		
Stage 1	40	30
Stage 2	Angle-tighten a further 90°	
Upper joint-to-suspension arm nut*:		
Stage 1	40	30
Stage 2	Angle-tighten a further 90°	
Mounting clamp nuts*	25	18
Hub bolt*:		
M14 bolt:		
Stage 1	115	85
Stage 2	Angle-tighten a further 180°	
M16 bolt:		
Stage 1	190	140
Stage 2	Angle-tighten a further 180°	
Lower suspension arms:		
Front lower arm-to-hub carrier balljoint nut*	100	74
Front lower arm-to-subframe nut*:		
Stage 1	90	66
Stage 2	Angle-tighten a further 90°	
Rear lower arm-to-hub carrier balljoint nut*	100	74
Rear lower arm-to-subframe nut*:		
Stage 1	90	66
Stage 2	Angle-tighten a further 90°	
Subframe:		
Front mounting bracket bolts*	60	44
Main mounting bolts*:		
Stage 1	110	81
Stage 2	Angle-tighten a further 90°	
Rear mounting bracket bolts*:		
Underside of bolt head plain	25	18
Underside of bolt head ribbed	75	55
Underside of bolt head and washer ribbed	30	22
Suspension strut:		
Lower mounting nut to suspension arm*	90	66
Piston rod nut*	50	37
Upper mounting nuts*	20	15
Upper suspension arms:		
Bracket-to-bodywork bolts	75	55
Front upper arm-to-bracket nut*:		
Stage 1	50	37
Stage 2	Angle-tighten a further 90°	
Hub carrier-to-upper arm clamp bolt nut*	40	30
Rear upper arm-to-bracket nut*:		
Stage 1	50	37
Stage 2	Angle-tighten a further 90°	

Torque wrench settings (continued)

	Nm	lbf ft
Rear suspension		
Axle pivot bolt and nut*:		
Stage 1	120	89
Stage 2	Angle-tighten a further 90°	
Axle pivot bracket securing bolts*:		
Stage 1	110	81
Stage 2	Angle-tighten a further 90°	
Hub/bearing bolts	60	44
Suspension strut:		
Lower mounting bolt nut*:		
Stage 1	50	37
Stage 2	Angle-tighten a further 90°	
Shock absorber piston nut*	25	18
Upper mounting bolts	45	33
Steering		
Power steering pump mounting bolts	20	15
Steering column:		
Mounting bolts	23	17
Universal joint pinch-bolt nut*	40	30
Steering gear:		
Hydraulic pipe union bolts:		
Supply pipe	40	30
Return pipe	50	37
Hydraulic pipe retaining bracket bolt	20	15
Centring hole plug	18	13
Mounting bolts	65	48
Steering damper-to-track rod nut	10	7
Steering damper-to-steering gear housing bolt	35	26
Steering wheel retaining bolt:		
Hexagon bolt*	75	55
Multi-point socket bolt (can be used 5 times)	60	44
Track rod:		
Adjustment locknut	40	30
Balljoint-to-hub carrier pinch-bolt/nut*	45	33
Toe curve adjustment bolt	7	5
Track rod to steering gear	100	74
Roadwheels		
Wheel bolts	120	89

* Use new fasteners.

1 General information

1 The front suspension is fully independent, utilising four transverse arms (two upper and two lower) and a solid upright (or hub carrier) in an unequal-length, double-wishbone configuration. Coil spring-over-telescopic shock absorber struts are connected between the front lower transverse arm and upper transverse arm mounting bracket. The hub carriers house the wheel bearings, brake calipers and the hub/disc assemblies, and are connected to the upper and lower transverse arms by means of balljoints. A front anti-roll bar is fitted to all models; the anti-roll bar is rubber-mounted onto the subframe, and is connected to the front lower transverse arms by a drop link. The subframe provides mountings for all the lower suspension components as well as the engine and transmission mountings.

2 The rear suspension comprises a torsion beam axle with trailing arms, which are connected to the body by rubber bushes. The axle is attached to the lower ends of the rear suspension telescopic shock absorbers, which are fitted behind the separate coil springs. A rear anti-roll bar is incorporated into the rear axle design to reduce body roll.

3 The suspension type code is stamped on the vehicle identification (VIN) plate and on the identification label in the spare wheel well, or luggage compartment floor.

4 The steering column has a flexible coupling at its lower end and is secured to the steering gear pinion by means of a clamp bolt.

5 The steering gear is mounted onto the vehicle body and is connected by two track rods, with balljoints at their outer ends, to bosses projecting rearwards from the suspension hub carriers. The track rod ends are threaded, to facilitate adjustment. The hydraulic steering system is powered by a belt-driven pump, which is driven off the crankshaft pulley.

2 Front hub bearings – renewal

Note: *The bearing is a sealed, pre-adjusted and pre-lubricated, double-row roller type, and is intended to last the car's entire service life without maintenance or attention. Never overtighten the hub bolt in an attempt to adjust the bearing.*

Note: *A hydraulic press will be required to dismantle and rebuild the assembly; if such a tool is not available, a large bench vice and spacers (such as large sockets) may serve as an adequate substitute. The bearing's inner races are an interference fit on the hub; if the inner race remains on the hub when it is pressed out of the hub carrier, a knife-edged bearing puller will be required to remove it.*

1 Park the vehicle on a level surface, switch off the ignition, apply the handbrake firmly and select first gear.

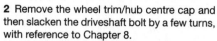

2.9 Undo the nut and remove the clamp bolt

2.11 Press the hub out of the bearing . . .

2.12 . . . and the bearing out of the carrier

2 Remove the wheel trim/hub centre cap and then slacken the driveshaft bolt by a few turns, with reference to Chapter 8.

3 Raise the front of the vehicle and rest it securely on axle stands. Remove the appropriate front roadwheel.

4 On vehicles equipped with electrical discharge headlamps, release the clip and disconnect the vehicle level sensor connecting rod from the front lower transverse arm; see Chapter 12 for details.

5 Refer to Chapter 9 and carry out the following:

a) *Unbolt the brake caliper, together with its mounting bracket, from the hub carrier and suspend it from the coil spring.*

b) *Remove the brake disc.*

c) *Remove the ABS wheel speed sensor from the base of the hub carrier. Release the ABS wheel sensor wiring from its retaining clips in the wheel arch. Pull the rubber grommet from the inner wheel arch to reveal the sensor connector. Disconnect the lead, and pull it through the hub carrier and away from the vehicle.*

6 Undo the screws and detach the brake disc shield from the hub carrier.

7 Undo the securing nuts, then separate the front and rear lower transverse arms from the base of the hub carrier, with the aid of a balljoint splitter (see Section 5). Avoid damaging the rubber gaiters.

8 Unbolt the track rod balljoint from the hub carrier, as described in Section 19.

9 Undo the securing nut and extract the clamp bolt from the top of the hub carrier (see Section 5). Separate the front and rear upper transverse arm balljoints from the top of the hub carrier, but do not force the slots apart with a screwdriver or similar, in an attempt to free the balljoint pins **(see illustration)**. Take care to avoid damaging the balljoint rubber gaiters.

10 Grasp the hub carrier and gradually draw it off the driveshaft. Use a hub puller if the driveshaft is a tight fit in the hub.

11 Support the base of the hub carrier securely on blocks or in a vice. Using a tubular spacer which bears only on the inner end of the hub flange, press the hub flange out of the bearing **(see illustration)**. If the bearing's inner race remains on the hub, remove it using a bearing puller (see note above).

12 Securely support the outer face of the hub carrier then, using a tubular spacer which bears only on the inner race, press the complete bearing assembly out from the carrier **(see illustration)**.

13 Thoroughly clean the hub and hub carrier, removing all traces of dirt and grease, and polish away any burrs or raised edges which might hinder reassembly. Check both for cracks or any other signs of wear or damage, and renew them if necessary. **Note:** *Note that as from Model Year 2002, the depth of the balljoint location at the top of the hub carrier has been reduced to 30.00 mm, and bushes are now incorporated to improve sealing of the joints. Only combi-type nuts should be used on the this type of carrier, whereas conventional nuts must be used on the earlier type.*

14 Securely support the inner face of the base of the hub carrier and locate the bearing in the carrier bore. Make sure the larger diameter inner race of the bearing is facing outwards (towards the hub flange) then press the bearing into position using a tubular spacer which bears only on the outer race. Ensure the bearing enters the hub carrier squarely and is pressed fully into position **(see illustrations)**.

15 Securely support the outer face of the hub flange, and locate the hub bearing inner race over the end of the hub flange. Using a tubular spacer which bears only on the inner race, press the bearing onto the hub until it seats against the shoulder **(see illustration)**.

16 Check that the hub flange rotates freely, without any sign of roughness or sticking.

17 Offer the hub carrier up to the wheel arch and pass the driveshaft through the centre of the hub. Fit the new driveshaft bolt, but hand tighten it only at this stage.

18 Reconnect the lower transverse arms to the base of the hub carrier as described in Section 5. Fit new self-locking nuts and tighten them to the specified torque.

19 Reconnect the upper transverse arms to the top of the hub carrier as described in Section 5. Refit the clamp bolt, together with a new self-locking nut and tighten it to the specified torque. Press down on both transverse arms as you tighten the nut, to ensure that the balljoints are properly seated in the hub carrier.

2.14a Fit the bearing into the carrier with the larger diameter of the inner race facing outwards . . .

2.14b . . . until it contacts the inner shoulder of the carrier

2.15 Press the hub squarely into the bearing, until it seats against the shoulder

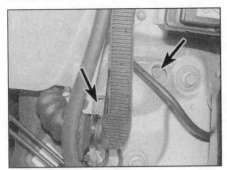

3.4 Prise out the grommets, and undo the strut upper mounting nuts (arrowed)

3.7 Remove the mounting bolt, and separate the strut from the lower arm

3.8 Disengage the strut upper mounting studs from the mounting bracket and withdraw the strut from the wheel arch

20 Reconnect the steering track rod balljoint to the hub as described in Section 19. Fit a new securing nut and tighten it, and the adjustment bolt, to their respective specified torque.

21 Refit the brake disc shield and tighten the retaining screws securely.

22 Carry out the following with reference to the appropriate sections of Chapter 9:
   a) *Refit the ABS wheel speed sensor to the hub carrier and secure the wiring with the clips in the wheel arch.*
   b) *Refit the brake disc.*
   c) *Refit the brake caliper.*

23 On vehicles equipped with electrical discharge headlamps, fasten the clip to reconnect the vehicle level sensor connecting rod to the front lower transverse arm; see Chapter 12 for details.

24 Refit the roadwheel, tighten the bolts to the specified torque and lower the vehicle to the ground.

25 Tighten the driveshaft bolt to the specified torque, as described in Chapter 8, then refit the hub cap/wheel trim.

26 On completion, it is essential that the front wheel alignment is checked and if necessary adjusted either by a VW dealer or a suitably-equipped tyre specialist.

3 Front suspension strut – removal and refitting

Removal

1 Remove the wheel trim/hub cap (as applicable) and slacken the wheel bolts by half a turn with the vehicle resting on its wheels.

2 Chock the rear wheels of the car, firmly apply the handbrake, then jack up the front of the car and support it securely on axle stands. Remove the appropriate front roadwheel.

3 On vehicles equipped with electrical discharge headlamps, release the clip and disconnect the vehicle level sensor connecting rod from the front lower transverse arm; see Chapter 12 for details.

4 The strut upper mounting nuts are accessed via two holes, located in the scuttle to the rear of the engine compartment and plugged with

rubber grommets. Support the underside of the hub carrier on a trolley jack or an axle stand, then prise out the grommets and unscrew the strut upper mounting nuts using a socket wrench and long extension bar **(see illustration)**.

5 Release the ABS wheel speed sensor from its mounting clips and position it away from the suspension strut (see Chapter 9).

6 Working in the wheel arch, undo the securing nut and extract the clamp bolt from the top of the hub carrier (see Section 5). Separate the front and rear upper transverse arm balljoints from the top of the hub carrier, but do not force the slots apart with a screwdriver or similar, in an attempt to free the balljoint pins. Take care to avoid damaging the balljoint rubber gaiters.

7 Undo the nut and remove the suspension strut lower mounting bolt from the transverse arm **(see illustration)**.

8 Disengage the strut upper mounting studs from the mounting bracket and withdraw the strut from the wheel arch **(see illustration)**.

Refitting

9 Offer up the suspension strut to the wheel arch and engage the upper mounting studs with the mounting bracket. Ensure that the alignment hole in the strut coil spring lower seat faces inwards towards the vehicle.

10 Bolt the strut lower mounting to the lower transverse arm, fit a new securing nut but hand-tighten it only at this stage.

11 Reconnect the upper transverse arms to the top of the hub carrier as described in Section 5. Refit the clamp bolt, together

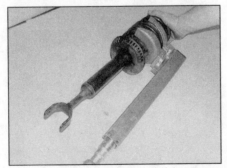

4.2 Compress the coil spring evenly and progressively until all tension is relieved from the spring seats

with a new self-locking nut and tighten it to the specified torque. Press down on both transverse arms as you tighten the nut, to ensure that the balljoints are properly seated in the hub carrier.

12 Fit new nuts to the strut upper mounting studs and tighten them to the specified torque. Refit the rubber grommets to the scuttle access holes.

13 Refit the ABS wheel speed sensor to its retaining clips.

14 On vehicles equipped with electrical discharge headlamps, fasten the clip to reconnect the vehicle level sensor connecting rod to the front lower transverse arm; see Chapter 12 for details.

15 Refit the road wheel and tighten the bolts to the specified torque, then lower the vehicle to the ground.

16 With the vehicle resting on its wheels, tighten the suspension strut lower mounting bolt nut to the specified torque.

4 Front suspension strut – overhaul

Warning: Before attempting to dismantle the front suspension strut, a suitable tool to hold the coil spring in compression must be obtained. Adjustable coil spring compressors are readily-available, and are recommended for this operation. Any attempt to dismantle the strut without such a tool is likely to result in damage or personal injury.

1 With the strut removed from the car, clean away all external dirt. If required, mount the strut upright in a vice to provide stability. Pad the vice jaws with wood or aluminium, to prevent damage to the strut lower mountings.

2 Fit the spring compressor and compress the coil spring evenly and progressively until tension is relieved from the spring seats **(see illustration)**.

3 Slacken the shock absorber piston nut whilst retaining the piston with a suitable Allen key **(see illustration)**. This can be achieved using either a spanner with an angled head, or by turning the socket with a 'crow's foot' adapter, or by using a socket with a centre

4.3 Slacken the shock absorber piston nut whilst retaining the piston with a suitable Allen key

4.4a Remove the nut . . .

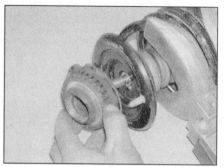

4.4b . . . then lift off the mounting plate . . .

4.4c . . . followed by the washer . . .

4.4d . . . the upper spring seat and upper spring support

5 Remove the dust gaiter, rubber bump stop and protective cap from the shock absorber piston, then lift off the coil spring (together with the compressors) **(see illustrations)**.

6 Remove the lower spring support **(see illustration)**, then if required, loosen the lower spring seat from the shock absorber body by tapping it lightly with a soft-faced mallet.

7 Examine the shock absorber for signs of fluid leakage. Check the piston rod for signs of pitting along its entire length, and check the shock absorber body for signs of damage or serious corrosion. While holding it in an upright position, test the operation of the shock absorber by moving the piston through a full stroke, and then through short strokes of 50 to 100 mm. In both cases, the resistance felt should be smooth and continuous. If the resistance is jerky, or uneven, or if there is any visible sign of wear or damage to the shock absorber, renewal will be necessary. **Note:** *Shock absorbers must be renewed in pairs, to preserve the handling characteristics of the vehicle.*

8 Inspect all other components for signs of damage or deterioration, and renew as required.

hole large enough to allow the Allen key to pass through and a hex fitting at the top; the socket can then be turned with an open-ended spanner.

4 Remove the nut, then lift off the mounting plate followed by the washer, the upper spring seat and upper spring support **(see illustrations)**.

9 Refit the lower spring seat to the shock absorber body, such that the alignment hole is positioned at 90° to the axis of the strut lower mounting bolt.

10 Refit the lower spring support, ensuring that it engages correctly with the recess in the lower spring seat.

11 Slide the protective cap, bump stop rubber and dust gaiter onto the end of the piston rod and press them firmly into position. Ensure the lower end of the dust gaiter is correctly engaged with the strut base.

12 Refit the compressed coil spring to the strut base, ensuring that the end of the coil bears against the corresponding stop on the spring support **(see illustration)**.

13 Fit the upper spring support and spring seat, washer and upper mounting to the top of the strut, such that the spring seat alignment hole is positioned at 11° to the longitudinal axis of the strut lower mounting bolt. If the assembly has been carried out correctly, the upper end of the coil spring should be positioned against the stop on the underside of the upper spring seat **(see illustrations)**.

4.5a Remove the dust gaiter, rubber bump stop and protective cap from the shock absorber piston . . .

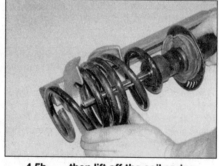

4.5b . . . then lift off the coil spring (together with the compressors)

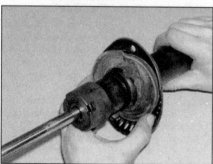

4.6 Remove the lower spring support

4.12 Ensure that the end of the coil spring bears against the stop (arrowed) on the spring support

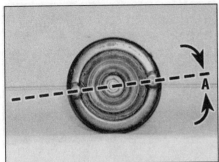

4.13a Fit the upper spring seat such that the alignment hole is positioned at an angle (A) of 11° to the longitudinal axis of the strut lower mounting bolt (shown by a length of welding rod)

14 Fit a new piston rod nut, then retain the shock absorber piston rod using the method employed during removal and tighten the nut to the specified torque.

15 Ensure all components are correctly seated and both spring ends are in contact with their stops then progressively release the spring compressor and remove it from the strut.

16 Refit the strut to the vehicle as described in Section 3.

5 Front suspension transverse arms – removal, overhaul and refitting

Upper arms

Removal

1 Chock the rear wheels, firmly apply the handbrake, then jack up the front of the vehicle and support on axle stands. Remove the appropriate front roadwheel. Whilst the wheel is removed, refit at least one wheel bolt to ensure the brake disc remains correctly positioned on the hub.

2 On vehicles equipped with electrical discharge headlamps, release the clip and disconnect the vehicle level sensor connecting rod from the front lower transverse arm; see Chapter 12 for details.

3 Carefully prise the ABS wheel speed sensor wiring from its retaining clips.

4 Undo the securing nut and extract the clamp bolt from the top of the hub carrier. Separate the front and rear upper transverse arm balljoints from the top of the hub carrier, but do not force the slots apart with a screwdriver, or similar, in an attempt to free the balljoint pins **(see illustrations)**. Take care to avoid damaging the balljoint rubber gaiters.

5 Undo the nut and remove the suspension strut lower mounting bolt from the front transverse arm (see Section 4).

6 The upper transverse arm mounting bracket bolts are located in the scuttle, to the rear of the engine compartment **(see illustration)**. Unscrew the three bolts and remove the

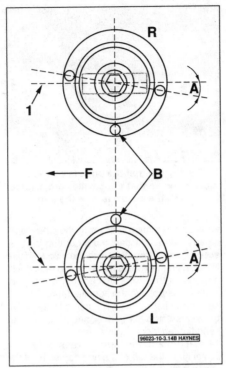

4.13b Note the difference in angle offset between the right and left-hand struts

A   Angle = 11° ± 2°
B   Lower spring seat alignment holes
F   Direction of travel
L   Left-hand strut
R   Right-hand strut
1   Axis of strut lower mounting bolt

5.4a Undo the securing nut . . .

5.4c Separate the balljoints from the top of the hub carrier

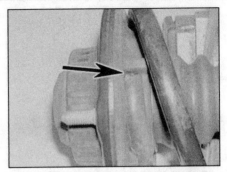

4.13c The upper end of the coil spring should be positioned against the stop (arrowed) on the underside of the upper spring seat

mounting bracket, the suspension strut and both upper transverse arms as an assembly. There may be plastic washers fitted to the underside of the bolts; these are factory assembly components which do not need to be refitted, once removed. **Note:** *Make a careful note of the fitted positions of any shims fitted underneath the heads of the transverse arm mounting bracket bolts; they must be refitted in the same positions to preserve the front suspension alignment settings.*

7 Mount the lower end of the strut in a bench vice, then slacken and remove the nut and bolt securing the appropriate upper transverse arm to the mounting bracket **(see illustration)**.

Overhaul

8 Thoroughly clean the arm and the area around the arm mountings, removing all

5.4b . . . and extract the clamp bolt from the top of the hub carrier

5.6 The upper transverse arm mounting bracket bolts (arrowed) are located in the scuttle, to the rear of the engine compartment

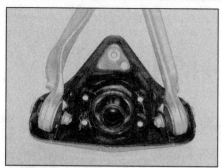

5.7 Upper transverse arm pivot bolts/nuts (shock absorber removed for clarity)

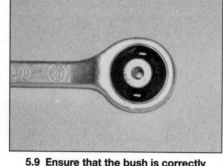

5.9 Ensure that the bush is correctly positioned so that the cavities are aligned with the centre axis of the arm

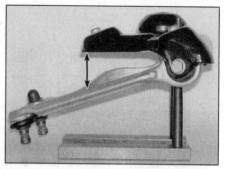

5.11 Position the transverse arm such that the vertical distance between the front of edge of the mounting bracket and the arm is 47 mm

traces of dirt, thread locking compound and underseal if necessary, then check carefully for cracks, distortion or any other signs of wear or damage, paying particular attention to the inner pivot bush and balljoint. The balljoint is an integral part of the lower arm and cannot be renewed separately. If the arm or balljoint are damaged then the complete assembly must be renewed.

9 Renewal of the inner pivot bush will require the use of a hydraulic press and several spacers and is therefore best entrusted to a VW dealer or garage with access to the necessary equipment. If such equipment is available, press out the old bush and install the new one using a spacer which bears only on the bush outer edge. Ensure the bush is correctly positioned so that the cavities are aligned with the centre axis of the arm **(see illustration)**.

Refitting

10 Offer up the transverse arm to the mounting bracket, insert a new securing bolt and screw on a new securing nut.

11 Position the transverse arm such that the vertical distance between the front edge of the mounting bracket and the arm is 47 mm **(see illustration)**. Hold the arm in this position and tighten the securing nut to the specified Stage 1 and 2 torque settings. This ensures that the rubber bush is not stressed when the vehicle is lowered onto its wheels.

12 Refit the suspension strut, transverse arms and mounting bracket to the wheel arch as an assembly. Insert the mounting bracket securing bolts, together with the shims (where fitted), using the notes made during removal to ensure that the shims are correctly positioned. Tighten the bolts to the specified torque.

13 Bolt the strut lower mounting to the lower transverse arm, fit a new securing nut but hand tighten it only at this stage.

14 Reconnect the upper transverse arm balljoints to the top of the hub carrier. Refit the clamp bolt, together with a new self-locking nut and tighten it to the specified torque **(see illustration)**. Press down on both transverse arms as you tighten the nut, to ensure that the balljoints are properly seated in the hub carrier.

15 Refit the ABS wheel speed sensor wiring to its retaining clips.

16 On vehicles equipped with electrical discharge headlamps, fasten the clip to reconnect the vehicle level sensor connecting rod to the front lower transverse arm; see Chapter 12 for details.

17 Refit the road wheel and tighten the bolts to the specified torque, then lower the vehicle to the ground.

18 With the vehicle resting on its wheels, tighten the suspension strut lower mounting bolt nut to the specified torque.

19 On completion, have the front wheel alignment checked and if necessary adjusted by a VW dealer or a suitably-equipped tyre specialist.

Rear lower arm

Removal

20 Chock the rear wheels, firmly apply the handbrake, then jack up the front of the vehicle and support on axle stands. Remove the appropriate front roadwheel. Whilst the wheel is removed, refit at least one wheel bolt to ensure the brake disc remains correctly positioned on the hub.

21 Undo the securing nut, then separate the transverse arm from the base of the hub carrier, with the aid of a balljoint splitter – avoid damaging the rubber gaiter **(see illustrations)**.

22 Slacken and remove the nut from the bolt at the inboard end of the transverse arm. To allow the bolt to be withdrawn, the corner of the subframe must be lowered slightly. To do this, unscrew and remove the two support plate bolts, then slacken and withdraw the subframe securing bolt. Note that the bolt is threaded through the inner of the two sets of subframe bolt holes.

23 Lower the subframe slightly, withdraw the transverse arm inboard securing bolt then remove the arm from the vehicle.

Overhaul

24 Thoroughly clean the arm and the area around the arm mountings, removing all traces of dirt, thread locking compound and underseal if necessary, then check carefully for cracks, distortion or any other signs of

5.14 Tighten the new clamp bolt nut to the specified torque

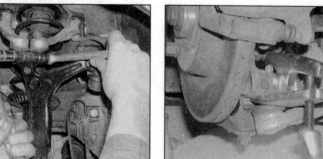

5.21a With the aid of a balljoint splitter . . .

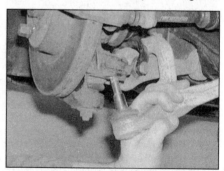

5.21b . . . separate the rear lower transverse arm from the base of the hub carrier

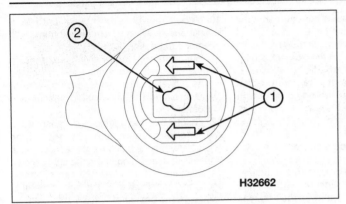

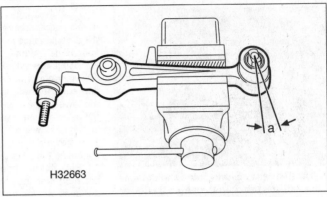

5.25 Ensure that the arrows on the hydro-mounting (1) or the central groove (2), point towards the balljoint

5.34 Position the mounting so that dimension (a) is 6° ± 3°

wear or damage, paying particular attention to the inner pivot bush and balljoint. Note that the inner bush has a hydraulic action; fluid leakage indicates that the bush has been damaged and must be renewed. The balljoint is an integral part of the lower arm and cannot be renewed separately. If the arm or balljoint are damaged then the complete assembly must be renewed.

25 Renewal of the inner pivot bush will require the use of a hydraulic press and several spacers and is therefore best entrusted to a VW dealer or garage with access to the necessary equipment. If such equipment is available, press out the old bush and install the new one using a spacer which bears only on the bush outer edge. Ensure the bush is correctly positioned so that the arrows or central groove points towards the balljoint **(see illustration).**

Refitting

26 Refitting is a reversal of removal noting the following points:
  a) *Use new transverse arm and subframe securing nuts and bolts.*
  b) *Delay tightening the transverse arm inboard securing bolt until the vehicle is resting on its roadwheels.*
  c) *Ensure that the transverse arm inboard securing bolt passes through the inner of the two sets of subframe bolt holes.*
  d) *Tighten all fixings to the correct torque, where specified.*

Front lower arm

Removal

27 Chock the rear wheels, firmly apply the handbrake, then jack up the front of the vehicle and support on axle stands. Remove the appropriate front roadwheel. Whilst the wheel is removed, refit at least one wheel bolt to ensure the brake disc remains correctly positioned on the hub.

28 On vehicles equipped with electrical discharge headlamps, release the clip and disconnect the vehicle level sensor connecting rod from the front lower transverse arm; see Chapter 12 for details.

29 Undo the securing nut, then separate the front lower transverse arm from the base of the hub carrier, with the aid of a balljoint splitter (avoid damaging the rubber gaiter).

30 Undo the nut and remove the suspension strut lower mounting bolt from the front transverse arm.

31 Remove the securing nut and detach the anti-roll bar drop link, from the transverse arm as described in Section 6.

32 Unscrew the nut and withdraw the transverse arm inboard securing bolt, then remove the transverse arm from the vehicle. Note that the bolt is threaded through the inner of the two sets of subframe bolt holes.

Overhaul

Note: *As from Model Year 2002, the front lower arm has been modified to accept anti-roll bar links with bonded rubber bushes.*

33 Thoroughly clean the arm and the area around the arm mountings, removing all traces of dirt, thread locking compound and underseal if necessary, then check carefully for cracks, distortion or any other signs of wear or damage, paying particular attention to the inner and strut pivot bushes and balljoint. The balljoint is an integral part of the lower arm and cannot be renewed separately. If the arm or balljoint are damaged then the complete assembly must be renewed.

34 Renewal of the inner and strut pivot bushes will require the use of a hydraulic press and several spacers and is therefore best entrusted to a VW dealer or garage with access to the necessary equipment. If such equipment is available, press out the old bush and install the new one using a spacer which bears only on the bush outer edge. Ensure the bush is correctly positioned **(see illustration).**

Refitting

35 Refitting is a reversal of removal noting the following points:
  a) *Use new transverse arm and strut securing nuts and bolts.*
  b) *To avoid damaging the bushes, delay tightening the transverse arm inboard securing nut the strut securing nut and the anti-roll bar drop link securing nut to*

their final torque settings until the vehicle is resting on its roadwheels.
  c) *Ensure that the transverse arm inboard securing bolt passes through the inner of the two sets of subframe bolt holes.*
  d) *Tighten all fixings to the correct torque, where specified*

6 Front suspension anti-roll bar – removal and refitting

Removal

1 The anti-roll bar must be removed/refitted with the vehicle resting on its wheels. For this reason the following operation will be much easier if the vehicle can be positioned over an inspection pit. Alternatively drive the vehicle onto ramps to increase the clearance between the front of the vehicle and the ground.

2 Remove the fasteners and retaining clips and remove the undercover from beneath the engine/transmission to gain access to the anti-roll bar mounting clamps.

3 Slacken and remove the nuts and bolts securing both the anti-roll bar mounting clamps to the subframe. Remove the clamps and discard the nuts; new ones should be used on refitting **(see illustration).**

4 Unscrew the securing nuts and detach the drop links from the lower transverse arms each side. Note that on later models with rubber bushed joints, rather than the balljoints fitted

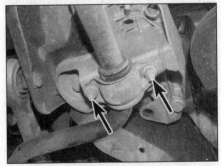

6.3 Slacken and remove the nuts securing the anti-roll bar clamps to the subframe

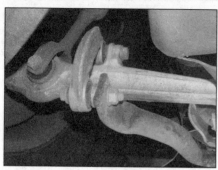

6.4 Undo the securing nuts and detach the anti-roll bar drop links from the lower transverse arm

to earlier models, the drop link is secured with separate nuts and bolts **(see illustration)**. On both versions, discard the nuts as new ones should be used on refitting.

5 Unscrew the nuts securing the anti-roll bar ends to the drop links and discard them; new nuts should be used on refitting. On later models the drop links are secured by separate nuts and bolts (refer to the note in the previous paragraph). Where applicable, remove the washer and rear bush from each end of the bar, noting their correct fitted positions.

6 As they are removed, note that the drop link-to-lower arm mounting bushes are fitted with their concave side facing the wishbone. On later models, the drop links have rubber bushes instead of balljoints; the arrow marked on the side of this version of the link must point towards the front of the vehicle when correctly fitted.

7 Lower the anti-roll bar, and remove it from under the vehicle.

8 Renew the anti-roll bar if it is damaged or distorted. Renew the mounting bushes if they are perished or worn.

Refitting

9 Mount the drop links onto the anti-roll bar, then fit the bolts (where applicable) and fit

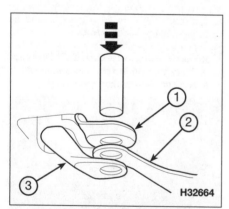

7.21 Pass a wooden dowel (arrowed) through each of the alignment holes in the front corners of the subframe

1 Bracket (upper)
2 Subframe
3 Bracket (lower)

new securing nuts – hand tighten them only at this stage. Ensure that the concave side of the drop link faces the front of the vehicle. On later models, the arrow on the side of the drop link points towards the front of the vehicle.

10 Manoeuvre the anti-roll bar into position and engage the ends of the drop links with the lower arms. Insert the securing bolts, or the balljoints studs (as applicable) through the lugs in the lower arms.

11 Screw on the new drop link retaining nuts, tightening them lightly only at this stage.

12 Refit the mounting clamps to the anti-roll bar mounting bushes. Ensure both clamps are correctly located on the bushes then fit the retaining bolts and new nuts. Tighten the retaining nuts lightly only at this stage.

13 Rock the vehicle from side-to-side, to settle the anti-roll bar in position. Tighten all four anti-roll bar drop link nuts to the specified torque settings. Also tighten the anti-roll bar mounting clamp bolt nuts to the specified torque.

14 Refit the undercover and tighten the fixings securely.

7 Front suspension subframe – removal and refitting

Removal

1 Chock the rear wheels, firmly apply the handbrake, then jack up the front of the vehicle and support on axle stands.

2 Remove both front roadwheels. Whilst the wheel is removed, refit at least one wheel bolt to ensure the brake discs remain correctly positioned on the hub.

3 Remove the fasteners and retaining clips and remove the undercover from beneath the engine/transmission unit.

4 Referring to Chapter 2A or 2B, attach a lifting bracket to the rear of the engine and support the weight of the engine/transmission unit, using either a lifting beam or an engine hoist.

5 On vehicles equipped with electrical discharge headlamps, release the clip and disconnect the ride height sensor connecting rod from the front lower transverse arm; see Chapter 12 for details.

6 Carefully prise the ABS wheel speed sensor wiring from its retaining clips.

7 Unbolt the anti-roll bar drop links from both lower suspension arms, with reference to Section 6.

8 Unbolt the inboard ends of both rear lower transverse arms from the subframe with reference to Section 5. Note that this will entail unbolting the rear corners of the subframe from the underside of the vehicle and lowering it slightly to allow the transverse arm bolts to be withdrawn.

9 Unbolt the lower ends of both suspension struts from the front lower transverse arms with reference to Section 3.

10 Unbolt the inboard ends of both front lower transverse arms from the subframe with reference to Section 5.

11 Suspend the hub carrier, suspension strut and transverse arms from the inside of the wheel arch using lengths of wire to avoid straining the suspension bushes and balljoints.

12 Ensure that the engine and transmission are securely suspended by the lifting equipment, then unbolt the right- and left-hand transmission mountings from the subframe.

13 Slacken and withdraw the two subframe securing bolts, located to the rear of the anti-roll bar clamp brackets.

14 Slacken the four subframe securing bolts located forward of the anti-roll bar clamps brackets, until the subframe can be released from its mountings. Do not remove the bolts completely.

15 Carefully lower the subframe and withdraw it from the underside of the vehicle.

Overhaul

16 Renewal of the bonded subframe bushes requires access to a hydraulic press and a number of specially-shaped extraction/fitment tools. Fabrication of alternative tools is not recommended due to the risk of damage to the subframe bush mountings. For this reason, it's best to entrust bush renewal work to a VW dealer.

Refitting

Note: *All subframe mounting nuts and bolts must be renewed.*

17 Offer the subframe up to the underside of the engine compartment and engage the front mountings with their respective brackets. Fit the new subframe front mounting bolts, but do not fully tighten them at this stage.

18 Reconnect the transmission mountings to the subframe.

19 Reconnect the lower end of the suspension strut to the front lower transverse arm with reference to Section 3, then reconnect the front and rear lower transverse arms to the subframe with reference to Section 5. Do not fully tighten the securing nuts and bolts at this stage.

20 Refit the electrical discharge headlamp ride height sensor pushrod to the front lower transverse arm with reference to Chapter 12 (where applicable).

21 Obtain two lengths of wooden dowel, each roughly 15 mm in diameter and 150 mm in length. Working through the wheel arches, pass a dowel through each of the alignment holes in the front corners of the subframe. Adjust the position of the subframe until both dowels pass through all three alignment holes on each side **(see illustration)**.

22 Refit the mounting brackets at the rear corners of the subframe, insert the new brackets securing bolts and tighten them lightly. With the brackets in place, fit new subframe rear mounting bolts and tighten them lightly.

23 Remove the engine hoist/support bar (as applicable) then tighten the subframe and suspension mounting bolts in the order given in the following paragraphs.

24 Tighten the four main subframe securing bolts to their specified first and second Stage torques **(see illustration)**.

25 Tighten the four subframe front mounting bracket bolts to their specified torques.

26 Tighten the four subframe rear mounting bracket bolts to their specified torques.

27 Tighten the transmission mounting bolts to their specified torques, with reference to Chapter 7A or 7B as applicable.

28 Tighten the front and rear lower transverse arm inboard securing bolts to their specified torques, with reference to Section 5.

29 Refit the anti-roll bar drop link with reference to Section 6. Use new securing nuts and tighten them to the specified torques.

30 Tighten the strut-to-front lower transverse arm securing nut to the specified torque (see Section 4).

31 Refit the ABS wheel speed sensor wiring to its retaining clips (see Chapter 9).

32 Securely refit the undercover then refit the roadwheels and lower the vehicle to the ground. Tighten the wheel bolts to the specified torque.

33 On completion, have the front wheel alignment and steering angles checked and if necessary adjusted at the earliest possible opportunity.

8 Rear hub, bearings and housing – renewal

1 The rear wheel hub bearings are housed in the rear brake disc/hub. The bearings are an integral assembly with the hub and housing, and are maintenance-free. If defective, the bearings must be renewed with the hub and housing as a complete unit.

2 Remove the rear brake disc as described in Chapter 9. Pull the ABS wheel sensor and retainer from the inboard end of the bearing housing assembly **(see illustration)**.

3 Unscrew the five hexagon socket-head bolts securing the bearing/hub assembly to the axle, and remove the assembly **(see illustration)**.

4 Clean the axle-to-bearing housing mating surfaces.

5 The remainder of refitting is a reversal of removal.

9 Rear suspension strut and spring – removal and refitting

Removal

1 Chock the front wheels, then jack up the rear of the car and support it on axle stands. Remove the relevant rear roadwheel.

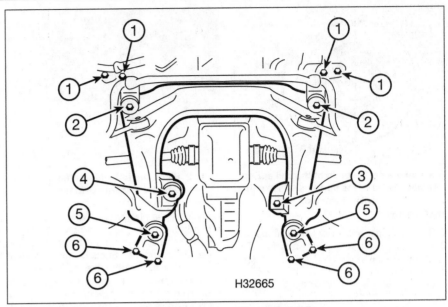

7.24 Subframe mounting bolt details

1 Rear mounting bracket bolts
2 Main mounting bolts
3 Transmission mounting bolts

4 Transmission mounting bolts
5 Main mounting bolts
6 Front bracket mounting bolts

2 Position a trolley jack underneath the rear axle and raise it until it is supporting the axle weight.

3 Slacken and remove the nut then withdraw the lower mounting bolt which secures the strut to the axle **(see illustration)**. Discard the nut and bolt; new items should be used on refitting.

4 Undo and remove the two upper strut mounting bolts from under the wheel arch **(see illustration)**.

5 Carefully lower the trolley jack until all the tension in the spring is released. Recover the spring and the strut.

6 Recover the upper and lower spring supports.

8.2 Release the retaining clip and pull the wheel sensor from the back of the hub assembly

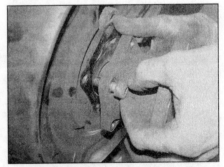

8.3 Undo the five securing bolts and remove the hub/bearing/housing

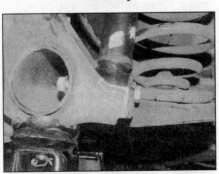

9.3 Remove the rear shock absorber lower mounting bolt

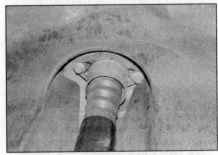

9.4 Remove the two rear shock absorber upper mounting bolts from under the wheel arch

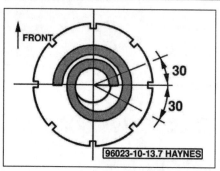

9.8 Make sure the ends of the coil springs are positioned in the spring seats like this when installed

Refitting

7 Refit the upper and lower spring supports.

8 Manoeuvre the spring into position. The spring must be orientated as shown (see illustration).

9 Position the strut, and finger-tighten the upper mounting bolts.

10 Raise the axle and locate the strut lower mounting on the axle brackets. Fit the new lower mounting bolt and screw on the new nut. Tighten to the specified torque.

11 Tighten the upper strut mounting bolts to the specified torque.

12 Refit the roadwheel then lower the vehicle to the ground and tighten the wheel bolts to the specified torque.

10 Rear suspension strut – overhaul

1 With the strut removed from the car, clean away all external dirt, then mount it upright in a vice.

2 Slacken the damper rod nut whilst retaining the damper rod with a suitable spanner (see illustration).

3 Remove the nut then lift off the upper mounting, stop buffer and protective tube (see illustration).

4 Examine the shock absorber for signs of fluid leakage. Check the piston for signs of pitting along its entire length, and check the shock

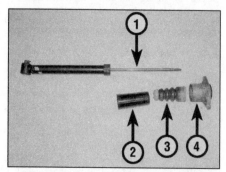

10.3 Rear shock absorber components

1 Damper
2 Protective cap
3 Stop buffer
4 Upper mounting

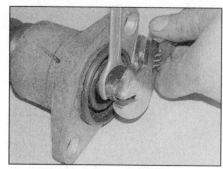

10.2 Slack the nut whist retaining the damper rod with a spanner

body for signs of damage. While holding it in an upright position, test the operation of the shock absorber by moving the piston through a full stroke, and then through short strokes of 50 to 100 mm. In both cases, the resistance felt should be smooth and continuous. If the resistance is jerky, or uneven, or if there is any visible sign of wear or damage to the shock absorber, renewal will be necessary.

Caution: Shock absorbers must be renewed in pairs. Different versions of shock absorbers are fitted to different models – ensure that you have the correct version for your vehicle.

5 Inspect all other components for signs of damage or deterioration, and renew any that are suspect.

6 Slide the protective tube over the damper rod then refit the stop buffer, followed by the upper mounting.

7 Fully extend the piston rod and screw on the new nut. Counter-hold the damper rod to prevent it from rotating and tighten the nut to the specified torque.

8 Refit the strut to the vehicle as described in Section 9.

11 Rear axle assembly – removal and refitting

Removal

1 Chock the front wheels, engage 1st gear (or P), then slacken the rear roadwheel bolts. Raise and support the vehicle at the rear on axle stands (see *Jacking and vehicle support*). Remove the rear roadwheels.

2 Remove the screws securing the heat shield above the exhaust system intermediate pipe. Slide the heat shield to one side to allow access to the handbrake cable adjustment collars. With reference to Chapter 9, disconnect the handbrake cables from each rear brake, then detach the cables from the clips securing it to the axle.

3 Clamp the rubber section of the rear brake pipes to minimise fluid loss, then unscrew the unions and disconnect the brake hydraulic lines from each rear brake. Plug the open unions to prevent the ingress of dirt.

4 On models fitted with electric discharge headlamps, disconnect the ride height sensor pushrod from the axle beam; refer to Chapter 12 for details.

5 Position jacks under the axle each side to support its weight. Where fitted, remove the rear undertray.

6 Unbolt and remove the strut lower mounting bolt each side, and detach the struts and springs from the axle, as described in Section 9 of this Chapter.

7 Disconnect the ABS wheel sensors from the rear of the axle as described in Chapter 9. Release the wiring from its clips to free it from the axle assembly then position it away from the work area.

8 Check that all associated fittings are clear of the axle. Cover the brake assemblies to ensure that they do not get damaged or dirty as the axle assembly is removed. Ensure that the axle is securely supported. If possible, engage the services of an assistant to help in steadying the axle assembly as it is detached and lowered from the vehicle.

9 Mark around the left-hand side axle bush housing with a felt tip pen or similar, and slacken the three mounting bolts.

10 Unscrew and remove the pivot bolt nut each side, then withdraw the bolts and lower the axle from the pivot/mountings. Lower and remove the axle assembly from under the vehicle.

11 If the mounting/pivot bushes are worn, they must be renewed. At the time of writing, the rubber bush was not available separately. Check with your VW dealer or specialist.

Refitting

12 Refitting is a reversal of the removal procedure. When the axle is raised into position, loosely assemble the retaining bolts and nuts until the axle is fully located before tightening them fully to the specified torque settings. The pivot bolt nuts must only be tightened when the vehicle is standing on its roadwheels.

13 When reconnecting the brake hydraulic lines, handbrake cables and ABS wiring, ensure that everything is correctly routed and secured. Bleed the hydraulic system, adjust the handbrake and refit the ABS wheel sensor as described in Chapter 9.

14 On models fitted with electric discharge headlamps, reconnect the ride height sensor pushrod to the axle beam with reference to Chapter 12.

15 On completion, the rear wheel alignment must be checked. The rear axle overall toe-out cannot be adjusted as the axle is a rigid assembly, but the toe-out at the individual wheels can be altered by slackening the securing bolts and repositioning the axle pivot mounting brackets. However, this should only be attempted if the appropriate wheel alignment checking equipment is available. For this reason it is recommended that the operation is carried out by a VW dealer, or a suitably-equipped tyre specialist.

12 Steering wheel –
removal and refitting

 Warning: Refer to the precautions given in Chapter 12 before handling airbag system components.

Removal

1 Remove the airbag unit as described in Chapter 12.

2 Position the front wheels in the straight-ahead position and engage the steering lock.

3 Slacken and remove the steering wheel securing nut/bolt, then mark the steering wheel and steering column shaft in relation to each other **(see illustration)**. On vehicles so equipped, the multi-spline nut may be used 5 times. We suggest that the nut is marked with a centre punch each time it is slackened. Hexagon bolts should always be renewed.

4 Lift the steering wheel off the column splines, taking care not to damage the contact unit wiring. Disconnect the wiring plugs as the wheel is withdrawn. **Do not** rotate the contact unit whilst the wheel is removed.

Refitting

5 Refitting is a reversal of removal, noting the following points:

a) Use the markings made during removal to ensure that the alignment between the steering wheel and column is correct.

b) If necessary, fit a new steering wheel securing bolt/nut and tighten it to the correct torque.

c) On completion, refit the airbag unit as described in Chapter 12.

13 Steering column –
removal, inspection and refitting

 Warning: Refer to the precautions given in Chapter 12, regarding the safe handling of airbag system components, before proceeding.

Removal

1 Disconnect the battery negative lead. **Note:**

12.3 Steering wheel and column shaft alignment marks

If the vehicle has a security-coded radio, check that you have a copy of the code number before disconnecting the battery. Refer to your VW dealer if in doubt.

2 Remove the driver's airbag from the steering wheel, as described in Chapter 12.

3 Remove the steering wheel from the steering column, as described in Section 12.

4 Undo the retaining screws and remove the upper and lower column shrouds. The upper shroud is retained by two cross-head screws inserted from the under side of the column, and the lower shroud is retained by two cross-head screws and a hexagon socket-head bolt. If necessary refer to Chapter 12, Section 5. Note that it will be necessary to undo the two screws and remove the steering column height adjustment lever grip.

5 Undo the socket-head bolt at the top of the column switch assembly, disconnect the wiring plugs and pull the switch over the end of the steering column along with the coil connector and slip ring.

6 Undo the cable ties and release the wiring harness from the steering column.

7 Detach and remove the lower facia trim/storage tray and insulation panels on the driver's side.

8 Disconnect the ignition switch/steering column lock wiring connector (see Section 14).

9 On models with automatic transmission, disconnect the transmission selector lock cable from the ignition switch as follows. Move the transmission selector lever to the Park position. Insert the ignition key and turn it clockwise to the first (On) position. Lift the

locking lever at the rear of the ignition switch housing up slightly, then withdraw the locking cable from the rear of the housing.

10 Remove the remaining trim panels underneath the driver's side of the facia, as necessary to gain access to the base of the steering column.

11 Secure the lower section of the steering column to the upper section using a length of wire. This is to ensure that, when the steering column is detached from the steering gear, the two sections of the column do not become separated **(see illustration)**.

Caution: Do not allow the upper and lower sections of the steering column to become separated whilst the steering column is detached from the steering gear, as this can cause the internal components to become detached and misaligned.

12 Unscrew the nut from the pinch-bolt securing the universal joint at the base of the steering column to the steering gear. Rotate the bolt clockwise through half turn and withdraw it from the joint **(see illustration)**.

13 Pull the steering column universal joint off the steering gear pinion and move it to one side.

14 Remove the four steering column mounting bolts and withdraw the column assembly from the vehicle **(see illustration)**.

15 Check the various components for excessive wear. If the column has been damaged in any way, it must be renewed as a unit.

16 If required, remove the ignition switch/steering column lock, as described in Section 14.

Refitting

17 Refitting is a reversal of the removal procedure, noting the following points:

18 Ensure that the protective plastic cap is still in place on the pivot bolt that protrudes from the left-hand side of the steering column. If the cap has been lost, cover the end of the bolt with thick adhesive tape to prevent the wiring harness from chafing.

19 Where applicable, refit the ignition switch/column lock as described in Section 14.

20 Fit the four steering column upper securing bolts, but do not tighten them yet.

13.11 Secure the lower section of the steering column to the upper section using a length of wire (arrowed)

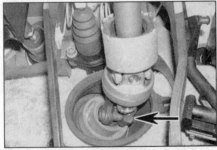

13.12 Unscrew the nut from the pinch-bolt (arrowed) securing the universal joint at the base of the steering column to the steering gear

13.14 Remove the four steering column mounting bolts (arrowed)

14.3 Unplug the wiring connector from the side of the key sensor ring

14.5 Insert a length of 2mm diameter welding rod with a chamfered point (arrowed) into the access hole until it is felt to contact the retaining tang

21 Insert the pinch-bolt that secures the universal joint at the base of the steering column to the steering gear, and secure by rotating it through half a turn anti-clockwise. Refit the nut and tighten it to the specified torque.

22 Now tighten the four upper steering column securing bolts to the specified torque.

23 Remove the wire that was used to secure the upper and lower sections of the steering column together.

24 On models with automatic transmission, to refit the selector lever locking cable, move the gear selector lever to the Park position, and turn the ignition key to the On position. Inserting the end of the locking cable into the rear of the ignition switch housing and push it firmly home, until the locking bar can be heard to engage. Test the operation of the cable as follows:

1) It should be only possible to move the selector lever from the Park position to other gear positions with the ignition key in the On position.

2) It should only be possible to remove the ignition key from the switch with the selector lever in the Park position and the ignition key in the Off position.

25 Refit the lower facia trim/storage tray and insulation panels on the driver's side.

26 Refit the combination switches as described in Chapter 12.

27 Refit the steering wheel as described in Section 12.

28 Refit the driver's airbag as described in Chapter 12.

29 As a safety precaution against accidental airbag detonation, ensure that no-one is inside the car then reconnect the battery negative cable.

30 On completion, ensure that the steering action, and the operation of the column switches, is satisfactory.

14 Ignition switch/ steering column lock – removal and refitting

Lock cylinder

Note: Removal of the lock cylinder requires the use of the vehicle's spare ignition key, which is fitted with a narrow-profile, moulded plastic grip. The grip fitted to the standard key, fitted with a built-in immobiliser transmitter and/or lock illumination torch is too bulky to be used in the removal procedure.

Removal

1 Remove the steering wheel (Section 12).

14.6 Withdraw the lock cylinder from its housing

14.15 Unplug the multi-way wiring connector from the rear of the ignition switch

2 Remove the steering column combination switches as described in Chapter 12.

3 Carefully unplug the wiring connector from the side of the key sensor ring (see illustration).

4 Insert the spare key (see note at the beginning of this sub-Section) into the ignition switch and turn it to the On position. In this position, a small hole which allows access to the lock cylinder retaining tang hole is exposed.

5 Insert a thin screwdriver or a length of 1.2 mm diameter welding rod (chamfered at the end) into the access hole until it is felt to contact the retaining tang (see illustration).

6 Hold the screwdriver/rod in position, then grasp the key and withdraw the lock cylinder from its housing (see illustration).

Refitting

7 Fit the key to the new lock cylinder and turn it to the On position.

8 Slide the new lock cylinder into position, until the retaining tang can be heard to engage with a click.

9 Pull lightly on the key to check that the cylinder is securely held in position.

10 Reconnect the wiring to the sensor ring, checking that the connector is pushed fully home.

11 Refit the steering column combination switches as described in Chapter 12.

12 Refit the steering wheel as described in Section 12.

Ignition switch

Note: The lock cylinder does not have to be removed to complete this procedure.

Removal

13 Remove the steering wheel, as described in Section 12.

14 Remove the steering column combination switches as described in Chapter 12.

15 Unplug the multi-way wiring connector from the rear of the ignition switch (see illustration).

16 Carefully scoop the locking compound

from the two bolt holes on the left-hand side of the lock cylinder housing, to expose the heads of the ignition switch securing screws.

17 Undo the ignition switch securing screws and withdraw the switch from the lock cylinder housing **(see illustrations).**

Refitting

18 Ensure the switch is correctly positioned (rotated as far anti-clockwise as possible) then refit it to the rear of the lock cylinder housing. Ensure the switch is correctly engaged with the lock and slide it fully into position.

19 Clean the threads of the retaining screws then apply a drop of locking compound to each screw. Refit the screws to the lock assembly and tighten them securely. Apply a drop of locking compound to the heads of both screws after they have been tightened.

20 Refit the wiring connector to the rear of the ignition switch.

21 Refit the steering column combination switches as described in Chapter 12.

22 Refit the steering wheel as described in Section 12.

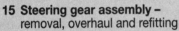
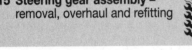

15 Steering gear assembly –
  removal, overhaul and refitting

Right-hand drive models

Removal

1 Remove the battery as described in Chapter 5A.

2 Unscrew the securing bolts and remove the battery tray.

3 Remove the air cleaner housing and its associated ducting, as described in the relevant part of Chapter 4.

4 Remove the trim panels underneath the driver's side of the facia to gain access to the base of the steering column. Turn the steering wheel so that the steering lock engages.

5 Secure the lower section of the steering column to the upper section using a length of wire. This is to ensure that when the steering column is detached from the steering gear, the two sections of the column do not become separated **(see illustration 13.11).**

Caution: Do not turn the steering wheel or allow the upper and lower sections of the steering column to become separated whilst the steering column is detached from the steering gear, as this can cause the column's internal components to become detached and misaligned.

6 Unscrew the nut from the pinch-bolt securing the universal joint at the base of the steering column to the steering gear. Rotate the bolt clockwise through half a turn and withdraw it from the joint.

7 Pull the steering column universal joint off the steering gear pinion and move it to one side. Detach the pinion plastic cowling from the bulkhead and withdraw it into the vehicle.

8 Firmly apply the handbrake then jack up

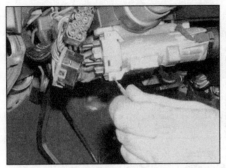

14.17a Undo the ignition switch securing screws . . .

the from of the vehicle and support it on axle stands. Remove both front roadwheels. Whilst the wheels are removed secure the discs to the hubs with a least one roadwheel bolt each.

9 Remove the right-hand hub carrier assembly as described in Section 2, paragraphs 1 to 10. Remove the left-hand track rod balljoint pinch-bolt and retaining bolt, and separate the balljoint from the hub carrier. Take care to avoid damaging the track rod bellows as you do this.

10 Unbolt the bottom of the right-hand suspension strut from the suspension lower arm as described in Section 3, but do not slacken or remove the strut upper mounting nuts.

11 Unscrew the three bolts and remove the upper transverse arm mounting bracket, the suspension strut and both upper transverse arms as an assembly from the right-hand wheel arch. Note that the bolts are accessible from the plenum chamber, to the rear of the engine compartment. There may be plastic washers fitted to the underside of the bolts; these are factory assembly components which do not need to be refitted, once removed. **Note**: *Make a careful note of the fitted positions of any shims fitted underneath the heads of the transverse arm mounting bracket bolts; they must be refitted in the same positions to preserve the front suspension alignment settings.*

12 Undo the plastic nut, prise out the clips and remove the section of the inner wheel arch liner that shrouds the point where the track rod end enters the engine compartment.

13 Using brake hose clamps, clamp both the supply and return hoses near the power steering fluid reservoir. This will minimise fluid loss during subsequent operations.

14 Mark the unions to ensure that they are correctly positioned on reassembly, then unscrew the feed and return pipe union bolts from the steering gear assembly; be prepared for fluid spillage, and position a suitable container beneath the pipes whilst unscrewing the union bolts. Disconnect both pipes and recover the sealing rings; discard the rings – new ones must be used on refitting. Plug the pipe ends and steering gear orifices, to prevent fluid leakage and to keep dirt out of the hydraulic system.

14.17b . . . and withdraw the switch from the lock cylinder housing

15 Free the power steering pipes from the retaining clips on the underside of the steering gear housing and position them clear of the underside of the steering gear.

16 Unbolt and remove the heat shield from the front of the steering gear.

17 On models with air conditioning, disconnect the wiring connector from the pressure switch on the steering gear housing.

18 Slacken and remove the bolts securing the steering gear in position. There are three bolts in total; two either side of the pinion housing at the right-hand side of the steering gear (one accessible from above the housing and one accessible from below), the third is located at the left-hand end of the steering gear, and is accessible from above via the plenum chamber.

19 Make a note of the correct routing of all wiring and hoses around the steering gear to ensure they are correctly positioned on refitting.

20 With the aid of an assistant, free the steering gear pinion from the bulkhead then manoeuvre the steering gear out of position via the right-hand wheel arch aperture. Take great care not to damage any wiring/hoses or the rubber gaiter as the steering gear is removed.

21 With the steering gear removed, check the pinion housing gaiter for signs of damage or deterioration and renew if necessary **(see illustration overleaf).**

Overhaul

22 Examine the steering gear assembly for signs of wear or damage, and check that the rack moves freely throughout the full length of its travel, with no signs of roughness or excessive free play between the steering gear pinion and rack. Inspect all the steering gear fluid unions for signs of leakage, and check that all union bolts are securely tightened.

23 It is possible to overhaul the steering gear assembly housing components, but this task should be entrusted to a VW dealer. The only components which can be renewed easily by the home mechanic are the steering gear gaiters (rubber bellows) and the track rod balljoints. Track rod balljoint and steering gear rubber bellows renewal procedures are covered elsewhere in this Chapter.

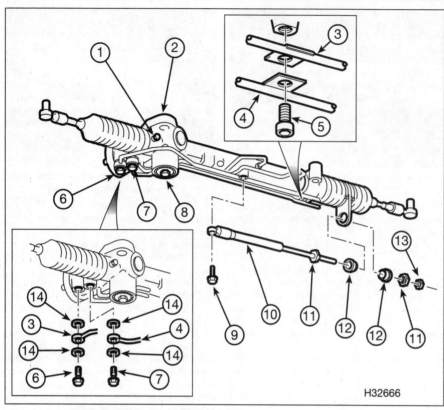

H32666

15.21 Steering gear and associated components – RHD models

1 Inspection hole and	5 Bolt	10 Damper
bolt	6 Banjo bolt	11 Bush
2 Steering gear	7 Banjo bolt	12 Bush
3 Supply pipe	8 Adjustment screw	13 Nut
4 Return pipe	9 Bolt	14 Sealing washer

Refitting

24 Before the steering gear can be refitted, it must be centred as follows. Remove the socket-head bolt from the tapped inspection hole at the side of the pinion gear housing. Move the right-hand track rod by hand until the alignment hole – drilled into the surface of the steering rack – is visible through the inspection hole. Obtain a bolt of the same thread as that removed from the inspection hole and file the end of it to a conical point. Thread the bolt into the inspection hole and turn it until the pointed end engages with the

drilled alignment hole in the steering rack; check that the rack is immobilised by trying to move the right-hand track rod end. The steering gear is now locked in the centre position **(see illustration)**.

25 With the aid of an assistant, carefully manoeuvre the steering gear into position, ensuring that the wiring/hoses are all correctly routed around the steering gear.

26 Fit the two steering gear securing bolts that are accessed from above, but only hand tighten them at this stage.

27 Fit the remaining steering gear securing

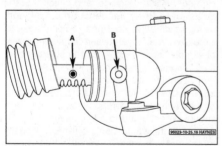

15.24 Steering rack centring details – align the hole in the rack (A) with the inspection hole (B) and thread the specially fabricated bolt into the hole

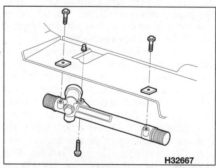

H32667

15.27 Steering gear securing bolt details – RHD models

bolt from below and tighten it to its specified torque. On completion, tighten the two upper securing bolts to their specified torque settings **(see illustration)**.

28 Position the rigid hydraulic pipes in their retaining clips on the underside of the steering gear, then reconnect the feed and return pipes to the steering gear, positioning a new sealing ring on each side of each end fitting, then screw in the union bolts. Ensure the pipes are correctly routed, then tighten both union bolts to their respective specified torque settings. Tighten the hydraulic pipe retaining clip bolt(s) securely. Remove the clamps from the fluid reservoir hoses.

29 Working inside the vehicle, from the driver's footwell, press the flexible gaiter over the steering gear pinion and into position on the bulkhead.

30 Reconnect the universal joint at the base of the steering column to the steering gear pinion. Insert the pinch-bolt and secure by rotating it through half a turn anti-clockwise. Refit the nut and hand tighten it.

31 Remove the wire that was used to secure the upper and lower sections of the steering column together.

32 Remove the home-made locking bolt from the inspection hole on the side of the steering gear, then refit the original socket head bolt to seal the inspection hole and tighten to the specified torque.

33 Now tighten the universal joint pinch-bolt at the base of the steering column to the specified torque.

34 Refit the trim panels to the underside of the driver's side of the facia.

35 Refit the plastic cover to the inside of the wheel arch, over the track rod end, and secure it with the press stud clips and the plastic nut(s). Reconnect the left-hand track rod balljoint and tighten the bolts to the specified torque.

36 Refit the upper suspension arm mounting bracket to the inside of the wheel arch, ensuring that the shims (if fitted) are refitted in their original positions, as noted during removal. Insert the three securing bolts and tighten them to the specified torque.

37 Refit the bottom of the right-hand suspension strut to the suspension lower arm as described in Section 3. Tighten the securing nut and bolt to the specified torque.

38 Refit the right-hand hub carrier assembly as described in Section 2, paragraphs 17 to 23. Take care to avoid damaging the track rod bellows as you do this.

39 Refit the heat shield panel to the front of the steering gear.

40 On models with air conditioning, reconnect the wiring to the pressure switch on the steering gear hydraulic pipe.

41 Refit the roadwheels then lower the vehicle to the ground and tighten the wheel bolts to the specified torque.

42 Tighten the driveshaft bolt to the specified torque, as described in Chapter 8, then refit the hub cap/wheel trim.

43 Refit the battery tray and tighten the retaining bolts securely, then refit the battery with reference to Chapter 5A. Refit the cover panel over the plenum chamber.

44 Refit the air cleaner and its associated ducting with reference to the relevant section of Chapter 4.

45 Top-up the power steering fluid and bleed the hydraulic system with reference to Section 17.

46 On completion, have the front wheel alignment checked by a VW dealer.

Left-hand drive models

Removal

47 Apply the handbrake and chock the rear wheels, then loosen the front roadwheel bolts. Raise and support the front of the vehicle on axle stands (see *Jacking and vehicle support*). Remove both front roadwheels.

48 Remove the battery from the engine compartment as described in Chapter 5A, then unbolt and remove the battery tray.

49 Turn the steering wheel to the centre position then remove the ignition key to engage the steering lock.

Caution: Ensure that the steering column and roadwheels remains in the straight-ahead position throughout the remainder of this procedure, or the airbag contact unit may become misaligned, leading to the failure of the airbag system.

50 Working inside the vehicle, detach and remove the lower facia trim/storage tray and insulation panels on the driver's side. Detach and remove the lower column/bulkhead cover.

51 Remove the remaining trim panels underneath the driver's side of the facia to gain access to the base of the steering column.

52 Secure the lower section of the steering column to the upper section using a length of wire. This is to ensure that when the steering column is detached from the steering gear, the two sections of the column do not become separated (see illustration 13.11).

Caution: Do not allow the upper and lower sections of the steering column to become separated whilst the steering column is detached from the steering gear, as this can cause the internal components to become detached and misaligned.

53 Unscrew the nut from the pinch-bolt securing the universal joint at the base of the steering column to the steering gear. Rotate the bolt clockwise through half turn and withdraw it from the joint.

54 Pull the steering column universal joint off the steering gear pinion and move it to one side. Unclip the pinion cover from the bulkhead and withdraw it into the vehicle.

55 Syphon the fluid from the power steering fluid reservoir. If a suitable implement is not readily available to syphon the fluid from the system, it can be drained into a container when the hydraulic lines are detached from the steering gear.

56 To minimise fluid leakage, apply hose clamps to the fluid pipes leading to and from the steering gear. Take care to avoid causing damage to the hoses by pinching.

57 Undo the plastic nut, prise out the clips and remove the section of the inner wheel arch liner that shrouds the point where the track rod end enters the engine compartment.

58 Unscrew the unions and disconnect the fluid supply and return lines from the steering gear. Clean the connections before they are detached. Drain any fluid remaining in the system into a container for disposal. Tie the lines back away from the work area, and seal off their ends to prevent further leakage and the possible ingress of dirt.

59 Refer to Section 19, and unbolt the track rod end balljoints from the hub carriers.

60 Unscrew and remove the steering gear mounting bolts from the bodywork – two bolts from above in the plenum chamber, and one from below.

61 Check that all connections are free and clear of the steering gear, then unclip the plastic collar from the pinion housing and withdraw the steering gear from the vehicle via the left-hand wheel arch.

62 If the steering gear is known to be damaged or worn beyond an acceptable level, it may have to be renewed. However, it is possible to have the steering gear overhauled – consult a VW dealer or specialist repairer for further advice (see illustration).

Refitting

63 Before the steering gear can be refitted, it must be centred as follows. Remove the socket-head bolt from the tapped inspection hole at the side of the pinion gear housing. Move the right-hand track rod by hand until the alignment hole – drilled into the surface of the steering rack – is visible through the inspection hole. Obtain a bolt of the same thread as that removed from the inspection hole and file the end of it to a conical point. Thread the bolt into the inspection hole and turn it until the pointed end engages with the drilled alignment hole in the steering rack; check that the rack is immobilised by trying to move the right-hand track rod end. The steering gear is now locked in the centre position (refer to illustration 15.24).

64 Manoeuvre the steering gear into position in the engine compartment. Insert the three securing bolts, then tighten them to their specified torques in the sequence

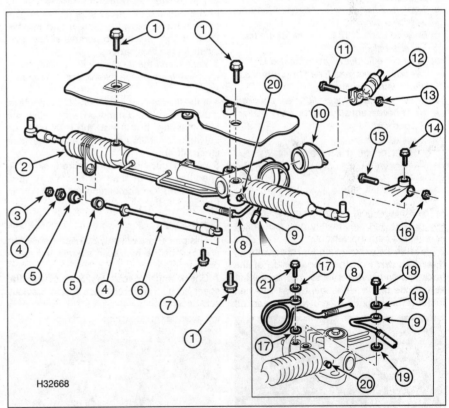

15.62 Steering gear and associated components – LHD models

1 Bolt	7 Bolt	12 Steering	17 Sealing ring
2 Steering gear	8 Supply pipe	column	18 Banjo bolt
3 Nut	9 Return pipe	13 Nut	19 Sealing ring
4 Bush	10 Gaiter	14 Bolt	20 Inspection hole
5 Bush	11 Eccentric pinch-	15 Bolt	and bolt
6 Damper	bolt	16 Nut	21 Banjo bolt

H32668

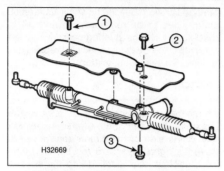

15.64 Steering gear securing bolt tightening sequence – LHD models

shown **(see illustration)**. On completion, remove the locking bolt from the alignment hole, then refit the original plug to seal the steering gear.

65 The remainder of the refitting procedure is a reversal of removal, noting the following points:

a) *The fluid lines will need to be connected as the steering gear is raised into position. Take care to keep the connections clean and tighten the unions to their specified torques, using new sealing washers where applicable.*

b) *Tighten all fixings to the specified torque wrench settings.*

c) *Refer to Section 19 to reconnect the track rod end balljoints.*

d) *Top-up the fluid level as described in 'Weekly checks' and bleed the system as described in Section 17.*

e) *Finally, have the wheel alignment checked and if necessary adjusted by a VW dealer or specialist.*

16 Steering gear rubber bellows – renewal

1 The steering gear bellows can be removed and refitted with the steering gear unit *in situ* or removed from the vehicle.

2 Measure the exposed amount of adjustment thread showing on the inboard side of the track rod end balljoint locknut. This will act as a guide to the adjustment position when refitting the balljoint to the rod. Loosen off

the locknut, and detach the balljoint from the track rod as described in Section 19.

3 Unscrew and remove the locking nut from the track rod.

4 Release the retaining clips and withdraw the bellows from the steering gear and track rod.

5 Refit in the reverse order of removal. Smear the inner bore of the bellows with lubricant prior to fitting to ease its assembly. Renew the balljoint locknuts. Use new clips to retain the bellows and ensure that the end of the bellows locates correctly in the groove machined into the track rod, without twisting.

6 On completion, have the front wheel alignment checked and if necessary adjusted (see Section 22).

17 Power steering system – level checking and bleeding

Level checking

1 Position the vehicle on level ground with the front wheels straight-ahead and the engine stopped. The level check may be made with the hydraulic fluid cold or hot.

2 The power steering fluid reservoir is located on the left-hand side of the engine compartment. Slowly unscrew and remove the filler cap, which incorporates a fluid level dipstick **(see illustration)**.

3 Wipe clean the dipstick with a clean cloth, then screw it onto the reservoir and unscrew it again.

4 If the fluid is cold (less than 50ºC), the level must be within 2.0 mm above or below the MIN marking. If it is hot, the level must be between the MIN and MAX markings **(see illustration)**.

5 Where topping-up is required, add the specified type of fluid as necessary **(see illustration)**. On completion refit and tighten the cap.

Bleeding

6 This procedure will only be necessary when any part of the hydraulic system has been disconnected.

7 Check and if necessary top-up with the specified fluid with reference to the previous sub-Section.

8 Jack up the front of the vehicle and support it on axle stands to remove the weight from the front wheels.

9 Start the engine and allow it to idle for 5 seconds, then switch it off. Check the fluid level, and if necessary top-up.

10 Repeat the procedure in paragraph 9, then start the engine and allow it to idle.

11 With the engine idling, turn the steering from lock-to-lock three times, then switch off the engine. Check the fluid level, and if necessary top-up.

12 Repeat the procedure in paragraph 11 two times, then leave the engine switched off for 2 to 3 minutes to allow any air bubbles to escape from the fluid.

13 Lower the vehicle to the ground, then start the engine and allow it to idle. Turn the steering from lock-to-lock five times.

14 Check that no more air bubbles are escaping from the fluid. If necessasary, repeat the bleeding procedure. When finished, fully tighten the filler cap.

18 Power steering pump – removal and refitting

Removal

1 Firmly apply the handbrake then jack up the front of the vehicle and support it on axle stands.

2 Remove the retaining screws and fasteners and remove the undercover from beneath the engine/transmission unit.

3 Move the lock carrier crossmember at the front of the engine compartment to the service position; refer to Chapter 11 for details.

4 Refer to the relevant part of Chapter 2 and remove the ribbed auxiliary drivebelt.

5 On petrol vehicles, remove the pulley from the coolant pump.

6 Using brake hose clamps, clamp both the supply and return hoses near the power steering fluid reservoir. This will minimise fluid loss during subsequent operations.

7 Wipe clean the area around the power steering pump fluid pipe unions and hose connections.

8 Unscrew the union bolt and disconnect fluid delivery pipe from the pump; be prepared for

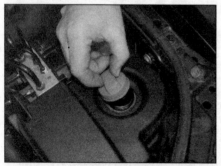

17.2 Unscrew the filler cap from the power steering fluid reservoir

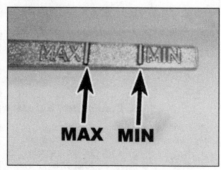

17.4 MIN and MAX markings on the fluid level dipstick

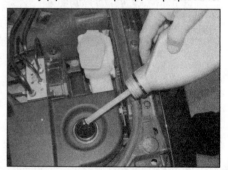

17.5 Topping-up the fluid level

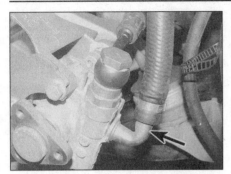

18.8 Disconnect the power steering pump fluid delivery pipe (arrowed)

fluid spillage, and position a suitable container beneath the pipe whilst unscrewing the union bolt **(see illustration)**. Disconnect the pipe and recover the sealing rings; discard the rings new ones must be used on refitting. Plug the pipe end and steering pump orifice, to minimise fluid leakage and to keep dirt out of the hydraulic system.

9 Slacken the clip and disconnect the fluid supply hose from the rear of the power steering pump. Plug the end of the hose and cover the pump fluid port to prevent contamination.

10 Using a strap wrench to prevent the pulley from rotating, undo the retaining bolts and remove the power steering pump pulley.

11 Slacken and remove the pump mounting bolts and withdraw the pump from its bracket **(see illustration)**.

12 If the power steering pump is faulty it must be renewed. The pump is a sealed unit and cannot be overhauled.

Refitting

13 If a new pump is to be fitted, it must be primed with fluid prior to fitting, to ensure adequate lubrication during its initial stages of operation. Failure to do this could cause noisy operation and may lead to early pump failure. To prime the pump, pour the specified grade of hydraulic fluid (see *Lubricants and fluids*) into the fluid supply port on the pump, and simultaneously rotate the pump pulley. When the fluid exits from the fluid delivery union, it is primed and ready for use.

14 Manoeuvre the pump into position, then refit its mounting bolts and tighten them to the specified torque. Refit the pump pulley.

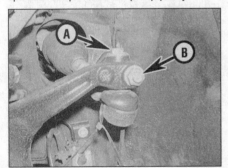

19.2 Track rod balljoint adjustment bolt (A) and securing nut and bolt (B)

15 Fit a new sealing ring to each side of the hydraulic delivery pipe end fitting then reconnect the pipe to the pump and screw in the union bolt. Ensure the pipe is correctly routed then tighten the union bolt to the specified torque.

16 Reconnect the supply hose to the pump and secure it in position with the retaining clip. Remove the hose clamps used to minimise fluid loss.

17 Where applicable, refit the pulley to the coolant pump.

18 Refit and tension the auxiliary drivebelt(s) as described in the relevant part of Chapter 2.

19 Refit the lock carrier crossmember to the front of the engine compartment, as described in Chapter 11.

20 Refit the engine compartment undercover, ensuring it is securely held by all its retaining screws and fasteners.

21 On completion, top up the hydraulic system as described in *Weekly Checks*, then bleed the system as described in Section 17.

19 Track rod balljoint – removal and refitting

Removal

1 Apply the handbrake, then jack up the front of the vehicle and support it on axle stands. Remove the appropriate front roadwheel. Whilst the wheel is removed, secure the brake disc to the hub with a roadwheel bolt.

2 Slacken and withdraw the adjustment bolt, followed by the pinch-bolt and nut then push down on the track rod to detach it from the rear of the hub carrier **(see illustration)**.

3 To give greater clearance, unscrew the plastic nuts and extract the press-fit clips then detach the plastic track rod cover from the wheel arch.

4 If the balljoint is to be re-used, use a straight-edge and a scriber, or similar, to mark its relationship to the track rod adjustment nut.

5 Hold the track rod adjustment flats, and unscrew the balljoint locknut by a quarter of a turn. Do not move the locknut from this position, as it will serve as a handy reference mark on refitting.

6 Counting the **exact** number of turns necessary to do so, unscrew the balljoint assembly from the track rod.

7 Carefully clean the balljoint and the threads. Renew the balljoint if its movement is sloppy or too stiff, if excessively worn, or if damaged in any way; carefully check the stud taper and threads. If the balljoint gaiter is damaged, the complete balljoint assembly must be renewed; it is not possible to obtain the gaiter separately.

Refitting

8 Screw the balljoint onto the track rod by the number of turns noted on removal. This

18.11 Slacken and remove the pump mounting bolts

should bring the balljoint locknut to within a quarter of a turn from the track rod, with the alignment marks that were made on removal (if applicable) lined up. Counter-hold the track rod adjustment flats and tighten the locknut to the specified torque **(see illustration)**.

9 Locate the balljoint spigot in the rear of the hub carrier then fit the pinch-bolt with a new nut, followed by the adjustment bolt and tighten them to the specified torque settings.

10 Refit the roadwheel, then lower the vehicle to the ground and tighten the roadwheel bolts to the specified torque.

11 Check and, if necessary, adjust the front wheel alignment as described in Section 22.

20 Track rod – removal and refitting

Removal

1 Apply the handbrake, then jack up the front of the vehicle and support it on axle stands. Remove the appropriate front roadwheel. Whilst the wheel is removed, secure the brake disc to the hub with a roadwheel bolt.

2 Slacken and withdraw the adjustment bolt, followed by the pinch-bolt and nut then push down on the track rod balljoint to detach it from the rear of the hub carrier (see previous Section).

3 Unscrew the plastic nuts and extract the press-fit clips, then detach the plastic track rod cover from the wheel arch.

4 Release the retaining clips and slide the

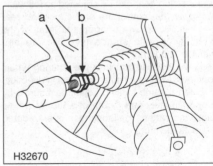

H32670

19.8 Track rod adjustment flats (b) and locknut (a)

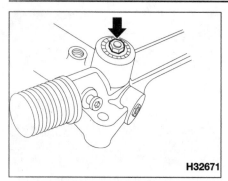

21.3 Steering gear adjustment screw (arrowed) – LHD model shown

rubber bellows towards the outboard end of the track rod; this will expose the large integral hex nut at the inner end of the track rod.

5 Hold the track rod hex nut securing using a large open-ended spanner, and unscrew the track rod from the end of the steering gear.

6 If the balljoint is to be re-used, use a straight-edge and a scriber, or similar, to mark its relationship to the track rod adjustment nut. Remove the balljoint from the track rod with reference to Section 19. **Note:** *If both track rods are to be removed, and the L and R markings on the track rod balljoints are no longer visible, mark the rods to avoid confusion on refitting.*

Refitting

7 Refitting is a reversal of removal noting the following points:

   a) *Tighten the track rod to the specified torque, using a suitable 'crow's foot' adapter.*
   b) *Ensure that the rubber bellows is securely refitted, using new clips where necessary.*
   c) *On completion have the front wheel alignment checked and if necessary adjusted.*

21 Steering gear – adjustment

1 With the vehicle stationary and the engine switched off, turn the steering wheel from side-to-side. If there is any undue slackness in the steering gear, resulting in noise or rattles the steering gear can be adjusted as follows.

2 Apply the handbrake and chock the rear wheels. Raise and support the front of the vehicle on axle stands (see *Jacking and vehicle support*).

3 Have an assistant turn the steering wheel back-and-forth by half a turn in each direction. Tighten the self-locking adjustment screw by approximately one eighth of a turn at a time until the rattling or looseness is eradicated (see illustration).

4 Lower the vehicle to the ground, then road test the car. If the steering fails to self-centre after cornering, loosen the adjustment screw a fraction at a time until it does.

5 If, when the correct self-centring point is reached, there is still excessive play in the steering, retighten the adjuster nut a fraction to take up the play.

6 If the adjustment procedures listed above do not provide satisfactory steering adjustment, it is probable that the steering gear is worn beyond an acceptable level, and it must be removed and overhauled.

22 Wheel alignment and steering angles – general information

Definitions

1 A car's steering and suspension geometry is defined in four basic settings – all angles are expressed in degrees; the steering axis is defined as an imaginary line drawn through the axis of the suspension strut, extended where necessary to contact the ground.

2 **Camber** is the angle between each roadwheel and a vertical line drawn through its centre and tyre contact patch, when viewed from the front or rear of the car. Positive camber is when the roadwheels are tilted outwards from the vertical at the top; negative camber is when they are tilted inwards. The individual front wheel camber angles cannot be adjusted, but the overall camber angle between both front wheels can be balanced out by repositioning the suspension subframe. The rear wheel camber angle is also specified but no adjustment is possible.

3 **Castor** is the angle between the steering axis and a vertical line drawn through each roadwheel's centre and tyre contact patch, when viewed from the side of the car. Positive castor is when the steering axis is tilted so that it contacts the ground ahead of the vertical; negative castor is when it contacts the ground behind the vertical. The castor angle is not adjustable.

4 **Toe** is the difference, viewed from above, between lines drawn through the roadwheel centres and the car's centre-line. Toe-in is when the roadwheels point inwards, towards each other at the front, while toe-out is when they splay outwards from each other at the front.

5 The front wheel toe setting is adjusted by screwing the track rod adjusters in or out of its balljoints, to alter the effective length of the track rod assembly. The overall rear wheel toe setting cannot be altered, but the individual toe angles can be balanced out by repositioning the rear axle assembly.

Checking and adjustment

6 Due to the special measuring equipment necessary to check the wheel alignment and steering angles, and the skill required to use it properly, the checking and adjustment of these settings is best left to a VW dealer or similar expert. Note that most tyre-fitting shops now possess sophisticated checking equipment. The following is provided as a guide, should the owner decide to carry out a DIY check.

Front wheel toe setting

7 To check the toe setting, a tracking gauge must first be obtained. Two types of gauge are available, and can be obtained from motor accessory shops. The first type measures the distance between the front and rear inside edges of the roadwheels with the vehicle stationary. The second type, known as a scuff plate, measures the actual position of the contact surface of the tyre, in relation to the road surface, with the vehicle in motion. This is achieved by pushing or driving the front tyre over a plate, which then moves slightly according to the scuff of the tyre, and shows this movement on a scale. Both types have their advantages and disadvantages, but either can give satisfactory results if used correctly and carefully.

8 For the measurements to be accurate it is important that the vehicle is unladen except for a full tank of fuel, the spare wheel and vehicle tool kit, and that the tyres are correctly inflated (see *Weekly checks*). Rock the vehicle several times to settle all suspension components in position and ensure the front wheels are positioned in the straight-ahead position before taking any measurements.

9 If adjustment is necessary, apply the parking brake then jack up the front of the vehicle and support it securely on axle stands.

10 First clean the track rod adjuster threads; if they are corroded, apply penetrating fluid before starting adjustment.

11 Hold the adjuster stationary and slacken the balljoint and track rod locknuts. Alter the length of the track rod by rotating the adjuster as necessary; shortening the track rod length will increase toe-out/decrease toe-in.

12 When the setting is correct, hold the track rod adjuster and tighten both locknuts to the specified torque setting.

13 If after adjustment, the steering wheel spokes are no longer horizontal when the wheels are in the straight-ahead position, remove the steering wheel and reposition it (see Section 12).

14 Check that the toe setting has been correctly adjusted by lowering the vehicle to the ground and rechecking the toe setting; re-adjust if necessary.

Chapter 11
Bodywork and fittings

Contents

Section number

Bonnet and strut – removal, refitting and adjustment 7
Bonnet lock and release cable – removal and refitting 8
Boot lid – removal and refitting 12
Boot lid lock and lock cylinder – removal and refitting 13
Boot lid/tailgate support strut(s) – removal and refitting 15
Bumpers – removal and refitting 9
Central locking system – general 18
Centre console – removal and refitting. 28
Door handles and lock cylinder – removal and refitting. 20
Door lock – removal and refitting 19
Door mirror components – removal and refitting 27
Door rattles – tracing and rectification 6
Door trim panel – removal and refitting 17
Door window glass – removal and refitting 21
Door window regulator – removal and refitting 22
Doors – removal and refitting. 24
Electrically-operated windows – general information and motor
  renewal. 23
Facia, associated panels and crossmember – removal and refitting . . 29
General description 1

Glovebox – removal and refitting 30
Grab handles – removal and refitting 37
Interior mirror – removal and refitting 31
Interior trim – removal and refitting 33
Lock carrier/front crossmember – removal and refitting 10
Maintenance – bodywork and underframe 2
Maintenance – upholstery and carpets 3
Major body damage – repair 5
Minor body damage – repair 4
Seat belt tensioning mechanism – general information 34
Seat belts – general, removal and refitting. 35
Seats – removal and refitting 32
Sunroof – general 26
Sunvisors – removal and refitting. 36
Tailgate (Estate models) – removal and refitting. 14
Tailgate lock and lock cylinder (Estate models) – removal and
  refitting 16
Wheel arch liners – removal and refitting 11
Windscreen, rear window glass and rear side window glass – general
  information 25

Degrees of difficulty

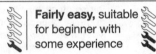

Easy, suitable for novice with little experience	**Fairly easy,** suitable for beginner with some experience	**Fairly difficult,** suitable for competent DIY mechanic	**Difficult,** suitable for experienced DIY mechanic	**Very difficult,** suitable for expert DIY or professional

Specifications

Torque wrench settings	Nm	lbf ft
Bonnet hinge bolts.	23	17
Bonnet lock bolts	12	9
Boot lid (Saloon) mounting bolts	22	16
Tailgate (Estate) mounting nuts	10	7
Door hinge bolts:		
Lower hinge bolts*:		
Stage one	20	15
Stage two	Angle-tighten a further 90°	
Upper hinge grub screw.	23	17
Door lock screws	20	15
Door mirror bolt	10	7
Front bumper mounting tube-to-bodywork bolts	40	30
Front bumper mounting bolts:		
Upper centre.	6	4
Side and bottom.	2	1
Lock carrier-to-body retaining bolts.	50	37
Rear bumper mounting bolts:		
Lower centre.	6	4
Side	2	1
Seat belt anchor bolts	40	30
Seat belt front stalk mounting bolt.	24	18
Seat belt inertia reel bolt	40	30
Rear centre seat belt inertia reel (Estate)	40	30
Tailgate (Estate) mounting nuts	22	16
Window component carrier-to-door bolts	8	6
Window motor to regulator	4	3

Use new fasteners.

1 General description

Two body types are produced – the four-door Saloon and the five-door Estate. The body is of all-steel construction, and incorporates calculated impact crumple zones at the front and rear, with a central safety cell passenger compartment.

During manufacture, the underbody is treated with underseal and, as a further anti-rust aid, some of the more exposed body panels are galvanised. The bumpers and wheel arch liners are plastic mouldings, for durability and strength.

2 Maintenance – bodywork and underframe

The general condition of a vehicle's bodywork is the one thing that significantly affects its value. Maintenance is easy, but needs to be regular. Neglect, particularly after minor damage, can lead quickly to further deterioration and costly repair bills. It is important also to keep watch on those parts of the vehicle not immediately visible, for instance the underside, inside all the wheel arches, and the lower part of the engine compartment.

The basic maintenance routine for the bodywork is washing – preferably with a lot of water, from a hose. This will remove all the loose solids which may have stuck to the vehicle. It is important to flush these off in such a way as to prevent grit from scratching the finish. The wheel arches and underframe need washing in the same way, to remove any accumulated mud which will retain moisture and tend to encourage rust. Paradoxically enough, the best time to clean the underframe and wheel arches is in wet weather, when the mud is thoroughly wet and soft. In very wet weather, the underframe is usually cleaned of large accumulations automatically, and this is a good time for inspection.

Periodically, except on vehicles with a wax-based underbody protective coating, it is a good idea to have the whole of the underframe of the vehicle steam-cleaned, engine compartment included, so that a thorough inspection can be carried out to see what minor repairs and renovations are necessary. Steam cleaning is available at many garages, and is necessary for the removal of the accumulation of oily grime, which sometimes is allowed to become thick in certain areas. If steam-cleaning facilities are not available, there are some excellent grease solvents available which can be brush-applied; the dirt can then be simply hosed off. Note that these methods should not be used on vehicles with wax-based underbody protective coating, or the coating will be removed. Such vehicles should be inspected annually, preferably just before Winter, when the underbody should be washed down, and any damage to the wax coating repaired. Ideally, a completely fresh coat should be applied. It would also be worth considering the use of wax-based protection for injection into door panels, sills, box sections, etc, as an additional safeguard against rust damage, where such protection is not provided by the vehicle manufacturer.

After washing paintwork, wipe off with a chamois leather to give an unspotted clear finish. A coat of clear protective wax polish will give added protection against chemical pollutants in the air. If the paintwork sheen has dulled or oxidised, use a cleaner/polisher combination to restore the brilliance of the shine. This requires a little effort, but such dulling is usually caused because regular washing has been neglected. Care needs to be taken with metallic paintwork, as special non-abrasive cleaner/polisher is required to avoid damage to the finish. Always check that the door and ventilator opening drain holes and pipes are completely clear, so that water can be drained out. Brightwork should be treated in the same way as paintwork. Windscreens and windows can be kept clear of the smeary film which often appears, by proprietary glass cleaner. Never use any form of wax or other body or chromium polish on glass.

3 Maintenance – upholstery and carpets

Mats and carpets should be brushed or vacuum-cleaned regularly, to keep them free of grit. If they are badly stained, remove them from the vehicle for scrubbing or sponging, and make quite sure they are dry before refitting. Seats and interior trim panels can be kept clean by wiping with a damp cloth. If they do become stained (which can be more apparent on light-coloured upholstery), use a little liquid detergent and a soft nail brush to scour the grime out of the grain of the material. Do not forget to keep the headlining clean in the same way as the upholstery. When using liquid cleaners inside the vehicle, do not over-wet the surfaces being cleaned. Excessive damp could get into the seams and padded interior, causing stains, offensive odours or even rot. If the inside of the vehicle gets wet accidentally, it is worthwhile taking some trouble to dry it out properly, particularly where carpets are involved. *Do not leave oil or electric heaters inside the vehicle for this purpose.*

4 Minor body damage – repair

Minor scratches

If the scratch is very superficial, and does not penetrate to the metal of the bodywork, repair is very simple. Lightly rub the area of the scratch with a paintwork renovator or a very fine cutting paste to remove loose paint from the scratch, and to clear the surrounding bodywork of wax polish. Rinse the area with clean water.

Apply touch-up paint to the scratch using a fine paint brush; continue to apply fine layers of paint until the surface of the paint in the scratch is level with the surrounding paintwork. Allow the new paint at least two weeks to harden, then blend it into the surrounding paintwork by rubbing the scratch area with a paintwork renovator or a very fine cutting paste. Finally, apply wax polish.

Where the scratch has penetrated right through to the metal of the bodywork, causing the metal to rust, a different repair technique is required. Remove any loose rust from the bottom of the scratch with a penknife, then apply rust-inhibiting paint to prevent the formation of rust in the future. Using a rubber or nylon applicator, fill the scratch with bodystopper paste. If required, this paste can be mixed with cellulose thinners to provide a very thin paste which is ideal for filling narrow scratches. Before the stopper-paste in the scratch hardens, wrap a piece of smooth cotton rag around the top of a finger. Dip the finger in cellulose thinners, and quickly sweep it across the surface of the stopper-paste in the scratch; this will ensure that the surface of the stopper-paste is slightly hollowed. The scratch can now be painted over as described earlier in this Section.

Dents

When deep denting of the vehicle's bodywork has taken place, the first task is to pull the dent out, until the affected bodywork almost attains its original shape. There is little point in trying to restore the original shape completely, as the metal in the damaged area will have stretched on impact, and cannot be reshaped fully to its original contour. It is better to bring the level of the dent up to a point which is about 3 mm below the level of the surrounding bodywork. In cases where the dent is very shallow anyway, it is not worth trying to pull it out at all. If the underside of the dent is accessible, it can be hammered out gently from behind, using a mallet with a wooden or plastic head. Whilst doing this, hold a suitable block of wood firmly against the outside of the panel, to absorb the impact from the hammer blows and thus prevent a large area of the bodywork from being 'belled-out'.

Should the dent be in a section of the bodywork which has a double skin, or some other factor making it inaccessible from behind, a different technique is called for. Drill several small holes through the metal inside the area – particularly in the deeper section. Then screw long self-tapping screws into the holes, just sufficiently for them to gain a good purchase in the metal. Now the dent can be pulled out by pulling on the protruding heads of the screws with a pair of pliers.

The next stage of the repair is the removal of the paint from the damaged area, and from an inch or so of the surrounding 'sound' bodywork. This is accomplished most easily by using a wire brush or abrasive pad on a power drill, although it can be done just as effectively by hand, using sheets of abrasive paper. To complete the preparation for filling, score the surface of the bare metal with a screwdriver or the tang of a file, or alternatively, drill small holes in the affected area. This will provide a good 'key' for the filler paste.

To complete the repair, see the Section on filling and respraying.

Rust holes or gashes

Remove all paint from the affected area, and from an inch or so of the surrounding 'sound' bodywork, using an abrasive pad or a wire brush on a power drill. If these are not available, a few sheets of abrasive paper will do the job most effectively. With the paint removed, you will be able to judge the severity of the corrosion, and therefore decide whether to renew the whole panel (if this is possible) or to repair the affected area. New body panels are not as expensive as most people think, and it is often quicker and more satisfactory to fit a new panel than to attempt to repair large areas of corrosion.

Remove all fittings from the affected area, except those which will act as a guide to the original shape of the damaged bodywork (eg headlight shells etc). Then, using tin snips or a hacksaw blade, remove all loose metal and any other metal badly affected by corrosion. Hammer the edges of the hole inwards, to create a slight depression for the filler paste.

Wire-brush the affected area to remove the powdery rust from the surface of the remaining metal. Paint the affected area with rust-inhibiting paint; if the back of the rusted area is accessible, treat this also.

Before filling can take place, it will be necessary to block the hole in some way. This can be achieved with aluminium or plastic mesh, or aluminium tape.

Aluminium or plastic mesh, or glass-fibre matting, is probably the best material to use for a large hole. Cut a piece to the approximate size and shape of the hole to be filled, then position it in the hole so that its edges are below the level of the surrounding bodywork. It can be retained in position by several blobs of filler paste around its periphery.

Aluminium tape should be used for small or very narrow holes. Pull a piece off the roll, trim it to the approximate size and shape required, then pull off the backing paper (if used) and stick the tape over the hole; it can be overlapped if the thickness of one piece is insufficient. Burnish down the edges of the tape with the handle of a screwdriver or similar, to ensure that the tape is securely attached to the metal underneath.

Filling and respraying

Before using this Section, see the Sections on dent, deep scratch, rust holes and gash repairs.

Many types of bodyfiller are available, but generally speaking, those proprietary kits which contain a tin of filler paste and a tube of resin hardener are best for this type of repair which can be used directly from the tube. A wide, flexible plastic or nylon applicator will be found invaluable for imparting a smooth and well-contoured finish to the surface of the filler.

Mix up a little filler on a clean piece of card or board – measure the hardener carefully (follow the maker's instructions on the pack), otherwise the filler will set too rapidly or too slowly. Using the applicator, apply the filler paste to the prepared area; draw the applicator across the surface of the filler to achieve the correct contour and to level the surface. When a contour that approximates to the correct one is achieved, stop working the paste – if you carry on too long, the paste will become sticky and begin to 'pick-up' on the applicator. Continue to add thin layers of filler paste at 20-minute intervals, until the level of the filler is just proud of the surrounding bodywork.

Once the filler has hardened, the excess can be removed using a metal plane or file. From then on, progressively-finer grades of abrasive paper should be used, starting with a 40-grade production paper, and finishing with a 400-grade wet-and-dry paper. Always wrap the abrasive paper around a flat rubber, cork, or wooden block – otherwise the surface of the filler will not be completely flat. During the smoothing of the filler surface, the wet-and-dry paper should be periodically rinsed in water. This will ensure that a very smooth finish is imparted to the filler at the final stage.

At this stage, the 'dent' should be surrounded by a ring of bare metal, which in turn should be encircled by the finely 'feathered' edge of the good paintwork. Rinse the repair area with clean water, until all the dust produced by the rubbing-down operation has gone.

Spray the whole area with a light coat of primer – this will show up any imperfections in the surface of the filler. Repair these imperfections with fresh filler paste or bodystopper, and again smooth the surface with abrasive paper. If bodystopper is used, it can be mixed with cellulose thinners, to form a thin paste which is ideal for filling small holes. Repeat this spray-and-repair procedure until you are satisfied that the surface of the filler, and the feathered edge of the paintwork, are perfect. Clean the repair area with clean water, and allow to dry fully.

The repair area is now ready for final spraying. Paint spraying must be carried out in a warm, dry, windless and dust-free atmosphere. This condition can be created artificially if you have access to a large indoor working area, but if you are forced to work in the open, you will have to pick your day very carefully. If you are working indoors, dousing the floor in the work area with water will help to settle the dust which would otherwise be in the atmosphere. If the repair area is confined to one body panel, mask off the surrounding panels; this will help to minimise the effects of a slight mismatch in paint colours. Bodywork fittings (e.g. chrome strips, door handles etc) will also need to be masked off. Use genuine masking tape, and several thickness of newspaper, for the masking operations.

Before starting to spray, agitate the aerosol can thoroughly, then spray a test area (an old tin, or similar) until the technique is mastered. Cover the repair area with a thick coat of primer; the thickness should be built up using several thin layers of paint, rather than one thick one. Using 400 grade wet-and-dry paper, rub down the surface of the primer until it is smooth. While doing this, the work area should be thoroughly doused with water, and the wet-and-dry paper periodically rinsed in water. Allow to dry before spraying on more paint.

Spray on the top coat, again building up the thickness by using several thin layers of paint. Start spraying at one edge of the repair area, and then, using a side-to-side motion, work until the whole repair area and about 2 inches of the surrounding original paintwork is covered. Remove all masking material 10 to 15 minutes after spraying on the final coat of paint.

Allow the new paint at least two weeks to harden, then, using a paintwork renovator or a very fine cutting paste, blend the edges of the paint into the existing paintwork. Finally, apply wax polish.

Plastic components

With the use of more and more plastic body components by the vehicle manufacturers (e.g. bumpers, spoilers, and in some cases major body panels), rectification of more serious damage to such items has become a matter of either entrusting repair work to a specialist in this field, or renewing complete components. Repair of such damage by the DIY owner is not feasible, owing to the cost of the equipment and materials required for effecting such repairs. The basic technique involves making a groove along the line of the crack in the plastic, using a rotary burr in a power drill. The damaged part is then welded back together, using a hot air gun to heat up and fuse a plastic filler rod into the groove. Any excess plastic is then removed, and the area rubbed down to a smooth finish. It is important that a filler rod of the correct plastic is used, as body components can be made of a variety of different types (e.g. polycarbonate, ABS, polypropylene).

Damage of a less serious nature (abrasions, minor cracks etc) can be repaired by the DIY owner using a two-part epoxy filler repair material which can be used directly from the

7.2 Disconnect the washer tubes and the wiring plug

tube. Once mixed in equal proportions, this is used in similar fashion to the bodywork filler used on metal panels. The filler is usually cured in twenty to thirty minutes, ready for sanding and painting.

If the owner is renewing a complete component himself, or if he has repaired it with epoxy filler, he will be left with the problem of finding a suitable paint for finishing which is compatible with the type of plastic used. At one time, the use of a universal paint was not possible, owing to the complex range of plastics met with in body component applications. Standard paints, generally speaking, will not bond to plastic or rubber satisfactorily, but professional matched paints, to match any plastic or rubber finish, can be obtained from some dealers. However, it is now possible to obtain a plastic body parts finishing kit which consists of a pre-primer treatment, a primer and coloured top coat. Full instructions are normally supplied with a kit, but basically the method of use is to first apply the pre-primer to the component concerned, and allow it to dry for up to 30 minutes. Then the primer is applied, and left to dry for about an hour before finally applying the special-coloured top coat. The result is a correctly coloured component, where the paint will flex with the plastic or rubber, a property that standard paint does not normally possess.

5 Major body damage – repair

Where serious damage has occurred, or large areas need renewal due to neglect, it means that complete new panels will need welding-in, and this is best left to professionals. If the damage is due to impact, it will also be necessary to check completely the alignment of the bodyshell, and this can only be carried out accurately by a VW dealer using special jigs. If the body is left misaligned, it is primarily dangerous, as the car will not handle properly, and secondly, uneven stresses will be imposed on the steering, suspension and possibly transmission, causing abnormal wear, or complete failure, particularly to such items as the tyres.

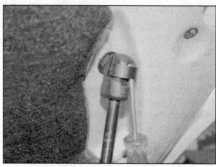

7.10 Prise off the circlip

6 Door rattles – tracing and rectification

1 Check first that the door is not loose at the hinges, and that the latch is holding the door firmly in position. Check also that the door lines up with the aperture in the body. If the door is out of alignment, adjust it with reference to Section 24.
2 If the latch is holding the door in the correct position, but the latch still rattles, the lock mechanism is worn and should be renewed.
3 Other rattles from the door could be caused by wear in the window operating mechanism, interior lock mechanism, loose glass channels or loose wiring.

7 Bonnet and strut – removal, refitting and adjustment

Bonnet

Removal

1 Fully open the bonnet, then place some cardboard or rags beneath the corners by the hinges to protect the bodywork.
2 Prise the grommets from the bonnet underside, and disconnect the windscreen washer tubes from the connecting piece. Unplug the heated jet wiring connectors and release the hose/loom from retaining clips **(see illustration)**.

8.1a Slacken and withdraw the securing bolts and move the lock mechanism away from the crossmember (arrowed)

3 Prop the bonnet open using two stout lengths of wood, one positioned at each corner. Alternatively, enlist the help of an assistant to support the bonnet.
4 Disconnect the gas strut from the bonnet, with reference to the information given later in this Section.
5 Mark the location of the hinges with a pencil, then loosen the four hinge-to-bonnet retaining bolts (two each side).
6 Support the bonnet as the securing bolts are unscrewed, then withdraw the bonnet from the car.

Refitting and adjustment

7 Refitting is a reversal of removal. Ensure that the hinges are adjusted to their original positions. Close the bonnet very carefully initially; misalignment may cause the edges of the bonnet to damage the bodywork. If necessary, adjust the hinges to their original positions and check that the bonnet is level with the surrounding bodywork. If necessary, adjust the height of the bonnet front edge by screwing the rubber buffers in or out.
8 Check that the bonnet lock operates in a satisfactory manner. In particular, check that the safety catch holds the bonnet after the bonnet release cable has been pulled.

Strut

Removal

9 Prop the bonnet open using two stout lengths of wood, one positioned at each corner. Alternatively, enlist the help of an assistant to support the bonnet.
10 Release the circlips from the strut upper and lower mountings, using a suitable screwdriver **(see illustration)**.
11 Withdraw the pivot pin from the upper mounting and slide the base of the strut off its lower mounting bracket spigot.

Refitting

12 Refitting is a reversal of removal, noting that the thicker end of the strut must face towards the bonnet.

8 Bonnet lock and release cable – removal and refitting

Removal

1 Open the bonnet and locate the bonnet lock mechanism, mounted underneath the crossmember at the front of the engine compartment. Slacken and withdraw the three securing bolts and move the lock mechanism away from the crossmember **(see illustrations)**. Lever up the safety catch handle retaining clip, prise apart the two arms, and detach the safety catch handle. Use a small screwdriver and prise off the micro-switch retaining clip. Remove the switch from the lock mechanism. Note that the switch locating pins locate in two holes in the mounting plate.

8.1b Lever up the safety catch handle retaining clip, prise apart the two arms, and detach the safety catch handle

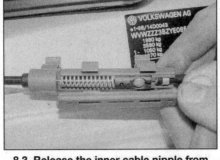

8.3 Release the inner cable nipple from the connecting piece

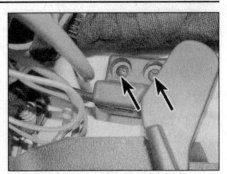

8.5 Undo the screws and remove the bonnet release handle

2 Slide out the two grommets and disengage the release cable inner from the lever in the lock mechanism, using a pair of thin-nosed pliers. Withdraw the cable from the lock mechanism.

3 Free the release cable from all its retaining clips in the engine compartment. Prise the cable junction from the right-hand side inner wing and, using a screwdriver, open the junction. Lift the inner cable nipple and separate the two halves of the release cable **(see illustration)**.

4 If required, working in the driver's footwell, unclip the cover panel from the right-hand end of facia. Remove the trim/storage tray beneath the steering column by undoing the two screws at the right-hand end of the facia, one screw next to the steering column, and one screw near the centre console.

5 Undo the securing screws and detach the

handle mechanism and its bracket from the bodywork **(see illustration)**.

6 Attach a suitable length of strong cord to the end of the release cable at the lock mechanism end, then carefully draw the cable through into the engine compartment.

7 Undo the cord from the cable, and leave the cord ends exposed in the engine compartment and footwell.

Refitting

8 Refit in the reverse order of removal. Tie the inner end of the cable to the exposed cord in the engine compartment, carefully pull the cable through to the release handle, then untie the cord.

9 When positioning the cable in the engine compartment, ensure that it is re-routed correctly to avoid kinks, sharp bends and chafing. Check

for satisfactory operation of the cable and the lock before closing the bonnet. Ensure that the bonnet locks properly when closed, and also that the safety catch operates correctly when the bonnet release cable is actuated.

9 Bumpers – removal and refitting

Front bumper

Removal

1 Undo the two upper screws securing the radiator grille to the front crossmember, then lift the grille upwards from the lower clips. The release lever must now be disconnected. To do this, use a screwdriver to open up the inner legs of the lever, and disconnect it from the pivot on the lock. Remove the radiator grille **(see illustrations)**.

2 Unscrew the front bumper upper centre mounting bolts **(see illustration)**.

3 From under the bumper, undo the three quick-fastening screws **(see illustration)**.

4 Working on each side at a time, undo the three screws securing the wheel arch liners to the front bumper **(see illustration)**.

5 With the help of an assistant, release the ends of the front bumper from the guides on each side, and withdraw it from the front of the car **(see illustration)**.

6 Disconnect the wiring from the foglamps, ambient temperature sensor or accessory components. If required, the securing strip and

9.1a Undo the upper screws and pull out the top of the radiator grille . . .

9.1b . . . lift the grille upwards from the lower clips . . .

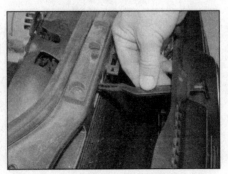

9.1c . . . then disconnect the release lever from the lock . . .

9.1d . . . and remove the radiator grille with the release lever

9.2 Front bumper upper centre mounting bolts

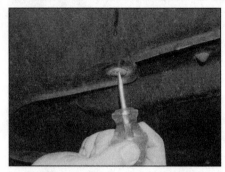

9.3 Unscrewing the quick-fastening screws under the front bumper

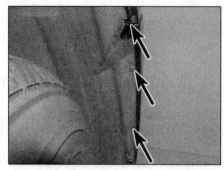

9.4 Screws securing the front bumper to the wheel arch liners on each side

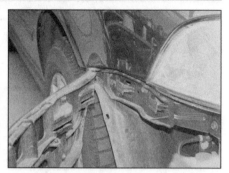

9.5 Release the ends of the front bumper from the guides on each side

9.6a Disconnecting the foglamp wiring

9.6b Removing the front bumper securing strip

9.9 Screws securing the wheel arch liners to the rear bumper

bumper bar can be removed by unscrewing the mounting bolts **(see illustrations)**. Also, the trim strips can be removed by releasing the securing tabs.

Refitting

7 Refitting is a reversal of removal. On completion, check for satisfactory operation of the accessory components as applicable.

Rear bumper

Removal

8 Remove both rear light units as described in Chapter 12.

9 Working at each rear wheel arch in turn, undo the three screws securing the wheel arch liners to the rear bumper **(see illustration)**.

10 From under the bumper, undo the centre and side securing screws **(see illustrations)**.

11 Undo the mounting bolts located beneath the rear light locations **(see illustration)**.

12 With the help of an assistant, release the ends of the rear bumper from the guides on each side, and withdraw it from the rear of the car **(see illustrations)**.

13 Disconnect the wiring from the parking aid or any accessory components located on the rear bumper. If required, the bumper bar can be removed by unscrewing the mounting bolts

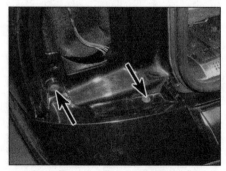

9.10a Rear bumper side securing screws . . .

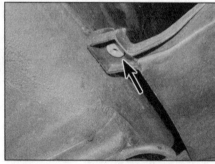

9.10b . . . and centre screws

9.11 Rear bumper mounting bolts

9.12a Release the ends of the rear bumper from the side guides . . .

9.12b . . . and withdraw the bumper

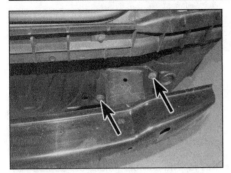

9.13 Rear bumper bar mounting bolts

(see illustration). Also, the trim strip at the upper edge of the bumper can be removed by releasing the securing tabs.

Refitting

14 Refit in the reverse order of removal. Loosely fit all retaining bolts and screws before fully tightening them. Tighten the retaining bolts to the specified torque.

10 Lock carrier/front crossmember – removal and refitting

General information

1 The lock carrier/front crossmember is the name given to the section of bodywork that is mounted across the front of the engine compartment. A number of major components, including the bonnet lock mechanism, front bumper, radiator, automatic transmission fluid cooler and front light clusters are mounted on the lock carrier. The construction of the VW Passat bodywork is such that the lock carrier and its associated components can be removed without being extensively dismantled. In addition, the lock carrier can be moved forward several centimetres to a 'service' position without having to disconnect the various hoses, pipes and wiring harnesses that serve the components mounted on it. In this position, access to components at the front of the engine compartment is greatly improved.

Removal

2 Disconnect the battery negative lead (see Chapter 5A). **Note:** *If the vehicle has a security-coded radio, check that you have a copy of the code number before disconnecting the battery. Refer to your VW dealer if in doubt.*
3 Refer to Section 9 and remove the front bumper and bumper bar.
4 Undo the screws and remove the engine undertray **(see illustration).**
5 With reference to Section 8, prise open the bonnet release cable connector in front of the driver's side bonnet hinge, and separate the two halves of the release cable.
6 Remove the securing screw(s) and detach the air inlet grille and ducting from the lock carrier **(see illustration).** Where applicable, loosen the clips and disconnect the air ducts from the intercooler.
7 Disconnect the wiring plugs for the headlight units, headlight beam aim control motors and, at the left-hand front corner of the engine compartment, lift the plastic cover and disconnect the five loom connectors **(see illustration).** Release the looms from their retaining clips.
8 Disconnect the wiring from the temperature sender/thermal switch located at the rear lower edge of the radiator, adjacent to the bottom hose stub pipe, the air conditioning compressor clutch wiring plug (to the right of the radiator), and the horn(s) wiring plug(s).
9 Drain the coolant as described in Chapter 1A or 1B, then disconnect the coolant hoses from the radiator as described in Chapter 3.
10 The air conditioning condenser must now be removed from the lock carrier and secured to a suitable point at the front of the engine compartment using cable ties or wire. To release the condenser from the lock carrier, press the lug in the end of the retaining pin, pull the pin from the mounting bracket either side of the condenser, and separate the two halves of the mounting brackets **(see illustration).** Undo the retaining screws and remove the rubber shrouds either side of the condenser **(see illustration).** Disconnect the pressure switch wiring as the condenser is removed.

 Warning: Do not disconnect the refrigerant pipes from the condenser (refer to the precautions in Chapter 3 regarding the dangers of air conditioning system refrigerant).

Caution: Do not allow the condenser to hang by its refrigerant pipes, as the strain may cause them to fracture.

11 Unbolt the power steering fluid cooler from the lock carrier and radiator **(see illustration).**
12 Release the ends of the lock carrier rubber

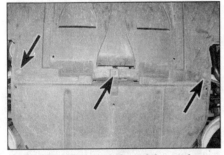

10.4 The front section of the engine undertray is secured to the rear section by three screws (arrowed)

10.6 Undo the screws and detach the air inlet duct from the lock carrier

10.7 Disconnect the wiring plugs and release the looms from the retaining clips

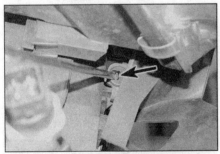

10.10a Depress the lug, and pull the condenser retaining pin from the mounting bracket (arrowed)

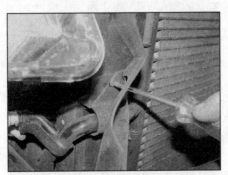

10.10b Undo the screws and remove the rubber shroud

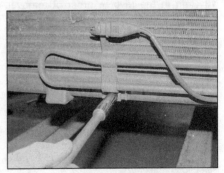

10.11 Unbolt the power steering fluid cooler from the lock carrier and radiator

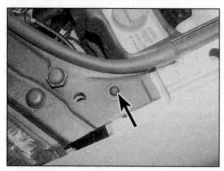

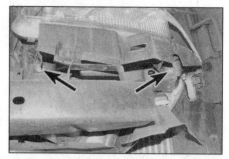

10.13a The lock carrier is secured by one bolt at the top of each wing . . .

10.13b . . . and one beside each headlamp

10.14a The bumper guides are secured by two bolts under each headlamp (arrowed) . . .

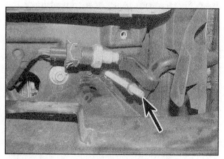

10.14b . . . and one under each wing (arrowed)

10.15 Unscrew the three bumper bar retaining bolts each side (one hidden under the bar)

10.22 Screw the home-made service tool into the hole vacated by the bumper bar mounting bolt

sealing strip from each front wing; there is no need to remove the strip from the lock carrier completely.

13 Unscrew and remove the bolts securing the lock carrier to the top of the front wing on each side of the vehicle **(see illustration)**. Unscrew the bolts alongside each headlamp **(see illustration)**.

14 Unscrew and remove the side-mounted bumper guides, located just below each headlamp, and unclip them from the front wings **(see illustrations)**.

15 Enlist the help of an assistant to support the lock carrier during this final stage. Unscrew and remove the front bumper bar bolts (three on the right-hand side, three on the left-hand side) then withdraw the lock carrier/crossmember from the front of the vehicle **(see illustration)**.

Refitting

16 Refit in the reverse order of removal. Check the operation of the front lights, and the bonnet lock and safety catch, on completion. Refill and bleed the cooling system as described in Chapter 1A or 1B, and have the headlights checked for correct beam alignment.

Setting the lock carrier in the 'service' position

Note: *To carry out this procedure, it will necessary to fabricate two service tools, using two 300 mm lengths of threaded rod and a selection of hex nuts.*

17 Disconnect the battery negative lead (see Chapter 5A). **Note:** *If the vehicle has a security-*

coded radio, check that you have a copy of the code number before disconnecting the battery. Refer to your VW dealer if in doubt.

18 Refer to Section 9 and remove the front bumper.

19 With reference to Section 8, prise open the bonnet release cable connector in front of the driver's side bonnet hinge, and separate the two halves of the release cable.

20 Undo the quick-release bolts and release the front edge of the engine compartment noise insulation panel from the underside of the lock carrier; there is no need to remove the panel completely.

21 Remove the securing screw(s) and detach the air inlet grille/ducting from the lock carrier. Where applicable, loosen the clips and disconnect the air ducts from the intercooler. Unscrew and remove the side-mounted bumper guides, just below each headlamp, and unclip them from the front wings.

22 Slacken and withdraw the right-hand uppermost bolt from the right-hand bumper mounting tube. Thread one of the home-made service tools into the hole vacated by the bolt and thread one of the hex nuts to the end of the tool. Thread the second tool into the hole located to the left of the bumper left-hand mounting tube **(see illustration)**.

23 Remove the remainder of the bolts securing the lock carrier in position.

24 With the help of an assistant, carefully draw the lock carrier approximately 10 cm away from the front of the engine. Adjust the hex nuts on the two home-made service tools so that the lock carrier is held securely.

25 The lock carrier can be refitted by following

the removal procedure in reverse. Ensure that all fixings are tightened to the correct torque wrench setting, where specified. On completion, have the headlights checked for correct beam alignment.

11 Wheel arch liners – removal and refitting

Removal

1 Loosen the relevant wheel bolts, then raise the front or rear of the car and support on axle stands (see *Jacking and vehicle support*). Remove the relevant roadwheel.

2 The liner is secured by expanding plastic rivets and screws. The rivets may be of the type that have to be prised out, or they may have a central pin that has to be pressed through the rivet body first, before the rivet is prised free.

3 Undo and remove the liner securing screws.

4 Lower the liner out of position, and manoeuvre it out from under the wing. Recover the rivet expander pins (where fitted), as necessary.

Refitting

5 Refitting is a reversal of removal. Renew any fasteners which were broken on removal. When fitting the expanding-type rivets, place the rivet body into position with the central pin retracted, then press pin into the rivet body until it is flush with the top of the rivet.

12 Boot lid –
removal and refitting

Removal

1 Raise the boot lid, then remove warning triangle from its holder **(see illustration)**.
2 Remove the securing screws and detach the warning triangle holder from the boot lid **(see illustration)**.
3 Undo the trim retaining screws from the hand grip recess, then carefully pull away the trim **(see illustrations)**. If necessary, use a wide-blade screwdriver to prise the clips from the boot lid.
4 Unplug the wiring connectors from the lock switch and number plate light units, then release the grommet and withdraw the wiring harness from the boot lid **(see illustration)**. Unclip the wiring from the guide channel clipped to the side of the hinge.
5 Prise the spring clips from the upper and lower balljoints using a small screwdriver, then release the gas struts from the boot lid hinges **(see illustrations)**.
6 Mark the relationship between the boot lid and the hinges by drawing around the outside of each hinge with a marker pen.
7 Place cloths or pieces of cardboard over the surfaces of the rear wings, to prevent damage during removal.
8 Enlist the aid of an assistant to support the boot lid, then unscrew and remove the hinge-to-boot lid retaining nuts **(see illustration)**, and lift the lid clear.

Refitting

9 Refit in the reverse order of removal. Check the lid for correct alignment, and if necessary loosen off the hinge bolts to adjust, then retighten them; there should be an even gap between the outside edge of the boot lid and the surrounding bodywork. The closed position of the boot lid must be set with a 2.0 mm pretension. To do this, use a 3.0 mm Allen key to loosen both supports, then set them to an initial dimension of 12.5 mm. Close the boot lid using light pressure while pulling on the handle, then open it – this sets the pretension. Now set the supports to a dimension of 25.0 mm. Check that the boot lid opens and closes correctly.

13 Boot lid lock
and lock cylinder –
removal and refitting

1 Remove the trim from inside the boot lid, as described in Section 12.

Lock cylinder housing and carrier

Removal

2 Disconnect the wiring for the number plate lights, central locking positioning motor **(see illustration)** and boot lid lock.
3 Detach the cable from the lock.

12.1 Warning triangle on the boot lid trim

12.2 Remove the warning triangle holder from the boot lid

12.3a Undo the screws in the hand grip . . .

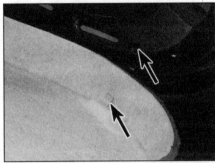

12.3b . . . then pull the trim away from the clips

4 Unscrew the mounting nuts, then withdraw the lock cylinder carrier from the boot lid **(see illustrations)**.
5 Disconnect the outer then inner cable, disconnect the wiring, and unclip the lock

cylinder housing from the carrier **(see illustrations)**.

Refitting

6 Refitting is a reversal of removal.

12.4 Disconnecting the wiring from the boot lid

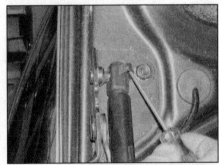

12.5a Prise the spring clips from the upper balljoints . . .

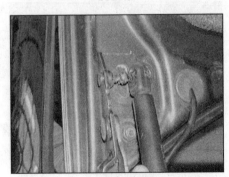

12.5b . . . then release the gas strut from the boot lid hinge

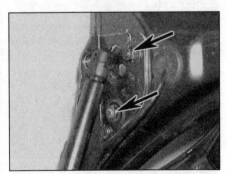

12.8 Unscrew and remove the hinge-to-boot lid retaining nuts (arrowed)

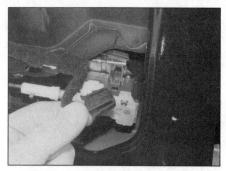

13.2 Disconnecting the wiring from the central locking positioning motor

13.4a Unscrew the mounting nuts . . .

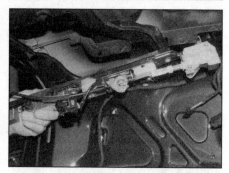

13.4b . . . and withdraw the lock cylinder carrier from the boot lid

13.5a Disconnect the outer cable . . .

13.5b . . . inner cable . . .

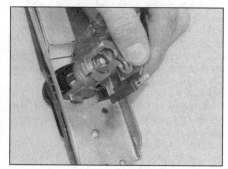

13.5c . . . disconnect the wiring . . .

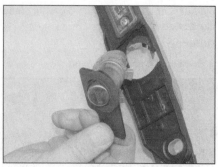

13.5d . . . and unclip the lock cylinder housing from the carrier

13.8 Disconnecting the cable from the boot lid lock

13.9 Boot lid lock

Lock unit

Removal

7 Disconnect the wiring from the lock.
8 Detach the cable from the lock **(see illustration)**.
9 Mark the fitted position of the lock with a marker pen, then unscrew the retaining nuts and withdraw the lock unit from the boot lid **(see illustration)**.

Refitting

10 Refit in the reverse order of removal.

14 Tailgate (Estate models) – removal and refitting

Removal

1 Open the tailgate, then unscrew the four

lower trim panel securing screws. Two are located under flaps in the grab handle recesses, and two outer edges of the trim **(see illustration)**.

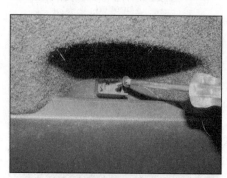

14.1 Two of the trim panel screws are located under flaps in the grab handle recesses

2 Carefully prise the lower section of the trim panel from the tailgate using just enough force to overcome the spring clips. Similarly, unclip the upper section of the trim panel from the tailgate rear window aperture.
3 Disconnect the wiring from the tailgate components (lock switch, wiper motor, number plate light units and demister element) at the connectors. Note the routing and attachment locations of the wires.
4 Mark the relationship between the tailgate and its hinges using a felt tip pen.
5 Enlist the aid of an assistant to help support the tailgate, then detach the tailgate struts with reference to Section 15.
6 Unscrew and remove the tailgate-to-hinge securing bolts, and lift the tailgate clear of the vehicle.

Refitting

7 Refit in the reverse order of removal. Check

that the tailgate is correctly aligned before fully tightening the tailgate hinge bolts.

8 The fit and closing tension of the tailgate can be adjusted by altering the positions of the rubber buffers at the upper and lower edges of the tailgate.

15 Boot lid/tailgate support strut(s) – removal and refitting

Removal

1 Open the boot lid or tailgate and support it in its open position, or have an assistant hold it open.

2 Disconnect the strut(s) at the upper and lower balljoints by lifting (not removing) the spring clips, and prising the joint free **(see illustrations)**.

3 If a strut is defective in operation, it must be renewed. Do not attempt to dismantle and repair the strut. Note that the struts are filled with pressurised gas, and so should not be punctured or disposed of by incineration.

Refitting

4 Refit in the reverse order of removal. The thinner, piston rod end of the strut(s) must be attached to the bodywork. Ensure that the strut is securely engaged with the balljoints.

16 Tailgate lock and lock cylinder (Estate models) – removal and refitting

1 Remove the trim from inside the tailgate, as described in Section 14.

Lock cylinder housing and carrier

Removal

2 Disconnect the wiring for the number plate lights, central locking positioning motor and tailgate lock.

3 Detach the cable from the lock.

4 Unscrew the mounting nuts, then withdraw the lock cylinder carrier from the boot lid.

5 Unclip the housing from the carrier.

Refitting

6 Refitting is a reversal of removal.

15.2a Use a screwdriver to prise off the strut circlip . . .

Lock unit

Removal

7 Disconnect the wiring from the lock.

8 Detach the cable from the lock.

9 Mark the fitted position of the lock with a marker pen, then unscrew the retaining nuts and withdraw the lock unit from the boot lid.

Refitting

10 Refit in the reverse order of removal.

17 Door trim panel – removal and refitting

Driver's door

Removal

1 Open the door and insert a thin-bladed

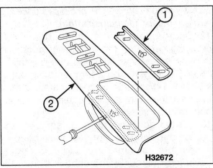

17.1 Separate the grip recess/switch panel (2) and grip trim (1)

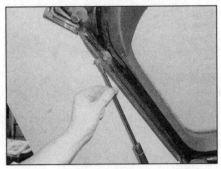

15.2b . . . and remove the strut balljoint from the stud

screwdriver between the door trim and the grip recess/switch panel. Push the screwdriver in and release the grip trim together with the grip recess/switch panel **(see illustration)**.

2 Disconnect the switch panel wiring plug **(see illustration)**.

3 Undo the three screws exposed by the removal of the grip recess **(see illustration)**.

4 Undo the two Torx screws along the lower edge of the door trim **(see illustration)**.

5 Using a flat-bladed screwdriver carefully prise the trim away from the door frame, releasing the retaining clips. Lift the trim panel up squarely, to disengage the trim from the lock button and the weatherstrip moulding between the trim and window.

6 Unhook the operating cable from the rear of the interior handle as it becomes accessible **(see illustration)**.

7 Unplug the wiring from the mirror/central locking switches/kerb light (where applicable).

17.2 Disconnect the switch panel wiring plug

17.3 Undo the exposed screws . . .

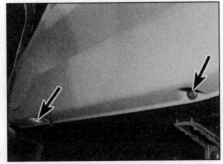

17.4 . . . and the two Torx screws along the lower edge of the door trim

17.6 Unhook the operating cable . . .

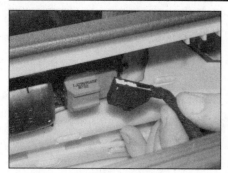

17.7 . . . and disconnect the wiring

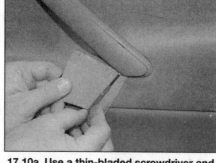

17.10a Use a thin-bladed screwdriver and cardboard protector . . .

17.10b . . . to remove the handle centre trim

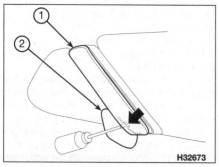

17.11 Use a piece of cardboard (2) to protect the door trim, and prise the centre trim (1) from the grip handle

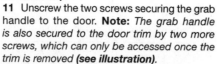

17.13a Unhooking the operating cable from the rear of the interior handle

Refitting

14 If necessary, pull the window slot seal from the door trim and insert it into the window slot.

15 Check the door trim for any missing or broken clips, and renew where necessary.

16 Refit in the reverse order of removal. Guide the door locking knob through the hole at the upper edge of the trim panel **(see illustration)**, and ensure that the wiring and connections are secure and correctly routed, clear of the window regulator and latch/lock components.

18 Central locking system – general

Refer to the information given in Chapter 12.

19 Door lock - removal and refitting

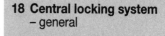

Release the wiring from its retaining clips on the rear of the door trim panel **(see illustration)**.

8 Lift the trim panel away from the door. If the window rubber seal becomes detached from the door, refit it.

Refitting

9 Refit in the reverse order of removal. Guide the door locking knob through the hole at the upper edge of the trim panel, and ensure that the wiring and connections are secure and correctly routed, clear of the window regulator and latch/lock components.

Passenger doors

Removal

10 Insert a thin-bladed screwdriver into the slot on the front side of the door grab handle,

and prise the handle centre trim out **(see illustrations)**.

11 Unscrew the two screws securing the grab handle to the door. **Note:** *The grab handle is also secured to the door trim by two more screws, which can only be accessed once the trim is removed* **(see illustration)**.

12 On the rear doors, undo the single retaining screw on the trim lower edge. On the front passenger door, the trim is retained by two screws. Using a trim removal tool or a wide flat-bladed screwdriver, carefully prise the door trim from the frame along the front, bottom and rear edges.

13 Lift the door trim upwards squarely and out of the window slot. As they become accessible, unclip the handle operating cable from its guide and unhook it from the lever, and unplug the wiring connectors **(see illustrations)**.

Front door

Removal

1 The door lock is removed together with the window component carrier, then separated on the bench **(see illustration)**.

2 Refer to Section 17 and remove the door trim panel.

3 Lever out the cap from the rear edge of the door, then insert a multi-spline screwdriver and unscrew the lock cylinder housing locking screw while holding the door exterior handle in its open position. **Do not** undo the screw completely or it will fall into the bottom of the door. Unscrewing the locking screw turns the housing locking ring on the inside of the lock cylinder housing.

4 Pull the lock cylinder housing with cap (the rear part of the door handle) directly out of the exterior door handle mounting bracket.

5 Detach the release cable end fitting from the slot in the exterior door handle.

6 Temporarily reconnect the window switch and lower the window until the glass retaining plastic clips are visible in the inner door panel access holes (remove the caps where fitted).

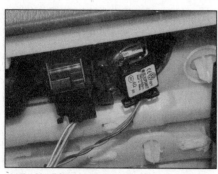

17.13b Disconnecting the wiring on the door trim panel

17.16 Guide the door locking knob through the hole in the trim panel

The window is attached to the regulator arms by an outer ring with a locking inner peg. Using a small drift, drive the inner pegs right through the outer rings until they drop to the bottom of the door. **Note:** *The peg length is such that it will contact the door outer skin panel, and great care is required to prevent damage to the panel.* On later models, the pegs can be removed with a 5.0 mm diameter bolt and the outer rings with an 8.0 mm diameter bolt.

7 Fully raise the window glass and secure it with adhesive tape.

8 Disconnect all wiring from the electric window motor.

9 Lever out the two caps (where fitted) and unscrew the lock mounting bolts from the rear edge of the door.

10 Unscrew the 10 mounting bolts securing the carrier to the door, then pull out the top of the carrier, lift it and withdraw towards the front of the door.

11 Disconnect the wiring from the door lock, and release all wiring from the back of the carrier.

12 Drive out the plastic clips, then lever off the lock unit, together with its baseplate from the carrier.

13 Turn the lock and disconnect the locking rod, then disconnect the release cable by turning the nipple through 90°.

Refitting

14 Refitting is a reversal of the removal procedure. Check that the door striker enters the lock centrally when the door is closed, and if necessary adjust the position of the striker **(see illustration)**.

Rear door

Removal

15 The door lock is removed together with the window component carrier, then separated on the bench.

16 Refer to Section 17 and remove the door trim panel.

17 Pull out the door weatherseal in the area of the exterior handle to expose the access hole, then insert a multi-spline screwdriver and unscrew the lock cylinder housing locking screw while holding the door exterior handle in its open position **(see illustration)**. Do

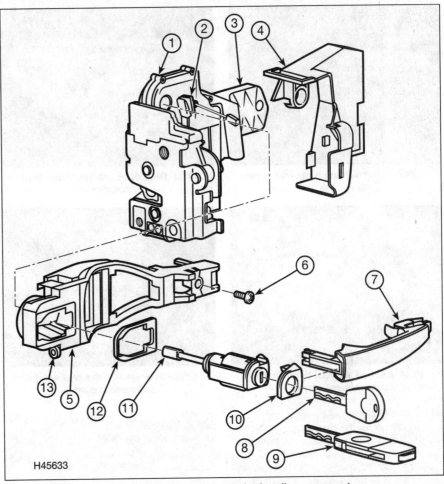

19.1 Front door lock and exterior handle components

1 Door lock	5 Baseplate	10 Cap
2 Cable	6 Screw	11 Lock cylinder
3 Bracket	7 Handle	housing
4 Security	8 Key (folding)	12 Gasket
cover	9 Key (non-folding)	13 Locking screw

H45633

not undo the screw completely or it will fall into the bottom of the door. Unscrewing the locking screw turns the housing locking ring on the inside of the lock cylinder housing.

18 Pull the lock cylinder housing (the rear part of the door handle) directly out of the exterior door handle mounting bracket, then detach

the release cable end fitting from the slot in the exterior door handle **(see illustration)**.

19 Temporarily reconnect the window switch and lower the window until the glass retaining plastic clip is visible in the inner door panel access hole (remove the cap where fitted). The window is attached to the regulator by

19.14 Door lock striker

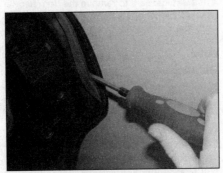

19.17 Unscrewing the locking element Allen screw in the door rear edge

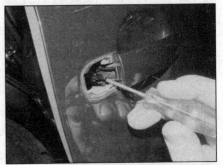

19.18 Disconnecting the cable end fitting from the slot in the exterior door handle

19.22 Lock mounting bolts on the rear edge of the door

19.23 Rear door window component carrier

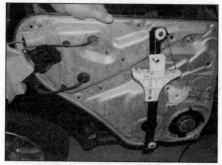

19.24 Back of the rear door window component carrier

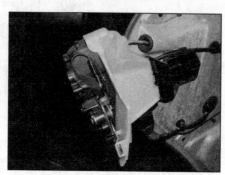

19.25 Door lock on the rear window component carrier

an outer ring with a locking inner peg. Using a small drift, drive the inner peg right through the outer ring until it drops to the bottom of the door. **Note:** *The peg length is such that it will contact the door outer skin panel, and great care is required to prevent damage to the panel.* On later models, the peg can be removed with a 5.0 mm diameter bolt and the outer ring with an 8.0 mm diameter bolt.

20 Fully raise the window glass and secure it with adhesive tape.

21 Disconnect all wiring from the electric window motor.

22 Lever out the two caps (where fitted) and unscrew the lock mounting bolts from the rear edge of the door **(see illustration).**

23 Unscrew the 7 mounting bolts securing the carrier to the door, then pull out the top of the carrier, lift it and withdraw towards the front of the door **(see illustration)**

24 Disconnect the wiring from the door lock, and release all wiring from the back of the carrier **(see illustration).**

25 Drive out the plastic clips, then lever off the lock unit, together with its baseplate from the carrier **(see illustration).**

26 Turn the lock and disconnect the locking rod, then disconnect the release cable by turning the nipple through 90°.

Refitting

27 Refitting is a reversal of the removal procedure. Check that the door striker enters the lock centrally when the door is closed, and if necessary adjust the position of the striker.

---

20 Door handles and lock cylinder – removal and refitting

Exterior handles

Removal

1 Pull out the exterior handle and hold. Prise out the cap and unscrew the locking element Allen screw in the door rear edge. As the Allen screw is rotated the lock cylinder will be released from the door exterior. **Note:** *On the rear doors, the Allen screw is covered by the door weatherstrip.* Remove the lock cylinder.

2 Unclip the door lock cable from the handle.

3 The handle can now be removed from the door.

4 If it is necessary to remove the door handle bracket, remove the door trim (Section 17), and the window component carrier (Section 21). The bracket is retained by a single screw.

Refitting

5 Refitting is a reversal of removal.

Lock cylinders

Removal

6 Remove the cap from the Allen screw nearest the external door handle on the rear end face of the door. On the rear doors, the screw is covered by the door weatherstrip.

7 Pull the external door handle to the 'open'

position and hold. Undo the screw until it is felt to reach a 'stop'. This releases the lock cylinder.

8 Withdraw the lock cylinder housing from the door.

Refitting

9 Refitting is a reversal of removal.

Interior handles

Removal

10 With reference to Section 17, remove the door trim panel.

11 Undo the cross-head screw, unclip the switch for the electric windows (except driver's side), and unclip the release handle from the door trim.

Refitting

12 Refitting is a reversal of removal.

---

21 Door window glass – removal and refitting

Front door

Removal

1 Remove the door trim as described in Section 17.

2 Temporarily reconnect the window switch and lower the window until the glass retaining plastic clips are visible in the inner door panel access holes.

3 The window is attached to the regulator arms by two outer rings with locking inner pegs. Working on each arm in turn, use a small drift to drive the inner pegs right through the outer rings until they drop to the bottom of the door. **Note:** *The peg length is such that it will contact the door outer skin panel, and great care is required to prevent damage to the panel.*

4 Starting at the rear corner, lift the window glass from the door.

5 If necessary, drive the outer rings from the window glass.

Refitting

6 Refitting is a reversal of removal, however, fit the outer rings and locking pegs to the glass before refitting it – the pegs will automatically locate on the regulator arms if the glass is carefully tapped downwards.

Rear door

Removal

7 Remove the door trim as described in Section 17.

8 Pull up and remove the window glass inner and outer weatherseals from the door **(see illustrations).**

9 Pull the glass guide channel from the front of the rear door, then undo the screws and remove the trim from the door frame. Similarly, pull the glass guide channel from the rear of the rear door, then undo

21.8a Prise off the inner . . .

21.8b . . . and outer weatherseals from the door

21.9a Pull the glass guide channel from the front . . .

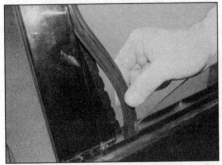

21.9b . . . and rear of the door . . .

21.9c . . . then undo the screws . . .

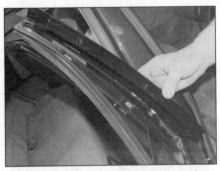

21.9d . . . and remove the trim from the door frame

the 2 hidden and outer lower screws, and remove the trim from the door frame **(see illustrations)**.

10 Pull out the door weatherseal in the area of the exterior handle to expose the access hole, then insert a multi-spline screwdriver and unscrew the lock cylinder housing locking screw while holding the door exterior handle in its open position **(see illustration)**. **Do not** undo the screw completely or it will fall into the bottom of the door. Unscrewing the locking screw turns the housing locking ring on the inside of the lock cylinder housing.

11 Pull the lock cylinder housing (the rear part of the door handle) directly out of the exterior door handle mounting bracket **(see illustration)**.

12 Temporarily reconnect the window switch and lower the window until the glass retaining plastic clip is visible in the inner door panel access hole **(see illustration)**.

13 The window is attached to the regulator by an outer ring with a locking inner peg. Use a small drift to drive the inner peg right through the outer ring until it drops to the bottom of the door **(see illustration)**. **Note:** *The peg length*

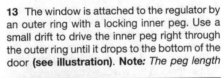

21.10 Unscrew the lock cylinder housing locking screw using a multi-spline screwdriver

is such that it will contact the door outer skin panel, and great care is required to prevent damage to the panel.

14 Lift the window glass upwards from the outside of the door **(see illustration)**.

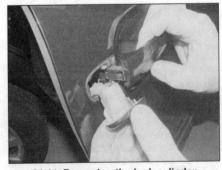

21.11 Removing the lock cylinder

21.12 Lower the window until the glass retaining plastic clips are visible in the inner door panel access holes

21.13 Use a small drift to drive the inner pegs right through the outer rings

21.14 Removing the window glass from the rear door

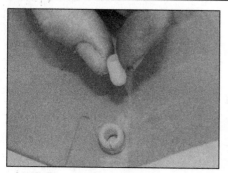

21.15 Rear window glass outer ring and locking peg

15 If necessary, drive the outer rings from the window glass **(see illustration)**.

Refitting

16 Refitting is a reversal of removal, however, fit the outer ring and locking peg to the glass before refitting it – the peg will automatically locate on the regulator arm if the glass is carefully tapped downwards.

22 Door window regulator – removal and refitting

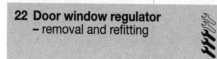

Removal

1 The window regulator is secured to the window component carrier by rivets **(see illustration)**, and, at the time of writing it was not available as a separate part. This Section describes removal of the carrier, together with details of the procedure to take if the motor fails.

2 Follow the procedure given in Section 19 for door lock removal, however there is no need to remove the lock from the carrier. If the motor has failed, the window glass may be moved as follows.

3 Unscrew the bolts and pull the armature housing off of the motor **(see illustration)**. On the front door it will be necessary to reach in behind the door inner skin.

4 On the Bosch-type motor, the window glass can now be pushed down until the retaining plastic clips are visible in the inner door panel access hole(s). On the Siemens-type motor, the armature can be turned anti-clockwise to lower the glass.

Refitting

5 Refit the window regulator and window component carrier to the door by following the removal procedure in reverse.

23 Electrically-operated windows – general information and motor renewal

Window switches

1 Refer to Chapter 12, Section 6.

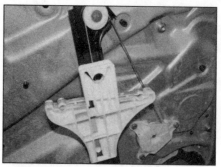

22.1 Window regulator on the window component carrier

Window motors

Removal

2 Remove the window component carrier as described in Section 22.

3 Remove the three motor securing screws. Carefully lift the motor from the carrier.

HAYNES HiNT *When removing or refitting the rear door motor, insert a hammer shaft beneath the window guide so that it presses against the carrier.*

Refitting

4 Fit the motor, aligning it with the regulator mechanism, and refit the retaining screws. Evenly and progressively tighten the retaining screws in a diagonal sequence to draw the motor squarely down onto the regulator then tighten them to the specified torque.

5 Refit the window carrier.

6 Prior to refitting the trim panel, reconnect the window switch and check the operation of the window. **Note:** *On models where the windows are equipped with a safety system which automatically opens the window should anything become trapped, it will be necessary to initiate the motor as follows. Switch the ignition On and then Off again then raise the window fully and hold the switch in the closed position for four seconds, then lower the window and check that it opens fully.*

7 Once the window operation is known to be correct, refit the inner trim panel as described in Section 17.

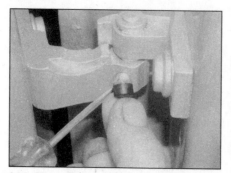

24.3 Prise off the plastic cap, and undo the grub screw

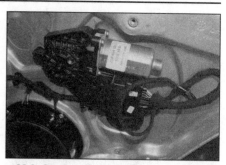

22.3 On the rear door the door window regulator motor is located on the outside of the carrier

24 Doors – removal and refitting

Removal

1 Remove the door trim as described in Section 17.

2 Unclip the trim panel from the lower A-pillar. Disconnect the door wiring harness at the multiway connector, pull the bellows between the pillar and door away from the A-pillar, and feed the door wiring loom through the aperture.

3 On the upper hinge, prise out the cap and remove the grub screw from the hinge element attached to the A-pillar **(see illustration)**.

4 Get an assistant to support the weight of the door, or support it with blocks. If blocks are used, make sure the door will be securely supported (it is a heavy and awkward component), and pad the blocks with some rag to prevent damage to the underside of the door.

5 Mark the relationship between the lower hinge and the door, using a marker pen.

6 Unscrew and remove the bolts that secure the lower hinge to the door.

7 Remove the door by lifting it upwards, to separate the upper hinge, and remove it from the vehicle.

8 Clean the bolt threads with a wire brush, and the nut threads with a tap, and treat them with thread-locking fluid when refitting the door.

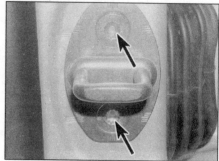

24.10 Slacken the screws to reposition the door striker

26.4a On Saloon models, the rear sunroof drain tubes terminate behind the leading edges of the rear bumper . . .

26.4b . . . but can also be accessed by removing the load space side trim panels . . .

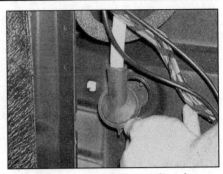

26.4c . . . and prising out the tube grommet

Refitting

9 Refitting is a reversal of the removal procedure. Use the markings made during removal to ensure that the lower hinge is positioned correctly on the door. Note that the hinges have elongated mounting holes to allow the position of the door to be adjusted.

10 On completion, shut the door and check it for closure and alignment. Check the depth at which the striker enters the lock. If adjustment is required, slacken the securing bolts and reposition the striker plate (see illustration).

25 Windscreen, rear window glass and rear side window glass – general information

The windscreen, rear window glass, and rear side window glass are directly bonded to the metalwork. Their removal and refitting requires the use of special tools not readily available to the home mechanic. This work should therefore be left to a VW dealer, or a specialist glass replacement company.

26 Sunroof – general

1 A sliding/tilting sunroof is fitted to some models. When fitted correctly, the roof panel in the fully closed position should be level with, or no more than 1.0 mm lower than, the roof panel at the leading edge. The rear edge must be level with, or no more than 1.0 mm higher than, the roof panel at the rear.

2 Removal and refitting, and adjustments to the roof panel, are best entrusted to a VW garage, as specialised tools are required.

3 The sunroof panel motor can be removed and refitted as described in Chapter 12. If the motor malfunctions when the roof panel is in the open position, it can be wound shut manually; refer to Chapter 12.

4 If the sunroof water drain hoses become blocked, they may be cleared by probing them with a length of suitable cable (an old speedometer drive cable is ideal). The

front drain tubes terminate just below the A-pillars, between the upper and lower front door hinges. The rear drain tubes on Saloon models terminate behind the leading edges of the rear bumper, but can also be accessed by removing the load space side trim panels and prising out the tube grommet (see illustrations). On Estate models, the rear drain tubes terminate in front of the rear wheel arch. Remove the rear wheel arch liner to gain access.

27 Door mirror components – removal and refitting

Mirror housing

Renewal

1 Fold the mirror forwards then adjust the position of the glass so that the mirror is vertical, otherwise when the housing is lifted off, the mirror could be damaged by the housing.

2 Remove the rubber grommet, and insert a thin-bladed screwdriver through the hole in the underside of the mirror carrier and into the clip. Push the handle of the screwdriver forward and release the housing.

3 Lift the housing up and away from the mirror body.

4 Fit the new mirror housing using a reversal of the removal procedure.

Mirror

Renewal

⚠ Warning: Wear gloves and eye protection when carrying out this operation, particularly if the mirror glass is broken.

5 Remove the mirror housing as described in the previous sub-Section.

6 Disconnect the heater element wiring plugs, and carefully prise the mirror glass from the mounting/retaining clip.

7 To refit, press firmly at the centre of the mirror glass to engage the retaining clip. On completion, check the operation of the mirror adjustment mechanism using the adjustment knob/buttons.

Complete assembly

Removal

8 Remove the door trim panel (Section 17).

9 Working inside the vehicle, carefully pull out the top of the triangular mirror internal trim.

10 Pull the trim up to release it from the two retaining clips.

11 Unplug the mirror wiring harness at the connector.

12 Undo the retaining bolt and withdraw the mirror from the door. Pass the wiring harness connector through the door aperture and recover the rubber seal.

13 To remove the mirror adjustment mechanism, first remove the mirror glass as described earlier in this Section. Undo the securing screws and remove the mechanism from the mirror body.

Refitting

14 Refitting the mirror is a reversal of the removal procedure. Check the operation of the mirror adjustment on completion.

28 Centre console – removal and refitting

Removal

1 Prise the plastic plugs from the lower edges of the console and remove the securing bolts beneath (see illustrations).

2 Fold up the armrest and pull out the oddments box (see illustration).

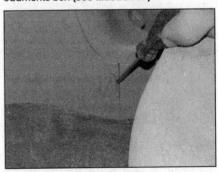

28.1a Prise out the plastic plugs . . .

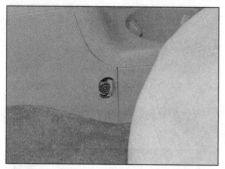

28.1b ... and unscrew the securing bolts

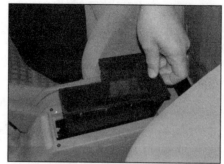

28.2 Removing the oddments box

28.3a Remove the rear ashtray ...

28.3b ... and unscrew the console rear mounting screws

28.4a Remove the console rear trim ...

28.4b ... and disconnect the wiring

3 Remove the rear ashtray and undo the 2 console rear mounting screws **(see illustrations)**.
4 Remove the console rear trim and disconnect the wiring **(see illustrations)**.
5 From the top of the console, undo the 3 mounting nuts **(see illustration)**.

6 Lift the rear of the console and release the rear section from the front section. Withdraw the rear console section upwards over the handbrake lever **(see illustrations)**.
7 On manual transmission models, unclip the gear lever gaiter from the top of the console **(see illustration)**, then unscrew the gear

lever knob and remove it together with the gaiter.
8 On all models, raise the rear of the console front section and withdraw it to the rear over the gear lever. Disconnect the wiring from the cigarette lighter and withdraw the console **(see illustrations)**.

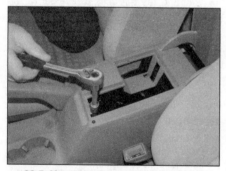

28.5 Unscrew the mounting nuts ...

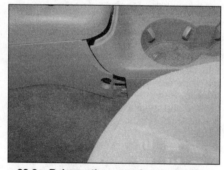

28.6a Release the console rear section from the front section ...

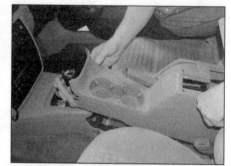

28.6b ... and withdraw it over the handbrake lever

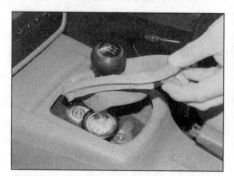

28.7 Unclip the gear lever gaiter from the top of the console

28.8a Withdraw the front section of the console from the facia ...

28.8b ... and disconnect the wiring from the cigarette lighter

29.7 Prise off the trim at the driver's end of the facia

29.8 The trim panel screw to the right of the steering column . . .

29.10 Unscrew the four steering column surround screws (arrowed)

Refitting

9 Refitting is a reversal of the removal procedure.

29 Facia, associated panels and crossmember – removal and refitting

Facia

Removal

1 Disconnect the battery negative lead (refer to Chapter 5A). **Note:** *If the vehicle has a security-coded radio, check that you have a copy of the code number before disconnecting the battery. Refer to your VW dealer if in doubt.*

2 Remove the centre console as described in Section 28.

3 Remove the switch panel and heater control panel as described in Chapter 3.

4 Remove the steering wheel as described in Chapter 10.

5 Remove the steering column stalk switches, as described in Chapter 12.

6 Prise out the caps, and remove the two screws securing the driver's side A-pillar trim beneath the facia. Unclip and remove the trim. Repeat this procedure on the passenger's side.

7 Unclip the trim panel from the driver's side end of the facia **(see illustration)**.

8 Unscrew the four bolts at the end of the facia, and the two bolts underneath securing the lower facia trim panel **(see illustration)**.

9 Unplug the wiring from the lighting switch and headlight range control adjuster as the panel is withdrawn.

10 Remove the four retaining screws and detach the steering column surround trim **(see illustration)**.

11 Undo the two retaining screws and remove the dash panel insert. Separate the electrical

connectors as the panel is withdrawn **(see illustrations)**.

12 Unscrew the two retaining Torx screws either side of the steering column under the facia.

13 With reference to Chapter 12, remove the radio/cassette/CD unit.

14 Unscrew the two screws in the corners of the storage compartment below the audio unit aperture, and two below the centre panel. Remove the two uppermost captive spire nuts from the panel aperture and pull out the dash centre panel cover **(see illustrations)**.

15 Working in the dash centre panel aperture, undo the three bolts in the top of the opening **(see illustration)**.

16 Unscrew and remove the Torx bolts beneath the passenger's storage compartment lid.

17 Open the passenger's storage compartment lid, and unscrew the five retaining bolts **(see illustration)**.

29.11a The instrument panel insert is retained by two screws

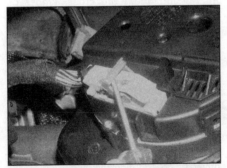

29.11b Unlock the instrument panel connector with a small screwdriver

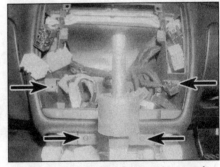

29.14a Remove the four centre panel screws (arrowed) . . .

29.14b . . . and the spire nuts

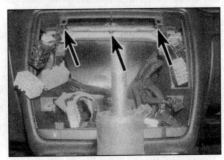

29.15 At the upper edge of the centre panel aperture, undo the three screws (arrowed)

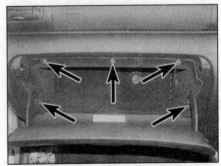

29.17 Undo the five glovebox screws (arrowed)

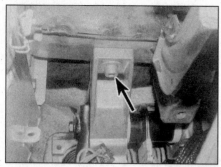

29.24 Remove the Allen bolt securing the pedal support bracket to the crossmember

29.25 After removing the four retaining screws, support the steering column with an axle stand

29.27 The fusebox is secured by two screws

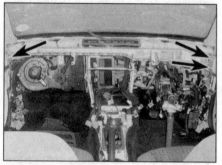

29.29 Crossmember is secured by one nut on the passenger side, and two on the driver's side (arrowed)

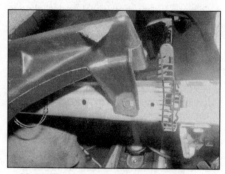

29.34 The windscreen centre vent can be unbolted as the crossmember is withdrawn

18 Starting at the top of the lens, carefully prise out the passenger's storage compartment light and disconnect the wiring plug. Pull the storage compartment from the facia.

19 Unclip the trim panel from the passenger's end of the facia, undo the four retaining Torx screws.

20 Where fitted, prise up the sunlight sensor fitted to the vent top centre of the facia, and disconnect the wiring plug. Push the wiring and plug back down the hole into the facia.

21 Make a final check to ensure that all wiring looms are released from their retaining clips and carefully withdraw the facia, disconnect the passenger air vent temperature sensor as the wiring plug becomes accessible.

Refitting

22 Refitting is a reversal of the removal process. Ensure that the heater control cables and all wiring harnesses are correctly routed and clipped in position.

Facia crossmember

Removal

23 Remove the facia as described above.

24 Unscrew the single Allen bolt securing the brake/clutch pedal support bracket to the crossmember **(see illustration)**.

25 Mark the relationship of the steering column to the crossmember, slacken and remove the four retaining bolts, and lower the steering column from the crossmember. Support the column on an axle stand. Do not allow it to hang down unsupported, or the

steering universal joint may be damaged **(see illustration)**.

26 Release the wiring loom retaining clips from the crossmember above the steering column.

27 Working under the crossmember on the driver's side, undo the two bolts and remove the fusebox. There is no need to disconnect any of the wiring connections **(see illustration)**.

28 Still working in the driver's footwell, undo the two retaining nuts and lower the relay plate from the crossmember. Again, there is no need to disconnect any wiring plugs. Release the wiring loom retaining clips from the crossmember in this area.

29 Undo the two nuts securing the crossmember to the vehicle body on the driver's side end, and the single nut on the passenger's side **(see illustration)**.

30 Disconnect the passenger airbag orange wiring connector. Undo the four retaining bolts and remove the airbag assembly.

31 On the passenger side, undo the two bolts securing the heater box to the crossmember, and the two bolts securing the heater box bracket. Release any wiring loom retaining clips.

32 Working in the engine compartment, undo the screws and remove the ECU cover from the plenum chamber. Prise off the retaining clip and remove the ECU from the box. Do not disconnect the ECU wiring plugs.

33 Working through the aperture exposed by the ECU removal, undo the two cross-head screws securing the wiring connector plate to

the crossmember. The plate is located on the bracket by two pegs.

34 Release the wiring loom from the retaining clips on the front side of the crossmember as it is withdrawn. The centre vent is bolted to the crossmember, but the retaining bolts can only be accessed once the crossmember has been partly withdrawn **(see illustration)**.

35 Make a final check to ensure all wiring connectors/loom retaining clips are released, and remove the crossmember.

36 If required, the centre bracket can be removed by carefully pulling the centre vent from the heater box, and remove the bracket securing bolts:

  a) *2 lower bolts each side.*
  b) *2 on the upper passenger side.*
  c) *2 on the driver's side upper (note the plastic cap on the threads to protect the wiring loom).*
  d) *2 on the driver's side into the heater box (one vertical, and one horizontal).*
  e) *1 bolt on the driver's side into the top of the heater box.*

37 Release any wiring loom retaining clips, and remove the bracket from the vehicle.

Refitting

38 Refitting is the reversal of removal, bearing in mind the following points:

  a) *Ensure all wiring looms are routed correctly, and secured properly.*
  b) *Tighten all fasteners securely.*

30 Glovebox – removal and refitting

Removal

1 Undo and remove the two screws below the storage compartment lid.

2 Open the glovebox lid and undo the five side retaining screws.

3 Prise out the top of the storage compartment light and disconnect the wiring plug.

4 Pull the storage compartment from the facia.

Refitting

5 Refit in the reverse order of removal.

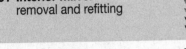

31 Interior mirror –
removal and refitting

 Warning: Use extreme care whilst attempting this procedure; the windscreen is easily cracked.

Mirror without rain sensor

Removal

1 Twist the mirror 90° anti-clockwise, and remove it from the mounting plate.

Refitting

2 To refit, position the support arm at 90° to the vertical, then carefully turn it clockwise to the point where the lock spring is felt to engage.

Mirror with rain sensor

Removal

3 Carefully prise apart the left- and right-hand covers from the base of the mirror.
4 Pull the wiring connector from the base, then separate it.
5 Pull the mirror downwards to release the clips, and withdraw the sensor.

Refitting

6 Refitting is a reversal of removal.

Mirror mounting plate

7 If the mirror mounting plate becomes detached, clean away the old glue, then apply a suitable glass-to-metal glue in accordance with the glue manufacturer's instructions, and refit the mounting plate into position. Ensure that the plate is correctly orientated, so that when the mirror is fully fitted to it, the mirror support arm is vertical.

32 Seats –
removal and refitting

Front seat

 Warning: Both front seats are equipped with side airbags. Prior to disconnecting the airbag wiring plug, it is essential you are electrostatically discharged by touching a door lock or vehicle body briefly.

Removal

1 Disconnect the battery negative cable (see Chapter 5A).
2 Move the seat forwards to the extent of its travel.
3 At the inner side of the seat, prise out the cap, undo the screw and prise up the rear of the inner seat rail cover and pull it backwards from the rail.
4 At the outer side of the seat, prise out the cap, undo the screw and prise up the rear of the outer seat rail cover and pull it forwards from the rail.

32.6 Squeeze the retaining clip lugs, and move the seat to the rear

5 Move the seat fully rearwards. At the front of the seat, unscrew and remove the two securing bolts.
6 Pinch together the lugs of the retaining clip at the from of the seat, and slide the seat to the rear and off the rails (see illustration).
7 Unplug the airbag wiring from the underside of the seat (see warning above), and where fitted the wiring plugs for the seat heating and motor systems and remove the seat from the vehicle.
Note: *Whilst the seat is removed from the vehicle, VW insist that the side airbag should still be earthed. This can be achieved with a VW adapter/loom (VAS 5094) plugged into the connector on the seat and the connector to the airbag module (see illustration). In the absence of the VW adapter/loom, connect a cable from the top right-hand terminal or the connector under the seat (nearest the adjustment handle) to a good chassis earth*

point. **Due to the risk of injury or component failure, no further dismantling of the seats is recommended.**

Refitting

8 Refit the seat in the reverse order of removal. **Note:** *If after refitting the seat(s), the airbag warning light on the dash signals a fault, take the vehicle to a VW dealer or suitably-equipped specialist, to have the self diagnosis system interrogated and the fault code erased.*

Rear seat bench (Saloon models)

Removal

9 Grasp the front lower edge of the seat and pull it upwards, to release the retaining pins from their plastic sockets. Note that plastic sockets may be removed from the floor during the seat removal – refit them before installing the seat bench.
10 Slide the seat bench forward and remove it from the vehicle.

Refitting

11 Refit the seat bench in the reverse order of removal.

Rear seat bench (Estate models)

Removal

12 Prise out the covers and undo the screws, then remove the covers from the two front hinges.
13 Using a pair of pliers, pull out the hinge pins.
14 Withdraw the rear seat bench from inside the car.

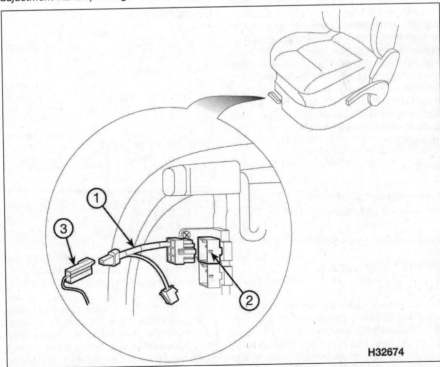

H32674

32.7 Plug the VW adapter/loom (1) into the connector nearest the adjustment handle (2) and the airbag module connector (3)

Refitting

15 Refitting is a reversal of removal.

Rear seat backrest (one-piece)

Removal

16 Remove the rear seat bench as described above.

17 Remove the head restraints, then push down the material around the head restraint guides, and release the locking tabs by pushing them forwards with a screwdriver. Pull out the guides.

18 Fold down the centre armrest, push the locking tabs outwards, and remove the frame.

19 Unscrew the rear seat backrest centre mounting bolt.

20 On models with a centre three-point seat belt, unbolt the centre stalk, then, at the top of the backrest, prise out the cover and unclip the belt guide.

21 Release the backrest from the clips located near the outer head restraints, then lift the backrest upwards from the sill panel clips.

Refitting

22 Refit the seat backrest in the reverse order of removal.

Rear seat backrest (split)

Removal

23 On models **without** a centre three-point seat belt, fold down the backrests, then unbolt the locking plate from the centre mounting bracket. Lift the inner end of the right-hand backrest and withdraw it from the outer pin. Similarly, lift the inner end of the left-hand backrest and withdraw it from the outer pin.

24 On models **with** a centre three-point seat belt, remove the rear seat bench as described previously in this section, then unbolt the centre seat belt. Fold down the backrests then unbolt the locking plate from the centre mounting bracket. Lift the inner end of the right-hand backrest and withdraw it from the outer pin. Similarly, lift the inner end of the left-hand backrest and withdraw it from the outer pin.

Refitting

25 Refit the seat backrest in the reverse order of removal.

33 Interior trim – removal and refitting

Interior trim panels

Removal

1 The interior trim panels are secured using either screws or various types of trim fasteners, usually studs or clips.

2 Check that there are no other panels overlapping the one to be removed; usually there is a sequence that has to be followed, and this will only become obvious on close inspection.

3 Remove all obvious fasteners, such as screws. If the panel will not come free, it is held by hidden clips or fasteners. These are usually situated around the edge of the panel and can be prised up to release them; note, however that they can break quite easily so new ones should be available. The best way of releasing such clips without the correct type of tool, is to use a large flat-bladed screwdriver. Note in many cases that the adjacent sealing strip must be prised back to release a panel.

4 When removing a panel, **never** use excessive force or the panel may be damaged; always check carefully that all fasteners or other relevant components have been removed or released before attempting to withdraw a panel.

Refitting

5 Refitting is the reverse of the removal procedure; secure the fasteners by pressing them firmly into place and ensure that all disturbed components are correctly secured to prevent rattles.

Carpets

6 The passenger compartment floor carpet is in one piece and is secured at its edges by screws or clips, usually the same fasteners used to secure the various adjoining trim panels.

7 Carpet removal and refitting is reasonably straightforward but very time-consuming because all adjoining trim panels must be removed first, as must components such as the seats, the centre console and seat belt lower anchorages.

Headlining

8 The headlining is clipped to the roof and can be withdrawn only once all fittings such as the grab handles, sunvisors, sunroof (if fitted), windscreen and rear quarter windows and related trim panels have been removed and the door, tailgate and sunroof aperture sealing strips (as applicable) have been prised clear.

9 Note that headlining removal requires considerable skill and experience if it is to be carried out without damage and is therefore best entrusted to an expert.

34 Seat belt tensioning mechanism – general information

All models are fitted with seat belt pretensioners that are integrated into the airbag control system. The system is designed to instantaneously take up any slack in the seat belt in the case of a direct or oblique frontal impact, therefore reducing the possibility of injury to the occupants. Each front seat inertia reel is fitted with its own tensioner, which is triggered by a frontal impact above a predetermined force. Lesser impacts and impacts to the rear of the vehicle will not trigger the system.

When the system is triggered, the explosive gas in the tensioner mechanism retracts and locks the seat belt. This prevents the seat belt moving and keeps the occupant firmly in position in the seat. Once the tensioner has been triggered, the seat belt will be permanently locked and the assembly must be renewed, together with the impact sensors.

The pretensioners are rendered safe to handle by loosening the inertia reel mounting bolts.

Note the following warnings before contemplating any work on the front seat belts.

Warning:
• *Do not expose the tensioner mechanism to temperatures in excess of 100°C (212°F).*
• *If the tensioner mechanism is dropped, it must be renewed, even it has suffered no apparent damage.*
• *Do not allow any solvents to come into contact with the tensioner mechanism.*
• *Do not attempt to open the tensioner mechanism as it contains explosive gas.*
• *Tensioners must be discharged before they are disposed of, but this task should be entrusted to a VW dealer.*

35 Seat belts – general, removal and refitting

Note: *Refer to the warnings in Section 34 before working on the front seat belts.*

General

1 Periodically check the belts for fraying or other damage. If evident, renew the belt.

2 If the belts become dirty, wipe them with a damp cloth, using a little liquid detergent only.

3 Check the tightness of the anchor bolts, and if they are ever disconnected, make quite sure that the original sequence of fitting of washers, bushes, and anchor plate is retained.

4 Access to the front belt height adjuster and inertia reel units can be made by removing the trim from the B-pillar on the side concerned.

5 The rear seat belt anchorages can be checked by removing the rear seat bench. Access to the rear seat inertia reel units is made by removing the rear seat backrest, parcel shelf and luggage area side trim.

6 The torque wrench settings for the seat belt anchor bolts and other attachments are given in the Specifications at the start of this Chapter.

7 Never modify the seat belts, or alter the attachments to the body, in any way.

Removal

Front seat belt

8 Pull away the door weatherstrip from the sill, A-pillar and B-pillar.

9 Remove the lower A-pillar trim. To do this, prise out the cap from the lower retaining screw, then unscrew the two screws and

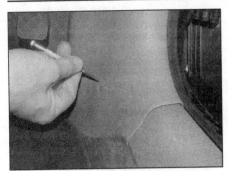

35.9a Prise out the cap . . .

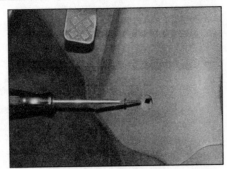

35.9b . . . undo the screw . . .

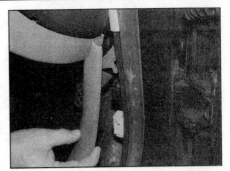

35.9c . . . and remove the lower A-pillar trim

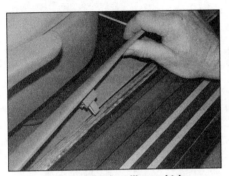

35.10 Unclip the sill panel trim

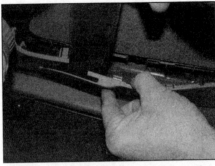

35.11a Disconnect the seat belt from the trim . . .

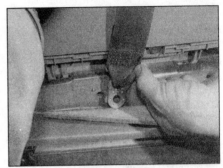

35.11b . . . then unscrew the front seat lower anchor bolt

unclip the small trim from the bottom of the A-pillar **(see illustrations)**.

10 Pull off (unclip) the sill panel trim from the front to behind the B-pillar **(see illustration)**.

11 Disconnect the belt from the trim, then unscrew the front seat lower anchor bolt **(see illustrations)**.

12 Pull off (unclip) the upper B-pillar trim, first at the sides then at the top. Feed the seat belt through the trim **(see illustration)**. If any of the clips remains in the body, use pliers to remove it and fit it to the trim.

13 Pull off (unclip) the lower B-pillar trim, starting at the top, then release the lower clips from the body with a screwdriver, and lift the trim upwards. Where necessary, disconnect the wiring from the switch mounted in the trim **(see illustrations)**.

14 Unbolt the seat belt anchor from the height adjuster, then unbolt the guide from the B-pillar **(see illustrations)**.

15 Unscrew the seat belt inertia reel mounting bolt and withdraw the reel unit and belt from the B-pillar **(see illustrations)**. **Note**: *The action of loosening the mounting bolt renders the reel pretensioner inactive and 'safe'.*

16 To remove the front seat belt stalk, first remove the front seat as described in Section 32. Unscrew the bolt, remove the washer, and withdraw the stalk from the seat followed by the spacer.

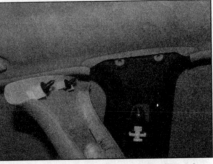

35.12 Unclipping the upper B-pillar trim

35.13a Disconnect the wiring from the switch . . .

35.13b . . . then unclip the lower B-pillar trim

35.14a Unbolt the seat belt anchor from the height adjuster . . .

35.14b . . . then unbolt the guide from the B-pillar

35.15a Front seat belt inertia reel and mounting bolt

35.15b Removing the front seat belt inertia reel unit

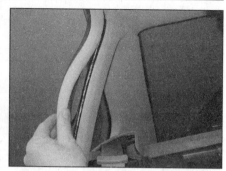

35.17 Pull away the door weatherstrip

35.19 Removing the backrest striker pin

35.21 Rear seat belt inertia reel unit

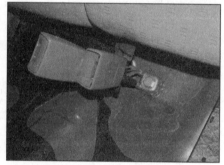

35.23 Rear seat belt stalks

Rear side seat belt

17 Pull away the door weatherstrip from the rear area of the rear door aperture **(see illustration)**.

18 Fold the rear seat backrest forwards.

19 Unscrew the nut and remove the backrest

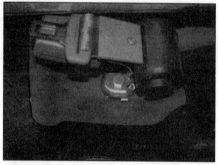

35.25 Rear centre seat belt inertia reel unit

striker pin from the side padding **(see illustration)**.

20 Pull the side padding from the body clip, press the lower locking lug from the sill strip, and pull the padding upwards.

21 Unscrew the mounting bolt and unhook the seat belt and inertia reel unit from the body **(see illustration)**. **Note:** *The action of loosening the mounting bolt renders the reel pretensioner inactive and 'safe'.*

22 Unscrew the rear seat belt upper anchor bolt, then open the guide and remove the inertia reel unit and belt.

23 To remove the rear seat belt stalk, first remove the bench (Section 32). Unbolt the stalk from the floor **(see illustration)**.

Rear centre seat belt

Note: *Removal of the backrest-mounted rear centre seat belt inertia reel requires removal of the backrest upholstery and is best left to a specialist.*

24 Remove the rear seat bench.

25 Unscrew the mounting bolt and withdraw the rear centre seat belt inertia reel unit from the floor **(see illustration)**.

Refitting

26 Refitting is a reversal of removal.

36 Sunvisors –
removal and refitting

Removal

1 Swing the sunvisor out of its retaining clip. Prise off the plastic cover to expose the clip retaining screw. Undo the screw and remove the retaining clip **(see illustration)**.

2 To remove the sunvisor/hinge, prise out the plastic cap, undo the retaining screw and remove the hinge/visor.

Refitting

3 Refitting is a reversal of removal.

37 Grab handles –
removal and refitting

Removal

1 Hold down the grab handle, and prise out the plastic caps. Undo the retaining screws and remove the handles **(see illustration)**.

Refitting

2 Refitting is a reversal of removal.

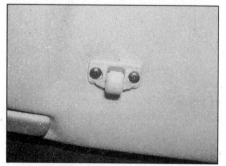

36.1 Prise off the plastic cover, and remove the sunvisor retaining clip screw

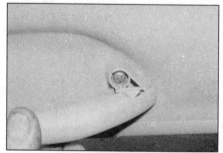

37.1 Hold the grab handle down, prise out the plastic cap and undo the retaining screw

Chapter 12
Body electrical system

Contents

Section number

Airbag system – general information and precautions. 22
Airbag system components – removal and refitting. 23
Anti-theft alarm system – general information 24
Central locking system – general information 17
Convenience system electronic control unit – removal and refitting . 25
Electrical discharge headlight system – component removal, refitting
    and adjustment. 10
Electrical fault finding – general information 2
Exterior light bulbs – renewal. 7
Exterior light units – removal, refitting and beam adjustment 9
Fuses and relays – general information 3
General information and precautions. 1
Horns – removal and refitting. 15

Section number

Ignition switch/steering column lock – removal and refitting. 4
Instrument panel – removal and refitting 11
Interior light bulbs – renewal 8
Parking aid components – general, removal and refitting 18
Radio aerial – removal and refitting 20
Radio/CD player – removal and refitting 19
Speakers – removal and refitting 21
Steering column combination switch – removal and refitting 5
Sunroof motor – removal and refitting 16
Switches – removal and refitting 6
Tailgate wiper motor – removal and refitting 14
Washer system – general. 13
Windscreen wiper components – removal and refitting. 12

Degrees of difficulty

Easy, suitable for novice with little experience	Fairly easy, suitable for beginner with some experience	Fairly difficult, suitable for competent DIY mechanic	Difficult, suitable for experienced DIY mechanic	Very difficult, suitable for expert DIY or professional

Specifications

System type.	12 volt, negative earth

Bulbs — Power rating (watts)

Direction indicators	21
Direction indicator side repeaters	5
Foglamp:	
Front.	55
Rear	21
Headlight:	
Dipped	55
Main	55
Number plate light	5
Reversing light	21
Sidelights	5
Stop and tail lights	21/5
Stop-light (separate).	21
Tail light (separate)	5

Torque wrench settings

	Nm	lbf ft
Driver's airbag securing plate-to-steering wheel screws.	4	3
Passenger airbag unit-to-facia screws.	4	3
Rear combination light	3	2
Rear window wiper arm nut	15	11
Rear window wiper mounting bracket nuts	8	6
Windscreen wiper arm nuts	16	12
Windscreen wiper linkage bolts	8	6

1 General information and precautions

⚠️ **Warning: Before carrying out any work on the electrical system, read through the precautions given in 'Safety first!' at the beginning of this manual, and in Chapter 5A.**

1 The electrical system is of 12 volt negative earth type. Power for the lights and all electrical accessories is supplied by a lead-acid type battery which is charged by the alternator.

2 This Chapter covers repair and service procedures for the various electrical components not associated with the engine. Information on the battery, alternator and starter motor can be found in Chapter 5A.

3 It should be noted that prior to working on any component in the electrical system, the battery negative terminal should first be disconnected to prevent the possibility of electrical short-circuits and/or fires. **Note:** *If the vehicle has a security-coded radio, check that you have a copy of the code number before disconnecting the battery. Refer to your VW dealer if in doubt.*

2 Electrical fault finding – general information

Note: *Refer to the precautions given in 'Safety first!' and in Chapter 5A before starting work. The following tests relate to testing of the main electrical circuits, and should not be used to test delicate electronic circuits (such as anti-lock braking systems), particularly where an electronic control unit is used.*

General

1 Typically, electrical circuit consists of an electrical component, any switches, relays, motors, fuses, fusible links or circuit breakers related to that component, and the wiring and connectors which link the component to both the battery and the chassis. To help to pinpoint a problem in an electrical circuit, wiring diagrams are included at the end of this Chapter.

2 Have a good look at the appropriate wiring diagram, before attempting to diagnose an electrical fault, to obtain a complete understanding of the components included in the particular circuit concerned. The possible sources of a fault can be narrowed down by noting if other components related to the circuit are operating properly. If several components or circuits fail at one time, the problem is likely to be related to a shared fuse or earth connection.

3 An electrical problem will usually stem from simple cause, such as loose or corroded connections, a faulty earth connection, a blown fuse, a melted fusible link, or a faulty relay (refer to Section 3 for details of testing relays). Visually inspect the condition of all fuses, wires and connections in a problem circuit before testing the components. Use the wiring diagrams to determine which terminal connections will need to be checked in order to pinpoint the trouble-spot.

4 The basic tools required for electrical fault finding include a circuit tester or voltmeter (a 12 volt bulb with a set of test leads can also be used for certain tests); a self-powered test light (sometimes known as a continuity tester); an ohmmeter (to measure resistance); a battery and set of test leads; and a jumper wire, preferably with a circuit breaker or fuse incorporated, which can be used to bypass suspect wires or electrical components. Before attempting to locate a problem with test instruments, use the wiring diagram to determine where to make the connections.

5 Sometimes, an intermittent wiring fault (usually caused to a poor or dirty connection, or damaged wiring insulation) can be pinpointed by performing a wiggle test on the wiring. This involves wiggling the wiring by hand to see if the fault occurs as the wiring is moved. It should be possible to narrow down the source of the fault to a particular section of wiring. This method of testing can be used in conjunction with any of the tests described in the following sub-Sections.

6 Apart from problems due to poor connections, two basic types of fault can occur in an electrical circuit: open-circuit, or short-circuit.

7 Largely, open-circuit faults are caused by a break somewhere in the circuit, which prevents current from flowing. An open-circuit fault will prevent a component from working, but will not cause the relevant circuit fuse to blow.

8 Low resistance or short-circuit faults are caused by a 'short'; a failure point which allows the current flowing in the circuit to 'escape' along an alternative route, somewhere in the circuit. This typically occurs when a positive supply wire touches either an earth wire, or an earthed component such as the bodyshell. Such faults are normally caused by a breakdown in wiring insulation, A short circuit fault will normally cause the relevant circuit fuse to blow.

9 Fuses are designed to protect a circuit from being overloaded. A blown fuse indicates that there may be problem in that particular circuit and it is important to identify and rectify the problem before renewing the fuse. Always renew a blown fuse with one of the correct current rating; fitting a fuse of a different rating may cause an overloaded circuit to overheat and even catch fire.

Finding an open-circuit

10 One of the most straightforward ways of finding an open-circuit fault is by using a circuit test meter or voltmeter. Connect one lead of the meter to either the negative battery terminal or a known good earth. Connect the other lead to a connector in the circuit being tested, preferably nearest to the battery or fuse. Switch on the circuit, bearing in mind that some circuits are live only when the ignition switch is moved to a particular position. If voltage is present (indicated either by the tester bulb lighting or a voltmeter reading, as applicable), this means that the section of the circuit between the relevant connector and the battery is problem-free. Continue to check the remainder of the circuit in the same fashion. When a point is reached at which no voltage is present, the problem must lie between that point and the previous test point with voltage. Most problems can be traced to a broken, corroded or loose connection.

Finding a short-circuit

11 Loading the circuit during testing will produce false results and may damage your test equipment, so all electrical loads must be disconnected from the circuit before it can be checked for short circuits. Loads are the components which draw current from a circuit, such as bulbs, motors, heating elements, etc.

12 Keep both the ignition and the circuit under test switched off, then remove the relevant fuse from the circuit, and connect a circuit test meter or voltmeter to the fuse connections.

13 Switch on the circuit, bearing in mind that some circuits are live only when the ignition switch is moved to a particular position. If voltage is present (indicated either by the tester bulb lighting or a voltmeter reading, as applicable), this means that there is a short-circuit. If no voltage is present, but the fuse still blows with the load(s) connected, this indicates an internal fault in the load(s).

Finding an earth fault

14 The battery negative terminal is connected to 'earth': the metal of the engine/transmission and the car body – and most systems are wired so that they only receive a positive feed, the current returning through the metal of the car body. This means that the component mounting and the body form part of that circuit. Loose or corroded mountings can therefore cause a range of electrical faults, ranging from total failure of a circuit, to a puzzling partial fault. In particular, lights may shine dimly (especially when another circuit sharing the same earth point is in operation), motors (eg, wiper motors or the radiator auxiliary cooling fan motor) may run slowly, and the operation of one circuit may have an apparently unrelated effect on another. Note that on many vehicles, earth straps are used between certain components, such as the engine/transmission and the body, usually where there is no metal-to-metal contact between components due to flexible rubber mountings, etc.

15 To check whether a component is properly earthed, disconnect the battery and connect one lead of an ohmmeter to a known good earth point. Connect the other lead to the wire or earth connection being tested.

3.2 The main fusebox is located behind a trim panel at the driver's end of the facia

3.11 The relays are located next to the steering column behind the lower facia trim panel

The resistance reading should be zero; if not, check the connection as follows.

16 If an earth connection is thought to be faulty, dismantle the connection and clean back to bare metal both the bodyshell and the wire terminal or the component earth connection mating surface. Be careful to remove all traces of dirt and corrosion, then use a knife to trim away any paint, so that a clean metal-to-metal joint is made. On reassembly, tighten the joint fasteners securely; if a wire terminal is being refitted, use serrated washers between the terminal and the bodyshell to ensure a clean and secure connection. When the connection is remade, prevent the onset of corrosion in the future by applying a coat of petroleum jelly or silicone-based grease or by spraying on (at regular intervals) a proprietary ignition sealer or a water dispersant lubricant.

3 Fuses and relays – general information

Main fuses

1 The fuses are located on a single panel at the right-hand end of the facia on RHD models, and at the left-hand end on LHD models.

2 Access to the fuses is gained by pulling open the cover panel **(see illustration)**.

3 Each fuse is numbered; the fuses' ratings and circuits they protect are listed on the rear face of the cover panel. A list of fuses is given with the wiring diagrams.

4 On some models (depending on specification), some additional fuses are located in separate holders next to the relays.

5 To remove a fuse, first switch off the circuit concerned (or the ignition), then pull the fuse out of its terminals. The wire within the fuse should be visible; if the fuse is blown the wire will have a break in it, which will be visible through the plastic casing.

6 Always renew a fuse with one of an identical rating; never use a fuse with a different rating from the original or substitute anything else. Never renew a fuse more than once without tracing the source of the trouble. The fuse rating is stamped on top of the fuse; note that the fuses are also colour-coded for easy recognition.

7 If a new fuse blows immediately, find the cause before renewing it again; a short to earth as a result of faulty insulation is most likely. Where a fuse protects more than one circuit, try to isolate the defect by switching on each circuit in turn (if possible) until the fuse blows again. Always carry a supply of spare fuses of each relevant rating on the vehicle, a spare of each rating should be clipped into the base of the fusebox.

Fusible links

8 On diesel models, the glow plug electrical supply circuit is protected by a fusible link. The link is located inside a protective plastic box at the rear of the engine compartment, next to the heater intake vent. A melted link indicates a serious wiring fault or a glow plug failure – renewing the link should **not** be attempted without first diagnosing the cause of the problem.

9 Prior to renewing the link, first disconnect the battery negative cable (see Chapter 5A). Unclip the cover to gain access to the metal link. Slacken the retaining screws, then slide the link out of position.

10 Fit the new link (noting the information given in paragraphs 6 and 7) then tighten its retaining screws securely and clip the cover into position.

Relays

11 The relays are mounted on common base, which is accessed by removing the trim panel from the underside of the steering column **(see illustration)**.

12 The relays are of sealed construction, and cannot be repaired if faulty. The relays are of the plug-in type, and may be removed by pulling directly from their terminals. In some cases, it will be necessary to prise the two plastic clips outwards before removing the relay.

13 If a circuit or system controlled by a relay develops a fault and the relay is suspect, operate the system; if the relay is functioning, it should be possible to hear it click as it is energised. If this is the case, the fault lies with the components or wiring of the system. If the relay is not being energised, then either the relay is not receiving a main supply or a switching voltage, or the relay itself is faulty. Testing is by the substitution of a known good unit, but be careful; while some relays are identical in appearance and in operation, others look similar but perform different functions.

14 To renew a relay, first ensure that the ignition switch is off. The relay can then simply be pulled out from the socket and the new relay pressed in. **Note:** *The direction indicator/ hazard warning relay is incorporated into the hazard warning light switch; see Section 6 for removal details.*

4 Ignition switch/ steering column lock – removal and refitting

Refer to the information given in Chapter 10.

5 Steering column combination switch – removal and refitting

Removal

1 Disconnect the battery negative lead (refer to Section 1 and Chapter 5A).

2 Refer to Chapter 10 and remove the steering wheel.

3 Undo the retaining screws and remove the upper and lower column shrouds. The upper shroud is retained by two cross-head screws inserted from the under side of the column,

5.3 Steering column upper and lower shroud retaining bolts (arrowed)

5.4 Slacken the column switch clamp screw

5.5a Use a small screwdriver . . .

5.5b . . . to carefully separate the column switch elements

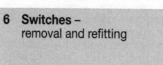

5.6 When refitting the column upper shroud, ensure that the locating lug engages correctly (arrowed)

and the lower shroud is retained by two cross-head screws and a hexagon socket-head bolt. Note that it will be necessary to undo the two screws and remove the steering column height adjustment lever grip **(see illustration)**.

4 Slacken the clamp sleeve screw and remove the combination switch assembly from the steering column, disconnecting the wiring plugs as the switch is withdrawn **(see illustration)**.

5 Release the retaining clips and detach the relevant section of the switch assembly **(see illustrations)**. **Note:** *Do not turn the spring contact assembly whilst the steering wheel is removed. On models equipped with ESP, the steering angle sensor can be detached from the combination switch, but after re-installation, specialist equipment is required*

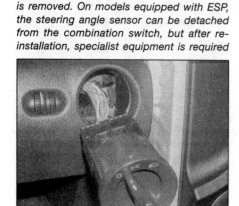

6.1 With the light switch in position O, press the switch centre inwards, turn it slightly to the right, and withdraw the switch from the panel

to perform a 'zero comparison'. Therefore we recommend that removal and refitting of the angle sensor is entrusted to a VW dealer or specialist.

Refitting

6 Refit the switch over the steering column, reconnecting the wiring plugs, but do not tighten the clamp sleeve screw at this stage. Temporarily refit the steering wheel, and position the switch so that there is a 3 mm gap between the steering wheel and switch. Tighten the clamp sleeve screw and remove the steering wheel. The remainder of refitting is a reversal of removal, noting that the upper column shroud engages with locating lugs at the front edge **(see illustration)**. Ensure that the wiring connections are securely made. Check for satisfactory operation on completion.

6 Switches – removal and refitting

Facia-mounted light switch

1 With the light switch in position O, press the switch centre inwards and turn it slightly to the right. Hold this position and pull the switch from the dash **(see illustration)**.

2 As the switch is withdrawn from the dash, disconnect the wiring plug.

3 To refit, reconnect the wiring plug.

4 Hold the switch and press the rotary part inwards and slightly to the right.

5 Insert the switch into the dash, turn the rotary part to position O and release. Check the switch for correct operation.

Door mirror adjuster

6 Remove the door inner trim panel, as described in Chapter 11.

7 Detach the wiring connector. Compress the retaining lugs on the underside of the switch and push it from the door trim panel.

8 Refit in the reverse order of removal.

Sunroof control

9 The sunroof control switch is only available as a complete unit with the interior light and switch panel. Carefully prise the trim from behind the control switch.

10 Remove the two cross-head screws **(see illustration)**.

11 Lift out the switch with the interior light, and disconnect the wiring plugs as the assembly is removed.

12 Refit in the reverse order of removal.

Courtesy light switches

13 The courtesy light are controlled by micro-switches incorporated into the door locks. The switches are not available separately. If defective, the door lock assembly must be renewed (see Chapter 11).

Handbrake warning switch

14 Remove the rear section of the centre console as described in Chapter 11.

15 Undo the screw and remove the switch from the lever. On some models the switch is

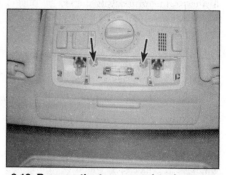

6.10 Remove the two cross-head screws (arrowed)

6.15 Unclip the handbrake warning switch from the lever

6.18 Carefully release the grip trim

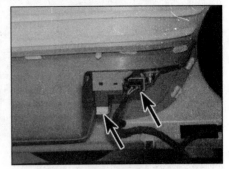

6.20a Disconnect the wiring . . .

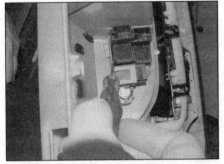

6.20b . . . then prise the switch to one side . . .

6.20c . . . and remove it from the trim panel

6.29 Squeeze in the retaining lugs either side of the range control/dash illumination adjuster, and pull it from the rear of the panel

simply clipped in place on the handbrake lever mounting bracket (see illustration).

16 Detach the wiring connector from the switch.

17 Refit in the reverse order of removal.

Window switches

Driver's door switch panel

Note: *The driver's side electric window switches cannot be removed individually, the complete door switch panel must be renewed*

18 Open the door and insert a thin-bladed screwdriver between the door trim and the grip recess/switch panel. Push the screwdriver in and release the grip trim (see illustration), then carefully prise the grip recess/switch panel up and away from the door trim.

19 Disconnect the wiring plug, then undo the three retaining screws and separate the switch block/control unit from the trim.

Individual door switch

20 Remove the door trim panel as described in Chapter 11, then disconnect the wiring and use a screwdriver to prise the switch sideways from the trim panel (see illustrations).

Passenger's door

22 The passenger's door window switch is mounted alongside the interior door handle. Remove the interior handle as described in Chapter 11, Section 20.

23 Remove the retaining screw and withdraw the switch.

Stop-light switch

24 Refer to Chapter 9.

Steering column switch

25 Refer to Section 5.

Headlight control/ dash illumination

26 Unclip the trim panel from the driver's side end of the facia. Undo the two screws securing the end of the lower trim panel.

27 Unscrew the two bolts securing the lower facia trim panel.

28 Unplug the wiring from the lighting switch and headlight range control/dash illumination adjuster as the panel is withdrawn.

29 Squeeze in the retaining lugs either side of the range control/dash illumination adjuster, and pull it from the rear of the panel (see illustration).

30 Refit in the reverse order of removal.

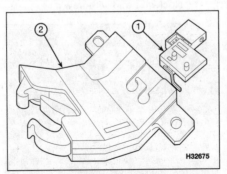

6.33 Push the luggage compartment light switch (1) down and release it from the lock assembly (2)

Luggage compartment light

31 The switch is incorporated into the tailgate/boot lid lock. Remove the tailgate/boot lid lock as described in Chapter 11.

32 Remove the switch protective cap from the lock.

33 Release the switch locking device and pull the switch from the lock (see illustration).

34 Refitting is a reversal of removal.

Heated rear window/hazard warning/seat heating/ESP/ASR

35 Using a screwdriver, carefully prise the switch from the trim (see illustration). Take great care not to damage the surrounding area.

36 Disconnect the wiring plug(s) from the switch.

6.35 Carefully prise the switch from the trim

6.38 Prise the fuel filler flap release switch from the centre console

37 To refit, reconnect the wiring plug(s), push the switch into the appropriate hole in the facia.

Fuel filler flap release

38 The fuel filler flap release switch is located under the handbrake lever in the centre console. Using a thin-bladed screwdriver, carefully prise the switch from the console, and disconnect the wiring plug **(see illustration)**

39 To refit the switch, reconnect the wiring plug and push the switch into the console.

7 Exterior light bulbs – renewal

1 Whenever a bulb is renewed, note the following points:
   a) *Remember that if the light has just been in use, the bulb may be extremely hot.*
   b) ***Do not*** *touch the bulb glass with the fingers, as the small deposits can cause the bulb to cloud over.*
   c) *Always check the bulb contacts and holder, ensuring that there is clean metal-to-metal contact. Clean off any corrosion or dirt before fitting a new bulb.*
   d) *Wherever bayonet-type bulbs are fitted, ensure that the live contacts bear firmly against the bulb contact.*
   e) *Always ensure that the new bulb is of the correct rating and that it is completely clean before fitting it.*

Headlight

Note: *Access to the rear of the headlights is very limited, and for the inexperienced home mechanic it may well be better to remove the headlight completely as described in Section 9. This section does not cover bulb renewal on models fitted with gas discharge headlights; refer to Section 10 for renewal details.*

Main beam

2 Remove the triangular plastic cover from the rear of the headlight unit **(see illustration)**.

3 Twist the bulbholder anti-clockwise and withdraw it from the rear of the headlight **(see illustration)**.

4 Pull the bulb directly from the bulbholder **(see illustration)**, noting which way round it is fitted. If the bulb is to be refitted, do not touch the glass with the fingers. If the glass is accidentally touched, clean it with methylated spirit.

5 Fit the new bulb using a reversal of the removal procedure. On completion have the beam adjustment checked at the earliest opportunity.

Dipped beam

6 Remove the round cover from the rear of the headlight unit **(see illustration)**.

7 Twist the bulbholder anti-clockwise and withdraw it from the rear of the headlight **(see illustration)**.

8 Pull the bulb directly from the bulbholder, noting which way round it is fitted **(see illustration)**. If the bulb is to be refitted, do not touch the glass with the fingers. If the glass is accidentally touched, clean it with methylated spirit.

9 Fit the new bulb using a reversal of the removal procedure. On completion have the beam adjustment checked at the earliest opportunity.

Sidelight

Note: *Access to the rear of the headlights is very limited, and for the inexperienced home mechanic it may well be better to remove the headlight completely as described in Section 9. This section does not cover sidelight bulb renewal on models fitted with gas discharge headlights; refer to Section 10 for renewal details.*

10 Remove the triangular plastic cover from the rear of the headlight unit.

11 Pull out the sidelight bulbholder and bulb from the reflector **(see illustration)**.

12 Pull the wedge-type bulb directly from the bulbholder **(see illustration)**.

13 Fit the new bulb using a reversal of the removal procedure.

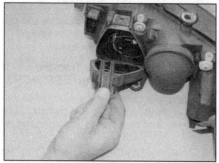

7.2 Remove the triangular plastic cover . . .

7.3 . . . then twist the bulbholder anti-clockwise and withdraw it . . .

7.4 . . . and pull the main beam bulb directly from the bulbholder, noting which way round it is fitted

7.6 Remove the round cover from the rear of the headlight unit . . .

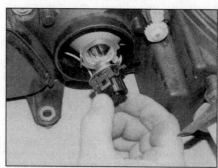

7.7 . . . twist the bulbholder anti-clockwise from the headlight . . .

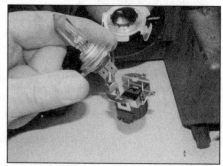

7.8 . . . then pull the dipped beam bulb directly from the bulbholder

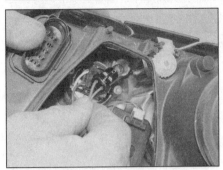

7.11 Pull out the sidelight bulbholder and bulb . . .

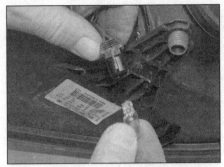

7.12 . . . then pull the wedge-type bulb directly from the bulbholder

7.15 Twist the cap from the rear of the foglamp . . .

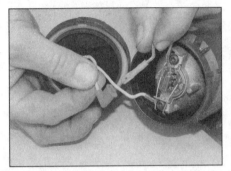

7.16 . . . disconnect the wiring at the connector . . .

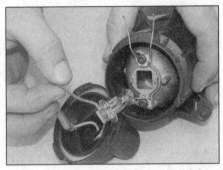

7.17 . . . then release the clip and withdraw the foglamp bulb

7.19 Twist the front direction indicator bulbholder anti-clockwise to remove it . . .

Front foglamp

14 Remove the front foglamp as described in Section 9.

15 Twist the cap from the rear of the foglamp **(see illustration)**.

16 Disconnect the wiring at the connector **(see illustration)**.

17 Release the retaining clip legs from the bar, and withdraw the front foglamp bulb, noting how it is located **(see illustration)**.

18 Fit the new bulb using a reversal of the removal procedure. On completion, have the beam adjustment checked at the earliest opportunity.

Direction indicator

Note: *This section does not cover sidelight bulb renewal on models fitted with gas discharge headlights; refer to Section 10 for renewal details.*

19 Reach down behind the front headlight unit and twist the front direction indicator bulbholder anti-clockwise to remove it **(see illustration)**.

20 Depress and twist the bulb to remove it from the bulbholder **(see illustration)**.

21 Fit the new bulb using a reversal of removal procedure.

Direction indicator side repeater

22 Note that some late models are fitted with LED side repeaters in the exterior door mirrors **(see illustration)**. At the time of writing, no information was available for this type of installation.

23 On the standard side repeater, push the lens towards the front of the vehicle, then tilt it out at the rear to release the lens from the bodywork **(see illustration)**. **Note:** *The side repeater can be fitted either way round, and*

7.20 . . . then depress and twist the bulb from the bulbholder

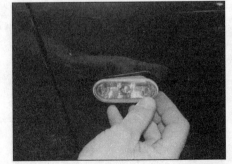

7.23 Push the lens towards the front of the vehicle . . .

it is impossible to determine how it is fitted. If difficulty is experienced, push the lens in the opposite direction.

24 Hold the side repeater in one hand then pull out the rubber bulbholder **(see illustration)**.

7.22 LED-type side repeater located in the exterior door mirrors

7.24 . . . pull out the rubber bulbholder . . .

7.25 . . . then pull the wedge-type bulb from the bulbholder

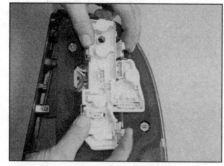

7.30 Squeeze the plastic tabs to withdraw the bulbholder from the rear light unit

7.31 Removing a bulb from the bulbholder

7.33a On Estate models, undo the screws . . .

7.33b . . . and remove the accessory rack/ tool kit holder

7.34 Removing the rear direction indicator bulb on Estate models

25 Pull the wedge-type bulb from the bulb-holder (see illustration).

26 Fit the new bulb using a reversal of the removal procedure.

Rear combination light

Saloon models

27 Note that it is necessary to remove the rear light completely (see Section 9) if renewing a bulb in the combination unit with the reversing light bulbholder.

28 Remove the clips and fold the inner trim panel away from the side of the load space, to expose the rear of the light unit.

29 Disconnect the wiring plug.

30 Squeeze the plastic tabs and withdraw the bulbholder from the rear light unit (see illustration).

31 Press and twist the relevant bulb anti-clockwise, and withdraw it from the bulbholder (see illustration).

32 Fit the new bulb using a reversal of the removal procedure.

Estate models

33 Open the storage compartment flap adjacent to the rear light, and disconnect the wiring plug from the light unit. Where applicable when working on the left-hand side of the vehicle, remove the tool kit, car phone transceiver unit and any other audio components mounted in the accessory rack behind the trim panel. Undo the securing screws and remove the accessory rack/tool kit holder (see illustrations).

34 The rear direction indicator bulb is mounted separate to the main rear light bulbholder, and is removed by twisting the bulbholder anti-clockwise, then depressing and twisting the bulb (see illustration).

35 To remove the remaining bulbs, depress the plastic tabs and withdraw the main bulbholder from the rear light unit, then

depress and twist the relevant bulb anti-clockwise (see illustrations).

36 Fit the new bulb using a reversal of the removal procedure.

Number plate light

37 The number plate lights are located in the boot lid or tailgate, just above the number plate. For better access to the retaining screws, open the boot lid or tailgate. Undo the two retaining screws and prise out the relevant lens/bulbholder (see illustrations).

38 Remove the festoon-type bulb from its holder (see illustration).

39 Fit the new bulb using a reversal of the removal procedure.

High-level stop-light

Saloon models

40 With the boot lid open, use a screwdriver to prise the high-level stop-light bulbholder

7.35a Depress the tabs . . .

7.35b . . . and withdraw the main bulbholder . . .

7.35c . . . then depress and twist the relevant bulb to remove it from the bulbholder

7.37a Undo the two retaining screws . . .

7.37b . . . and prise out the number plate lens/bulbholder

7.38 Removing the festoon-type bulb from the number plate light

7.42 Remove the tailgate trim panels on Estate models . . .

7.43a . . . then undo the screws . . .

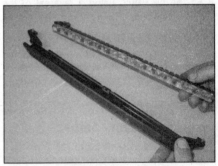

7.43b . . . withdraw the high-level stop-light and disconnect the wiring

from the bracket. Note that LEDs are soldered to a printed circuit board and it is not possible to renew a single LED. Where an LED is not functioning, the complete stop-light unit must be renewed.

41 Press the new stop-light bulbholder into position until retained by the clips.

Estate models

42 Remove the tailgate trim panels as described in Chapter 11 **(see illustration)**.
43 Undo the screws, withdraw the high-level stop-light and disconnect the wiring **(see illustrations)**.
44 Depress the locking lugs and separate the lens from the light unit **(see illustrations)**. Note that LEDs are soldered to a printed circuit board and it is not possible to renew a single LED. Where an LED is not functioning, the complete stop-light unit must be renewed.
45 Fit the new stop-light bulbholder using a reversal of the removal procedure.

7.44a Depress the locking lugs . . .

ensure that the live contact(s) bear firmly against the bulb contact.
d) *Always ensure that the new bulb is of the correct rating and that it is completely clean before fitting it.*

Interior/reading lights

Front

2 Unclip the lens from the light unit.
3 Remove the bulb from its holder. The courtesy light is fitted with a festoon bulb which can be prised from its spring contacts. The map reading lights are equipped with push-fit bulbs.
4 Fit the new bulb using a reversal of the removal procedure.

Rear

5 Prise free the light lens/unit, then twist and withdraw the combined bulb and bulbholder.
6 Fit the new bulb using a reversal of the removal procedure.

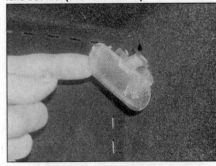

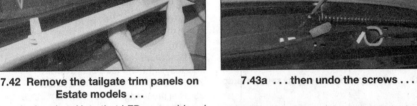

8 Interior light bulbs – renewal

1 Whenever a bulb is renewed, note the following points:
a) *Remember that if the light has just been in use, the bulb may be extremely hot.*
b) *Always check the bulb contacts and holder, ensuring that there is clean metal-to-metal contact between the bulb and its live and earth. Clean off any corrosion or dirt before fitting a new bulb.*
c) *Wherever bayonet-type bulbs are fitted,*

7.44b . . . and separate the high-level stop-light lens from the light unit

Luggage area and glovebox lights

7 Prise free the light lens/unit and extract the festoon bulb from its holder. When removing the glovebox light unit, prise the top of the lens out first **(see illustration)**.

8.7 When removing the glovebox light, prise the top of the lens out first

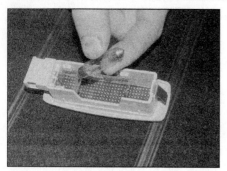

8.9 Prise the festoon bulb from its holder

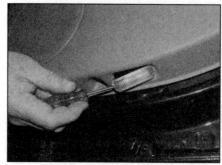

8.20 Prise the courtesy light from the bottom of the front door . . .

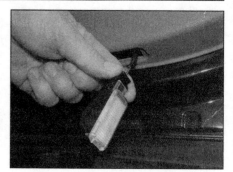

8.21 . . . disconnect the wiring . . .

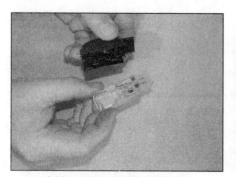

8.22 . . . prise off the lens . . .

8.23 . . . then pull out the wedge-type bulb

17 Pull the rotary switch centre section from the control panel.

18 Pull the bulb from its holder.

19 Fit the new bulb using a reversal of the removal procedure, noting that the switch centre section will only fit in one position.

Front door courtesy light

20 Use a screwdriver to prise the light from the bottom of the front door **(see illustration)**.

21 Disconnect the wiring and remove the courtesy light unit **(see illustration)**.

22 Prise off the lens **(see illustration)**.

23 Pull the wedge-type bulb from its contacts **(see illustration)**.

24 Fit the new bulb using a reversal of the removal procedure.

8 Fit the new bulb using a reversal of the removal procedure.

Sunvisor/vanity mirror light

9 Prise free the lens from the headlining above the sunvisor. The festoon bulbs can be extracted from their holders **(see illustration)**.

10 Fit the new bulb using a reversal of the removal procedure.

Instrument panel bulbs

11 On all models covered by this Manual, it is not possible to renew the instrument panel bulbs individually as they are of LED design and soldered to a printed circuit board. It is not possible to renew a single LED. Where an LED is not functioning, the complete instrument panel must be renewed.

Cigar lighter illumination

12 Open the ashtray, depress the locking tabs

and withdraw the ashtray from its housing. Disconnect the wiring plug.

13 Leaving the cigar lighter in the panel, pull free the bulbholder from the rear of the lighter, and extract the bulb from the holder.

14 Fit the new bulb using a reversal of the removal procedure.

Switch illumination

15 Switch illumination bulbs are usually built into the switch itself, and cannot be renewed separately. Refer to Section 6 and remove the switch – bulb renewal should then be self-evident, if it is possible; otherwise, renew the switch.

Heater control panel illumination

16 Only models fitted with conventional heating system (non-air conditioned) and controls are equipped with renewable bulbs.

| 9 | Exterior light units – removal, refitting and beam adjustment | |

Headlight unit

Note: *This section does not cover dipped beam bulb renewal on models fitted with gas discharge headlights; refer to Section 10 for renewal details.*

Removal

1 Remove the front bumper and plastic reinforcement strip as described in Chapter 11.

2 Mark the three headlight unit mounting bolts in relation to the crossmember in order to maintain the identical beam adjustment.

3 Using a screwdriver, prise out the protective cover concealing the innermost mounting bolt, then unscrew and remove the four mounting bolts **(see illustrations)**.

4 Slide the headlight unit forwards, disconnect the wiring plug and withdraw it from the front of the car **(see illustrations)**.

Refitting

5 Refitting is a reversal of the removal procedure. If a new unit is being fitted, align it so that the gap between the headlight and surrounding bodywork is even. On completion check for satisfactory operation, and have the headlight beam adjustment checked as soon as possible.

9.3a Remove the protective cover . . .

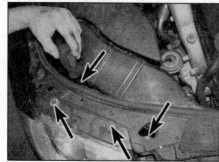

9.3b . . . then unscrew the mounting bolts . . .

9.4a ... slide the headlight unit forwards ...

9.4b ... disconnect the wiring ...

9.4c ... and withdraw the unit from the front of the car

9.6 Unclip the foglamp grille ...

9.7a Undo the mounting screws ...

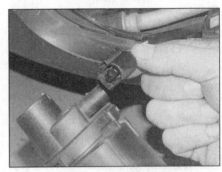

9.7b ... then withdraw the foglamp and disconnect the wiring

Front foglamp

Removal

6 Unclip the foglamp grille by releasing its innermost end first **(see illustration)**.

7 Undo the three mounting screws, withdraw the foglamp from the front bumper, and disconnect the wiring **(see illustrations)**.

Refitting

8 Refitting is a reversal of removal, but have the foglamp beam setting checked at the earliest opportunity. An approximate adjustment can be made by positioning the car 10 metres in front of a wall marked with the centre point of the foglamp lens. Turn the adjustment screw as required. Note that only height adjustment is possible – there is no lateral adjustment.

Direction indicator side repeater

Removal and refitting

9 The procedure is as described for bulb renewal in Section 7.

Range control motor

Removal

10 Remove the headlight unit.

11 Remove the triangular plastic cover from the rear of the headlight unit.

12 Disconnect the wiring from the range control motor.

13 Rotate the motor unit (clockwise for the left-hand headlight, anti-clockwise for right-hand headlight) until it is felt to disengage from the rear of the headlight unit.

14 Tilt the unit to one side so that the balljoint at the end of the adjustment shaft disengages from the socket at the of the lens, then withdraw the motor from the headlight unit **(see illustration)**.

Refitting

15 Refitting is a reversal of removal. It may be necessary to lift the reflector to allow the adjustment shaft balljoint to engage with its socket. On completion, check for satisfactory operation, and have the headlight beam adjustment checked as soon as possible.

Rear combination light (Saloon)

Removal

16 With the boot lid open, remove the clips and fold the inner trim panel away from the side of the load space, to expose the rear of the light unit.

17 Disconnect the wiring plug.

18 Depress the plastic tabs and withdraw the bulbholder from the rear light unit.

19 Undo the mounting nuts and withdraw the rear combination light from the rear of the car **(see illustrations)**.

9.14 Removing the range control motor from the headlight

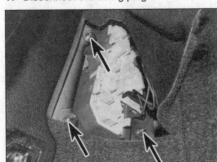

9.19a Undo the mounting nuts ...

9.19b ... and remove the rear combination light unit

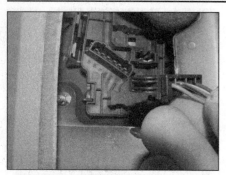

9.21 Disconnecting the wiring plug from the rear combination light on Estate models

Refitting

20 Refitting is a reversal of removal, but only tighten the mounting nuts to the specified torque, and ensure that the seal is correctly positioned.

Rear combination light (Estate)

Removal

21 Open the storage compartment flap adjacent to the rear light, and disconnect the wiring plug from the light unit **(see illustration)**. Where applicable when working on the left-hand side of the vehicle, remove the tool kit and holder, car phone transceiver unit and any other audio components mounted in the accessory rack behind the trim panel. Undo the securing screws and remove the accessory rack/tool kit holder .

22 Undo the mounting nuts and withdraw the rear combination light from the rear of the car **(see illustration)**.

23 Depress the plastic tabs and withdraw the bulbholder from the rear light unit.

Refitting

24 Refitting is a reversal of removal, but only tighten the mounting nuts to the specified torque, and ensure that the seal is correctly positioned.

Number plate light

Removal and refitting

25 The procedure is as described for bulb renewal in Section 7.

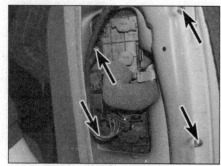

9.22 Rear combination light mounting nuts on Estate models

High-level stop-light

Removal and refitting

26 The procedure is as described for bulb renewal in Section 7.

Beam adjustment

Halogen headlights

27 Accurate adjustment of the headlight beam is only possible using optical beam setting equipment, and this work should therefore be carried out by a VW dealer or suitably-equipped workshop. Tyre pressures must correct, the car must be loaded with the driver (or equivalent of 75 kg), and the fuel tank should be at least 90% full. If the fuel tank is only half full, an additional weight of 30 kg must be positioned in the luggage compartment.

28 For reference, the headlights can be adjusted using the adjuster screws, accessible via the top of each light unit.

29 Some models are equipped with an electrically-operated headlight beam adjustment system which is controlled through the switch in the facia. On these models, ensure that the switch is set to the basic O position before adjusting the headlight aim.

---

10 Electrical discharge headlight system – component removal, refitting and adjustment

---

General information

1 Electrical discharge headlights were available as an optional extra on all models covered in this manual. The headlights are fitted with bulbs that produce light by means of an electric arc, rather than by heating a metal filament as in conventional halogen bulbs. The arc is generated by a control circuit which operates at voltages of above 28 000 volts. The intensity of the emitted light means that the headlight beam has to be controlled dynamically to avoid dazzling other road users. An electronic control unit monitors the vehicle's pitch and overall ride height by sensors mounted on the front and rear suspension and adjusts the beam range accordingly, using the range control motors built into the headlight units.

⚠ *Warning: The discharge bulb starter circuitry operate at extremely high voltages. To avoid the risk of electric shock, ensure that the battery negative cable is disconnected before working on the headlight units, then additionally switch the dipped beam on and off to discharge any residual volatage.*

Bulb renewal

Note: *Access to the rear of the headlights is very limited, and for the inexperienced home mechanic it may well be better to remove the headlight completely as described in Section 9.*

Headlight main beam

2 Reach down behind the headlight and remove the small plastic cover by releasing the clip and pulling the tab from the guide.

3 Twist the bulbholder anti-clockwise from the reflector. It is not necessary to undo the bulbholder screws.

4 Pull the bulb directly from the bulbholder, noting which way round it is fitted. If the bulb is to be refitted, do not touch the glass with the fingers. If the glass is accidentally touched, clean it with methylated spirit.

5 Fit the new bulb using a reversal of the removal procedure. On completion have the beam adjustment checked at the earliest opportunity.

Headlight dipped beam

Caution: The dipped beam bulb is under gas pressure of at least 10 bars, therefore it is recommended that protective glasses are worn during this procedure.

6 Remove the headlight as described in Section 9.

7 Undo the bolts and remove the triangular plastic cover.

8 Turn the wiring connector 90° anti-clockwise and remove it.

9 Pull the bulb directly from the bulbholder, noting which way round it is fitted. If the bulb is to be refitted, do not touch the glass with the fingers. If the glass is accidentally touched, clean it with methylated spirit.

10 Fit the new bulb using a reversal of the removal procedure. On completion have the beam adjustment checked at the earliest opportunity.

Sidelight

11 Reach down behind the headlight and remove the small plastic cover by releasing the clip and pulling the tab from the guide.

12 Pull out the sidelight bulbholder and bulb from the reflector.

13 Pull the wedge-type bulb directly from the bulbholder.

14 Fit the new bulb using a reversal of the removal procedure.

Bulb control unit

Removal

15 Remove the headlight as described in Section 9.

16 Undo the single screw securing the control unit retainer.

17 Release the retaining clip and withdraw the control unit from its location.

18 Undo the retaining screws and remove the triangular plastic cover from the rear of the headlight unit.

19 Turn the wiring connector 90° anti-clockwise and remove the lead from the dipped beam bulb. The control unit can now be removed from the headlight.

Refitting

20 Refitting is a reversal of removal.

Front ride height sensor

Removal

21 The sensor is mounted on the anti-roll bar in the front left-hand wheel housing. Apply the handbrake, then jack up the front of the vehicle and support it on axle stands (see *Jacking and vehicle support*).

22 Unplug the wiring connector from the sensor.

23 Unscrew the link retaining nut while counter-holding the flats on the ball-head pin with a further spanner.

24 Unscrew the Torx mounting bolts and remove the front ride height sensor.

Refitting

25 Refitting is a reversal of removal.

Rear ride height sensor

Removal

26 The sensor is secured to the left-hand side of the rear axle. Chock the front wheels, then jack up the rear of the vehicle and support it on axle stands (*see Jacking and vehicle support*).

27 Undo the screws and remove the cover from below the rear axle.

28 Unplug the wiring connector from the sensor.

29 Unscrew the link retaining nut while counter-holding the flats on the ball-head pin with a further spanner.

30 Unscrew the Torx mounting bolts and remove the rear ride height sensor.

Refitting

31 Refitting is a reversal of removal.

Direction indicator

Removal

32 Reach down behind the headlight and remove the small plastic cover by releasing the clip and pulling the tab from the guide.

33 Twist the bulbholder anti-clockwise from the reflector.

34 Pull the bulb directly from the bulbholder, noting which way round it is fitted. If the bulb is to be refitted, do not touch the glass with the fingers. If the glass is accidentally touched, clean it with methylated spirit.

Refitting

35 Fit the new bulb using a reversal of the removal procedure.

Setting-up for left- or right-hand drive

36 On models equipped with gas discharge headlights, the 'dipping' characteristics of the unit can be set-up for countries who drive on the left or right. Remove the small cover from the centre rear of the headlight for access to the setting lever.

37 *Press* the lever upwards for driving on the left, and down for driving on the right. Note that the lever has a hexagon socket for inserting an Allen key, however, the key

must not be *turned* as this will damage the lever.

Beam adjustment

38 The headlight range is controlled dynamically by an electronic control unit which monitors the ride height of the vehicle by sensors fitted to the front and rear suspension. Beam adjustment can only be carried out using VW test equipment.

Range control electronic control unit

Removal

39 The electronic control unit is located behind the trim on the left-hand side of the rear luggage compartment. Remove the trim with reference to Chapter 11. Where necessary, also remove the CD changer and bracket.

40 Disconnect the wiring, then undo the retaining screws and remove the unit.

Refitting

41 Refitting is a reversal of removal, but have the system settings checked by a VW dealer at the earliest opportunity.

Range control positioning motor

Removal

42 Remove the relevant headlight as described in Section 9.

43 Remove the large plastic cover from the rear of the headlight unit.

44 Disconnect the wiring.

45 Undo the mounting screws, then swivel the shaft ball head out of the guide on the reflector, and remove the motor.

Refitting

46 Refitting is a reversal of removal. On completion have the beam adjustment checked at the earliest opportunity.

---

11 Instrument panel – removal and refitting

Note: *The instrument panel includes the immobiliser control unit and its function is included in the vehicle's self-diagnosis program. If the instrument panel has a fault, it would be prudent to have the vehicle's fault code memory interrogated by a VW dealer or specialist, prior to removing the panel.*

Note: *If the instrument panel is being substituted with a new or exchange unit, the assistance of a VW dealer or specialist is required to initialise/adapt the various instrument panel functions.*

Removal

1 Disconnect the battery negative lead (see Chapter 5A).

2 Remove the steering wheel as described in Chapter 10.

11.3 Undo the steering column shroud retaining screws (arrowed)

3 Undo the retaining screws and remove the upper and lower column shrouds. The upper shroud is retained by two cross-head screws inserted from the under side of the column, and the upper shroud is retained by two cross-head screws and a hexagon socket-head bolt. Note that it will be necessary to lower the steering column height adjustment lever, and undo the two retaining screws to remove the handle grip **(see illustration)**.

4 Slacken the clamp sleeve screw and remove the combination switch assembly from the steering column, disconnecting the wiring plugs as the switch is withdrawn **(see illustration)**.

5 Prise out the caps, and remove the two screws securing the driver's side A-pillar trim beneath the facia. Unclip and remove the trim.

6 Unclip the trim panel from the driver's side end of the facia.

7 Refer to Chapter 11 and unscrew the two bolts securing the lower facia trim panel.

8 Unplug the wiring from the lighting switch and headlight range control/dash illumination adjuster as the panel is withdrawn.

9 Remove the four retaining screws and detach the steering column surround trim **(see illustration)**.

10 Undo the two retaining screws and remove the dash panel insert. Separate the electrical connectors as the panel is withdrawn **(see illustrations)**.

11 Remove the instrument panel from the facia.

11.4 Slacken the clamp screw, and disconnect the wiring plugs as the switch assembly is withdrawn

11.9 The steering column surround trim is retained by four screws (arrowed)

11.10a Undo the instrument panel screws . . .

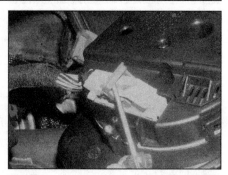

11.10b . . . lever up the lock and disconnect the wiring plugs as the panel is withdrawn

Refitting

12 Refitting is a reversal of removal, but see the note at the beginning of this section.

12 Windscreen wiper components – removal and refitting

Wiper blades

1 Refer to *Weekly checks.*

Wiper arms

2 If the wipers are not in their parked position, switch on the ignition, and allow the motor to automatically park.

3 Before removing an arm, mark its parked position on the glass with a strip of adhesive tape. Prise off the cover and unscrew the spindle nut **(see illustration)**. Note that on Estate models, the cover incorporates the

tailgate window washer jet. Remove the washer and ease the arm from the spindle by rocking it slowly from side-to-side.

4 Refitting is a reversal of removal, but before tightening the spindle nuts, position the wiper blades as marked before removal.

Wiper motor

Removal

5 Disconnect the battery negative terminal (see Chapter 5A).

6 Remove the wiper arms as described in the previous sub-Section.

7 Release the right (left on LHD models) and centre retaining clips and the single cross-head screw, securing the cowl panel to the panel edge below the windscreen **(see illustrations)**. Carefully prise the windscreen cowl panel up and out of the groove at the base of the windscreen.

8 Unscrew the five self-tapping screws securing the control unit housing cover.

9 The protective housing is secured by one nut inside the housing, and one nut outside the housing. Remove the nuts, carefully remove the housing from the rubber mounting, and push it forwards to allow access to the wiper motor and linkage **(see illustration)**. There is no need to disconnect any of the electrical connectors.

10 Slacken and remove the three mounting bolts and manoeuvre the wiper motor assembly out of position, disconnecting the wiring connector as it becomes accessible **(see illustration)**.

11 To separate the motor from the linkage, carefully prise the linkage arms off from the motor balljoint then undo the three retaining bolts and remove the motor **(see illustration)**.

Refitting

12 Refitting is the reverse of removal ensuring the mounting bolts are tightened securely. Also ensure that the cowl panel is correctly clipped in position.

12.3 Unscrew the wiper spindle nut

12.7a Release the cowl retaining clips . . .

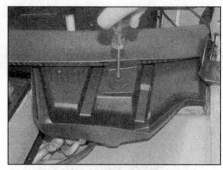

12.7b . . . and retaining screw

12.9 The protective housing is secured by one nut inside the housing, and one nut outside the housing (arrowed)

12.10 Slacken and remove the three mounting bolts (arrowed) and manoeuvre the wiper motor assembly out of position

12.11 Carefully prise the linkage arms off from the motor balljoint then undo the three retaining bolts and remove the motor

13 Washer system – general

1 All models are fitted with a windscreen washer system. Estate models also have a tailgate washer, and some models are fitted with headlight washers.

2 The fluid reservoir for the windscreen/headlight washer is located behind the left-hand side of the front bumper. The windscreen washer fluid pump is attached to the side of the reservoir body, as is the level sensor **(see illustrations)** and where headlight washers are fitted, a lift cylinder/accumulator is located in the supply tube, behind the front bumper. Access to the reservoir, pump and lift cylinder is achieved by removing either the left-hand front wheel arch liner or front bumper.

3 The tailgate washer is fed by the same reservoir and pump, operating in the reverse direction.

4 The reservoir fluid level must be regularly topped-up with windscreen washer fluid containing an antifreeze agent, but not cooling system antifreeze – see *Weekly checks*.

5 The supply hoses are attached by rubber couplings at their various connections, and if required, can be detached by simply pulling them free from the appropriate connector.

6 The windscreen washer jets can be adjusted by pushing the jet up or down in the holder with a finger. When adjusted correctly, the jets should be aimed at a point just above the centre of the wiper swept area. To remove a washer jet, pull off the hose, disconnect the wiring plug, push the jet forward and pull it downwards.

7 The headlight washer jets are best adjusted using the VW tool, and should therefore be entrusted to a VW garage to set.

14 Tailgate wiper motor – removal and refitting
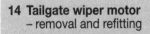

Removal

1 Make sure the tailgate wiper is switched off and in its rest position, then disconnect the battery negative lead (see Chapter 5A).

2 Remove the tailgate trim panel as described in Chapter 11.

3 Remove the wiper arm and blade as described in Section 12.

4 Detach the wiring connector from the wiper motor, then disconnect the washer jet hose.

5 Undo the three wiper motor mounting bolts and remove the wiper motor from the tailgate. Check the condition of the spindle rubber grommet in the tailgate, and if necessary, renew it.

Refitting

6 Refit in the reverse order of removal. Refit the wiper arm and blade so that the arm is parked correctly.

13.2a The windscreen washer fluid reservoir is located behind the left-hand side of the front bumper

15 Horns – removal and refitting

Removal

1 The horns are located at the front end of the vehicle, on the right- and left-hand corners between the front bumper and the inner wing. Access to the horns is achieved by removing the front bumper (see Chapter 11) **(see illustration)**.

2 With the bumper removed, undo the horn unit retaining bolt(s) and disconnect the wiring connector(s).

Refitting

3 Refit in the reverse order of removal. Check for satisfactory operation on completion.

16 Sunroof motor – removal and refitting

Closing sunroof manually

1 If the motor malfunctions when the roof panel is in the open position, it can be wound shut manually. To do this, unclip the trim from the overhead interior light switches by pulling down at the front of the trim, then release the manual cranking tool which is clipped to the inner surface of the trim. Insert the cranking tool into the hole at the end of the motor

15.1 Horn and mounting bracket

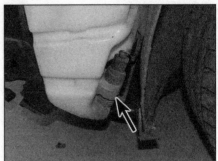

13.2b The washer motor fits into a grommet in the washer reservoir

shaft. The tool can then be turned to close the sunroof as required **(see illustration)**.

Motor

Removal

2 Ensure that the sunroof is fully closed – refer to paragraph 1 if the motor has failed. Disconnect the battery negative lead (refer to Chapter 5A).

3 Remove the cover from immediately behind the interior courtesy/map light unit.

4 Unplug the wiring connector from the motor assembly.

5 Undo and remove the mounting bolts and pull out the motor assembly.

6 The motor assembly is only available as a complete unit, no further dismantling is recommended.

Refitting

7 Refit in the reverse order of removal, noting the following points:

a) As with removal, it is important that the roof panel be in the closed position to ensure correct engagement. If the motor was activated whilst it was removed, or if a new motor is being fitted, it must be set for correct engagement before fitting. To do this, connect up the switch wiring to it and turn the switch to the closed position. This will activate the motor so that it is set at the closed position, ready for fitting.

b) Use new motor securing bolts and clean the threads of the corresponding mounting holes before refitting.

c) Check for satisfactory operation of the sunroof on completion.

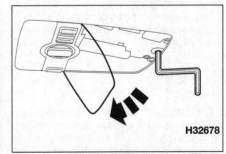

16.1 Unclip the plastic panel from behind the interior light switches, then release the sunroof manual cranking tool

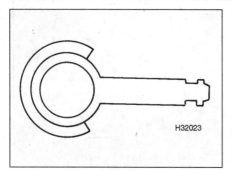

19.1 Radio/CD player removal tool

17 Central locking system
– general information

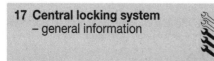

1 All models are equipped with a central door locking system, which automatically locks all doors and the rear tailgate/boot lid in unison with the manual locking of the driver's front door. The system is operated electronically with motors/switches incorporated into the door lock assemblies. The system is controlled by an electronic control unit located under the carpet in front of the left-hand front seat.
2 The control unit is equipped with a self-diagnosis capability. Should the system develop a fault, have the control unit interrogated by a VW dealer or suitably-equipped specialist. Once the fault has been established, refer to the relevant Section of Chapter 11 to renew a door lock or tailgate/boot lid lock as applicable.

18 Parking aid components
– general, removal and refitting

General information

1 The parking aid system is available on all models. Four ultrasound sensors located in the rear bumper measure the distance to the closest object behind the car, and inform the driver using acoustic signals from a buzzer located under the rear luggage compartment trim. The nearer the object, the more frequent the acoustic signals.
2 The system includes a control unit and self-diagnosis program, and therefore, in the event of a fault, the vehicle should be taken to a VW dealer.

Control unit

Removal

3 The control unit is located behind the right-hand trim in the rear luggage compartment. On Saloon models, pull back the trim but do not remove it. On Estate models, remove the trim completely.
4 Check that the ignition and all electrical consumers are switched off.

19.4 Slide the removal tools in fully until they click into place . . .

5 On Saloon models, disconnect the wiring plugs, then pull off the securing pins. Press together the side clips and remove the control unit.
6 On Estate models, release the lower securing clip holding the control unit and warning buzzer. Disconnect the wiring plugs, then pull off the securing pins, press together the side clips and remove the control unit from the mounting bracket.

Refitting

7 Refitting is a reversal of removal.

Range/distance sensor

Removal

8 It is not necessary to remove the rear bumper. Reach under the bumper and squeeze the retaining clips on the top and bottom of the sensor. Now press out the sensor inwards from the outside of the bumper.
9 Disconnect the wiring and remove the sensor.

Refitting

10 Refitting is a reversal of removal. Press the sensor firmly into position until the retaining clips engage.

Warning buzzer

Removal

11 On Saloon models, the warning buzzer is located beneath the rear shelf in the rear luggage compartment. First, switch off the ignition and all electrical consumers. Unclip the buzzer from its location and disconnect the wiring.

19.5 . . . then withdraw the radio/CD player

12 On Estate models, the warning buzzer is located behind the right-hand rear luggage compartment trim. Remove the trim, then unclip the control unit and buzzer assembly. Pull off the securing pins. press together the clips, remove the assembly from the mounting plate, and disconnect the wiring.

Refitting

13 Refitting is a reversal of removal.

19 Radio/CD player –
removal and refitting

Note: *This Section applies only to standard-fit audio equipment.*

Removal

1 The radio/CD player is fitted with special mounting clips, requiring the use of special removal tools, which should be supplied with the vehicle, or may be obtained from an in-car entertainment specialist. Alternatively, it may be possible to make up some removal tools **(see illustration)**.
2 Disconnect the battery negative lead (refer to Chapter 5A).
3 Insert the removal rods in the holes provided on the lower, or upper and lower edges of the radio/CD player unit (depending on model). **Note:** *It is necessary to remove the radio prior to removing the CD player.*
4 Slide the removal tools fully into the slots until they locate **(see illustration)**.
5 Withdraw the radio/CD player from the mounting case **(see illustration)**, then disconnect the loudspeaker, supply and aerial plugs. Note that some radio units also have a fuse fitted on the rear face.

Refitting

6 Refitting is a reversal of removal, but push the radio fully into its case until the spring clips are engaged. If the radio is of the security code type, it will be necessary to enter the code number before using the radio.

20 Radio aerial –
removal and refitting

Removal

1 The aerial mast can be unscrewed from the base by twisting anti-clockwise.
2 If the aerial base is to be removed, the rear of the headlining must be lowered for access (refer to Chapter 11).
3 Once the headlining has been lowered, disconnect the aerial lead at the connector, then unscrew the securing nut, and withdraw the aerial base from the roof. Hold the aerial base as the nut is being unscrewed to prevent the base from rotating and scratching the roof panel **(see illustrations)**. Recover the rubber spacer.

Refitting

4 Refitting is a reversal of removal.

21 Speakers –
removal and refitting

1 The audio system speakers are fitted in the front and rear door trim panels. Separate mid-range and high frequency tweeters are fitted in the front and rear door trim panels.

Low frequency speaker

2 To remove a door-mounted speaker, remove the appropriate door trim as described in Chapter 11.
3 Drill out the rivets securing the speaker, detach the wiring connectors and remove the speaker **(see illustration)**.
4 Refit in the reverse order of removal.

High frequency speaker

5 Remove the appropriate door trim as described in Chapter 11. The treble loudspeaker is permanently attached to the triangular exterior mirror cover.
6 Disconnect the wiring plug to the speaker, pull the top of the triangular cover out, then carefully slide the cover upwards and remove it **(see illustration)**.
7 Refit in the reverse order of removal.

22 Airbag system –
general information
and precautions

⚠ *Warning: Before carrying out any operations on the airbag system, disconnect the battery negative terminal (see Chapter 5A). When operations are complete, make sure no one is inside the vehicle when the battery is reconnected.*
• *Note that the airbag(s) must not be subjected to temperatures in excess of*

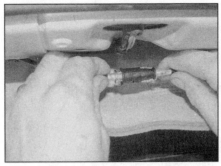

20.3a Once the rear of the headlining has been lowered, disconnect the aerial wiring plug . . .

90°C (194°F). When the airbag is removed, ensure that it is stored the correct way up to prevent possible inflation.
• *Do not allow any solvents or cleaning agents to contact the airbag assemblies. They must be cleaned using only a damp cloth.*
• *The airbags and control unit are both sensitive to impact. If either is dropped or damaged they should be renewed.*
• *Disconnect the airbag control unit wiring plug prior to using arc-welding equipment on the vehicle.*

Both a driver's and passenger's airbag were fitted as standard equipment to models in the Passat range. The driver's airbag is fitted to the centre of the steering wheel. The passenger's airbag is fitted to the upper surface of the facia, above the glovebox. The airbag system comprises the airbag unit(s) (complete with gas generators), an impact sensor, the control unit and a warning light in the instrument panel. Seat mounted side airbags and overhead curtain airbags are also fitted on certain models, and seat belt tensioners are incorporated in the front seat belt reels.

The airbag system is triggered in the event of a direct or offset frontal impact above a predetermined force. The airbag is inflated

20.3b . . . and unscrew the aerial base nut

within milliseconds, and forms a safety cushion between the driver and the steering wheel or (where applicable) the passenger and the facia. This prevents contact between the upper body and the steering wheel, column and facia, and therefore greatly reduces the risk of injury. The airbag then deflates almost immediately through vents in the side of the airbag.

Every time the ignition is switched on, the airbag control unit performs a self-test. The self-test takes approximately 3 seconds, and during this time the airbag warning light on the facia is illuminated. After the self-test has been completed, the warning light should go out. If the warning light fails to come on, remains illuminated after the initial 3-second period, or comes on at any time when the vehicle is being driven, there is a fault in the airbag system. The vehicle should then be taken to a VW dealer for examination at the earliest possible opportunity.

23 Airbag system components
– removal and refitting

Note: *Refer to the warnings in Section 21 before carrying out the following operations.*

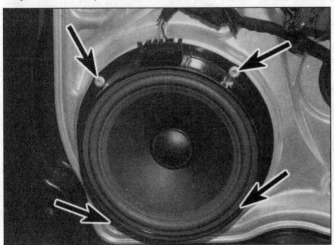

21.3 Drill out the rivets, and remove the door-mounted speaker

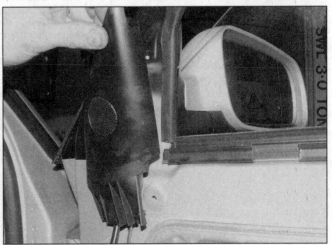

21.6 Pull the top of the triangular cover out, then carefully slide the cover up

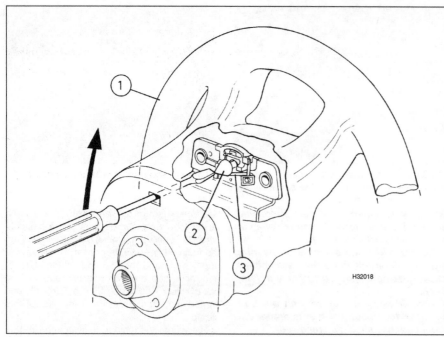

23.3a Insert a screwdriver approximately 45 mm and release the air bag retaining clip – four-spoked steering wheel . . .

1 *Steering wheel*	2 *Retaining clip*	3 *Locking lug*

1 Disconnect the battery negative terminal (see Chapter 5A).

Driver's airbag

2 Set the steering wheel to straight-ahead, then turn it 90° to the left or right. Release the steering column adjustment lever, and pull the wheel out and down as far as possible.
3 Locate the access hole in the reverse side

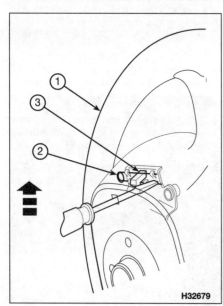

23.3b . . . and three-spoked steering wheel

1 *Steering wheel*
2 *Retaining clip*
3 *Locking catch*

of the steering wheel, and insert a long, flat-bladed screwdriver approximately 45 mm into the hole. Move the handle of the screwdriver upwards to release the airbag retaining clip **(see illustrations)**. Turn the airbag 180° and release the second retaining clip on the opposite side.
4 Temporarily touch the striker plate of the front door to discharge any electrostatic electricity. Return the steering wheel to the straight-ahead position, then carefully lift the airbag assembly away from the steering wheel and disconnect the wiring connector(s) from the rear of the unit **(see illustration)**. Note that the airbag must not be knocked or dropped, and should be stored the correct way up with its padded surface uppermost.
5 On refitting, reconnect the wiring connector(s) and locate the airbag unit in the steering wheel, making sure the wire does not become trapped. Switch on the ignition, **then** reconnect the battery negative lead.

23.4 Disconnect the wiring plug from the underside of the airbag

Passenger airbag

6 The passenger side airbag is located under a cover above the glovebox. Carefully pull the cover away from the facia and out of its retaining clips. Unscrew the three retaining nuts and detach it from the hinge plate.
7 Temporarily touch the striker plate of the front door to discharge any electrostatic electricity. Remove the four securing bolts, and lift the airbag upwards from its support brackets. Disconnect the wiring plug as the airbag is withdrawn **(see illustration)**. Note that the airbag must not be knocked or dropped, and should be stored the correct way up with its hinged surface uppermost.
8 Refitting is a reversal of removal. Ensure that the wiring connector is securely reconnected **(see illustration)**.
9 Ensure that no-one is inside the vehicle. Switch on the ignition, then reconnect the battery negative lead.

Airbag wiring contact unit

10 Set the front wheels in the straight-ahead position, then remove the steering wheel as described in Chapter 10.
11 Undo the retaining screws and remove the upper and lower column shrouds. The upper shroud is retained by two cross-head screws inserted from the under side of the column, and the upper shroud is retained by four cross-head screws and a hexagon socket-head bolt. Note that it will be necessary to lower the steering column height adjustment lever, undo the two securing screws and remove the adjustment lever grip.
12 Models without ESP (Electronic Stability Program), disconnect the wiring plug on the underside of the contact unit, and release the three locking clips. Remove the contact unit from the steering column switch **(see illustration)**.
13 On models fitted the ESP, the steering wheel angle sensor is incorporated into the contact unit. With the wheels in the straight-ahead position, a yellow spot must be visible in the top right-hand corner of the contact unit, and the markings must align **(see illustration)**. Release the four retaining clips and lift the contact unit from the column. Disconnect the wiring plug as the contact unit is removed.
14 Refitting is a reversal or removal, bearing in mind the following points:
a) *Ensure that the front wheels are in the straight-ahead position.*
b) *Ensure that the wiring plug is securely reconnected.*
c) *On models with ESP, if a new contact unit/steering angle sensor has been fitted, it must be initialised/adapted. Access to specialised diagnostic equipment is required. Consult your VW dealer or specialist.*
d) *Ensure that no-one is inside the vehicle, switch on the ignition, then reconnect the battery negative lead.*

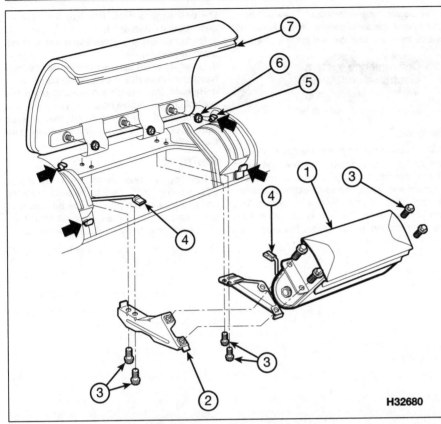

23.8 Passenger airbag connector

23.12 Release the three locking clips, and remove the contact unit from the steering column switch

23.7 Passenger airbag components

1	Airbag	3	Bolt
2	Support bracket	4	Connector

5	Retaining clip	6	Nut
		7	Cover

Airbag control unit

15 Refer to Chapter 11 and remove the dash panel and centre console.

16 The control unit is located beneath the heater housing (**see illustration**). Release the locking device and disconnect the wiring plug for the control unit.

17 Undo the retaining nuts and remove the control unit.

18 Refitting is a reversal of removal.

Side airbags

19 The side airbags are incorporated into the side of the front seats. Removal of the units requires the seat upholstery to be removed. This is a specialist task, which we recommend should be entrusted to a VW dealer or specialist.

Crash sensors for side airbags

20 The sensors are located under each front seat, immediately behind the floor crossmember. Remove the appropriate seat with reference to Chapter 11.

21 Carefully prise up the sill trim on the left-hand side, to enable the carpet to be lifted.

22 Disconnect the wiring plug from the sensor, and unscrew the two retaining Allen bolts. Remove the sensor (**see illustration**).

23 Refitting is a reversal of removal. After refitting, switch on the ignition, close all doors, and **then** reconnect the battery negative lead.

24 Anti-theft alarm system
– general information

An anti-theft alarm and immobiliser system is fitted as standard equipment. Should the system become faulty, the vehicle should be taken to

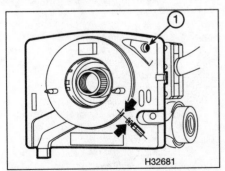

23.13 With the wheels straight-ahead, the yellow dot (1) should be visible, and the marks align

23.16 Airbag control unit

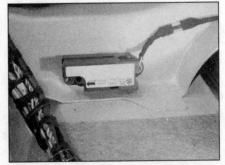

23.22 The side airbag crash sensors are secured by two Allen screws

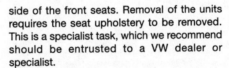

25.5 The convenience system control unit is housed in a plastic box in front of the passenger seat under the carpet

a VW dealer for examination. They will have access to a special diagnostic tester which will quickly trace any fault present in the system.

25 Convenience system electronic control unit
– removal and refitting

Removal

1 The convenience system electronic control unit (ECU) is responsible for the operation of the central locking, mirror adjustment, electric windows, heated exterior mirror, control panel illumination, anti-theft alarm, and interior lights. The ECU is located behind the floor crossmember, under the carpet on the passenger's side. Remove the seat as described in Chapter 11.

2 Undo the retaining screw and unclip footwell trim from the A-pillar.

3 Carefully prise up the sill trim on the left-hand side, to enable the carpet to be lifted.

4 Release the retaining clips and open the control unit protective box.

5 Disconnect the wiring plugs, and release the ECU from the retaining clips **(see illustration)**.

Refitting

6 Refitting is a reversal of removal. If a new ECU is being fitted, it will be necessary for the unit to be initialised prior to use by means of dedicated test equipment. Consult your local VW dealer or suitably-equipped specialist.

VW PASSAT wiring diagrams

Diagram 1

Key to symbols

Bulb	⊗	Item no.	**2**
Flashing bulb	⊗	Single speed pump/motor	Ⓜ
Switch		Twin speed motor	Ⓜ
Multiple contact switch (ganged)		Gauge/meter	⊘
Fuse/fusible link with rating	F28 15A	Earth point location	E4
Resistor		Diode	▸|
Variable resistor		Light emitting diode (LED)	
Variable resistor		Solenoid actuator	
Wire splice, unspecified connector or soldered joint		Heating element	
Connecting wires		Plug and socket connection	
Wire colour (green with yellow tracer)		Gn/Ge	

Dashed component outline denotes part of a larger item. Connectors may be shown in two ways;

Multiple connectors — 32a/1

Single connector — 2

32a/1   32 way connector A, pin 1
2   single connector, pin 2

Key to circuits

Diagram 1	Information for wiring diagrams
Diagram 2	Starting, charging, horn, cigar lighter & heater blower
Diagram 3	Side, tail, number plate lights, stop & reversing lights, headlights
Diagram 4	Direction indicators & hazard warning lights, front & rear foglights, headlight levelling
Diagram 5	Interior lighting, front & rear wash/wipe
Diagram 6	Instrument cluster
Diagram 7	Electric windows
Diagram 8	Central locking
Diagram 9	Electric mirrors, sunroof & heated rear window
Diagram 10	Audio system, ABS/TCS system

Earth locations

E1	Battery to body
E2	Next to relay plate
E3	Lower RH 'A' pillar
E4	Lower LH 'A' pillar
E5	Lower RH 'B' pillar
E6	Lower LH 'B' pillar
E7	At luggage compartment light
E8	LH front footwell
E9	LH rear pillar
E10	LH side of bulkhead
E11	RH rear pillar
E12	Rear roof rail
E13	Under rear shelf
E14	Below centre console
E15	On hydraulic unit

Passenger compartment fusebox 5

Fuse	Rating	Circuit protected
F1	5A	Heated washer jets
F2	10A	Direction indicators
F3	5A	Heated screen
F4	5A	Number plate lights
F5	10A	Heated seats, air conditioning, telematics system, multi-function steering wheel, solar roof, mirrors
F6	5A	Convenience system control unit
F7	10A	ABS/TCS, stop light switch, cruise control, engine management
F8	5A	Automatic headlight levelling
F9	5A	Parking light
F10	5A	CD changer, telephone, telematics system, multi-function steering wheel, navigation system, audio system
F11	5A	Memory seats, convenience system control unit
F12	10A	Diagnostic connector supply
F13	10A	Stop lights
F14	10A	Convenience system control unit
F15	10A	Instrument cluster, air conditioning, automatic gearbox
F16	5A	ABS/TCS, steering angle sensor
F17	10A	Special vehicles, two-way radio socket, ABS/TCS
	15A	Telematics system (USA)
F18	10A	RH main beam
F19	10A	LH main beam
F20	15A	RH dip beam
F21	15A	LH dip beam
F22	5A	RH side light
F23	5A	LH side light
F24	25A	Wiper system
F25	30A	Heater blower, air recirculation system, air conditioning, solar roof
F26	30A	Heated rear window
F27	15A	Rear wiper
F28	20A	Fuel pump, supplementary Diesel pump
F29	20A	Engine management, radiator cooling fan
F30	20A	Electric sunroof
F31	15A	Reversing lights, automatic gearbox, mirror, diagnostic connector
F32	20A	Engine management
F33	15A	Cigar lighter
F34	15A	Engine management
F35	30A	12V socket, tow bar
F36	15A	Fog lights
F37	20A	Audio system, navigation system, convenience system control unit
F38	15A	Convenience system control unit, door control unit
F39	15A	Hazard warning light system
F40	25A	Horn
F41	25A	Telematics system (USA)
F42	25A	ABS/TCS
F43	15A	EGR, coolant temperature sensor, engine management
F44	30A	Heated seats, convenience system control unit

H33202

Wire colours

Bl	Blue	Li	Purple
Br	Brown	Ws	White
Ge	Yellow	Or	Orange
Gr	Grey	Ro	Red
Gn	Green	Sw	Black

Key to items

1 Battery
2 Ignition switch
3 Starter motor
4 Alternator
5 Passenger compartment fusebox
6 Relay plate
  a = horn relay
  b = 'x' contact relay
7 Steering wheel clock springs

8 Horn switch
9 Low tone horn
10 High tone horn
11 Cigar lighter
12 Heater blower switch
  a = fresh air/recirc. flap switch
  b = fresh air/recirc. flap warning lamp
  c = switch illumination
  d = heater blower switch

13 Heater blower motor
14 Fresh air/recirc. flap motor
15 Heater blower resistors
16 Dash panel vent illumination

Diagram 2

H33203

Starting and charging

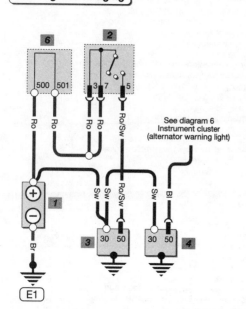

See diagram 6
Instrument cluster
(alternator warning light)

Horn

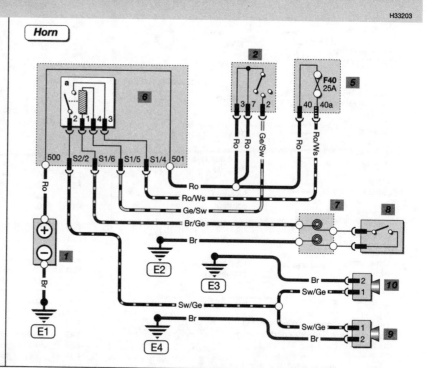

Cigar lighter

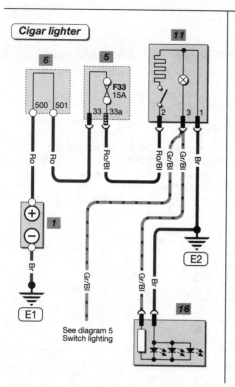

See diagram 5
Switch lighting

Heater blower

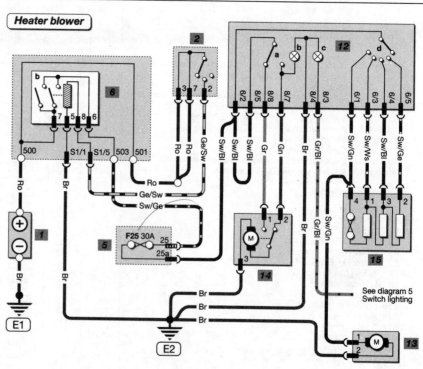

See diagram 5
Switch lighting

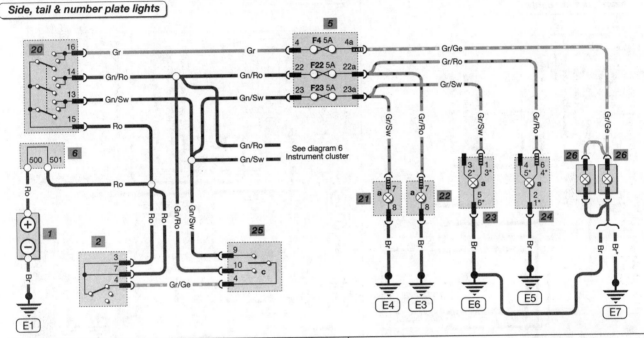

Wire colours

Bl	Blue	**Li**	Purple
Br	Brown	**Ws**	White
Ge	Yellow	**Or**	Orange
Gr	Grey	**Ro**	Red
Gn	Green	**Sw**	Black

* Estate models

Key to items

1 Battery
2 Ignition switch
5 Passenger compartment fusebox
6 Relay plate
20 Lighting switch
  a = side/headlight
21 LH headlight unit
  a = side light
  b = dip beam
  c = main beam
22 RH headlight unit
  (as above)

23 LH rear light unit
  a = side/tail light
  b = stop light
  c = reversing light
24 RH rear light unit
  (as above)
25 Multi-function switch
  a = headlight flash
  b = main/dip switch
  c = parking light/direction
    indicator switch
26 Number plate light

27 Stop light switch
28 Reversing light switch
29 High level stop light

Diagram 3

H33204

Side, tail & number plate lights

Headlights

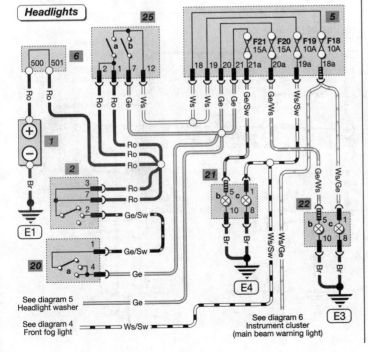

Stop & reversing lights

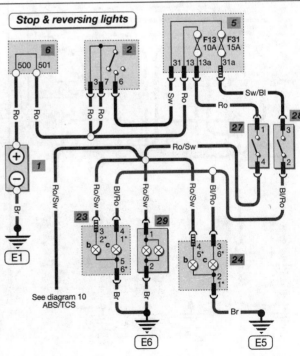

Wire colours

Bl	Blue	**Li**	Purple
Br	Brown	**Ws**	White
Ge	Yellow	**Or**	Orange
Gr	Grey	**Ro**	Red
Gn	Green	**Sw**	Black

* Estate models

Key to items

1 Battery
2 Ignition switch
5 Passenger compartment fusebox
6 Relay plate
  b = 'x' contact relief relay
20 Lighting switch
  a = side/headlight
  b = front/rear foglight
21 LH headlight unit
  d = direction indicator
  e = headlight levelling

22 RH headlight unit
  d = direction indicator
  e = headlight levelling
23 LH rear light unit
  d = direction indicator
  e = rear foglight
24 RH rear light unit
  d = direction indicator
25 Multi-function switch
  c = parking light/direction
    indicator switch

33 LH indicator side repeater
34 RH indicator side repeater
35 Hazard warning switch
36 Front foglight relay
37 LH front foglight
38 RH front foglight
39 Headlight levelling/lighting rheostat

Diagram 4

H33205

Direction indicators & hazard warning lights

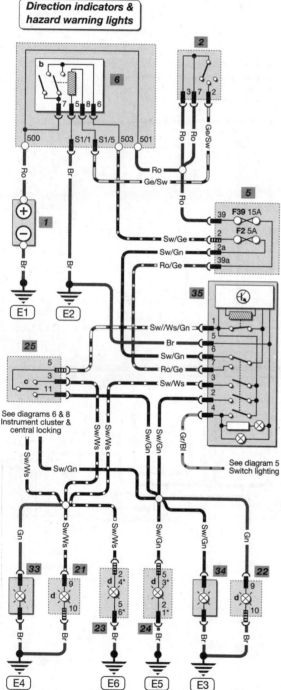

Front & rear foglights

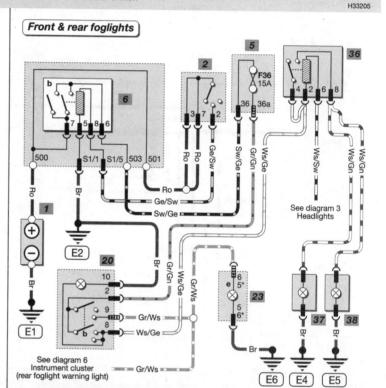

Headlight levelling

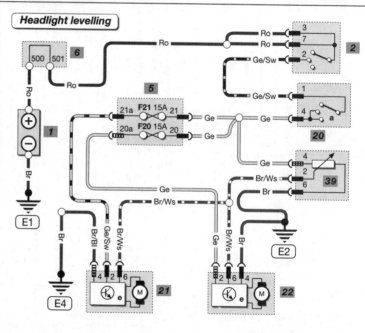

Wire colours

Bl	Blue	Li	Purple
Br	Brown	Ws	White
Ge	Yellow	Or	Orange
Gr	Grey	Ro	Red
Gn	Green	Sw	Black

* Estate models

Key to items

1 Battery
2 Ignition switch
5 Passenger compartment fusebox
6 Relay plate
  b = 'X' contact relief relay
20 Lighting switch
  a = side/headlight
  c = switch illumination
39 Headlight levelling/lighting rheostat
42 Convenience system control unit

43 Glovebox light/switch
44 Front interior light
  a = LH reading light
  b = interior light
  c = RH reading light
45 LH rear reading light
46 RH rear reading light
47 Vanity mirror light
48 Vanity mirror cover switch
49 Luggage compartment light

50 Luggage compartment light switch
51 Wash/wipe switch
  a = front wash/wipe
  b = rear wash/wipe
  c = intermittent wiper rheostat
52 Wash/wipe relay
53 Front/rear washer pump
54 Front wiper motor
55 Headlight washer pump
56 Rear wiper motor

Diagram 5

H33206

Interior lighting

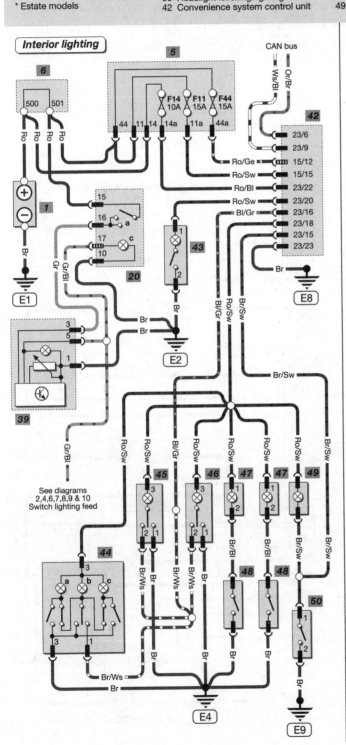

Front & rear wash/wipe

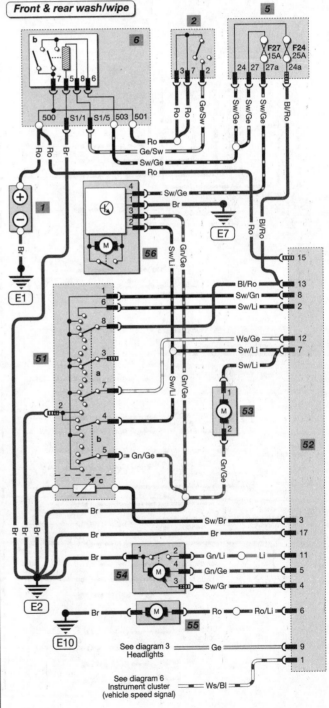

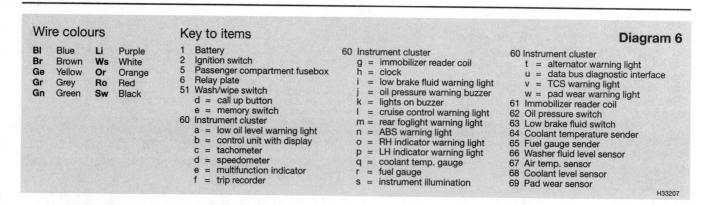

Wire colours

Bl	Blue	**Li**	Purple
Br	Brown	**Ws**	White
Ge	Yellow	**Or**	Orange
Gr	Grey	**Ro**	Red
Gn	Green	**Sw**	Black

Key to items

1 Battery
2 Ignition switch
5 Passenger compartment fusebox
6 Relay plate
51 Wash/wipe switch
  d = call up button
  e = memory switch
60 Instrument cluster
  a = low oil level warning light
  b = control unit with display
  c = tachometer
  d = speedometer
  e = multifunction indicator
  f = trip recorder

60 Instrument cluster
  g = immobilizer reader coil
  h = clock
  i = low brake fluid warning light
  j = oil pressure warning buzzer
  k = lights on buzzer
  l = cruise control warning light
  m = rear foglight warning light
  n = ABS warning light
  o = RH indicator warning light
  p = LH indicator warning light
  q = coolant temp. gauge
  r = fuel gauge
  s = instrument illumination

60 Instrument cluster
  t = alternator warning light
  u = data bus diagnostic interface
  v = TCS warning light
  w = pad wear warning light
61 Immobilizer reader coil
62 Oil pressure switch
63 Low brake fluid switch
64 Coolant temperature sender
65 Fuel gauge sender
66 Washer fluid level sensor
67 Air temp. sensor
68 Coolant level sensor
69 Pad wear sensor

Diagram 6

H33207

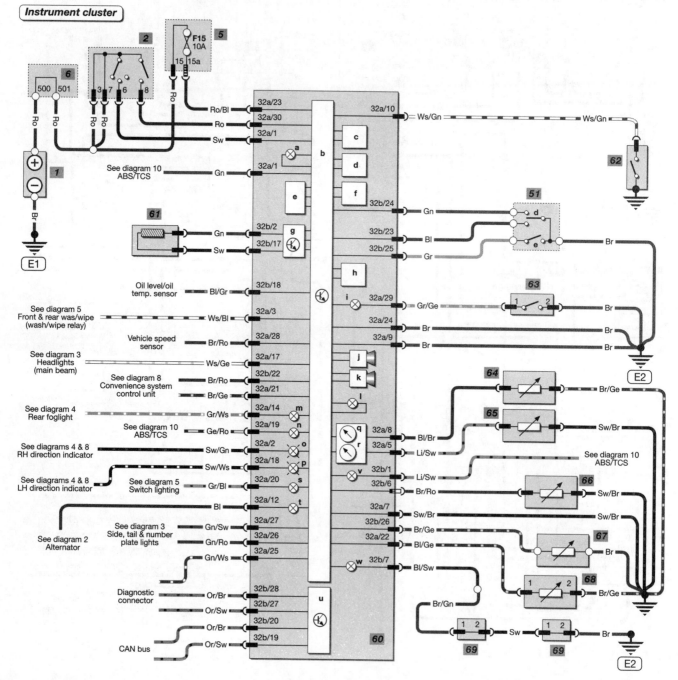

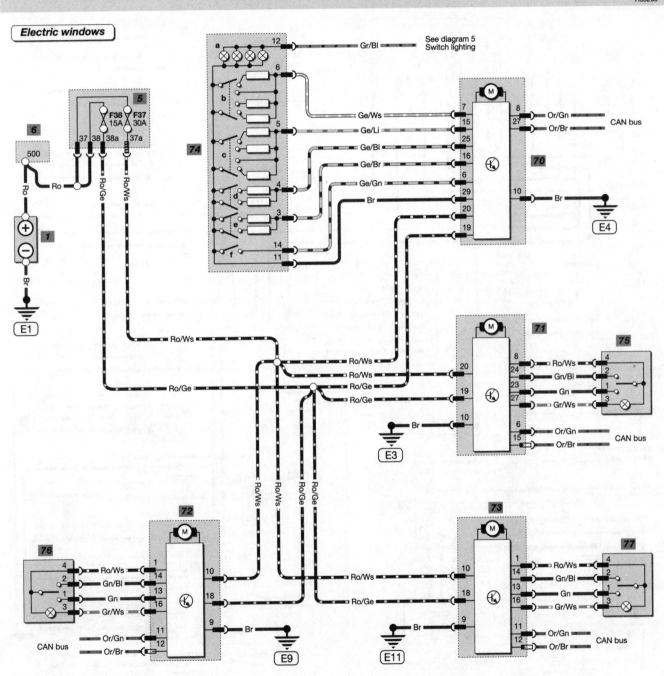

H33208

Wire colours

Bl	Blue	**Li**	Purple
Br	Brown	**Ws**	White
Ge	Yellow	**Or**	Orange
Gr	Grey	**Ro**	Red
Gn	Green	**Sw**	Black

* Estate models

Key to items

1 Battery
2 Ignition switch
5 Passenger compartment fusebox
6 Relay plate
42 Convenience system control unit
70 Driver's door control unit
71 Front passenger's door control unit
72 LH rear door control unit
73 RH rear door control unit

74 Driver's door window switch
  a = switch illumination
  g = interior locking switch
80 Central locking warning light
81 Driver's door lock
82 Driver's door courtesy light
83 Front passenger's door lock
84 Front passenger's door courtesy light
85 LH rear door losk

86 LH rear door courtesy light
87 RH rear door lock
88 RH rear door courtesy light
87 Tailgate/boot lid lock motor
88 Tailgate/boot lid lock switch
89 Filler cap release switch
90 Filler cap release motor

Diagram 8

H33209

Central locking

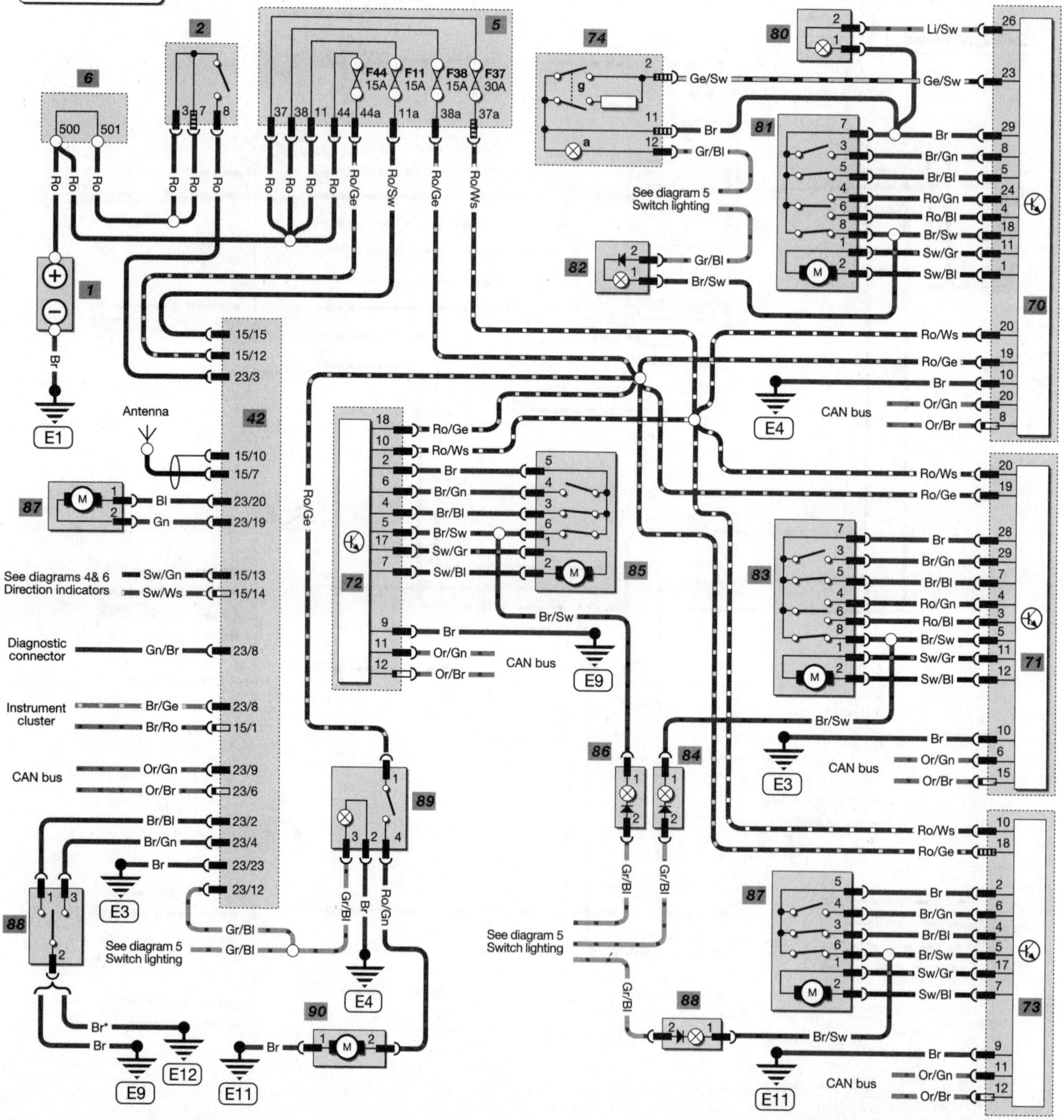

Wire colours

Bl	Blue	**Li**	Purple
Br	Brown	**Ws**	White
Ge	Yellow	**Or**	Orange
Gr	Grey	**Ro**	Red
Gn	Green	**Sw**	Black

* Estate models

Key to items

1 Battery
2 Ignition switch
5 Passenger compartment fusebox
6 Relay plate
  b = 'X' contact relief relay
70 Driver's door control unit
71 Front passenger's door control unit
93 Driver's mirror assembly
  a = mirror adjustment motor
  b = folding mirror motor
  c = folding mirror contact switch
  d = heating element

94 Passenger's mirror assembly
  a = mirror adjustment motor
  b = folding mirror motor
  c = folding mirror contact switch
  d = heating element
95 Mirror control switch
  a = mirror heating switch
  b = adjustment switch
  c = change-over switch
  d = folding mirror switch
  e = switch illumination

96 Sunroof motor
97 Sunroof control switch
  a = adjustment regulator
  b = lift/lower switch
98 Heated rear window switch
99 Heated rear window

Diagram 9

H33210

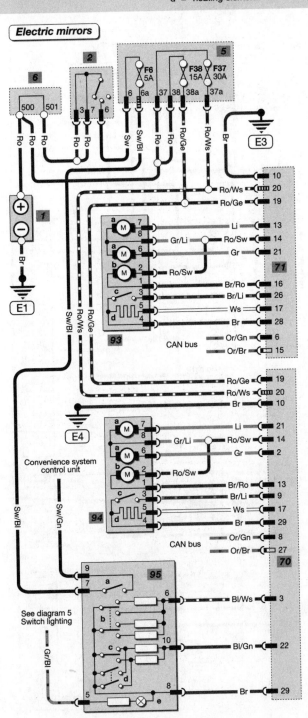

Electric mirrors

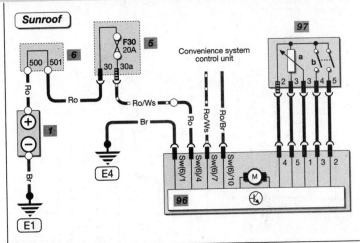

Sunroof

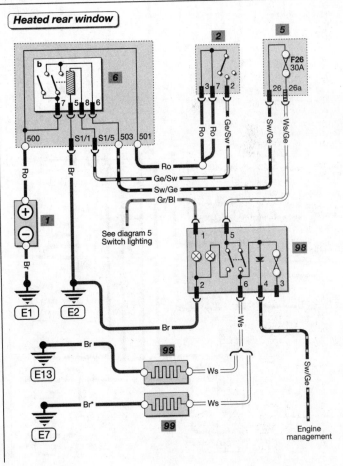

Heated rear window

Wire colours

Bl	Blue	**Li**	Purple
Br	Brown	**Ws**	White
Ge	Yellow	**Or**	Orange
Gr	Grey	**Ro**	Red
Gn	Green	**Sw**	Black

Key to items

1   Battery
2   Ignition switch
5   Passenger compartment fusebox
6   Relay plate
100 Audio unit
101 CD changer
102 LH front bass speaker
103 LH front tweeter
104 LH rear bass speaker
105 LH rear tweeter
106 RH front bass speaker
107 RH front tweeter
108 RH rear bass speaker

109 RH rear tweeter
110 ABS hydraulic unit
  a = control unit
  b = LH rear outlet valve
  c = LH rear inlet valve
  d = RH rear inlet valve
  e = RH rear outlet valve
  f = RH front inlet valve
  g = RH front outlet
  g = RH front outlet
  h = LH front inlet
  i = LH front outlet
  j = LH front EDL outlet

  k = RH front EDL outlet
  l = LH front EDL change over valve
  m = RH front EDL change over valve
  n = ABS solenoid valve relay
  o = return pump relay
  p = return pump
111 LH front wheel sensor
112 LH rear wheel sensor
113 RH front wheel sensor
114 RH rear wheel sensor
115 TCS switch

Diagram 10

H33211

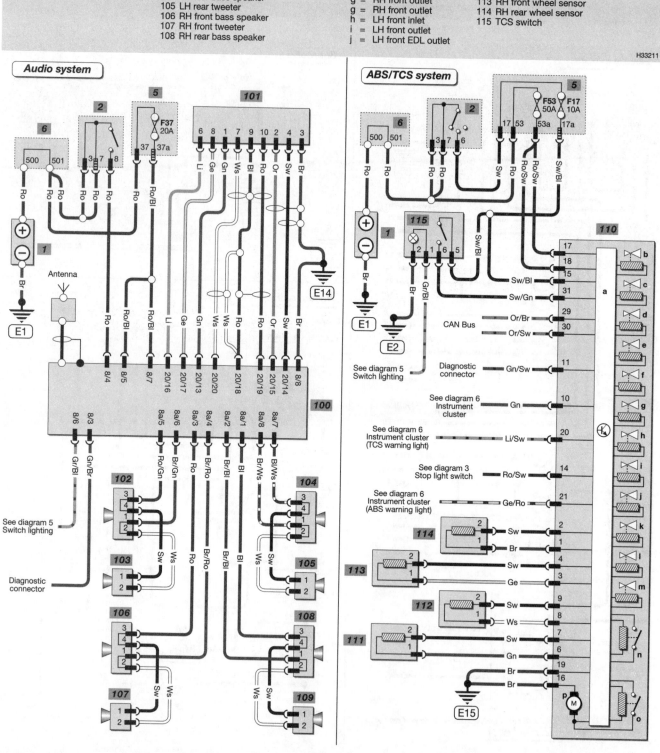

Audio system

ABS/TCS system

Dimensions and weights . . . . **REF•1**
Conversion factors . . . . **REF•2**
Jacking and vehicle support . . . . **REF•3**
Radio/CD/cassette unit anti-theft system –
 precaution . . . . **REF•3**
General repair procedures . . . . **REF•4**
Buying spare parts . . . . **REF•5**

Vehicle identification . . . . **REF•5**
Tools and working facilities . . . . **REF•6**
MOT test checks . . . . **REF•8**
Fault finding . . . . **REF•12**
Glossary of technical terms . . . . **REF•20**
Index . . . . **REF•24**

Dimensions and weights

Note: *All figures are approximate, and may vary according to model. Refer to manufacturer's data for exact figures.*

Dimensions

Overall length:
  Saloon . . . .   4703 mm
  Estate . . . .   4682 mm
Overall width . . . .   1746 mm
Overall height (unladen):
  Saloon . . . .   1462 mm
  Estate . . . .   1498 mm
Turning circle . . . .   11.4 m

Weights

Kerb weight:
  Petrol engine models:
    1.8 litre:
      Saloon . . . .   1375 kg (manual) or 1385 kg (automatic)
      Estate . . . .   1399 kg (manual) or 1451 kg (automatic)
    2.0 litre:
      Saloon . . . .   1354 kg (manual) or 1406 kg (automatic)
      Estate . . . .   1375 kg (manual) or 1396 kg (automatic)
  Diesel engine models:
    Saloon . . . .   1361 kg (manual) or 1389 kg (automatic)
    Estate . . . .   1411 kg (manual) or 1437 kg (automatic)
Maximum towing weight:
  Trailer without brakes . . . .   630 to 650 kg
  Trailer with brakes . . . .   1400 to 1700 kg
Maximum roof rack load . . . .   100 kg

Conversion factors

Length (distance)

Inches (in)	x 25.4	= Millimetres (mm)	x 0.0394	= Inches (in)
Feet (ft)	x 0.305	= Metres (m)	x 3.281	= Feet (ft)
Miles	x 1.609	= Kilometres (km)	x 0.621	= Miles

Volume (capacity)

Cubic inches (cu in; in³)	x 16.387	= Cubic centimetres (cc; cm³)	x 0.061	= Cubic inches (cu in; in³)
Imperial pints (Imp pt)	x 0.568	= Litres (l)	x 1.76	= Imperial pints (Imp pt)
Imperial quarts (Imp qt)	x 1.137	= Litres (l)	x 0.88	= Imperial quarts (Imp qt)
Imperial quarts (Imp qt)	x 1.201	= US quarts (US qt)	x 0.833	= Imperial quarts (Imp qt)
US quarts (US qt)	x 0.946	= Litres (l)	x 1.057	= US quarts (US qt)
Imperial gallons (Imp gal)	x 4.546	= Litres (l)	x 0.22	= Imperial gallons (Imp gal)
Imperial gallons (Imp gal)	x 1.201	= US gallons (US gal)	x 0.833	= Imperial gallons (Imp gal)
US gallons (US gal)	x 3.785	= Litres (l)	x 0.264	= US gallons (US gal)

Mass (weight)

Ounces (oz)	x 28.35	= Grams (g)	x 0.035	= Ounces (oz)
Pounds (lb)	x 0.454	= Kilograms (kg)	x 2.205	= Pounds (lb)

Force

Ounces-force (ozf; oz)	x 0.278	= Newtons (N)	x 3.6	= Ounces-force (ozf; oz)
Pounds-force (lbf; lb)	x 4.448	= Newtons (N)	x 0.225	= Pounds-force (lbf; lb)
Newtons (N)	x 0.1	= Kilograms-force (kgf; kg)	x 9.81	= Newtons (N)

Pressure

Pounds-force per square inch (psi; lbf/in²; lb/in²)	x 0.070	= Kilograms-force per square centimetre (kgf/cm²; kg/cm²)	x 14.223	= Pounds-force per square inch (psi; lbf/in²; lb/in²)
Pounds-force per square inch (psi; lbf/in²; lb/in²)	x 0.068	= Atmospheres (atm)	x 14.696	= Pounds-force per square inch (psi; lbf/in²; lb/in²)
Pounds-force per square inch (psi; lbf/in²; lb/in²)	x 0.069	= Bars	x 14.5	= Pounds-force per square inch (psi; lbf/in²; lb/in²)
Pounds-force per square inch (psi; lbf/in²; lb/in²)	x 6.895	= Kilopascals (kPa)	x 0.145	= Pounds-force per square inch (psi; lbf/in²; lb/in²)
Kilopascals (kPa)	x 0.01	= Kilograms-force per square centimetre (kgf/cm²; kg/cm²)	x 98.1	= Kilopascals (kPa)
Millibar (mbar)	x 100	= Pascals (Pa)	x 0.01	= Millibar (mbar)
Millibar (mbar)	x 0.0145	= Pounds-force per square inch (psi; lbf/in²; lb/in²)	x 68.947	= Millibar (mbar)
Millibar (mbar)	x 0.75	= Millimetres of mercury (mmHg)	x 1.333	= Millibar (mbar)
Millibar (mbar)	x 0.401	= Inches of water (inH_2O)	x 2.491	= Millibar (mbar)
Millimetres of mercury (mmHg)	x 0.535	= Inches of water (inH_2O)	x 1.868	= Millimetres of mercury (mmHg)
Inches of water (inH_2O)	x 0.036	= Pounds-force per square inch (psi; lbf/in²; lb/in²)	x 27.68	= Inches of water (inH_2O)

Torque (moment of force)

Pounds-force inches (lbf in; lb in)	x 1.152	= Kilograms-force centimetre (kgf cm; kg cm)	x 0.868	= Pounds-force inches (lbf in; lb in)
Pounds-force inches (lbf in; lb in)	x 0.113	= Newton metres (Nm)	x 8.85	= Pounds-force inches (lbf in; lb in)
Pounds-force inches (lbf in; lb in)	x 0.083	= Pounds-force feet (lbf ft; lb ft)	x 12	= Pounds-force inches (lbf in; lb in)
Pounds-force feet (lbf ft; lb ft)	x 0.138	= Kilograms-force metres (kgf m; kg m)	x 7.233	= Pounds-force feet (lbf ft; lb ft)
Pounds-force feet (lbf ft; lb ft)	x 1.356	= Newton metres (Nm)	x 0.738	= Pounds-force feet (lbf ft; lb ft)
Newton metres (Nm)	x 0.102	= Kilograms-force metres (kgf m; kg m)	x 9.804	= Newton metres (Nm)

Power

Horsepower (hp)	x 745.7	= Watts (W)	x 0.0013	= Horsepower (hp)

Velocity (speed)

Miles per hour (miles/hr; mph)	x 1.609	= Kilometres per hour (km/hr; kph)	x 0.621	= Miles per hour (miles/hr; mph)

Fuel consumption*

Miles per gallon, Imperial (mpg)	x 0.354	= Kilometres per litre (km/l)	x 2.825	= Miles per gallon, Imperial (mpg)
Miles per gallon, US (mpg)	x 0.425	= Kilometres per litre (km/l)	x 2.352	= Miles per gallon, US (mpg)

Temperature

Degrees Fahrenheit = (°C x 1.8) + 32

Degrees Celsius (Degrees Centigrade; °C) = (°F - 32) x 0.56

** It is common practice to convert from miles per gallon (mpg) to litres/100 kilometres (l/100km), where mpg x l/100 km = 282*

The jack supplied with the vehicle tool kit should only be used for changing the roadwheels – see *Wheel changing* at the front of this manual. When carrying out any other kind of work, raise the vehicle using a hydraulic trolley jack, and always supplement the jack with axle stands positioned under the vehicle jacking points.

When using a trolley jack or axle stands, always position the jack head or axle stand head under, or adjacent to one of the relevant wheel changing jacking points under the sills **(see illustration)**. Use a block of wood between the jack or axle stand and the sill.

Do not attempt to jack the vehicle under the front crossmember, the sump, or any of the suspension components.

The jack supplied with the vehicle locates in the jacking points on the underside of the sills – see *Wheel changing* at the front of this manual. Ensure that the jack head is correctly engaged before attempting to raise the vehicle.

Never work under, around, or near a raised vehicle, unless it is adequately supported in at least two places.

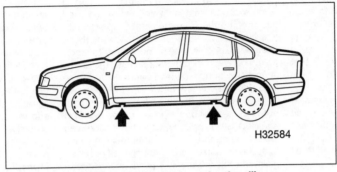

Vehicle jacking points under the sills

Radio/CD/cassette unit anti-theft system – precaution

The radio/CD/cassette unit fitted as standard equipment by VW is equipped with a built-in security code to deter thieves. If the power source to the unit is cut, the anti-theft system will activate. Even if the power source is immediately reconnected, the unit will not function until the correct security code has been entered. Therefore, if you do not know the correct security code for the unit, do not disconnect the battery negative lead, or remove the unit from the vehicle.

Whenever servicing, repair or overhaul work is carried out on the car or its components, observe the following procedures and instructions. This will assist in carrying out the operation efficiently and to a professional standard of workmanship.

Joint mating faces and gaskets

When separating components at their mating faces, never insert screwdrivers or similar implements into the joint between the faces in order to prise them apart. This can cause severe damage which results in oil leaks, coolant leaks, etc upon reassembly. Separation is usually achieved by tapping along the joint with a soft-faced hammer in order to break the seal. However, note that this method may not be suitable where dowels are used for component location.

Where a gasket is used between the mating faces of two components, a new one must be fitted on reassembly; fit it dry unless otherwise stated in the repair procedure. Make sure that the mating faces are clean and dry, with all traces of old gasket removed. When cleaning a joint face, use a tool which is unlikely to score or damage the face, and remove any burrs or nicks with an oilstone or fine file.

Make sure that tapped holes are cleaned with a pipe cleaner, and keep them free of jointing compound, if this is being used, unless specifically instructed otherwise.

Ensure that all orifices, channels or pipes are clear, and blow through them, preferably using compressed air.

Oil seals

Oil seals can be removed by levering them out with a wide flat-bladed screwdriver or similar implement. Alternatively, a number of self-tapping screws may be screwed into the seal, and these used as a purchase for pliers or some similar device in order to pull the seal free.

Whenever an oil seal is removed from its working location, either individually or as part of an assembly, it should be renewed.

The very fine sealing lip of the seal is easily damaged, and will not seal if the surface it contacts is not completely clean and free from scratches, nicks or grooves. If the original sealing surface of the component cannot be restored, and the manufacturer has not made provision for slight relocation of the seal relative to the sealing surface, the component should be renewed.

Protect the lips of the seal from any surface which may damage them in the course of fitting. Use tape or a conical sleeve where possible. Lubricate the seal lips with oil before fitting and, on dual-lipped seals, fill the space between the lips with grease.

Unless otherwise stated, oil seals must be fitted with their sealing lips toward the lubricant to be sealed.

Use a tubular drift or block of wood of the appropriate size to install the seal and, if the seal housing is shouldered, drive the seal down to the shoulder. If the seal housing is unshouldered, the seal should be fitted with its face flush with the housing top face (unless otherwise instructed).

Screw threads and fastenings

Seized nuts, bolts and screws are quite a common occurrence where corrosion has set in, and the use of penetrating oil or releasing fluid will often overcome this problem if the offending item is soaked for a while before attempting to release it. The use of an impact driver may also provide a means of releasing such stubborn fastening devices, when used in conjunction with the appropriate screwdriver bit or socket. If none of these methods works, it may be necessary to resort to the careful application of heat, or the use of a hacksaw or nut splitter device.

Studs are usually removed by locking two nuts together on the threaded part, and then using a spanner on the lower nut to unscrew the stud. Studs or bolts which have broken off below the surface of the component in which they are mounted can sometimes be removed using a stud extractor. Always ensure that a blind tapped hole is completely free from oil, grease, water or other fluid before installing the bolt or stud. Failure to do this could cause the housing to crack due to the hydraulic action of the bolt or stud as it is screwed in.

When tightening a castellated nut to accept a split pin, tighten the nut to the specified torque, where applicable, and then tighten further to the next split pin hole. Never slacken the nut to align the split pin hole, unless stated in the repair procedure.

When checking or retightening a nut or bolt to a specified torque setting, slacken the nut or bolt by a quarter of a turn, and then retighten to the specified setting. However, this should not be attempted where angular tightening has been used.

For some screw fastenings, notably cylinder head bolts or nuts, torque wrench settings are no longer specified for the latter stages of tightening, "angle-tightening" being called up instead. Typically, a fairly low torque wrench setting will be applied to the bolts/nuts in the correct sequence, followed by one or more stages of tightening through specified angles.

Locknuts, locktabs and washers

Any fastening which will rotate against a component or housing during tightening should always have a washer between it and the relevant component or housing.

Spring or split washers should always be renewed when they are used to lock a critical component such as a big-end bearing retaining bolt or nut. Locktabs which are folded over to retain a nut or bolt should always be renewed.

Self-locking nuts can be re-used in non-critical areas, providing resistance can be felt when the locking portion passes over the bolt or stud thread. However, it should be noted that self-locking stiffnuts tend to lose their effectiveness after long periods of use, and should then be renewed as a matter of course.

Split pins must always be replaced with new ones of the correct size for the hole.

When thread-locking compound is found on the threads of a fastener which is to be re-used, it should be cleaned off with a wire brush and solvent, and fresh compound applied on reassembly.

Special tools

Some repair procedures in this manual entail the use of special tools such as a press, two or three-legged pullers, spring compressors, etc. Wherever possible, suitable readily-available alternatives to the manufacturer's special tools are described, and are shown in use. In some instances, where no alternative is possible, it has been necessary to resort to the use of a manufacturer's tool, and this has been done for reasons of safety as well as the efficient completion of the repair operation. Unless you are highly-skilled and have a thorough understanding of the procedures described, never attempt to bypass the use of any special tool when the procedure described specifies its use. Not only is there a very great risk of personal injury, but expensive damage could be caused to the components involved.

Environmental considerations

When disposing of used engine oil, brake fluid, antifreeze, etc, give due consideration to any detrimental environmental effects. Do not, for instance, pour any of the above liquids down drains into the general sewage system, or onto the ground to soak away. Many local council refuse tips provide a facility for waste oil disposal, as do some garages. If none of these facilities are available, consult your local Environmental Health Department, or the National Rivers Authority, for further advice.

With the universal tightening-up of legislation regarding the emission of environmentally-harmful substances from motor vehicles, most vehicles have tamperproof devices fitted to the main adjustment points of the fuel system. These devices are primarily designed to prevent unqualified persons from adjusting the fuel/air mixture, with the chance of a consequent increase in toxic emissions. If such devices are found during servicing or overhaul, they should, wherever possible, be renewed or refitted in accordance with the manufacturer's requirements or current legislation.

Note: It is antisocial and illegal to dump oil down the drain. To find the location of your local oil recycling bank, call this number free.

Spare parts are available from many sources, including maker's appointed garages, accessory shops, and motor factors. To be sure of obtaining the correct parts, it will sometimes be necessary to quote the vehicle identification number. If possible, it can also be useful to take the old parts along for positive identification. Items such as starter motors and alternators may be available under a service exchange scheme – any parts returned should be clean.

Our advice regarding spare parts is as follows.

Officially appointed garages

This is the best source of parts which are peculiar to your car, and which are not otherwise generally available (eg, badges, interior trim, certain body panels, etc). It is also the only place at which you should buy parts if the vehicle is still under warranty.

Accessory shops

These are very good places to buy materials and components needed for the maintenance of your car (oil, air and fuel filters, light bulbs, drivebelts, greases, brake pads, touch-up paint, etc). Components of this nature sold by a reputable shop are usually of the same standard as those used by the car manufacturer.

Besides components, these shops also sell tools and general accessories, usually have convenient opening hours, charge lower prices, and can often be found close to home. Some accessory shops have parts counters where components needed for almost any repair job can be purchased or ordered.

Motor factors

Good factors will stock all the more important components which wear out comparatively quickly, and can sometimes supply individual components needed for the overhaul of a larger assembly (eg, brake seals and hydraulic parts, bearing shells, pistons, valves). They may also handle work such as cylinder block reboring, crankshaft regrinding, etc.

Tyre and exhaust specialists

These outlets may be independent, or members of a local or national chain. They frequently offer competitive prices when compared with a main dealer or local garage, but it will pay to obtain several quotes before making a decision. When researching prices, also ask what extras may be added – for instance fitting a new valve and balancing the wheel are both commonly charged on top of the price of a new tyre.

Other sources

Beware of parts or materials obtained from market stalls, car boot sales or similar outlets. Such items are not invariably sub-standard, but there is little chance of compensation if they do prove unsatisfactory. in the case of safety-critical components such as brake pads, there is the risk not only of financial loss, but also of an accident causing injury or death.

Second-hand components or assemblies obtained from a car breaker can be a good buy in some circumstances, but this sort of purchase is best made by the experienced DIY mechanic.

Vehicle Identification

Modifications are a continuing and unpublicised process in vehicle manufacture, quite apart from major model changes. Spare parts manuals and lists are compiled upon a numerical basis, the individual vehicle identification numbers being essential to correct identification of the component concerned.

When ordering spare parts, always give as much information as possible. Quote the car model, year of manufacture, body and engine numbers as appropriate.

The *vehicle identification plate* is situated at the rear of the engine compartment **(see illustration)**. A further *vehicle identification sticker* is located under the rear luggage compartment floor covering or on the luggage compartment floor **(see illustration)**. The *vehicle identification number* is also repeated in the form of plate visible through the windscreen on the passenger's side **(see illustration)**.

The *engine number* is stamped on the left-hand side of the cylinder block. The *engine code* can also be found on the vehicle data sticker in the spare wheel recess or luggage compartment floor, and on a sticker on the toothed belt or valve cover.

Other identification numbers or codes are stamped on major items such as the gearbox, etc. These numbers are unlikely to be needed by the home mechanic.

Vehicle identification plate

Vehicle Identification Number

Vehicle identification sticker

Introduction

A selection of good tools is a fundamental requirement for anyone contemplating the maintenance and repair of a motor vehicle. For the owner who does not possess any, their purchase will prove a considerable expense, offsetting some of the savings made by doing-it-yourself. However, provided that the tools purchased meet the relevant national safety standards and are of good quality, they will last for many years and prove an extremely worthwhile investment.

To help the average owner to decide which tools are needed to carry out the various tasks detailed in this manual, we have compiled three lists of tools under the following headings: *Maintenance and minor repair*, *Repair and overhaul*, and *Special*. Newcomers to practical mechanics should start off with the *Maintenance and minor repair* tool kit, and confine themselves to the simpler jobs around the vehicle. Then, as confidence and experience grow, more difficult tasks can be undertaken, with extra tools being purchased as, and when, they are needed. In this way, a *Maintenance and minor repair* tool kit can be built up into a *Repair and overhaul* tool kit over a considerable period of time, without any major cash outlays. The experienced do-it-yourselfer will have a tool kit good enough for most repair and overhaul procedures, and will add tools from the *Special* category when it is felt that the expense is justified by the amount of use to which these tools will be put.

Maintenance and minor repair tool kit

The tools given in this list should be considered as a minimum requirement if routine maintenance, servicing and minor repair operations are to be undertaken. We recommend the purchase of combination spanners (ring one end, open-ended the other); although more expensive than open-ended ones, they do give the advantages of both types of spanner.

☐ *Combination spanners:*
   Metric - 8 to 19 mm inclusive
☐ *Adjustable spanner - 35 mm jaw (approx.)*
☐ *Spark plug spanner (with rubber insert) - petrol models*
☐ *Spark plug gap adjustment tool - petrol models*
☐ *Set of feeler gauges*
☐ *Brake bleed nipple spanner*
☐ *Screwdrivers:*
   Flat blade - 100 mm long x 6 mm dia
   Cross blade - 100 mm long x 6 mm dia
   Torx - various sizes (not all vehicles)
☐ *Combination pliers*
☐ *Hacksaw (junior)*
☐ *Tyre pump*
☐ *Tyre pressure gauge*
☐ *Oil can*
☐ *Oil filter removal tool*
☐ *Fine emery cloth*
☐ *Wire brush (small)*
☐ *Funnel (medium size)*
☐ *Sump drain plug key (not all vehicles)*

Repair and overhaul tool kit

These tools are virtually essential for anyone undertaking any major repairs to a motor vehicle, and are additional to those given in the *Maintenance and minor repair* list. Included in this list is a comprehensive set of sockets. Although these are expensive, they will be found invaluable as they are so versatile - particularly if various drives are included in the set. We recommend the half-inch square-drive type, as this can be used with most proprietary torque wrenches.

The tools in this list will sometimes need to be supplemented by tools from the *Special* list:

☐ *Sockets (or box spanners) to cover range in previous list (including Torx sockets)*
☐ *Reversible ratchet drive (for use with sockets)*
☐ *Extension piece, 250 mm (for use with sockets)*
☐ *Universal joint (for use with sockets)*
☐ *Flexible handle or sliding T "breaker bar" (for use with sockets)*
☐ *Torque wrench (for use with sockets)*
☐ *Self-locking grips*
☐ *Ball pein hammer*
☐ *Soft-faced mallet (plastic or rubber)*
☐ *Screwdrivers:*
   Flat blade - long & sturdy, short (chubby), and narrow (electrician's) types
   Cross blade - long & sturdy, and short (chubby) types
☐ *Pliers:*
   Long-nosed
   Side cutters (electrician's)
   Circlip (internal and external)
☐ *Cold chisel - 25 mm*
☐ *Scriber*
☐ *Scraper*
☐ *Centre-punch*
☐ *Pin punch*
☐ *Hacksaw*
☐ *Brake hose clamp*
☐ *Brake/clutch bleeding kit*
☐ *Selection of twist drills*
☐ *Steel rule/straight-edge*
☐ *Allen keys (inc. splined/Torx type)*
☐ *Selection of files*
☐ *Wire brush*
☐ *Axle stands*
☐ *Jack (strong trolley or hydraulic type)*
☐ *Light with extension lead*
☐ *Universal electrical multi-meter*

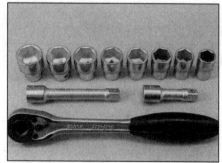

Sockets and reversible ratchet drive

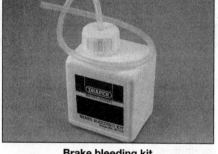

Brake bleeding kit

Torx key, socket and bit

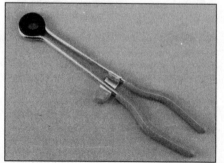

Hose clamp

Angular-tightening gauge

Special tools

The tools in this list are those which are not used regularly, are expensive to buy, or which need to be used in accordance with their manufacturers' instructions. Unless relatively difficult mechanical jobs are undertaken frequently, it will not be economic to buy many of these tools. Where this is the case, you could consider clubbing together with friends (or joining a motorists' club) to make a joint purchase, or borrowing the tools against a deposit from a local garage or tool hire specialist. It is worth noting that many of the larger DIY superstores now carry a large range of special tools for hire at modest rates.

The following list contains only those tools and instruments freely available to the public, and not those special tools produced by the vehicle manufacturer specifically for its dealer network. You will find occasional references to these manufacturers' special tools in the text of this manual. Generally, an alternative method of doing the job without the vehicle manufacturers' special tool is given. However, sometimes there is no alternative to using them. Where this is the case and the relevant tool cannot be bought or borrowed, you will have to entrust the work to a dealer.

- [ ] Angular-tightening gauge
- [ ] Valve spring compressor
- [ ] Valve grinding tool
- [ ] Piston ring compressor
- [ ] Piston ring removal/installation tool
- [ ] Cylinder bore hone
- [ ] Balljoint separator
- [ ] Coil spring compressors (where applicable)
- [ ] Two/three-legged hub and bearing puller
- [ ] Impact screwdriver
- [ ] Micrometer and/or vernier calipers
- [ ] Dial gauge
- [ ] Stroboscopic timing light
- [ ] Dwell angle meter/tachometer
- [ ] Fault code reader
- [ ] Cylinder compression gauge
- [ ] Hand-operated vacuum pump and gauge
- [ ] Clutch plate alignment set
- [ ] Brake shoe steady spring cup removal tool
- [ ] Bush and bearing removal/installation set
- [ ] Stud extractors
- [ ] Tap and die set
- [ ] Lifting tackle
- [ ] Trolley jack

Buying tools

Reputable motor accessory shops and superstores often offer excellent quality tools at discount prices, so it pays to shop around.

Remember, you don't have to buy the most expensive items on the shelf, but it is always advisable to steer clear of the very cheap tools. Beware of 'bargains' offered on market stalls or at car boot sales. There are plenty of good tools around at reasonable prices, but always aim to purchase items which meet the relevant national safety standards. If in doubt, ask the proprietor or manager of the shop for advice before making a purchase.

Care and maintenance of tools

Having purchased a reasonable tool kit, it is necessary to keep the tools in a clean and serviceable condition. After use, always wipe off any dirt, grease and metal particles using a clean, dry cloth, before putting the tools away. Never leave them lying around after they have been used. A simple tool rack on the garage or workshop wall for items such as screwdrivers and pliers is a good idea. Store all normal spanners and sockets in a metal box. Any measuring instruments, gauges, meters, etc, must be carefully stored where they cannot be damaged or become rusty.

Take a little care when tools are used. Hammer heads inevitably become marked, and screwdrivers lose the keen edge on their blades from time to time. A little timely attention with emery cloth or a file will soon restore items like this to a good finish.

Working facilities

Not to be forgotten when discussing tools is the workshop itself. If anything more than routine maintenance is to be carried out, a suitable working area becomes essential.

It is appreciated that many an owner-mechanic is forced by circumstances to remove an engine or similar item without the benefit of a garage or workshop. Having done this, any repairs should always be done under the cover of a roof.

Wherever possible, any dismantling should be done on a clean, flat workbench or table at a suitable working height.

Any workbench needs a vice; one with a jaw opening of 100 mm is suitable for most jobs. As mentioned previously, some clean dry storage space is also required for tools, as well as for any lubricants, cleaning fluids, touch-up paints etc, which become necessary.

Another item which may be required, and which has a much more general usage, is an electric drill with a chuck capacity of at least 8 mm. This, together with a good range of twist drills, is virtually essential for fitting accessories.

Last, but not least, always keep a supply of old newspapers and clean, lint-free rags available, and try to keep any working area as clean as possible.

Micrometers

Dial test indicator ("dial gauge")

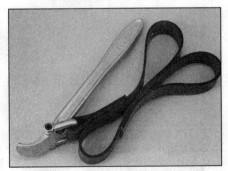

Strap wrench

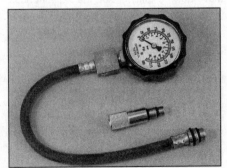

Compression tester

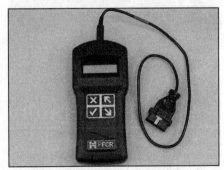

Fault code reader

This is a guide to getting your vehicle through the MOT test. Obviously it will not be possible to examine the vehicle to the same standard as the professional MOT tester. However, working through the following checks will enable you to identify any problem areas before submitting the vehicle for the test.

It has only been possible to summarise the test requirements here, based on the regulations in force at the time of printing. Test standards are becoming increasingly stringent, although there are some exemptions for older vehicles.

An assistant will be needed to help carry out some of these checks.

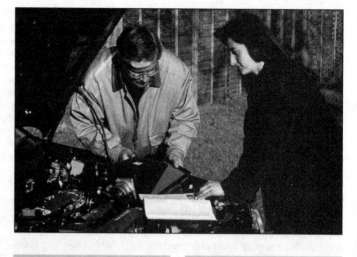

The checks have been sub-divided into four categories, as follows:

1 Checks carried out **FROM THE DRIVER'S SEAT**

2 Checks carried out **WITH THE VEHICLE ON THE GROUND**

3 Checks carried out **WITH THE VEHICLE RAISED AND THE WHEELS FREE TO TURN**

4 Checks carried out on **YOUR VEHICLE'S EXHAUST EMISSION SYSTEM**

---

1 Checks carried out **FROM THE DRIVER'S SEAT**

Handbrake

☐ Test the operation of the handbrake. Excessive travel (too many clicks) indicates incorrect brake or cable adjustment.
☐ Check that the handbrake cannot be released by tapping the lever sideways. Check the security of the lever mountings.

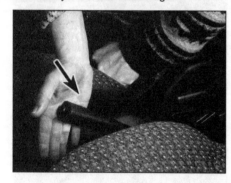

Footbrake

☐ Depress the brake pedal and check that it does not creep down to the floor, indicating a master cylinder fault. Release the pedal, wait a few seconds, then depress it again. If the pedal travels nearly to the floor before firm resistance is felt, brake adjustment or repair is necessary. If the pedal feels spongy, there is air in the hydraulic system which must be removed by bleeding.

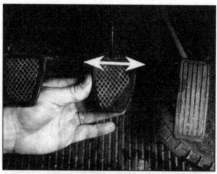

☐ Check that the brake pedal is secure and in good condition. Check also for signs of fluid leaks on the pedal, floor or carpets, which would indicate failed seals in the brake master cylinder.
☐ Check the servo unit (when applicable) by operating the brake pedal several times, then keeping the pedal depressed and starting the engine. As the engine starts, the pedal will move down slightly. If not, the vacuum hose or the servo itself may be faulty.

Steering wheel and column

☐ Examine the steering wheel for fractures or looseness of the hub, spokes or rim.
☐ Move the steering wheel from side to side and then up and down. Check that the steering wheel is not loose on the column, indicating wear or a loose retaining nut. Continue moving the steering wheel as before, but also turn it slightly from left to right.
☐ Check that the steering wheel is not loose on the column, and that there is no abnormal

movement of the steering wheel, indicating wear in the column support bearings or couplings.

Windscreen, mirrors and sunvisor

☐ The windscreen must be free of cracks or other significant damage within the driver's field of view. (Small stone chips are acceptable.) Rear view mirrors must be secure, intact, and capable of being adjusted.

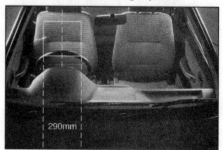

☐ The driver's sunvisor must be capable of being stored in the "up" position.

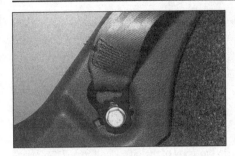

Seat belts and seats

Note: *The following checks are applicable to all seat belts, front and rear.*

☐ Examine the webbing of all the belts (including rear belts if fitted) for cuts, serious fraying or deterioration. Fasten and unfasten each belt to check the buckles. If applicable, check the retracting mechanism. Check the security of all seat belt mountings accessible from inside the vehicle.

☐ Seat belts with pre-tensioners, once activated, have a "flag" or similar showing on the seat belt stalk. This, in itself, is not a reason for test failure.

☐ The front seats themselves must be securely attached and the backrests must lock in the upright position.

Doors

☐ Both front doors must be able to be opened and closed from outside and inside, and must latch securely when closed.

2 Checks carried out WITH THE VEHICLE ON THE GROUND

Vehicle identification

☐ Number plates must be in good condition, secure and legible, with letters and numbers correctly spaced – spacing at (A) should be at least twice that at (B).

☐ The VIN plate and/or homologation plate must be legible.

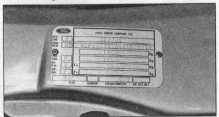

Electrical equipment

☐ Switch on the ignition and check the operation of the horn.

☐ Check the windscreen washers and wipers, examining the wiper blades; renew damaged or perished blades. Also check the operation of the stop-lights.

☐ Check the operation of the sidelights and number plate lights. The lenses and reflectors must be secure, clean and undamaged.

☐ Check the operation and alignment of the headlights. The headlight reflectors must not be tarnished and the lenses must be undamaged.

☐ Switch on the ignition and check the operation of the direction indicators (including the instrument panel tell-tale) and the hazard warning lights. Operation of the sidelights and stop-lights must not affect the indicators - if it does, the cause is usually a bad earth at the rear light cluster.

☐ Check the operation of the rear foglight(s), including the warning light on the instrument panel or in the switch.

☐ The ABS warning light must illuminate in accordance with the manufacturers' design. For most vehicles, the ABS warning light should illuminate when the ignition is switched on, and (if the system is operating properly) extinguish after a few seconds. Refer to the owner's handbook.

Footbrake

☐ Examine the master cylinder, brake pipes and servo unit for leaks, loose mountings, corrosion or other damage.

☐ The fluid reservoir must be secure and the fluid level must be between the upper (**A**) and lower (**B**) markings.

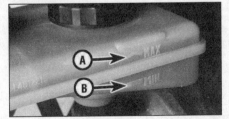

☐ Inspect both front brake flexible hoses for cracks or deterioration of the rubber. Turn the steering from lock to lock, and ensure that the hoses do not contact the wheel, tyre, or any part of the steering or suspension mechanism. With the brake pedal firmly depressed, check the hoses for bulges or leaks under pressure.

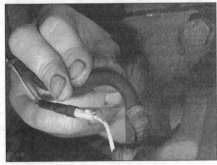

Steering and suspension

☐ Have your assistant turn the steering wheel from side to side slightly, up to the point where the steering gear just begins to transmit this movement to the roadwheels. Check for excessive free play between the steering wheel and the steering gear, indicating wear or insecurity of the steering column joints, the column-to-steering gear coupling, or the steering gear itself.

☐ Have your assistant turn the steering wheel more vigorously in each direction, so that the roadwheels just begin to turn. As this is done, examine all the steering joints, linkages, fittings and attachments. Renew any component that shows signs of wear or damage. On vehicles with power steering, check the security and condition of the steering pump, drivebelt and hoses.

☐ Check that the vehicle is standing level, and at approximately the correct ride height.

Shock absorbers

☐ Depress each corner of the vehicle in turn, then release it. The vehicle should rise and then settle in its normal position. If the vehicle continues to rise and fall, the shock absorber is defective. A shock absorber which has seized will also cause the vehicle to fail.

Exhaust system

☐ Start the engine. With your assistant holding a rag over the tailpipe, check the entire system for leaks. Repair or renew leaking sections.

3 Checks carried out **WITH THE VEHICLE RAISED AND THE WHEELS FREE TO TURN**

Jack up the front and rear of the vehicle, and securely support it on axle stands. Position the stands clear of the suspension assemblies. Ensure that the wheels are clear of the ground and that the steering can be turned from lock to lock.

Steering mechanism

☐ Have your assistant turn the steering from lock to lock. Check that the steering turns smoothly, and that no part of the steering mechanism, including a wheel or tyre, fouls any brake hose or pipe or any part of the body structure.

☐ Examine the steering rack rubber gaiters for damage or insecurity of the retaining clips. If power steering is fitted, check for signs of damage or leakage of the fluid hoses, pipes or connections. Also check for excessive stiffness or binding of the steering, a missing split pin or locking device, or severe corrosion of the body structure within 30 cm of any steering component attachment point.

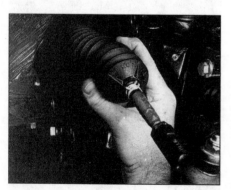

Front and rear suspension and wheel bearings

☐ Starting at the front right-hand side, grasp the roadwheel at the 3 o'clock and 9 o'clock positions and rock gently but firmly. Check for free play or insecurity at the wheel bearings, suspension balljoints, or suspension mountings, pivots and attachments.

☐ Now grasp the wheel at the 12 o'clock and 6 o'clock positions and repeat the previous inspection. Spin the wheel, and check for roughness or tightness of the front wheel bearing.

☐ If excess free play is suspected at a component pivot point, this can be confirmed by using a large screwdriver or similar tool and levering between the mounting and the component attachment. This will confirm whether the wear is in the pivot bush, its retaining bolt, or in the mounting itself (the bolt holes can often become elongated).

☐ Carry out all the above checks at the other front wheel, and then at both rear wheels.

Springs and shock absorbers

☐ Examine the suspension struts (when applicable) for serious fluid leakage, corrosion, or damage to the casing. Also check the security of the mounting points.

☐ If coil springs are fitted, check that the spring ends locate in their seats, and that the spring is not corroded, cracked or broken.

☐ If leaf springs are fitted, check that all leaves are intact, that the axle is securely attached to each spring, and that there is no deterioration of the spring eye mountings, bushes, and shackles.

☐ The same general checks apply to vehicles fitted with other suspension types, such as torsion bars, hydraulic displacer units, etc. Ensure that all mountings and attachments are secure, that there are no signs of excessive wear, corrosion or damage, and (on hydraulic types) that there are no fluid leaks or damaged pipes.

☐ Inspect the shock absorbers for signs of serious fluid leakage. Check for wear of the mounting bushes or attachments, or damage to the body of the unit.

Driveshafts (fwd vehicles only)

☐ Rotate each front wheel in turn and inspect the constant velocity joint gaiters for splits or damage. Also check that each driveshaft is straight and undamaged.

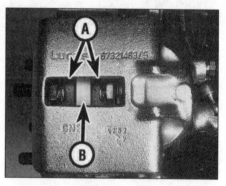

Braking system

☐ If possible without dismantling, check brake pad wear and disc condition. Ensure that the friction lining material has not worn excessively, (A) and that the discs are not fractured, pitted, scored or badly worn (B).

☐ Examine all the rigid brake pipes underneath the vehicle, and the flexible hose(s) at the rear. Look for corrosion, chafing or insecurity of the pipes, and for signs of bulging under pressure, chafing, splits or deterioration of the flexible hoses.

☐ Look for signs of fluid leaks at the brake calipers or on the brake backplates. Repair or renew leaking components.

☐ Slowly spin each wheel, while your assistant depresses and releases the footbrake. Ensure that each brake is operating and does not bind when the pedal is released.

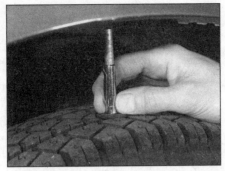

☐ Examine the handbrake mechanism, checking for frayed or broken cables, excessive corrosion, or wear or insecurity of the linkage. Check that the mechanism works on each relevant wheel, and releases fully, without binding.

☐ It is not possible to test brake efficiency without special equipment, but a road test can be carried out later to check that the vehicle pulls up in a straight line.

Fuel and exhaust systems

☐ Inspect the fuel tank (including the filler cap), fuel pipes, hoses and unions. All components must be secure and free from leaks.

☐ Examine the exhaust system over its entire length, checking for any damaged, broken or missing mountings, security of the retaining clamps and rust or corrosion.

Wheels and tyres

☐ Examine the sidewalls and tread area of each tyre in turn. Check for cuts, tears, lumps, bulges, separation of the tread, and exposure of the ply or cord due to wear or damage. Check that the tyre bead is correctly seated on the wheel rim, that the valve is sound and properly seated, and that the wheel is not distorted or damaged.

☐ Check that the tyres are of the correct size for the vehicle, that they are of the same size

and type on each axle, and that the pressures are correct.

☐ Check the tyre tread depth. The legal minimum at the time of writing is 1.6 mm over at least three-quarters of the tread width. Abnormal tread wear may indicate incorrect front wheel alignment.

Body corrosion

☐ Check the condition of the entire vehicle structure for signs of corrosion in load-bearing areas. (These include chassis box sections, side sills, cross-members, pillars, and all suspension, steering, braking system and seat belt mountings and anchorages.) Any corrosion which has seriously reduced the thickness of a load-bearing area is likely to cause the vehicle to fail. In this case professional repairs are likely to be needed.

☐ Damage or corrosion which causes sharp or otherwise dangerous edges to be exposed will also cause the vehicle to fail.

4 Checks carried out on YOUR VEHICLE'S EXHAUST EMISSION SYSTEM

Petrol models

☐ The engine should be warmed up, and running well (ignition system in good order, air filter element clean, etc).

☐ Before testing, run the engine at around 2500 rpm for 20 seconds. Let the engine drop to idle, and watch for smoke from the exhaust. If the idle speed is too high, or if dense blue or black smoke emerges for more than 5 seconds, the vehicle will fail. Typically, blue smoke signifies oil burning (engine wear); black smoke means unburnt fuel (dirty air cleaner element, or other fuel system fault).

☐ An exhaust gas analyser for measuring carbon monoxide (CO) and hydrocarbons (HC) is now needed. If one cannot be hired or borrowed, have a local garage perform the check.

CO emissions (mixture)

☐ The MOT tester has access to the CO limits for all vehicles. The CO level is measured at idle speed, and at 'fast idle' (2500 to 3000 rpm). The following limits are given as a general guide:

At idle speed – Less than 0.5% CO
At 'fast idle' – Less than 0.3% CO
Lambda reading – 0.97 to 1.03

☐ If the CO level is too high, this may point to poor maintenance, a fuel injection system problem, faulty lambda (oxygen) sensor or catalytic converter. Try an injector cleaning treatment, and check the vehicle's ECU for fault codes.

HC emissions

☐ The MOT tester has access to HC limits for all vehicles. The HC level is measured at 'fast idle' (2500 to 3000 rpm). The following limits are given as a general guide:

At 'fast idle' – Less then 200 ppm

☐ Excessive HC emissions are typically caused by oil being burnt (worn engine), or by a blocked crankcase ventilation system ('breather'). If the engine oil is old and thin, an oil change may help. If the engine is running badly, check the vehicle's ECU for fault codes.

Diesel models

☐ The only emission test for diesel engines is measuring exhaust smoke density, using a calibrated smoke meter. The test involves accelerating the engine at least 3 times to its maximum unloaded speed.

Note: On engines with a timing belt, it is VITAL that the belt is in good condition before the test is carried out.

☐ With the engine warmed up, it is first purged by running at around 2500 rpm for 20 seconds. A governor check is then carried out, by slowly accelerating the engine to its maximum speed. After this, the smoke meter is connected, and the engine is accelerated quickly to maximum speed three times. If the smoke density is less than the limits given below, the vehicle will pass:

Non-turbo vehicles: 2.5m-1
Turbocharged vehicles: 3.0m-1

☐ If excess smoke is produced, try fitting a new air cleaner element, or using an injector cleaning treatment. If the engine is running badly, where applicable, check the vehicle's ECU for fault codes. Also check the vehicle's EGR system, where applicable. At high mileages, the injectors may require professional attention.

Engine

- [ ] Engine fails to rotate when attempting to start
- [ ] Engine rotates, but will not start
- [ ] Engine difficult to start when cold
- [ ] Engine difficult to start when hot
- [ ] Starter motor noisy or excessively-rough in engagement
- [ ] Engine starts, but stops immediately
- [ ] Engine idles erratically
- [ ] Engine misfires at idle speed
- [ ] Engine misfires throughout the driving speed range
- [ ] Engine hesitates on acceleration
- [ ] Engine stalls
- [ ] Engine lacks power
- [ ] Engine backfires
- [ ] Oil pressure warning light illuminated with engine running
- [ ] Engine runs-on after switching off
- [ ] Engine noises

Cooling system

- [ ] Overheating
- [ ] Overcooling
- [ ] External coolant leakage
- [ ] Internal coolant leakage
- [ ] Corrosion

Fuel and exhaust systems

- [ ] Excessive fuel consumption
- [ ] Fuel leakage and/or fuel odour
- [ ] Excessive noise or fumes from exhaust system

Clutch

- [ ] Pedal travels to floor – no pressure or very little resistance
- [ ] Clutch fails to disengage (unable to select gears)
- [ ] Clutch slips (engine speed increases, with no increase in vehicle speed)
- [ ] Judder as clutch is engaged
- [ ] Noise when depressing or releasing clutch pedal

Manual transmission

- [ ] Noisy in neutral with engine running
- [ ] Noisy in one particular gear
- [ ] Difficulty engaging gears
- [ ] Jumps out of gear
- [ ] Vibration
- [ ] Lubricant leaks

Automatic transmission

- [ ] Fluid leakage
- [ ] General gear selection problems
- [ ] Transmission will not downshift (kickdown) with accelerator pedal fully depressed
- [ ] Engine will not start in any gear, or starts in gears other than Park or Neutral
- [ ] Transmission slips, shifts roughly, is noisy, or has no drive in forward or reverse gears

Driveshafts

- [ ] Vibration when accelerating or decelerating
- [ ] Clicking or knocking noise on turns (at slow speed on full-lock)

Braking system

- [ ] Vehicle pulls to one side under braking
- [ ] Noise (grinding or high-pitched squeal) when brakes applied
- [ ] Excessive brake pedal travel
- [ ] Brake pedal feels spongy when depressed
- [ ] Excessive brake pedal effort required to stop vehicle
- [ ] Judder felt through brake pedal or steering wheel when braking
- [ ] Pedal pulsates when braking hard
- [ ] Brakes binding
- [ ] Rear wheels locking under normal braking

Steering and suspension

- [ ] Vehicle pulls to one side
- [ ] Wheel wobble and vibration
- [ ] Excessive pitching and/or rolling around corners, or during braking
- [ ] Wandering or general instability
- [ ] Excessively-stiff steering
- [ ] Excessive play in steering
- [ ] Lack of power assistance
- [ ] Tyre wear excessive

Electrical system

- [ ] Battery will not hold a charge for more than a few days
- [ ] Ignition/no-charge warning light remains illuminated with engine running
- [ ] Ignition/no-charge warning light fails to come on
- [ ] Lights inoperative
- [ ] Instrument readings inaccurate or erratic
- [ ] Horn inoperative, or unsatisfactory in operation
- [ ] Windscreen/tailgate wipers inoperative, or unsatisfactory in operation
- [ ] Windscreen washers inoperative, or unsatisfactory in operation
- [ ] Electric windows inoperative, or unsatisfactory in operation

Introduction

The vehicle owner who does his or her own maintenance according to the recommended service schedules should not have to use this section of the manual very often. Modern component reliability is such that, provided those items subject to wear or deterioration are inspected or renewed at the specified intervals, sudden failure is comparatively rare. Faults do not usually just happen as a result of sudden failure, but develop over a period of time. Major mechanical failures in particular are usually preceded by characteristic symptoms over hundreds or even thousands of miles. Those components which do occasionally fail without warning are often small and easily carried in the vehicle.

With any fault-finding, the first step is to decide where to begin investigations. Sometimes this is obvious, but on other occasions, a little detective work will be necessary. The owner who makes half a dozen haphazard adjustments or replacements may be successful in curing a fault (or its symptoms), but will be none the wiser if the fault recurs, and ultimately may have spent more time and money than was necessary. A calm and logical approach will be found to be more satisfactory in the long run. Always take into account any warning signs or abnormalities that may have been noticed in the period preceding the fault – power loss, high or low gauge readings, unusual smells, etc – and remember that failure of components such as fuses or spark plugs may only be pointers to some underlying fault.

The pages which follow provide an easy-reference guide to the more common problems which may occur during the operation of the vehicle. These problems and their possible causes are grouped under headings denoting various components or systems, such as Engine, Cooling system, etc. The general

Chapter which deals with the problem is also shown in brackets; refer to the relevant part of that Chapter for system-specific information. Whatever the fault, certain basic principles apply. These are as follows:

Verify the fault. This is simply a matter of being sure that you know what the symptoms are before starting work. This is particularly important if you are investigating a fault for someone else, who may not have described it very accurately.

Don't overlook the obvious. For example, if the vehicle won't start, is there fuel in the tank? (Don't take anyone else's word on this particular point, and don't trust the fuel gauge either!) If an electrical fault is indicated, look for loose or broken wires before digging out the test gear.

Cure the disease, not the symptom. Substituting a flat battery with a fully-charged one will get you off the hard shoulder, but if the underlying cause is not attended to, the new battery will go the same way. Similarly, changing oil-fouled spark plugs for a new set will get you moving again, but remember that the reason for the fouling (if it wasn't simply an incorrect grade of plug) will have to be established and corrected.

Don't take anything for granted. Particularly, don't forget that a new component may itself be defective (especially if its been rattling around in the boot for months), and don't leave components out of a fault diagnosis sequence just because they are new or recently-fitted. When you do finally diagnose a difficult fault, you'll probably realise that all the evidence was there from the start.

Engine

Engine fails to rotate when attempting to start

- ☐ Battery terminal connections loose or corroded (see *Weekly checks*).
- ☐ Battery discharged or faulty (Chapter 5A).
- ☐ Broken, loose or disconnected wiring in the starting circuit (Chapter 5A).
- ☐ Defective starter solenoid or switch (Chapter 5A).
- ☐ Defective starter motor (Chapter 5A).
- ☐ Starter pinion or flywheel/driveplate ring gear teeth loose or broken (Chapter 2 and 5A).
- ☐ Engine earth strap broken or disconnected (Chapter 5A).

Engine rotates, but will not start

- ☐ Fuel tank empty.
- ☐ Battery discharged (engine rotates slowly) (Chapter 5A).
- ☐ Battery terminal connections loose or corroded (see *Weekly checks*).
- ☐ Ignition components damp or damaged – petrol models (Chapters 1A and 5B).
- ☐ Broken, loose or disconnected wiring in the ignition circuit – petrol models (Chapters 1A and 5B).
- ☐ Worn, faulty or incorrectly-gapped spark plugs – petrol models (Chapter 1A).
- ☐ Preheating system faulty – diesel models (Chapter 5C).
- ☐ Fuel injection system fault – petrol models (Chapter 4A).
- ☐ Air in fuel system – diesel models (Chapter 4B).
- ☐ Major mechanical failure (e.g. timing belt) (Chapter 2).

Engine difficult to start when cold

- ☐ Battery discharged (Chapter 5A).
- ☐ Battery terminal connections loose or corroded (see *Weekly checks*).
- ☐ Worn, faulty or incorrectly-gapped spark plugs – petrol models (Chapter 1A).
- ☐ Preheating system faulty – diesel models (Chapter 5C).
- ☐ Fuel injection system fault – petrol models (Chapter 4A).
- ☐ Other ignition system fault – petrol models (Chapters 1A and 5B).
- ☐ Low cylinder compressions (Chapter 2).

Engine difficult to start when hot

- ☐ Air filter element dirty or clogged (Chapter 1).
- ☐ Fuel injection system fault – petrol models (Chapter 4A).
- ☐ Low cylinder compressions (Chapter 2).

Starter motor noisy or excessively-rough in engagement

- ☐ Starter pinion or flywheel ring gear teeth loose or broken (Chapter 2 and 5A).
- ☐ Starter motor mounting bolts loose or missing (Chapter 5A).
- ☐ Starter motor internal components worn or damaged (Chapter 5A).

Engine starts, but stops immediately

- ☐ Loose or faulty electrical connections in the ignition circuit – petrol models (Chapters 1A and 5B).
- ☐ Vacuum leak at the throttle body or inlet manifold – petrol models (Chapter 4A).
- ☐ Blocked injector/fuel injection system fault – petrol models (Chapter 4A).

Engine idles erratically

- ☐ Air filter element clogged (Chapter 1).
- ☐ Vacuum leak at the throttle body, inlet manifold or associated hoses – petrol models (Chapter 4A).
- ☐ Worn, faulty or incorrectly-gapped spark plugs – petrol models (Chapter 1A).
- ☐ Uneven or low cylinder compressions (Chapter 2).
- ☐ Camshaft lobes worn (Chapter 2).
- ☐ Timing belt incorrectly fitted (Chapter 2).
- ☐ Blocked injector/fuel injection system fault – petrol models (Chapter 4A).
- ☐ Faulty injector(s) – diesel models (Chapter 4B).

Engine misfires at idle speed

- ☐ Worn, faulty or incorrectly-gapped spark plugs – petrol models (Chapter 1A).
- ☐ Faulty spark plug HT leads – petrol models (Chapter 1A).
- ☐ Vacuum leak at the throttle body, inlet manifold or associated hoses – petrol models (Chapter 4A).
- ☐ Blocked injector/fuel injection system fault – petrol models (Chapter 4A).
- ☐ Faulty injector(s) – diesel models (Chapter 4B).
- ☐ Uneven or low cylinder compressions (Chapter 2).
- ☐ Disconnected, leaking, or perished crankcase ventilation hoses (Chapter 4C).

Engine misfires throughout the driving speed range

- ☐ Fuel filter choked (Chapter 1).
- ☐ Fuel pump faulty, or delivery pressure low – petrol models (Chapter 4A).
- ☐ Fuel tank vent blocked, or fuel pipes restricted (Chapter 4).
- ☐ Vacuum leak at the throttle body, inlet manifold or associated hoses – petrol models (Chapter 4A).
- ☐ Worn, faulty or incorrectly-gapped spark plugs – petrol models (Chapter 1A).
- ☐ Faulty spark plug HT leads – petrol models (Chapter 1A).
- ☐ Faulty injector(s) – diesel models (Chapter 4B).
- ☐ Faulty ignition coil – petrol models (Chapter 5B).
- ☐ Uneven or low cylinder compressions (Chapter 2).
- ☐ Blocked injector/fuel injection system fault – petrol models (Chapter 4A).

Engine (continued)

Engine hesitates on acceleration

- ☐ Worn, faulty or incorrectly-gapped spark plugs – petrol models (Chapter 1A).
- ☐ Vacuum leak at the throttle body, inlet manifold or associated hoses – petrol models (Chapter 4A).
- ☐ Blocked injector/fuel injection system fault – petrol models (Chapter 4A).
- ☐ Faulty injector(s) – diesel models (Chapter 4B).

Engine stalls

- ☐ Vacuum leak at the throttle body, inlet manifold or associated hoses – petrol models (Chapter 4A).
- ☐ Fuel filter choked (Chapter 1).
- ☐ Fuel pump faulty, or delivery pressure low – petrol models (Chapter 4A).
- ☐ Fuel tank vent blocked, or fuel pipes restricted (Chapter 4).
- ☐ Blocked injector/fuel injection system fault – petrol models (Chapter 4A).
- ☐ Faulty injector(s) – diesel models (Chapter 4B).

Engine lacks power

- ☐ Timing belt incorrectly fitted or tensioned (Chapter 2).
- ☐ Fuel filter choked (Chapter 1).
- ☐ Fuel pump faulty, or delivery pressure low – petrol models (Chapter 4A).
- ☐ Uneven or low cylinder compressions (Chapter 2).
- ☐ Worn, faulty or incorrectly-gapped spark plugs – petrol models (Chapter 1A).
- ☐ Vacuum leak at the throttle body, inlet manifold or associated hoses – petrol models (Chapter 4A).
- ☐ Blocked injector/fuel injection system fault – petrol models (Chapter 4A).
- ☐ Faulty injector(s) – diesel models (Chapter 4B).
- ☐ Brakes binding (Chapters 1 and 9).
- ☐ Clutch slipping (Chapter 6).
- ☐ Air filter element clogged (Chapter 1).

Engine backfires

- ☐ Timing belt incorrectly fitted or tensioned (Chapter 2).
- ☐ Vacuum leak at the throttle body, inlet manifold or associated hoses – petrol models (Chapter 4A).
- ☐ Blocked injector/fuel injection system fault – petrol models (Chapter 4A).

Oil pressure warning light illuminated with engine running

- ☐ Low oil level, or incorrect oil grade (Weekly checks).
- ☐ Faulty oil pressure switch (Chapter 5A).
- ☐ Worn engine bearings and/or oil pump (Chapter 2).
- ☐ High engine operating temperature (Chapter 3).
- ☐ Oil pressure relief valve defective (Chapter 2).
- ☐ Oil pick-up strainer clogged (Chapter 2).

Engine runs-on after switching off

- ☐ Excessive carbon build-up in engine (Chapter 2).
- ☐ High engine operating temperature (Chapter 3).
- ☐ Fuel injection system fault – petrol models (Chapter 4A).
- ☐ Faulty stop solenoid – diesel models (Chapter 4B).

Engine noises

Pre-ignition (pinking) or knocking during acceleration or under load

- ☐ Ignition system fault – petrol models (Chapters 1A and 5B).
- ☐ Incorrect grade of spark plug – petrol models (Chapter 1A).
- ☐ Vacuum leak at the throttle body, inlet manifold or associated hoses – petrol models (Chapter 4A).
- ☐ Excessive carbon build-up in engine (Chapter 2).
- ☐ Blocked injector/fuel injection system fault – petrol models (Chapter 4A).

Whistling or wheezing noises

- ☐ Leaking inlet manifold or throttle body gasket – petrol models (Chapter 4A).
- ☐ Leaking exhaust manifold gasket or pipe-to-manifold joint (Chapter 4).
- ☐ Leaking vacuum hose (Chapters 4 and 9).
- ☐ Blowing cylinder head gasket (Chapter 2).

Tapping or rattling noises

- ☐ Worn valve gear or camshaft (Chapter 2).
- ☐ Ancillary component fault (coolant pump, alternator, etc) (Chapters 3, 5, etc).

Knocking or thumping noises

- ☐ Worn big-end bearings (regular heavy knocking, perhaps less under load) (Chapter 2).
- ☐ Worn main bearings (rumbling and knocking, perhaps worsening under load) (Chapter 2).
- ☐ Piston slap (most noticeable when cold) (Chapter 2).
- ☐ Ancillary component fault (coolant pump, alternator, etc) (Chapters 3, 5, etc).

Cooling system

Overheating

☐ Insufficient coolant in system (*Weekly checks*).
☐ Thermostat faulty (Chapter 3).
☐ Radiator core blocked, or grille restricted (Chapter 3).
☐ Electric cooling fan or thermostatic switch faulty (Chapter 3).
☐ Inaccurate temperature gauge sender unit (Chapter 3).
☐ Airlock in cooling system.
☐ Expansion tank pressure cap faulty (Chapter 3).

Overcooling

☐ Thermostat faulty (Chapter 3).
☐ Inaccurate temperature gauge sender unit (Chapter 3).

External coolant leakage

☐ Deteriorated or damaged hoses or hose clips (Chapter 1).
☐ Radiator core or heater matrix leaking (Chapter 3).
☐ Pressure cap faulty (Chapter 3).
☐ Coolant pump internal seal leaking (Chapter 3).
☐ Coolant pump-to-housing seal leaking (Chapter 3).
☐ Boiling due to overheating (Chapter 3).
☐ Core plug leaking (Chapter 2).

Internal coolant leakage

☐ Leaking cylinder head gasket (Chapter 2).
☐ Cracked cylinder head or cylinder block (Chapter 2).

Corrosion

☐ Infrequent draining and flushing (Chapter 1).
☐ Incorrect coolant mixture or inappropriate coolant type (see *Weekly checks*).

Fuel and exhaust systems

Excessive fuel consumption

☐ Air filter element dirty or clogged (Chapter 1).
☐ Fuel injection system fault – petrol models (Chapter 4A).
☐ Faulty injector(s) – diesel models (Chapter 4B).
☐ Ignition system fault – petrol models (Chapters 1A and 5B).
☐ Tyres under-inflated (see *Weekly checks*).

Fuel leakage and/or fuel odour

☐ Damaged fuel tank, pipes or connections (Chapter 4).

Excessive noise or fumes from exhaust system

☐ Leaking exhaust system or manifold joints (Chapters 1 and 4).
☐ Leaking, corroded or damaged silencers or pipe (Chapters 1 and 4).
☐ Broken mountings causing body or suspension contact (Chapter 1).

Clutch

Pedal travels to floor – no pressure or very little resistance

☐ Faulty master or slave cylinder (Chapter 6).
☐ Faulty hydraulic release system (Chapter 6).
☐ Broken clutch release bearing or arm (Chapter 6).
☐ Broken diaphragm spring in clutch pressure plate (Chapter 6).

Clutch fails to disengage (unable to select gears)

☐ Faulty master or slave cylinder (Chapter 6).
☐ Faulty hydraulic release system (Chapter 6).
☐ Clutch disc sticking on gearbox input shaft splines (Chapter 6).
☐ Clutch disc sticking to flywheel or pressure plate (Chapter 6).
☐ Faulty pressure plate assembly (Chapter 6).
☐ Clutch release mechanism worn or incorrectly assembled (Chapter 6).

Clutch slips (engine speed increases, with no increase in vehicle speed)

☐ Faulty hydraulic release system (Chapter 6).
☐ Clutch disc linings excessively worn (Chapter 6).
☐ Clutch disc linings contaminated with oil or grease (Chapter 6).
☐ Faulty pressure plate or weak diaphragm spring (Chapter 6).

Judder as clutch is engaged

☐ Clutch disc linings contaminated with oil or grease (Chapter 6).
☐ Clutch disc linings excessively worn (Chapter 6).
☐ Faulty or distorted pressure plate or diaphragm spring (Chapter 6).
☐ Worn or loose engine or gearbox mountings (Chapter 2).
☐ Clutch disc hub or gearbox input shaft splines worn (Chapter 6).

Noise when depressing or releasing clutch pedal

☐ Worn clutch release bearing (Chapter 6).
☐ Worn or dry clutch pedal pivot (Chapter 6).
☐ Faulty pressure plate assembly (Chapter 6).
☐ Pressure plate diaphragm spring broken (Chapter 6).
☐ Broken clutch friction plate cushioning springs (Chapter 6).

Manual transmission

Noisy in neutral with engine running

- [ ] Input shaft bearings worn (noise apparent with clutch pedal released, but not when depressed) (Chapter 7A).*
- [ ] Clutch release bearing worn (noise apparent with clutch pedal depressed, possibly less when released) (Chapter 6).

Noisy in one particular gear

- [ ] Worn, damaged or chipped gear teeth (Chapter 7A).*

Difficulty engaging gears

- [ ] Clutch fault (Chapter 6).
- [ ] Worn or damaged gear linkage (Chapter 7A).
- [ ] Worn synchroniser units (Chapter 7A).*

Jumps out of gear

- [ ] Worn or damaged gear linkage (Chapter 7A).
- [ ] Worn synchroniser units (Chapter 7A).*
- [ ] Worn selector forks (Chapter 7A).*

Vibration

- [ ] Lack of oil (Chapter 1).
- [ ] Worn bearings (Chapter 7A).*

Lubricant leaks

- [ ] Leaking oil seal (Chapter 7A).
- [ ] Leaking housing joint (Chapter 7A).*
- [ ] Leaking input shaft oil seal (Chapter 7A).

*Although the corrective action necessary to remedy the symptoms described is beyond the scope of the home mechanic, the above information should be helpful in isolating the cause of the condition, so that the owner can communicate clearly with a professional mechanic.

Automatic transmission

Note: Due to the complexity of the automatic transmission, it is difficult for the home mechanic to properly diagnose and service this unit. For problems other than the following, the vehicle should be taken to a dealer service department or automatic transmission specialist. Do not be too hasty in removing the transmission if a fault is suspected, as most of the testing is carried out with the unit still fitted.

Fluid leakage

- [ ] Automatic transmission fluid is usually dark in colour. Fluid leaks should not be confused with engine oil, which can easily be blown onto the transmission by airflow.
- [ ] To determine the source of a leak, first remove all built-up dirt and grime from the transmission housing and surrounding areas using a degreasing agent, or by steam-cleaning. Drive the vehicle at low speed, so airflow will not blow the leak far from its source. Raise and support the vehicle, and determine where the leak is coming from.

General gear selection problems

- [ ] Chapter 7B deals with checking and adjusting the selector mechanism on automatic transmissions. The following are common problems which may be caused by a poorly-adjusted mechanism:
  - a) Engine starting in gears other than Park or Neutral.
  - b) Indicator panel indicating a gear other than the one actually being used.
  - c) Vehicle moves when in Park or Neutral.
  - d) Poor gear shift quality or erratic gear changes.
- [ ] Refer to Chapter 7B for the selector mechanism adjustment procedure.

Transmission will not downshift (kickdown) with accelerator pedal fully depressed

- [ ] Low transmission fluid level (Chapter 1).
- [ ] Incorrect selector mechanism adjustment (Chapter 7B).

Engine will not start in any gear, or starts in gears other than Park or Neutral

- [ ] Incorrect selector mechanism adjustment (Chapter 7B).

Transmission slips, shifts roughly, is noisy, or has no drive in forward or reverse gears

- [ ] There are many probable causes for the above problems, but unless there is a very obvious reason (such as a loose or corroded wiring plug connection on or near the transmission), the car should be taken to a franchise dealer for the fault to be diagnosed. The transmission control unit incorporates a self-diagnosis facility, and any fault codes can quickly be read and interpreted by a dealer with the proper diagnostic equipment.

Driveshafts

Vibration when accelerating or decelerating

- ☐ Worn inner constant velocity joint (Chapter 8).
- ☐ Bent or distorted driveshaft (Chapter 8).

Clicking or knocking noise on turns (at slow speed on full-lock)

- ☐ Worn outer constant velocity joint (Chapter 8).
- ☐ Lack of constant velocity joint lubricant, possibly due to damaged gaiter (Chapter 8).

Braking system

Note: *Before assuming that a brake problem exists, make sure that the tyres are in good condition and correctly inflated, that the front wheel alignment is correct, and that the vehicle is not loaded with weight in an unequal manner. Apart from checking the condition of all pipe and hose connections, any faults occurring on the anti-lock braking system should be referred to a VW dealer for diagnosis.*

Vehicle pulls to one side under braking

- ☐ Worn, defective, damaged or contaminated front or rear brake pads on one side (Chapters 1 and 9).
- ☐ Seized or partially-seized front or rear brake caliper (Chapter 9).
- ☐ A mixture of brake pad lining materials fitted between sides (Chapter 9).
- ☐ Brake caliper or rear brake backplate mounting bolts loose (Chapter 9).
- ☐ Worn or damaged steering or suspension components (Chapters 1 and 10).

Noise (grinding or high-pitched squeal) when brakes applied

- ☐ Brake pad friction lining material worn down to metal backing (Chapters 1 and 9).
- ☐ Excessive corrosion of brake disc – may be apparent after the vehicle has been standing for some time (Chapters 1 and 9).
- ☐ Foreign object (stone chipping, etc) trapped between brake disc and shield (Chapters 1 and 9).

Excessive brake pedal travel

- ☐ Faulty master cylinder (Chapter 9).
- ☐ Air in hydraulic system (Chapter 9).
- ☐ Faulty vacuum servo unit (Chapter 9).
- ☐ Faulty vacuum pump, where fitted (Chapter 9).

Brake pedal feels spongy when depressed

- ☐ Air in hydraulic system (Chapter 9).
- ☐ Deteriorated flexible rubber brake hoses (Chapters 1 and 9).
- ☐ Master cylinder mountings loose (Chapter 9).
- ☐ Faulty master cylinder (Chapter 9).

Excessive brake pedal effort required to stop vehicle

- ☐ Faulty vacuum servo unit (Chapter 9).
- ☐ Disconnected, damaged or insecure brake servo vacuum hose (Chapters 1 and 9).
- ☐ Faulty vacuum pump, where fitted (Chapter 9).
- ☐ Primary or secondary hydraulic circuit failure (Chapter 9).
- ☐ Seized brake caliper (Chapter 9).
- ☐ Brake pads incorrectly fitted (Chapter 9).
- ☐ Incorrect grade of brake pads fitted (Chapter 9).
- ☐ Brake pads contaminated (Chapter 9).

Judder felt through brake pedal or steering wheel when braking

- ☐ Excessive run-out or distortion of brake disc(s) (Chapter 9).
- ☐ Brake pad linings worn (Chapters 1 and 9).
- ☐ Brake caliper mounting bolts loose (Chapter 9).
- ☐ Wear in suspension or steering components or mountings (Chapters 1 and 10).

Pedal pulsates when braking hard

- ☐ Normal feature of ABS – no fault

Brakes binding

- ☐ Seized brake caliper piston(s) (Chapter 9).
- ☐ Incorrectly-adjusted handbrake mechanism (Chapter 9).
- ☐ Faulty master cylinder (Chapter 9).

Rear wheels locking under normal braking

- ☐ Rear brake pad linings contaminated (Chapters 1 and 9).
- ☐ Rear brake discs warped (Chapters 1 and 9).

Steering and suspension

Note: *Before diagnosing suspension or steering faults, be sure that the trouble is not due to incorrect tyre pressures, mixtures of tyre types, or binding brakes.*

Vehicle pulls to one side

- ☐ Defective tyre (see *Weekly checks*).
- ☐ Excessive wear in suspension or steering components (Chapters 1 and 10).
- ☐ Incorrect front wheel alignment (Chapter 10).
- ☐ Accident damage to steering or suspension components (Chapters 1 and 10).

Wheel wobble and vibration

- ☐ Front roadwheels out of balance (vibration felt mainly through the steering wheel) (Chapter 10).
- ☐ Rear roadwheels out of balance (vibration felt throughout the vehicle) (Chapter 10).
- ☐ Roadwheels damaged or distorted (Chapter 10).
- ☐ Faulty or damaged tyre (*Weekly checks*).
- ☐ Worn steering or suspension joints, bushes or components (Chapters 1 and 10).
- ☐ Wheel bolts loose (Chapter 1 and 10).

Excessive pitching and/or rolling around corners, or during braking

- ☐ Defective shock absorbers (Chapters 1 and 10).
- ☐ Broken or weak coil spring and/or suspension component (Chapters 1 and 10).
- ☐ Worn or damaged anti-roll bar or mountings (Chapter 10).

Wandering or general instability

- ☐ Incorrect front wheel alignment (Chapter 10).
- ☐ Worn steering or suspension joints, bushes or components (Chapters 1 and 10).
- ☐ Roadwheels out of balance (Chapter 10).
- ☐ Faulty or damaged tyre (*Weekly checks*).
- ☐ Wheel bolts loose (Chapter 10).
- ☐ Defective shock absorbers (Chapters 1 and 10).

Excessively-stiff steering

- ☐ Seized track rod end balljoint or suspension balljoint (Chapters 1 and 10).
- ☐ Broken or incorrectly adjusted auxiliary drivebelt (Chapter 1).
- ☐ Incorrect front wheel alignment (Chapter 10).
- ☐ Steering gear damaged (Chapter 10).

Excessive play in steering

- ☐ Worn steering column universal joint(s) (Chapter 10).
- ☐ Worn steering track rod end balljoints (Chapters 1 and 10).
- ☐ Worn steering gear (Chapter 10).
- ☐ Worn steering or suspension joints, bushes or components (Chapters 1 and 10).

Lack of power assistance

- ☐ Broken or incorrectly-adjusted auxiliary drivebelt (Chapter 1).
- ☐ Incorrect power steering fluid level (*Weekly checks*).
- ☐ Restriction in power steering fluid hoses (Chapter 10).
- ☐ Faulty power steering pump (Chapter 10).
- ☐ Faulty steering gear (Chapter 10).

Tyre wear excessive

Tyres worn on inside or outside edges

- ☐ Incorrect camber or castor angles (Chapter 10).
- ☐ Worn steering or suspension joints, bushes or components (Chapters 1 and 10).
- ☐ Excessively-hard cornering.
- ☐ Accident damage.

Tyre treads exhibit feathered edges

- ☐ Incorrect toe setting (Chapter 10).

Tyres worn in centre of tread

- ☐ Tyres over-inflated (*Weekly checks*).

Tyres worn on inside and outside edges

- ☐ Tyres under-inflated (*Weekly checks*).
- ☐ Worn shock absorbers (Chapter 10).

Tyres worn unevenly

- ☐ Tyres/wheels out of balance (*Weekly checks*).
- ☐ Excessive wheel or tyre run-out (Chapter 10).
- ☐ Worn shock absorbers (Chapters 1 and 10).
- ☐ Faulty tyre (*Weekly checks*).

Electrical system

Note: *For problems associated with the starting system, refer to the faults listed under Engine earlier in this Section.*

Battery will not hold a charge more than a few days

- ☐ Battery defective internally (Chapter 5A).
- ☐ Battery electrolyte level low – where applicable (*Weekly checks*).
- ☐ Battery terminal connections loose or corroded (*Weekly checks*).
- ☐ Auxiliary drivebelt worn – or incorrectly adjusted, where applicable (Chapter 1).
- ☐ Alternator not charging at correct output (Chapter 5A).
- ☐ Alternator or voltage regulator faulty (Chapter 5A).
- ☐ Short-circuit causing continual battery drain (Chapters 5 and 12).

Ignition/no-charge warning light remains illuminated with engine running

- ☐ Auxiliary drivebelt broken, worn, or incorrectly adjusted (Chapter 1).
- ☐ Internal fault in alternator or voltage regulator (Chapter 5A).
- ☐ Broken, disconnected, or loose wiring in charging circuit (Chapter 5A).

Ignition/no-charge warning light fails to come on

- ☐ Broken, disconnected, or loose wiring in warning light circuit (Chapter 12).
- ☐ Alternator faulty (Chapter 5A).

Electrical system (continued)

Lights inoperative

- ☐ Bulb blown (Chapter 12).
- ☐ Corrosion of bulb or bulbholder contacts (Chapter 12).
- ☐ Blown fuse (Chapter 12).
- ☐ Faulty relay (Chapter 12).
- ☐ Broken, loose, or disconnected wiring (Chapter 12).
- ☐ Faulty switch (Chapter 12).

Instrument readings inaccurate or erratic

Instrument readings increase with engine speed

- ☐ Faulty voltage regulator (Chapter 12).

Fuel or temperature gauges give no reading

- ☐ Faulty gauge sender unit (Chapters 3 and 4).
- ☐ Wiring open-circuit (Chapter 12).
- ☐ Faulty gauge (Chapter 12).

Fuel or temperature gauges give continuous maximum reading

- ☐ Faulty gauge sender unit (Chapters 3 and 4).
- ☐ Wiring short-circuit (Chapter 12).
- ☐ Faulty gauge (Chapter 12).

Horn inoperative, or unsatisfactory in operation

Horn operates all the time

- ☐ Horn contacts permanently bridged or horn push stuck down (Chapter 12).

Horn fails to operate

- ☐ Blown fuse (Chapter 12).
- ☐ Cable or cable connections loose, broken or disconnected (Chapter 12).
- ☐ Faulty horn (Chapter 12).

Horn emits intermittent or unsatisfactory sound

- ☐ Cable connections loose (Chapter 12).
- ☐ Horn mountings loose (Chapter 12).
- ☐ Faulty horn (Chapter 12).

Windscreen/tailgate wipers inoperative, or unsatisfactory in operation

Wipers fail to operate, or operate very slowly

- ☐ Wiper blades stuck to screen, or linkage seized or binding (*Weekly checks* and Chapter 12).
- ☐ Blown fuse (Chapter 12).
- ☐ Cable or cable connections loose, broken or disconnected (Chapter 12).
- ☐ Faulty relay (Chapter 12).
- ☐ Faulty wiper motor (Chapter 12).

Wiper blades sweep over too large or too small an area of the glass

- ☐ Wiper arms incorrectly positioned on spindles (Chapter 12).
- ☐ Excessive wear of wiper linkage (Chapter 12).
- ☐ Wiper motor or linkage mountings loose or insecure (Chapter 12).

Wiper blades fail to clean the glass effectively

- ☐ Wiper blade rubbers worn or perished (*Weekly checks*).
- ☐ Wiper arm tension springs broken, or arm pivots seized (Chapter 12).
- ☐ Insufficient windscreen washer additive to adequately remove road film (*Weekly checks*).

Windscreen washers inoperative, or unsatisfactory in operation

One or more washer jets inoperative

- ☐ Blocked washer jet (Chapter 12).
- ☐ Disconnected, kinked or restricted fluid hose (Chapter 12).
- ☐ Insufficient fluid in washer reservoir (*Weekly checks*).

Washer pump fails to operate

- ☐ Broken or disconnected wiring or connections (Chapter 12).
- ☐ Blown fuse (Chapter 12).
- ☐ Faulty washer switch (Chapter 12).
- ☐ Faulty washer pump (Chapter 12).

Washer pump runs for some time before fluid is emitted from jets

- ☐ Faulty one-way valve in fluid supply hose (Chapter 12).

Electric windows inoperative, or unsatisfactory in operation

Window glass will only move in one direction

- ☐ Faulty switch (Chapter 12).

Window glass slow to move

- ☐ Regulator seized or damaged, or in need of lubrication (Chapter 11).
- ☐ Door internal components or trim fouling regulator (Chapter 11).
- ☐ Faulty motor (Chapter 11).

Window glass fails to move

- ☐ Blown fuse (Chapter 12).
- ☐ Faulty relay (Chapter 12).
- ☐ Broken or disconnected wiring or connections (Chapter 12).
- ☐ Faulty motor (Chapter 12).

Central locking system inoperative, or unsatisfactory in operation

Complete system failure

- ☐ Blown fuse (Chapter 12).
- ☐ Faulty relay (Chapter 12).
- ☐ Broken or disconnected wiring or connections (Chapter 12).

Latch locks but will not unlock, or unlocks but will not lock

- ☐ Faulty switch (Chapter 12).
- ☐ Broken or disconnected latch operating rods or levers (Chapter 11).
- ☐ Faulty relay (Chapter 12).

One lock fails to operate

- ☐ Broken or disconnected wiring or connections (Chapter 12).
- ☐ Faulty motor (Chapter 11).
- ☐ Broken, binding or disconnected lock operating rods or levers (Chapter 11).
- ☐ Fault in door lock (Chapter 11).

A

ABS (Anti-lock brake system) A system, usually electronically controlled, that senses incipient wheel lockup during braking and relieves hydraulic pressure at wheels that are about to skid.

Air bag An inflatable bag hidden in the steering wheel (driver's side) or the dash or glovebox (passenger side). In a head-on collision, the bags inflate, preventing the driver and front passenger from being thrown forward into the steering wheel or windscreen.

Air cleaner A metal or plastic housing, containing a filter element, which removes dust and dirt from the air being drawn into the engine.

Air filter element The actual filter in an air cleaner system, usually manufactured from pleated paper and requiring renewal at regular intervals.

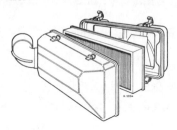

Air filter

Allen key A hexagonal wrench which fits into a recessed hexagonal hole.

Alligator clip A long-nosed spring-loaded metal clip with meshing teeth. Used to make temporary electrical connections.

Alternator A component in the electrical system which converts mechanical energy from a drivebelt into electrical energy to charge the battery and to operate the starting system, ignition system and electrical accessories.

Ampere (amp) A unit of measurement for the flow of electric current. One amp is the amount of current produced by one volt acting through a resistance of one ohm.

Anaerobic sealer A substance used to prevent bolts and screws from loosening. Anaerobic means that it does not require oxygen for activation. The Loctite brand is widely used.

Antifreeze A substance (usually ethylene glycol) mixed with water, and added to a vehicle's cooling system, to prevent freezing of the coolant in winter. Antifreeze also contains chemicals to inhibit corrosion and the formation of rust and other deposits that would tend to clog the radiator and coolant passages and reduce cooling efficiency.

Anti-seize compound A coating that reduces the risk of seizing on fasteners that are subjected to high temperatures, such as exhaust manifold bolts and nuts.

Asbestos A natural fibrous mineral with great heat resistance, commonly used in the composition of brake friction materials.

Asbestos is a health hazard and the dust created by brake systems should never be inhaled or ingested.

Axle A shaft on which a wheel revolves, or which revolves with a wheel. Also, a solid beam that connects the two wheels at one end of the vehicle. An axle which also transmits power to the wheels is known as a live axle.

Axleshaft A single rotating shaft, on either side of the differential, which delivers power from the final drive assembly to the drive wheels. Also called a driveshaft or a halfshaft.

B

Ball bearing An anti-friction bearing consisting of a hardened inner and outer race with hardened steel balls between two races.

Bearing The curved surface on a shaft or in a bore, or the part assembled into either, that permits relative motion between them with minimum wear and friction.

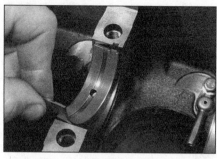

Bearing

Big-end bearing The bearing in the end of the connecting rod that's attached to the crankshaft.

Bleed nipple A valve on a brake wheel cylinder, caliper or other hydraulic component that is opened to purge the hydraulic system of air. Also called a bleed screw.

Brake bleeding Procedure for removing air from lines of a hydraulic brake system.

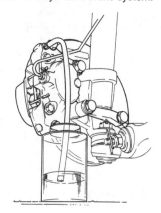

Brake bleeding

Brake disc The component of a disc brake that rotates with the wheels.

Brake drum The component of a drum brake that rotates with the wheels.

Brake linings The friction material which contacts the brake disc or drum to retard the vehicle's speed. The linings are bonded or riveted to the brake pads or shoes.

Brake pads The replaceable friction pads that pinch the brake disc when the brakes are applied. Brake pads consist of a friction material bonded or riveted to a rigid backing plate.

Brake shoe The crescent-shaped carrier to which the brake linings are mounted and which forces the lining against the rotating drum during braking.

Braking systems For more information on braking systems, consult the *Haynes Automotive Brake Manual*.

Breaker bar A long socket wrench handle providing greater leverage.

Bulkhead The insulated partition between the engine and the passenger compartment.

C

Caliper The non-rotating part of a disc-brake assembly that straddles the disc and carries the brake pads. The caliper also contains the hydraulic components that cause the pads to pinch the disc when the brakes are applied. A caliper is also a measuring tool that can be set to measure inside or outside dimensions of an object.

Camshaft A rotating shaft on which a series of cam lobes operate the valve mechanisms. The camshaft may be driven by gears, by sprockets and chain or by sprockets and a belt.

Canister A container in an evaporative emission control system; contains activated charcoal granules to trap vapours from the fuel system.

Canister

Carburettor A device which mixes fuel with air in the proper proportions to provide a desired power output from a spark ignition internal combustion engine.

Castellated Resembling the parapets along the top of a castle wall. For example, a castellated balljoint stud nut.

Castor In wheel alignment, the backward or forward tilt of the steering axis. Castor is positive when the steering axis is inclined rearward at the top.

Catalytic converter A silencer-like device in the exhaust system which converts certain pollutants in the exhaust gases into less harmful substances.

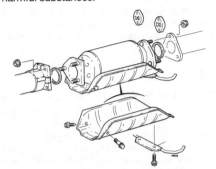

Catalytic converter

Circlip A ring-shaped clip used to prevent endwise movement of cylindrical parts and shafts. An internal circlip is installed in a groove in a housing; an external circlip fits into a groove on the outside of a cylindrical piece such as a shaft.

Clearance The amount of space between two parts. For example, between a piston and a cylinder, between a bearing and a journal, etc.

Coil spring A spiral of elastic steel found in various sizes throughout a vehicle, for example as a springing medium in the suspension and in the valve train.

Compression Reduction in volume, and increase in pressure and temperature, of a gas, caused by squeezing it into a smaller space.

Compression ratio The relationship between cylinder volume when the piston is at top dead centre and cylinder volume when the piston is at bottom dead centre.

Constant velocity (CV) joint A type of universal joint that cancels out vibrations caused by driving power being transmitted through an angle.

Core plug A disc or cup-shaped metal device inserted in a hole in a casting through which core was removed when the casting was formed. Also known as a freeze plug or expansion plug.

Crankcase The lower part of the engine block in which the crankshaft rotates.

Crankshaft The main rotating member, or shaft, running the length of the crankcase, with offset "throws" to which the connecting rods are attached.

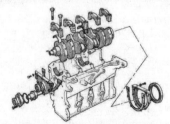

Crankshaft assembly

Crocodile clip See Alligator clip

D

Diagnostic code Code numbers obtained by accessing the diagnostic mode of an engine management computer. This code can be used to determine the area in the system where a malfunction may be located.

Disc brake A brake design incorporating a rotating disc onto which brake pads are squeezed. The resulting friction converts the energy of a moving vehicle into heat.

Double-overhead cam (DOHC) An engine that uses two overhead camshafts, usually one for the intake valves and one for the exhaust valves.

Drivebelt(s) The belt(s) used to drive accessories such as the alternator, water pump, power steering pump, air conditioning compressor, etc. off the crankshaft pulley.

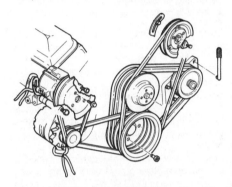

Accessory drivebelts

Driveshaft Any shaft used to transmit motion. Commonly used when referring to the axleshafts on a front wheel drive vehicle.

Drum brake A type of brake using a drum-shaped metal cylinder attached to the inner surface of the wheel. When the brake pedal is pressed, curved brake shoes with friction linings press against the inside of the drum to slow or stop the vehicle.

E

EGR valve A valve used to introduce exhaust gases into the intake air stream.

Electronic control unit (ECU) A computer which controls (for instance) ignition and fuel injection systems, or an anti-lock braking system. For more information refer to the *Haynes Automotive Electrical and Electronic Systems Manual.*

Electronic Fuel Injection (EFI) A computer controlled fuel system that distributes fuel through an injector located in each intake port of the engine.

Emergency brake A braking system, independent of the main hydraulic system, that can be used to slow or stop the vehicle if the primary brakes fail, or to hold the vehicle stationary even though the brake pedal isn't depressed. It usually consists of a hand lever that actuates either front or rear brakes mechanically through a series of cables and linkages. Also known as a handbrake or parking brake.

Endfloat The amount of lengthwise movement between two parts. As applied to a crankshaft, the distance that the crankshaft can move forward and back in the cylinder block.

Engine management system (EMS) A computer controlled system which manages the fuel injection and the ignition systems in an integrated fashion.

Exhaust manifold A part with several passages through which exhaust gases leave the engine combustion chambers and enter the exhaust pipe.

F

Fan clutch A viscous (fluid) drive coupling device which permits variable engine fan speeds in relation to engine speeds.

Feeler blade A thin strip or blade of hardened steel, ground to an exact thickness, used to check or measure clearances between parts.

Feeler blade

Firing order The order in which the engine cylinders fire, or deliver their power strokes, beginning with the number one cylinder.

Flywheel A heavy spinning wheel in which energy is absorbed and stored by means of momentum. On cars, the flywheel is attached to the crankshaft to smooth out firing impulses.

Free play The amount of travel before any action takes place. The "looseness" in a linkage, or an assembly of parts, between the initial application of force and actual movement. For example, the distance the brake pedal moves before the pistons in the master cylinder are actuated.

Fuse An electrical device which protects a circuit against accidental overload. The typical fuse contains a soft piece of metal which is calibrated to melt at a predetermined current flow (expressed as amps) and break the circuit.

Fusible link A circuit protection device consisting of a conductor surrounded by heat-resistant insulation. The conductor is smaller than the wire it protects, so it acts as the weakest link in the circuit. Unlike a blown fuse, a failed fusible link must frequently be cut from the wire for replacement.

G

Gap The distance the spark must travel in jumping from the centre electrode to the side electrode in a spark plug. Also refers to the spacing between the points in a contact breaker assembly in a conventional points-type ignition, or to the distance between the reluctor or rotor and the pickup coil in an electronic ignition.

Adjusting spark plug gap

Gasket Any thin, soft material - usually cork, cardboard, asbestos or soft metal - installed between two metal surfaces to ensure a good seal. For instance, the cylinder head gasket seals the joint between the block and the cylinder head.

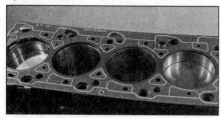

Gasket

Gauge An instrument panel display used to monitor engine conditions. A gauge with a movable pointer on a dial or a fixed scale is an analogue gauge. A gauge with a numerical readout is called a digital gauge.

H

Halfshaft A rotating shaft that transmits power from the final drive unit to a drive wheel, usually when referring to a live rear axle.

Harmonic balancer A device designed to reduce torsion or twisting vibration in the crankshaft. May be incorporated in the crankshaft pulley. Also known as a vibration damper.

Hone An abrasive tool for correcting small irregularities or differences in diameter in an engine cylinder, brake cylinder, etc.

Hydraulic tappet A tappet that utilises hydraulic pressure from the engine's lubrication system to maintain zero clearance (constant contact with both camshaft and valve stem). Automatically adjusts to variation in valve stem length. Hydraulic tappets also reduce valve noise.

I

Ignition timing The moment at which the spark plug fires, usually expressed in the number of crankshaft degrees before the piston reaches the top of its stroke.

Inlet manifold A tube or housing with passages through which flows the air-fuel mixture (carburettor vehicles and vehicles with throttle body injection) or air only (port fuel-injected vehicles) to the port openings in the cylinder head.

J

Jump start Starting the engine of a vehicle with a discharged or weak battery by attaching jump leads from the weak battery to a charged or helper battery.

L

Load Sensing Proportioning Valve (LSPV) A brake hydraulic system control valve that works like a proportioning valve, but also takes into consideration the amount of weight carried by the rear axle.

Locknut A nut used to lock an adjustment nut, or other threaded component, in place. For example, a locknut is employed to keep the adjusting nut on the rocker arm in position.

Lockwasher A form of washer designed to prevent an attaching nut from working loose.

M

MacPherson strut A type of front suspension system devised by Earle MacPherson at Ford of England. In its original form, a simple lateral link with the anti-roll bar creates the lower control arm. A long strut - an integral coil spring and shock absorber - is mounted between the body and the steering knuckle. Many modern so-called MacPherson strut systems use a conventional lower A-arm and don't rely on the anti-roll bar for location.

Multimeter An electrical test instrument with the capability to measure voltage, current and resistance.

N

NOx Oxides of Nitrogen. A common toxic pollutant emitted by petrol and diesel engines at higher temperatures.

O

Ohm The unit of electrical resistance. One volt applied to a resistance of one ohm will produce a current of one amp.

Ohmmeter An instrument for measuring electrical resistance.

O-ring A type of sealing ring made of a special rubber-like material; in use, the O-ring is compressed into a groove to provide the sealing action.

Overhead cam (ohc) engine An engine with the camshaft(s) located on top of the cylinder head(s).

Overhead valve (ohv) engine An engine with the valves located in the cylinder head, but with the camshaft located in the engine block.

Oxygen sensor A device installed in the engine exhaust manifold, which senses the oxygen content in the exhaust and converts this information into an electric current. Also called a Lambda sensor.

P

Phillips screw A type of screw head having a cross instead of a slot for a corresponding type of screwdriver.

Plastigage A thin strip of plastic thread, available in different sizes, used for measuring clearances. For example, a strip of Plastigage is laid across a bearing journal. The parts are assembled and dismantled; the width of the crushed strip indicates the clearance between journal and bearing.

Plastigage

Propeller shaft The long hollow tube with universal joints at both ends that carries power from the transmission to the differential on front-engined rear wheel drive vehicles.

Proportioning valve A hydraulic control valve which limits the amount of pressure to the rear brakes during panic stops to prevent wheel lock-up.

R

Rack-and-pinion steering A steering system with a pinion gear on the end of the steering shaft that mates with a rack (think of a geared wheel opened up and laid flat). When the steering wheel is turned, the pinion turns, moving the rack to the left or right. This movement is transmitted through the track rods to the steering arms at the wheels.

Radiator A liquid-to-air heat transfer device designed to reduce the temperature of the coolant in an internal combustion engine cooling system.

Refrigerant Any substance used as a heat transfer agent in an air-conditioning system. R-12 has been the principle refrigerant for many years; recently, however, manufacturers have begun using R-134a, a non-CFC substance that is considered less harmful to the ozone in the upper atmosphere.

Rocker arm A lever arm that rocks on a shaft or pivots on a stud. In an overhead valve engine, the rocker arm converts the upward movement of the pushrod into a downward movement to open a valve.

Rotor In a distributor, the rotating device inside the cap that connects the centre electrode and the outer terminals as it turns, distributing the high voltage from the coil secondary winding to the proper spark plug. Also, that part of an alternator which rotates inside the stator. Also, the rotating assembly of a turbocharger, including the compressor wheel, shaft and turbine wheel.

Runout The amount of wobble (in-and-out movement) of a gear or wheel as it's rotated. The amount a shaft rotates "out-of-true." The out-of-round condition of a rotating part.

S

Sealant A liquid or paste used to prevent leakage at a joint. Sometimes used in conjunction with a gasket.

Sealed beam lamp An older headlight design which integrates the reflector, lens and filaments into a hermetically-sealed one-piece unit. When a filament burns out or the lens cracks, the entire unit is simply replaced.

Serpentine drivebelt A single, long, wide accessory drivebelt that's used on some newer vehicles to drive all the accessories, instead of a series of smaller, shorter belts. Serpentine drivebelts are usually tensioned by an automatic tensioner.

Serpentine drivebelt

Shim Thin spacer, commonly used to adjust the clearance or relative positions between two parts. For example, shims inserted into or under bucket tappets control valve clearances. Clearance is adjusted by changing the thickness of the shim.

Slide hammer A special puller that screws into or hooks onto a component such as a shaft or bearing; a heavy sliding handle on the shaft bottoms against the end of the shaft to knock the component free.

Sprocket A tooth or projection on the periphery of a wheel, shaped to engage with a chain or drivebelt. Commonly used to refer to the sprocket wheel itself.

Starter inhibitor switch On vehicles with an automatic transmission, a switch that prevents starting if the vehicle is not in Neutral or Park.

Strut See MacPherson strut.

T

Tappet A cylindrical component which transmits motion from the cam to the valve stem, either directly or via a pushrod and rocker arm. Also called a cam follower.

Thermostat A heat-controlled valve that regulates the flow of coolant between the cylinder block and the radiator, so maintaining optimum engine operating temperature. A thermostat is also used in some air cleaners in which the temperature is regulated.

Thrust bearing The bearing in the clutch assembly that is moved in to the release levers by clutch pedal action to disengage the clutch. Also referred to as a release bearing.

Timing belt A toothed belt which drives the camshaft. Serious engine damage may result if it breaks in service.

Timing chain A chain which drives the camshaft.

Toe-in The amount the front wheels are closer together at the front than at the rear. On rear wheel drive vehicles, a slight amount of toe-in is usually specified to keep the front wheels running parallel on the road by offsetting other forces that tend to spread the wheels apart.

Toe-out The amount the front wheels are closer together at the rear than at the front. On front wheel drive vehicles, a slight amount of toe-out is usually specified.

Tools For full information on choosing and using tools, refer to the *Haynes Automotive Tools Manual.*

Tracer A stripe of a second colour applied to a wire insulator to distinguish that wire from another one with the same colour insulator.

Tune-up A process of accurate and careful adjustments and parts replacement to obtain the best possible engine performance.

Turbocharger A centrifugal device, driven by exhaust gases, that pressurises the intake air. Normally used to increase the power output from a given engine displacement, but can also be used primarily to reduce exhaust emissions (as on VW's "Umwelt" Diesel engine).

U

Universal joint or U-joint A double-pivoted connection for transmitting power from a driving to a driven shaft through an angle. A U-joint consists of two Y-shaped yokes and a cross-shaped member called the spider.

V

Valve A device through which the flow of liquid, gas, vacuum, or loose material in bulk may be started, stopped, or regulated by a movable part that opens, shuts, or partially obstructs one or more ports or passageways. A valve is also the movable part of such a device.

Valve clearance The clearance between the valve tip (the end of the valve stem) and the rocker arm or tappet. The valve clearance is measured when the valve is closed.

Vernier caliper A precision measuring instrument that measures inside and outside dimensions. Not quite as accurate as a micrometer, but more convenient.

Viscosity The thickness of a liquid or its resistance to flow.

Volt A unit for expressing electrical "pressure" in a circuit. One volt that will produce a current of one ampere through a resistance of one ohm.

W

Welding Various processes used to join metal items by heating the areas to be joined to a molten state and fusing them together. For more information refer to the *Haynes Automotive Welding Manual.*

Wiring diagram A drawing portraying the components and wires in a vehicle's electrical system, using standardised symbols. For more information refer to the *Haynes Automotive Electrical and Electronic Systems Manual.*

Note: *References throughout this index are in the form* "**Chapter number**" • "**Page number**". *So, for example, 2C•15 refers to page 15 of Chapter 2C.*

A

Accelerator position sender – 4B•3
Accessory shops – REF•5
Acknowledgements – 0•5
Aerial – 12•16
Air conditioning system – 3•11, 3•12
Air filter – 1A•13, 1B•15, 4A•4, 4B•2
Air intake charge pressure/temperature
  sensor – 4B•8
Air mass meter – 4B•8
Air temperature sensor – 4A•5, 4A•8
Airbags – 0•6, 1A•12, 1B•14, 12•17
Airflow meter – 4A•5, 4A•8
Alarm system – 12•19
Alternator – 5A•3, 5A•4
Altitude sensor – 4B•9
Antifreeze – 0•13, 0•17, 1A•10, 1A•17,
  1B•12, 1B•18
Anti-lock braking system (ABS) – 9•16, 9•17
Anti-roll bar – 10•9
Anti-theft alarm system – 12•19, REF•4
Asbestos – 0•6
ASR switch – 12•5
Automatic transmission – 7B•1 *et seq*
  fault finding – REF•16
  fluid – 0•17, 1A•14, 1A•15, 1B•15, 1B•16
Auxiliary drivebelt – 1A•10, 1A•14, 1B•12,
  1B•15, 2A•8, 2B•10

B

Balancer shaft – 2A•16
Battery – 0•6, 0•15, 1A•12, 1B•14, 5A•2,
  5A•3
Big-end bearings – 2C•24, 2C•27
Bleeding
  brakes – 9•2
  clutch – 6•2
  power steering – 10•18
Blower motor – 3•9, 3•12, 3•13
Body corrosion – REF•11
Body electrical system – 12•1 *et seq*
Bodywork and fittings – 11•1 *et seq*
Bonnet – 11•4
Bonnet lock and release cable – 11•4
Boot lid – 11•9, 11•11
Bosch Motronic engine management
system – 4A•5
Braking system – 1A•11, 1A•13, 1B•14,
  9•1 *et seq*, REF•8, REF•9, REF•10
  brake fluid – 0•13, 0•17, 1A•16, 1B•17
  fault finding – REF•17
  hydraulic circuit – 1B•12
  pedal – 4B•9
Brush holder (alternator) – 5A•5
Bulbs – 12•6, 12•9
Bumpers – 11•5
Burning – 0•6
Buying spare parts – REF•5

C

Cables
  bonnet release – 11•4
  handbrake – 9•15
  locking (automatic transmission) – 7B•5
  selector (automatic transmission) – 7B•3
Calipers – 9•8, 9•10
Camshaft – 2C•15
Camshaft cover – 2A•9, 2B•10
Camshaft hub – 2B•9
Camshaft oil seal – 2A•9, 2B•11
Camshaft position sensor – 4B•9
Camshaft sprocket – 2A•7, 2A•8, 2B•9
Carpets – 11•2, 11•22
Cassette unit anti-theft system –
  precaution – REF•4
Catalytic converter – 4C•5, 4C•6
CD player – 12•16, REF•4
Central locking system – 12•16
Centre console – 11•17
Change-over valve – 4B•12
Charcoal canister – 4C•2
Charge pressure control valve – 4B•8
Charging – 5A•3
Cigar lighter illumination – 12•10
Climatronic air conditioning – 3•13
Clutch – 6•1 *et seq*
  fault finding – REF•15
  fluid – 0•13, 0•17, 1A•16, 1B•17
  pedal – 4B•9
Coil(s) – 5B•3
Compression test – 2A•4, 2B•6
Compressor – 3•12
Connecting rod assemblies – 2C•19, 2C•27
Console – 11•17
Control unit parking aid – 12•16
Convenience system electronic control
  unit – 12•20
Conversion factors – REF•2
Coolant – 0•13, 0•17, 1A•10, 1A•16, 1B•17
Coolant temperature sensor – 4A•5, 4A•8,
  4B•7
Cooler unit (fuel cooling system) – 3•14
Cooling pump (fuel cooling system) – 3•14
*Cooling, heating and ventilation
  systems* – 3•1 *et seq*
  fault finding – REF•15
Courtesy light – 12•10
  switches – 12•4
Crankcase – 2C•23
Crankcase emission control – 4C•2
Crankshaft – 2C•22, 2C•25
Crankshaft oil seals – 2A•10, 2B•11
Crankshaft sprocket – 2A•8, 2B•9
Crash sensors (side airbags) – 12•19
Crossmember – 11•7
Crushing – 0•6
Cylinder block – 2C•23
Cylinder head – 2A•11, 2B•12, 2C•11, 2C•15

D

Dash illumination switch – 12•5
Dents – 11•2
Depressurisation (fuel injection system) –
  4A•13
Diesel engine in-car repair procedures –
  2B•1 *et seq*
Diesel engine management system – 4B•7
Diesel injection equipment – 0•6
Dimensions – REF•1
Dipped beam – 12•6, 12•12
Direction indicators – 12•7, 12•11, 12•13
Discs – 9•7, 9•8
Distance sensor parking aid – 12•16
Door courtesy light – 12•10
Door mirror adjuster – 12•4
Doors – 11•11, 11•12, 11•14, 11•16, REF•9
Door rattles – 11•4
Drivebelt – 1A•10, 1A•14, 1B•12, 1B•15,
  2A•8, 2B•10
Driveplate – 2A•13, 2B•15
Driveshafts – 8•1 *et seq*, REF•10
  flange oil seals – 7A•5
  gaiter – 1A•11,– 1B•13
  fault finding – REF•17
Drivetrain – 1A•13, 1B•14

E

Earth fault – 12•2
Electric auxiliary cooling fan – 3•5
Electric shock – 0•6
Electric windows – 11•16
Electrical equipment – 0•15, 1A•13, 1B•14,
  REF•9
  fault finding – 12•2, REF•18, REF•19
Electronic control unit (ECU)
  convenience system – 12•20
  diesel fuel injection – 4B•8
  ESP – 9•18
  fuel injection system – 4A•7, 4A•9
Emission control and exhaust systems –
  4C•1 *et seq*, REF•11
Engine fault finding – REF•13, REF•14
Engine management system – 4A•5, 4A•8,
  4B•7
  self-diagnosis memory fault check –
    1A•12, 1B•14
  temperature sensor – 3•7
Engine oil – 0•12, 0•17, 1A•8, 1B•8
Engine removal and overhaul procedures –
  2C•1 *et seq*
Engine speed sensor – 4A•5, 4A•8, 4B•8
Environmental considerations – REF•4
ESP switch – 12•5
ESP system – 9•18
Evaporative emission control – 4C•2
Evaporator/heater matrix housing – 3•12

Note: *References throughout this index are in the form* "**Chapter number**" • "**Page number**". *So, for example, 2C•15 refers to page 15 of Chapter 2C.*

Exhaust emissions – 1A•13, 1B•14, 4C•2
Exhaust Gas Recirculation (EGR) system – 4C•3
Exhaust manifold – 4C•4
Exhaust specialists – REF•5
Exhaust system – 1A•10, 1B•10, 4C•2, 4C•4, REF•10, REF•11

F

Facia – 11•19
Facia-mounted light switch – 12•4
Fan – 3•5
Fan thermostatic switch – 3•6
Fault finding – REF•12 *et seq*
   automatic transmission – REF•16
   braking system – REF•17
   clutch – REF•15
   cooling system – REF•15
   driveshafts – REF•17
   electrical system – 12•2, REF•18, REF•19
   engine – REF•13, REF•14
   fuel and exhaust systems – REF•15
   manual transmission – REF•16
   steering and suspension – REF•18
Filling – 11•3
Filters
   air – 1A•13, 1B•15, 4A•4, 4B•2
   fuel – 1B•9, 1B•11, 1B•15, 4A•9
   oil – 1A•8, 1B•8
   pollen – 1A•11, 1B•12
Final drive fluid – 1A•15, 1B•16
Fire – 0•6
Fluid leaks – 1A•10, 1B•10
Fluids – 0•17
Flywheel – 2A•13, 2B•15
Foglamp – 12•7, 12•11
Fresh/recirculating air flap valve motor – 3•11, 3•13
Friction disc – 6•5
Fuel cooling system – 3•13, 3•14
Fuel filler flap release switch – 12•6
Fuel filter – 1B•9, 1B•11, 1B•15, 4A•9
Fuel gauge sender unit – 4A•10, 4B•3
Fuel injection system – 4A•14
Fuel injectors – 4A•6, 4A•8, 4B•5
Fuel pressure regulator – 4A•7, 4A•9
Fuel pump – 4A•10, 4B•11
Fuel rail – 4A•6, 4A•8
Fuel system – diesel – 4B•1 *et seq*
Fuel system – petrol injection – 4A•1 *et seq*
Fuel system – REF•11
   fault finding – REF•15
Fuel tank – 4A•11, 4B•4
Fuel temperature sensor – 3•15, 4B•9
Fume or gas intoxication – 0•6
Fuses – 4B•9, 12•3
Fusible links – 12•3

G

Gaiters
   driveshaft – 1A•11, 1B•13
   steering gear – 10•18
Garages – REF•5
Gashes – 11•3
Gaskets – REF•4
Gearchange linkage – 7A•3
General repair procedures – REF•4
Glossary of technical terms – REF•20 *et seq*
Glovebox – 11•20
Glovebox lights – 12•9
Glow plug – 5C•2
Glow plug fusebox – 4B•9
Grab handles – 11•23

H

Hall sender – 4A•7, 4A•9
Handbrake – 9•14, 9•15, REF•8
Handbrake warning switch – 12•4
Handles door – 11•14
Hazard warning switch – 12•5
Headlight – 1A•11, 1B•12, 12•6, 12•10, 12•12, 12•13
Headlight control switch – 12•5
Headlight washer system – 1A•12, 1B•14
Headlining – 11•22
Heated rear window switch – 12•5
Heater – 3•10, 3•11, 3•12
Heater control panel illumination – 12•10
Heating and ventilation system – 3•8
High-level stop-light – 12•8, 12•12
Hinge lubrication – 1A•12, 1B•14
Horns – 12•15
Hose leaks – 1A•10, 1B•10
Hoses – 3•2, 9•3
HT coil(s) – 5B•3
Hub bearings – 10•3, 10•11
Hydraulic pipes and hoses – 9•3
Hydraulic pump (ESP) – 9•19
Hydraulic tappets – 2A•13, 2B•15
Hydraulic unit (ABS) – 9•17
Hydrofluoric acid – 0•6

I

Identifying leaks – 0•10
Ignition switch – 10•14
Ignition system – petrol engines – 5B•1 *et seq*
Ignition timing – 5B•3
Indicators – 12•7, 12•11, 12•13
Injectors – 4A•6, 4A•8, 4B•5
Inlet ducts – 4A•4, 4B•2
Inlet manifold – 4A•13, 4B•11
Inlet manifold change-over flap and valve – 4B•12
Input shaft oil seal – 7A•6

Instrument panel – 12•13
Instrument panel bulbs – 12•10
Instruments – 1A•13, 1B•14
Intercooler – 4A•15, 4B•10
Interior lights – 12•9

J

Jacking and vehicle support – REF•3
Joint mating faces – REF•4
Jump starting – 0•8

K

Knock sensors – 5B•3

L

Lateral acceleration sensor (ESP) – 9•18
Leakdown test – 2B•7
Leaks – 0•10, 1A•10, 1B•10
Light units – 12•10
Lock carrier – 11•7
Lock lubrication – 1A•12, 1B•14
Locking cable (automatic transmission) – 7B•5
Locknuts, locktabs and washers – REF•4
Locks
   automatic transmission – 7B•5
   bonnet – 11•4
   boot lid – 11•9
   door – 11•12, 11•14
   steering – 10•14
   tailgate – 11•11
Lower arm – 10•8, 10•9
Lubricants and fluids – 0•17
Luggage area lights – 12•9
Luggage area light switch – 12•5

M

Main beam – 12•6, 12•12
Main bearings – 2C•24, 2C•25
Manifolds – 2B•13
   exhaust – 4C•4
   inlet – 4A•13, 4B•11, 4B•12
Manual transmission – 7A•1 *et seq*
   fault finding – REF•16
   oil – 0•17, 1A•11, 1B•12
Master cylinder
   brake – 9•11
   clutch – 6•3, 6•8
Mirrors – 11•17, 11•21, 12•4, REF•8
Mirror light – 12•10
MOT test checks – REF•8 *et seq*
Motor factors – REF•5
Motronic engine management system – 4A•5
Mountings – 2A•13, 2B•16
Multi-function switch – 7A•5

Note: *References throughout this index are in the form "Chapter number" • "Page number". So, for example, 2C•15 refers to page 15 of Chapter 2C.*

N

Number plate light – 12•8, 12•12

O

Oil filter – 1A•8, 1B•8
Oil level sensor – 5A•7
Oil pressure warning light switch – 5A•6
Oil pump and pick-up – 2A•16, 2B•17
Oil seals – 7A•5, REF•4
    camshaft – 2A•9, 2B•11
    crankshaft – 2A•10, 2B•11
    driveshaft flange – 7A•5
    input shaft – 7A•6
    selector shaft – 7A•7
Oil temperature sensor – 2A•16, 5A•7
Oils
    engine – 0•12, 0•17, 1A•8, 1B•8
    manual transmission – 0•17, 1A•11, 1B•12
Open-circuit – 12•2
Oxygen sensors – 4A•7, 4A•9

P

Pads – 1A•9, 1B•9, 9•4, 9•6
Parking aid components – 12•16
Parts – REF•5
Pedals
    brake – 4B•9, 9•12, 9•16
    clutch – 4B•9, 6•3, 6•8
Petrol engine in-car repair procedures –
    2A•1 *et seq*
Pipes – 9•3
Piston rings – 2C•27
Pistons – 2C•19, 2C•27
Plastic components – 11•3
Poisonous or irritant substances – 0•6
Pollen filter – 1A•11, 1B•12
Power steering – 10•18
Power steering fluid – 0•17, 10•18
Pre/post-heating systems – diesel
    models – 5C•1 *et seq*
Pressure plate – 6•5
Pressure regulator (fuel) – 4A•7, 4A•9
Pressure sensor (fuel system) – 4B•8
Pressure sensor (ESP) – 9•19
Project vehicles – 0•5
Pump injector rocker shaft – 2B•10
Puncture repair – 0•9
Purge valve – 4C•2

R

Radiator – 1A•16, 1B•17, 3•3
Radiator (fuel cooling system) – 3•14
Radio – 12•16
Radio aerial – 12•16
Radio anti-theft system – precaution –
    REF•4
Range control – 12•13
Range control motor – 12•11
Range/distance sensor parking aid – 12•16
Reading lights – 12•9
Rear axle – 10•12
Rear combination light – 12•8, 12•11,
    12•12
Rear window – 11•17
Recirculation flap motor – 3•11, 3•13
Regulator (window) – 11•16
Relays – 12•3
    diesel fuel injection – 4B•9
Release bearing and lever – 6•7
Respraying – 11•3
Ride height sensor – 12•13
Road test – 1A•13, 1B•14
Roadside repairs – 0•7 *et seq*
Roadspeed sensor – 4A•5, 4A•8, 7A•5
Rocker shaft – 2B•10
Routine maintenance – bodywork and
    underframe – 11•2
Routine maintenance – upholstery and
    carpets – 11•2
Routine maintenance and servicing
    – diesel models – 1B•1 *et seq*
Routine maintenance and servicing
    – petrol models – 1A•1 *et seq*
Rust holes – 11•3

S

Safety first! – 0•6, 0•13
Scalding – 0•6
Scratches – 11•2
Screw threads and fastenings – REF•4
Seat belts – 11•22
Seat heating switch – 12•5
Seats – 11•21
Secondary air injection system – 4C•6
Selector cable (automatic transmission) –
    7B•3
Selector shaft oil seal – 7A•7
Sensors
    air intake charge pressure/temperature –
    4B•8

    air temperature – 4A•5, 4A•8
    altitude – 4B•9
    brake pressure – 9•19
    camshaft position – 4B•9
    coolant temperature – 4A•5, 4A•8, 4B•7
    engine management system temperature –
      3•7
    engine speed – 4A•5, 4A•8, 4B•8
    fuel temperature – 4B•9
    knock – 5B•3
    lateral acceleration – 9•18
    oil level – 5A•7
    oil temperature – 5A•7
    oxygen – 4A•7, 4A•9
    roadspeed – 4A•5, 4A•8, 7A•5
    steering angle – 9•19
    temperature – 4A•5, 4A•8, 4B•7, 4B•8,
      4B•9, 5A•7
    temperature gauge/warning
      light – 3•6
    yaw rate – 9•18
Service interval display – 1A•9, 1B•10
Service position – 11•8
Servo unit – 9•14
Shock absorbers – REF•9, REF•10
Short-circuit – 12•2
Shut-off valve (fuel cooling
    system) – 3•14
Side airbags – 12•19
Side window – 11•17
Sidelight – 12•6, 12•12
Silencer – 4C•5
Simos engine management
    system – 4A•8
Slave cylinder – 6•5
Spare parts – REF•5
Spark plugs – 1A•13
Speakers – 12•17
Springs – 10•11, REF•10
Starting and charging systems –
    5A•1 *et seq*
Start-up after overhaul and reassembly –
    2C•29
Steering – 1A•12, 1A•13, 1B•13, 1B•14,
    REF•9, REF•10
Steering angle sensor (ESP) – 9•19
Steering angles – 10•20
Steering column – 10•13, REF•8
Steering column combination switch –
    12•3
Steering gear – 10•15, 10•20
Steering wheel – 10•13, REF•8
Stop-light – 12•8, 12•12
Stop-light switches – 9•16

Note: *References throughout this index are in the form* **"Chapter number"** • **"Page number"**. *So, for example, 2C•15 refers to page 15 of Chapter 2C.*

Strut
    bonnet – 11•4
    boot lid – 11•11
    suspension – 10•5, 10•11, 10•12
    tailgate – 11•11
Subframe – 10•10
Sump – 2A•14, 2B•16
Sunlight photo-sensor – 3•13
Sunroof – 1A•12, 1B•14, 11•17, 12•15
Sunroof control switch – 12•4
Sunvisor – 11•23
Sunvisor light – 12•10
Suspension – 1A•12, 1A•13, 1B•13, 1B•14,
    REF•9, REF•10
Suspension and steering – 10•1 et seq
    fault finding – REF•18
Switch illumination – 12•10
Switches – 12•4
    brake – 9•16
    brake pedal – 4B•9
    clutch pedal – 4B•9, 6•8
    fan thermostatic – 3•6
    ignition – 10•14
    manual transmission multi-function – 7A•5
    oil pressure warning light – 5A•6
    steering column combination – 12•3

T

Tailgate – 11•10, 11•11, 12•15
Tailgate washer system – 1A•12, 1B•14
Tailgate wiper motor – 12•15
Tandem fuel pump – 4B•11
Tappets – 2A•13, 2B•15
TDC on No 1 cylinder – 2A•4, 2B•4
Technical terms – REF•20 et seq

Temperature gauge/warning light sensor –
    3•6
Temperature sensor – 2A•16, 3•13, 3•15,
    4A•5, 4A•8, 4B•7, 4B•8, 4B•9, 5A•7
Tensioner – 2A•7, 2A•8, 2B•8
Thermostat – 3•3
Throttle body – 4A•6, 4A•8
Throttle valve positioner – 4A•5
Throttle valve potentiometer – 4A•5, 4A•8
Timing (ignition) – 5B•3
Timing belt – 1A•16, 1B•10, 2A•4, 2B•7
Tools – REF•4
Tools and working facilities – REF•6 et seq
Torque arm – 2A•14, 2B•16
Towing – 0•10
Track rod – 10•19
Transverse arms – 10•7
Trim panels – 11•11, 11•22
Turbocharger – 4A•15, 4B•9
Tyre condition and pressure – 0•14
Tyre pressures – 0•17
Tyre specialists – REF•5
Tyres – REF•11

U

Underbody protection – 1A•11, 1B•13
Underbonnet check points – 0•11
Underframe – 11•2
Upholstery – 11•2
Upper arms – 10•7

V

Vacuum pump – 9•18
Vacuum servo unit – 9•14
Valve timing marks – 2A•3, 2B•3
Valves – 2C•15

Vanity mirror light – 12•10
Vehicle Identification – REF•5, REF•9
Vehicle support – REF•3
Ventilation system – 3•8
Viscous-coupled cooling fan – 3•5
Voltage regulator – 5A•5
VW Passat Manual – 0•5

W

Warning buzzer parking aid – 12•16
Washer fluid – 0•16
Washer system – 1A•12, 1B•14, 12•15
Water pump – 3•7
Weekly checks – 0•11 et seq
Weights – REF•1
Wheel alignment – 10•20
Wheel arch liners – 11•8
Wheel bearings – 10•3, 10•11, REF•10
Wheel changing – 0•9
Wheel sensor (ABS) – 9•17, 9•18
Wheels – REF•11
Window regulator – 11•16
Window switches – 12•5
Windows – 11•14, 11•16
Windscreen – 11•17, REF•8
Windscreen washer system – 1A•12, 1B•14
Windscreen wipers – 12•14
Wiper arms – 12•14
Wiper blades – 0•16
Wiper motor – 12•14, 12•15
Wiring diagrams – 12•21 et seq
Working facilities – REF•6

Y

Yaw rate sensor (ESP) – 9•18

Haynes Manuals – The Complete UK Car List

Title	Book No.
ALFA ROMEO Alfasud/Sprint (74 - 88) up to F *	0292
Alfa Romeo Alfetta (73 - 87) up to E *	0531
AUDI 80, 90 & Coupe Petrol (79 - Nov 88) up to F	0605
Audi 80, 90 & Coupe Petrol (Oct 86 - 90) D to H	1491
Audi 100 & 200 Petrol (Oct 82 - 90) up to H	0907
Audi 100 & A6 Petrol & Diesel (May 91 - May 97) H to P	3504
Audi A3 Petrol & Diesel (96 - May 03) P to 03	4253
Audi A4 Petrol & Diesel (95 - 00) M to X	3575
Audi A4 Petrol & Diesel (01 - 04) X to 54	4609
AUSTIN A35 & A40 (56 - 67) up to F *	0118
Austin/MG/Rover Maestro 1.3 & 1.6 Petrol (83 - 95) up to M	0922
Austin/MG Metro (80 - May 90) up to G	0718
Austin/Rover Montego 1.3 & 1.6 Petrol (84 - 94) A to L	1066
Austin/MG/Rover Montego 2.0 Petrol (84 - 95) A to M	1067
Mini (59 - 69) up to H *	0527
Mini (69 - 01) up to X	0646
Austin/Rover 2.0 litre Diesel Engine (86 - 93) C to L	1857
Austin Healey 100/6 & 3000 (56 - 68) up to G *	0049
BEDFORD CF Petrol (69 - 87) up to E	0163
Bedford/Vauxhall Rascal & Suzuki Supercarry (86 - Oct 94) C to M	3015
BMW 316, 320 & 320i (4-cyl) (75 - Feb 83) up to Y *	0276
BMW 320, 320i, 323i & 325i (6-cyl) (Oct 77 - Sept 87) up to E	0815
BMW 3- & 5-Series Petrol (81 - 91) up to J	1948
BMW 3-Series Petrol (Apr 91 - 99) H to V	3210
BMW 3-Series Petrol (Sept 98 - 03) S to 53	4067
BMW 520i & 525e (Oct 81 - June 88) up to E	1560
BMW 525, 528 & 528i (73 - Sept 81) up to X *	0632
BMW 5-Series 6-cyl Petrol (April 96 - Aug 03) N to 03	4151
BMW 1500, 1502, 1600, 1602, 2000 & 2002 (59 - 77) up to S *	0240
CHRYSLER PT Cruiser Petrol (00 - 03) W to 53	4058
CITROËN 2CV, Ami & Dyane (67 - 90) up to H	0196
Citroën AX Petrol & Diesel (87 - 97) D to P	3014
Citroën Berlingo & Peugeot Partner Petrol & Diesel (96 - 05) P to 55	4281
Citroën BX Petrol (83 - 94) A to L	0908
Citroën C15 Van Petrol & Diesel (89 - Oct 98) F to S	3509
Citroën C3 Petrol & Diesel (02 - 05) 51 to 05	4197
Citroën C5 Petrol & Diesel (01-08) Y to 08	4745
Citroën CX Petrol (75 - 88) up to F	0528
Citroën Saxo Petrol & Diesel (96 - 04) N to 54	3506
Citroën Visa Petrol (79 - 88) up to F	0620
Citroën Xantia Petrol & Diesel (93 - 01) K to Y	3082
Citroën XM Petrol & Diesel (89 - 00) G to X	3451
Citroën Xsara Petrol & Diesel (97 - Sept 00) R to W	3751
Citroën Xsara Picasso Petrol & Diesel (00 - 02) W to 52	3944
Citroen Xsara Picasso (03-08)	4784
Citroën ZX Diesel (91 - 98) J to S	1922
Citroën ZX Petrol (91 - 98) H to S	1881
Citroën 1.7 & 1.9 litre Diesel Engine (84 - 96) A to N	1379
FIAT 126 (73 - 87) up to E *	0305
Fiat 500 (57 - 73) up to M *	0090
Fiat Bravo & Brava Petrol (95 - 00) N to W	3572
Fiat Cinquecento (93 - 98) K to R	3501
Fiat Panda (81 - 95) up to M	0793
Fiat Punto Petrol & Diesel (94 - Oct 99) L to V	3251
Fiat Punto Petrol (Oct 99 - July 03) V to 03	4066
Fiat Punto Petrol (03-07) 03 to 07	4746
Fiat Regata Petrol (84 - 88) A to F	1167
Fiat Tipo Petrol (88 - 91) E to J	1625
Fiat Uno Petrol (83 - 95) up to M	0923
Fiat X1/9 (74 - 89) up to G *	0273
FORD Anglia (59 - 68) up to G *	0001

Title	Book No.
Ford Capri II (& III) 1.6 & 2.0 (74 - 87) up to E *	0283
Ford Capri II (& III) 2.8 & 3.0 V6 (74 - 87) up to E	1309
Ford Cortina Mk I & Corsair 1500 ('62 - '66) up to D*	0214
Ford Cortina Mk III 1300 & 1600 (70 - 76) up to P *	0070
Ford Escort Mk I 1100 & 1300 (68 - 74) up to N *	0171
Ford Escort Mk I Mexico, RS 1600 & RS 2000 (70 - 74) up to N *	0139
Ford Escort Mk II Mexico, RS 1800 & RS 2000 (75 - 80) up to W *	0735
Ford Escort (75 - Aug 80) up to V *	0280
Ford Escort Petrol (Sept 80 - Sept 90) up to H	0686
Ford Escort & Orion Petrol (Sept 90 - 00) H to X	1737
Ford Escort & Orion Diesel (Sept 90 - 00) H to X	4081
Ford Fiesta (76 - Aug 83) up to Y	0334
Ford Fiesta Petrol (Aug 83 - Feb 89) A to F	1030
Ford Fiesta Petrol (Feb 89 - Oct 95) F to N	1595
Ford Fiesta Petrol & Diesel (Oct 95 - Mar 02) N to 02	3397
Ford Fiesta Petrol & Diesel (Apr 02 - 07) 02 to 57	4170
Ford Focus Petrol & Diesel (98 - 01) S to Y	3759
Ford Focus Petrol & Diesel (Oct 01 - 05) 51 to 05	4167
Ford Galaxy Petrol & Diesel (95 - Aug 00) M to W	3984
Ford Granada Petrol (Sept 77 - Feb 85) up to B *	0481
Ford Granada & Scorpio Petrol (Mar 85 - 94) B to M	1245
Ford Ka (96 - 02) P to 52	3570
Ford Mondeo Petrol (93 - Sept 00) K to X	1923
Ford Mondeo Petrol & Diesel (Oct 00 - Jul 03) X to 03	3990
Ford Mondeo Petrol & Diesel (July 03 - 07) 03 to 56	4619
Ford Mondeo Diesel (93 - 96) L to N	3465
Ford Orion Petrol (83 - Sept 90) up to H	1009
Ford Sierra 4-cyl Petrol (82 - 93) up to K	0903
Ford Sierra V6 Petrol (82 - 91) up to J	0904
Ford Transit Petrol (Mk 2) (78 - Jan 86) up to C	0719
Ford Transit Petrol (Mk 3) (Feb 86 - 89) C to G	1468
Ford Transit Diesel (Feb 86 - 99) C to T	3019
Ford Transit Diesel (00-06)	4775
Ford 1.6 & 1.8 litre Diesel Engine (84 - 96) A to N	1172
Ford 2.1, 2.3 & 2.5 litre Diesel Engine (77 - 90) up to H	1606
FREIGHT ROVER Sherpa Petrol (74 - 87) up to E	0463
HILLMAN Avenger (70 - 82) up to Y	0037
Hillman Imp (63 - 76) up to R *	0022
HONDA Civic (Feb 84 - Oct 87) A to E	1226
Honda Civic (Nov 91 - 96) J to N	3199
Honda Civic Petrol (Mar 95 - 00) M to X	4050
Honda Civic Petrol & Diesel (01 - 05) X to 55	4611
Honda CR-V Petrol & Diesel (01-06)	4747
Honda Jazz (01 - Feb 08) 51 - 57	4735
HYUNDAI Pony (85 - 94) C to M	3398
JAGUAR E Type (61 - 72) up to L *	0140
Jaguar MkI & II, 240 & 340 (55 - 69) up to H *	0098
Jaguar XJ6, XJ & Sovereign; Daimler Sovereign (68 - Oct 86) up to D	0242
Jaguar XJ6 & Sovereign (Oct 86 - Sept 94) D to M	3261
Jaguar XJ12, XJS & Sovereign; Daimler Double Six (72 - 88) up to F	0478
JEEP Cherokee Petrol (93 - 96) K to N	1943
LADA 1200, 1300, 1500 & 1600 (74 - 91) up to J	0413
Lada Samara (87 - 91) D to J	1610
LAND ROVER 90, 110 & Defender Diesel (83 - 07) up to 56	3017
Land Rover Discovery Petrol & Diesel (89 - 98) G to S	3016
Land Rover Discovery Diesel (Nov 98 - Jul 04) S to 04	4606
Land Rover Freelander Petrol & Diesel (97 - Sept 03) R to 53	3929
Land Rover Freelander Petrol & Diesel (Oct 03 - Oct 06) 53 to 56	4623

Title	Book No.
Land Rover Series IIA & III Diesel (58 - 85) up to C	0529
Land Rover Series II, IIA & III 4-cyl Petrol (58 - 85) up to C	0314
MAZDA 323 (Mar 81 - Oct 89) up to G	1608
Mazda 323 (Oct 89 - 98) G to R	3455
Mazda 626 (May 83 - Sept 87) up to E	0929
Mazda B1600, B1800 & B2000 Pick-up Petrol (72 - 88) up to F	0267
Mazda RX-7 (79 - 85) up to C *	0460
MERCEDES-BENZ 190, 190E & 190D Petrol & Diesel (83 - 93) A to L	3450
Mercedes-Benz 200D, 240D, 240TD, 300D & 300TD 123 Series Diesel (Oct 76 - 85)	1114
Mercedes-Benz 250 & 280 (68 - 72) up to L *	0346
Mercedes-Benz 250 & 280 123 Series Petrol (Oct 76 - 84) up to B *	0677
Mercedes-Benz 124 Series Petrol & Diesel (85 - Aug 93) C to K	3253
Mercedes-Benz A-Class Petrol & Diesel (98-04) S to 54	4748
Mercedes-Benz C-Class Petrol & Diesel (93 - Aug 00) L to W	3511
Mercedes-Benz C-Class (00-06)	4780
MGA (55 - 62) *	0475
MGB (62 - 80) up to W	0111
MG Midget & Austin-Healey Sprite (58 - 80) up to W *	0265
MINI Petrol (July 01 - 05) Y to 05	4273
MITSUBISHI Shogun & L200 Pick-Ups Petrol (83 - 94) up to M	1944
MORRIS Ital 1.3 (80 - 84) up to B	0705
Morris Minor 1000 (56 - 71) up to K	0024
NISSAN Almera Petrol (95 - Feb 00) N to V	4053
Nissan Almera & Tino Petrol (Feb 00 - 07) V to 56	4612
Nissan Bluebird (May 84 - Mar 86) A to C	1223
Nissan Bluebird Petrol (Mar 86 - 90) C to H	1473
Nissan Cherry (Sept 82 - 86) up to D	1031
Nissan Micra (83 - Jan 93) up to K	0931
Nissan Micra (93 - 02) K to 52	3254
Nissan Micra Petrol (03-07) 52 to 57	4734
Nissan Primera Petrol (90 - Aug 99) H to T	1851
Nissan Stanza (82 - 86) up to D	0824
Nissan Sunny Petrol (May 82 - Oct 86) up to D	0895
Nissan Sunny Petrol (Oct 86 - Mar 91) D to H	1378
Nissan Sunny Petrol (Apr 91 - 95) H to N	3219
OPEL Ascona & Manta (B Series) (Sept 75 - 88) up to F *	0316
Opel Ascona Petrol (81 - 88)	3215
Opel Astra Petrol (Oct 91 - Feb 98)	3156
Opel Corsa Petrol (83 - Mar 93)	3160
Opel Corsa Petrol (Mar 93 - 97)	3159
Opel Kadett Petrol (Nov 79 - Oct 84) up to B	0634
Opel Kadett Petrol (Oct 84 - Oct 91)	3196
Opel Omega & Senator Petrol (Nov 86 - 94)	3157
Opel Rekord Petrol (Feb 78 - Oct 86) up to D	0543
Opel Vectra Petrol (Oct 88 - Oct 95)	3158
PEUGEOT 106 Petrol & Diesel (91 - 04) J to 53	1882
Peugeot 205 Petrol (83 - 97) A to P	0932
Peugeot 206 Petrol & Diesel (98 - 01) S to X	3757
Peugeot 206 Petrol & Diesel (02 - 06) 51 to 06	4613
Peugeot 306 Petrol & Diesel (93 - 02) K to 02	3073
Peugeot 307 Petrol & Diesel (01 - 04) Y to 54	4147
Peugeot 309 Petrol (86 - 93) C to K	1266
Peugeot 405 Petrol (88 - 97) E to P	1559
Peugeot 405 Diesel (88 - 97) E to P	3198
Peugeot 406 Petrol & Diesel (96 - Mar 99) N to T	3394
Peugeot 406 Petrol & Diesel (Mar 99 - 02) T to 52	3982

* Classic reprint

Title	Book No.
Peugeot 505 Petrol (79 - 89) up to G	0762
Peugeot 1.7/1.8 & 1.9 litre Diesel Engine (82 - 96) up to N	0950
Peugeot 2.0, 2.1, 2.3 & 2.5 litre Diesel Engines (74 - 90) up to H	1607
PORSCHE 911 (65 - 85) up to C	0264
Porsche 924 & 924 Turbo (76 - 85) up to C	0397
PROTON (89 - 97) F to P	3255
RANGE ROVER V8 Petrol (70 - Oct 92) up to K	0606
RELIANT Robin & Kitten (73 - 83) up to A *	0436
RENAULT 4 (61 - 86) up to D *	0072
Renault 5 Petrol (Feb 85 - 96) B to N	1219
Renault 9 & 11 Petrol (82 - 89) up to F	0822
Renault 18 Petrol (79 - 86) up to D	0598
Renault 19 Petrol (89 - 96) F to N	1646
Renault 19 Diesel (89 - 96) F to N	1946
Renault 21 Petrol (86 - 94) C to M	1397
Renault 25 Petrol & Diesel (84 - 92) B to K	1228
Renault Clio Petrol (91 - May 98) H to R	1853
Renault Clio Diesel (91 - June 96) H to N	3031
Renault Clio Petrol & Diesel (May 98 - May 01) R to Y	3906
Renault Clio Petrol & Diesel (June '01 - '05) Y to 55	4168
Renault Espace Petrol & Diesel (85 - 96) C to N	3197
Renault Laguna Petrol & Diesel (94 - 00) L to W	3252
Renault Laguna Petrol & Diesel (Feb 01 - Feb 05) X to 54	4283
Renault Mégane & Scénic Petrol & Diesel (96 - 99) N to T	3395
Renault Mégane & Scénic Petrol & Diesel (Apr 99 - 02) T to 52	3916
Renault Megane Petrol & Diesel (Oct 02 - 05) 52 to 55	4284
Renault Scenic Petrol & Diesel (Sept 03 - 06) 53 to 06	4297
ROVER 213 & 216 (84 - 89) A to G	1116
Rover 214 & 414 Petrol (89 - 96) G to N	1689
Rover 216 & 416 Petrol (89 - 96) G to N	1830
Rover 211, 214, 216, 218 & 220 Petrol & Diesel (Dec 95 - 99) N to V	3399
Rover 25 & MG ZR Petrol & Diesel (Oct 99 - 04) V to 54	4145
Rover 414, 416 & 420 Petrol & Diesel (May 95 - 98) M to R	3453
Rover 45 / MG ZS Petrol & Diesel (99 - 05) V to 55	4384
Rover 618, 620 & 623 Petrol (93 - 97) K to P	3257
Rover 75 / MG ZT Petrol & Diesel (99 - 06) S to 06	4292
Rover 820, 825 & 827 Petrol (86 - 95) D to N	1380
Rover 3500 (76 - 87) up to E *	0365
Rover Metro, 111 & 114 Petrol (May 90 - 98) G to S	1711
SAAB 95 & 96 (66 - 76) up to R *	0198
Saab 90, 99 & 900 (79 - Oct 93) up to L	0765
Saab 900 (Oct 93 - 98) L to R	3512
Saab 9000 (4-cyl) (85 - 98) C to S	1686
Saab 9-3 Petrol & Diesel (98 - Aug 02) R to 02	4614
Saab 9-3 Petrol & Diesel (02-07) 52 to 57	4749
Saab 9-5 4-cyl Petrol (97 - 04) R to 54	4156
SEAT Ibiza & Cordoba Petrol & Diesel (Oct 93 - Oct 99) L to V	3571
Seat Ibiza & Malaga Petrol (85 - 92) B to K	1609
SKODA Estelle (77 - 89) up to G	0604
Skoda Fabia Petrol & Diesel (00 - 06) W to 06	4376
Skoda Favorit (89 - 96) F to N	1801
Skoda Felicia Petrol & Diesel (95 - 01) M to X	3505
Skoda Octavia Petrol & Diesel (98 - Apr 04) R to 04	4285
SUBARU 1600 & 1800 (Nov 79 - 90) up to H *	0995

Title	Book No.
SUNBEAM Alpine, Rapier & H120 (67 - 74) up to N *	0051
SUZUKI SJ Series, Samurai & Vitara (4-cyl) Petrol (82 - 97) up to P	1942
Suzuki Supercarry & Bedford/Vauxhall Rascal (86 - Oct 94) C to M	3015
TALBOT Alpine, Solara, Minx & Rapier (75 - 86) up to D	0337
Talbot Horizon Petrol (78 - 86) up to D	0473
Talbot Samba (82 - 86) up to D	0823
TOYOTA Avensis Petrol (98 - Jan 03) R to 52	4264
Toyota Carina E Petrol (May 92 - 97) J to P	3256
Toyota Corolla (80 - 85) up to C	0683
Toyota Corolla (Sept 83 - Sept 87) A to E	1024
Toyota Corolla (Sept 87 - Aug 92) E to K	1683
Toyota Corolla Petrol (Aug 92 - 97) K to P	3259
Toyota Corolla Petrol (July 97 - Feb 02) P to 51	4286
Toyota Hi-Ace & Hi-Lux Petrol (69 - Oct 83) up to A	0304
Toyota RAV4 Petrol & Diesel (94-06) L to 55	4750
Toyota Yaris Petrol (99 - 05) T to 05	4265
TRIUMPH GT6 & Vitesse (62 - 74) up to N *	0112
Triumph Herald (59 - 71) up to K *	0010
Triumph Spitfire (62 - 81) up to X	0113
Triumph Stag (70 - 78) up to T *	0441
Triumph TR2, TR3, TR3A, TR4 & TR4A (52 - 67) up to F *	0028
Triumph TR5 & 6 (67 - 75) up to P *	0031
Triumph TR7 (75 - 82) up to Y *	0322
VAUXHALL Astra Petrol (80 - Oct 84) up to B	0635
Vauxhall Astra & Belmont Petrol (Oct 84 - Oct 91) B to J	1136
Vauxhall Astra Petrol (Oct 91 - Feb 98) J to R	1832
Vauxhall/Opel Astra & Zafira Petrol (Feb 98 - Apr 04) R to 04	3758
Vauxhall/Opel Astra & Zafira Diesel (Feb 98 - Apr 04) R to 04	3797
Vauxhall/Opel Astra Petrol (04 - 08)	4732
Vauxhall/Opel Astra Diesel (04 - 08)	4733
Vauxhall/Opel Calibra (90 - 98) G to S	3502
Vauxhall Carlton Petrol (Oct 78 - Oct 86) up to D	0480
Vauxhall Carlton & Senator Petrol (Nov 86 - 94) D to L	1469
Vauxhall Cavalier Petrol (81 - Oct 88) up to F	0812
Vauxhall Cavalier Petrol (Oct 88 - 95) F to N	1570
Vauxhall Chevette (75 - 84) up to B	0285
Vauxhall/Opel Corsa Diesel (Mar 93 - Oct 00) K to X	4087
Vauxhall Corsa Petrol (Mar 93 - 97) K to R	1985
Vauxhall/Opel Corsa Petrol (Apr 97 - Oct 00) P to X	3921
Vauxhall/Opel Corsa Petrol & Diesel (Oct 00 - Sept 03) X to 53	4079
Vauxhall/Opel Corsa Petrol & Diesel (Oct 03 - Aug 06) 53 to 06	4617
Vauxhall/Opel Frontera Petrol & Diesel (91 - Sept 98) J to S	3454
Vauxhall Nova Petrol (83 - 93) up to K	0909
Vauxhall/Opel Omega Petrol (94 - 99) L to T	3510
Vauxhall/Opel Vectra Petrol & Diesel (95 - Feb 99) N to S	3396
Vauxhall/Opel Vectra Petrol & Diesel (Mar 99 - May 02) T to 02	3930
Vauxhall/Opel Vectra Petrol & Diesel (June 02 - Sept 05) 02 to 55	4618
Vauxhall/Opel 1.5, 1.6 & 1.7 litre Diesel Engine (82 - 96) up to N	1222
VW 411 & 412 (68 - 75) up to P *	0091
VW Beetle 1200 (54 - 77) up to S	0036
VW Beetle 1300 & 1500 (65 - 75) up to P	0039

Title	Book No.
VW 1302 & 1302S (70 - 72) up to L *	0110
VW Beetle 1303, 1303S & GT (72 - 75) up to P	0159
VW Beetle Petrol & Diesel (Apr 99 - 07) T to 57	3798
VW Golf & Jetta Mk 1 Petrol 1.1 & 1.3 (74 - 84) up to A	0716
VW Golf, Jetta & Scirocco Mk 1 Petrol 1.5, 1.6 & 1.8 (74 - 84) up to A	0726
VW Golf & Jetta Mk 1 Diesel (78 - 84) up to A	0451
VW Golf & Jetta Mk 2 Petrol (Mar 84 - Feb 92) A to J	1081
VW Golf & Vento Petrol & Diesel (Feb 92 - Mar 98) J to R	3097
VW Golf & Bora Petrol & Diesel (April 98 - 00) R to X	3727
VW Golf & Bora 4-cyl Petrol & Diesel (01 - 03) X to 53	4169
VW Golf & Jetta Petrol & Diesel (04 - 07) 53 to 07	4610
VW LT Petrol Vans & Light Trucks (76 - 87) up to E	0637
VW Passat & Santana Petrol (Sept 81 - May 88) up to E	0814
VW Passat 4-cyl Petrol & Diesel (May 88 - 96) E to P	3498
VW Passat 4-cyl Petrol & Diesel (Dec 96 - Nov 00) P to X	3917
VW Passat Petrol & Diesel (Dec 00 - May 05) X to 05	4279
VW Polo & Derby (76 - Jan 82) up to X	0335
VW Polo (82 - Oct 90) up to H	0813
VW Polo Petrol (Nov 90 - Aug 94) H to L	3245
VW Polo Hatchback Petrol & Diesel (94 - 99) M to S	3500
VW Polo Hatchback Petrol (00 - Jan 02) V to 51	4150
VW Polo Petrol & Diesel (02 - May 05) 51 to 05	4608
VW Scirocco (82 - 90) up to H *	1224
VW Transporter 1600 (68 - 79) up to V	0082
VW Transporter 1700, 1800 & 2000 (72 - 79) up to V *	0226
VW Transporter (air-cooled) Petrol (79 - 82) up to Y *	0638
VW Transporter (water-cooled) Petrol (82 - 90) up to H	3452
VW Type 3 (63 - 73) up to M *	0084
VOLVO 120 & 130 Series (& P1800) (61 - 73) up to M *	0203
Volvo 142, 144 & 145 (66 - 74) up to N *	0129
Volvo 240 Series Petrol (74 - 93) up to K	0270
Volvo 262, 264 & 260/265 (75 - 85) up to C *	0400
Volvo 340, 343, 345 & 360 (76 - 91) up to J	0715
Volvo 440, 460 & 480 Petrol (87 - 97) D to P	1691
Volvo 740 & 760 Petrol (82 - 91) up to J	1258
Volvo 850 Petrol (92 - 96) J to P	3260
Volvo 940 petrol (90 - 98) H to R	3249
Volvo S40 & V40 Petrol (96 - Mar 04) N to 04	3569
Volvo S40 & V50 Petrol & Diesel (Mar 04 - Jun 07) 04 to 07	4731
Volvo S60 Petrol & Diesel (01-08)	4793
Volvo S70, V70 & C70 Petrol (96 - 99) P to V	3573
Volvo V70 / S80 Petrol & Diesel (98 - 05) S to 55	4263

DIY MANUAL SERIES

Title	
The Haynes Air Conditioning Manual	4192
The Haynes Car Electrical Systems Manual	4251
The Haynes Manual on Bodywork	4198
The Haynes Manual on Brakes	4178
The Haynes Manual on Carburettors	4177
The Haynes Manual on Diesel Engines	4174
The Haynes Manual on Engine Management	4199
The Haynes Manual on Fault Codes	4175
The Haynes Manual on Practical Electrical Systems	4267
The Haynes Manual on Small Engines	4250
The Haynes Manual on Welding	4176

* Classic reprint

All the products featured on this page are available through most motor accessory shops, cycle shops and book stores. Our policy of continuous updating and development means that titles are being constantly added to the range. For up-to-date information on our complete list of titles, please telephone: (UK) +44 1963 442030 • (USA) +1 805 498 6703 • (Sweden) +46 18 124016 • (Australia) +61 3 9763 8100

CL24.08/09

Preserving Our Motoring Heritage

< *The Model J Duesenberg Derham Tourster. Only eight of these magnificent cars were ever built – this is the only example to be found outside the United States of America*

Almost every car you've ever loved, loathed or desired is gathered under one roof at the Haynes Motor Museum. Over 300 immaculately presented cars and motorbikes represent every aspect of our motoring heritage, from elegant reminders of bygone days, such as the superb Model J Duesenberg to curiosities like the bug-eyed BMW Isetta. There are also many old friends and flames. Perhaps you remember the 1959 Ford Popular that you did your courting in? The magnificent 'Red Collection' is a spectacle of classic sports cars including AC, Alfa Romeo, Austin Healey, Ferrari, Lamborghini, Maserati, MG, Riley, Porsche and Triumph.

A Perfect Day Out

Each and every vehicle at the Haynes Motor Museum has played its part in the history and culture of Motoring. Today, they make a wonderful spectacle and a great day out for all the family. Bring the kids, bring Mum and Dad, but above all bring your camera to capture those golden memories for ever. You will also find an impressive array of motoring memorabilia, a comfortable 70 seat video cinema and one of the most extensive transport book shops in Britain. The Pit Stop Cafe serves everything from a cup of tea to wholesome, home-made meals or, if you prefer, you can enjoy the large picnic area nestled in the beautiful rural surroundings of Somerset.

John Haynes O.B.E., Founder and Chairman of the museum at the wheel of a Haynes Light 12. >

< *Graham Hill's Lola Cosworth Formula 1 car next to a 1934 Riley Sports.*

The Museum is situated on the A359 Yeovil to Frome road at Sparkford, just off the A303 in Somerset. It is about 40 miles south of Bristol, and 25 minutes drive from the M5 intersection at Taunton.
Open 9.30am - 5.30pm (10.00am - 4.00pm Winter) 7 days a week, *except Christmas Day, Boxing Day and New Years Day*
Special rates available for schools, coach parties and outings Charitable Trust No. 292048